Itinera Fiduciae

Trust and Treuhand in Historical Perspective

Comparative Studies
in Continental and Anglo-American Legal History

Vergleichende Untersuchungen zur kontinentaleuropäischen
und anglo-amerikanischen Rechtsgeschichte

Herausgegeben von

Helmut Coing, Richard Helmholz, Knut Wolfgang Nörr
und Reinhard Zimmermann

Band 19

Itinera Fiduciae

Trust and Treuhand in Historical Perspective

Edited by

Richard Helmholz
Reinhard Zimmermann

Duncker & Humblot · Berlin

Gedruckt mit Unterstützung der Gerda Henkel Stiftung, Düsseldorf

Die Deutsche Bibliothek – CIP-Einheitsaufnahme

Itinera Fiduciae : trust and Treuhand in historical perspective / ed. by Richard Helmholz ; Reinhard Zimmermann. – Berlin : Duncker und Humblot, 1998
(Comparative studies in continental and Anglo-American legal history ; Bd. 19)
ISBN 3-428-09614-2

Fremddatenübernahme und Druck:
Berliner Buchdruckerei Union GmbH, Berlin
Printed in Germany

ISSN 0935-1167
ISBN 3-428-09614-2

Gedruckt auf alterungsbeständigem (säurefreiem) Papier
entsprechend ISO 9706 ♾

Preface

A person may hold property for a variety of purposes. The most common situation is that he wants to use and enjoy it for his own benefit. But he may also have agreed to administer the property either for the benefit of someone else or to further some particular purpose. Thus, in a broad and untechnical sense of the word, he may hold it "in trust". This kind of arrangement has been resorted to for many different reasons, both legitimate and illegitimate. From very early on, European legal systems have been faced with the need to establish rules and, eventually, institutions to deal with the resulting legal problems. *Fiducia, fideicommissum, Treuhand,* foundation, executorship and, of course, the trust: they all provided, at some time or other and in some place or other, the legal framework that was required.

The present volume attempts to present a comparative historical analysis of these devices. It seeks to trace the paths of the idea of "holding for others" or of holding property in a fiduciary capacity: *itinera fiduciae.* The intellectual objectives pursued by the editors and contributors to this volume are set out in the Introduction ("Views of Trust and Treuhand"). We have met twice to discuss these objectives: once in November 1995 in Regensburg before we began the project and then in April 1997 in Halle when most of us had written their papers. Both meetings, and also the publication of this volume, were sponsored by the Gerda Henkel Stiftung. We are very grateful for this support. We would also like to express our sincere thanks to Knut Wolfgang Nörr for his encouragement, Paul Farlam for his editorial assistance, and Gabriele Schmitt, secretary at the Lehrstuhl in Regensburg, for her unfailing support and commitment.

February 1998

Richard Helmholz
Chicago

Reinhard Zimmermann
Regensburg

Summary of Contents

Table of Contents

Abbreviations

a.	= anno
A. 2d	= Atlantic Reporter, 2nd Series
ABGB	= Allgemeines Bürgerliches Gesetzbuch
A.C.	= Appeal Cases, Law Reports
AcP	= Archiv für die civilistische Praxis
APS	= Acts of the Parliaments of Scotland 1124 - 1707 (ed. Thomas Thomson, Cosmo Innes)
Add.	= Addendum
Add. Ms.	= Additional Manuscript
AktG	= Aktiengesetz
All E.R.	= All England Law Reports
Am. Dec.	= American Decisions
Art.	= Artikel
art.	= article
Atk.	= Atkyn's Reports, Chancery
B.	= Baron of the Exchequer
B. Mon.	= Kentucky Reports, Ben Monroe (Court of Appeals)
BGB	= Bürgerliches Gesetzbuch
BGBl	= Bundesgesetzblatt
BGH	= Bundesgerichtshof
BGHZ	= Entscheidungen des Bundesgerichtshofs für Zivilsachen
BIHR	= Borthwick Institute of Historical Research, York
BL	= British Library
BNB	= Bracton's Note Book
BW	= Burgerlijk Wetboek
Barb.	= Barbour's Reports (Supreme Court of New York)
BayGVBl	= Bayerisches Gesetz- und Verordnungsblatt
BayObLG	= Bayerisches Oberstes Landesgericht
Bod. Lib.	= Bodleian Library
Bro. C.C.	= W. Brown's Chancery Reports
Bro. P.C.	= J. Brown's Cases in Parliament
C	= Chancery
C 33	= Chancery Entry Books of Decrees and Orders
C 78	= Chancery and Supreme Court of Judicature, Chancery Division: Six Clerks' Office and successors: Decree Rolls
C.	= Justinian's Code
c.	= canon

C.B.	= Chief Baron
CCA	= Canterbury Cathedral Archive, Canterbury
C.C.Pa.	= Circuit Court of Appeals (Pennsylvania cases)
C.J.	= Chief Justice
COM	= EC Commission, Documents
CP	= Common Pleas
CP 25	= Common Pleas Feet of Fines
CP 40	= Court of Common Pleas De Banco Rolls
C. Th.	= Codex Theodosianus
CUL	= Cambridge University Library
cap.	= capitulum
Carth.	= Carthew's Reports, King's Bench
Ch.	= Law Reports, Chancery
Ch. Cas.	= Cases in Chancery
Ch.D.	= Law Reports, Chancery Division
Chan.	= Court of Chancery
Cl. & F.	= Clark and Finelly's House of Lords Report
Co. Rep.	= Sir Edward Coke's Reports
Col. LS MS.	= Columbia Law School, Manuscript
Columbia L.R.	= Columbia Law Review
Comb.	= Comberback's Reports, King's Bench
Cornell L.R.	= Cornell Law Review
D	= Dunlop's Series of the Court of Session Reports
D.	= Justinian's Digest
DJZ	= Deutsche Juristen-Zeitung
dec.	= decisio
E I	= Erster Entwurf eines Bürgerlichen Gesetzbuches für das Deutsche Reich
E.C.R.	= European Court Reports
EDR	= Ely Diocesan Office
E.R.	= English Reports
ed.	= edidit, editor
Eng. Judg.	= The Decisions of the English Judges during the Usurpation
Ex. Ch.	= Exchequer Chamber
Exch. AB.	= Act Book of the Court of Exchequer, York
F	= Fraser's Series of the Court of Session Reports; Federal Reporter
F. 2d	= Federal Reporter, 2nd Series
Fac. Coll.	= Faculty Collection (Court of Session)
Fed. Cas.	= Federal Cases
Fount.	= Fountainhall's Decisions, Court of Session
Free. Ch.	= Freeman's Reports, Chancery
Freem.	= Freeman's Reports, Chancery

Gai. Inst.	= Gaius's Institutes
Gilb. Rep.	= Gilbert's Reports, Chancery
H, Hil.	= Hilary
H.L.	= House of Lords
HLS MS.	= Harvard Law School, Manuscript
HRG	= Handwörterbuch zur deutschen Rechtsgeschichte
HansOLG	= Hanseatisches Oberlandesgericht
Hants. R.O.	= Hampshire Record Office, Winchester
Hard.	= Hardres' Reports, Exchequer
Harg.	= Hargrave (MS. collection)
Harl.	= Harleian (MS. collection)
Harvard L.R.	= Harvard Law Review
Hg.	= Herausgeber (editor)
Holt K.B.	= Sir John Holt's Reports, King's Bench
Iav.	= Iavolenus
Inst.	= Justinian's Institutes
Iul.	= Iulianus
JCP	= Juris Classeur Periodique
J.L.H.	= Journal of Legal History
JW	= Juristische Wochenschrift
JZ	= Juristenzeitung
JhJb	= Jherings Jahrbücher für die Dogmatik des bürgerlichen Rechts; zuvor: Jahrbücher für die Dogmatik des heutigen römischen und deutschen Privatrechts
JUST	= Rolls of the Justices in Eyre in the Public Record Office
John & H.	= Johnson and Hemming's Reports, Chancery
K. & W. Dict.	= Kames' and Woodhouselee's Dictionary of Decisions (Court of Session)
KAO	= Kent Archives Office, Maidstone
K.B.	= King's Bench; Law Reports, King' s Bench Division
KTS	= Zeitschrift für Konkurs-, Treuhand- und Schiedsgerichtswesen
Kames Sel. Dec.	= Kames' Select Decisions
Keb.	= Keble's Reports
Ky.	= Kentucky Reports (Court of Appeals)
L.C.	= Lord Chancellor
L.K.	= Lord Keeper
L.Q.R.	= Law Quarterly Review
L.R. Eq.	= Law Reports, Equity Cases
L.R. Ir.	= Law Reports, Ireland
L.T.	= Law Times
LZ	= Leipziger Zeitschrift
Lans.	= Lansdowne (MS. collection)

Ld. Raym.	= Lord Raymond's Reports, King's Bench and Common Pleas
Lev.	= Levinz's Reports, King's Bench and Common Pleas
Lib. Ass.	= Liber Assisarum
Lutw.	= Sir E. Lutwyche's Entries and Reports, Common Pleas
M	= Macpherson's Series of the Court of Session Reports
M, Mich.	= Michaelmas
M. & Cr.	= Mylne and Craig's Chancery Reports
M.R.	= Master of the Rolls
MS., Ms.	= Manuscript
MSS., Mss.	= Manuscripts
Marcell.	= Marcellus
March N.R.	= Reports, or New cases, collected by John March
Marci.	= Marcianus
Mass.	= Massachusetts Reports (Supreme Judicial Court of Massachusetts)
Mer.	= Merivale's Chancery Reports
Mod.	= Modern Reports in King's Bench
Moore K.B.	= Sir F. Moore's Reports, King's Bench
Mor.	= Morison's Dictionary of Decisions
N.E.	= North Eastern Reporter
N.H.	= New Hampshire Reports (Supreme Court)
NJW	= Neue Juristische Wochenschrift
N.S.W.L.R.	= New South Wales Law Reports
N.W. 2d	= North Western Reporter, 2nd Series
N.Y.S. 2d	= New York Supplement, 2nd Series
Nels.	= Nelson's Reports, Chancery
Nov.	= Justinian's Novels
Nov. Marc.	= Novellae Marciani
OLG	= Oberlandesgericht
P.	= Pacific Reporter
P, Pas.	= Easter
P. Wms.	= Peere Williams' Chancery Reports
Pat. App.	= Paton's House of Lords Appeal Cases
pl.	= plea
Plowd.	= Plowden's Reports
Pomp.	= Pomponius
Poph.	= Popham's Reports, King's Bench
PrALR	= Preußisches Allgemeines Landrecht
Pre. Ch.	= Precedents in Chancery
Quaest.	= Quaestio
R	= Rettie's Series of the Court of Session Reports
RGZ	= Entscheidungen des Reichtsgerichts in Zivilsachen

RIDA	= Revue internationale des droits de l'antiquité
ROHG	= Reichsoberhandelsgericht
ROHGE	= Entscheidungen des Reichsoberlandesgerichts
RabelsZ	= Zeitschrift für ausländisches und internationales Privatrecht, begründet von Ernst Rabel
Rawl.	= Rawlinson (MS. collection)
Rob.	= Robertson's House of Lords Appeal Cases
Rz.	= Randziffer
S	= Shaw's Series of the Court of Session Reports
S. & M.	= P. Shaw and Maclean's House of Lords Appeal Cases
S.C.	= Court of Session Cases
SC	= senatus consultum
S.L.T.	= Scots Law Times
Salk.	= Salkeld's Reports, King's Bench
ser. lat.	= series latina
Sh. Ct.	= Sheriff Court
Show. K.B.	= Shower's Reports, King's Bench
Show. P.C.	= Shower's Cases in Parliament
So.	= Southern Reporter
Som. R.O.	= Somerset Record Office
St. Tr.	= State Trials
t.	= tomus
T, Trin.	= Trinity
T.R.	= Tijdschrift voor rechtsgeschiedenis
trans.	= translated by
Tulane L.R.	= Tulane L.R.
U.S.	= Reports of Cases in the Supreme Court of the United States of America
Ulp.	= Ulpianus
University of Chicago L.R.	= University of Chicago Law Review
V. & B.	= Vesey and Beames's Reports, Chancery
V.-C.	= Vice Chancellor
Va.	= Virginia Reports (Supreme Court)
Vent.	= Ventris' King's Bench Reports
Vern.	= Vernon's Reports, Chancery
Ves.	= Vesey's Reports, Chancery
Ves. Sen.	= Vesey Senior's Reports, Chancery
Vt.	= Vermont Reports (Supreme Court)
W. & S.	= Wilson and Shaw's House of Lords Reports
W.N.	= Weekly Notes (Law Reports)
WM	= Wertpapiermitteilungen
X	= Liber Extra (Corpus Juris Canonici)
Y.B.	= Yearbook

Yale L.J.	= Yale Law Journal
ZDR	= Zeitschrift für deutsches Recht und deutsche Rechtswissenschaft
ZEuP	= Zeitschrift für Europäisches Privatrecht
ZGB	= Zivilgesetzbuch
ZHR	= Zeitschrift für das gesamte Handels- und Wirtschaftsrecht
ZIP	= Zeitschrift für Wirtschaftsrecht
ZRG	= Zeitschrift für Rechtsgeschichte
ZSS (GA)	= Zeitschrift der Savigny-Stiftung für Rechtsgeschichte (Germanistische Abteilung)
ZSS (KA)	= Zeitschrift der Savigny-Stiftung für Rechtsgeschichte (Kanonistische Abteilung)
ZSS (RA)	= Zeitschrift der Savigny-Stiftung für Rechtsgeschichte (Romanistische Abteilung)

RICHARD HELMHOLZ and REINHARD ZIMMERMANN

Views of Trust and *Treuhand:* An Introduction

I. Adoption of the Trust in Civil Law Countries

"I do not understand your law of trusts" – so *Otto von Gierke* is said to have remarked about this characteristic English institution. His words were long remembered by the great English legal historian, *F. W. Maitland,* who quoted them more than once[1]. According to this view – the traditional view and probably still the prevailing one – the trust is a distinctive institution of Anglo-American law[2]. It is a special child of the English common law. Nothing like it occurred elsewhere.

In *Maitland's* hands, *Gierke's* puzzlement about the trust became an example, and eventually a symbol, of a wall of incomprehension that separated the English common law from the law of the Continent. Indeed trusts were only the most dramatic example of a quite fundamental divide. No matter the possible coincidence in origins of the Germanic *Salmann* and the English feoffee to uses, trusts were strange creatures to lawyers versed in the civil law. *Maitland* concluded that trusts always required substantial modification, as well as an extended period of adjustment, whenever they were taken over into a civilian legal regime.

Maitland would have been surprised to find that in recent times the trust has been adopted in many civil law countries, and apparently without fundamental difficulty. The perceived adaptability of this institution to meet so many different needs has caused it to burst the bounds of whatever geographical isolation it once

---

1 *F. W. Maitland,* The Unincorporate Body, in: H. A. L. Fisher (ed.), The Collected Papers of Frederic William Maitland, vol. 3, 1911, p. 272. In *F. W. Maitland,* Equity, 1909, p. 23, the same remark is given as " 'I can't understand your trust', said *Gierke* to me".

2 *W. W. Buckland, Arnold D. McNair,* Roman Law and Common Law: A Comparison in Outline, 2nd ed. by *F. H. Lawson,* 1965, p. 177: "It has long been recognised that the trust is not derived from Roman law, nor has Roman law influenced its development to any extent". The trust is described as a distinctive feature ("stiltypisches Institut") of the English common law in: *Konrad Zweigert, Hein Kötz,* Einführung in die Rechtsvergleichung, 3rd ed., 1996, pp. 71, 186. It should be noted, however, that only two brief remarks have remained of what once (*Konrad Zweigert, Hein Kötz,* Einführung in die Rechtsvergleichung, 1st ed., 1971, pp. 328 ff.) constituted an entire chapter. Both the concept of "distinctive features" and the notion of "legal families" (that can be characterized with reference to their "distinctive features") seem to be regarded as more problematic today than in the 1970s. For discussion, see *Hein Kötz,* Abschied von der Rechtskreislehre?, ZEuP 6 (1998) 493 ff.

suffered. Trusts have been taken up widely[3]. For the most part this has occurred by the familiar process of purposeful reception or transplantation. Civil law countries have sought to incorporate the English trust into their own legal systems.

Perhaps the most conspicuous means of adopting the English trust is the invitation contained in the Hague Convention on Private International Law in 1985[4]. The Convention declared that trusts created in accordance with its terms were to be recognized and protected by all signatory states[5]. Trust property was to be treated as a separate fund and "placed under the control of a trustee for the benefit of a beneficiary or for a specified purpose"[6]. By January 1998, Italy and the Netherlands were the only civil law countries to have fully ratified the Convention[7]. It has received an enthusiastic welcome there, however[8], and other countries have given it preliminary assent[9].

---

3 For a review of the overall situation, current as of 1982, see: *Adair Dyer, Hans van Loon,* Report on Trusts and Analogous Institutions, in: Conférence de La Haye de droit international privé, Actes et documents de la Quinzième session 8 au 20 octobre 1984, vol. 2: Trust, 1985, pp. 26 ff. See generally: the contributions in J. Herbots, D. Philippe (eds.), Le trust et la fiducie, implications pratiques, 1997; *Antonio Gambaro,* Trust in Continental Europe, in: Alfredo Mordechai Rabello (ed.), Aequitas and Equity, 1997, pp. 777 ff.; *Donovan W. M. Waters,* The Institution of the Trust in Civil and Common Law, in: Recueil des cours: Collected Courses of the Hague Academy of International Law, vol. 252, 1995, pp. 113 ff.; W. A. Wilson (ed.), Trusts and Trust-Like Devices, 1981; *William F. Fratcher,* Trust, in: International Encyclopedia of Comparative Law, vol. VI, chapter 11, 1973, nn. 101 ff.; *Christian de Wulf,* The Trust and Corresponding Institutions in the Civil Law, 1965; *Kevin W. Ryan,* The Reception of the Trust in the Civil Law, 1959, pp. 264 ff.

4 Convention on the Law Applicable to Trusts and on their Recognition, 1985, Ch. I, art. 2, in: Hague Conference on Private International Law, Collection of Conventions 1951 - 1988, vol. XXX, pp. 315 ff. For the English and French versions, cf. also RabelsZ 50 (1986) 698 ff.; for the German version, see Praxis des Internationalen Privat- und Verfahrensrechts (IPRax) 1987, 55 ff. or *Heinrich Dörner,* in: Staudinger, Kommentar zum Bürgerlichen Gesetzbuch mit Einführungsgesetz, Einführungsgesetz zum Bürgerlichen Gesetzbuch / IPR, 13. Aufl., 1995, Vorbem. zu Art. 25 f. EGBGB, n. 141.

5 *Loc. cit.,* Ch. III, art. 11.

6 *Loc. cit.,* Ch. I, art. 2.

7 Italy signed the Convention on 1 July 1985, ratified it on 21 February 1990, and it entered into force on 1 January 1992. For the Netherlands, the respective dates are: 1 July 1985 (signature), 28 November 1995 (ratification) and 1 February 1996 (entry into force). Information kindly supplied by the Bureau Permanent de la conférence de la Haye de droit international privé on 4 February 1998.

8 Particularly in Italy; see *Maurizio Lupoi,* Trusts, 1997; Ilaria Beneventi (ed.), I trusts in Italia oggi, 1996. For the Netherlands, where the Convention has only been in force since two years, see the contributions in Frans Sonneveldt, Harrie L. van Mens (eds.), The Trust: Bridge or Abyss Between Common and Civil Law Jurisdictions?, 1992; D. J. Hayton, S.C.J.J. Kortmann *et al.* (ed.), Vertrouwd met de trust, 1996; *Margaretha Elizabeth Koppenol-Laforce,* Het Haagse trustverdrag, 1997.

9 So far, it has been signed by France (26 November 1991) and Luxembourg (1 July 1985); same source of information as in n. 7. Cf. also Table of Signatures and Ratifications of the Hague Convention, (1993) 42 International and Comparative Law Quarterly 650 ff. and (1994) 43 International and Comparative Law Quarterly 654.

The immediate results of the 1985 Convention do not tell the whole story. Other signs of a movement of opinion in the same direction are visible. For example, an International Working Group has been convened by the *Onderzoekcentrum Onderneming & Recht* at the University of Nijmegen to elaborate common principles of European trust law[10]. Moreover, some civilian systems have followed the Convention's lead even without fully ratifying the Hague Convention. Liechtenstein, for example, has received a form of the trust[11]. So has Mexico[12]. The Roman-Dutch law of South Africa has adopted the testamentary trust from English law, changing some of its features in the process[13], and other regimes with "mixed systems" of law – Scotland[14], and Québec[15], for example – have taken the same step. Even

---

10 "Principles of European Trust Law" (unpublished MS.). See generally *Ugo Mattei,* Comparative Law and Economics, 1997, pp. 147 ff. including abundant references to other literature; *Michel Grimaldi, François Barrière,* Trust and Fiducie, in: Towards a European Civil Code, 2nd ed., 1998, pp. 567 ff.

11 Art. 897 PRG, in: Personen und Gesellschaftsrecht mit dem Gesetz über das Treuunternehmen, 1986, p. 331. It reads: "Treuhänder (Trustee oder Salmann) im Sinne dieses Gesetzes ist diejenige Einzelperson, Firma oder Verbandsperson, welcher ein anderer (der Treugeber) bewegliches oder unbewegliches Vermögen oder ein Recht (als Treugut), welcher Art auch immer, mit der Verpflichtung zuwendet, dieses ais Treugut in eigenem Namen als selbständiger Rechtsträger zu Gunsten eines oder mehrerer Dritter (Begünstigter) mit Wirkung gegen jedermann zu verwalten oder zu verwenden". This provision was obviously inspired by the trust; but it attempts to place the institution within the conceptual framework of the civil law. Trustee and beneficiary are not both owners; there is merely an obligation to administer on behalf of the beneficiary. For a detailed doctrinal analysis, see *Harald Bösch,* Die liechtensteinische Treuhänderschaft zwischen trust und Treuhand, 1995, pp. 64 ff. and 246 ff.; *Klaus Biedermann,* The Trust in Liechtenstein Law, trans. *H. Gerald Crossland,* 1984, pp. 59 ff.

12 *Roberto Molina Pasquel,* The Mexican Fideicomiso: The Reception, Evolution and Present Status of the Common Law Trust in a Civil Law Country, (1969) 8 Columbia Journal of Transnational Law 54 ff.; *Lupoi* (n. 8) 358 ff.

13 *Tony Honoré,* Trust, in: Reinhard Zimmermann, Daniel Visser (eds.), Southern Cross: Civil Law and Common Law in South Africa, 1996, pp. 849 ff. For comparison between South African and Scots trust law, see *Tony Honoré,* Obstacles to the Reception of Trust Law?, in: Rabello (n. 3) 793 ff. The standard work on South African trust law is *Tony Honoré, Edwin Cameron,* Honoré's South African Law of Trusts, 4th ed., 1992.

14 See the paper by *George Gretton* in the present volume; cf. also *idem,* Trust and Patrimony, in: Scots Law into the 21st Century: Essays in Honour of W.A. Wilson, 1996, pp. 182 ff. (discussing the various ways of conceptualizing the trust from a civilian point of view); *Daniela Krantz,* Trusts im schottischen Recht, 1997.

15 See the treatment of "fiducie" in arts. 1256 - 1298 of its new code civil, 1994. For comparative analysis, see *Lupoi* (n. 8) 362 f.; *Donovan W. M. Waters,* Unification or Harmonization? Experience with the Trust Concept, in: Conflicts and Harmonization: Mélanges von Overbeck, 1990, pp. 591 ff.; *Justin Thorens,* Le trust de common law dans les systèmes de droit civil et l'arrêt Tucker de la Cour Supreme du Canada, in: Festschrift für Walter J. Habscheid, 1989, pp. 325 ff.; *D. B. Walters,* Analogues of the Trust and of its Constituents in French Law, approached from the Standpoint of Scots and English Law, in: Wilson (n. 3) 124 ff. Louisiana is another interesting case in point; see *Joachim Zekoll,* Zwischen den Welten – Das Privatrecht von Louisiana als europäisch-amerikanische Mischrechtsordnung, in: Reinhard Zimmermann (ed.), Amerikanische Rechtskultur und europäisches Privatrecht, 1995, pp. 28 ff. on the reception of the trust in that state.

France, the civil law system proudest of its independence, has advanced to the point of introducing the *fiducie* into its civil code[16]. A *fiducie* is at least a close cousin of the trust. Forty years ago such a step was regarded by many commentators as utterly impossible[17]. Yet it has happened, and the heavens have not fallen.

II. The Inquiry

These developments make it of both interest and practical significance to ask whether there have been historical connections between the English trust and Continental legal traditions. Is the trust really so alien to the civilian experience, or is there a "common core" that unites them? The aim of the series, Comparative Studies in Continental and Anglo-American Legal History, is to examine questions like this one, and under its auspices, a Working Group was organized to explore the history of the trust. This volume is the result. The authors have examined various aspects of the subject in the hope that they will shed light on the larger inquiry.

Such comparative examination of the history of the law of trusts is not, of course, a wholly new endeavor. Indeed some of the questions addressed by our contributors have been of interest, and have even given rise to sharp dispute, among historians of the law for more than 100 years. About the law of the Middle Ages, for example, it was long ago asked whether the medieval use, the parent or at least a lineal ancestor of the modern English trust, had its origins in the Germanic *Salmann,* or instead in the Roman law's *fideicommissum.*

These debates tended to proceed from premises that have since been discredited: from somewhat dogmatic ideas about the "nature" of Medieval law, from partial views on the phenomenon of the "Reception" of Roman law and also, occasionally, from the unacknowledged desire to see the past in terms of present concerns. Thus,

---

16 The standard work arguing that the institution already existed and still exists in French private law is *Claude Witz,* La fiducie en droit privé français, 1981 (historical analysis nn. 36 ff.; cf. also *Helmut Coing,* Europäisches Privatrecht, vol. II, 1989, pp. 423 f.). A definition of "fiducie" is contained in the draft art. 2062 I code civil: "La fiducie est un contrat par lequel un constituant transfère tout ou partie de ses biens et droits à un fiduciaire qui, tenant ces biens et droits séparés de son patrimoine personnel, agit dans un but déterminé au profit d'un ou plusieurs béneficiaires aux stipulations du contrat". The project has been shelved for some time but it has not been abandoned. See *Claude Witz,* La fiducie-sûreté en droit français: Chronique d'une réforme ajourneé, in: Lebendiges Recht – Von den Sumerern bis zur Gegenwart: Festschrift für Reinhold Trinkner, 1995, pp. 795 ff. and, most recently, *idem,* La fiducie en Europe: France, Suisse, Luxembourg, Allemagne, Liechtenstein. Analyse des lois existantes et des projects en cours, in: Herbots/Philippe (n. 3) 63 ff.; *Grimaldi/Barrière* (n. 10) 567 ff.

17 See *Henri Motulsky,* De l'impossibilité juridique de constituer un "Trust" anglo-saxon sous l'empire de la loi française, Revue critique de droit international 37 (1948) 467. See also *Frans Sonneveldt,* The Trust – An Introduction, in: Sonneveldt/van Mens (n. 8) 13 ff.

it is not surprising that the focus of scholarship on trust and *Treuhand* shifted away from legal history and predominantly adopted either a functional or analytical approach[18]. Believing that the time for a reassessment of the historical evidence has come, and that there is something more to be discovered about this subject, the contributors to this volume came together to investigate several of its aspects. We realized that no comprehensive study of the history of trust law has yet been attempted, and we cannot pretend to have provided one. However, we have found and examined a variety of legal institutions that fit most common definitions of a trust. They shed some new light on old questions.

III. Prior Scholarship

1. England

Before the end of the 19th century, it seems to have been broadly assumed among English lawyers that the origins of the use, ancestor of the trust, by which land was granted to one person to be held for the benefit of another, lay in the Roman law's *fideicommissum.* In his celebrated "Reading on the Statute of Uses", *Sir Francis Bacon* (d. 1626) had asserted the English use's civilian pedigree as a fact[19], and lawyers who came after him found *Bacon's* account of the genesis of the use both convincing and congenial. Of course no one had any direct evidence. Indeed all that existed was evidence of the most circumstantial sort. But the undeniable similarity in the institutions, the common usage of Romano-canonical procedure in the court where trusts found their home, the Court of Chancery, and the references to Roman law that had appeared here and there in the case law[20], all made it seem logical that, in its origins, the English use should have been taken over from the Roman law.

---

[18] Cf., in particular, *Hein Kötz,* Trust und Treuhand: Eine rechtsvergleichende Darstellung des anglo-amerikanischen trust und funktionsverwandter Institute des deutschen Rechts, 1963, taking a strictly functional approach. See also *Vera Bolgár,* Why No Trusts in the Civil Law?, (1953) 2 American Journal of Comparative Law 204 ff. For important modern studies adopting a predominantly functional and / or analytical approach, see the works by *Lupoi* (n. 8) and *Mattei* (n. 10); *Michele Graziadei,* Diritti nell'interesse altrui: Undisclosed agency e trust nell'esperienza giuridica inglese, 1995; *John Langbein,* The Contractarian Basis of the Law of Trusts, (1995) 105 Yale L. J. 625 ff.; *Henry Hansmann, Ugo Mattei,* The Functions of Trust Law: A Comparative Legal and Economic Analysis, (1998) 73 New York University Law Review 434 ff.

[19] *Francis Bacon,* Reading on the Statute of Uses, 1st ed. 1642, in: Law Tracts, London, 1737, pp. 314 ff. See also *Lord Nottingham's* Chancery Cases, no. 77 (1674) (= Selden Society, vol. 73), ed. *D. E. C. Yale,* 1954, 37 - 38: "... in legacies the chancery governs itself by the civil law".

[20] See, e.g., *Attorney General v. Platt,* Finch 221, 23 E.R. 122 (Chan. 1675); *Hicks v. Pendarvis,* 2 Freeman 41, 22 E.R. 1046 (Chan. 1678); *Harvey v. Aston,* 1 Atk. 361, 26 E.R. 364 (Chan. 1737).

Bacon's explanation may also have seemed convincing because it fit the temper of the immediately following centuries, particularly the 18th. Englishmen were used to having their churches made to look like classical temples, and even to seeing statutes of their kings dressed in Roman togas. The classical tastes of the upper classes which prevailed for so long must have made ascription of the English trust's origins to the law of the Romans seem altogether natural.

Whatever the cause, the unanimity and persistence of opinion on the point is quite impressive. *Sir William Blackstone* (d. 1780) concluded that English trusts were "in their original of a nature very similar, or rather exactly the same" as the fiduciary institutions of the Roman law, chiefly the *fideicommissum*[21]. *Sir Geoffrey Gilbert* (d. 1720), prolific treatise writer and chief baron of the Court of the Exchequer, took the view that legacies in wills had themselves originally been *fideicommissa,* going on to describe the English executor as a *fideicommissarius*[22]. *William Cruise* (d. 1824), author of standard works on real property, summed up what was by then the widely accepted position: "The idea of a use and the rules by which it was first regulated, are now generally admitted to have been borrowed by the ecclesiasticks [*sic*] from the *fidei-commissum* of the civil law"[23].

This view of the origins of the use was called into question during the last years of the 19th century[24]. Indeed it was overthrown, and at least a part of the overthrow

21 *William Blackstone,* Commentaries on the Laws of England, 1st ed., vol. 2, 1766, p. 327.

22 *Geoffrey Gilbert,* The History and Practice of the High Court of Chancery, 1st ed. 1756, Washington, D.C., 1874, p. 262. See also *Geoffrey Gilbert,* The Law of Uses and Trusts, London, 1734, p. 3: "The original of uses was from a title under the Civil Law, which allows of an usufructuary possession, distinct from the substance of the thing itself; and 'twas brought over to us from thence by the clergy, who were masters of the civil law". Other examples: *William Nelson* (d. 1653), Lex Testamentaria or a Compendious System of all the Laws of England ... concerning Last Wills and Testaments, London, 1714, p. 157; *Francis S. Sullivan* (d. 1776), Historical Treatise on the Feudal Law and the Constitution and Laws of England, London, 1772, p. 423; *Henry H. (Lord) Kames* (d. 1782), Principles of Equity, Edinburgh, 1760, Book I, Part 3, pp. 168 ff.; *J. H. Thomas* (b. 1788/89), Systematic Arrangement of Lord Coke's First Institute of the Laws of England, Philadelphia, vol. 2, 1836, p. 460.

23 *William Cruise,* An Essay on Uses, Dublin, 1796, p. 3. See also *Joseph Story* (d. 1845), Commentaries on Equity Jurisprudence as administered in England and America, Boston, vol. 2, 1836, § 965: "It is in the highest degree probable, that those Trusts ... were in their origin, derived from the Roman Law"; George Spence (d. 1850), The Equitable Jurisdiction of the Court of Chancery, Philadelphia, 1846, vol. 1, p. 435: "For its [the trust's] source, we must look to the Roman jurisprudence ..."; *John Norton Pomeroy* (d. 1885), A Treatise on Equity Jurisprudence, San Francisco, 1881, vol. 1, p. 31: "[U]ses were derived, with much modification, from the Roman law ..."; *Alfred H. Marsh* (d. 1909), History of the Court of Chancery and of the Rise and Development of the Doctrines of Equity, Toronto, 1890, p. 70: "The principal doctrines so borrowed from the Roman Law and incorporated into the English Equity Jurisprudence, in a more or less modified form, are the doctines relating to trusts ...". See also *Michele Graziadei,* Changing Images of the Law in XIX Century English Legal Thought (The Continental Impulse), in: Mathias Reimann (ed.), The Reception of Continental Ideas in the Common Law World 1820 - 1920 (= Comparative Studies in Continental and Anglo-American Legal History, vol. 17), 1993, pp. 122 ff.

can be attributed to the influence of German scholarship. *O. W. Holmes, Jr.*, author of "The Common Law" (1st ed. 1881) as a young man and later a Justice of the U. S. Supreme Court, seems to have been the initiator in effecting the change. Citing the work on the subject by *Georg Beseler* (d. 1888)[25], *Holmes* concluded that the English trust, like the *Treuhand,* had actually sprung from Germanic roots. He concluded that, "[t]he feoffee to uses of the early English law corresponds point by point to the *Salman* of the early German law"[26].

With remarkable speed, *Holmes'* conclusion became the *communis opinio* among English speaking historians of law. For instance, in 1908 the influential Harvard law professor, *James Barr Ames* (d. 1910), began his essay on the subject by stating, "It may be conceded that the feoffee to uses, down to the beginning of the fifteenth century, was the German Salman or Treuhand under another name"[27]. *Sir William Holdsworth* (d. 1944), author of the standard multi-volume history of English law, adopted only a slightly modified form of this approach[28]. The leading modern American authority on the law of trusts cited *Holmes'* position as the "generally accepted" view, noting that the English use took root from the Germanic institution, but that it developed thereafter along wholly independent lines[29]. The tie to the Roman law tradition, which *Sir Francis Bacon* had asserted centuries before, disappeared very quickly.

In part, its quick disappearance occurred because this newer position's most influential exponent was not *Holmes.* It was *F. W. Maitland,* the English legal historian whose work, now over 100 years old, continues to furnish the starting point for a great deal of our understanding of the history of English law. Like *Holmes, Maitland* was in touch with contemporary German scholarship and, together with

---

24 That Roman law had provided the model for uses was stated to be "the common explanation" in *D. M. Kerly,* An Historical Sketch of the Equitable Jurisdiction of the Court of Chancery, Cambridge, 1890, p. 78. However, he also took note of the (then) new derivation by *O. W. Holmes.* See also *David Johnston,* The Roman Law of Trusts, 1988, pp. 284 ff.

25 *Georg Beseler,* Die Lehre von den Erbverträgen, Göttingen, 1835 - 40, vol. 1, §§ 15 - 16. *Holmes* also cited *Andreas Heusler,* Die Gewere, Weimar, 1872.

26 *O. W. Holmes, Jr.*, Early English Equity, (1885) 1 L.Q.R. 162 ff., revised and reprinted in: Select Essays in Anglo-American Legal History, vol. 2, 1908, pp. 705 ff.

27 *James Barr Ames,* The Origin of Uses and Trusts, (1908) 21 Harvard L. R. 261 ff., at 263, reprinted in: Select Essays (n. 27) vol. 2, 737 ff., at 740.

28 *William Holdsworth,* A History of English Law, 3rd ed., vol. 4, 1945, p. 417: "Though we must look to the Salman or Treuhand for the origin [of the institution], the shape which that idea took in English law is wholly the result of [the manner in which the beneficiary's interest] was protected by the Chancery."

29 *Austin Wakeman Scott,* The Law of Trusts, 3rd ed., 1967, § 29. To the same effect are: *George Gleason Bogert, George Taylor Bogert,* Handbook of the Law of Trusts, 5th ed., 1973, pp. 5 ff.; *George W. Keeton, L. A. Sheridan,* Equity, 1969, pp. 143 ff.; and *T. F. T. Plucknett,* A Concise History of the Common Law, 5th ed., 1956, pp. 575 ff., who rejects any connection with Roman law but notes the existence of parallels between it and English developments.

Holmes, he could say that he had "long been persuaded that every attempt to discover the genesis of our *use* in Roman law breaks down"[30]. *Maitland* was willing to concede the possibility that there had once been "a momentary contact" between the English use and the *ius commune*[31]. However, in his opinion, that contact could only have been a chance encounter and in the end quite unimportant in its consequences. No real relationship therefore existed between the English use and the Continental *fideicommissum.* The institutions had too few features in common. Indeed, here as elsewhere, for *Maitland,* a chasm separated the English common law from the legal systems that prevailed across the Channel[32].

In his fullest treatment of the subject, *Maitland* therefore reached the conclusion that the English trust could only have been "a natural outcome of ancient English elements"[33]. Those elements probably had Germanic roots, but it was in England alone that they flowered. Only there did they give rise to the trust. This was, moreover, a cause for celebration. For him, the trust was "the greatest feat that men of our race [had] performed in the field of jurisprudence"[34]. *Maitland* imagined that the first thing an English lawyer would notice upon perusing the (then) new German Civil Code (BGB) would be the absence in it of a section on the law of trusts[35]. Similarly, he supposed that any Continental lawyer would stand in puzzled amazement before treatises devoted to the English law of trusts. Mutual incomprehension would prevail.

2. Germany

This volume is not limited to German legal thought and institutions. Contributors have taken up aspects of the place of *fiducia* in Italy, France, the Low Countries, and Austria, not to speak of trust-like devices in the *ius commune* more generally. It was, however, among German jurists that the scientific investigation of the nature of trust and *Treuhand* first took place. In turn, they influenced French and Italian lawyers. And of course it was the work of German jurists that *Holmes* and *Maitland* read. It is appropriate, therefore, and indeed almost inevitable, that one should pay particular attention, both here and in the volume's essays, to developments in German scholarship. The rediscovery of the subject in modern German

30 *F. W. Maitland,* The Origin of Uses, (1894) 8 Harvard L. R. 127, reprinted in: Collected Papers (n. 1) vol. 2, 1911, 403.

31 *Maitland,* (1894) 8 Harvard L. R. 136; Collected Papers (n. 1) 416.

32 See *R. H. Helmholz,* The Learned Laws in "Pollock and Maitland", in: John Hudson (ed.), The History of English Law: Centenary Essays on "Pollock and Maitland" (= Proceedings of the British Academy, vol. 89), 1996, pp. 153 ff.

33 *Maitland,* Equity (n. 1) 6.

34 From a letter to John Chipman Gray (15 November 1903), in: C. H. S. Fifoot (ed.), The Letters of Frederic William Maitland, 1965, no. 366.

35 *Idem,* Trust and Corporation, in: Collected Papers (n. 1) vol. 2, 323.

legal literature[36], and in particular the strengthening of the position of the *Treugeber* as against third parties to the point where it is possible to describe his rights as "quasi-dinglich"[37], provides an additional reason for devoting the closest attention to German thought on the subject.

Such an investigation of the place of the trust (or of the principles inherent in *fiducia)* in Germany contains parallels with the English experience in some respects, but it also responded to a more fundamental divide in German historiography – that between the Germanist and the Romanist schools. This subject was most commonly approached as one part of the attempt to discover the roots of the German *Treuhand*[38]. Was it, at bottom, a Germanic institution, or did its features derive from Roman law? The depth of feeling over this question – extending to the point where there occurred what can be called a "Wettstreit zwischen Pandektisten und Germanisten"[39], and which of course extended well beyond the *Treuhand* – has marked the course of German legal scholarship to this day.

Some of this scholarship, particularly the more recent, has taken a more nuanced position. It is now more generally recognized that the lack of systematic treatment among jurists during the Middle Ages makes it difficult, even impossible, to speak with assurance about the *Treuhand's* origins. A somewhat larger role would today probably be given to the role played by the law of the Church in the development of trust-like institutions, and more would be made of the importance of customary law and legal practice as against the exclusive claims of legal dogmatics. It is even possible to speak of a certain *Verbindung* between Germanic institutions and principles drawn from the Romanists' *fiducia*[40]. Such a position would not have seemed possible 100 years ago.

German scholars have also long taken note of the English trust, just as *Maitland* and others paid attention to Germanic institutions. When the subject of the origins

---

36 *Helmut Coing,* Die Treuhand kraft privaten Rechtsgeschäfts, 1973; *Martin Henssler,* Treuhandgeschäft – Dogmatik und Wirklichkeit, AcP 196 (1996) 37 ff.; *Stefan Grundmann,* Der Treuhandvertrag im System des deutschen Zivilrechts, 1997; for Austria, see Peter Apathy (ed.), Die Treuhandschaft, 1995.

37 This is significant where the *Treuhänder* becomes insolvent or where his creditors seek to reach the assets held in a fiduciary capacity. In the first case, the *Treugeber* may demand segregation of "his" property in terms of § 43 Insolvency Act and in the second case the *Treugeber* may avail himself of § 771 Code of Civil Procedure on the basis of having a right over the object "which prevents its alienation". It does not, however, prevent the *Treuhänder* from transferring the goods to a third party. For an overview, see *Helmut Koziol,* Grundlagen und Streitfragen der Gläubigeranfechtung, 1991, pp. 7, 46 f., 53; *Henssler* (n. 36) 47 ff.; *Joachim Gernhuber,* Die fiduziarische Treuhand, Juristische Schulung 1988, 355 ff.; as well as the analysis by *Stefan Grundmann* in the present volume.

38 *Coing* (n. 36) 28 ff.; *idem,* Die Treuhandtheorie als Beispiel der geschichtlichen Dogmatik des 19. Jahrhunderts, RabelsZ 37 (1973) 202 ff.

39 *Karl Otto Scherner,* Treuhand, in: Handwörterbuch zur deutschen Rechtsgeschichte, 34th part, 1992, col. 343.

40 See the essay by *Sibylle Hofer* in this volume, at II. 2 (b).

of the *Treuhand* was first taken up in earnest in Germany during the 19th century, parallels between the English trust and the *Salmann* or *Treuhand* were immediately noticed. In broad outline, the two looked alike. Both embodied a fiduciary relationship in which one person held property for the benefit of another. Complete identity there may not have been, but the *Treuhand* served many of the same purposes that the English trust did. And, like the trust, it had assumed a variety of forms depending on what those specific purposes happened to be.

Reasons for comparing the two therefore seemed self-evident. If the two institutions were related, for example, the Germanistic School could find support for its position in the existence of the trust in England despite the absence of any real reception of Roman law there[41]. This would be strong evidence that the *Treuhand* itself had existed naturally before the Reception of Roman law in Germany. On the other hand, if the English use had itself felt the shaping hand of Roman law, this would be an argument in favor of the Romanist school. It would make it more likely that the *Treuhand* had sprung from and been nourished by civilian soil.

3. The Contemporary Situation

So has the subject of this volume remained controversial. Despite movement towards a more nuanced position, the question has not disappeared. On the English side, a few recent students of the subject have revived a new form of the English position prevalent in the 18th century, suggesting that the trust belongs within the ambit of the European *ius commune*[42]. Others, and probably the majority, continue to regard the trust as an institution typical of an insular English tradition[43]. Although they acknowledge that the trust has become a part of the law in many lands outside the common law world, they none the less insist that such trusts sit "like a cuckoo in the nest of the Civil Law" – interlopers at best, and certainly no natural dwellers there[44].

Looking at Continental developments, many scholars, English or Continental, would very likely agree that there is no *necessary* opposition between trust and

---

41 See *Graziadei* (n. 23) 146 ff.

42 *H. Patrick Glenn*, Le trust et le jus commune, in: Pierre Legrand (ed.), Common Law d'un siècle l'autre, 1992, pp. 87 ff., also published in an English version in: Aequitas and Equity (n. 1) 775 ff.; *Stephen W. DeVine*, The Franciscan Friars, the Feoffment to Uses, and Canonical Theories of Property Enjoyment before 1535, (1989) 10 J.L.H. 1 ff., 14; *Vincert R. Vasey*, Fideicommissa and Uses: the Clerical Connection Revisited, (1982) 42 The Jurist 1 ff.

43 See e.g., from an English perspective, *J. M. W. Bean*, The Decline of English Feudalism, 1215 - 1540, 1968, pp. 126 ff. See also *James Gordley*, Common law und civil law: eine überholte Unterscheidung, ZEuP 1 (1993) 516, where the trust is described as an exception to the vanishing structural differences between the two "families of law". The subject of origins is approached with characteristic circumspection by *William F. Fratcher* (n. 3) nn. 7 ff.

44 *Maurice Sheldon Amos*, The Common Law and the Civil Law in the British Commonwealth of Nations, (1937) 50 Harvard L.R. 1249 ff., at 1264.

Treuhand. They recognize the parallels that exist, as they recognize regional and temporal variations within civilian systems themselves. Variations between civilian regimes have long been a fact of life, and they have not prevented correspondence[45]. However, it is another matter to decide whether there has been anything more than the sort of parallel that exists whenever similar social needs and roughly analogous legal problems come together. And whether a tie can be made from the English trust to the traditions of the *ius commune* remains a difficult question. That is the question we hope the papers in this volume will help answer. At least it is the question we have sought to address.

IV. The Problem of Definition

Much, of course, depends upon definition. Just what is a trust? *Maitland* wrestled with the question[46], and German scholars have themselves found that defining *Treuhand* is a task not free from ambiguity[47]. The question is important[48]. Some definition is required; otherwise a trust will be indistinguishable from a bailment or an agency relationship. Too strict a definition, however, will inevitably exclude all possibility of establishing intellectual relationships between trust-like institutions across legal and geographical boundaries. That would not be realistic. Absorption of an institution or a legal rule from without has undeniably occurred, and it virtually always changes the institution or legal rule itself. Such changes should not keep us from seeing the realities.

Today English law assumes that the trust requires that legal ownership of the trust property be vested in the trustee. A divided title between beneficiary and trustee appears to some to constitute the essence of the trust[49], and Anglo-American lawyers have continued to speak easily of legal title and equitable title long after the amalgamation of legal and equitable jurisdictions[50]. For purposes of this volume,

45 E.g. *Lupoi* (n. 8) 13 ff. and *passim; Pierre Lepaulle,* Civil Law Substitutes for Trusts, (1927) 36 Yale L.J. 1126 ff.

46 *F. W. Maitland,* Equity (n. 1) 43: "But I know not where to find an authoritative definition".

47 See, e.g. *Henssler* (n. 36) 41 ff.

48 The problem is discussed in *Donovan W. M. Waters* (n. 3) 123.

49 Professor *Waters* takes this view; for example, see *idem* (n. 43) 448: "[O]nce that notion of a person 'owning' – or being vested with title – is gone, the trust as the common law now knows it is also gone".

50 For criticism see, in particular, section I. of *George Gretton's* contribution to the present volume. The main reason why civil lawyers find it difficult to understand the trust is that it straddles the civilian categories of property and contract; see, e.g. *Maitland,* in: Collected Papers (n. 1) 323 ff. However, the position of a modern German *Treugeber,* at least in certain respects, looks like a real right (see *supra,* n. 37). At the same time, attempts have been made to argue for the primacy of the contractual model in explaining trust law; see, especially, *Langbein,* (1995) 105 Yale L.J. 625 ff.; and "[w]hat is explicable in contractual terms is

however, we have purposely avoided a definition tied to the modern English trust. In our view, the English trust has itself been a product of evolution. It was a practical device, evolved out of the needs of clients, not fixed by its modern definition.

Too narrow a definition would, moreover, be false to the protean nature of institutions that have always been acknowledged to be trusts. It would be false to the flexible nature of the institutions and to the wide variety of purposes the trust and *Treuhand* have served[51]. It would, for instance, preclude the possibility of influence simply because the trust was so closely connected in England with the equitable jurisdiction of the Court of Chancery, a court that had no exact analogue on the Continent[52]. Moreover, within English law itself, adopting too narrow a definition of trusts would make it difficult to find any relationship between a charitable trust and the dynastic trust that was part of a family settlement. The latter required that beneficiaries be named; the former did not. Yet we know that a connection between them did exist.

This Working Group has therefore thought it right to adopt a relatively general definition. Such a choice accords with that repeatedly made by most modern writers.[53] It is essentially the approach adopted by *Helmut Coing*[54]. It is at one in its major particulars with the definition adopted by the American Restatement of Trusts[55], and also with the Hague Convention on Private International Law in 1985[56]. Individual contributors to the volume have added to or subtracted from this

---

already close to what is comprehensible in civilian ones" (*David Johnston* in his review of *Graziadei's* book (n. 18), 1998 Cambridge Law Journal 217).

51 For details concerning the flexibility of the trust, see *Kötz* (n. 18) 38 ff.; *Georg Wittuhn*, Das internationale Privatrecht des trust, 1987, pp. 14 ff.; *Hayton*, Trusts, in: Hayton / Kortmann (n. 8) 32 ff.; and see the 26 different purposes listed by *Fratcher* (n. 3) n. 1 as well as the remark by *Lepaulle*, (1927) 36 Yale L.J. 1126: "[Trusts] are like those extraordinary drugs curing at the same time toothache, sprained ankles, and baldness sold by peddlers on the Paris boulevards". On commercial trusts, see John H. Langbein, The Secret Life of the Trust: The Trust as an Instrument of Commerce, (1997) 107 Yale L.J. 165 ff. For the *Treuhand*, see *Coing* (n. 36) 54 ff.; *Henssler* (n. 36) 38 ff.; *Grundmann* (n. 36) 11 ff.

52 See *Margaret Avery*, An Evaluation of the Effectiveness of the Court of Chancery under the Lancastrian Kings, (1970) 86 L.Q.R. 84 ff.; *Charles J. Reid, Jr.*, The Seventeenth-Century Revolution in the English Land Law, (1995) 43 Cleveland State Law Review 281 ff.

53 See *Bogert/Bogert* (n. 29) § 1: "A trust may be defined as a fiduciary relationship in which one person holds a property interest subject to an equitable obligation to keep or use that interest for the benefit of another". See also *David Hayton*, The Irreducible Core Content of Trusteeship, in: A. J. Oakley (ed.), Trends in Contemporary Trust Law, 1996, p. 47. The International Working Group on Trusts (n. 10) takes a very similar line.

54 *Helmut Coing* (n. 36) 1 ff.

55 Restatement (Third) of the Law, 1996, Trusts § 2: "A trust ... is a fiduciary relationship with respect to property, arising as a result of a manifestation of an intention to create that relationship and subjecting the person who holds title to the property to duties to deal with it for the benefit of charity or for one or more persons, at least one of whom is not the sole trustee".

56 Convention on the Law Applicable to Trusts and on their Recognition (1985) (n. 4) 315: "For the purposes of this Convention, the term 'trust' refers to the legal relationships

definition, according to the special needs of their subject. But they have made their exceptions clear.

With these exceptions, a trust is defined in this volume as a relationship in which one or more persons (the trustees) hold property, but administer it either for the benefit of someone else (the beneficiary)[57] or to further some particular purpose. No special terminology is required, as long as the substance is present. Properly speaking, the relationship must have more than a momentary duration, for otherwise it serves a purely remedial purpose. Some specific asset (real property or chattels) is also required before one can speak of a trust; an obligation to act in the interests of another person may be an agency relationship or even a partnership. A trust must have a lawful purpose, though lawful purposes may be widely conceived and may vary over time. There must also be a remedy against the trustee for breach of his duties as a fiduciary. Under the definition adopted, a moral duty to hold property for another does not qualify as a trust unless there is a realistic way of enforcing it. Finally, it may be useful to state that the object of our investigations has been the express trust, not the constructive or the resulting trust[58]. These are remedial devices.

V. The Contributions

The editors of this volume have made no attempt to require contributors to toe a party line, and they have not toed one. This is a series of comparative studies, and the first duty of any such series is to present the evidence from which legitimate comparisons can be drawn. The editors have therefore asked the contributors to produce a paper that would contain their own research on the subject of trusts, *fiducia,* or *Treuhand,* and then to consider what they had discovered in the light of

---

created – *inter vivos* or on death – by a person, the settlor, when assets have been placed under the control of a trustee for the benefit of a beneficiary or for a specified purpose.

A trust has the following characteristics –

a) the assets constitute a separate fund and are not a part of the trustee's own estate;
b) title to the trust assets stands in the name of the trustee or in the name of another person on behalf of the trustee;
c) the trustee has the power and the duty, in respect of which he is accountable, to manage, employ or dispose of the assets in accordance with the terms of the trust and the special duties imposed upon him by law".

57 See also the treatment and authorities cited by *Fratcher* (n. 3) nn. 2 ff.

58 A constructive trust takes the title to property from a person who would be unjustly enriched if he were allowed to retain it and transfers it to the person wrongly deprived of it. A resulting trust comes into being when an express trust fails or is incomplete; commonly it exists in favor of the settlor and requires that the trustee hold for his benefit or reconvey the property to him. See *Austin Wakeman Scott,* Abridgment of the Law of Trusts, 1960, §§ 404 ff. and 460 ff.; *Lupoi* (n. 8) 21 ff. For a recent analysis of constructive trusts, from the Scottish point of view, see *George Gretton,* Constructive Trusts, (1997) 1 Edinburgh Law Review 281 ff., 408 ff. On resulting trusts, see *Robert Chambers,* Resulting Trusts, 1997.

the comparative aims of the series. Accordingly, although there are links between the contributions in this volume – many of them noted in the contributions themselves – the authors do not play upon a single note.

Characteristic features of German and English scholarship in legal history are readily apparent in the essays. The historians of the common law begin with the cases. The historians of German law begin with legal dogmatics. Of course there are points of contact between these approaches. Theories have practical consequences. Cases make use of legal rules. The intersections should become apparent. There is, however, more in the way of contact between them than these necessary points of intersection. The contributions are linked by at least four common themes. These themes in turn link Anglo-American legal development with the civilian tradition. Variations on them recur thoughout the contributions.

1. The Slow Emergence of the Concept of the Trust

Both on the Continent and in England, the existence of trusts antedates by centuries the concept of the trust. "Trusts are various," concludes *Neil Jones* in discussing the characteristics of the English trust in the 16th and 17th centuries, adding that the word "trust" is itself rather like a chameleon, changing its colors to fit its environment[59]. The same comment might easily have been made about the *fiducia* in Italy or France, or even the *Treuhand* in Germany. For example, *Bartolus* and *Baldus,* the greatest of the medieval civilians, made use of the idea of *fiducia* to solve particular legal problems, but to all appearances they had no fixed legal category in their minds when they did so[60]. That approach had a long life.

No titles devoted explicitly to *fiducia* appeared in either the Justinianic compilations of Roman law or the medieval *Corpus iuris canonici.* In a legal tradition based upon texts, this absence discouraged the creation of a distinct concept of the trust. It was legal practice, more than the schools, that provided the impetus for development of trust-like devices. As a result, it is natural to find that the legal elements of many trust-like institutions in Germany "seem strangely intertwined" with each other when they are examined closely[61]. Conceptual clarity was not the starting point. Likewise, the exact legal position of the testamentary executor, an obvious fiduciary in some sense, was "not easy to conceptualize before the modern era"[62]. There was no trust concept, although there were trusts.

59 See the paper by *Neil Jones* in this volume, at II.

60 See the contribution by *Michele Graziadei* in this volume: see also *Maria Carla Zorzoli,* Della famiglia e del suo patrimonio: riflessioni sull'uso del fedecommesso in Lombardia tra cinque e seicento, in: Lloyd Bonfield (ed.), Marriage, Property, and Succession (= Comparative Studies in Continental and Anglo-American Legal History, vol. 10), 1992, pp. 155 ff.

61 See the paper by *Stefan Grundmann* in this collection, in the second paragraph of his introduction.

62 See the chapter by *Reinhard Zimmermann* in this volume, at VI. 1.

Only in the 19th century did a concerted effort to extract a true law of trusts from a myriad of individual trust-like devices occur. It is surprising to discover that this occurred in England, as it did in Germany, although there was less contention and less conscious innovation involved among English lawyers. In any event, the idea that there was *a* law of trusts in England, rather than separate legal entities – executors, feoffees to uses, custodians of charities, and guardians of minors – emerged slowly. It was only in the 19th century that treatises devoted to the trust as a separate body of law began to be written[63]. Only then did what now appear to be basic theoretical questions, such as determining the exact nature of the beneficiary's interest in a trust, need finally to be confronted.

2. Mining the Civilian Tradition

Most of the trust-like devices that existed for so long in England and on the Continent depended in some measure upon Roman law. This is perhaps the most surprising theme of parallel development in the contributions to this volume. Continental legal historians are surprised to find that, quite apart from the question of the trust's origins, the *ius commune* played a significant part in the development of the English trust. English legal historians are surprised to find that trust-like institutions, making use of civilian sources, were in place on the Continent, and that they were not simply the *fideicommissa* of the Roman law. In both legal arenas, similar institutions drew from Roman law sources, even though Roman law itself contained no concept of the trust.

This process of selection, making use of what seem to have been quite unpromising sources, happened from a very early date. The *fideicommissum* was given an expanded interpretation by the Roman jurists themselves, and at least some of the potentialities of the law of *fiducia* were exploited in the law of testaments[64]. Canon law also played a part in the medieval development. Where the interests of the Church coincided with the desirability of fiduciary responsibility – a common enough situation – trust-like institutions arose to meet the need. Men administered property of the Church under principles drawn from the law of *fiducia.* The Canon law itself had no proper law of trusts, but it did contain texts and principles from which rules useful in creating trust-like institutions could be fashioned.

The resources of the Roman and Canon laws were thus a continuing factor in the creation and regulation of trusts. In medieval Italy, a new doctrine of *fiducia* was "built upon Roman law sources" without being controlled by them[65]. This was

---

63 See *Waters* (n. 3) 207 ff.

64 See, e.g., *Philippe Godding,* Le droit au service du patrimoine familial: les Pays-Bas méridionaux (12e-18e siècles), in: Bonfield (n. 60) 15 ff.; *Robert Feenstra,* Family, Property and Succession in the Province of Holland during the sixteenth, seventeenth and eighteenth centuries, in: Bonfield (n. 60) 37 ff.

65 See the chapter by *Michele Graziadei* in this volume, at III.

a pattern. Some of this was pure "gap-filling" to meet the needs of legal practice. Customary law also played an important part. But the resources of the *ius commune* proved useful in a wide variety of circumstances, influencing the interpretation of statutes and documents even when they were not the primary source. The identical idea took differing forms, depending upon local needs and conditions, without ceasing to be linked to the texts that gave it life[66].

3. Circumventing Legal Restrictions

When English lawyers say that the parents of the trust are fraud and fear[67], they are (perhaps unknowingly) repeating a maxim of great antiquity. Some form of the maxim goes back at least to the 4th century[68], and it captures a continuing feature of the history of the trust, one that is common to both Anglo-American and Continental law. Put more neutrally, the maxim means that trusts have made it possible lawfully to accomplish objectives that could not be achieved otherwise. Avoiding taxes and circumventing restrictive rules of the law of succession, for instance, may be said to entail fraud in one sense. They permit violation of a positive law. But there is nothing necessarily unethical or immoral about either goal. The example of the Franciscans and other religious orders, for whom the use or trust became a legal way of controlling enough property to sustain a spiritual life for their followers, is perhaps the most striking example. A "fraud" on the principles of *St. Francis* only in the minds of the most zealous of his followers, such trust-like devices permitted realization of a goal most observers regarded as entirely admirable. The examples of the trust-like devices grouped under the concept of *fiduziarische Rechtsgeschäfte*[69] perhaps skate a little closer to the line, but in principle they too were simply ways to avoid inconveniences in existing law.

Whatever one's assessment of the merits, it is certain that trust-like devices were commonly used in similar ways to circumvent existing legal restrictions both in England and on the Continent. This is evident above all in the law of testamentary succession. The pattern is the same. Jurists in Germany, France or Italy would have recognized what English lawyers were doing in employing uses to avoid the common law's rules against freedom of testation or in order to exclude the liability of the heir to pay the father's debts. At least they would have recognized the purpose once someone had explained to them the basic features of English inheritance law. Similarly, English lawyers would have recognized quite well what was being done

---

66 See, e.g., *David Johnston,* The Renewal of the Old, (1997) 56 Cambridge Law Journal 80 ff.

67 So stated by *Atkyns J.* in *Attorney General v. Sandres,* Hard. 488 (491), 145 E.R. 563 (Exchequer, 1668).

68 *Jerome,* Epistolae 52, 6, cited in *David Johnston's* chapter in this book, at II. 1.

69 The concept was devised by *Ferdinand Regelsberger,* Zwei Beiträge zur Lehre von der Cession, AcP 63 (1880) 157 ff. See also *Helmut Coing* (n. 36) 35 ff.

when the law of *fiducia* was used to circumvent the heir's ability to subtract the *quarta Trebellianica.* At least they would have recognized it once someone had explained to them what the *quarta Trebellianica* was.

4. Trust Purposes

It is remarkable how close a coincidence in trust purposes is revealed by the early evidence[70]. Quite apart from the pattern of circumventing inconvenient restrictions in the law, the typical beneficiaries of trusts prove to have been remarkably alike in England and on the Continent. This does not, of course, prove the existence of a legal connection. A distinction must be drawn between parallel development and the reception of legal rules and ideas. The social, religious, and economic conditions common to medieval and early modern Europe gave rise to similar conditions encouraging men and women to entrust their property to third parties for the benefit of their families or for charitable purposes. None the less, the factual coincidence in trust purposes does show that, in this area, the barriers between the legal systems were not high. If they had discussed the reasons for employing trust-like devices, English and Continental lawyers would have understood one another.

The frequent use of trusts in order to pass family property from one generation to the next upon terms different from those established by the customary law of succession has just been noted. It was a common feature wherever these devices were used, and it linked English with Continental legal practice[71]. A second example is the trust for the benefit of the poor and disadvantaged. Either in a formal sense of the charitable foundation or in less formal institutions set up to benefit vulnerable individuals, the trust form was particularly appropriate for charitable purposes broadly defined. With reason were the earliest English statutes on the subject called statutes of "charitable uses"[72]. Using different words, one finds substantially identical trust-like devices created to give effect to gifts *ad pias causas* on the Continent. It is therefore only to be expected that the institution of the trust

70 See, e.g., *Karl Otto Scherner's* paper in this volume, at V.

71 These devices are explored, in greater detail, in the contributions to vol. 10 of this series, edited by Lloyd Bonfield (n.60). The standard treatise on family settlement in the German territories was *Philipp Knipschildt,* Tractatus de Fideicommissis Familiarum Nobilium, von Stamm-Gütern, 1626. It is analysed by *Klaus Luig* in his contribution to the present volume. On the relationship between family settlements in Great Britain and on the Continent, see *Luig's* paper, at I. 2 and now also *Jörn Eckert,* Use, Trust, Strict Settlement – Fideikommißähnliche Bindungen des Grundbesitzes in England, in: Wirkungen europäischer Rechtskultur: Festschrift für Karl Kroeschell, 1997, pp. 187 ff. On the abolition of the family settlements in Germany, see the very comprehensive (and comparative) study by *Jörn Eckert,* Der Kampf um die Familienfideikommisse in Deutschland, 1992.

72 See the discussion in *Gareth Jones,* History of the Law of Charity 1532 - 1827, 1969, 22 ff.

should figure in the evidence relating to charitable gifts in so many of the essays in this volume. It is equally worthy of note that trust-like devices established for the benefit of women, minor children, and others without full legal capacity – trusts that would not fully qualify as charitable – should appear in the historical record in so many different places.

VI. A Final Word

The question posed at the start of this Introduction was whether historical connections can be drawn between the English trust and Continental legal traditions. The editors conclude that they can. More than simple parallels reflecting similar social conditions are evident in the history of *fiducia*. The common features and the common sources evident on both sides of the Channel mean that no wall of incomprehension separated the English trust from analogous institutions on the Continent. On this account *Otto von Gierke's* oft quoted words give a misleading impression.

It does seem undeniable, and it should be stated, that there was no exact equivalent to the English use or trust in the early historical record of Continental law[73]. The English division between legal title and equitable title, each the source of rights enforceable in different courts and each eventually a fundamental feature of English trust law, was no part of Continental jurisprudence[74]. But does this require us to suppose that the English trust would have been incomprehensible to a civilian? We do not think so. Continental jurisprudence relating to *fiducia* was not homogeneous in itself, but the differences in detail did not present insuperable obstacles to understanding and even to influence. So it was with trust and *Treuhand*. If, as seems to be happening today, modern European law incorporates the trust, there is much to suggest that it will be building upon historical foundations.

73 *Helmut Coing* (n. 36) 11 ff.

74 Even though, as *Robert Feenstra* points out in his contribution to this volume (*sub* I), "[t]his difference is not essential from an historical point of view: the exclusion of dual ownership has not always been a part of Continental law"; cf. also *Bolgar*, (1953) 2 American Journal of Comparative Law 204 ff.

DAVID JOHNSTON

Trusts and Trust-like Devices in Roman Law

I. Introduction

It is a common-place that Roman law and the civil systems which remain faithful to it do not know the trust. This paper does not challenge that view: there does not appear to be a concept "the trust" in Roman law. Although it is not necessary here to consider the question of defining "the trust" or "trust-like devices"[1], at the outset it may be said that the central feature of Roman trust-like devices is that property is committed or entrusted by one person to another, who is under a duty to convey it, to hold it or to apply it for the benefit of a person other than himself. Just as there are signs in Roman law of trust-like devices, so too there are signs of trustee-like persons.

The subject of trust-like devices in Roman law can be approached in two different ways. The first is as an account of how the Romans actually employed them: that would amount principally to a record of Roman legal history. The second approach is to provide an account of the structure and the central features of such devices: that would illustrate what the Roman sources offered by way of example and inspiration to the jurists of later generations. In this paper some attention is paid to each of these approaches, but the second is the more central concern. The next section deals with the various legal institutions which in one way or another resemble trusts. For reasons which will become obvious, most attention is devoted to the *fideicommissum*. There are, however, other legal institutions such as *fiducia* which require attention. The third section covers the same ground in relation to trustees. The final section does no more than sum up the most material similarities and differences which emerge from the discussion.

II. Trust-like Devices

1. *Fideicommissum*

The *fideicommissum* was a method of transferring property on death. Instead of making a legacy of a thing directly to an intended beneficiary, a testator could en-

---

1 For this, see the introduction to this volume.

trust (*committere)* to the faith (*fides)* of an intermediary, most often his heir, that property should be conveyed to the beneficiary[2]. It is not unlikely that as a legal institution the *fideicommissum* developed out of the practice of death-bed *commendatio,* in which a person entrusted his family or property to the protection of others after his death[3]. *Commendatio* created a purely moral obligation. Initially too *fideicommissa* were not recognized by the law, and the only entitlement the beneficiary had was a moral one which was not enforceable in the courts. That changed when the emperor *Augustus* introduced a jurisdiction charged with the enforcement of such trusts[4]; initially it was the consuls, magistrates who did not otherwise normally concern themselves with matters of civil litigation, who were responsible for this jurisdiction. Later on, a special praetor (*praetor fideicommissarius)* performed the same role[5]. An institution which had depended on *fides* and on *amicitia* came to depend on legal obligation.

The *fideicommissum,* as a newcomer to the Roman legal order, enjoyed certain freedoms which the legacy did not. In the days when it had generated a purely moral obligation, the *fideicommissum* had clearly been used to transfer property to beneficiaries who as a matter of civil law were disqualified from receiving legacies. Although it is hard to believe that this freedom remained wholly untrammelled once *fideicommissa* were actionable, there is none the less evidence of their being used for avoidance of civil law restrictions; and the series of measures closing loopholes plainly confirms the – albeit diminishing – utility of the *fideicommissum* for getting round inconvenient rules of civil law[6]. Even as late as *Jerome,* the *fideicommissum* retained its reputation as a technique for avoidance: he wrote "by *fideicommissa* we cheat the law"[7].

Although the *fideicommissum* remained an institution of the law of succession, available only for dispositions *mortis causa,* it soon expanded its role beyond that of an "indirect legacy" to a more significant case: a *fideicommissum* of the whole inheritance received by the heir, or a part of it. The heir therefore acquired the inheritance, but was under a duty imposed by the *fideicommissum* to make it over to a third person. It is important to note that this possibility was not restricted to the heir under a will, since *fideicommissa* were capable also of operating on intestacy[8]. The full potential of this liberation of the *fideicommissum* from the confines of a

---

2 *Gai.* Inst. I, 248, 260; *W. W. Buckland,* Textbook of Roman Law, 3rd ed. by *P. Stein,* Cambridge, 1963, pp. 353 ff.

3 See *D. Johnston,* The Roman Law of Trusts, Oxford, 1988, pp. 22 ff.; for the canonistic practice of *commendatio,* see the paper by *Herman* in the present volume.

4 *Just.* Inst. II, 23.1; see *Johnston* (n. 3) 9, 21 ff., 271 ff.

5 *Johnston* (n. 3) 4, 222: I take the opportunity to correct a statement on p. 4 of the book which may be misleading: it is the *praetor fideicommissarius,* who had jurisdiction over trusts, rather than the urban praetor, who presided in a special private-law jurisdiction.

6 *Johnston* (n. 3) 29 ff.

7 *Jerome,* Epistolae 52, 6: "per fideicommissa legibus inludimus".

8 *Johnston* (n. 3) 117 ff., 213.

will was never realized in Roman times: it never found a place in the Roman law of property or obligations; and it remained in the law of succession, restricted to dispositions *mortis causa*. But that restriction was one of practice or mere traditionalism; it did not rest on any compelling legal principle.

(a) Structure

The structure of the *fideicommissum* is tripartite: the parties to the arrangement are the truster or settlor; the trustee or *fiduciarius;* and the beneficiary or *fideicommissarius*. This terminology finds certain resonances in the later legal tradition[9]. Once the *fideicommissum* has become operative on the death of the settlor, it is the fiduciary, the trustee, who is the owner of the property affected. Roman law does not recognize a division of ownership into legal and equitable interests: here quite simply, the trustee, *fiduciarius,* is the owner[10]. It follows that the beneficiary cannot enforce the trust by using the proprietary remedy of *vindicatio*. There will be more to say about the nature of the beneficiary's right (section (d) below).

While, as already noted, the *fidecommissum* never emerged beyond the law of succession, it is important to note that the intermediary upon whom it was charged need not be the heir. It could be charged on any person who acquired a benefit from the deceased, even if the benefit was very modest and essentially transitory, most of it being passed on to the ultimate beneficiary[11]. As we shall see (section (c) below), the fact that the *fideicommissum* was not restricted to the deceased's immediate heir meant that it was able to serve purposes going beyond the generation of the deceased's immediate successors.

(b) Content

The content of the *fideicommissum* might be very various: money; land; movable property. It might also extend to the whole or part of an inheritance, which clearly might include all or any of those things. The only restriction is that the property must be acquired by way of succession[12]. That brings out one important difference between the *fideicommissum* and the modern trust: the *fideicommissum* was not a commercial arrangement; it was essentially a domestic one, a device for disposing of family property and securing succession to it.

---

9 See the chapters by *Graziadei, Herman,* and *Macnair* in this volume. In keeping the respective influences of *fideicommissum* and *fiducia* distinct, some difficulty arises from the fact that the term *fiduciarius* is also employed in the later civil law tradition in connexion with *fiducia*.

10 For restrictions on his ownership, see (c) (i) below.

11 *Johnston* (n. 3) 15 ff.

12 *Johnston* (n. 3) 15 ff.

The early history of *fideicommissa*, as already mentioned, is a history of evading civil law rules, notably about testamentary capacity. There is an interesting parallel here with the later history both of trusts and *Treuhand*[13]. Equally clear is one difference in function: *fideicommissa* were not used to hold property for those under the legal age of majority or for the insane; instead the normal regime of tutors and curators applied to these cases[14].

(c) Duration

In the simplest case, the *fideicommissum* would be of brief duration: it would become enforceable on death of the deceased, and it would impose an obligation on the trustee (usually the heir) to convey property to the ultimate beneficiary. As soon as the conveyance was made, the *fideicommissum* would be spent. This is therefore no more than a bare trust for conveyance. In such a case no interesting questions arise about the trustee's duties of investment or administration. But this was not the only case.

(i) The trustee might be charged with making over the whole inheritance or part of it (*fideicommissum hereditatis). Gaius* deals with this case in his Institutes: "cum igitur scripserimus L. TITIUS HERES ESTO, possumus adicere ROGO TE L. TITI PETOQUE A TE UT CUM PRIMUM POSSIS HEREDITATEM MEAM ADIRE C. SEIO REDDAS RESTITUAS. Possumus autem et de parte restituenda rogare; et liberum est vel sub condicione vel pure relinquere fideicommissa, vel ex die certa"[15]. In this case too, if the transfer was to be immediate and unconditional, there would be no particular duties in the trustee other than delivery. But, as *Gaius* makes clear, the transfer need not take place at once. There is no shortage of cases in the Digest where the trustee is required only to make the estate over to the fideicommissary after an interval[16]. A common case is where the transfer is to be *cum morieris,* on the trustee's death: in such a case the trustee is owner of the inheritance during his lifetime, but is under a duty to transfer it to a beneficiary after a potentially lengthy interval. In this case it is clear that there is scope for developing rules about the trustee's duties towards the trust property during the period of his ownership.

---

13 See the papers by *Biancalana, Jones, Macnair,* and *Scherner* in the present volume.

14 For this, see *Buckland* (n. 2) 142 ff., 168 ff.

15 *Gai.* Inst. II, 250 "When we have written 'Let L. Titius be heir' we can add 'I ask and pray of you, L Titius, that as soon as you are able to enter my inheritance you should make it over and restore it to C. Seius. But we can also ask for a part to be made over; and it is possible to leave a conditional, or unconditional *fideicommissum* or one to operate from an appointed day".

16 See, e.g., D. 35, 1, 102; D. 36, 1, 56, 60, 8; D. 42, 8, 19; for the legislation which protected the trustee's right to retain a benefit from the estate, see *U. Manthe,* Das SC Pegasianum, Berlin, 1989.

It would have been possible for such questions to be dealt with by detailed regulation of the trustee's duties to invest and safeguard the property. But that was not the Roman approach. Instead, what we find is the notion that the property received, the inheritance, should be treated as a fund; the trustee's duties arise therefore only in relation to maintaining the value of the fund. Rules about how far the value of the fund could be reduced were developed; rules about how the specific items of trust property were to be treated were not. Probably this owes something to a reluctance to dictate to an owner what he should do with his property[17].

(ii) It will be clear that the facts that *fideicommissa* need not be imposed on heirs[18], and could be made to operate at the death of a trustee, made it possible to set up fideicommissary arrangements of the nature of perpetuities. These are normally referred to as fideicommissary substitutions. Under such arrangements, the settlor appointed the beneficiary (for example) of land under his will as a *fiduciarius* under a *fideicommissum* in favour of a further beneficiary, whether a named individual or simply a member of the family. Here is one example, provided by *Scaevola:* "pater filium heredem praedia alienare seu pignori ponere prohibuerat sed conservari liberis ex iustis nuptiis et ceteris cognatis fideicommiserat ..."[19]. This was one way of setting up a life interest in property[20]: the initial beneficiary would enjoy the land during his lifetime but would have to die intestate with respect to it, since although he was the owner, it was not his to dispose of; its fate was already regulated by the settlor's will. The same arrangement might extend over several generations, the only limiting factor being the rule that each beneficiary must be determinate. In classical law the most remote beneficiaries who were still regarded as determinate appear to have been the immediate issue of those living at the date of the settlor's death[21]. In these cases, therefore, each successive beneficiary was at the same time trustee with respect to his or her successor. While classical Roman law imposed no further restrictions on the time such fideicommissary arrangements might last, under *Justinian* a clear rule was established that they should not exceed four generations[22]. In later legal history, this four generation limit is mentioned rather frequently.

17 Accordingly, the Romans employ no such term as *dominus fiduciarius,* the quality of the fiduciary's ownership not being regarded as conceptually different from the normal case. The term *heres fiduciarius* makes two appearances, in D. 36, 1, 48 and 69, and *hereditas fiduciaria* makes one, in D. 12, 1, 9, 1; for discussion, see the chapters by *Graziadei* and *Zimmermann* in this volume. In usufruct, by contrast, there were detailed rules on permissible activities, considerations of maximizing capital against income, and so forth: see *D. Johnston,* Successive Rights and Successful Remedies, in: Peter Birks (ed.), New Perspectives in the Roman Law of Property, Oxford, 1989, pp. 153 ff.

18 See *Gai.* Inst. 2, 271; D. 32, 5, 1; D. 32, 6 pr.

19 *Scaevola* 19 dig. D. 32, 38 pr. "A father prohibited his son and heir from alienating or mortgaging lands and imposed a *fideicommissum* on him to conserve them for legitimate children and other cognates ...".

20 Another method would be usufruct; cf. *Johnston* (n. 17) 154 ff., 166 f.

21 See D. 31, 32, 6; *Johnston* (n. 3) 79 f., 109 ff.

22 Nov. 159 (AD 555); *Johnston* (n. 3) 111 ff.

Accordingly, although there is not in fact much evidence that this was done[23], these *fideicommissa familiae relicta* could be used in order to restrict the free powers of disposal over property which future generations would normally have. Abuse of such powers in later legal history made the whole institution notorious.

(iii) Purposes of a charitable nature – such as to provide games, heat public baths, pave roads, build buildings – or in memory of the deceased seem to have been dealt with in a different manner. The evidence suggests that they were not typically constructed as *fideicommissa.* Instead they were legacies *sub modo,* that is, for specific purposes to be carried out[24]. A typical instance is the following: "Lucius Titius testamento patriae suae civitati Sebastenorum centum legavit, uti alternis annis ex usuris eiusdem certamina sub nomine ipsius celebrarentur ..."[25]. In order to ensure the durability of such arrangements, the legatee chosen would be a non-natural person, such as a municipality: in principle therefore the legatee, so long as it existed, was liable to perform the purpose for which the legacy had been left. In classical law, such arrangements suffered from the weakness that the *modus,* the purpose, could not be specifically enforced. In later law, however, there is some reason to believe that the *modus* would have been specifically enforced if there was a public interest; furthermore, also in later law, *modus* came to be interpreted as a *fideicommissum,* which offered enhanced protection; and finally *Justinian* provided that *modus* could be specifically enforced[26]. While we do therefore find a certain amount of material on the carrying on of charitable or public purposes, none the less it is true to say that the Roman sources do not provide much significant material in this area, and what they do provide certainly does not amount to a clear doctrine for dealing with the special case of public trusts[27].

(d) Remedies and Third Parties

In high classical law – during the age of the formulary system of procedure – the beneficiary of a *fideicommissum* enjoyed an advantage over his counterpart who had been left a legacy. The reason was simple: in formulary procedure, to

---

23 *Johnston* (n. 3) 87 f.

24 See *D. Johnston,* Munificence and Municipia: Bequests to Towns in Classical Roman Law, (1985) 75 Journal of Roman Studies 105 ff.; and on memorials to the deceased: *idem,* Trusts and Tombs, Zeitschrift für Papyrologie und Epigraphik 72 (1988) 81 ff.

25 *Scaevola* 22 dig. D. 33, 1, 21, 3 "Lucius Titius left a legacy in his will of 100 to his hometown, Sebaste, so that from the interest on it games should be celebrated in his name every other year ...".

26 *Johnston* (n. 3) 245, 248 f.; Nov. 1 (AD 535).

27 An example of intervention is in the regulation of bequests to towns for building: here some imperial involvement can be found, but it is directed not so much at securing that the settlor's intentions are observed (as in the modern cy-près jurisdiction) but at making sure that a town does not take on too many new buildings while its existing ones crumble: see my 1985 paper (n. 24) 121 ff.

which a legatee must resort, only money judgments could be pronounced, so that the legatee could never be assured of obtaining *in specie* the property bequeathed. In the jurisdiction responsible for *fideicommissa,* however, which is known generically as *cognitio extra ordinem,* specific performance could be ordered[28]. This is just one example of the sort of flexibility from which, owing to its origins outside the established scheme of civil law, the *fideicommissum* benefited.

The beneficiary of a *fideicommissum* was not owner and therefore had no *vindicatio.* But neither was he reliant purely on rights *in personam* against the fiduciary. He enjoyed what is in Roman law terms plainly anomalous: that is, a right which was enforceable not merely against the fiduciary but also against certain third parties. That right consisted in his having a *missio in rem,* the ability to obtain an order from the magistrate granting him possession of the property subject to the *fideicommissum.* This order would enable him to recover the property from most people, but not from a purchaser in good faith for value who had notice of the *fideicommissum*[29].

The beneficiary enjoyed a similar sort of protection if the fiduciary, while in possession of the property subject to the *fideicommissum,* became insolvent: in such circumstances the beneficiary had priority over ordinary creditors of the fiduciary[30].

Under *Justinian,* the classical *missio in rem* was castigated as a *tenebrosissimus error* and abolished; in its place came an *actio in rem*[31]. The result was that the beneficiary of a *fideicommissum* became its owner as soon as succession to the deceased opened. His right was a straightforward real right; the classical intricacies of a *ius ad rem* asserted by *missio in rem* were a thing of the past. So far as the future was concerned, we must note too that, while many traces of the classical *missio* remained in the texts, they were not prominent: to piece together the classical doctrine would, although possible, have been a task of some difficulty.

It will be clear from what has been said that the role of the Roman courts, as attested in the sources, lay in protecting the property subject to the *fideicommissum* and enabling its beneficiary to recover it. Apart from a few hints about enforcement in cases where there was a public interest, we do not find in Roman law any substantial traces of the sort of intervention by the court to supervise trusts which is routine in common law jurisdictions.

---

28 *Johnston* (n. 3) 223 - 7.

29 See, e.g., Pauli sententiae 4, 1, 15; also *D. Johnston,* Prohibitions and Perpetuities: Family Settlements in Roman Law, ZSS (RA) 102 (1985) 220, 262 ff.; also *Johnston* (n. 3) 230 ff.

30 *Johnston* (n. 3) 234 ff. For similar considerations in uses and trusts, see the papers by *Biancalana* and *Macnair* in the present volume.

31 C. 6, 43, 1 (AD 529); C. 6, 43, 3, 2 (AD 531); *Buckland* (n. 2) 358.

2. *Fiducia*

Fiducia was in essence an agreement which qualified a conveyance by providing what was to be done with the thing conveyed. It is to be found both in the law of persons, attached to the formal dispositions by which persons might be freed or adopted, and in the law of property[32]. Only the second of these categories is considered here. Within that context, in the Institutes of *Gaius,* it is divided into two: *cum amico* and *cum creditore*[33]. In the first of these, *fiducia cum amico,* the property was conveyed to a friend, the purpose often being safe-keeping; other purposes attested are the setting up of a gift *mortis causa,* where the *fiducia* operated as a resolutive condition so that the donor could recover if his death did not ensue[34]; the manumission of a slave, where there might be advantages in the slave's being freed by the transferee rather than the transferor[35]. The second type, *fiducia cum creditore,* was a form of security in which the debtor transferred ownership of some property to the creditor. The creditor undertook to reconvey the property when the debt was repaid, and that was the substance of the *fiducia,* together possibly with other provisions as to when the creditor might sell the property.

Fiducia is a trust-like device in the sense that there is a division of title and interest in the thing: where it operates like a deposit with a friend, the "depositee" has the title, while the depositor retains his interest in reconveyance; where it is a security transaction with a creditor, the creditor has the title, while the debtor retains his interest in reconveyance. The owner for the time being has an ownership which is qualified in the sense that he must satisfy a standard of care of the thing; he cannot sell it; and he must offset profits made through the thing against the debt owed[36]. In neither case of *fiducia,* however, does the arrangement go much beyond a bare trust for reconveyance: the creditor does not necessarily bear any other duties. Furthermore, the debtor has rights only *in personam* against the creditor, so that, although the creditor's ownership is qualified, if he breaches the *fiducia* and conveys the property to a third party, the debtor has no right to recover it. Nor does there appear to be any evidence that, if the third party knew of the existence of the *fiducia,* the debtor would be able to assert any right against him: the *fiducia* itself did not impress any real right in the debtor on the thing.

---

32 For a full account of both aspects, see *A. Pernice,* Labeo, Halle, 1892, 3. 10. 120 ff. See, e.g., *Just.* Inst. 3, 2, 8.

33 *Gai.* Inst. II, 60. For examples from practice, see *P. Girard,* Textes de droit romain, 5th ed., Paris, 1923, pp. 825 f.

34 D. 39, 6, 42.

35 Advantages: for the transferor if he was under-age for performing manumission (D. 40, 9, 7, 1); for the transferee, since his freeing of the slave would make him patron. Cases involving freedom raise special considerations, as to which see *W. W. Buckland,* The Roman Law of Slavery, Cambridge, 1908, pp. 632 ff.

36 See, e.g., D. 13, 7, 22 pr.; 6 pr., 8, 4; Pauli sententiae 2, 13, 6. (Note that many of the Digest texts now speaking of *pignus* were originally written of *fiducia.*)

Fiducia is not prominent in the Roman sources: in its security form, it was largely suppressed by Justinianic interpolation[37]. In its form *cum amico* it survives, but its appearances are no more than sporadic[38]. Furthermore, the brief but clear account provided by *Gaius's* Institutes disappeared after antiquity until that work was rediscovered in 1816. What these points amount to is this: as a model for adoption or adaptation in later legal history, *fiducia* is unlikely to have been of great utility[39]. The sources provided only a meagre account, and it was in any event an account of a legal institution which created only contractual rights and gave its beneficiary no preference in bankruptcy or in competition with third parties having real rights.

3. Usufruct and *usus*

For completeness a word about usufruct and *usus* may be in order, although these institutions differ from those considered so far in that they do not impose any fiduciary duties on the person holding the property affected[40]. In the present context, their significance is that they are cases in which title and enjoyment of property are divided, either for a term of years or for a life: in usufruct the owner *(dominus)* of the property has a bare title only, while the usufructuary has the right to use and to take the fruits of the property; in *usus* the usuary's right is to use alone. These devices are particularly common in connexion with land; and it is clear that the most frequent application of usufruct was the grant by a testator of a life interest in land to his widow, the title to the property being conveyed to the children. Accordingly, although the owner's rights in the property are not protected by way of fiduciary duties imposed on the usufructuary or usuary but instead by means of a contractual guarantee *(cautio usufructuaria)*, the functions served by these institutions and the manner in which they divided title from beneficial interest explain their appearance in later legal history in discussion about trusts[41].

III. Trustees

Although the law of *fideicommissa* provides the most detailed and sustained instance of a trust-like device in Roman law, the same is not true in the law relating to trustees. The *fiduciarius* in the law of *fideicommissa* did not provide a very interesting model for the trustee, viewed as a person occupying a particular office

---

37 It appears in the Theodosian rather than the Justinianic Code: C. Th. 15, 14, 9 (AD 395).

38 See the references in nn. 34 - 35; also Fragmenta Vaticana 334a (but this was discovered only in 1821).

39 See the paper by *Graziadei* in this volume.

40 For a brief account, *Buckland* (n. 2) 268 ff.; also *Johnston* (n. 17) 154 ff.

41 See the papers by *Herman* and *Macnair* in the present volume.

and subject to specific duties with respect to the trust property. The reason for this has already been mentioned: even where the *fiduciarius* was more than a bare trustee for conveyance, he was subject only to a general duty to maintain the value of the trust fund. That meant that there was no need to regulate specifically acts which he might and acts which he might not perform in relation to the property under *fideicommissum*. So far as *fiducia* is concerned, the same point recurs: there arose only a contractual duty to make reconveyance. Accordingly, other potentially trustee-like figures in Roman law require to be considered.

1. Executors and the *familiae emptor*

There appears to be no trace of the notion of the executor in Roman law[42]. Instead, it was the heir who took charge of attempting to secure that the testator's will was done, and of recovering property and debts due to the estate[43]. Even in less straightforward cases it was again the heir who acted: for example, where a legacy was left to a beneficiary to carry out a specific purpose, even if the heir had no direct interest in performance, he could indirectly achieve the desired result by refusing to pay the bequest until the legatee had given him a promise to make due performance[44]. The heir therefore performed the role which in some other systems falls to be performed by the executor.

It does not seem that the shadowy figure of the *familiae emptor* functioned as an executor. The old Roman mancipatory will was made by formally conveying the estate as a whole to a *familiae emptor*. According to *Gaius's* Institutes, that person was in the position of an heir[45]. The details are obscure: whether, originally, the *familiae emptor* took title to the estate, subject to directions given to him by the testator as to its disposal, or whether he was something in the nature of a trustee, is unclear. In classical law he became a mere formality, participating in the making of the will, but having no responsibility for carrying out its provisions[46]. There is little basis here for detecting an executor discharging a duty imposed on him by the deceased.

2. *Tutor*

The closest that Roman law comes to the notion of trusteeship is that of *tutela*, tutorship. Here the tutor does occupy an office with recognized duties to his pupil

42 See, above all, *L. Mitteis*, Römisches Privatrecht bis auf die Zeit Diokletians, Leipzig, 1908, 105, n. 30, and the paper by *Zimmermann* in this volume.

43 *Buckland* (n. 2) 316 f.

44 See, e.g., D. 32, 19.

45 *Gai.* Inst. II, 103.

46 *Buckland* (n. 2) 284; *M. Kaser*, Das römische Privatrecht, Erster Abschnitt, 2nd ed., München, 1971, pp. 108, 679.

and in particular to his pupil's property. Naturally, the pupil retained ownership in the property but, so far as the pupil's interests were concerned, the tutor was sometimes regarded as being in the position of owner[47]. This does not amount to any legal division of title and interest in property, but it does constitute a practical recognition of the tutor's standing – and the pupil's temporary lack of standing – in relation to it.

The main duties inherent in the office of tutor, so far as relevant to this discussion, may conveniently be summarized: (a) Security: the tutor must provide security that the ward's property would be safe (*cautio rem salvam pupillo fore*), although a tutor appointed in a will might be relieved by the testator from this obligation. (b) Inventory: the tutor must make an inventory of the ward's property. What is interesting about both of these duties is that the magistrates exercised powers of supervision to ensure that they were complied with[48]. (c) Investment: this has many aspects, among them the duties to invest money promptly; to sell perishable goods without delay; to refrain in general from selling land; to demonstrate the same care for the pupil's as for one's own affairs[49]. (d) Accounting: the tutor must provide accounts of dealings with the pupil's property[50]. In addition rules grew up to regulate cases where the tutor's own interest and the pupil's interest conflicted, the tutor being described in such cases as acting as *auctor in rem suam*[51]: here the normal practice was to appoint a *curator* to act for the particular transaction. Breaches in any of the tutor's duties could be redressed by the *actio tutelae* or, for the particular case of embezzlement of the pupil's property, by an *actio de rationibus distrahendis*[52].

Many of these points about investments and accounting will seem familiar from the modern law of trustees. Here it is enough to say that, while Roman law knew the concept of an office in which there inhered duties to administer the property of another person, that concept was never generalized beyond the special circumstances of those who lacked legal capacity.

IV. Conclusions

Roman law knew two devices which enjoyed trust-like characteristics: *fideicommissum* and *fiducia*. *Fiducia* represents an example of ownership which is qualified

47 D. 26, 7, 27 "Tutor qui tutelam gerit quantum ad providentiam pupillarem domini loco haberi debet". Cf. D. 41, 4, 7, 3; D. 43, 24, 11, 7 = D. 50, 17, 157 pr.; D. 47, 2, 57, 4.

48 Security: D. 27, 8 (in general; and see e.g. fr. 1.11); inventory (the evidence is mainly late): C. 5, 37, 24 (AD 396); C. 5, 51, 13, 2 (AD 530); cf. D. 26, 7, 7 pr.

49 D. 26, 7, 7, 3 - 4; D. 26, 7, 7, 1; D. 27, 9, 1; D. 27, 3, 1 pr. and D. 16, 3, 32.

50 D. 27, 3, 1, 3.

51 This appears to be the origin of the same doctrine in the Scottish law of trusts.

52 *Buckland* (n. 2) 163 ff.; *Kaser* (n. 46) 364 - 5.

in the interests of another: that is an important element in trusts, but it cannot be maintained that the rules of *fiducia*, so far as they are known, provide much detailed regulation of a trust-like nature. While this was an institution and a juristic achievement of importance, the fact that its consequences were analysed purely in terms of contract meant that it was not liable to make a significant impact on property law.

In the case of *fideicommissa*, on the other hand, the detailed rules were particularly well-developed. They exhibit a number of points which are generally associated with trusts: a tripartite structure in which property is entrusted by one person to another for the benefit of a third; a grounding in the notion of *fides;* a flexibility as against parallel institutions of the established civil law, sometimes amounting to avoidance of established legal rules; a potential for creating perpetuities, since the trustee need not be born during the settlor's lifetime; a preference in the trustee's insolvency for the beneficiary; and a right to follow the property into the hands of all but purchasers in good faith for value without notice of the *fideicommissum*.

The differences between the trust and the *fideicommissum* are well-known. But they can be exaggerated. To give but one example: it is regularly stressed that the *fideicommissum*, unlike the trust, could be set up only *mortis causa*. That is true, but to insist upon it is misleading, since the *fideicommissum* to a large extent freed itself from the restraints of the Roman law of wills and inheritance and developed a role as an extra-testamentary means of disposing of property. While it is true that this remained a function exercised only *mortis causa*, the fact that the *fideicommissum* in no way depended on a will shows that its confinement to applications *mortis causa* was to some degree an artificial restriction. More significant differences between trusts and *fideicommissa* are these: first, that the Roman device lacked any commercial dimension and operated purely in the context of family and domestic property; second, that while the Romans did employ institutions which functioned like trusts, they lacked the concept of the trust. These two points are not unconnected: the *fideicommissum* was developed for its own particular domestic purposes; the opportunity was not taken to abstract from it a concept of trust which might be applied in wider fields. In the absence of the abstract concept, the legal institution remained confined to its original quarters.

Much the same has to be said of trustees. While neither *fiducia* nor the *fideicommissum* led to the development of any detailed rules on a fiduciary's powers, precisely such rules were developed to circumscribe the activities of the tutor. But here too the detailed rules were confined to the area in which they had been developed; the great step of turning from the particular notion of the tutor to the general notion of the trustee was never taken.

What the Roman law knew, therefore, was no more than a fiduciary institution and a fiduciary office, each developed and employed in its own delimited sphere of the law. For the purposes of later law Roman law could provide impulses towards, and examples of, the workings of the trust and the role of the trustee. But the forging of an abstract fiduciary concept – the trust – lay in the future.

HARALD SIEMS

Von den *piae causae* zu den Xenodochien

I. Einleitung

Die folgende Untersuchung befaßt sich mit der Fortdauer wohltätiger Einrichtungen von der Spätantike zum frühen Mittelalter. Zu überprüfen ist die rechtliche Ausgestaltung dieser Einrichtungen, die gewöhnlich als Stiftungen eingestuft werden. Justinianische Rechtsquellen kennen die Ausdrücke *piae causae*[1] und *domus* oder *loci venerabiles* für Fremdenherbergen (*xenodochia)*, Armen-, Kranken-, Waisen-, Findel- und Altenhäuser[2]. Die untechnischen Bezeichnungen lassen die

---

1 Aus der Literatur zu den *piae causae: Ludovicus Thomassinus,* Vetus et nova ecclesiae disciplina circa beneficia et beneficiarios in tres partes distributa, 1766, pars I, liber II, cap. 89 f., 93; pars III, liber III, cap. 26 - 31; *Christian Friedrich Mühlenbruch, Chr. Fr. v. Glück,* Ausführliche Erläuterung der Pandecten, 39. Teil, 1870, S. 442 ff.; *Edgar Loening,* Geschichte des deutschen Kirchenrechts, 1. Band, 1878, S. 250 f.; *Aemilius Ludwig Richter, Richard Dove, Wilhelm Kahl,* Lehrbuch des katholischen und evangelischen Kirchenrechts, 8. Auflage, 1886, 2. Band, S. 1301 ff.; *August Knecht,* System des Justinianischen Kirchenvermögensrechtes, 1905 (Nachdruck, 1963), S. 43 ff., 102 ff., 114 ff.; *Uhlhorn-Hauck,* Wohltätigkeitsanstalten, in: A. Hauck (Hg.), Realencyklopädie für protestantische Theologie und Kirche, 3. Auflage, 21. Band, 1908, S. 435 - 452; *Pierre Gillet,* La personnalité juridique en droit ecclesiastique, 1927, S. 26 ff.; *Siegfried Reicke,* Stiftungsbegriff und Stiftungsrecht im Mittelalter, ZSS (GA) 53 (1933) 247 - 276; *Gerda Krüger,* Die Rechtsstellung der vorkonstantinischen Kirche, 1935 (Nachdruck, 1969), S. 216 ff.; *Jean Imbert,* Les Hôpitaux en droit canonique, 1947, S. 16 ff.; *Dieter Pleimes,* Irrwege der Dogmatik im Stiftungsrecht, 1954, S. 8 ff.; *Hans-Rudolf Hagemann,* Die Stellung der Piae Causae nach justinianischem Recht, 1953; *idem,* Die rechtliche Stellung der christlichen Wohltätigkeitsanstalten in der östlichen Reichshälfte, RIDA 3 (1956) 265 - 283; *Eberhard F. Bruck,* Die Stiftungen für die Toten in Recht, Religion und politischem Denken der Römer, in: *idem,* Über römisches Recht im Rahmen der Kulturgeschichte, 1954, S. 70 ff.; *Jean Gaudemet,* Les fondations en Occident au Bas Empire, RIDA 2 (1955) 275 - 286; *idem,* L'église dans l'empire romain (IVe-V^{e} siécles), 1958, S. 303 f.; *Robert Feenstra,* Le concept de fondation du droit romain classique jusqu'à nos jours: théorie et pratique, in: RIDA 3 (1956) 245 - 263; *idem,* L'histoire des fondations, T.R. 24 (1956) 381 - 448 (beide Arbeiten von *Feenstra* sind zum Thema methodisch grundlegend); *Hans Liermann,* Handbuch des Stiftungsrechts, 1963, 1. Band, S. 24 ff.; *Reinhard Zimmermann,* „Cy-près", in: Iuris professio, Festgabe für Max Kaser zum 80. Geburtstag, 1986, S. 402 ff.; *Fabrizio Fabbrini,* La personalità giuridica degli enti di assistenza (detti „piae causae") in diritto romano, Utrumque ius 11 (1990) 57 - 121. Allgemein zum kirchlichen Vermögensrecht jetzt: *Peter Landau,* Kirchengut, in: Theologische Realenzyklopädie, Band 18, S. 560 - 575.

2 C. Justinianus 1, 2, 19; C. Justinianus 1, 3, 45, 1; Nov. 7,1.

Nähe zu frommen christlichen Zielen und zu kirchlichen Institutionen erkennen. Zur rechtlichen Einordnung geben die Quellen unterschiedliche Hinweise. Errichtet durch Testament oder Schenkung erscheinen die *piae causae* einmal als erbfähig, sind Grundeigentümer und schließen Verträge, dann sind sie Kirchen und Klöstern einverleibt oder gehören einem Grundherrn oder der Verwalter und Vorsteher ist Eigentümer, gebunden durch die Zielsetzung der Einrichtung, und schließlich werden Zuwendungen und Legate sogar an die Armen selbst gerichtet. Außerdem nehmen Schenker und Erblasser auf Verwaltung und Zwecke der von ihnen bedachten Einrichtung Einfluß. Man mag in den verschiedenen Aussagen den durchgängigen Wunsch nach Absicherung einer durch Zwecksetzung individualisierten Vermögensmasse sehen. Die geringe Technizität und das Fehlen eines Begriffes werden dahin gedeutet, daß die römischen Juristen an einer dogmatischen Erfassung nicht interessiert waren. Dennoch werden die *piae causae* überwiegend als Stiftungen, als juristische Personen mit anstaltlichem oder korporativem Charakter eingeordnet. Brucks Bezeichnung dieser Stiftungen als Produkt des Vulgarrechts mit dem Parfüm von Chianti und Salami[3] fand Anklang, wohl wegen des assoziationsreichen Bildes und der fehlenden Falsifizierbarkeit. Dunkel bleiben auch die Herleitung aus dem Volke[4] und die Feststellung, daß die *piae causae* ihrem Wesen nach Stiftungen waren[5]. Frühere Kritik[6] an der Einordnung als juristische Person fand kaum Resonanz. Grundsätzlich wurde in letzter Zeit die Angemessenheit dieser Rechtsfigur bezweifelt und mit mentalitätsgeschichtlichten Erwägungen bis zum 18. Jahrhundert eine fortwirkende Rechtsträgerschaft des verstorbenen Stifters vorgeschlagen[7]. Beachtlich erscheint die methodische Kritik, daß bei der Suche nach dogmatischer Erfassung der *piae causae* zu sehr auf die juristische Person gesehen wurde, statt historisch-rechtsvergleichend andere Modelle der europäischen Rechtsentwicklung einzubeziehen[8].

Eine Fortdauer der *piae causae,* d. h. der frommen Stiftungen sieht man durch die Briefe *Papst Gregors* und ein Urkundenformular für die Errichtung eines *xenodochium* oder Klosters in der Sammlung *Marculfs* als gegeben an. Über die eigentliche Wortbedeutung hinaus erscheinen Xenodochien im Frühmittelalter als Häuser für Arme, Fremde und sonstige Bedürftige[9]. Die Verbreitung in Italien und Frank-

---

3 *Bruck* (Fn. 1) 72.

4 *Bruck* (Fn. 1) 72.

5 *Zimmermann* (Fn. 1) 403, Anm. 68

6 *Loening* (Fn. 1).

7 *Michael Borgolte,* Die Stiftungen des Mittelalters in rechts- und sozialhistorischer Sicht, ZSS (KA) 105 (1988) 71 - 94.

8 *Feenstra* (Fn. 1).

9 Zu den frühmittelalterlichen Xenodochien außer der in Fn. 1 und 7 genannten Literatur: *Loening* (Fn. 1) 2. Band, S. 648 ff.; *Siegfried Reicke,* Das deutsche Spital und sein Recht im Mittelalter, 1. Teil, 1932, S. 3 ff.; *Augustinus Thiele,* Studien zur Vermögensbildung und Vermögensverwertung der Kirche im Merowingerreich (6. Jhdt.), 1969, S. 91 ff.; *Egon Boshof,* Untersuchungen zur Armenfürsorge im fränkischen Reich des 9. Jahrhunderts, Archiv für

reich hat insbesondere *W. Schönfeld*[10] untersucht. Trotz schwankender, untechnischer Ausdrucksweise zur Rechtsträgerschaft und oft unklarem Verhältnis zum sonstigen Kirchengut wurden auch die Xenodochien als Stiftungen angesehen. Wenn in den Quellen etwa die Armen als Empfänger einer Schenkung genannt werden, soll dem keine juristische Bedeutung zukommen. Vielmehr habe es im Rechtsbewußtsein des Volkes die lebendige Vorstellung einer eigenen Stiftungspersönlichkeit gegeben[11]. „Der Begriff lebte, aber war noch nicht gefaßt."[12] Unter Berücksichtigung der veränderten allgemeinen Verhältnisse des Mittelalters, insbesondere im Kirchenvermögen, erschienen *Liermann* die *piae causae* als juristische Personen erloschen. An ihre Stelle sei das Sondervermögen als grundlegendes Institut des germanischen Rechts getreten[13]. Damit wird eine Kategorie behauptet, auf die bezeichnenderweise nicht näher eingegangen wird.

Im Folgenden soll nicht der naheliegende Versuch unternommen werden, auf möglichst breiter Quellenbasis und mit neuer kritisch-methodischer Zurüstung die rechtliche Qualität der *piae causae* und der Xenodochien auszuleuchten. Es soll lediglich am Beispiel gängiger Quellen untersucht werden, ob Rechtsvorstellungen, die in der Spätantike zu den *piae causae* entwickelt wurden, im Frühmittelalter für die Xenodochien übernommen und dabei vielleicht sogar weiter ausgeformt wurden. Zu dieser Fragestellung regt an, daß in beiden Fällen, bei den *piae causae* wie bei den Xenodochien, ähnliche Probleme zu bewältigen waren, nämlich der Schutz des Vermögens gegen Entfremdung, Durchsetzung des Zwecks der Zuwendung und Effizienz der geschaffenen Einrichtungen. Rückgriffe auf antikes Traditionsgut wie die Entwicklung von Funktionsäquivalenten sind hier gleichermaßen interessant. Zu würdigen sind die Quellenaussagen vor dem Hintergrund veränderter Kulturumstände, etwa dem Verlust an Urbanität in weiten Gebieten des ehemals römischen Reiches, der sich wandelnden Bedeutung und Verfaßtheit der Kirche und dem schwindenden Bildungsstand, besonders im Bereich des Rechts.

Kulturgeschichte 58 (1976) 265 - 339; *idem,* Armenfürsorge im Frühmittelalter: Xenodochium, matricula, hospitale pauperum, Vierteljahrschrift für Sozial- und Wirtschaftsgeschichte 71 (1984) 153 - 174.

10 *Walther Schönfeld,* Die Xenodochien in Italien und Frankreich im frühen Mittelalter, ZSS (KA) 12 (1922) 1 - 54.

11 *Reicke* (Fn. 1) 272 f.

12 *Reicke* (Fn. 1) 273. Die schwer nachvollziehbare Aussage ist wohl eine Konsequenz der Quellen, die zwar modernen Konstruktionsdrang herausfordern, aber selbst untechnisch sprechen. *Imbert* (Fn. 1) 42 Anm. 3 drückt den Eindruck von *Reicke* so aus: „Ce n'est qu'avec le progrès du droit romain et du droit canonique, au XIIe siècle, que la notion de personnalité se fera jour dans le domaine des idées, après avoir déjà une longue existence dans les faits."

13 *Liermann* (Fn. 1) 58 f.

II. Das Nachwirken römischer Rechtstexte im Frühmittelalter

Voraussetzung für das Aufgreifen früherer Rechtstexte des eigenen oder eines fremden Rechtskreises ist neben der Motivation, etwa durch entsprechende Konfliktlagen und Regelungsbedürfnisse, die Verfügbarkeit der benötigten Vorlagen. Grundsätzlich waren dem Frühmittelalter jene spätantiken Rechtstexte vorausgegangen, die Regelungen zu den *piae causae* enthielten, unabhängig davon, welchen Aussagewert moderne Forschung ihnen zubilligt. Für die Vermittlung römischen Rechts im lateinischen Westen, namentlich Gallien, kommt der *Lex Romana Visigothorum*, d. h. den dort aufgenommenen spätantiken Rechtstexten, besondere Bedeutung zu[14]. Entscheidend ist, daß in dieser Quellenmasse anscheinend keine Texte zu den *piae causae* oder allgemein zu Wohlfahrtseinrichtungen enthalten sind[15]. Ein Gesetz von 434 läßt den Nachlaß von intestat verstorbenen Bischöfen und Priestern an die Kirche oder Klöster fallen[16]. Der Text ist in der *Lex Romana Visigothorum* enthalten, findet aber dort und in der Breviarliteratur keine Ausweitung auf wohltätige Einrichtungen[17]. Entsprechend verhält es sich mit einer Novelle *Marcians* zu letztwilligen Verfügungen von Nonnen[18]. Aus der im spätantiken Gallien zu lokalisierenden Rechtsliteratur läßt sich die sog. *Consultatio veteris cuiusdam iurisconsulti* mit einer „domus cum membris suis vel hospitiis circumiectis“ zitieren[19], doch bleiben die genaueren Verhältnisse im Dunkeln. Ergiebiger sind die Texte des justinianischen Gesetzgebungswerkes. Deren frühmittelalterliche Verbreitung im Westen dürfte primär Italien erfaßt haben. Relevante Aussagen zu den *piae causae* finden sich im *Codex* und in den Novellen.

Der justinianische *Codex* lag im Frühmittelalter nach überkommener Ansicht nur in verkürzter Form vor[20]. Deshalb war der Zugriff auf Texte zu *piae causae* begrenzt. Der zweite Titel des ersten Buches „De sacrosanctis ecclesiis et de rebus et privilegiis earum“ fehlt trotz inhaltlicher Bedeutung anscheinend völlig und der besonders einschlägige dritte Titel „De episcopis et clericis et orphanotrophis et brephotrophis ... et privilegio eorum ...“ ist erheblich verkürzt[21]. Tatsächlich war der Zugriff auf die fraglichen Titel im Frühmittelalter erschwert, da das erste Buch

---

14 Lex Romana Visigothorum, ed. *Gustavus Haenel*, 1849 (Nachdruck, 1962), der Text wird auch als *Breviarium Alarici* bezeichnet.

15 *Hagemann*, Piae Causae (Fn. 1) 26, Anm. 5; überprüft wurden die einschlägigen Wortverzeichnisse.

16 C. Theodosianus V, 3,1. Der Text ist rekonstruiert.

17 Lex Romana Visigothorum, C.Th. V, 3,1 (Fn. 14) 140 ff.

18 Novellae Marciani V; Lex Romana Visigothorum, Novellae Marciani V (Fn. 14) 304 f.

19 Consultatio II,1.

20 *Paul Krüger*, Kritik des justinianischen Codex, 1867, S. 242 ff.; *Carlo Guido Mor*, Epitome Codicis, in: *idem*, Scritti di storia giuridica altomedievale, 1977, S. 25 - 62; kritisch: *Ennio Cortese*, Il diritto nella storia medievale, 1. Band, 1995, S. 239.

21 *Paul Krüger*, Codex Iustinianus (editio maior) 1877, S. 49 ff.; *Mor* (Fn. 20) 42.

des *Codex* in der *Lex Romana canonice compta* und der *Collectio Anselmo dedicata,* die bekanntlich große Auszüge des römischen Rechtes vermittelten, übergangen wurde[22]. Die diesen Sammlungen nahe stehenden *Excerpta Bobiensia* verwerten zwar den dritten Titel des ersten Buches, übergehen aber die relevanten Regelungen[23].

Ähnlich gering ist die Resonanz in den Kanonessammlungen. Ein allerdings auch nur begrenztes Interesse spürt man bei *Anselm II. von Lucca.* In dessen *Collectio canonum* aus den achtziger Jahren des 11. Jahrhunderts finden sich: *C. Justinianus* 1, 2,12 mit dem Hinweis, daß „pauperibus alimenta non desint" und der Zuweisung von „salaria de publico"[24]; *C. Justinianus* 1, 2, 22 wo unter detaillierter Aufzählung den wohltätigen Einrichtungen Abgabenfreiheit bzgl. der ihnen gemachten Zuwendungen gewährt wird („lucrativorum inscriptionibus liberas immunesque esse")[25]; *C. Justinianus* 1, 2, 23 läßt Ansprüche wohltätiger Einrichtungen auf das ihnen Zugewandte in 100 Jahren verjähren[26]; *C. Justinianus* 1, 3, 34 pr. bestätigt den wohltätigen Einrichtungen, die dem Priester Nico unterstehen, ihre Privilegien[27]. Wie auch immer die Texte verstanden wurden[28], sie waren nunmehr in eine verbreitete Sammlung gelangt und hätten von da übernommen werden können. Tatsächlich gibt es nur geringe Spuren, die auf ein Interesse deuten könnten. Aus *Anselms* Sammlung übernimmt die unbedeutende *Collectio canonica Beneventana* allein *C. Justinianus* 1, 2, 12 und 1, 3, 34[29]. *C. Justinianus* 1, 3, 34 pr. taucht verkürzt in der *Collectio in CLXXXIII titulos digesta* auf[30]. Die Kanonessammlung *Polycarpus* enthält *C. Justinianus* 1, 2, 12 und 23[31]. Unter Verkürzung

---

22 *Carlo Guido Mor,* Lex Romana canonice compta, 1927, S. 25 f.; *Jean-Claude Besse,* Histoire des textes du droit de l'église au moyen-age de Denys à Gratien. Collectio Anselmo dedicata, 1960, S. 91; *Giuseppe Russo,* Tradizione manoscritto di leges romanae, 1980, S. 252.

23 *Carlo Guido Mor,* Bobbio, Pavia e gli „Excerpta Bobiensia", in: Contributi alla Storia dell'Università di Pavia, 1925, S. 72. Die Excerpta Bobiensia enthalten aus dem C. Justinianus 1, 3 die Konstiutionen 5, 7, 8, 9, 10, 13, 14, 20, 34, 54.

24 *Anselm II.* Bischof von Lucca, Collectio canonum, ed. *Fr. Thaner,* 2 Bände, 1906 - 1915; hier: IV, 53.

25 *Anselm* (Fn. 24) IV, 19.

26 *Anselm* (Fn. 24) IV, 38.

27 *Anselm* (Fn. 24) IV, 55.

28 Insbesondere für C. Justinianus 1, 3, 34 = *Anselm* IV, 5 bleibt fraglich, wie man diese Regelung im frühmittelalterlichen Italien umsetzten wollte wegen ihres Bezugs auf den Priester Nico.

29 *Ottorino Bertolini,* La collezione canonica Beneventa del Vat. lat. 4939, in: Collectanea Vaticana in honorem Anselmi M. Card. Albareda, 1962, S. 134 f.

30 Liber canonum diversorum sanctorum patrum sive Collectio in CLXXXIII titulos digesta, ed. *Joseph Motta* (Monumenta iuris canonici, ser. B, Band 7) 1988; hier: Titel 146 c. 13 der Text endet bei „... custodiri decernimus". Die Sammlung wird der gregorianischen Reform und der Toskana zugewiesen: *Motta,* S. XXVI ff.

31 Polycarpus III, 15, 17 und III, 12, 37. *Uwe Horst,* Die Kanonessammlung Polycarpus des Gregor von S. Grisogono (Monumenta Germaniae Historica, Hilfsmittel 5) 1980, S. 215.

des ersten Textes auf das Wesentliche finden sich beide Stellen auch bei *Deusdedit*, der auch *C. Justinianus* 1, 3, 32 mit der Lastenbefreiung für wohltätige Einrichtungen und ihre Verwalter zitiert[32]. *Gratian* greift nur auf *C. Justinianus* 1, 2, 22 zurück[33]. Die geringe Auswertung des *Codex* läßt sich nur zum Teil mit dem Fehlen ausreichender Textvorlagen erklären, denn neben der frühmittelalterlichen Epitomefassung muß es auch vollständigere Texte gegeben haben, aus denen die Epitome aufgefüllt wurde, so daß in bologneser Zeit wieder der Volltext vorlag.

Zum justinianischen *Codex* gibt es Bearbeitungen, die aus vorbologneser Zeit stammen sollen. Die frühen Glossen zum *Codex epitomatus* lassen – soweit sie ediert vorliegen – allerdings keine eindringliche Beschäftigung mit den Regelungen betreffend die *piae causae* erkennen[34]. Etwas ergiebiger ist die *Summa Perusina*[35], die dem 7. Jh. zugewiesen wird. Sie faßt die einzelnen Konstitutionen in nur einem Satz zusammen. Das hat zu der Erklärung geführt, die Summen hätten ursprünglich als Orientierungshilfe am Rande einer Codexhandschrift gestanden. Immerhin setzt die Bildung der Summen eine inhaltliche Beschäftigung mit den Texten voraus, wenn dabei auch gravierende Qualitätsschwankungen feststellbar sind[36]. Der *Summa Perusina* fehlt bereits *C. Justinianus* 1, 2, und von *C. Justinianus* 1, 3 werden nur die lateinischen Konstitutionen behandelt[37]. *C. Justinianus* 1, 3, 24 wird brauchbar zusammengefaßt: „Quod pauperibus per testamentum relinquitur, firmum est", allerdings unter Übergehung des rechtlichen Problems der Unbestimmtheit der Bedachten. *C. Justinianus* 1, 3, 28 lautet: „Captivorum redemptionem per testamentum aut in verbum reliquerit, adimpleatur. Curas episcopi sit exigendi, et iudici ratione edat." Damit wird zutreffend die Rolle der Bischöfe und die Fremdnützigkeit ihres Handelns herausgestellt, was bei der Nähe von letztwilligen Verfügungen für wohltätige Einrichtungen und solchen zum Freikauf von Gefangenen bedeutsam werden konnte. Bei *C. Justinianus* 1, 3, 31 klingt in der Zusammenfassung wieder der Gesichtspunkt der Fremdnützigkeit an: „Orphanotrophiis est que fideiussore res minorum et omnem utilitatem vindicet, que et notum faciat iudici et

---

32 Die Kanonessammlung des Kardinals Deusdedit, ed. *Victor Wolf von Glanvell*, 1905 (Nachdruck, 1967), I, 317; III, 166; III, 173; IV, 285, S. 186, 340, 343 f., 551 f. *Jean Gaudemet*, Le droit romain dans la Collectio canonum du Cardinal Deusdedit, in: *idem*, La doctrine canonique médiévale, 1994, Nr. IV.

33 Decretum Gratiani, Causa 23, Quaest. 8, c. 23.

34 *Luigi Chiappelli*, La glossa pistoiese al Codice giustinianeo tratta dal manoscritto capitolare di Pistoia, in: Memorie della Reale Accademia della Scienze di Torino, seria II, 37, 1886, S. 31, 40, 56; *Enrico Besta*, Le glosse di Monteprandone e di Pesaro al Codice giustinianeo, in: Mélanges Fitting, 1. Band, 1907, S. 92. Da es sich um Epitome-Fassungen handelt, fehlen Glossen zu C. Justinianus 1, 2.

35 *Friderico Patetta*, Adnotationes Codicum domini Justiniani (Summa Perusina), Bulletino dell'Istituto di diritto romano 12 (1900). Dazu *Detlef Liebs*, Die Jurisprudenz im spätantiken Italien, 1987, S. 276 ff.; *Cortese* (Fn. 20) 240 ff.

36 *Harald Siems*, Handel und Wucher im Spiegel frühmittelalterlicher Rechtsquellen, 1992, S. 176, 312 ff.

37 Summa Perusina (Fn. 35) 7 - 11.

civium". Allerdings ist der Text bei „que" anscheinend gestört, und es wurde eine Emendation in „absque" erwogen[38]. *C. Justinianus* 1, 3, 34 wird sinnvoll generalisiert: „Omnes privilegias locis venerabilibus serventur". Daran läßt sich ablesen, daß man im Frühmittelalter Rechtstexte mit einer konkreten Einzelfallregelung durch Verallgemeinerung fruchtbar machen konnte. Nicht der Wortlaut, sondern die allgemeine Intention, oder was man dafür hielt, wurde als Regelungsgehalt herangezogen. *C. Justinianus* 1, 3, 48 wird durch die *Summa Perusina* in seinen Aussagen über letztwillige Verfügungen nicht erfaßt und hinsichtlich der Lex Falcidia sogar verkehrt, will man den Text nicht emendieren[39]. *C. Justinianus* 1, 3, 53 betrifft die Frauenräuber „Raptores sacrarum mulierum decollentur, et qui se ibi commiscuerunt. Res raptorum loca venerabilia, in qua fuerat dedicata, abeant in perpetuum, et exinde usumfructum mulier consequatur." Die Anordnung zum Vermögen des *raptor* generalisiert wieder einen Spezialfall der Vorlage. Damit wird für *venerabilia loca* die dauernde Vermögensträgerschaft bei gleichzeitiger Zweckbindung durch *ususfructus* zugunsten der Frau festgeschrieben. Diese tatsächliche Konstellation scheint dem Verfasser der *Summa Perusina* nicht fremd gewesen zu sein. Zu einer Präzisierung der Rechtsstellung von *venerabilia loca* bot die *Summa Perusina* keine Gelegenheit und man wird angesichts ihrer geringen Technizität die Befähigung des Verfassers bezweifeln dürfen. Zur Vermittlung eines eindringenden Verständnisses von Institutionen des römischen Rechts kommt die *Summa Perusina* kaum in Betracht. Ihre Funktion als Orientierungshilfe zum *Codex* und die vermutlich geringe Verbreitung dürften dem entgegen gestanden haben.

Eine deutlichere Vermittlung der rechtlichen Ausgestaltung von *piae causae* an das Mittelalter lassen die justinianischen Novellen erwarten. Gerade hier finden sich Texte, die der rechtshistorischen Forschung zur Rekonstruktion der *piae causae* dienten: Über ihre Errichtung durch letztwillige Verfügung, deren Auslegung und Durchsetzung, zum Einfluß des Erblassers auf die Verwaltung, über Aufsicht und Einwirkung der Bischöfe, Entfremdungsverbote und Maßgaben für die Verwaltung. Die Novellen waren im Frühmittelalter durch die *Juliani Epitome* bekannt. Es handelt sich um einen lateinischen Novellenauszug aus den Jahren 556/57, der auf den Antezessor *Julian* zurückgehen soll[40]. Die *Juliani Epitome* ist im Westen verbreitet und wird von kirchenrechtlichen Sammlungen häufig benutzt. Die *Lex Romana canonice compta* aus dem 9. Jahrhundert enthält wohl alle für die *piae causae* einschlägigen Texte[41]. Angesichts der weitgreifenden Auszüge aus der *Juliani Epitome* dort ist damit noch kein gezieltes Interesse bezeugt, sondern nur

---

38 *Patetta* (Fn. 35) 10, Anm. 2.

39 Summa Perusina (Fn. 35) 11 mit Anm. 1: „Lex 37 (48) Impr. Iustinianus a. Johannes pp. Ecclesia vel episcopus qui tota bona sua pauperes aut pro captivis erogandas per testamentum gessit, filius exinde falcidia consequatur. Episcopis sit distributio." *Patetta* schlägt für „filius" „nullus" vor.

40 *Gustav Haenel*, Juliani Epitome latina Novellarum Iustiniani, 1873 (Nachdruck, 1965); *Liebs* (Fn. 35) 220 ff., 269 ff.

41 *Supra*, Fn. 22, S. 29 ff.

erwiesen, daß die Texte bereit lagen. Aussagekräftiger sind die Übernahmen in Kanonessammlungen.

Juliani Epitome VII, 1 kann als zentrale Vorschrift gegen Entfremdung von Gütern der *venerabilia loca* gelten, mit Aufzählung der wohltätigen Einrichtungen und Sanktionen gegen den *oeconomus*, den *tabellio* und sonstige Beteiligte[42]. Der Text ist als vermeintliches Kapitular in der Sammlung des *Ansegis*[43] enthalten. Die nur fragmentarisch überlieferte *Summa De ordine ecclesiastico* konzentriert die Regelung sinnvoll auf das Wesentliche[44]. Diese Fassung übernimmt *Benedictus Levita* in seine gefälschte Kapitulariensammlung[45]. Aus *Ansegis* schöpft *Regino*[46]. Verkürzt, unter Auslassung aller Bezüge auf die wohltätigen Einrichtungen, somit allein als Schutzvorschrift für Kirchengut, hat *Regino* in seinen Büchern über die Sendgerichtsbarkeit die Stelle angeführt[47]. Diese unspezifische Fassung übernimmt *Burchard von Worms* in sein Dekret, allerdings unter der gefälschten Überschrift „Ex concil. apud Silvanectim praesente Ludovico rege, cap. 5"[48]. Vielleicht war der Text in der reduzierten Form uninteressant geworden[49]. Jedenfalls erscheint der ursprüngliche Text aus der *Juliani Epitome* gleich zweimal in *Ivos* Dekret[50]. Auf den vollen Text nehmen anscheinend auch die Bearbeiter des sog. *Liber Papiensis* in der *Expositio* Bezug[51]. *Gratians* Dekret gibt eine völlig abweichende

42 Juliani Epitome VII, 1 (Fn. 40) 32.

43 *Gerhard Schmitz*, Die Kapitulariensammlung des Ansegis, 1996, II, 29, S. 549 ff.; siehe auch ebenda S. 26 f.

44 Summa De ordine ecclesiastico, 22. *Max Conrat*, Der Novellenauszug De ordine ecclesiastico, eine Quelle des Benedikt Levita, Neues Archiv der Gesellschaft für ältere deutsche Geschichtskunde 24 (1898) 341 - 348.

45 Benedicti Capitularia, Additio III, 56, ed. *Georgius Henricus Pertz*, in: Monumenta Germaniae Historica, Leges in folio II, 2, 1837 (Nachdruck, 1965), S. 141.

46 *Gerhard Schmitz*, Ansegis und Regino, ZSS (KA) 74 (1988) 95 - 132; *idem* (Fn. 43) 330 f.

47 *F.G.A. Wasserschleben*, Reginonis libri duo de synodalibus causis, 1840 (Nachdruck, 1964), I, 372, S. 171.

48 *Burchard von Worms*, Decretorum libri XX, 1548, Nachdruck herausgegeben von: *Gérard Fransen, Theo Kölzer*, 1992, III, 164, S. 72 recto. Zu Burchards Textbehandlung: *Horst Fuhrmann*, Einfluß und Verbreitung der pseudoisidorischen Fälschungen, 2. Band, 1973, S. 479 ff.

49 *Seckel* hat in der Sammlung der Handschrift von Santa Croce, die er auf das 11. Jahrhundert datiert, den Text Juliani Epitome VII, 1 identifiziert, diesen jedoch so unvollständig mitgeteilt, daß eine Beurteilung der Textfassung nicht möglich ist. *Emil Seckel*, Zu den Acten der Triburer Synode 895. Zweite Abhandlung, Neues Archiv der Gesellschaft für ältere deutsche Geschichtskunde 20 (1895) 320. Zur Kanonessammlung der Handschrift von Santa Croce: *Paul Fournier*, Un groupe de recueils canoniques italiens des Xe et XIe siècles, in: Theo Kölzer (Hg.), Mélanges de droit canonique, 2. Band, 1983, S. 310 ff.; *Paul Fournier, Gabriel Le Bras*, Histoire des collections canoniques en occident, 1. Band, 1931 (Nachdruck, 1972), S. 445 f.

50 *Ivo*, Decretum III, 183; XVII, 137, in: Migne, Patrologiae cursus completus, ser. lat., Band 161, Sp. 241, 1022. *Ivo* orientiert sich beide Male am *Julianus*, doch fehlt dem ersten Text das Ende und dem zweiten der Anfang.

Fassung der Novelle[52]. Er greift nicht auf die *Juliani Epitome* und das inzwischen vorliegende *Authenticum*[53] zurück, sondern übernimmt die Authentica „Hoc ius porrectum“[54], die bei intensiver Umgestaltung aus den Novellen 7 und 120 gebildet wurde. Dieses Produkt der jungen Rechtswissenschaft[55] dürfte erst in einem späteren Arbeitsgang ins Dekret gekommen sein[56]. Im *Liber Extra* wird unter der Inscription „Ex concilio apud Silvanectim“ der bei *Regino*[57] verkürzte Text mit der von *Burchard*[58] gefälschten Zuweisung wiedergegeben[59].

Das Beispiel zeigt die verschlungenen Wege der Textübermittlung. Was daraus im Hinblick auf ein Interesse an Regelungen über wohltätige Einrichtungen zu entnehmen ist, bedarf der Interpretation. Man möchte annehmen, daß die aufgezeigte Verbreitung von *Juliani Epitome* VII, 1 eine Folge von der tatsächlichen inhaltlichen Bedeutung des Textes ist. Zweifel daran entstehen, da die folgende Stelle, *Juliani Epitome* VII, 2 mit der mageren Aussage, der *princeps* dürfe Liegenschaften mit den heiligen Orten tauschen, in der gleichen Weise verbreitet ist[60]. In dieser Regelung fehlen spezifische Hinweise auf wohltätige Einrichtungen. Daß die Wirkungsgeschichte von *Juliani Epitome* VII, 1 von einem Informationsbedarf über *piae causae* getragen war, muß bezweifelt werden wegen der Verkürzungen in der

51 Liber Papiensis, Astulfus 7, Expositio § 3, ed. *Alfred Boretius*, in: Monumenta Germaniae Historica, Leges in folio IV. Band, 1868 (Nachdruck, 1984), S. 481. Die Kenntnis des Julianus wird durch die vorausgehende Nennung von Xenodochien nahegelegt. Zur Quelle: *Giovanni Diurni*, L'expositio ad Librum Papiensem e la scienzia giuridica preirneriana, Rivista di storia del diritto italiano 49 (1976) 5 - 277.

52 Causa 10, Quaest. 2, c. 2.

53 Authenticum. Novellarum constitutionum Iustiniani versio vulgata, ed. *Gustav Ernst Heimbach*, 1846 - 1851 (Nachdruck, 1974), 1. Band, S. 67 ff.

54 C. Justinianus 1, 2, 14 Authentica Hoc ius porrectum, ed. *Aemilius Herrmann*, in: Albertus Kriegel, Mauritius Kriegel (Hg.), Corpus iuris civilis, 2. Band, 12. Auflage, 1868, S. 18.

55 Die Authentica *Hoc ius porrectum* wird auf *Irnerius* zurückgeführt. Dazu *E. Besta*, L'opera d'Irnerio, 1. Band 1896, S. 1129. Vgl. *Azo*, Lectura super Codicem 1577 (Nachdruck, 1966) zu C. Justinianus 1, 2, 14 Authentica Hoc ius, S. 12. Den Text hat bereits *Vacarius*, Liber Pauperum I, 2 als Glosse, ed. *Francis de Zulueta*, The Liber Pauperum of Vacarius, 1927, S. 6.

56 *Adam Vetulani*, Gratien et le droit romain, in: *idem*, Sur Gratien et les Décrétales, 1990, Nr. III, S. 24; *Stephan Kuttner*, New Studies on the Roman Law in Gratian's Decretum, in: *idem*, Gratian and the Schools of Law 1140 - 1234, 1983, Nr. IV, S. 38 f. Grundsätzlich zur Entstehung des Dekrets jetzt: *Anders Winroth*, The Two Recensions of Gratian's Decretum, ZSS (KA) 83 (1997) 22 - 31.

57 *Supra*, Fn. 47.

58 *Supra*, Fn. 48.

59 X 3, 13, 5; Compilatio prima 3, 11, 4, *Aemilius Friedberg*, Quinque Compilationes antiquae, 1882, S. 30; Collectio Lipsiensis XVI, 11, ebenda, S. 194.

60 *Ansegis* (Fn. 43) II, 30; *Regino* (Fn. 47) I, 373 ungekürzt; *Burchard* (Fn. 48) III, 165 unter Fortführung der gefälschten Inscription von III, 164 (siehe Fn. 48); *Ivo* (Fn. 50) III, 184; *Gratian*, Causa 10, Quaest. 2, c. 2 § 4 aus Authentica „Sed et permutare“ zu C. Justinianus 1, 2, 14 (Fn. 54); Compilatio prima 3, 16, 1 (Fn. 59); X 3, 19, 1 unter Verwendung der genannten Authentica.

Summa De ordine ecclesiastico, bei *Benedictus Levita, Regino Burchard,* der Authentica, bei *Gratian* und im *Liber Extra,* wodurch wesentliche Aussagen verloren gingen. Dieser Eindruck geringen oder gar mangelnden Interesses wird verstärkt durch unterbliebene Übernahmen. Natürlich sind Mutmaßungen in diesem Bereich unsicher, doch lassen sich konkrete Beobachtungen treffen. Obwohl der vollständige Text in *Ivos* Dekret zu finden war, wird er von *Gratian* nicht übernommen, sondern erst später ergänzt man die blasse Version der Authentica. Wie bemerkt, ist *Juliani Epitome* VII, 1 im Zusammenhang dieser Novelle auch in der *Lex Romana canonice compta* enthalten[61]. Von hier aus wäre eine Übernahme in die bedeutenden italienischen Kanonessammlungen möglich gewesen. Dies ist nicht geschehen, obwohl einzelne Sammlungen andere Regelungen aus *Juliani Epitome* VII aufgreifen. Entscheidend war, daß die wegen ihrer Vermittlungswirkung bedeutende *Collectio Anselmo dedicata* zwar *Juliani Epitome* VII, 11 enthält, unseren Text aber nicht übernimmt[62]. Er fehlt auch den *Excerpta Bobiensia*[63], die ebenfalls umfangreich die *Juliani Epitome* ausschreiben. Die *Collectio canonum Regesto Farfensi inserta*[64] und *Deusdedit*[65] haben Texte aus *Juliani Epitome* VII aber nicht VII, 1. Bedeutsam ist das Fehlen in den nur als Rubrikenverzeichnis überlieferten *Capitula ex lege Iustiniana*[66], denn aus dieser Zusammenstellung bedienten sich die *9 Bücher-Sammlung Vaticanus latinus 1349*[67] und die *5 Bücher-Sammlung Vaticanus latinus 1339*[68] mit den zahlreichen von ihr abhängigen Sammlungen[69]. Nur erwähnt sei das Fehlen in kleineren Sammlungen, wie dem *Brevis libellus de rebus ecclesiae*[70].

61 Lex Romana canonice compta 96 (Fn. 22) 70 f.

62 Collectio Anselmo dedicata (Fn. 22) VI, 139 bietet Juliani Epitome VII, 11.

63 Die Angabe *Mors* (Fn. 23) 71, daß Excerpta 1 den Text Juliani Epitome VII, 1 enthalte, dürfte ein Druckfehler für richtig VI, 1 sein, vgl. ebenda S. 79 f.

64 Ed. *Theo Kölzer,* Monumenta iuris canonici, series B, vol. 5, 1982, siehe S. 265.

65 *Deusdedit* (Fn. 32) III, 167, S. 341 enthält Juliani Epitome VII, 7.

66 *Federico Patetta,* Contributi alla storia del diritto romano nel medio evo I, in: *idem,* Studi sulle fonti giuridiche medievali, 1967, S. 1 ff., bes. S. 8 ff. Immerhin enthalten die Capitula Juliani Epitome VII, 7 und 8. Vgl. zum Folgenden auch *Giovanni Santini,* Ricerche sulle „Exceptiones legum romanarum", 1969, S. 183 - 195.

67 *Patetta* (Fn. 66) 14 ff.

68 *Patetta* (Fn. 66) 17 ff.; *Fournier* (Fn. 49) 277 ff., 300 ff. Edition von Buch I-III: *Mario Fornasari,* Collectio canonum in V libris, Corpus Christianorum, Continuatio mediaevalis VI, 1970; Buch IV: *Davide Cito,* Collectio canonum in quinque libris, libro IV, Centro accademico romano della Santa Croce, sezione romana della Facoltà di diritto canonico dell'Università di Navarra, 1989.

69 *Fournier* (Fn. 49) 308 - 325; *Roger E. Reynolds,* The South-Italian Canon Law Collection in Five Books and its Derivatives: New Evidence on its Origins, Diffusion, and Use, in: *idem,* Law and Liturgy in the Latin Church, 5th-12th Centuries, 1994, Nr. XIV.

70 Ed. *Elisabeth Meyer-Marthaler,* in: Lex Romana Curiensis, Sammlung Schweizer Rechtsquellen, 15. Abteilung, 1. Teil, 1. Band, 2. Auflage 1966, S. 620 - 643 unter dem Titel: Constitutiones domini Iustiniani imperatoris pro diversis capitulis episcoporum, monachorum, clericorum vel ea, que ad pias pertinent causas ecclesiae. Weitere kleine Sammlungen sind mit Nachweisen genannt bei *Siems* (Fn. 36) 181, Anm. 102; 321, Anm. 771. Einen Rekonstruktionsversuch unternimmt *Adelheid Krah,* Lex episcoporum et ceteris clericorum,

Insgesamt ergibt sich trotz der beachtlichen Nachwirkung von *Juliani Epitome* VII, 1 der Eindruck, als habe man nach einem Text dieses Inhaltes nicht gerade gesucht. Eher gelegentlich wird die Stelle übernommen und man nimmt auch nicht jede Gelegenheit wahr. Die Kürzungen zeigen, daß man nähere Angaben zu den *piae causae* für verzichtbar hielt.

Die zur frühmittelalterlichen Verbreitung von *Juliani Epitome* VII, 1 getroffenen Feststellungen sollen knapp an der Übernahme weiterer einschlägiger Novellentexte überprüft werden. *Juliani Epitome* XIV gibt eine abgestufte Regelung, unter welchen Voraussetzungen ein *locus venerabilis* Liegenschaften zur Begleichung von Schulden veräußern darf. Den Text hat wohl nur die *Lex Romana canonice compta*[71]. Den Grundstückstausch zwischen *venerabilia loca* behandelt *Juliani Epitome* XLVIII, 2. Das findet sich in der *Lex Romana canonice compta*[72], in *Ivos Decretum* in sinnvoller Verkürzung[73] und ist den Bearbeitern des *Liber Papiensis* bekannt[74]. Die 40jährige Verjährungsfrist zugunsten der *piae causae* in *Juliani Epitome* CIV wird übernommen durch die *Lex Romana canonice compta*[75], *Hinkmar von Reims* zitiert den Text in einem eherechtlichen Traktat[76], die *Excerpta Bobiensia*[77] enthalten ihn und die Bearbeiter des *Liber Papiensis* argumentieren damit[78]; *Deusdedit* übernimmt die Regelung[79], allerdings nicht aus dem *Julianus*, sondern aus dem *Authenticum*[80] mit einigen Änderungen. *Juliani Epitome* CXI, 1 - 5 befassen sich u. a. mit der Entfremdung von Kirchengütern oder des Vermögens wohltätiger Einrichtungen, den Voraussetzungen für Veräußerung und Verpfändung und äußern sich zur Verwaltung. Die *Lex Romana canonice compta* übernimmt wieder alle Regelungen[81]. Die *Anselmo dedicata*[82] und die *Excerpta Bobiensia*[83]

Abhandlungen der sächsischen Akademie der Wissenschaften zu Leipzig, philosophisch-historische Klasse 73, 5, 1993.

71 Lex Romana canonice compta 120 (Fn. 22) 87.

72 Lex Romana canonice compta 122 (Fn. 22) 88.

73 *Ivo,* Decretum III, 189 (Fn. 50) Spalte 243.

74 Siehe den Nachweis Fn. 51.

75 Lex Romana canonice compta 107 (Fn. 22) 77.

76 *Letha Böhringer,* Der eherechtliche Traktat im Paris. Lat. 12445, einer Arbeitshandschrift *Hinkmars von Reims,* Deutsches Archiv für Erforschung des Mittelalters 46 (1990) 32.

77 Excerpta Bobiensia 81 (Fn. 23) 110 f.

78 Liber Papiensis, Liutprandus 69, Expositio § 7 (Fn. 51) 437. Die Stelle wird genau angegeben.

79 *Deusdedit,* Kanonessammlung (Fn. 32) III, 176, S. 345. Die Benutzung des *Authenticum* neben der *Juliani Epitome* bemerkte in anderem Zusammenhang bereits *Hermann Fitting,* Über die Stellen des römischen Rechts in einer Streitschrift des Cardinals Deusdedit, ZSS (RA) 9 (1888) 376 ff.

80 Authenticum 106 (Fn. 53) 2. Band, 823 ff.

81 Lex Romana canonice compta enthält Juliani Epitome 111, 1 - 9 in gleicher Abfolge Nr. 128 - 135 (Fn. 22) 94 - 101, ausgenommen Juliani Epitome 111, 3. Dieser Text wurde versetzt als Nr. 161, S. 110 f. Es handelt sich um jene Regelung, die von der Collectio Anselmo dedicata übernommen wurde, siehe folgende Fn.

haben jeweils nur einen Text. Der *Brevis libellus de rebus ecclesiae* entnimmt dem *Julianus* hier einen Textblock[84]. *Juliani Epitome* CXV, 26 verbietet, daß die Verwalter von *piae causae* ihr Amt gegen Geld erhalten. Der folgende Text erlaubt den Verwaltern Schenkungen aus ihren Vermögen *pro salute animae.* Beide Regelungen stehen in dieser Abfolge in der *Lex Romana canonice compta*[85], den *Excerpta Bobiensia*[86], der 5 Bücher-Sammlung[87] und der *Collectio canonum Regesto Farfensi inserta*[88], der letzte Text auch bei *Deusdedit*[89] und in den *Capitula ex lege iustiniana*[90]. *Juliani Epitome* CXV, 40 bestimmt, daß der Verwalter von *piae causae* Rechnung legen muß und CXV, 41 trifft eine Ergänzungsregelung für dessen Erben. Die *Lex Romana canonice compta* hat die Abfolge der Vorschriften unverständig umgekehrt[91] und der *Brevis libellus de rebus ecclesiae*[92] begnügt sich wenig sinnvoll mit dem Text für den Erben. Weitere Resonanz fehlt. Stärkere Verbreitung erfuhren *Juliani Epitome* CXIX 5 und 6. Die erste Regelung gibt eine Steuer- und Lastenbefreiung. Das übernehmen die *Summa De ordine ecclesiastico*[93] und von dort mit Verkürzung *Benedictus Levita*[94], der *Brevis libellus de rebus ecclesiae*[95], die *Lex Romana canonice compta*[96], die *Excerpta Bobiensia*[97] und *Abbo von Fleury*[98], dabei wird so getan, als gäbe es die spätantiken Steuern und *sordida munera* noch. Die 40jährige Verjährung in *Juliani Epitome* CXIX, 6 findet wieder breite Aufnahme. *Hinkmar von Reims* zitiert sie[99], sie steht in der *Summa De or-*

---

82 Collectio Anselmo dedicata VI 134 enthält Juliani Epitome 111, 3; *Besse* (Fn. 22) 40; *Russo* (Fn. 22) 122.

83 Excerpta Bobiensia 78 (Fn. 23) 109 f. gibt Juliani Epitome 111, 4 wieder.

84 Brevis libellus 1 - 4, ed. *Meyer-Marthaler* (Fn. 70) 623 ff. enthält mit Auslassungen, aber in gleicher Abfolge Juliani Epitome 111, 3 - 9.

85 Lex Romana canonice compta 19, 20 (Fn. 22) 46 f.

86 Excerpta Bobiensia 32, 33 (Fn. 23) 93.

87 Collectio canonum in V libris, I 172, I 173 ed. *Fornasari* (Fn. 68) 113. Da die Capitula ex lege Iustiniana nur den 2. Text bieten (vgl. Fn. 90), bleibt die Frage, woher der erste Text genommen und richtig zugeordnet wurde.

88 Collectio canonum Regesto Farfensi inserta 4, 2 und 4, 3, ed. *Kölzer* (Fn. 64) 245 f.

89 *Deusdedit* III, 172 (Fn. 32) 343.

90 *Patetta* (Fn. 66) 11.

91 Lex Romana canonice compta 46 = Juliani Epitome 115, 41; Lex Romana canonice compta 47 = 115, 40: *Mor* (Fn. 22) 55.

92 Brevis libellus de rebus ecclesiae 10, *Meyer-Marthaler* (Fn. 70) 629.

93 Summa De ordine ecclesiastico 29, *Conrat* (Fn. 44) 343.

94 Benedictus Levita II, 109, *Pertz* (Fn. 45) 79. Dazu *Emil Seckel,* Studien zu Benedictus Levita VII, Neues Archiv der Gesellschaft für ältere deutsche Geschichtskunde 34 (1909) 360.

95 Brevis libellus de rebus ecclesiae 24, 2. Teil, *Meyer-Marthaler* (Fn. 70) 639.

96 Lex Romana canonice compta 112 (Fn. 22) 78.

97 Excerpta Bobiensia 82, *Mor* (Fn. 23) 111.

98 *Abbo von Fleury,* Collectio canonum, c. 5 (3. Text), in: Migne, Patrologiae cursus completus, ser. lat. Band 139, Sp. 479 f.

dine ecclesiastico[100], bei *Benedictus Levita*[101], im *Brevis libellus de rebus ecclesiae*[102], in der *Lex Romana canonice compta*[103], bei *Polycarpus*[104] und *Gratian*[105]. Die Regelungen *Juliani Epitome* CXIX, 9 - 12 betreffen zentrale Fragen der Errichtung und Verwaltung von *piae causae:* Die Auslegung letztwilliger Verfügungen, Einsetzung eines Verwalters und dessen Kontrolle durch den Bischof, Legate für die Armen und deren Verwaltung, deren Durchsetzung gegenüber den Erben. So wichtig diese Regelungen sind, sie finden sich nur in der *Lex Romana canonice compta*[106] und dem unbedeutenden *Brevis libellus de rebus ecclesiae*[107].

Der bisherige Eindruck verfestigt sich. Übernommen werden Texte über die verlängerte Verjährung, über Privilegien und die Entfremdung von Vermögen der *venerabilia loca.* Die typischen Belange der *piae causae,* ihre Verwaltung, finden kaum Resonanz und bei diesen Texten werden auch Kürzungen vorgenommen. Bedenkt man, daß insbesondere die häufig übernommenen Texte in den Überschriften allgemein auf *venerabilia loca*[108] bezogen, und damit auf Kirchenvermögen insgesamt anwendbar sind, so deutet das auf ein Verständnis hin, das die wohltätigen Einrichtungen als Teile des Kirchengutes sieht. Eine solche Sichtweise war durchaus naheliegend, denn seit *Gelasius* war ein Viertel des Kirchenvermögens für die Armen bestimmt[109]. Häuser für Arme, Kranke und Fremde werden zumal bei den Klöstern fest eingerichtet und die Äbte überwachen die Verwaltung. Ein Muster der Aufgabenbestimmung und Organisation für Armen-, Kranken- und Fremdenfürsorge im Rahmen einer Klosterwirtschaft ist in den Statua *Adalhards von Cor-*

---

99 *Böhringer* (Fn. 76).

100 Summa De ordine ecclesiastico 52, *Conrat* (Fn. 44) 344.

101 Benedictus Levita I, 389, *Pertz* (Fn. 45) 69. *Emil Seckel,* Studien zu Benedictus Levita VI, Neues Archiv der Gesellschaft für ältere deutsche Geschichtskunde 31 (1906) 128.

102 Brevis libellus de rebus ecclesiae 25, *Meyer-Marthaler* (Fn. 70) 639.

103 *Mor* (Fn. 22) 78.

104 Polycarpus III, 12, 34, *Horst* (Fn. 31) 214.

105 Causa 16, Quaest. 4, c. 3. *Gratian* dürfte den Text der Juliani Epitome aus einer früheren Kanonessammlung entnommen haben. Immerhin hat er *Polycarpus* benutzt: *Peter Landau,* Neue Forschungen zu vorgratianischen Kanonessammlungen und den Quellen des gratianischen Dekrets, in: *idem,* Kanones und Dekretalen, 1997, Nr. 7, S. 199*.

106 Lex Romana canonice compta 82 - 86 (Fn. 22) 66 ff.

107 Brevis libellus de rebus ecclesiae 26 - 29, *Meyer-Marthaler* (Fn. 70) 639 ff.

108 Juliani Epitome VII, 1 und 2; CXI, 1; CXV, 26 und 27; CXIX, 5 und 6.

109 *Philippus Jaffé,* Regesta pontificum romanorum, 2. Auflage, herausgegeben von: S. Löwenfeld, F. Kaltenbrunner, P. Ewald (JK 636), 1. Band, 1885, S. 85; *Gelasius* epistula 14, ad universos episcopos per Lucaniam, Brutios, et Siciliam constitutos, a. 494, c. 27: „Quatuor tam de reditu quam de oblatione fidelium ... convenit fieri portiones: quarum sit una pontificis, altera clericorum, pauperum tertia, quarta fabriciis applicanda", ed. *Andreas Thiel,* Epistolae romanorum pontificum genuinae et quae ad eos scriptae sunt a S. Hilario usque ad Pelagium II, 1868, S. 378. Zur intensiven Verbreitung des Textes *Friedrich Maassen,* Geschichte der Quellen und der Literatur des canonischen Rechts im Abendlande, 1870 (Nachdruck, 1956), S. 281 f. Grundsätzlich zur kirchlichen Armenfürsorge im Frühmittelalter die Aufsätze von *Boshof* (Fn. 9).

bie[110] überliefert. Sie enthalten einen Abschnitt „De hospitio pauperum" mit sehr detaillierten Anweisungen an den *hospitalarius* über die Darreichungen an die Bedürftigen. Hatte man solche Erscheinungen vor Augen, so mußten antike Rechtstexte über wohltätige Einrichtungen ganz selbstverständlich als Aussagen über Teile des Kirchenvermögens rezipierbar werden.

III. Die Briefe *Gregors des Großen*

Für die frühe Verbreitung der *piae causae* im Westen des versunkenen römischen Reiches wird auf die Briefe *Gregors des Großen* verwiesen[111]. Deren Bedeutung für die mittelalterliche Rechtsentwicklung ist leicht daran abzulesen, daß *Gratian* von keinem Papst so viele Texte übernimmt, wie aus den Briefen *Gregors*[112]. Aussagen *Gregors* zu Recht und Verwaltung der Kirche mußte wegen seiner Autorität und der Verbreitung seiner Briefe[113] große Bedeutung zukommen. Tatsächlich enthält das *Decretum Gratiani* drei im vorliegenden Zusammenhang interessierende Texte, die auf *Gregor den Großen* zurückgehen. „Sacrilegium et contra legem est, si quis quod venerabilibus locis relinquitur pravae voluntatis studiis temptaverit conpendiis retinere."[114] Der griffige Satz war ursprünglich auf ein nicht ausgefolgtes Legat zugunsten einer Kirche bezogen. Durch die Herauslösung aus dem Kontext erfaßte er jetzt auch wohltätige Einrichtungen als Empfänger. Die Anordnung, keine Almosen von unrechtmäßig erworbenem Gut zu geben[115], nennt als Empfänger einmal die Armen, dann die Klöster und Xenodochien. Gemeint war jeweils das gleiche und die Wortwahl wird dem Stilgefühl und nicht einem Drang nach juristischer Korrektheit gefolgt sein. Die Regelung, daß kein Abt oder Priester eines Xenodochium oder Klosters Bischof werden soll, damit diese Einrichtungen und die dort lebenden Armen und Fremden keine Not leiden[116], ist

---

110 *Adalhardi* abbatis Corbeiensis Statuta seu Brevia, ed. *Josef Semmler*, in: K. Hallinger (Hg.), Corpus consuetudinum monasticarum, 1. Band, 1963, S. 365 - 408; *Brigitte Kasten*, Adalhard von Corbie, 1986, S. 110 - 137, besonders S. 125 ff.; *Dieter Hägermann*, Der Abt als Grundherr. Kloster und Wirtschaft im frühen Mittelalter, in: F. Prinz (Hg.), Herrschaft und Kirche, 1988, besonders S. 351 - 369; *Martina Stratmann*, Schriftlichkeit in der Verwaltung von Bistümern und Klöstern, in: R. Schieffer (Hg.), Schriftkultur und Reichsverwaltung unter den Karolingern, 1996, bes. S. 90 ff.

111 Zuletzt etwa *Borgolte* (Fn. 7) 81.

112 Vgl. die Aufstellung bei *Aemilius Friedberg*, Corpus iuris canonici, 1. Teil 1879 (Nachdruck, 1959), Spalte XXV-XXXI.

113 *Gregorius I Papa*, Registrum epistolarum, ed. *Paulus Ewald*, *Ludovicus M. Hartmann*, Monumenta Germanicae Historica, Epistolae Band 1 und 2, 1887 - 1899 (Nachdruck, 1978), diese Ausgabe wird benutzt; ed. *D. Norberg*, 2 Bände, 1982; *Ernst Pitz*, Papstreskripte im frühen Mittelalter. Diplomatische und rechtsgeschichtliche Studien zum Brief-Corpus Gregors des Großen, 1990.

114 *Gregor* (Fn. 113) IX, 89; *Gratian*, Causa 17, Quaest. 4, c. 4.

115 *Gregor* (Fn. 113) IX, 218; *Gratian*, Causa 1, Quaest. 1, c. 27.

116 *Gregor* (Fn. 113) XIII, 11.

bei *Gratian* stärker auf die Klöster ausgerichtet[117]. Hinter der Vorschrift stehen grundsätzliche Probleme der Vermögenssicherung.

Die Aussagen zu den wohltätigen Einrichtungen in den Briefen *Gregors* sind geprägt durch konkrete Probleme. Sie erscheinen bestimmt durch fallbezogene Pragmatik und nicht als Deduktionen aus fester Begrifflichkeit. *Gregor* verwendet den Ausdruck *piae causae* unterschiedlich. Einmal steht er umgangssprachlich flach für fromme-religiöse Angelegenheiten[118], dann läßt die Abfolge Kirchen, Klöster, *piae causae*[119] an die überkommene Bezeichnung wohltätiger Einrichtungen denken. *Gregor* verwendet in letzterem Zusammenhang sonst das Wort Xenodochia. In anderen Briefen ist die genaue Bedeutung von *piae causae* offen.

Wie sich bereits abzeichnet, ist der gängige Ausdruck für wohltätige Einrichtungen bei *Gregor* Xenodochia und damit sind über die ursprüngliche Bedeutung hinaus auch Armenhäuser gemeint[120]. Immer wieder ist der Papst mit Angelegenheiten der Xenodochien befaßt und seine Briefe geben Einblick in deren alltägliche Probleme[121]. Xenodochien werden durch Legate errichtet oder zusätzlich ausgestattet. Selbst wenn einem Xenodochium nur 10 Stuten und ein Hengst vermacht werden, kann die Durchsetzung eine Initiative des Papstes erforderlich machen[122]. Daß Legate von den Erben auch tatsächlich ausgefolgt werden, war anscheinend ein durchgängiges Problem[123], und es ist daher nicht zufällig, daß *Gratian* sich zur Erzwingung auf einen Satz *Gregors* beruft[124]. Dringt der Papst auf Erfüllung des Erblasserwillens, so zeigt er sich gleichzeitig sehr souverän in der Auslegung dieses Willens. Ein gewisser Isidor hatte letztwillig angeordnet, in Palermo ein Xenodochium zu errichten, und der Papst schreibt dem *defensor* Fantino, dessen Erben zur Durchführung anzuhalten[125]. Sollten die hinterlassenen Mittel dazu nicht ausreichen – man mag vermuten, daß die Erben dies behauptet haben, um von ihrer Verpflichtung frei zu werden – dann sollen diese Mittel dem Xenodochium Sancti Theodori, das ein gewisser Petrus in der gleichen Stadt errichtet hat, zugewiesen werden. *Gregor* erklärt das unbeschwert zur „voluntas defuncti", durch dessen Einhaltung auch die Erben von ihrer Pflicht befreit würden. Legate zugunsten von Xenodochien sollten allerdings nicht im Sinne moderner Begrifflichkeit als Nachweis

---

117 Causa 16, Quaest. 1, c. 39.

118 *Gregor* (Fn. 113) IV, 12; XIII, 11.

119 *Gregor* (Fn. 113) XIV, 2. Es werden Regelungen getroffen über die Verwaltung der Xenodochien auf Sardinien.

120 *Gregor* (Fn. 113) XIII, 11; IX, 63. Zu den Griechischkenntnissen im Mittelalter: *Walter Berschin*, Griechisch-Lateinisches Mittelalter, 1980.

121 *Gregor* (Fn. 113) I, 42; II, 38; IV, 8; IV, 24; IX, 8; IX, 35; IX, 63; IX, 66a; IX, 82; IX, 130; IX ,170; XIII, 7; XIII, 11 - 13.

122 *Gregor* (Fn. 113) IX, 8.

123 *Gregor* (Fn. 113) IX, 35; IX, 170.

124 *Supra*, Fn. 114.

125 *Gregor* (Fn. 113) IX, 35.

einer Rechtsträgerschaft der Xenodochien verstanden werden. Im Jahre 598 schreibt *Gregor*[126], daß der *numerarius* Bonifatius dem bei St. Peter gelegenen Xenodochium testamentarisch einen Teil seines Vermögens hinterlassen habe und nennt es einige Zeilen später ganz selbstverständlich ein Vermächtnis zugunsten der Armen. Beide Male ist derselbe Sachverhalt gemeint und dürfte auch verstanden worden sein, so wie man heute die Aussage, eine deutsche Gewerkschaft habe Grundstücke erworben, versteht, ohne daß damit der rechtliche Vorgang bezeichnet werden sollte.

Wiederholt ist *Gregor* mit Verwaltungsangelegenheiten der Xenodochien befaßt[127]. Verwalter oder Leiter sollen in jeder Hinsicht untadelige und eifrige Leute sein, die keinem *iudex* unterstehen, auf daß die Güter keinen Schaden nehmen[128]. Die Verwalter haben dem Bischof Rechnung zu legen[129]. Im Jahre 598 bekräftigt der Papst eine Vereinbarung zwischen dem Abt eines Klosters in Palermo und dem Subdiakon Antonius *praepositus* des Xenodochium Valerii in Rom. Die Vereinbarung soll einen Streit zwischen Kloster und Xenodochium über Besitzungen im Gebiet von Palermo beenden[130]. Ihre Verbindlichkeit erlangt die Vereinbarung anscheinend aus dem Handeln des Abtes und des *praepositus.* Ein erforderliches Mitwirken weiterer Personen hätte *Papst Gregor,* der an der Streitbeilegung sehr interessiert ist, erwähnt oder herbeigeführt. Der *praepositus*[131] kann danach allein für das Xenodochium handeln und auch gewichtige Verträge schließen.

Gefahren, die einem Xenodochium drohen konnten, lassen sich aus einem Privileg *Gregors* für ein von der Königin Brunichild in Autun gegründetes Xenodochium ablesen[132]. Der Papst gewährt ungestörten Besitz und Schutz gegen Entfremdung. Der Abt soll vom König im Einverständnis mit den Mönchen gewählt

126 *Gregor* (Fn. 113) IX, 63.

127 *Gregor* (Fn. 113) I, 42; II, 38; IV, 24; IX, 66a; IX, 82.

128 *Gregor* (Fn. 113) IV, 24.

129 *Supra,* Fn. 128.

130 *Gregor* (Fn. 113) IX, 66a; IX, 82.

131 „Praepositus" muß kein fester Begriff sein. Inhaber der gleichen Funktion nennt *Gregor* (Fn. 130) kurz zuvor „amministratores".

132 *Gregor* (Fn. 113) XIII, 7 enthält die Antwort an Brunichild; XIII, 11 das Privileg für das Xenodochium und XIII, 12 und XIII, 13 Privilegien für Klöster in Autun. Die drei Privilegien entsprechen sich über weite Strecken, was die Annäherung von Kloster und Xenodochium in ihrer Organisation zeigt. Zum frühmittelalterlichen Autun und diesem Xenodochium: *Carlrichard Brühl,* Palatium und civitas, 1. Band, Gallien, 1975, S. 111 ff.; *Jean Richard,* Autun, in: Lexikon des Mittelalters, 1. Band, Sp. 1274 ff. Das Privileg XIII, 11 ist als Fälschung verdächtigt worden wegen Übereinstimmung der Pönformel mit einer Abhandlung *Hinkmar von Reims* „Quae exsequi debeat episcopus ...", in: Migne, Patrologiae cursus completus, ser. lat., Band 125, Spalte 1091. Dazu *Loening* (Fn. 1) 2. Band, 392 ff., Anm. 2; *Brühl,* Die Urkunden Karls des Einfältigen und Rudolfs von Westfranken für das Nonnenkloster St. Andoche zu Autun, in: *idem,* Aus Mittelalter und Diplomatik, 2 Bände, 1989, S. 839. Keine Bedenken bei *Eugen Ewig,* Beobachtungen zu den Klosterprivilegien des 7. und 8. Jahrhunderts, in: *idem,* Spätantikes und fränkisches Gallien, 2 Bände, 1979, S. 414; *Friedrich Prinz,* Frühes Mönchtum im Frankenreich, 1965, S. 161; *Pitz* (Fn. 113).

werden. Weder der König noch eine andere Person soll für die Wahl etwas aus dem Vermögen des Xendochium erhalten. Der Abt kann nur nach einem besonders gesicherten Verfahren abgesetzt werden. Kein Abt oder Priester des Xenodochium soll zum Bischofsamt gelangen, auf daß dem Xenodochium kein Vermögen entzogen wird und die Armen, Fremden und sonstigen dort Lebenden in Not geraten. Die letzte Anordnung hat, wie gezeigt, *Gratian* übernommen[133] und damit verallgemeinert.

Gregor gewährt das Privileg auf Bitten der Königin. Es sollte also allgemeinen Befürchtungen vorgebeugt werden. Gefährdet war das Vermögen durch Übergriffe von außen aber auch von innen, etwa dadurch, daß man einen mißliebigen Abt durch einen willfährigen ersetzte. Wenn der zum Bischofsamt gelangte frühere Abt oder Priester des Xenodochium weiter auf dessen Güter zugreifen kann, so weist das auf eine unzureichende Verselbständigung dieses Vermögens hin, mit der Folge einer Gefährdung der Zwecksetzung, nämlich die Armenversorgung. *Gregor* sieht die Probleme und sucht pragmatische Lösungen unter anderem durch Ämtertrennung. Wenn schon nicht die Vermögensmassen entsprechend ihrer Zweckbestimmung voneinander abgehoben werden können, so werden wenigstens die Funktionsträger voneinander getrennt und gegen Eingriffe abgeschirmt.

Wie auch bei der Behandlung wirtschaftlicher Probleme seiner Zeit[134] zeigt *Gregor* hier eine beachtliche Aufgeschlossenheit für Alltagsschwierigkeiten und sucht nach praktischen Lösungen. Bei dieser Ausrichtung ist die Entwicklung abstrakter Rechtsfiguren wie eine begriffliche Erfassung der Xenodochien nicht zu erwarten. Von Fall zu Fall werden Recht und Verwaltung des Kirchenvermögens weiter entwickelt.

IV. Merowingische Formulare und Testamente

Als Beleg für eine frühmittelalterliche Stiftung mit eigener Rechtspersönlichkeit wird ein Formular bei *Marculf* angeführt[135]. Gemeint ist das fränkische Formularbuch des Mönchs *Marculf* vom Ende des 7. Jahrhunderts. Es enthält eine Sammlung von Mustern *(formulae)* für unterschiedliche Geschäfte. Für die Errichtung eines Xenodochium steht ein Formular mit der Überschrift: „Ista de magna rem, qui vult exsinodocio aut monasterio construere“[136] bereit. Die Parallele zur kirchlichen Einrichtung macht wieder deutlich, welchem Rechts- und Lebenskreis wohltätige Einrichtungen bis in die Institutionen und Hierarchie hinein zugeordnet sind. Der

133 *Supra,* Fn. 116 f.

134 Bemerkenswert sind die unvoreingenommenen sachorientierten Entscheidungen, vgl. *Siems* (Fn. 36) 662 ff.

135 *Schönfeld* (Fn. 10) 30; *Boshof* (Fn. 9) 158 f.

136 *Marculfi* Formulae II, 1, ed. *Karl Zeumer,* Formulae merowingici et karolini aevi, in: Monumenta Germaniae Historica, 1886 (Nachdruck, 1963), S. 70 ff.

außergewöhnlich umfangreiche Prolog variiert immer wieder das Grundthema des Formulars, daß man für Gaben an die Armen himmlischen Lohn empfangen soll. Deshalb errichtet der Schenker ein oratorium oder eine cellola für 12 Arme und überträgt Liegenschaften und weitere Güter an die Armen oder Kleriker, die dort dienen „... de meo iure in eorum dominatione et potestate lego, trado, transmitto atque transfundo ...". Lastenfreiheit wird gewährt und alles soll dem Oratorium und den Armen zustehen „... in iure oraturio sanctae Mariae et predictorum pauperum ...", so wird wiederholt gesagt. Insbesondere soll der örtliche Bischof keine Macht haben, das Vermögen zu mindern. Schließlich vertraut der Schenker aber dem Bischof den Schutz der Güter und die Herrschaft über die Armen an und übergibt ihm die Urkunde „... defensionem rerum vel gubernationem ipsorum pauperum ... episcopo ... committo et strumenta ... per manibus tradedi ...".

Die sich abzeichnenden Probleme sind aus den Briefen *Gregors*, namentlich seinem Privileg für das Xenodochium in Autun[137], bekannt. Es drohen Zugriffe auf das für die Armen bestimmte Vermögen von innerhalb und außerhalb der Kirche. Deshalb soll sicher gestellt werden, daß alles dem Oratorium oder den Armen ausschließlich zusteht. Doch reicht das nicht, nach außen benötigt man den Schutz des Bischofs, der auch für die Leitung Sorge tragen muß. Gleichzeitig soll seine Macht nach innen begrenzt werden, um Übergriffe auf das Vermögen seinerseits zu verhindern. Hinzu kommt ein weiteres Problem. Das Xenodochium sollte erst errichtet werden. Es bedurfte aber schon eines Empfängers der Zuwendung. Hierfür und zur Durchsetzung des Schenkerwillens bot sich wiederum der Bischof an. Zur Bewertung des Gesamtvorganges kann es nicht darauf ankommen, welche Rechtsfigur man heute aus modernen Arsenalen auswählen würde. Aufzudecken sind die Gedanken der Damaligen. Die Gestaltung des Geschäfts läßt ein entwickeltes Problembewußtsein vermuten. Eine Lösung suchte man darin, daß das Vermögen den Armen oder dem Oratorium zugewiesen wurde. Dafür stehen Ausdrücke wie „in iure" oder „in potestate". Dazu paßt es, daß dem Bischof die Güter des künftigen Xenodochium nur anvertraut und die Urkunde übergeben wird. Es will eher scheinen, als habe man sich zu Vorstellungen von Treuhandschaft vorgetastet, als daß man die Kategorie der Stiftung mit eigener Rechtspersönlichkeit beherrscht hätte.

Welche Vorstellungen in merowingischer Zeit von Rechtsinhaberschaft bestanden, ist unsicher. Jedenfalls wechseln die Bezeichnungen[138]. In den *Formulae Andecavenses* vom Ende des 6. Jahrhunderts wird bei einer Schenkung an ein Kloster gleichzeitig von einer Zuwendung an die Basilika, an die Kongregation der Mönche und an deren „rector" gesprochen[139]. *Marculf* kennt die *dominatio sancti loci*[140] und meint ein Kloster. Bei Zuwendungen an Kirchen und Klöster heißt es „in

---

137 *Supra*, Fn. 132.

138 Zum Folgenden: *Franz Dorn*, Die Landschenkungen der fränkischen Könige, 1991, S. 177 - 213, besonders S. 200 ff.

139 Formulae Andecavenses 46, ed. *Zeumer* (Fn. 136) 20.

140 *Marculf* I, 35 (Fn. 136) 65.

potestate et dominatione monasterii illi, in honore illi ... transfundimus..." oder „in iure et dominatione sancte ecclesiae illius" u.s.w.[141]. In einer Urkunde kann der gleiche Vorgang aber auch einmal mit „in substantia pauperum conferimus", dann „ad prefata baselica volo esse donatum" beschrieben werden und schließlich soll der Abt die Güter in seine Herrschaft bringen[142]. Man nahm keinen Anstoß an der Vielfalt der Ausdrucksweise, die deshalb nicht zur Rückprojizierung moderner Institutionen dienen darf, ist doch zu bezweifeln, daß man sich die möglichen Unterschiede bewußt gemacht hat[143]. Je mehr man aber nicht nur den *locus sanctus,* sondern den Heiligen selbst als Inhaber der zugewandten Güter sah, desto deutlicher mußte die Zweckbindung des Vermögens werden.

Der im Formular *Marculfs* angetroffenen Gestaltungsmöglichkeit seien zwei Testamente des 7. Jahrhunderts gegenübergestellt[144]. Aus dem Jahre 616 haben wir das umfangreiche Testament des *Bischofs Berthramn von Le Mans*[145] mit einer Fülle von Verfügungen. Dabei zeigen sich durchaus Nachwirkungen des römischen Rechts. *Berthramn* setzt die Kirche von Le Mans und die Basilika der Apostel Petrus und Paulus zu Erben ein mit der Formel: „... heredes michi estote, heredesque meos vos esse constituo ac jubeo; caeteri ve exheredes sint toti"[146]. Aus dem großen Vermögen *Berthramns* erhalten die Armen keine unmittelbaren Zuwendungen. *Berthramn* verfährt in der Art, daß er alle Vermögensposten den Erben oder einer Vielzahl von Vermächtnisnehmern jeweils einzeln zuweist. Diese Verfügungen sind gelegentlich mit Auflagen verbunden, die den Armen bestimmte Erträge zuweisen, wie z. B.: „... quicquid exinde aut in tributum aut in suffragium annis singulis poterit obvenire, medietas ex hoc, quando fuerit mea commemoratio, pauperibus aut in vestimentum aut in aurum erogetur"[147]. Gemessen am Gesamtvermögen halten sich diese wohltätigen Zuwendungen sehr in Grenzen[148].

---

141 *Marculf* II, 3 - 6 (Fn. 136) 74 ff.

142 *Marculf* II, 6 (Fn. 136) 78 f.

143 *Dorn* (Fn. 138) 208.

144 Dazu *Ulrich Nonn,* Merowingische Testamente. Studien zum Fortleben einer römischen Urkundenform im Frankenreich, Archiv für Diplomatik 18 (1972) 1 - 129; *Goswin Spreckelmeyer,* Zur rechtlichen Funktion frühmittelalterlicher Testamente, in: P. Classen (Hg.), Recht und Schrift im Mittelalter (Vorträge und Forschungen, 23), 1977, S. 91 - 113.

145 *Thiele* (Fn. 9) 49 ff. und 138 ff.; *Michael Borgolte,* Felix est homo ille, qui amicos bonos relinquit. Zur sozialen Gestaltungskraft letztwilliger Verfügungen am Beispiel Bischof Berthrams von Le Mans (616), in: H. Maurer, H. Patze (Hg.), Festschrift für Berent Schwineköper zum 70. Geburtstag, 1982, S. 5 - 18; und jetzt umfassend *Margarete Weidemann,* Das Testament des Bischofs Berthramn von Le Mans vom 27. März 616. Untersuchungen zu Besitz und Geschichte einer fränkischen Familie im 6. und 7. Jahrhundert, 1986, dort S. 7 - 49 eine Edition des Testaments.

146 *Weidemann* (Fn. 145) 7.

147 *Weidemann* (Fn. 145) 11.

148 In der Zählung von *Weidemann* (Fn. 145) sind die Verfügungen Nr. 4, 25, 33, 36, 39 mit solchen Auflagen beschwert. Verfügung 36 etwa, stellt den Fischhändlern der Kirchen von Le Mans, die nach Bordeaux kommen, eine Unterkunft zur Verfügung.

Berthramn scheint auf die Einhaltung der Auflagen vertraut zu haben. Nur zweimal bittet er seine Nachfolger im Bischofsamt oder den Abt von St. Peter und Paul um Durchführung und wird dabei recht drastisch[149]. Ein Xenodochium in Pontlieue für Arme und Fremde soll künftig 16 Arme, Blinde und Gebrechliche beherbergen und täglich versorgen. Sollte der Abt darin nachlässig sein, habe er vor dem Gericht Christi Rechnung zu legen. Keiner seiner Nachfolger im Bischofsamt soll dem Ort oder den Armen das ihnen Zugewandte entziehen. Andernfalls soll er vor dem göttlichen Gericht als *necator pauperum* verurteilt werden. *Berthramn* bezieht sich auf das aktuelle Kirchenrecht. Das Konzil von Agde a. 506 hat jedem, der das der Kirche Vermachte zurückhielt oder entzog, als *necator pauperum* aus der Kirche ausgestoßen[150]. Dieser außerordentlich verbreitete Kanon, der ins *Decretum Gratiani* gelangte[151], wurde in merowingischen Konzilien mit dem Begriff des *necator pauperum* immer wieder aufgegriffen und allgemein auf den Schutz von Kirchengut erstreckt[152]. Zur Absicherung des von ihm bedachten Xenodochium bemühte *Berthramn* sich nicht um entsprechende rechtliche Konstruktion, wie dies im Formular *Marculfs* versucht wird. Dem mag schon die fehlende Selbständigkeit des Xenodochium entgegen gestanden haben. Zwar war es rein tatsächlich eine eigene Einrichtung, die aber der kirchlichen Hierarchie, konkret einem Kloster, zugeordnet war. Zur Sicherung seiner Zuwendung vertraut *Berthramn* auf kirchenrechtliche – religiöse Sanktionen.

Aus dem Jahre 634 kennen wir das Testament eines reichen Grundbesitzers, des Diakon *Adalgisel-Grimo* aus Verdun[153]. Zum Erben hat er das *monasterium* der heiligen Agatha in Longuyon eingesetzt neben einer Reihe von Legaten. Die zugewandten Güter sollen „suo iure“ oder „suo iure et dominatione“ besessen werden. Das als Erbe bedachte Kloster wird unterschiedlich benannt: „Confero monasterio sive xenodochio vel pauperibus Longagionis ...“ oder „monasterium Longagionense vel clericis seu pauperibus ...“ oder „sancto monasterio seu congregatio Longagionense, quos mihi heredes constitui ...“. Gemeint war stets dasselbe; veranschaulicht wird, was *Adalgisel* bei seiner Zuwendung vor Augen hat: Das Kloster, die Gemeinschaft, die Mönche, die dort versorgten Armen. Juristisch-technische Präzision wurde nicht angestrebt. Die Armen wollte *Adalgisel* selbstverständ-

149 *Weidemann* (Fn. 145) 26.

150 Concilium Agathense a. 506, c. 4, ed. *Charles Munier,* Concilia Galliae a. 314 – a. 506, Corpus Christianorum, ser. lat. 148, 1963, S. 194.

151 Causa 13, Quaest. 2, c. 11.

152 Concilium Aurelianense a. 549, c. 13, c. 15, c. 16; Concilium Arelatense a. 554, c. 6; Concilium Turonense a. 567, c. 25, c. 26; Concilium Parisiense a. 556 - 573, c. 1; Concilium Valentinum a. 583 - 585; Concilium Parisiense a. 614, c. 9; Concilium Clippiacense a. 626 - 627, c. 12, c. 24; Concilium Cabilonense a. 647 - 653, c. 6, ed. *Carolus de Clercq,* Concilia Galliae a. 511 – a. 695, Corpus Christianorum, ser. lat. 148 A, 1963, S. 152 - 154, 172, 192 f., 205, 235, 277, 294, 296, 304.

153 *Wilhelm Levison,* Das Testament des Diakon Adalgisel-Grimo vom Jahre 634, in: *idem,* Aus rheinischer und fränkischer Frühzeit, 1948, S. 118 - 138, Edition des Testaments S. 124 - 136.

lich versorgt wissen, doch hat er sie nicht als Empfänger seines Vermögens gesehen. Vielmehr hat er dem Abt die Sorge um das Xenodochium auferlegt. Stets sollten 16 Arme dort unterhalten werden. Eine Absicherung dieses Wunsches unterbleibt, von einer Verselbständigung des Xenodochium ist nichts zu spüren. Läßt man außer Betracht, daß die Kirche durch Hierarchie und moralische Prinzipien andere Rahmenbedingungen hatte, so bietet sich als Vergleich *Adalgisels* Vermächtnis von 4 Mühlen an den „molinarius" Erpo an, mit der Auflage „pauperes illos quos in villa Marciaco institui nutriat et gubernet". Eine eigene Rechtsposition gab ihnen das nicht.

Unsicher ist auch die rechtliche Beurteilung der Vermächtnisse an die Aussätzigen in Maastricht „leprosi Treiectenses" und Metz „leprosi Metenses", denn hier fehlen Hinweise auf die institutionellen und organisatorischen Umstände. Vielleicht war ganz selbstverständlich an entsprechende Verhältnisse gedacht, wie sie für die Aussätzigen in Verdun genannt werden „basilica sancti domni Petri et domni Vitoni oppidi Virdunensis, ubi leprosi resident ..." Die Leprosen waren Nutznießer des von der tragenden Einrichtung, einem Kloster etwa, gehaltenen Vermächtnisses.

Adalgisel bedenkt schließlich auch die *matricularii* in Trier, Huy und von St. Martin in Tours. Es soll sich um Arme einer Kirche handeln, die in ein Verzeichnis (*matricula*) aufgenommen und mit der Zeit privilegiert waren[154]. Ein gewisses Vermögen scheinen die *matricularii* in Trier gehabt zu haben, denn *Adalgisel* hatte ihnen früher ein Haus abgekauft, das er ihnen im Testament zurückgewährt. Auch die *matricularii* in Huy und St. Martin in Tours werden bedacht. Man hat die *matricularii* als Korporation mit Geschäftsfähigkeit eingestuft und das u. a. auf den erwähnten Hausverkauf in Trier gestützt[155]. Doch sagt das Testament dafür zu wenig. Es bleibt offen, wer gehandelt hat und man erfährt auch nicht, wie sich der Erwerb vermachter Güter vollziehen sollte, welche Rolle etwa die Kirche oder das Kloster, in deren *matricula* die Armen geführt wurden, dabei spielten. Immerhin gibt es zwei Formulare in denen die *matricularii* gemeinsam handelnd ein an ihrer Kirche ausgesetztes Kind verkaufen[156].

Während die Formula *Marculfs* zur Absicherung des Xenodochium, seines Vermögens und seiner Zwecke eine rechtliche Konstruktion, die nach außen den Schutz des Bischofs gewinnt, diesen aber am Zugriff auf das Vermögen hindert, zu entwickeln sucht, gehen die Testamente *Berthramns* und *Adalgisel-Grimos* von einer anderen Situation aus. Die Armenfürsorge ist kirchlichen Institutionen angegliedert und erfährt von diesen Ausstattung, Schutz und Aufsicht. Konsequent wer-

---

154 *Boshof* (Fn. 9) 163 ff.; zu einer Gleichsetzung von Xenodochium und matricula kommt *Imbert* (Fn. 1) 39, Anm. 3.

155 *Boshof* (Fn. 9) 166.

156 Formulae Andecavenses 49, hier wird die Zustimmung eines Priesters erwähnt; Formulae Turonenses 11 mit Zitat von Lex Romana Visigothorum C. Th. V, 8, 1, ed. *Zeumer* (Fn. 136) 21, 141.

den die künftigen Bischöfe und Äbte um die fürsorgliche Wahrnehmung ihrer Aufgaben gebeten. Der Satz aus dem Testament *Berthramns* „Felix est homo ille, qui amicos bonos relinquid"[157] hat danach eine größere Bedeutung als *Berthramn* unmittelbar ausdrücken wollte.

V. Merowingische Konzilien, *Leges* und Kapitularien

Aus dem Bisherigen war zu sehen, daß zum Schutz des Vermögens der wohltätigen Einrichtungen zwei Wege betreten werden konnten, eine rechtliche Ausgestaltung, die das Vermögen verselbständigte und mit Rechnungslegung gegen unberechtigten Zugriff abschirmte, oder sanktionsbewehrte Verbote. Auf *Gregor* geht die Einstufung vorenthaltener Legate als Sacrileg zurück[158] und der Ausschluß des *necator pauperum* aus der Kirche wurde auf merowingischen Konzilien beständig wiederholt[159]. Daraus ergibt sich die Frage nach frühmittelalterlichen Rechtsnormen zum Schutz, aber auch zur rechtlichen Gestaltung wohltätiger Einrichtungen. Wenige Hinweise müssen genügen.

Seit dem Konzil von Agde a. 506 zieht sich der Kirchenausschluß des *necator pauperum* durch das Bewußtsein merowingischer Konzilsteilnehmer. Den Schutz der Armen gegen Bedrückung durch „iudices aut potentes" spricht das Konzil von Tours 567 aus und droht diesen Exkommunikation an, falls sie sich auf Ermahnung des Bischofs nicht bessern[160]. Immerhin war es eine Norm, die sich vielfältiger Anwendung öffnen konnte. An die Unterstützung der Armen denkt das bedeutende Konzil von Orléans 511, das Bischöfe des gesamten Reiches vereinigte. Grundsätzlich wird festgelegt, daß ein Teil der Erträge aus königlichen Schenkungen an die Kirchen den Armen und dem Freikauf Gefangener zukommen soll[161]. Den Bischöfen wird es zur Pflicht gemacht, Arme und Kranke, die nicht arbeiten können, nach Möglichkeit mit Nahrung und Kleidung zu versorgen[162]. Im Jahre 549 tagt wieder ein Konzil in Orléans und die Teilnehmer sind betroffen vom Schicksal der Aussätzigen, die von ihrer schweren Krankheit in unerträgliche Not gedrückt werden. Die Bischöfe sollen ihnen deshalb aus den Mitteln der Kirche, soweit möglich, Nahrung und Kleidung geben[163]. 567 auf dem Konzil in Tours wird eine neue Dimension der Not sichtbar. Die Armen ziehen von Ort zu Ort in der Hoffnung auf Hilfe. Jede Stadt soll deshalb nach Kräften ihre Armen ernähren, auf das sie nicht herumvagieren. Mit der gleichen Zielrichtung gibt das Konzil von Lyon 583 den

157 *Supra,* Fn. 114.

158 *Supra,* Fn. 152.

159 Concilium Turonense a. 567, c. 27, *de Clercq* (Fn. 152) 194.

160 Concilium Aurelianense a. 511, c. 5, *de Clercq* (Fn. 152) 6.

161 Concilium Aurelianense a. 511, c. 16, *de Clercq* (Fn. 152) 9.

162 Concilium Aurelianense a. 549, c. 21, *de Clercq* (Fn. 152) 156.

163 Concilium Turonense a. 567, c. 5, *de Clercq* (Fn. 152) 178.

Bischöfen auf, den Aussätzigen Nahrung und Kleidung zu geben und sie am Herumziehen zu hindern[164]. Dies mag die Schaffung von Armen- und Leprosenhäusern nahegelegt haben. Die genannten Maßnahmen selbst schaffen allerdings keine dauernden wohltätigen Einrichtungen mit eigenen Mitteln.

Ein Xenodochium wird erstmals auf dem gleichen Konzil erwähnt, als Gründung durch König Childebert und Königin Vulthrogotho zu Lyon[165]. Die Situation ähnelt der Privilegierung des Xenodochium in Autun durch *Gregor* auf Bitten der Gründerin Königin Brunichild[166]. Jetzt bekräftigen die Konzilsväter die Errichtung des Xenodochium in Lyon und bemühen sich um dessen Absicherung. Insbesondere sollen die Bischöfe nichts von dem entfremden, was dem Xenodochium zugewandt wurde „. . .nihil exinde ad se . . . aut ad ius ecclesiae transferat . . .“. Vielmehr soll der Bestand gegen jedwede Minderung gesichert werden. Als *praepositi* sollen tüchtige und gottesfürchtige Leute eingesetzt werden, die Sorge für die Kranken und Fremden stets sichergestellt sein. Bei Verstößen und Übergriffen auf das Vermögen des Xenodochium droht dem *necator pauperum* das Anathem.

Schönfeld[167] sah hier wieder eine Stiftung mit eigener Rechtspersönlichkeit, das Stiftungsvermögen wäre völlig selbständig und auch für den Bischof unantastbar gewesen. Es läßt sich vermuten, daß man derartiges angestrebt hätte, wäre man zu solchen rechtlichen Konstruktionen in der Lage gewesen. Tatsächlich war das Vermögen des Xenodochium sehr wohl antastbar und seiner Minderung sucht man durch Bannandrohung vorzubeugen. Aufmerksamkeit verdient, daß wie beim Privileg *Papst Gregors* für das Xenodochium in Autun, die Initiative für die Absicherung der Einrichtung von den Gründern, also der königlichen Familie, ausging und Beweggrund war jedesmal, Befürchtungen vor Übergriffen auf das Vermögen von innerhalb – „ad ius ecclesiae transferat . . .“, sagte das Konzil von Orléans 549 – und außerhalb der Kirche. Auch die getroffene Vorsorge entspricht sich, wenn auch *Papst Gregor* mit wesentlich hinterhältigeren Angriffen auf das Xenodochium rechnet. Beide Male hofft man auf tüchtige Vorsteher und untersagt Eingriffe des Bischofs.

Die Sorge um das Vermögen der Xenodochien war damit nicht behoben. Das Konzil von Chalon 647 - 653 verbietet Bischof und Archidiakon nach dem Tode eines Priesters oder Abtes das Vermögen der Pfarrkirche, des Xenodochium oder des Klosters zu mindern[168]. Reichlich blaß wird für diese Fälle die Anwendung der *statuta canonum* in Aussicht gestellt. Der Kanon läßt jedenfalls erkennen, daß es inzwischen Xenodochien gab und vielleicht von nicht zu geringer Zahl. Sie waren kirchlichen Einrichtungen zugeordnet und von daher Übergriffen ausgesetzt.

---

164 Concilium Lugdunense a. 583, c. 6, *de Clercq* (Fn. 152) 232 f.

165 Concilium Aurelianense a. 549, c. 15, *de Clercq* (Fn. 152) 153.

166 *Supra*, Fn. 132.

167 *Schönfeld* (Fn. 10) 31 f.

168 Concilium Cabilonense a. 647 - 653, c. 7, *de Clercq* (Fn. 152) 304.

Von den Rechtsaufzeichnungen der germanischen Eroberer, den *Leges*, befaßt sich anscheinend nur das langobardische Recht mit den Xenodochien. Erwähnt werden sie allerdings erst in den Gesetzen *König Luitprands* (712 - 744) und *König Aistulfs* (749 -756). Beide Könige behandeln sie als bereits etablierte Größen, denen ein *praepositus* vorsteht[169]. Schon *Luitprand* gewährt den Xenodochien mit den heiligen Stätten Privilegien. Der übliche Schutz der noch nicht Achtzehnjährigen wird eingeschränkt, wenn sie in Todesgefahr für ihr Seelenheil einem Xenodochium etwas vermachen[170]. Das zur Gültigkeit von Schenkungen grundsätzlich erforderliche „launigild" oder eine „thingatio" sind bei Schenkungen „pro anima" an „loca sanctorum" oder an Xenodochien verzichtbar[171]. *Aistulf* bestätigt die Bestandskraft von strafbewehrten Vereinbarungen auch über Liegenschaften mit dem *praepositus* eines Xenodochium[172]. Bußen an Xenodochien, die unter dem Schutz des Palastes stehen, sollen nicht wie die Bußen an den König verdoppelt werden[173].

Die wenigen Regelungen sagen Bedeutendes über die Position der Xenodochien. Die Befreiung von den Formerfordernissen bei Schenkungen dürfte Zuwendungen erheblich erleichtert haben und ganz allgemein wird sich die durchgängige Tendenz, Gaben *pro anima* zu Wirksamkeit zu verhelfen, im Rechtsalltag lukrativ ausgewirkt haben. Wie der Schutz durch den Palast konkret ausgestaltet war, welche Einflußnahmen sich vielleicht damit verbanden, ist nicht zu entnehmen. Immerhin bestand die Möglichkeit, daß Eingriffen von außen oder durch Kirchenobere seitens des Palastes entgegengetreten wurde.

Das fast völlige Schweigen der *Leges* zu den Xenodochien läßt sich damit erklären, daß deren Regelungsprogramm sich im wesentlichen auf die allgemeine Friedensordnung konzentrierte. Daß der Gestaltungwille der Karolinger umfassender war, zeigt die Behandlung der wohltätigen Einrichtungen durch die Kapitularien[174]. Die Fülle der Regelungen kann nur in den Tendenzen angedeutet werden. Die programmatische *Admonito generalis* von 789 gibt das Ziel vor: „... hospites, peregrini et pauperes susceptiones regulares et canonicas per loca diversa habeant ..."[175]. Die Bezeichnung für solche Einrichtungen ist ganz überwiegend Xenodo-

---

169 *Aistulf* 16, ed. *Friedrich Bluhme*, Edictus Langobardorum, in: Monumenta Germaniae Historica, Leges in fol. IV, 1868 (Nachdruck, 1984), S. 201 f.

170 *Luitprand* 19, ed. *Bluhme* (Fn. 169) 116 f.

171 *Luitprand* 73, ed. *Bluhme* (Fn. 169) 137.

172 *Aistulf* 16, ed. *Bluhme* (Fn. 169) 201 f.

173 *Aistulf* 17, ed. *Bluhme* (Fn. 169) 202.

174 Im Vorfeld einer neuen Edition der Kapitularien gibt es derzeit eine intensive Forschung zu diesen Quellen, die wesentlich von *Hubert Mordek* getragen und angeregt wird. Literaturstand und Textkritik bei *Mordek*, Bibliotheca capitularium regum Francorum manuscripta, Monunenta Germaniae Historica, Hilfsmittel 15, 1995.

175 Admonitio generalis c. 75, ed. *Alfred Boretius*, Capitularia regum Francorum 1. Band, 1883 (Nachdruck, 1960) = Capitularia I, S. 60. – 2. Band, ed. *Alfred Boretius, Victor Krause*, 1897 = Capitularia II.

chium. Vielleicht war das Wort aber nicht überall geläufig, denn in einem westfränkischen Kontext wird es durch das insgesamt weniger verwandte Wort „hospitalia“ erklärt. Auffällig ist weiterhin ein regionaler Schwerpunkt. Die Xenodochien werden ganz überwiegend in Kapitularien, die sich auf Italien beziehen, behandelt. Dabei steht nicht etwa die Neuerrichtung im Vordergrund, sondern Bestandsaufnahme und Wiederherstellung. Schon bald nach der Eroberung Italiens wird im *Capitulare Mantuanum* festgelegt „de sinodochiis volumus adque precipimus ut restaurata fiant“[176]. Den *missi* wird aufgegeben „ut inquirant de singulis monasteriis vel senedochiis, qualiter a conditoribus ordinata sunt vel quomodo nunc permaneant et a quibus personis detineantur“[177] oder „... abbates senodochia circumeant ..., ubi sunt neglecta, ad pristinum statum revocent; hospitales vero pauperum tam in montanis, quam et ubicumque fuisse noscuntur, pleniter et diligenti cura restaurentur“[178]. Für die Verwaltung wird das Ziel der Armenfürsorge eingeschärft. Nur solche Personen sollen eingesetzt werden, die den Armen nichts entziehen. Falls sie in der Versorgung der Armen nachlässig sind, werden andere an ihre Stelle gesetzt[179]. Maßgeblich für den Betrieb der Xenodochien ist die Anordnung des Gründers: „De senodochiis precipimus, ut secundum possibilitatem vel temporis fertilitatem testamentorum scripta sequantur.“[180] Konkret soll das Testament entscheidend sein. Enthält dieses keine entsprechende Regelung, wird festgelegt, daß die Armen den fünften Teil der Erträge erhalten[181]. Übergriffen weltlicher und geistlicher Großer durch unberechtigtes Erheben von Abgaben o.ä. wird entgegengetreten[182]. Zwar gab es Xenodochien in Schutz und Gewalt von Bischöfen, Kirchen, aber auch weltlichen Großen[183], doch beanspruchen die karolingischen Herrscher ihren bestimmenden Einfluß „... senodochia que ad mundio palatii pertinet aut pertinere debent ...“[184]. Sie knüpfen an die langobardischen Könige an, die bereits Xenodochien unter den Schutz des Palastes stellten[185]. Damit wird eine weitere Möglichkeit zur Sicherung wohltätiger Einrichtungen, ihres Vermögens, ihres Zweckes und einer tatkräftigen Organisation erkennbar. Entsprechend den christlichen Herrschertugenden, für die Armen zu sorgen, verstehen es die Karolinger als

176 Capitularia I 90, capitulum 12, S. 191 (Fn. 175).

177 Capitularia II 202, capitulum 1, S. 63 (Fn. 175).

178 Capitularia II 217, capitulum 5, S. 94 (Fn. 175).

179 Capitularia I 92, capitulum 3, S. 195 (Fn. 175); Capitularia I 95, capitulum 1, S. 200; Capitularia I 164, capitulum 7, S. 328 f.

180 Capitularia I 164, capitulum 4, S. 328 (Fn. 175); Capitularia I 179, capitulum 6, S. 369; Capitularia II 202, capitulum 1, S. 63; Capitularia II 228, capitulum 15 und capitulum 16, S. 121.

181 Capitularia I 166, capitulum 3, S. 332 (Fn. 175).

182 Capitularia I 103, S. 211 (Fn. 175); Capitularia I 166, capitulum 1, S. 332.

183 Capitularia I 95, capitulum 6, S. 201 (Fn. 175): „... senodochia qui per diversos comites esse videntur, ut regales sint ...“; Cap II 228, capitulum 15, S. 121.

184 Capitularia I 89 capitulum 5, S. 189 (Fn. 175); Capitularia I 92, capitulum 3, S. 195; Capitularia II 228, capitulum 16, S. 121.

185 *Supra*, Fn. 173.

ihre Aufgabe, die Funktionsfähigkeit der Xenodochien zu erhalten. Dabei orientieren sie sich für die Zwecksetzung am Willen der Gründer, drängen auf effiziente Verwaltung und suchen unberechtigte Eingriffe abzuwehren. Das Neue in dieser herrscherlichen Aufgabenbestimmung wird deutlich im Verlgeich zu den Merowingern. Zur Sicherung der von ihnen gegründeten Xenodochien bemühen sie sich um Privilegien *Papst Gregors* oder eines Konzils. Die Karolinger fühlen sich verpflichtet und in der Lage, Funktionsfähigkeit der Xenodochien selbst durchzusetzen.

VI. Zusammenfassung

Die knappe Durchsicht weniger Quellen mag glücklichenfalls einige allgemeine Tendenzen berührt haben. Der Niederschlag, den die wohltätigen Einrichtungen von der Spätantike bis zur Karolingerzeit in den Rechtsquellen gefunden haben, zeigt eine Kontinuität der Konfliktlagen. Eigenständigkeit und Zweckerreichung sind immer wieder gefährdet durch Übergriffe auf das Vermögen jener Institutionen, die seit dem Ende des 6. Jahrhunderts als Xenodochia bezeichnet werden. Und es wiederholen sich die Probleme: Die Erben wollen letztwillige Zuwendungen an die Xenodochien hintertreiben, weltliche Große oder kirchliche Obere suchen das Vermögen der Xenodochien eigenen Zwecken zuzuführen und die Verwalter orientieren ihre Tätigkeit zu wenig am Wohl der letztlich bedachten Armen. Zur Bewältigung dieser Schwierigkeiten wird man auf verschiedenen Ebenen tätig: Im Bereich der Kirche treten *Papst Gregor* und Konzilien hervor, eigene Initiativen zeigen langobardische und karolingische Herrscher und schließlich suchen die Gründer ihr Xenodochium zu sichern. Die Kirche ist in der Lage, durch Bischöfe und Äbte für Aufsicht, innere Ordnung und Schutz nach außen zu sorgen. Dem Zugriff durch diese Personen sollen kirchliche Strafandrohungen vorbeugen und *Papst Gregor* wird bei Mißständen unermüdlich selbst tätig. Dem entspricht die Tatkraft der Karolinger. Um ihren Bemühungen Nachhaltigkeit zu geben, hoffen beide auf gottesfürchtige Verwalter, deren Eigenständigkeit gestärkt wird. Insgesamt bleiben diese Anstrengungen primär im administrativen – politischen Bereich. Eine rechtliche Organisationsform, die etwa durch Zweckbindung des Vermögens oder Beschränkungen der Handlungsmacht die Xenodochien sichert, wird nicht vorgegeben. Die noch bei *Gregor* anzutreffende Pflicht des Verwalters zur Rechnungslegung wirkt wie ein Nachklang aus der Antike.

Die Suche nach geeigneter rechtlicher Gestaltung spürt man in merowingischen Testamenten und dem Formular *Marculfs*. Bei *Marculf* zeichnen sich immerhin Überlegungen ab, die bei konsequenter Fortentwicklung darauf hätten hinauslaufen können, den Bischof als Treuhänder des Vermögens einzusetzen.

In allen Quellen ging es nicht um eine grundsätzliche Erfassung der Xenodochien, und weit war man davon entfernt, diese theoretisch-abstrakt zu definieren, um dann aus der gefundenen Rechtsfigur heraus die anstehenden Probleme zu lösen. Von Fall zu Fall, und das nicht als Konsequenz einer Methode, suchte man Mißständen entgegenzuwirken und vorzubeugen. Die jeweiligen Konflikte bestimmen die Ausdrucksweise in einer Sprache, die nicht juristisch-technisch ist. Bezeichnenderweise legte man bei einer Zuwendung an die Armen einer Kirche keinen Wert darauf zu präzisieren, wie sich das rechtlich genau vollziehen soll und es ist fraglich, ob man dazu überhaupt in der Lage war. Was erreicht werden sollte, wußte man.

Es erscheint verfehlt, hinter der häufig sinnfälligen Ausdrucksweise Begriffe und Rechtsfiguren zu unterstellen, zu deren Entwicklung sich erst die moderne Rechtswissenschaft genötigt sah. Die Annahme, die Rechtsvorstellung habe gelebt vor dem Begriff, oder das Hineingeheimnissen in das Rechtsbewußtsein des Volkes, ist Erkenntnis hindernd, schafft Beliebigkeit und Quellenresistenz. So kann auch dieser Beitrag mit einem Gedanken *Brucks* enden: „In der Regel fehlt ein Wort ... nur dann, wenn die Sache selbst nicht bekannt ist“[186].

---

186 *Bruck* (Fn. 1) 71.

SHAEL HERMAN

The Canonical Conception of the Trust

I. Prelude: The Medieval Church's Dilemma

Although medieval artists typically portrayed Christ's early followers as an impoverished brotherhood, his medieval disciples suffered an embarrassment of riches: in apparent disregard of its own teachings on the sinfulness of earthly riches[1], the Church, during its first millennium, had become a wealthy proprietor. Medieval church leaders recognized that their spiritual program for the hereafter depended paradoxically upon material possessions in the here-and-now[2]. An expanding flock of faithful Christians required shrines, altars, and places of worship; deceased Christians were buried in exclusively Christian cemeteries[3]; and religious orders needed quarters and substantial financing to carry on their good works. While one might regard as extreme *John Wyclif's* characterization of clerical property-holding as a scriptural violation, Christian doctrine was still clear in its message that material wealth by itself opened no path to spiritual salvation[4]. This lesson was implicit in *Peter's* message to *Simon* that money secured none of God's gifts[5]. *Thomas Aquinas* echoed *Peter's* message that the Church's earthly lieutenants could not sell spiritual things because they were not theirs to sell[6].

---

1 See, e.g., *Henrici de Segusio Cardinalis Hostiensis* In Primum Decretalium librum Commentaria (1581; facsimile) 8 (De Constitutionibus) ("Cupiditas est radix omnium malorum; Pecuniae amor est mater quasi omnium criminum".) This essay abbreviates themes more fully explored in *Shael Herman,* Utilitas Ecclesiae: The Canonical Conception of the Trust, (1996) 70 Tulane L.R. 2239 ff.; and *Shael Herman,* Trusts Sacred and Profane: Clerical, Secular, and Commercial Uses of the Medieval Commendatio, (1997) 71 Tulane L.R. 869 ff.

2 For an array of perspectives on the paradox, see generally W. J. Sheils, Diana Wood (eds.), The Church and Wealth: Papers Read at the 1986 Summer Meeting and 1987 Winter Meeting of the Ecclesiastical History Society, 1987.

3 See *infra,* nn. 48 - 53.

4 For an account of canonical efforts to reconcile ecclesiastical wealth with apostolic poverty, see generally *Janet Coleman,* The Two Jurisdictions: Theological and Legal Justifications of Church Property in the Thirteenth Century, in: Sheils / Woods (n. 2) 75 ff.

5 Acts 8:20. "Simony was so-called from Simon Magus, a New Testament villain, who tried to bribe St. Peter to give him the power to confer the Holy Spirit through the laying on of hands (Acts 8:9 - 24). In the language of *[church]* reformers, simony covered a broad variety of sins: any transaction that involved the exchange of money or other worldly goods in return for ecclesiastical office or power was apt to be classed as simony, as was any other sort

1. The Trust: A Solution to the Church's Dilemma

To reconcile inconsistencies between the Church's acquisitive appetite and her admonitions against the spiritual dangers of wealth, the churchmen required a morally principled conceptualization of the church's mission and the clergy's role in fulfilling it. According to one appealing image, the pope and his clerical lieutenants, far from owning church assets, actually held them in trust for beneficiaries variously identified as Christ, the meek and poor, the community of faithful, and the eternal church. With such a trust construct the churchmen sought to avoid dissipation of the church's patrimony. As the church's loyal stewards clerics could maintain the church estate intact and even increase it. A sharp differentiation of a cleric's personal belongings from his benefice could put church assets beyond the grasp of a cleric's kinsmen who might claim his possessions at his death.

2. The Pope as Trustee; the Church as Primary Beneficiary of the Papal Trust

In a trust arrangement, Jesus Christ was the sovereign lord over church patrimony. No man, not even a pope, could own the Church's property. Inspired by *Aquinas's* slogan from the *Summa Theologica, Benedict XIV* declared church property "for the pope as principal steward, not lord and possessor" ("Res ecclesiae sunt papae, ut principalis dispensatoris non ut domini et possessoris"[7]). For this basic principle *Cajetan* fashioned a corollary: "The Pope cannot give church goods to whomsoever he chooses [not] even blood relatives, but is bound to dispense them prudently and as right reason counsels". ("[N]on possit bona Ecclesiae dare cui voluerit, aut consanguineis. ... Sed tenetur prudenter dispensare, ut recta ratio suadet"[8].) In such traditional canonical formulations, a guiding administrative prin-

---

of arrangement that threatened to compromise the independence of the clergy from secular control": *James A. Brundage,* Medieval Canon Law, 1995, pp. 35 ff.

6 On the sin of simony, see *Henrici de Segusio Cardinalis Hostiensis* In Quintum Decretalium librum Commentaria (1581; fascimile) 14a-16a (De Simonia); *Georges Duby,* Féodalité, 1996, pp. 360 ff. Within the church, misappropriation of spiritual gifts, typically classified as sins of simony and *laesa majestas,* constituted betrayals of the enduring mission of the Church: *Glen Olsen,* The Definition of the Ecclesiastical Benefice in the Twelfth Century: The Canonists' Discussion of Spiritualia, Studia Gratiana II (1967) 440 ff.

7 *Raoul Naz,* Traité de Droit Canonique: Lieux et Temps Sacrés, vol. III, 2nd ed., 1954, pp. 233 ff. (quoting Summa Theologiae IIa-IIae, q.c, art. 1, ad 7). Rooted firmly in church doctrine, the Pope's role as principal steward of church wealth seems to have been solidified in *Pope Gregory VII's* Dictatus Papae and the Concordat of Worms (1122): *Harold J. Berman,* Law and Revolution: The Formation of the Western Legal Tradition, 1983, pp. 98 ff.

8 *Naz* (n. 7) 233 ff. (quoting S. Rotae decisiones, T. III, 405 n. 24). By means of a distinction between jurisdiction and property, the canonists underscored the fiduciary character of the clergy's relationship to the church's patrimony. "[A] prelate was said to exercise jurisdiction over his church without owning its property. Hence he could not alienate his church's

ciple for both papacy and church hierarchy was exploitation of the church's wealth in this world to advance spiritual goals in the next.

II. Possible Objections to the Proposed Canonical Trust Conception

For a number of reasons, an attentive reader, especially one who may take his bearings by reference to doctrines of English trusteeship, could find a little too convenient the proposed canonical conception of the trust. First, the canonical conception seems to be missing the familiar trio of trust actors, namely, a settlor, a trustee and a beneficiary. Second, even if these three figures are present in the canonical conception, they seem to have arbitrarily acquired their roles. To these objections a brief response could be that the English trust does not require three different persons; the essence of trust is a tripartite configuration of interests animated by a duty of loyalty. A single person in the configuration could have two interests. For example, a settlor might settle property upon himself as beneficiary provided he confided title and control of the property to a loyal steward who appreciated his altruistic role.

Our hypothetical reader might further object that while a pope could conceivably be seen as a trustee, the other members of the trio may seem to secular minds rather metaphysical, even fictional; indeed, though the existence of God is widely regarded as undemonstrable in our age of secular rationalism, God seems to be on both ends of the canonical trust transaction. Boiled down to essentials, the proposed canonical conception would explain that God as divine creator settled the universe upon his own spiritual proxies, i.e. the meek and poor, Jesus Christ, and *utilitas ecclesiae*. Our hypothetical reader might consider it too convenient to view the present church leadership in the temporal here-and-now as collective trustee for the advantage *(utilitas)* of the eternal church in the hereafter. Even assuming the pope and his clerical lieutenants could qualify as feoffees to uses, the *cestui que use* would still be an elusive figure.

To these last objections, a short response might be that English law would not allow a charitable or public trust to fail for indefiniteness of the beneficiary even if the *cestuis* of such trusts were defined vaguely as the "poor" or a class of persons not yet in existence. This principle of English law seems to be anchored in Roman foundations[9]. As early as 1830, the United States Supreme Court recognized the general indebtedness of the law of charitable trusts to Roman sources. To explain the court's decisions in landmark American decisions, *Justice Joseph Story* analo-

---

goods or dispose of them as his own. Rather, he was a steward, a dispensator of communal wealth. Jurisdiction was ... linked with rightful dispensation, rightful ruling of what was not one's own private material goods ...": *Coleman* (n. 4) 77 ff.

[9] *H. F. Jolowicz*, Roman Foundations of Modern Law, 1957, p. 139.

gized charitable trusts to "legacies to pious uses, which included all legacies destined for works of charity". According to *Story,* "the high authority of the Roman law, coinciding with religious notions of the times could hardly fail to introduce the principles of pious legacies into the common law of England"[10].

Beyond these particularistic responses to our hypothetical reader's objections, we should note that criteria of modern secular rationalism are inappropriate measures of the faith of medieval men; in an agnostic era, the present project requires a leap of faith and imagination, or in *Coleridge's* memorable phrase, a "willing suspension of disbelief"[11]. This study suggests that the church fathers could have found appealing the proposed canonical trust conception as a coherent explanation of the church's mission. Recognizing that the church's own stability was at stake, medieval churchmen surely had motivation for embracing such a conception. They could not deny the church's growing wealth. "From an early stage in its development the church had become the largest landowner in Europe, creating its own princes, and from the proprietary churches of the medieval system to the lavish endowment of churches with treasures ... the Church ... often seemed ... the outward and visible sign of an aristocracy at prayer"[12]. If medieval churchmen seem to have enjoyed church riches for their own account and to the prejudice of their flock, then perhaps they might redeem their apparent acquisitiveness by depicting themselves as temporal stewards of church possessions for eternal spiritual purposes. If church wealth could not be turned to spiritual virtue, then the churchmen risked dissipation of the patrimony and defection of the flock. For the flock would not follow where the shepherds did not lead. To promote the flock's impulse to philanthropy and to cut down selfishness, the clerics themselves had to supply examples of charitable and righteous conduct as well as good works.

III. Clerical Efforts to Legitimate Church Wealth

Legitimating its material wealth seems to have bedevilled the church from its earliest days. Pastors probably bewildered their flocks with instructions to avoid the pitfalls of wealth by confiding their property to the church. Churchmen sometimes betrayed an uneasiness about the credibility of their paradoxical instructions. When, for example, in the 1370s, *John Wyclif* characterized earthly wealth as "the dung of the church"[13], his goal was to make the church's enjoyment of wealth seem virtuous, not to condemn it. To offer a credible explanation for having

10 17 U.S. (4 Wheat.) 341 (1819). On this theme see generally *Shael Herman,* The Contribution of Roman Law to the Jurisprudence of Antebellum Louisiana, (1995) 56 Louisiana Law Review 257, 289; *idem,* Der Einfluß des römischen Rechts auf die Rechtswissenschaft Louisianas vor dem amerikanischen Bürgerkrieg, ZSS (RA) 113 (1996) 293 ff., 322 - 24.

11 *S. T. Coleridge,* Biographia Literaria, ed. J. Shawcross, 1907, p. 6.

12 *Michael Wilks,* Thesaurus Ecclesiae (Presidential Address), in: Sheils / Woods (n. 2) xv.

13 *Wilks* (n 12), xvii, n.47.

wealth, one must first acquire it. But an acquirer should exploit his wealth philanthropically, not selfishly.

1. Apostolic *collegium*

Separating the virtuous uses of wealth from its venal ones could be understood in terms of an intellectual distinction between ownership and stewardship. Employing a metaphor that would intrigue directors of a modern corporation, *John Wyclif* taught that Christ's apostles, though barred by their vows from owning wealth for their own accounts, constituted a corporate body *(collegium)* in which the eternal church's patrimony was vested. In *Wyclif's* view, each apostle was a steward *(dispensator)* of Christ's fortune *(thesaurus ecclesiae)*. Images of the *dispensator* and the apostolic *collegium* would be evoked often in explanations of the role of the clergy as stewards rather than owners of church assets[14].

Wyclif did not originate the metaphor of the apostolic *collegium*. Centuries before *Wyclif*, churchmen had employed the *collegium* metaphor to distinguish ownership from stewardship and thereby to allay doubts about the virtue and legitimacy of church wealth. For example, *St. Augustine* taught that wealth itself was not necessarily a moral problem. If applied to good works and charity, *Augustine* said, wealth could be a source of virtue and piety. "What [the church fathers] criticized was the abuse of riches, the concentration of fortunes and the poverty of the masses, love of money, an attachment to earthly goods and their selfish exploitation. Wealth itself was not evil because God in his wisdom never created anything evil. Poverty was not good itself, nor wealth a crime. Sin consisted in the evil use of wealth"[15].

A hallmark of the English trust, the concept of divided title seems to have figured implicitly in *Augustine's* view of church property. Invoking the Roman contract of *depositum*, in which an owner retained title to an asset and vested its control in a trustee or bailee, *Augustine* said:

> "If one regards himself as a simple depositary of goods created for everyone, charged to manage them and to use them to the advantage of the community, then the property is legitimate. But this [property] implicates a spirit of justice, the sense of human brotherhood, the will to correct social inequalities. One could arrive at justifying wealth by a moderate use of riches and the practice of charity. Giving to the poor is just rendering them their due. Not giving [them] alms is theft"[16].

---

14 *Wilks* (n. 12) xvii, n. 47.

15 "Ce que les Pères critiquent c'est l'abus des richesses, la concentration d'immenses fortunes et la pauvreté de la masse, l'amour de l'argent et l'attachement aux biens terrestres, leur emploi égoïste. La richesse ne peut être mauvaise, car Dieu n'a rien créé de mauvais. La pauvreté n'est pas un bien en soi, ni la fortune un crime. C'est le mauvais usage de la fortune qui est péché": *Jean Gaudemet*, L'église dans L'Empire Romain, vol. III, p. 571.

16 "Si l'on se tient au contraire pour un simple dépositaire de biens créés pour tous, chargé de les gérer et d'en disposer au profit de l'ensemble, alors 'la propriété' est légitime. Mais

2. The Metaphoric Hostelry: Use the World, But Do Not Use it Up

Augustine's views on the ethical disposition of wealth conformed with his conviction that God was both first and final cause of the world; the world had originated in God and ultimately it belonged to him. Such views conformed with our earlier observations that the canonical conception of the trust viewed God as both settlor and ultimate beneficiary of creation. In *Augustine's* view, the Christian faithful did not own the world. Instead they merely occupied it as lodgers or pilgrims on a temporary sojourn in a vast metaphoric hostelry. By means of this metaphoric image, *Augustine* invited the faithful to "[put] ... up ... then in the hostelry of this life as travelers, passing on ..."[17]. By depicting life on earth as a hostelry, *Augustine* warned men of the risks of their selfish attachment to riches. With such a metaphor, *Augustine* also linked themes of trusteeship, pilgrimage, and hospitality to Christian salvation:

> "Use the world: *let not the world hold thee captive* ... Thou art passing on thy journey, and *this life is but a wayside inn.* Use money as the traveler at an inn uses table, cup, pitcher, and couch, with the purpose not of remaining but of leaving them behind"[18].

Between *Augustine's* hostelry metaphor and his view of property the links were implicit but reasonably clear:

> "[W]hile anyone may rightfully (*iure privato)* acquire possessions – 'private property', to use the traditional pleonasm – this *ius divinum* allows no man to claim them as exclusively and unreservedly his. Rather, he must always recollect that both in the first instance and in the last resort, '*the earth is the Lord's*', and its treasures come to him from God as to a steward or dispenser. ... on this account ... he should be ever ready to 'communicate', viz. to distribute to others in their need"[19].

3. Clerical Innkeeper as *usuarius*

If the temporal world were a vast hostelry and the faithful its temporary sojourners, then the clergy, as spiritual innkeepers, had a special mission to maintain for all time accommodations for those who sought sanctuary. Given *Christ's* teaching on hospitality toward strangers and the duties of caring for the poor and the sick,

---

elle implique l'esprit de justice, le sens de la fraternité humaine, la volonté de corriger les inégalités sociales. C'est par un usage modéré des richesses et par la pratique de la charité que l'on parviendra à justifier la propriété. Donner aux pauvres n'est que leur rendre ce qui leur revient. Ne pas faire l'aumône est un vol": *Gaudemet* (n. 15) 571.

17 Cf. *Herbert A. Deane,* The Political and Social Ideas of St. Augustine, 1963, pp. 266 ff., n. 22.

18 Cf. *Deane* (n. 17) 44.

19 *D.J. MacQueen,* St. Augustine's Concept of Property Ownership, Recherches Augustiniennes, 1972, pp. 187, 213 ff.

the church-as-hostelry was an apt formulation of the ecclesiastical mission. As the church urged the faithful on both pilgrimages and crusades, hostelries situated along the Christian travellers' paths offered them spiritual consolation, material comfort, and security.

It is difficult to locate authoritative texts that precisely characterize clerical hosts or innkeepers as trustees. For such clerical figures, an appealing Roman sobriquet was the *usuarius*, which may have links to the English use. The term *usuarius* or *usuary* designated someone who held an *usus*[20], a nonowner's enjoyment of premises subject to rather strict limitations. Unlike a *ususfructus*, in which the *usufructuary* could take fruits and revenues for his own profit, an *usus*, according to Roman law, denied an occupant's exploitation of the estate for profit[21]. An *usus* conferred upon an individual only a purely personal right, neither heritable nor transferable. To highlight the restrictive character of *usus* the Romans qualified the right as *nudus usus, id est sine fructu* ("naked use, i.e. without fruits").

Although the *usus* played no particular religious role for the Romans, the churchmen adroitly adapted this Roman institution to their own needs. A vision of a *usuarius* as a host of his family and guests fits comfortably with church teachings on the sanctity of showing hospitality to strangers and depictions of earthly life as a hostelry. Yet the churchmen seem to have recognized the impracticability of an *usus* utterly *nudus* and *sine fructu*. To provide for his guests and lodgers (*hospitum victum)* a hospitable innkeeper had to make at least a limited use of fruits from the *usus* (*usum quotidianum)*. Even a humble Franciscan friar bound by his vow of absolute poverty could make limited use of wealth raised through charity provided he applied the funds to the care of a fellow friar who had become ill[22]. Transplanted to England to serve the church, the Italian prelate *Hostiensis* extended *usum quotidianum* so that an *usuarius* of woodlands might harvest plants and wood for his own use and that of his family[23].

---

20 On the *usus* generally, see D. 7, 8 (On *Usus* and *Habitatio)*; *W. W. Buckland*, A Textbook of Roman Law From Augustus to Justinian, 1921, pp. 272 - 73 ff. For a canonical treatment of *ususfructus* and clerical *usus*, see generally F. Lucii Ferraris, Prompta Bibliotheca Canonica, Juridica, Moralis, Theologica, vol. 7, 1865, pp. 89 - 91 ff., 1515 *passim*. For discussion of *beneficium* as a grant or concession of use, i.e. a real right less than full ownership, and illumination of links among *beneficium, usus,* and *commendam*, see generally *Ernesto Sestan*, Per la Storia della Città nell'alto Medioevo, in: Studi in Onore di Armando Sapore, 1957, pp. 113, 117 - 23 ff.

21 Oxford Latin Dictionary, ed. *P. G. W. Glare*, 1982, p. 2110.

22 *Giovanni Tarello*, Profili Giuridici della Questione della Povertà nel Francescanesimo prima di Ockham, Scritti in Memoria di Antonio Falchi, 1964, pp. 338, 347. For these and subsequent references to *Tarello's* work, I am indebted to my colleague, *Michele Graziadei*, University of Torino. *Dr. Graziadei* generously supplied me information on the clerical *usus* and the Franciscan doctrine from *Paolo Grossi*, Il Dominio e le Cose: Percezioni Medievali e Moderne dei Diritti Reali, 1992, pp. 22 - 189.

23 *Hostiensis* (n. 1) 204a.

For other reasons *usuarius* was an apt clerical designation. Bent on maintaining the integrity of its patrimony in clerical possession, the church could shield its assets from the grasp of a cleric's relatives and heirs. If, as in Roman law, an *usus* conferred only a purely personal right, neither heritable nor transferable, by implication a clerical *usuary* could not transfer to a relative his interest in a church asset[24]. Furthermore, as the *usus* in Roman law expired at the *usuary's* death, it could be said that the clerical *usus* automatically expired at death and the asset affected by the *usus* reverted to Christ's *thesaurus ecclesiae.* Even if the term *usuarius* did not fully characterize a cleric's function, there seems little doubt that a cleric's interest was coterminous with his sacred office. With an *usus* churchmen, by their own examples, could instill humility and compassion in their flocks and communicate to them the fleeting character of man's sojourn on earth. What was good for the pastor held good for the flock. If the cleric's interest terminated with his office, a layman's estate was no less fragile. Perhaps for this reason, medieval church grants in favor of laymen were only exceptionally made *in feodum et hereditatem.* "Because *feodum* increasingly implied full and heritable property the clergy were sometimes wary of allowing anyone holding property from the churches to hold it as *fief*"[25].

IV. Clerical *usus,* Feoffments *ad usus,* and the Franciscan Friars

1. Clerical *usus* and the Franciscan Friars

Although the theme of wealth animated much church doctrine, medieval churchmen generally counted wealth a phenomenon to be reconciled with Christ's teachings on poverty. In *St. Francis'* teaching, such a reconciliation was crucial. Resolving doubts in favor of a standard of absolute poverty, *Francis'* Rule of 1223 (*Regula Bullata)* enjoined his followers to live "in obedience, without property and in chastity"[26]. In 1226 another of his injunctions invoked familiar images of righteous Christians as pilgrims, strangers, and lodgers:

---

24 "As early as 1102 Archbishop Anselm's council at Westminster ruled ... that sons of priests should not be heirs of their fathers' churches, but the practice persisted throughout the twelfth century. In some parts of England there were parish churches richly endowed with lands where the lord of the manor was not merely patron of the church but parson as well. He married although he was a priest and transmitted his church to a son who also took Orders. ... [C]ountless other livings descended from father to son by the tolerance of the patron or by the family's absorption of the patronage. ... A very large number of letters were directed to England by Alexander III and his successors to eradicate the custom whereby, as Alexander said, men sought to gain possession of God's sanctuary by hereditary right": *C. R. Cheney,* From Becket to Langton: English Church Government 1170 - 1213, 1956, pp. 125 - 26 ff.

25 *Susan Reynolds,* Fiefs and Vassals: The Medieval Evidence Reinterpreted, 1994, pp. 327 ff.

26 *Stephen W. DeVine,* The Franciscan Friars, the Feoffment to Uses, and Canonical Theories of Property Enjoyment before 1535, (1989) 10 J.L.H. 1, 2.

> "Let the brothers take care that churches, humble lodgings and all other things that will be built for them are never accepted unless they are in harmony with holy poverty, which we have promised in the Rule [of 1223], always living there as strangers and pilgrims"[27].

Bound by the dictates of *St. Francis'* Rule, the Franciscan friars could not hold property as a *collegium* or a *communitas*, even though early Christians had employed such forms of property holding. A vow of absolute poverty required the Franciscan friars to account for their use of all worldly goods, even those required for their own shelter and sustenance. To put worldly goods beyond their reach and themselves above reproach, the Franciscan friars relied upon feoffments to uses in various forms. For example, a Franciscan leader might enfeoff a town or a spiritual friend with property *ad usus* or *ad opus* his brotherhood. Such a feoffee held and administered the assets and directed its revenues for the benefit of the friars. Richard Ingworth is reported to have created "a compound for friars, but instead of giving it to the friars, he gave it to the people of the city of Oxford to hold for the use of the brotherhood (*ad opus fratrum*)"[28]. In this arrangement the Oxford community assumed the role of spiritual innkeeper, and the Franciscan brotherhood the role of lodgers. In the technical language of uses and trusts, a feoffee held assets for the benefit of a third party at the instance of the feoffor.

Toward the third party beneficiary a feoffee to uses had a duty of loyalty akin to that owed by a spiritual friend to a clerical *usuarius*. As in a clerical *usus*, the feoffment contemplated a distribution into different hands of ownership and administration. Between a feoffment *ad usus* and a clerical *usus* there were differences that it would be unreasonable to ignore. For example, unlike a clerical *usuarius*, a beneficiary in a standard feoffment had not taken a poverty vow. A clerical *usuary* disciplined his own appetites or risked discipline from those charged with administration of the estate. By contrast, in a feoffment in favor of non-clerics, a feoffee imposed a regimen of loyalty and discipline on behalf of his *cestuis*. But the fiduciary character of the two devices, along with the coincidence of the word *usus*, prompts us to ask if there were links between the institutions.

Although the question of such links is not novel, it is complicated: *usus*, *utilitas*, *utile* and a host of other terms connoting beneficial usage pervaded Roman and canonical lexicons. Perhaps the popularity of the terms may be traced to an ancient view that in a state of innocence men enjoyed only an *usus* of things. According to this view, ownership or *dominium* originated in Eden with loss of innocence and original sin[29]. According to *Bonagrazia*, *dominium* derived from laws of men, not God[30]. Among men living in a state of innocence, ideas of ownership, poverty, and wealth were supposed irrelevant. Men did not need to own anything as long as

27 *DeVine* (n. 26) 1, 2.

28 *DeVine* (n. 26) 1, 2.

29 *Tarello* (n. 22) 426 - 28.

30 *Tarello* (n. 22) 426 - 28.

there was enough for their shelter and sustenance. The laws of nature assured men only *usus in facti,* the actual use of items in their natural state. *Bonagrazia's* view was consistent with *Augustine's* injunction to Christians to "use the world; let not the world hold thee captive".

To reconcile their apparent wealth with their avowed poverty various Franciscan thinkers developed an elaborate and subtly refined continuum of property interests. Their goal seems to have been to protest even slight interest in worldly goods, though observers such as *Gerard of Abbeville* thought some friars protested too much. According to *Gerard,* the Franciscans had created "a vacuous legal fiction" by claiming that the pope owned considerable churches, buildings and goods over which they had only an *usus*[31]. Using as a springboard a familiar Roman division of property into *dominium, usus* and *fructus,* some papal decrees such as *Quo Elongati* (1230)[32] and *Ordinem vestrum* (1245)[33] distinguished property from use of goods. Reserving to the Apostolic See *dominium* in material things, this last decree granted the Franciscans a bare *usus* of things put before them for their spiritual journey. Such an intellectual division of property permitted the Franciscans to claim that they had not violated *Francis's* rule. Still, the Franciscans had immediately available for shelter and sustenance assets confided to a spiritual proxy. Consistent with *Augustine's* injunction, this intellectual division of property fit comfortably into *Bonaventure's* classification of property into *proprietas, possessio, usus fructus* and *simplex usus*[34], this last being for the Franciscans the most restrictive clerical interest and hence the easiest to accommodate to *Francis'* rule of absolute poverty. In 1279 *Nicolas III's Exiit qui seminat* further refined *Bonaventure's* property classification by splitting the *simplex usus* into *ius utendi* and *simplex usus facti*[35]. Like the *simplex usus,* the *simplex usus facti* was fragile; for it was a "license to use certain goods, revocable at the will of the conceder"[36].

A Franciscan archbishop and *King Edward's* influential adviser, *John Pecham,* elaborated the *usus pauper*[37]. Even more limited than the *simplex usus,* this property interest restricted the friars' use of things to the barest daily necessities. It is difficult to demonstrate that *Pecham* exerted considerable influence upon the Franciscans' understanding of the clerical *usus* as a device different from a Roman *usus,* though contemporary writings indicate that the friars were sensitive to this distinction. What we do know is that the Franciscans' acceptance of only a fragile

31 *Tarello* (n. 22) 418. In particular, *Gerard* denied that there was a way to distinguish *usus* and ownership of consumables because their use required them to be used up.

32 *Giovanni Tarello,* Novissimo Digesto Italiano, diretto da A. Azara e Ernesto Eula, vol. 13, 1966, pp. 520, 522.

33 *Tarello* (n. 32) 520, 522.

34 *Tarello* (n. 32) 522.

35 *Tarello* (n. 32) 522 - 23.

36 *M. D. Lambert,* Franciscan Poverty: The Doctrine of The Absolute Poverty of Christ and the Apostles in the Franciscan Order, 1961, p. 144.

37 *Tarello* (n. 22) 398 - 99.

usus distanced them from material wealth and prompted their need for procurators, agents, and intermediaries to conduct their affairs and administer their goods. In case of a legal dispute regarding administration of the goods, such intermediaries litigated in the name of the *dominus,* i.e. the Papacy, and not the friars. Within the church hierarchy, the figure most evocative of a trustee and a feoffee to uses was the *syndacus.* This was an office established in 1283 by *Martin IV* to represent the Holy See, the true owner of all Franciscan property, in its disposition of movables and immovables. The *syndacus* administered the friars' benefactions and turned the income from them to the use of the convent, at times indeed to the use of an individual brother. Such convents lived from their incomes and estates even as they preserved an appearance of utter poverty[38]. Perhaps the *syndacus*' office suggested to Sir John Rocliff of Calthorpe the template of a transaction in which he instructed his feoffees to give the profits of the enfeoffed lands to the grey friars of York in perpetuity. In exchange the Friars established a chantry where they were to pray for *John's* soul and those of his family and to bury him next to his father in the friars' church in York[39].

2. The Feoffment to Uses: A "Completely English Institution"

With this conclusion, *Stephen DeVine* ended his important recent inquiry into links among Franciscan practices, the feoffment to uses, and canonical distinctions between *dominium* and *usus.* According to *DeVine,* the Church had a "canon law framework" to accommodate its Franciscan members in England as elsewhere. Furthermore, "the canonical response, as well as its Roman law antecedents, could not but have been in the minds of high ranking ecclesiastics who shaped the development of the feoffment to uses as medieval chancellors of England"[40]. Nevertheless, *DeVine* concluded that the feoffment to uses was of English provenance. Though the feoffment, according to *DeVine,* seemed analogous to the Roman *usus,* these institutions lacked common roots. To this last point we may respond that our own modest research discloses that feoffments to uses, far from being completely English, were popular investment devices among Norman French monasteries. Indeed the terms fief and feoffment to uses were known throughout medieval Europe. Known in England in at least a primitive form before the Norman Conquest, the feoffment to uses owed its popularity in Norman England partly to Norman clerics who settled there after the Conquest[41].

On the absence of links between the Roman *usus* and the feoffment to uses, *DeVine* may be correct. As we have indicated, the *usus* in Roman law conferred a

38 *Lambert* (n. 36) 161 - 63.

39 *DeVine* (n. 26) 10.

40 *DeVine* (n. 26) 14.

41 See *infra,* text accompanying notes 64 - 75.

strictly personal real right, and thus could have thrust upon the Franciscans a greater interest in the material world than *Francis'* rule warranted. But the clerical *usus* was not a Roman *usus*. Whether as *usus simplex, usus facti,* or *usus pauper,* the clerical *usus* was reasonably consistent with a strict poverty vow, and its operation imported a fiduciary duty. If the Franciscans single-handedly did not invent the clerical *usus* to justify their poverty, they contributed generously to its elaboration. Though not precisely an English style beneficiary, a clerical *usuarius* enjoyed a narrow sliver of property. If, as in the Franciscan case, the *dominus* of the estate was the Papacy and its agent the *syndacus,* then perhaps a friar could see himself as a dependent beneficiary. More than a Roman *usus,* a clerical *usus,* because of duties of loyalty and a division of enjoyment and administration, could have suggested to English imaginations the feoffment to uses and the trust. *Professor Milsom* could perhaps have further investigated the clerical *usus* instead of concluding that the friars' *usus* was a Roman right of use and enjoyment[42]. Although *DeVine* noticed a distinction betweem *usus facti* and *usus iuris*[43] he may have too lightly dismissed it for the Franciscans had practically an allergy to *usus iuris* and prayed for *usus facti,* i.e. a license to use something in fact without any legal right. But more research into the sources will be required to turn this speculation into a reliable claim.

V. Influence of Roman Law upon the Concept of Trust

A hallmark of classical Roman law, the sharp contrast between ownership and possession equipped canonists to distinguish the Church's enduring interest in its patrimony from the temporary and fragile interests of her earthly lieutenants. According to church doctrine, the spiritual Church and Christ enjoyed ownership or *dominium* over the church patrimony. A bishop was *custos* of a church that he held in *custodia.* Because an individual churchman enjoyed no more than a limited occupancy or an *usus* of church assets, he could not sell the assets or pocket their revenues to build his estate. From such entrusted assets, the clerical *usuarius* was bound to gather revenues and spend them for his modest sustenance, his congregation's needs, and the Church's ultimate benefit.

A vocabulary redolent of trusteeship also permeated canonical depictions of the Pope's function. When churchmen did not characterize the Pope as a *dispensator* or a steward, they deemed him a guardian, and the Church his ward[44]. Evoking the

---

42 *S. F. C. Milsom,* Historical Foundations of the Common Law, 2nd ed., 1981, p. 203. *DeVine* seems justified in questioning *Milsom's* conclusions on the Roman *usus, DeVine* (n. 26) 17, nn. 31 - 34

43 *DeVine* (n. 26) 22, n. 105.

44 *Naz* (n. 7) 214 ff. On the treatment of churches as minor children and pastors as their guardians, see *Richard H. Helmholz,* The Spirit of Classical Canon Law, 1996, pp. 97 - 98 ff. As the Pope held the Church in wardship, the Church in turn held in wardship its faithful

patriarchal figure elaborated by Roman jurists, churchmen depicted the Pope as a *bonus paterfamilias,* dedicated to advancing *"utilitas ecclesiae et salus animarum* [the advantage of the Church and the welfare of the soul] ... not the self interests of individuals"[45].

The churchmen's imaginative excavation of Roman juridical strata may be illustrated by reference to the term *dispensator,* translated as steward and dispenser. We must take care not to read into the term *dispensator* a venality sometimes suggested in the word "dispensation". To a medieval Christian well-versed in Latin, the word *dispensator* was likely evocative of an enduring Roman social vision in which every man, no matter how high his social standing, owed someone else homage. A Roman's most trustworthy and competent slave, though fully subject to the authority of his *dominus,* served as *dispensator* of the latter's property and finances. Once manumitted, the slave must become a freedman *(libertus)* of his former master, now a *patronus.* As a freedman without his own resources, a former slave often continued as *dispensator* of his former master's affairs, and performing such financial and personal services became a common way for a *libertus* to pay homage to his *patronus.* "It was perhaps part of the domestic *officium* that the freedman should perform the duties of a client or accept the position of *dispensator* or *procurator* according to the patron's desire"[46]. In a Christian moral vision ani-

---

unfortunates. These included *personae miserabiles* such as orphans and widows too vulnerable to protect themselves. For further background on *personae miserabiles,* see *infra,* text at n. 27.

45 *J. A. Watt,* The Use of the Term 'Plenitudo Potestatis' in Hostiensis, in: Stephen Kuttner, J. Joseph Ryan (eds.), Proceedings of the Second International Congress of Medieval Canon Law, 1965, pp. 168 ff. These Latin standards formulated a spiritual ideal with which material reality could collide, for the self-interest of some clerics made clerical efforts to legitimate church wealth even more problematic. English churchmen often depicted themselves as vigilant shepherds who defended their flocks from jackals and wolves masking as clerics within the Church. Concerning the phenomenon of clerical materialism in the Middle Ages, *Robert Brentano* has observed: "To some men, significant ones, in each generation's stratum of reform, it [sc.: gross matter] seemed a repulsive perversion of Christian leadership. They fought to free religion from the filth of wealth without at the same time making ... religion, impotent or shrilly proud. ... [C]onventional Franciscans and Dominicans, like [Thomas] Pecham and Aquinas, constantly worried about the problem of poverty, fought about its implications against the remembered picture of Christ and his apostles, and did what they could ... to free themselves from the prison of property" (*Robert Brentano,* Two Churches: England and Italy in the Thirteenth Century, 1968, pp. 181 - 82 ff. Equating the Roman Church with unbridled avarice, English clerics sometimes depicted the English church as Rome's virtuous opponent or hapless victim. The theme of the vigilant shepherd was also woven into depictions of the Franciscan *Thomas Pecham,* the 13th century Archbishop of Canterbury, who decisively influenced the policies of the English church. According to *Decima Douie, Pecham* was a dutiful trustee at war with subordinate clerics for filling their pockets at their parishioners' expense. "[Pecham] never lost the conviction of his Paris days that the wealth of the Church was a trust, and his debts do not seem to have affected his almsgiving. ... He was scrupulous in reserving his generosity to his own flock, and his old order apparently benefited little materially from his elevation ...": *Decima L. Douie,* Archbishop Pecham, 1952, pp. 70 ff.

46 *Arnold Duff,* Freedmen in the Early Empire, 1928, pp. 40 ff.

mated by enduring Roman ideas of homage, the term *dispensator* may have conveyed the idea that the Pope, no matter how lofty his station in the spiritual hierarchy, always remained God's humble and obedient servant. Like a Roman *dispensator,* the Pope enjoyed sovereignty over the church's assets *vis-à-vis* inferior prelates; but to Jesus Christ, the Pope remained a humble servant and vassal. Even though the Pope occupied a lofty station in the church hierarchy, he performed his *officium* at the pleasure of his divine lord and patron.

VI. Forms of Trusteeship in the Early Christian Church

1. Christian Custodians

A *leitmotif* of trusteeship, although sometimes merely an ornamental or rhetorical figure in theological discourse, often had a programmatic function as well. With images of an equitable *dispensator* and a *bonus paterfamilias,* the church fathers signalled an innovative technique for achieving autonomy and self-sufficiency for their fledgling church. Such goals supposed a distinct patrimony fully within church control and separate from the private resources of individual clerics[47]. In hindsight, we may consider such a programmatic goal easy to attain, or perhaps even divinely ordained. Although the early Church's lack of juridical personality made the phrase "church property" seem a legal impossibility[48], the Church still required the advantages of property. We have already noticed briefly that the churchmen's self-depiction as a *collegium* allowed clerical exploitation of church property for spiritual or philanthropic purposes. With similar devices, early Christians reinforced the separation of ownership and administration and communicated the idea that church property was consistent with Christ's teachings so long as the property served spiritual purposes.

2. Cemetery Custodian

Some property holding techniques could be explained in terms of the material circumstances that early Christians faced. For example, post mortem segregation of Christians from non-Christians seems to have been a main *raison d'être* for a brotherhood of cemetery keepers. "Among Christians there developed very early a practice of attending to common burial plots where their bodies would repose next to each other, united among brothers in death as in life, to await the resurrection"[49].

---

47 See *infra,* text at n. 56.

48 On the Church's acquisition of legal personality by means of the Edict of Milan, see *infra,* text at n. 53.

49 "De très bonne heure la coutume s'introduisit chez les chrétiens de se ménager des lieux de sépulture communs, où leurs corps reposeraient les uns près des autres, unis entre frères

Evocative of the apostolic *collegium,* a brotherhood of the Christian faithful held and maintained burial places for the benefit of the Christian community. By safeguarding Christian souls confided to his care, a cemetery custodian symbolized spiritual continuity among the faithful, whether deceased, alive, or yet unborn.

3. Custodian of Holy Places

Lacking legal personality until the 4th century, the church was no more than a brotherhood on the fringes of Roman society. Making a virtue of its legal non-recognition among Roman authorities[50], the brotherhood placed control of Christian holy places in a righteous Christian. Like a *bonus paterfamilias,* this Christian figure retained custody of the asset on behalf of the Christian community. Such a property-holding vehicle was undependable: a Christian custodian who strayed from the path of righteousness by apostasizing and by renouncing his fiduciary duty to the church community might dispossess the congregants. Deprived of both juridical personality and a secure means of regaining physical possession of its holy place, the Christian community had as its only weapon against an apostate custodian the hollow threat of excommunication from the institution he had already betrayed. To *Raoul Naz,* the function of the interposed clerical custodian evoked the role of a trustee or fiduciary:

> "During its earliest history, the church had to rely upon a system of an interposed person, running the risk associated with [this approach]. A Christian is here owner in his own right; if he happened either to apostasize or to renounce the fiduciary character of his role, the church suffered eviction and had only spiritual means to defend itself against this eviction"[51].

According to *Neubecker,* collectively held church property was vested in a nominal owner who administered it in accordance with a pact of *fiducia.* Taking a cue

---

comme ils l'étaient de leur vivant, dans l'attente de la résurrection": *R. Saleilles,* L'organisation juridique des premières communautés chrétiennes, in: Mélanges Paul Frédéric Girard, 1912, pp. 472 ff.

50 Imperial Roman pronouncements sometimes betrayed an awareness that early Christians had experimented with secret or concealed trusts. During the 4th century, for example, constitutions of the late Empire expressly denied the heterodox a capacity to participate in trusts as trustees and beneficiaries to make secret trusts. Judging by the remarks of *Jerome,* such bans on secret trusts were not fully effective. A letter of *Jerome* "complaine[d] bitterly of the restrictions on the testamentary capacity of the Church imposed by emperors, but at the same time [Jerome] confide[d] that 'by trust we cheat the law' *(per fideicommissum legibus inludimus)*": *David Johnston,* The Roman Law of Trusts, 1988, pp. 73 ff.

51 "Dans les premiers temps de son histoire, n'ayant pas d'existence légale, l'Église a dû recourir au système de la personne interposée, en s'exposant à tous les dangers qu'il comporte. Un chrétien est ici propriétaire, à titre individuel: qu'il vienne à apostasier ou à renier le caractère fiduciaire de son rôle, dépossession effective s'ensuit pour l'Église, qui n'a d'autres moyens de défense contre cette éviction que les moyens spirituels": *Naz* (n. 7) 227 ff.

from *Neubecker's* findings, *Saleilles* suggested that practical necessity had impelled the Church to adapt the *fiducia* and *collegium tenuiorum* to permit it to hold property indirectly:

> "Collective property, when it is prohibited, can disguise itself under two contrasting forms: it either borrows the juridical form of a licit association, or it is concentrated in the hands of a fiduciary proprietor, who is purely apparent [i.e. not the real owner]. We wished to pay tribute to the first Christians with the first expedient, thanks to the fiction of *collegia tenuiorum* ... Now we wish to refer to the other, that of the pact of *fiducia*. The Roman devices would thus have anticipated the history of English trusts. The ground, catacomb, cemetery, or meeting place would have been put in the hands of an owner bound by a pact of *fiducia* to safeguard the immovable for its intended uses. For a sepulchre, the perpetuity of the designation would be better assured by the common clause revealed in inscriptions which excluded this category of property from testamentary succession, to leave it in perpetuity to the decedent's family ... We can suppose that money and movables were confided to a leader of the community, e.g., the bishop, who administered them for the account of the community and distributed them in alms. In reality ... the assets belonged to the community and in current language, one could say that [the community] possessed them and owned them, as it would be later said in England that, one would transfer a fief to a purely apparent title holder, subject to a direction that it [the community] was really the owner in equity, [while] the other party, the trustee, had only legal and purely nominal ownership"[52].

Neubecker's hypothesis and *Saleilles'* remarks accord with the view that clerical nominees laid a foundation for episcopal administration of church assets. As an apparent owner of the assets, the bishop, like a deputy *dispensator*, "was bound not to avail himself of these assets unless they were for the use of the community," the rightful beneficial owner[53]. In Christian imaginations, such nominal owners prefi-

---

52 "La propriété collective, quand elle est interdite, ne peut, en effet, se dissimuler que sous ces deux formes opposées; ou bien elle emprunte le moule juridique d'une association licite, ou bien elle se concentre aux mains d'un propriétaire fiduciaire, purement apparent. On a voulu faire honneur aux premiers chrétiens du premier expédient, grâce á la fiction des collegia tenuiorum; nous avons repoussé cette hypothèse. On veut maintenant qu'ils aient eu recours à l'autre, celui du pacte de fiducie. Ils auraient ainsi devancé l'histoire des trusts anglais. Le terrain, catacombe, cimetière, lieu de réunion, aurait été aux mains d'un propriétaire qui se serait engagé par un pacte de fiducie à laisser l'immeuble à l'usage auquel il était affecté. Lorsqu'il s'agissait de lieu de sépulture, la perpétuité de leur affectation aurait pu être encore mieux assurée par la clause si fréquente en pareil cas que nous révèlent les inscriptions, et qui avait pour objet d'excepter cette catégorie de propriété de la succession testamentaire, afin de la laisser à perpétuité dans la famille du défunt ... Pour l'argent et les meubles on pouvait supposer qu'ils étaient confiés à l'un des chefs de la communauté, l'épiscope par exemple, qui les administrait pour le compte de la communauté et les distribuait en aumônes. En réalité, ... c'est à elle que ces biens appartenaient, et, dans le langage courant, on pouvait dire qu'elle les possédait et qu'elle en était propriétaire, comme plus tard, en Angleterre, on dira de celui qui devait avoir le bénéfice de fiefs cédés à un titulaire purement apparent, avec charge d'affectation, qu'il en était vraiment le propriétaire équite ... et purement nominale": *Saleilles* (n. 49) 494 ff.

53 *Saleilles* (n. 49) 495 ff.

gured medieval trustee figures such as clerical executors, and leaders of religious foundations and monasteries[54].

4. *Corpus Christianorum*

During the 3rd century, Christian communities began to earn recognition and legitimacy from their Roman neighbors. From the era of emperor *Alexander Severus* (222 - 35), Christians were permitted to hold their sacred places in *de facto* corporate form. In 313, the Edict of Milan legitimated church property-holding in an institution known as *Corpus Christianorum*[55]. Thereafter the edict enhanced the church's autonomy in several ways. First, *Corpus Christianorum* itself permitted the Church to extend and stabilize its holdings. Second, the Edict of Milan authorized a Christian brotherhood to segregate and hold church assets separate from those belonging to individual Christians. Third, the edict granted a cadre of faithful followers a juridical personality and attributed a faculty of possession to each church constituted around a bishop. Church assets thenceforth came to be envisioned as a patrimony, i.e. an autonomous mass subdivided and distributed functionally into dioceses. The assets' revenues assured maintenance of the clergy, payment of oblations, and distribution of alms and services to *miserabiles personae* such as widows, orphans, and other unfortunates too vulnerable to care for themselves[56].

---

54 See *Herman*, (1996) 70 Tulane L. R. 2256 ff.

55 *Émile Chenon*, Les Consequences Juridiques de l'Édit de Milan, Nouvelle Revue Historique de Droit Français et Étranger (1914) 255, 260 ff. The edict ordered restoration to Christians of assets *corpori christianorum*, that is, property enjoyed by Christians in an institutional or corporate capacity, rather than as individuals: *Chenon*, at 260 - 63 ff. The impact of *corpus christianorum* seems not to have been felt fully until the 5th century. "Dès le ve s., on a remarqué que si l'évêqué était l'administrateur des biens de son Église, c'était le corpus christianorum, considéré comme une personne morale, d'après l'edit de Milan, qui en était le propriétaire": *R. Naz*, Dictionnaire de Droit Canonique 7 (1965) 378 ff.

56 According to *Professor Helmholz*, canonical texts imposed on the church "a special solicitude for widows and children. ... Orphans and widows were treated as unfortunates for whom the church had a special protective responsibility. ... [A]lthough clerics were ordinarily forbidden to assume the burdens of acting in secular affairs, an exception was made for guardianship (cura and tutela) of minor children. In fact, clerics were required to assume this special responsibility under orders from their bishop": *Helmholz* (n. 44) 124 ff. Animated by a notion of the monarch as "universal guardian to infants", this special clerical solicitude may have inspired the English chancery to develop a jurisprudence of guardianship to address the spiritual and material welfare of children. The phrase quoted in the preceding sentence appears in *Henry Ballow*, A Treatise on Equity, 3rd ed., 1807, pp. 223 ff. When guardianship entailed supervision of both a minor's estate and his personal welfare, English courts approached articulation of classical trust doctrine: *Ballow*, at 239 - 46. For links among Roman tutorship, English guardianship, and English trusteeship see *Ballow*, at 249 - 50.

5. Bishops as Earthly Dwellers and Spiritual Guides to Life Everlasting

As depicted in both canonical and secular texts, bishops, by assuming duties originally fulfilled by righteous Christian custodians, came to enjoy wide latitude in administering diocesan property. Yet, segregating a bishop's personal estate from that of his church posed a vexing problem: confusion over whether a certain asset was enjoyed by a bishop personally or had been confided to him as steward of his religious community might spark a dispute between his next-of-kin and his church. To remain above reproach, the bishop ideally should have adopted the ethic of an impoverished brotherhood by regarding himself as his community's trustee and all assets in his hands as having vested in the Church as beneficial owner. But the title to assets in a bishop's hands was seldom explicit, and the bishop's next of kin probably took little risk in claiming a volume of the decedent's possessions in hopes of wresting some assets from the local religious community. Accurate identification of church property was further complicated by a common episcopal practice of confiding holy places to *oeconomes*. These were trustees or managers who temporarily administered church property and rendered periodic accounts of receipts and disbursements. Although some prelates deplored a severance of their sacred ministry from their property-managing function, expansion of the Church's estate, coupled with progressive fragmentation of its holdings, assured the appointment of such property trustees[57].

VII. Church Doctrines and Practices Assist Consolidation of Church Patrimony

1. Wills

Having struggled in the Church's early centuries for autonomous legal personality and ecclesiastical authority to hold property, church leaders also articulated doctrines that helped tighten and extend the Church's grip over its material assets. By suggesting that a Christian decedent's intestacy signified that he had died unconfessed, churchmen encouraged gifts *mortis causa*. Such a suggestion made a will crucial for a Christian who had reflected upon the prospect of dying with his

57 *Gaudemet* (n. 15) 307 - 308 ff. In the 4th century, *St. Augustine*, among the earliest Christian missionaries in England, confided administration of church assets to clerics who rendered him an annual accounting of income and expenses. A practice of appointing *oeconomes* as church administrators seems to have originated among popes who sought to save church properties from deteriorating in the hands of neglectful clerics (*Gaudemet*, at 309). The Western Church seems gradually to have abandoned the practice of appointing oeconomes in favor of granting benefices in commendam. See *Herman*, (1997) 71 Tulane L. R. *passim*. On links among *oeconomes, utilitas ecclesiae*, and *benefices in commendam*, see *Hostiensis* (n. 1) 159A-160 (*De officio iudiciis ordinarii)*.

soul's destiny in doubt[58]. The Church provided the testator a priest to safeguard his soul[59] and incidentally to assure that certain testamentary bequests went to the church, usually for pious works *(ad pias causas)* [60]. At a time when wills were oral acts and associated writings memorialized the testator's oral desires, a clerical intermediary conveniently corroborated a testator's intention to give. In a sense, the cleric solemnized and formalized a testator's amorphously uttered wishes as sealing wax might formalize contractual promises. When a testator died and the moment had arrived for carrying out his wishes, church courts supervised the probate proceeding and furnished clerical executors to carry out the dead man's wish that a brotherhood of faithful pray for his soul and commend it to God[61].

---

58 Abundant evidence suggests that intestacy under any circumstances was a grave evil in the popular mind: "... [I]t was understood that to die without a will, with full intention, was tantamount to rejecting the ministry of the Church; the consequences were burial in unconsecrated ground and confiscation of property by the lay authority. References to intestacy appearing in chronicles, royal letter books, reports of juries, and canon and civil law show that those free to make a will were expected to do so": *Michael M. Sheehan,* The Will In Medieval England: From The Conversion of the Anglo-Saxons to The End of the Thirteenth Century, 1963, pp. 232 ff. A decisive Roman preference for testation, and a corresponding "horror of intestacy," perhaps helped clerics to impress upon early Christians the importance of willmaking. See *Henry Sumner Maine,* Ancient Law: Its Connection With the Early History of Society, and its Relation to Modern Ideas, 1864, pp. 216 ff.; *David Daube,* Roman Law: Linguistic, Social and Philosophical Aspects, 1969, pp. 71 - 75 ff. But a pervasive Roman-Christian emphasis on testation did not mean that a Roman vision of the afterlife had become engraved upon the Christian spirit. Concerned with the continuing maintenance of the *sacra,* the family's religious sites, as well as the proper settlement of his estate in favor of creditors and loved ones, a Roman testator made a will to assure his *heres* would continue his good name and reputation. In a Christian testator's heart, by contrast, salvation was uppermost. A Christian made his will primarily to assure that his path to salvation was not blocked by his dying unconfessed.

59 The ecclesiastical hierarchy collectively constituted an intermediary between a Christian's earthly abode and life everlasting; *Duby* (n. 6) 328 ff. A priest's reception of a dying man's last words was likened naturally to the Church's function as spiritual intermediary.

60 A papal decretal of *Gregory IX* urged the faithful to seek salvation by bequeathing part of their wealth for pious causes. "The day of harvest should be anticipated with works of great mercy, and, for the sake of things eternal, to sow on earth what we should gather in Heaven, the Lord returning it with increased fruit": *Gareth Jones,* History of the Law of Charity, 1969, pp. 3 ff. (quoting Letter of Authorisation for Collectors for Charitable Institutions, approved in 1215 by the Fourth Lateran Council). For omitting the Church from his will, a testator could be denied the Eucharist and could be buried in unconsecrated ground; *Jones,* at 3 ff. "A similar fate might befall the person who died intestate, for he too had failed to make provision for works of great mercy before death, but to ensure his salvation, the Church obtained the right to administer his estate and to distribute a portion of it ad pias causas": *Jones,* at 3 ff.

61 *A. Hamilton Thompson,* The English Clergy and Their Organization in the Later Middle Ages, 1947, pp. 132 ff.

2. Chantry Foundations

As if to project against a medieval backdrop early images of an impoverished Christian *collegium* in service to a community of the faithful, "[r]eligious houses furnished benefactors with letters of confraternity, admitting them to share vicariously in the works of piety and the suffrages of the community"[62]. A portion of the benefactor's goods might be used to endow a chantry chapel in which a chaplain and his clerical congregation recited regular masses and prayers *ad opus* the benefactor's salvation. Intestacy provided no escape from a Christian's duty to serve the Church; to the contrary, intestacy, by raising spiritual doubts about the destiny of one's soul, itself justified paying a premium to the Church in exchange for clerical assurances of spiritual welfare. After paying an intestate's just debts, his clerical representative was to distribute his decedent's remaining assets in "charitable deeds for the soul's health of the dead ..."[63]. *Inter vivos* transfers to the Church appear to have been commonplace among crusaders and pilgrims who sought to safeguard their estates during long absences[64]. In such feoffments, a clerical feoffee to uses usually administered assets for the welfare of the feoffors' children and kin.

3. Monastic Finances and Feoffments to Uses

To medieval clerics under a strict poverty vow, the clerical *usus* was an appealing way to enjoy property. Conferring upon such clerics *dominium* over church property would have given them too great a stake in the material world. It would have also made them, in *Augustine's* view, captives of the temporal sphere. The most effective way to safeguard *res ecclesiae* was by vesting *dominium* of the Church estate in Christ. Even *ususfructus* of a church benefice would have compromised Christ's estate by giving the clerics more than charity and virtue required. It was true that a *usufructuary*, under Roman law, had no *dominium*. Nevertheless he could take fruits and revenues of his estate for his own enrichment and

---

62 *Thompson* (n. 61) 132 ff. Evocations of the apostles' *collegium, supra*, n. 14. Such religious confraternities existed in England by the 8th century; *K. L. Wood-Legh*, Perpetual Chantries in Britain, 1965, pp. 3 ff.

63 *William Lyndwood*, Provinciale, ed. J. V. Bullard, H. C. Bell, 1929, pp. 68 ff.

64 Reminiscent of the *fiducia cum amico* – see *Herman*, (1996) 70 Tulane L.R. 2273 ff. – such transfers to the Church were often revocable; depending upon circumstances (e.g., whether a donor's life was out of danger), transferred assets might either revert to a donor or descend to a third party. During the Anglo-Saxon period, English churchmen served as intermediaries and trustees for soldiers setting out for war and pilgrims going "over sea"; *Sheehan* (n. 58) 42 ff. Contemplating the possibility that he would not return home, a traveler provided that a third party, often a cleric, should care for his property during his absence: *Sheehan*, at 42 ff. The cleric often pledged himself to restore the property to the traveler upon his return or to see to its distribution upon his death; *Sheehan*, at 42 ff.

luxury. By constrast a mere *usus* in property gave the cleric all he needed; though he could not luxuriate in worldly goods acquired with revenues from his benefice, he could as a faithful steward use a measure of the fruits modestly for *usum quotidianum.* Furthermore, Roman doctrine, by making the *usus* non-heritable, non-transferable and terminable at the death of the usuary, made the cleric a temporary trustee of property confided to him; he could thus use the world as a temporary sojourner and a pilgrim. Though he could spend revenues *ad usus* his flock's needs, the *usus* itself would ideally cut down his *superbia.* However, this clerical ideal collided with financial reality, and feoffments to uses became appealing investment vehicles for monastic orders.

For secular imaginations forged in a crucible of post-Enlightenment learning, a medieval monastery's essential feature was its cloister: here, a devout brotherhood, in retreat from the material world, sought spiritual rewards in contemplative life[65]. Although this characterization of a monastery is surely accurate, it is incomplete, for it veils the monastery's role as a sophisticated business. Engineered to ease application of material wealth to *utilitas ecclesiae,* the machinery of a medieval monastery resembled that of other trust-like institutions that we have considered. On a spiritual plane, a monastic order epitomized the *corpus christianorum.* Subject to a poverty vow, the monks trained their gaze on ideal ways of carrying out *Christ's* teaching. Yet the monastic financial organization seems to have followed the familiar principle that the whole was greater than the sum of its parts. Although each monk was impoverished, his monastic order was paradoxically a mortgage banker *par excellence.* A monastic order poignantly reflected the church's dilemma: practitioners of simony, the monks projected piety. Here we focus briefly on how the monastery's dual character, symbolized in the cloister and mortgage bank, led it to a deft application of the use, the ancestor of the trust[66].

Like a chantry, a monastery was a foundation dedicated to pious causes. In a chantry charter, a donor enfeoffed a chapel to the use of a clerical brotherhood for the benefit of his eternal salvation. A monastery's financial and spiritual organization depended upon large accumulations of enfeoffments to uses. Like a chantry donor, a secular donor, by means of a generous gift, acquired symbolic membership in a monastic fraternity. Like a clerical brotherhood in charge of a chantry chapel, a monastery promised the donor *confraternitas*[67], prayers, masses, and burial in a communal cemetery. To a monastic foundation, a wealthy donor might contribute a tenement whose yield in crops and rents sustained the order. Such a transaction resembled a gift to a modern university that might invest the funds in en-

---

65 For an account of monastic experience centered on the cloister, see generally *C. H. Lawrence,* Medieval Monasticism: Forms of Religious Life in Western Europe in the Middle Ages, 2nd ed., 1989, pp. 111 - 48.

66 For an account of medieval monasteries as bankers, see generally *R. Génestal,* Rôle des Monastères comme Établissements de Crédit, 1901; *Shael Herman,* Medieval Usury and the Commercialization of Feudal Bonds, 1993, *passim.*

67 *Génestal* (n. 66) 165.

dowment, segregate revenues from the corpus, and spend the revenues for ongoing programs earmarked by the donor. Monastic revenues from a particular gift might be applied to the monastery's physical plant. With surplus crops and revenues, monks performed God's work by giving alms to the poor and by caring for the sick unable to care for themselves. Yet, a prudent abbot tried to maintain the corpus intact and avoided exhaustion of the order's revenues.

As a monastery prospered, its capital reserves grew; and by the 11th century, monastic orders systematically invested surplus resources in interest-bearing loans. An order's borrowers collateralized such loans by means of gages and encumbered estates. Though, for a time, these monasteries showed a preference for gaged loans, their preference soon shifted to perpetual rents. Formulated as enfeoffments to use of the monastery, these rents resembled annuities in the sense that they produced a regular cash flow. In contrast with a gaged loan, however, a loan represented by a rent was not exigible: that is, the loan represented by a perpetual rent never matured. According to *Génestal's* study of medieval monasteries, monastic charters stipulated irredeemable rents because a redemption of rent amounted to alienating a church asset, a doctrinally prohibited activity[68].

A perpetual rent payable to a monastery had twin virtues: because the loan represented by a rent never matured, there was little need for a centralized administration to tend to fiscal monitoring. Second, if the monks were routinely subject to a poverty vow, then the rent's structure permitted them to avoid the issue of whether ownership of the principal of the loan violated their vow. By the canonically approved division of ownership into *dominium, usus,* and *fructus, dominium* of the loan was vested in the church; a monastic payee conceived himself as an investment's *usuarius,* not its *dominus*[69].

4. Feoffments to Uses Applied to Specific Spiritual Needs

Utilizing perpetual feoffments to uses, the order collected the cash flow and applied it to specific needs within the monastery. In a sense, the rent feoffment represented a miniaturization of the monastery's financial structure. Having set up his budget for a year, an abbot acquired a rent, by either loan or donation, and he then allocated the rent's cash flow to a specific monastic function or office. By making a rent directly payable to a monastic officer, the abbot sidestepped centralized fiscal administration. The payment's particular application or *usus* was implied in the

68 *Génestal* (n. 66) 130.

69 Among the Franciscans, the term *commendam,* meaning in classical Latin "to entrust", sometimes designated a *usus.* Subject to a poverty vow, the Franciscans could not be *domini* by title *(titulatio)*; they only used goods commended to them *(commendata).* For background on the *commendatio* as an entrusting device, see generally *Herman,* (1997) 71 Tulane L. R. 869.

title of the officer who received it. A large rent might be stipulated *ad usus* the *eleemosinarius* to be distributed in alms; for healing the sick, a more modest rent might be stipulated *ad usus* the *infirmarius;* earmarked for the *luminarius,* a tiny rent might allow a purchase of candles for a chapel altar[70]. If the rent were donated, its donor likely had some latitude in dictating application of revenues. By contrast rents from a rent seller (i.e. a borrower who had received a capital advance), were likely applied in an abbot's discretion. As *Génestal* showed, donors and borrowers were often difficult to distinguish[71]: to conceal usury and simony and to project "noble sentiments", a monastic charter drafter might use gift language for a transaction in which the "donor" was a borrower.

Authorized by a rent charter to redirect cash flow, the abbot acted as a modern trustee with discretion to reallocate income. But he lacked authority to invade the corpus because *dominium* of the loan was vested in the church patrimony. A cash yield from such a discretionary application might be spent for celebration of a mass, to buy candles, or to pay for an additional meal on a special occasion[72]. As *feoffments to uses* took hold and became prevalent, a monastic officer who received a particular rent came to see himself as a benefice holder endowed with both *officium* and *temporalia.* His role blended aspects of beneficiary and trustee. A monastery had *dominium utile vis-à-vis* a church with *dominium directum. Vis-à-vis* the abbot, a monastic *infirmarius* had *dominium utile* of his particular allocation of revenues. Forbidden to luxuriate in these revenues, an *infirmarius* could still lose sight of the fact that he was to minister to the sick with *temporalia* flowing from the *use.* He could readily have mistaken himself for his rightful beneficiaries, in much the way that a government bureaucrat today might confuse his personal status and welfare with those of his constituents[73].

Although our remarks about rents have thus far concerned Norman practice, we may reasonably conclude that uses had a similar career in England. Monastic orders were found on both sides of the Channel: until the early 1200s, England and Normandy were administratively like Siamese twins joined at the hip. Both territories were subject to Anglo-Norman custom. A number of English rent charters represented imaginative application of feoffments to uses. One can guess at the fi-

70 Contemporaneously, a monastery could segregate its estates and earmark its revenues for precise needs to insulate them from a feudal lord's long reach: *Sheehan* (n. 58) 252. Designated for precise monastic needs, the estates probably were readily classified as *spiritualia.* By acquiescing in the designation of these assets as *spiritualia,* a lay leader behaved as a modern creditor whose acquiescence in a debtor's designation of his "tools of trade" results in their exemption from the creditor's seizure.

71 *Génestal* (n. 66) 128 - 129.

72 *Génestal* (n. 66) 174.

73 Fascination with private wealth was a common frailty of the abbots themselves. Church texts regularly denied abbots the right to private holdings and to make wills, but the abbot could ignore the bans if he had obtained royal and papal consent: *Sheehan* (n. 58) 255 - 256. Even when consent was granted, the machinery of consent allowed both monarch and church to maintain surveillance over a cleric's activities.

nancial factors that impelled a York archbishop in 1241 to enter a trust with a religious order that contemplated successive transfers of a tenement on condition that the chapter would convey it to successive archbishops. According to the charter, each archbishop would pay a rent to the cathedral treasurer who in turn expended the rent to maintain a chantry. According to *Pollock* and *Maitland*, this financial arrangement resembled a usufruct for the cathedral treasurer. Hence, these scholars speculated on links between usufruct and use. Though they discounted their speculation as far-fetched, a case can be made that the structure of this financial arrangement resembled that of a classical benefice with a shift of *temporalia* and *spiritualia* for a succession of bishops. As the revenues supported a chantry, one may surmise that the rent was granted by a secular donor who desired masses for his eternal salvation. The donor's gift charter assured proper collection and application of the revenues by having the archbishop act as a conduit to the cathedral treasurer, who in turn expended funds for masses and prayers. Our interpretation of this transaction conforms with our understanding that chantry charters typically stipulated *ad usus* the chantry chapter[74].

Other early English arrangements recalled the institution of the righteous custodian who held a holy place when the infant church had no legal personality. A conceptual split of *dominium directum* and *dominium utile* gave these arrangements flexibility as the monastic orders confronted rising royal hostility toward their growing wealth. The Mortmain Statute was enacted to check this growth. After 1279, the date of the statute's enactment, division of an estate into a title in favor of a third person, a spiritual friend, and a monastery's interest *ad usus* seems to have allowed the monastery to maintain an appearance of poverty and to sidestep limitations upon transfers of estates into mortmain.

The "spiritual friend" just described could have found inspiration in the ancient institution of the faithful custodian of holy places. A device resembling a *fiducia cum amico* received papal sanction in the 12th century as a way of accommodating the Franciscans' absolute poverty vow. *St. Francis* had expressly forbidden the brethren to own buildings and to touch money. But there was a paradox inherent in *St. Francis'* policy: "[an] attempt to reconcile absolute poverty with the practical needs of a pastoral ministry involved heroic gymnastics of conscience"[75]. In 1230, provincial ministers sought a papal interpretation of *St. Francis'* requirement of

---

74 Paid a regular rent, a coalition of feoffees to uses might do a double duty, serving as both a decedent feoffer's executors and as trustees to a chantry chaplain who recited masses for the testator's welfare. This arrangement might have made it easy to avoid having to pay for a costly mortmain license. "In the course of the fourteenth century it had become customary to grant estates to groups of feoffees so that after the grantor's death they should pay his debts and execute his charitable bequests, and it was soon realized that such a group of feoffees could hold that estate indefinitely, using the income to pay a priest or for any other object which had been agreed upon between them and the grantor": *Wood-Legh* (n. 62) 49. For further background on the royal mortmain policy in England, see *Herman* (n. 66) 59 - 63. For a discussion of contemporary French mortmain policy, see *Herman* (n. 66) 43 - 45.

75 *Coleman* (n. 4) 79.

absolute poverty. The papal interpretation allowed the Franciscans to appoint as trustee an *amicus spiritualis* or "spiritual friend" who held money and property on behalf of the brethren. Beneficiaries of this arrangement, the brethren could apply to their spiritual friend for necessities. Franciscans were thus enabled to accept gifts of money, notably legacies showered upon them by their grateful penitents. "The papal privilege *Quo Elongati* authorising this concession represent[ed] the beginning of an inevitable retreat from *St. Francis's* uncompromising ideal of absolute poverty"[76].

VIII. Conclusion

As both faithful papal deputy and temporary steward of the monastery, a monastic leader in the company of his monks evoked images of Christ and his disciples as well as cemetery custodians whose vigilance promised the Church a measure of *de facto* autonomy before it had achieved juridical personality. From the days of the early Christians, separation of an asset's beneficial ownership from its administration allowed consolidation of church patrimony and its separation from a cleric's personal assets. Animated by an ideal of *utilitas ecclesiae*[77], popes and their clerical deputies replicated their trusteeship patterns for a variety of purposes including executorship, clerical feoffments, and foundation of chantries and monasteries.

By helping a testator make gifts to pious causes, a clerical executor sought to assure the welfare of the man's soul until judgment day. By assisting a testator to arrange his worldly goods, the clerical executor assured the welfare of the testator's family after his death. Eschewing his own needs, an abbot looked after his religious order, church assets confided to him, and the neediest parishioners of the local community. In accordance with instructions from a feoffor about to set out on pilgrimage or crusade, a clerical feoffee to uses administered assets for his *cestui's* moral and material welfare. Recognizing that spiritual rents were impressed with a trust, a monastic *luminarius* spent them for chapel candles. A chantry chaplain sang masses *ad usus* his founder's salvation. Called to account by clerical supervisors, all these trustee figures justified their conduct on the basis that they had elevated their beneficiaries' welfare above their own. As if inspired by a Christian version of a utilitarian calculus, each clerical trustee, by promoting the spiritual welfare of his immediate community, could be seen as contributing to the spiritual welfare of all Christendom. Services *ad utilitatem ecclesiae* enhanced God's glory, and each spiritual exercise advanced God's divine project for his faithful flock.

---

76 *Lawrence* (n. 65) 250.

77 For discussion of this standard of clerical stewardship, see *Herman*, (1996) 70 Tulane L. R. 2239 ff., n. 1.

JOSEPH BIANCALANA

Medieval Uses

Medieval uses transformed English law and participated in the transformation of English society. Uses were the precursors to early modern and modern trusts[1]. Uses permitted landholders to tap their landed revenues in making their last wills and to make last wills of land. The development of uses was entwined with the development of Chancery as a court of equity. Feoffments to uses were also instruments, along with the indenture of retainer and the letter patent, of the social ordering which historians have christened, misleadingly, bastard feudalism[2]. Yet, for all their importance, much about medieval uses, their invention, development, and employment, remains mysterious. The valuable work of *Bean*[3] provides a general map of a largely unexplored territory. Much of the territory remains *terra incognita* because, as *Milsom* has observed, the details are lacking[4]. Understandably, better knowledge of the details will require filling in or redrawing the earlier more general map. This essay begins to consider some of the details. It might be viewed, to change metaphors, as a footnote to *Bean* were it not that at significant points the footnote is in gentle war with the text.

A landholder created a use by conveying land to a group of persons to hold the land for a purpose other than, or in addition to, their own benefit. The landholder making the conveyance was called the feoffor; the recipients were called feoffees to uses or simply feoffees; the beneficiary was called the *cestui que use*. Uses had two defining features. First, the feoffees were said to have the freehold. This feature distinguished a feoffee from a bailiff or a lessee. This feature also distinguished uses from similar arrangements in the 13th century. Second, uses pertained primarily to land as opposed to chattels. This feature distinguished uses from various agency or trust relationships recognized by the common law as bailments or receiverships[5].

---

1 For a discussion of early modern trusts see the essays by *N. G. Jones* and *M. McNair* in this volume.

2 E.g., *P. R. Coss*, Bastard Feudalism Revised, (1989) 125 Past & Present 27 - 64; *K. B. McFarland*, Bastard Feudalism, in: England in the Fifteenth Century: Collected Essays of K. B. McFarland, 1981, pp. 23 - 43; *J. G. Bellamy*, Bastard Feudalism and the Law, 1989.

3 *J. M. W. Bean*, The Decline of English Feudalism, 1215 - 1540, 1968, pp. 104 - 234.

4 *S. F. C. Milsom*, Historical Foundations of the Common Law, 2nd ed., 1981, pp. 211 - 12.

5 *A. W. B. Simpson*, A History of the Land Law, 2nd ed., 1986, p. 173.

This barebones and somewhat technical definitional description of a use is designed to fit a wide variety of uses. For uses were created in various ways for various purposes. Uses varied in point of the estate given the feoffees, the relation, if any, prescribed between feoffor and feoffee, and the terms used to impose duties on the feoffees. More importantly, uses varied in point of their purpose or function. Medieval uses can be divided into two great classes, those which transmitted land from one generation to the next and those which did not. Uses of the latter class were created to secure debts or other obligations[6], to avoid creditors[7], to evade litigation[8], and to circumvent the Statute of Mortmain[9]. Parliament frowned on uses created for the last three purposes[10]. Uses of this class are tangential to this essay, which is concerned mainly with uses that transmitted land from one generation to the next. Uses of this class, intergenerational uses, were the more numerous and the more important legally and socially. In some uses of this class, the feoffees were to perform a single task and then convey the land to the feoffor's heir. The single task might be to give alms for the soul of the feoffor[11], to accumulate marriage portions for the feoffor's daughters[12], or to pay the feoffor's debts[13]. In other uses of this class, the feoffees were to perform several such tasks, frequently spelled out in the feoffor's last will, and then convey the land to the feoffor's heir. Whether single purpose or multi-purpose, intergenerational uses were created to achieve a delayed transfer of land to the feoffor's heir, the delay being the time it took after the feoffor's death for the feoffees to perform their designated tasks. Another type of use straddled the two main classes of uses. These were uses created when the feoffor was about to go overseas in the King's military service in France. They usually provided for the feoffor to receive the land back if he returned and for the feoffees to act as in an intergenerational use if the feoffor died while overseas[14].

The history of medieval uses, their invention and development, combines four stories: a story about their invention, a story about their increased employment, a

---

6 B.L. Harleian Charter 46 F 11 (1337); Calendar of Patent Rolls, 1348 - 50, p. 374 (1349); *ibid.*, 1374 - 77, p. 191 (1375). The Langley Cartulary, no. 157 (1471) (Ed. P. R. Coss, 32 Pub. of the Dugdale Soc. 1980).

7 Stat. 50 Edw. III, c.6 (1376).

8 Stat. 1 Ric. II, c.9 (1377); Stat. 4 Hen. IV, c.7 (1402); Stat. 11 Hen. VI, c.3 (1433); Y.B. Mich. 9 Hen. IV, f.8, pl.23 (1407); Y.B. Mich.10 Hen. IV, f.6, pl.9 (1408).

9 Stat. 15 Ric. II, c.5 (1391).

10 See *supra* nn. 7 - 9.

11 A Calendar of the Cartularies of John Pyel and Adam Fraunceys, ed. S. J. O'Connor, 2 Camden Society 5th Series, 1993, p. 120, no. 49 (1350).

12 Beauchamp Cartulary, B.L. Add. Ms. 28024, ff. 15 - 15v, Calendar of Patent Rolls, 1343 - 45, pp. 517 - 18 (1345).

13 The Langley Cartulary (n. 6) no. 157 (1471).

14 E.g., 3 Calendar of Miscellaneous Inquisitions, no. 78; Calendar of Close Rolls, 1374 - 77, pp. 286 - 88.

story about the tension between uses and a lord's right to wardship, and a story about their protection in Chancery as a court of equity.

I. The Invention of Uses

Isolated instances of feoffments to uses appear as early as the 1320s[15]. Uses became more frequent, though not very numerous, in the 1330s and 1340s[16]. Thereafter, the employment of uses increased steadily until by the end of *Edward III's* reign a feoffment to uses had become part of the conveyancer's standard repertoire of techniques for establishing family settlements[17].

1. Precursors

Historians have looked for earlier examples of uses, but their hunt for precursors has been largely in vain. It is no doubt frequently convenient to be able to give land to another person in order to accomplish a purpose of one's own. It is not, therefore, surprising to find arrangements similar to uses at various times and in various places. But rough resemblance, however interesting, does not make for historical connection. Neither the *Salmann,* which caught *Holmes'* eye, nor the few 12th century conveyances collected by *Bean* are connected to the later use[18].

An arrangement frequently discussed as a precursor to uses involved the Franciscans[19]. The Franciscan order was dedicated to poverty as long as the poverty was not real. One device which permitted the Franciscans to enjoy property while maintaining apostolic poverty was to have others own property for the benefit or use of the Franciscans. These arrangements were not precursors of intergenerational uses. They foreshadow both uses created to circumvent the Statute of Mort-

15 E.g., Calendar of Inquisitions Post Mortem, vol. 7, no. 281 (1326); *ibid.* no. 343 (before 1331).

16 Calendar of Patent Rolls, 1338 - 40, p. 101 (1338); *ibid.*, p. 216 (1339); Beauchamp Cartulary, B.L. Add. Ms. 28024, ff. 15 - 15v, Calendar of Patent Rolls, 1343 - 45, pp. 517 - 18 (1345); B.L. Harleian Charter 46 E 8 (1349). See *Bean* (n. 3) 116 - 18.

17 E.g., The Hylle Cartulary, ed. R. Dunning, 68 Somerset Records Society, 1968, p. 6, no. 11 (1350); A Calendar of the Cartularies of John Pyel and Adam Fraunceys (n. 11), p. 120, no. 49 (1350); *ibid.*, p. 123, no. 59, 62 (1363). See *Bean* (n. 3) 118.

18 *O.W. Holmes,* Early English Equity, I, Uses, (1885) 1 L.Q.R. 163 - 64; *Bean* (n. 3) 106 - 07. For the Germanic *Treuhand* and *Salmann* see the essay by *Karl Otto Scherner* in this volume.

19 *F. Pollock, F. W. Maitland,* History of English Law, 2nd ed., vol. 2, 1968, pp. 231, 237 - 8; *T. Plucknett,* A Concise History of the Common Law, 5th ed., 1956, p. 577; *Bean* (n. 3) 129; *A. W. B. Simpson* (n. 5) 174; *S. DeVine,* The Franciscan Friars, the Feoffment to Uses, and Canonical Theories of Property Enjoyment before 1535, (1989) 10 J.L.H. 1 - 22. See also the essay by *Shael Herman* in this volume.

main[20] and uses created as legitimate endowments of religious establishments[21]. The feoffees could make sure that the purpose of the endowment was being fulfilled[22]. On the other hand, there could also be disputes whether the original endowment was sufficient for the stated purpose[23].

Historians have also viewed seignorial wardship of underage heirs as foreshadowing uses[24]. There were, however, two important legal differences between a guardian and a feoffee: the guardian did not have seisin and his wardship was a chattel. The method by which royal administration in the later 12th century enforced norms of inheritance required that guardians, whether the lord in the case of military tenure or the next friend in the case of socage tenure, not have seisin of the heir's land. The Assize of Northampton had provided that the lord was to take the homage of the underage heir, who was to remain in the seisin his father had enjoyed on the day of his death[25]. Various statutory provisions on the duties of guardians are consistent with the heir, not the guardian, having seisin[26]. So, too, is Chapter 17 of the Statute of Marlborough, which gave heirs of land in socage tenure an action of account against their guardians[27]. The statute treated the guardian as a bailiff who does not have seisin of the land in his charge. In the 14th century, a wardship was classified as a chattel in that executers of the guardian could sue for its recovery[28]. By the 15th century, a wardship had become that expedient hybrid and monstrosity, a chattel real[29].

The most important precursors to uses were 13th century arrangements in which a man gave land to a donee to hold for the benefit of the donor. A man gives land to another to hold while he is away on business or goes to the Holy Land[30]. A man

---

20 Stat. 15 Ric. II, c. 5 (1391); Y.B. Mich. 8 Hen. IV f.15, pl.17 (1406). See *J. L. Barton,* The Medieval Use, (1965) 81 L.Q.R. 564 - 67.

21 A Calendar of the Norris Deeds, ed. *J. H. Lumley,* 93 Records Society of Lancashire & Cheshire, 1938, p. 167, no. 923 (1484).

22 *R. Palmer,* English Law in the Age of the Black Death, 1993, p. 113.

23 For such a dispute which was settled by arbitration see *supra* n. 21.

24 *Bean* (n. 3) 111.

25 Assize of Northampton, § 4 in: W. Stubbs, Select Charters and Other Illustrations of English Constitutional History, 9th ed., 1925, pp. 179 - 80; Magna Carta, c 3. *Bracton* said that a lord had seisin in the name of the heir only if he had taken the heir's homage. *Bracton,* De Legibus et Consuetudinibus Angliae, ed. G. Woodbine, tr. *S. E. Thorne,* vol. 2, 1968, pp. 135 - 6.

26 E.g., Magna Carta, c.5; Stat. 3 Edw. I, c.21, c.48 (1275).

27 Stat. 52 Hen. III, c.17 (1267).

28 Y.B. (Rolls Series) 17 - 18 Edw. III, p. 472 pl.15 (1344).

29 Y.B. Hil. 14 Hen. IV, f.24, pl.3 (1413).

30 Langley Cartulary (n. 6) no. 369 (1217 - 23) (Holy Land); Rolls of the Justices on Eyre for Lincolnshire and Worcestershire, ed. D. Stenton, Selden Society, vol. 68, 1949, no. 981 (1221) (business); Bracton's Note Book (BNB), ed. F. W. Maitland, 1887, no. 999 (1224) (Holy Land); Early Records of Medieval Coventry, ed. P. R. Coss, Records of Social and Economic History, new series, vol. 11, 1986, no. 708 (1235) (Rome); JUST 1/365, m.17

gives land to another to give to the grantor's child when the child comes of age or to manage for the child until he reaches majority[31]. A man arranges a marriage for his underage child and gives the child with some land to the father of the other party to the planned marriage[32]. These 13th century arrangements are noteworthy chiefly for their difference from later uses. A feoffor created a use by transferring seisin to his feoffees. Frequently, a 13th century arrangement worked because the donor did not transfer seisin to his donee. Thus, in a 1221 case a man had given his land to another while he went off to pursue his trade as a mason[33]. He died on his travels and his heir successfully brought *mort d'ancestor.* The court held that the mobile mason had died seised, no doubt because he had not transferred seisin to anyone before his departure. Unlike a feoffor in the creation of a use, the mason did not have to specify what the holder of the land was to do with the land in the event that the mason returned or did not return. Not having transferred seisin, the mason, if he returned, could take back the land without committing a disseisin. If the mason did not return, the land would descend to his heir.

In a 1233 case, a man wished to prefer his younger son by his second wife over his older son by his first wife[34]. He transferred seisin to his younger son, aged 7, and gave the land to successive guardians to the use of his younger son. He was careful not to transfer seisin to the guardians. Yet he had to transfer, in some sense, the land to the guardians for two reasons. First. doing so made clear that he did not retain seisin. Second, although *Bracton* thought that a child could receive seisin of land, he also thought that a child did not have the capacity to retain land transferred to him[35]. A guardian had such capacity on behalf of the child. When the man died, his lord gave the land to the elder son. The younger son brought novel disseisin. Upon hearing the story from the jurors, the court ruled that the younger son had been seised and was disseised by his elder brother. Thus recognizing the transfer of seisin to the younger son effectuated the father's transaction.

In a 1201 case, one Thurstan gave his son and some land to Gilbert Port on the understanding that Thurstan's son was to marry Gilbert's daughter[36]. The intended

(1271) (Holy Land); Y.B. (Rolls Series) 20 - 21 Edw. I, p. 218 - 21 (1292) (Holy Land). Calendar of Inquisitions Post Mortem, vol. III, no. 65 (Holy Land) (1293). See *Bean* (n. 3) 107 - 11.

31 BNB (n. 30) no. 754 (1233); Calendar of Close Rolls, 1242 - 47, 405.

32 Cases involving underage daughters are 1 Curia Regis Rolls, 309 (1200); 12 Curia Regis Rolls, nos. 828, 2511 (1225, 1226); The Rolls of the Shropshire Eyre, ed. A. Harding, Selden Society, 1980, no. 210. Cases involving underage sons are 2 Pleas Before the King or his Justices, ed. D. Stenton, Selden Society, vol. 68, 1949, no. 675 (1201); 17 Curia Regis Rolls, no. 1514 (1243); JUST 1 / 1045, m.2 (1246).

33 Rolls of the Justices on Eyre for Lincolnshire and Worcestershire (n. 19), no. 981 (1221).

34 BNB (n. 30) no. 754 (1233).

35 *Bracton* (n. 25) 252.

36 2 Pleas Before the King or his Justices (n. 21) no. 675 (1201).

marriage did not take place. On Thurstan's death, his son recovered the land from Gilbert in an assize of *mort d'ancestor.* Thurstan had remained seised, and his son's recovery effectuated Thurstan's intent. The court could not say that Thurstan's son had been seised, which would have required his bringing novel disseisin instead of *mort d'ancestor,* because the point of the transaction was probably to enable Gilbert to give the land to Thurstan's son in *maritagium* with Gilbert's daughter. Until the grant *in maritagium* was made, it was best to think of seisin remaining with Thurstan or returning to Thurstan upon failure of condition – the grant *in maritagium,* which never took place.

In these and other similar cases, the court looked to see whether and to whom a grantor had transferred seisin[37]. There was no rule of law, Bractonian or otherwise, as to where seisin was or had to be. Whether or not to transfer seisin was a choice a grantor made, or was supposed to have made, depending upon the purpose he wished to achieve. The court's job was to discover and to respect his choice. A 1271 case nicely illustrates how everything turned on whether there had been a transfer of seisin[38]. One Margery brought *mort d'ancestor* on the death of her father, Joseph, for ten acres of land. On his departure for the Holy Land, Joseph had given five acres to his wife as free bench and had given the other five acres to two neighbors for a term of three years in exchange for a sum of money[39]. Joseph died on his voyage. Margery recovered the five acres given to the wife but not the five acres leased to the neighbors. Joseph had died seised of the one, but not of the other.

When creating a use in the 14th century, a feoffor ordinarily made sure that he transferred seisin to his feoffees. In recognizing as much, 14th century courts were acting pretty much as 13th century courts had acted. The difference lies in the fact that the purpose of many 13th century arrangements could only be achieved by not transferring seisin to the donee who would hold the land, but the purposes of intergenerational uses could only be achieved by transferring seisin to the feoffees. Donors in 13th century arrangements, except those made to effectuate marriage grants, were not to perform tasks or make grants of land for the benefit of third parties. Feoffees frequently had obligations to third parties. And frequently, feoffees could fulfill their obligations to third parties only if the heir were, at least for a while, disinherited. Only by transferring seisin to the feoffees would the feoffor's heir be excluded from immediate inheritance upon the feoffor's death or, if the heir were underage, would the feoffor's lord be excluded from wardship. And only by excluding both the heir and the lord could intergenerational uses function as intended.

---

37 E.g., Rolls of the Justices in Eyre for Gloucestershire, Warwickshire and Straffordshire, ed. D. Stenton, Selden Society, vol. 59, 1940, no. 257 (1221); *ibid.*, no. 1013 (1221); BNB (n. 30) no. 1683 (1225).

38 JUST 1/365, m.17 (1271).

39 In his grant of a lease to his neighbors, probably made to finance his voyage, Joseph had provided that if he failed to return his lord was to grant them the fee.

Great changes in social circumstance, social attitudes, and legal culture, beyond the scope of this essay, lay behind the reversal in whether to transfer seisin.

2. Origins

In the 14th century 3 practices converged to create intergenerational uses. The first, as *Bean* observed, was the fairly well developed practice of making testaments and appointing executors to carry out the terms of the testament[40]. *Sheehan* has traced the rise of the executor within the developing practice of making testaments in the 13th century[41]. By the middle of the 14th century, testaments and executors and, in the case of intestacy, administrators marked a well-developed set of practices. In his testament, a testator could instruct his executors to arrange for his burial[42], to pay his debts[43], to give alms for the benefit of his soul[44], to carry out bequests, and to give his daughter a marriage portion[45]. Testators whose children were underage also left the residuum of their goods to their wives for the sustenance of their children[46]. Although there were exceptions, it was generally thought that an executor's authority was limited to the chattels of his testator[47]. One device to increase the chattels available to executors was to hold land under a term of years, which was classified as a chattel. There were two methods of doing so besides holding a simple leasehold. One could take a life estate plus a stated number of months or years.[48] The additional months or years counted as a

---

40 *Bean* (n. 3) 131 - 32.

41 *M. Sheehan*, The Will in Medieval England (1963) pp. 148 - 62. For the executor on the Continent see *Reinhard Zimmerman's* essay in this volume.

42 E.g., Testamenta Vetusta, ed. N. H. Nicolas, 1826, vol. I, pp. 50 - 51 (William de Beauchamp, 1268), pp. 52 (William de Beauchamp, 1296), pp. 53 - 54 (Guy de Beauchamp, 1315).

43 E.g., Testamenta Eboracensia, publications of Surtees Society, vols. IV, XXX and XLV, 1836, 1855 and 1865, vol. I, p. 5 (Christina Rous, 1342), pp. 7 - 9 (Richard de le Pole, 1345), pp. 38 - 39 (Hugh de Hastings, 1347), pp. 40 - 41 (Herbert de St. Quentin, 1347), pp. 41 - 45 (John de Warenne, Earl of Surrey, 1347).

44 E.g., Testamenta Vetusta (n. 42) 50 - 51 (William de Beauchamp, 1268).

45 E.g., Testamenta Vetusta (n. 42) 73 (Michael de Poynings, 1368), p. 79 (Thomas Earl of Warwick, 1369), Testamenta Eboracensia (n. 43), pp. 7 - 9 (Richard de le Pole, 1345), pp. 105 - 06 (John Constable of Frysmersk, 1378), pp. 128 - 29 (John Bigod, 1388), p. 132 (Robert Haunsard, 1390).

46 E.g., Testamenta Eboracensia (n. 43) pp. 6 - 7 (William Percy, 1344), p. 21 (William de Gathorne, 1346), pp. 52 - 53 (Thomas Pickering, 1348), p. 138 (William Aldeburgh, 1390), pp. 254 - 55 (Philip Darcy, 1399).

47 In 1219, William Marshall bequeathed his manor of Caversham to his executors until certain of his debts were paid: Testamenta Vetusta (n. 42) 47. In 1268, William de Beauchamp bequeathed his daughter SY.B.il land in Britlomton until she married "and no longer"; *ibid.* pp. 50 - 51.

48 A Calendar of the Cartularies of John Pyel and Adam Fraunceys (n. 11) 360 - 61, no. 928 (1334); Y.B. (Rolls Series) Mich. 15 Edw. III, pp. 434 - 37 (1341); Y.B. (Rolls Series)

term of years and would be available to executors. A variation on this method was to take a life estate but to provide that in no event should possession cease before a stated number of years[49]. A creditor would take the life estate and use the revenues to repay his loan. If the creditor died before the guaranteed number of years had elapsed, his executors would enjoy the balance of the term. Income received in repayment of their testators' loan could be used to carry out their testator's will.

An executor in possession of land looks very much like a feoffee. Conversely, a feoffee looks very much like an executor in possession of land. In a case in 1339 a defendant explains that the land sought by plaintiff had been given to her and her husband and the heirs of her husband[50]. On his death-bed, her husband had granted the land, effective after the death of defendant, to his executors to sell and otherwise deal with it for the good of his soul. Having thus portrayed herself as a life tenant with the remainder in her husband's executors, defendant prayed aid of the executors. Her aid prayer was denied. But the husband's grantees, called executors, are indistinguishable from feoffees. *Chief Justice Stonore* observed that it would have been difficult for her husband to have granted the reversion, especially to persons who were to sell and deal with it for the good of the grantor's soul. No doubt he thought that the heir could not be displaced. But *Justice Shardelowe* made a point of declining to say whether the reversion was in the heir or the executors / feoffees. The discussion is significant, given its date, because it suggests that the earliest feoffees were executors given additional resources.

Bean treated the relation of executor to feoffee as one of analogy: each did similar things in two different realms[51]. But the 1339 case shows that the connection between executors and feoffees was closer than analogy. In later wills, some testators directed their executors to hold their lands for stated purposes or to enfeoff others with the testator's land[52]. For example, in 1387 Richard Lord Poynings instructed that certain manors be retained by his executor for the payment of his debts and the marriages of his younger children[53]. In other wills, testators bequeathed land without specifying whether their executors or their feoffees were to carry out the instructions or appointed executors to carry out both their testament and their last will[54]. In 1379, Walter Paveley in his testament appointed feoffees to

---

Pas. 17 Edw. III, pp. 408 - 11 (1343); Y.B. Mich. 46 Edw. III, f.31, pl.32 (1372); Testamenta Eboracienasia (n. 43) 67 - 68.

49 B.L. Add. Charters 21771 - 7 (1357); Y.B. (Rolls Series) 18 - 19 Edw. III, p. 528, pl.44 (1345); A Calendar of the Cartularies of John Pyel and Adam Fraunceys (n.11) pp. 168 - 69, no. 186 (1359); Calendar of Close Rolls, 1364 - 1368, p. 298 (1366).

50 Y.B. (Rolls Series) 12 - 13 Edw. III, p. 172, pl.4 (1339).

51 *Bean* (n. 3) 131 - 32.

52 E.g., Testamenta Vetusta (n. 42) vol. I, pp. 81 - 82 (Joan Lady Cobham, 1369); *ibid.*, p. 66 (Humphrey as Bohun, Earl of Hereford, 1361); Testamenta Eboracensia (n. 43) vol. I, 147 (Roger de Fauconbergh, 1391).

53 Testamenta Vetusta (n. 42) vol. I, pp. 122 - 23.

deal with his lands and an executor to deal with his chattels[55]. The much more common practice, of course, was to convey land to feoffees during life so as not to die seised of the land. But where, as in Walter Paveley's case, it was not thought to be important to exclude both lord and heir, the appointment of feoffees in a testament would be as effective as a grant to them during life[56]. The distinction between executors and feoffees is sharper in the minds of historians than in the minds of 14th century landholders.

The second practice which converged on the creation of uses was the practice of granting land to strawmen who would grant the land back. A grant-regrant was necessary to change the terms on which one held land, because at common law one could not grant land to oneself. As *Bean* has observed, the statute *Quia Emptores*[57] no doubt simplified in point of tenurial relationships a grant-regrant transaction[58]. Historians have seen a connection between grant-regrant transactions and intergenerational uses, but they have not realized the full significance of what they saw[59]. *Milsom,* however, when he spoke of a grantor who desired a reconveyance to himself for life with remainder to a son, came within a quibble of getting it right[60]. A landholder could use a grant-regrant to change his fee simple into a fee tail. But two more interesting grant-regrants were undertaken. The regrant could give the landholder and his wife jointly a fee simple or fee tail and thus create a marital joint tenancy or jointure. A grant-regrant transaction would not always be necessary to create a jointure because a purchaser of land could take title jointly with his wife in fee simple or fee tail. More interesting still, and along the lines of *Milsom's* thinking, the regrant could give either the landholder or the landholder and his wife jointly a life estate and settle a remainder on the grantor's heir or other child in fee simple or fee tail. The life estate-fee tail form of settlement, studied by historians of the strict settlement in the early modern period, was very much alive in the early 14th century[61]. A life estate-fee simple form of settlement was also not uncommon.

---

54 E.g., Testamenta Vetusta (n. 42) vol. I, pp. 114 - 15 (William d'Uflord Earl of Suffolk, 1381); *ibid.*, p. 110 (John Cavendish, 1380); *ibid.*, p. 83 (John Delves); *ibid.*, pp. 76 - 77 (Bartholomew Burghersh, 1369). For testaments appointing executors to perform both testament and last will see Testamenta Eboracensia (n. 43) vol. I, pp. 19 - 20 (Ralph de Hastings, 1346); *ibid.*, pp. 38 - 39 (Hugh de Hastings, 1347); *ibid.*, pp. 47 - 49 (Thomas de Chaworth, 1347); *ibid.*, pp. 113 - 16 (William de Latymer, 1380).

55 Testamenta Vetusta (n. 42) vol. I, p. 106.

56 Paveley instructed his feoffees to convey the manor of Cotton Ditton, co. Kent, to his wife "and the heirs of Paveley". It would seem that his wife's enjoyment of the manor would depend upon the graciousness of the Paveley heirs.

57 Stat. 18 Edw. I, St.1 (1290).

58 *Bean* (n. 3) 113.

59 *T. Plucknett* (n. 35) 577 - 78; *S. F. C. Milsom* (n. 4) 205 - 08; *Bean* (n. 3) 111 - 14; *Barton* (n. 36) 566 - 68.

60 *S. F. C. Milsom* (n. 4) 207.

The table below sets forth the result of surveying some 1,600 final concords from the counties of Derby, Somerset, and Sussex for the period from 1320 to 1369, divided into 10-year periods[62]. Although final concords in the Court of Common Pleas were only an unknown fraction of the conveyances during any of the 5 periods, there is no reason to believe that they were not representative of the larger class in point of the form of settlement.

Table 1

Final Concords: Derbyshire, Somerset, Sussex
1320 - 1369

	Simple / Tail	Life Estate / Fee	Jointure	Other[63]	Total
1320 - 29[64]	94 (28.96%)	76 (22.6%)	132 (39.40%)	30 (8.96%)	335
1330 - 39	146 (35.18%)	96 (23.13%)	159 (38.31%)	14 (3.37%)	415
1340 - 49	162 (41.33%)	86 (21.94%)	129 (32.91%)	15 (3.83%)	392
1350 - 59	132 (52.59%)	32 (12.75%)	70 (27.89%)	17 (6.77%)	251
1360 - 69	163 (59.71%)	19 (6.96%)	72 (26.37%)	19 (6.96%)	*273*

Simple conveyances, whether grants or releases, in fee simple or fee tail to an individual or to a group of individuals none of whom was married to another member of the group, rose from 29 per cent of the final concords in the decade 1320 - 29 to 60 per cent in the decade 1360 - 69. Most of these plain conveyances were probably sales of land, which tell us little directly about forms of family settlements. Some of these conveyances in the later decades are to groups of men who look suspiciously like feoffees. Final concords creating jointures declined from 39 per cent to 26 per cent during the same period. Most telling, however, is that grants creating life estate-remainder settlements, whether the remainder was fee simple or fee tail, declined from about 23 per cent to about 7 per cent. The first substantial decline in this form of settlement occurred in the decade 1350 - 59. The following decade saw another, similarly substantial decline. Shortly thereafter, they disappear almost entirely. In these decades intergenerational uses became more common than

61 *L. Bonfield,* Marriage Settlements, 1601 - 1740: The Adoption of the Strict Settlement, 1983, pp. 46 - 54; *J. Habakkuk,* Marriage, Debt, and the Estates System: English Landownership 1650 - 1950, 1994, pp. 9 - 12.

62 Feet of Derbyshire Fines 1323 - 1546 (H. J. H. Garratt, 2 Derbyshire Records Society, 1985); Pedes Finium for the County of Somerset 1307 - 1346 (Emanuel Green, 12 Somerset Records Society 1898); *ibid.* 1347 - 1399 (Emanuel Green, 17 Somerset Records Society, 1902); An Abstract of Feet of Fines Relating to the County of Sussex 1326 - 1507 (L. F. Salzman, Sussex Records Society, 1916).

63 These are grants for life and grants to the church.

64 Derbyshire fines for this decade are not included.

they had been in the previous two decades. It is hard to explain the decline in life estate-remainder settlements other than to say that the grant-regrant transaction to create a life estate-remainder settlement was transformed into the intergenerational use. An intergenerational use permitted the feoffor to enjoy the land for his life, then have his feoffees hold the land for some period of time. They were then to convey the land to the feoffor's heir. The difference between a life estate-remainder settlement and an intergenerational use was the presence in a use of feoffees (executor?) between the functional equivalent of a life estate in the feoffor and the functional equivalent of a remainder in his heir. From a technical or conveyancer's point of view, an intergenerational use broke the life estate-remainder into two parts and inserted an executor / feoffee between the two parts. The development would not appear startling to men accustomed both to establishing life estate-remainder settlements and to using testaments to instruct executors.

The emergence of intergenerational uses out of grant-regrant transactions creating life estate-remainder settlements might help to explain the employment of life estates in creating intergenerational uses. One method of creating an intergenerational use was to grant feoffees a life estate. This form of feoffment was probably early and experimental. Intergenerational uses in this form seldom appear after the 1350s, but a definitive conclusion must await an exhaustive search of the surviving records[65]. Conveyancers and their clients at first might well have been uncomfortable granting feoffees fee simple. Instead of the traditional life estate-remainder settlement in which the grantor receives back a life estate and settles a remainder on his heir, the life estate form of feoffment simply put the life estate in the feoffees. The feoffor either retained the reversion, which would descend to his heir, or settled it as a remainder on his heir. Another way of employing a life estate in creating an intergenerational use was for the feoffor to grant his feoffees fee simple and take back a life estate[66]. This method of creating an intergenerational use broke the traditional regrant of a life estate / remainder into two parts. The life estate would be regranted immediately and the remainder to the feoffor's heir after the feoffees had completed their designated duties. If a royal license or pardon were necessary, the feoffees could wait until the feoffor died and receive the necessary license for the feoffments over to the feoffor's wife and designated remainderman[67].

The transformation of the intergenerational use out of practice of grant-regrant transactions permits a suggestion about the way in which lawyers might have learned how to create intergenerational uses. Lawyers might well have discovered

---

65 Calendar of Inquisitions Post Mortem, vol. 7, no. 281 (1326); *ibid.*, vol. 8, no. 386 (1339); Beauchamp Cartulary (n. 12) ff. 15 - 15v. (1345); The Hylle Cartulary (n. 17) p. 6, no. 11 (1350); A Calendar of the Cartulary of John Pyel and Adam Fraunceys (n. 11) p. 120, no. 49 (1350); Testamenta Eboraciensia (n. 43) pp. 67 - 68 (1355); Calendar of Patent Rolls, 1338 - 1340, p. 101 (1385); *ibid.* p. 216 (1339); *ibid.* 1340 - 1343, p. 273 - 4 (1341).

66 Calendar of Patent Rolls, 1374 - 77, pp. 72, 78 (1375).

67 Calendar of Patent Rolls, 1374 - 77, p. 289.

the possibility of extending a grant-regrant transaction beyond the life of the grantor by accident. At first, the death of the grantor before the regrant might not have been part of the plan. On 30 January 1344, Robert de Clifford, Earl of Suffolk, received royal license to enfeoff three men of several manors and for them to re-enfeoff him in tail male with various remainders over[68]. On 24 February, Clifford granted the lands to his feoffees[69]. The feoffees later said that Clifford wanted the regrant to be by final concord[70]. Before they could take seisin of the manors and arrange for the final concord, Clifford died leaving an heir underage. On 10 November, the King ordered an inquisition as to why the feoffees were depriving him of his wardship of Clifford's lands and heir[71]. The feoffees might well have remained in seisin of the manors after Clifford's death because they did not know what else to do. As a result of the royal inquisition, they were ousted. When they asked what would happen to the intended entail, they were told that it was lost because of their negligence in failing to reconvey to Clifford in time. The difficulty in determining whether Clifford's death was part of the planned transaction is itself suggestive. It would have been a short step from having a grant-regrant transaction upset by the grantor's death to planning for the regrant not to take place until after the grantor's executors could perform his will.

The third practice which converged on the creation of the intergenerational use was the practice of making conditional grants in order to secure the grantee's performance of an agreement. This form of transaction was the reverse of the typical mortgage in which a grantor conveyed land to his creditor as security for his own repayment of the debt[72]. The conveyance to the creditor would become void upon the grantor's full payment. A conditional grant made to secure the grantee's performance was the form used to secure regrants in a grant-regrant transaction. It was a satisfactory method of protecting the grantor against a wayward strawman[73]. Conditional grants were also made to secure other kinds of performance by grantees. For example, one Robert engaged one John for a fee to teach Robert a trade[74]. In order to secure both Robert's payment and John's performance, Robert conveyed land to John on condition that John keep his side of the bargain. A woman granted land to a man on condition that he marry her[75]. His failure to do so permitted her to take back the land. In creating an intergenerational use, feoffors frequently

68 *Ibid.*, 1343 - 45, pp. 188 - 89.

69 Calendar of Close Rolls, 1343 - 46, pp. 633 - 34.

70 *Ibid.*; Y.B. (Rolls Series) 18 - 19 Edw. III, p. 492, pl. 30 (1345).

71 Calendar of Close Rolls, 1343 - 46, pp. 633 - 34.

72 See, e.g., Y.B. (Rolls Series) 30 - 31 Edw. I, pp. 210 - 13 (1302); *ibid.*, pp. 208 - 11 (1302); Y.B. Hil. 42 Edw. III, f.1, pl.3 (1368).

73 *Barton* (n. 36) 566 - 68.

74 Y.B. Pas. 21 Edw. III, f.11, pl.2 (1347).

75 Y.B. (Rolls Series) 20 - 21 Edw. I, pp. 366 - 67 (1292); Y.B. (Rolls Series) 21 - 22 Edw. I, pp. 498 - 99 (1294). Similarly, a father might grant land to a man on condition that the man marry his daughter: Y.B. (Rolls Series) 20 - 21 Edw. I, pp. 258 - 61 (1292).

spoke of the tasks to be performed by their feoffees as conditions on the feoffment. Since it was frequently the case that feoffees were instructed both to perform one or more tasks and then to convey the land to the feoffor's heir or his widow, or his widow for life remainder to the heir, the conditions applied to both the feoffees' duties to creditors and other beneficiaries and to their duty to regrant the land. The language of conditions became dangerous, because, as we will see, words of condition came to be taken as evidence that the feoffment was meant to deprive the feoffor's lord of wardship. But even after it became dangerous to do so, feoffors continued to use the language of conditions. Even a feoffor who put his instructions to his feoffees in an indenture separate from his charter of feoffment could describe his instructions as conditions on his feoffment[76].

The three practices of appointing executors, making grants out to receive back a life estate-remainder settlement, and making conditional grants combined to form a feoffment to uses. For a feoffment to uses was a grant to feoffees on condition that they perform the tasks of executors and then regrant the land.

II. The Increased Employment of Uses

Whether a particular landholder would create an intergenerational use depended, of course, on the facts of his particular situation, the vicissitudes of his family, his relations with his lords, his financial position, his willingness to trust feoffees. Historians ordinarily explain the increased employment of uses during the latter half of the 14th and the 15th centuries by pointing to the advantages uses had over common law rules of inheritance. The standard account says that uses enabled feoffors to make last wills in which they could pay their debts, give alms, and provide for spouse, daughter and younger son in ways not permitted by the inflexible common law. But this sort of general statement requires one to specify the advantages of a use over common law rules and arrangements.

The major reason why landholders increasingly created intergenerational uses can be stated in two words: preservation and control. Other conveyancing strategies permitted a landholder to provide for his wife and his children. An intergenerational use had two advantages over other conveyancing strategies. A use permitted a landholder to preserve his landed property by using its revenues free of wardship to satisfy his obligations to his creditors, his children, his friends and servants, and his own soul. A use also afforded landholders greater ability to provide against future contingencies in his own life and in the lives of the members of his family. Circumstances beginning in the middle of the 14th century made these advantages of an intergenerational use rather attractive. The increasing financial burdens on landholders, burdens exasperated by the Black Death, elicited the employ-

76 B.L. Additional Charter 22213 (charter of feoffment) and 22214 (indenture that the feoffment was made "sub condicionibus subscriptis" [John de Seyton, 1383]).

ment of new strategies for landholders to preserve their landed property. The devastation of the plague probably moved survivors toward employing new strategies of attempting to assert control over their affairs in the face of great uncertainty. The military expeditions to France also were occasions to employ strategies which facilitated raising money to finance the journey and which could take into account the possibility of death overseas.

In this section, I focus on debtors and daughters. That is to say, I consider how uses better enabled feoffors to pay their debts and to provide for their daughters.

1. The Debtor Feoffor

The standard account says that uses better enabled feoffors to pay their debts. Thus *Bean* wrote that "the exclusion of the heir from the administration of the affairs of a deceased, and the growth of the total responsibility of the executors for these, meant that the revenues from the lands of the inheritance could no longer be employed for the payment of debts"[77]. To right the balance, as it were, feoffors conveyed land to feoffees with the instructions to pay the debts of the feoffor after his death. *Palmer* also asserts that because land descended to the heir, it was not available to pay debts and that "uses extended the assets available to pay debts"[78].

This argument is founded on a mistake and distorts the effect of uses. The heir was neither excluded nor relieved as a matter of law from liability for his father's debts. In the 15th century, creditors sued their debtors' heirs[79]. Nor did the fact that a debtor had appointed executors relieve his heir of legal liability for his debts. In 1353 and again in 1405 an heir made precisely this argument: that he should not have to answer his father's creditor in an action of debt because his father had appointed executors who were still alive and well[80]. The Justices rejected the heir's argument. An heir's liability for his father's debts was limited to the assets, including land, which had descended to the heir at the time his father's creditor obtained his writ[81]. This meant that by creating an intergenerational use, a debtor feoffor made sure that his heir would not be liable for his debts, because at his death his lands would be in the hands of his feoffees and would not descend to his heir. Not the law, but feoffors excluded the heir from liability for his father's debt. An in-

77 *Bean* (n. 3) 132.

78 *Palmer* (n. 38) 121.

79 E.g., Y.B. Hil. 6 Hen. IV, f.2, pl.14 (1405) ; Y.B. Pas. 7 Hen. IV, f.14, pl.11 (1406); Y.B. Pas. 12 Hen. IV, f.21, pl.11 (1411).

80 Y.B. Trin. 27 Edw. III, f.6, pl.23 (1353); Y.B. Pas. 7 Hen. IV, f.14, pl.11 (1405). Conversely, an executor's acquittance barred the heir from recovering from his ancestor's debtor. Y.B. (Rolls Series) Pas. 14 Edw. III, pp. 94 - 101 (1340).

81 Y.B. (Rolls Series) Mich. Edw. III, pp. 180 - 85 (1337); Y.B. Hil. Edw. III, f.9, pl.28 (1347); Y.B. Pas. 27 Edw. III, f.2, pl.16 (1353); Y.B. Pas. 28 Edw. III, f.17, pl.20 (1354) ; Y.B. Pas. 42 Edw. III, f.10, pl.13 (1368).

struction to feoffees to pay the debts of the deceased feoffor could make up for a feoffor thus removing assets from the reach of his creditors. But a careful creditor, with sufficient bargaining power, would get his debtor to agree not to alienate lands away from his heir[82].

No doubt the world depends upon most persons acting responsibly. And, no doubt, most feoffees were responsible and, if instructed to do so, paid the debts of their deceased feoffors. The trouble came, of course, where the feoffee, for good or bad reasons, did not pay in a fashion satisfactory to persons claiming, rightly or wrongly, to be the feoffor's creditor. Creditors had two lines of attack – against the heir and against the feoffee.

(a) Pursuing the Heir

Against the heir, creditors tried two arguments. First, a creditor might argue that lands in the hands of feoffees should count as lands available to the heir to pay his father's debts. In 1368, a plaintiff creditor pleaded that the defendant heir was seised "a sa volunte" of assets which had been his father's[83]. The defendant made sport of the phrase "a sa volunte," but the phrase fit defendant who was in possession of land seisin of which was in his father's or his own feoffees; he could be seised pretty much when he wished. *Fincheden* seems ready to hold that if someone is taking the profits for the heir, the heir will be deemed to be seised, therefore, liable. *Moubray* does not go so far. He asks the defendant whether he has freehold or is in possession of his father's lands. The defendant takes care not to deny that he is in possession but only to deny that he has fee simple, life estate, or term of years. Plaintiff had to take as the issue for the jury that defendant was seised in fee simple. The report of a case six years later in 1374 is again not clear as to whether the defendant's father or the defendant had put the land relied upon by the plaintiff creditor into the hands of feoffees[84]. In this case, the creditor, more aggressive, alleged that defendant had fraudulently put or left assets in the hands of feoffees. The defendant brazenly answered that no law required him to respond to the allegation of fraud. Two years later there was such a law. A statute in 1376 allowed a creditor to recover against land given to feoffees if he could prove that the feoffment was collusive for the purpose of avoiding liability[85]. The 1376 statute, however, would be of little help to a creditor where his debtor's feoffees had not yet conveyed the land to the debtor's heir.

A second way of getting at the heir would be to say that lands an heir received from his father's feoffees counted as lands received by descent from his father. I

---

82 E.g. Y.B. (Rolls Series) Mich. 14 Edw. III, pp. 68 - 71 (1340); Calendar of Close Rolls, 1364 - 1368, pp. 313 - 14.

83 Y.B. Pas. 42 Edw. III, f.10, pl.12 (1268).

84 Y.B. Mich. Edw. III, f.32, pl.22 (1374).

85 Stat. 50 Edw. III, c.6 (1376).

could not find a case in the printed Yearbooks in which a creditor tried this line of argument. But another case suggests that the argument would not have worked. A woman brought *cui in vita* to recover land which she had received by grant and which her late husband had granted away[86]. Defendant objected that she should have used a writ which described the land as her inheritance. Both forms of writ were available in Chancery. The woman argued that she could not use the writ urged by the defendant because she had not inherited the land. She had received it from her father's feoffees. The justices agreed: she was in by purchase, not by inheritance. Since the defendant did not suggest a writ describing the land as her *maritagium,* perhaps she was an heiress. If so, the learning of the case is more readily transferable to a case of an heir. Lands received from his father's feoffees were probably not assets an heir received by descent. A father who created an intergenerational use isolated his heir from liability.

(b) Pursuing the Feoffees

Creditors also pursued their deceased debtors' feoffees by characterizing them as executors or administrators of the decedent's estate. If the decedent had left a testament, he would have appointed executors, but if the decedent had died intestate, then the Bishop's Ordinary would appoint administrators. By statute in 1357, administrators could sue and be sued as well as executors[87]. But the statute posed an obstacle to a creditor who characterized his debtor's feoffee as an administrator if the feoffee had not been appointed administrator of his feoffor's estate. Creditors said that the feoffee was administrator "on his own head" or "on his own wrong" as opposed to being administrator by commission from the Ordinary[88]. But in cases from 1370 to 1421 the Justices held that only those who were appointed administrators could be held liable as administrators[89].

The same was not true for executors. The proper way for a creditor to sue someone, other than the heir, who had goods of the deceased debtor but was neither appointed executor in the debtor's testament nor administrator by the Ordinary was to sue the holder of the debtor's goods as the debtor's executor[90]. To be precise,

86 Y.B. Mich. 7 Hen. IV, f.5, pl. 28 (1405).

87 Stat. 31 Edw. III, St. 1 c.11 (1357).

88 Y.B. Trin. 11 Hen. IV, f.72, pl.11 (1410); Y.B. Pas. 9 Hen. V, f.6, pl.20 (1421). The printed Yearbooks use the phrases "de son teste demesne" and "de son tort demesne" interchangeably. The more frequent phrase is "de son tort demesne".

89 Y.B. Trin. 44 Edw. III, f.16, pl.1 (1370); Y.B. Hil. 50 Edw. III, f.19, pl.18 (1376); Y.B. Hil. 7 Hen. IV, f.10, pl. 18 (1406); Y.B. Trin. 11 Hen. IV, f.72, pl.11 (1410); Y.B. Pas. 9 Hen. V, f.6, pl.20 (1421).

90 For complications where the deceased had died intestate and the Ordinary had appointed an administrator see Y.B. Mich. 21 Hen. VI, f.8, pl.18 (1442); Y. B. Hil. 21 Hen. VI, f.13, pl.5 (1443); Y.B. Trin. 32 Hen. VI, f.6, pl.10 (1454).

merely holding goods of a deceased debtor was not sufficient to incur liability to his creditors. One had to administer his goods as would an executor[91]. This rule was a matter of pleading. A defendant sued as a debtor's executor could not answer that he was not executor, he had to answer that he never administered the goods of the deceased as executor or that he had fully administered the goods of the deceased on the day plaintiff sued out his writ[92]. Before the 1357 statute, which made administrators as liable for debts as executors, this pleading rule prevented *de facto* administrators of intestate debtors from escaping liability. In 1344, when a defendant answered that the deceased had died intestate and defendant was not executor, *Justice Willoughby* ruled that the allegation of intestacy would not be entered on the Roll[93]. It would thus not be part of the issue for the jury. The pleading rule, however, did not change after the statute of 1357[94]. In 1367, for example, a defendant denied that she was executrix to the deceased debtor[95]. She was held liable when the jury found that, although not executrix, she had the administration of the deceased's goods worth £10 in the manner of an executrix and not to "sa propre oeps". The recognition of *de facto* executors provided a reason for limiting liability as administrator to only those who had been appointed as such[96].

As late as 1376, *Chief Justice Belknap* thought of the pleading rule as permitting recovery against the officious intermeddler who took assets which should be left for the executors[97]. Not until the 1380s dc the printed Yearbook reports clearly show creditors using the pleading rule to recover against their deceased debtors' feoffees as *de facto* executors. In 1385, defendants explained that they had not administered as executors because the deceased had granted them all his goods and chattels, they had permitted him to use them during his life, but upon his death they had taken what was theirs[98]. *Justice Holt* suggested to plaintiff's sergeant that he try to plead some collusion. Plaintiff pleaded instead that defendants had administered other goods of the deceased as his executors. In a similar, later case plaintiff pleaded that the grant to defendant was collusive to avoid liability[99].

A feoffee who was administering the lands and goods of his deceased feoffor could not answer that the feoffor had given him the goods outright. He was and was meant to be a *de facto* executor. But whether he should be treated as executor for the purpose of liability in debt was not obvious. In 1401, *Justices Markham* and

---

91 Y.B. Trin. Hen. VI, f.6, pl.10 (1454).

92 Y.B. (Rolls Series) 12 - 13, Edw. III, p. 142, pl.41 (1339); *ibid.*, p. 162, pl.51 (1339); Y.B. (Rolls Series) 20(1) Edw. III, p. 188, pl.18 (1346).

93 Y.B. (Rolls Series) 18 Edw. III, p. 124, pl.28 (1344).

94 Y.B. Pas. 40 Edw. III, f.15, pl.1 (1366).

95 Y.B. Mich. 41 Edw. II, f.31 pl.38 (1367).

96 Y.B. Hil. 50 Edw. III, f.19, pl.18 (1376).

97 *Ibid.*

98 Y.B. (Ames Soc., Vol. 4) 8 Ric. II, p. 215, pl.17 (1385).

99 Y.B. Mich. 13 Hen. IV, f.4, pl.9 (1411). See Y.B. Pas. 11 Hen. VI, f.35, pl.27 (1433).

Rickhill were divided over whether a feoffee could be held liable because he administered assets of the feoffor as an executor[100]. Plaintiff alleged that his debtor enfeoffed defendants with a manor on condition that if he return from overseas they re-enfeoff him and if he did not return they should sell the manor and use the proceeds to benefit his soul. He did not return and defendants sold the manor for 200 marks. Although the case was decided for defendants on a point of process, *Markham* and *Rickhill* debated the substantive issue of liability. *Markham* argued that the defendants' receiving the 200 marks made them their feoffor's executor for the purpose of liability to plaintiff. *Rickhill* saw the proceeds as belonging to the defendants. *Rickhill* also argued that defendants were not liable because they would not have to account to the Ordinary. Some twenty years later, feoffees were held liable for the debts of their feoffor[101]. In this case, the jury found that defendants were enfeoffed by plaintiff's debtor to the intent that after the debtor's death they sell certain land and use the proceeds to benefit his soul. They had the proceeds in their hands on the day plaintiff obtained his writ. The Court did not accept the argument that feoffees could be liable only to the extent they had chattels which were chattels of their feoffor during his life. If they had revenues from the testator-feoffor's lands, they could be held liable for his debts as his *de facto* executors. It seems that the liability of feoffees was limited to the chattels of the deceased and the revenues from his lands. A creditor might, of course, sue his debtor's feoffee as his debtor's executor because the feoffee had also been appointed executor. Feoffors sometimes named the same persons both as executor and as feoffee[102].

That feoffees were liable from the early 15th century at common law for the feoffor's debts as if they were his executors might help to explain the nature of Chancery petitions brought by creditors against feoffees. Creditors in Chancery tended to characterize their debtors' feoffees as executors as they would at common law[103]. They are in Chancery, however, because they lack a writing as evidence of the debt which was required at common law to hold executors liable[104]. Feoffors sometimes instructed their feoffees to make assets available to their executors[105]. Such instructions could be the basis for a petition in Chancery by executors against feoffees[106].

---

100 Y.B. Trin. 2 Hen. IV, f.21, pl.2 (1401).

101 Y.B. Mich. 3. Hen. VI, f.3, pl.4 (1424).

102 Testamenta Eboracensia (n. 43) vol. I, pp. 116 - 17 (Peter Mauley, 1381); *ibid.*, p. 222 (Richard Byton, 1397).

103 *W. T. Barbour,* The History of Contract in Early English Equity, in: Oxford Studies in Social and Legal History, vol. 4, 1914, pp. 102 - 05. For exceptions see C1/38/17, 18; C1/50/94, 95.

104 *W. T. Barbour* (n. 103) 102 - 05.

105 Testamenta Vetusta (n. 42) vol. I, 108 (William Lord Latamer, 1380); Testamenta Eboracensia (n. 43) p. 222 (Richard Byton, 1397); Calendar of Ancient Deeds, vol. I, p. 412 (C273) (1462).

106 E.g., C1/6/270; C1/7/54, 55, 56; C1/16/5; C1/38/21; C1/50/45, 46; C1/50/96, 97.

The statements by *Bean* and *Palmer* that conveying land to feoffees with an instruction to pay the debts of the feoffor made additional assets available to creditors is too simple. The easiest way to make assets available to creditors was not to create an intergenerational use but to let the land descend to the heir. Not until the early 15th century was it clear that feoffees could be held liable for the debts of their feoffors as if they were his executors. Yet by creating intergenerational uses most feoffors were not trying to evade their creditors, although some probably were. They were trying to control the payment of their debts for the sake of protecting their lands. If a debtor let his lands descend to his heir, his creditors could collect their debts against the heir and, ultimately, against the family lands. The creditor could choose which lands of his debtor would be occupied to satisfy his debt. By creating an intergenerational use, a debtor wrested that choice from his creditors and gave it to his feoffees. Even when his feoffees became liable as if they were his executors, their liability was limited to the chattels and revenues of their feoffors in their hands as *de facto* executors. Unless their feoffor had given them specific instructions, they could choose the revenues of which lands would be used and, if need be, which lands would be sold to pay debts. The payment of debts could be timed according to the receipt of revenues, not the desire of creditors. If the debtor had entered into a recognizance, his creditor could collect against the land made subject to the recognizance[107]. But here, too, the debtor chose, within the limits of his bargaining power, which lands would be subject to the recognizance. Intergenerational uses permitted debts to be paid in such a manner as was consistent with preserving the integrity of the inheritance.

2. Daughters

Historians have also observed that landholders increasingly employed intergenerational uses because uses permitted them to circumvent the rigid common law rule of primogeniture[108]. By means of uses, for instance, a father could provide for his daughters. This sort of statement exaggerates the rigidity of the common law and thus obscures the advantages afforded by an intergenerational use.

A father could provide for his daughter by granting her land. He could grant her land in fee tail so that upon the failure of her issue the land would return to the father's heir. A father could also arrange to have the grant not take effect until after his death. He could do so either by granting out to a strawman who would grant back an estate for life, remainder in tail to the daughter, or by granting the land to his daughter who would grant back a life estate. In 1307 Richard Kembald chose the latter course[109]. He and his wife Maud granted land to their daughter Juliana.

107 Y.B. (Ames Soc., vol. 3) Trin. 7 Ric. II, p. 48 pl.19 (1383).

108 E.g., *C. Given-Wilson,* The English Nobility in the Late Middle Ages, 1987, pp. 140 - 41.

109 Bohun Cartulary, B.L. Harleian Ms. 2201, ff0.34 - 37.

She then granted the land back to Richard and Maud for their lives. In her grant she provided that if her parents survived her and she died without an heir of her body, she wished the land to remain to her parents and their heirs. The common law did not prevent fathers from providing for their daughters.

Increasingly in the 14th century fathers preferred to provide their daughters with money rather than with land. The shift to money changed the terms in which a father reconciled the two conflicting demands of a medieval landholder. On the one hand, he had to provide for his children other than his heir; on the other, he had to preserve the integrity of the inheritance[110]. In response to greater financial demands on the inheritance, which militated against its dispersal, fathers satisfied their obligations to their daughters with money rather than with land. In many 14th century testaments, fathers bequeathed sums of money to their daughters[111]. Although many bequests to daughters mention their marriage, many do not.

A testamentary bequest to a daughter competed with the claims of creditors, bequests to friends and servants, and the gifts to benefit the testator's soul for the chattels the testator had accumulated by the time of his death. At this point the common law was inflexible. An executor's ability to carry out bequests was limited to the money and chattels the testator had accumulated at his death. They might well fall short of the amount a father thought proper for his daughter given the social standing or pretensions of the family. It would have been difficult at common law to arrange for a daughter to receive a particular sum out of the revenues of the inheritance after her father's death. A father could achieve his goal by giving land to his executors to accumulate revenues for a provision for his daughter. A feoffment to uses to take real effect after the feoffor's death was the equivalent of putting land in the hands of an executor. In one of the earlier feoffments to a use Thomas Beauchamp, Earl of Warwick, in 1345 conveyed a number of manors to feoffees for their lives[112]. They agreed to grant him back a rent, probably equal to the revenues, for his life, then to accumulate specified marriage portions for each of his daughters, then to convey the manors to his heir. Other fathers did not specify a sum of money for their daughters but instructed executor or feoffee to see that their daughters were well married or married without disparagement[113]. This flexibility, which permitted feoffees to vary a marriage portion as marriage bargaining might require, was impossible under common law arrangements. Beau-

---

110 *N. Saul,* Scenes from Provencial Life: Knightly Families in Sussex 1280 - 1400, 1986, pp. 22 - 23; *Given-Wilson* (n. 108) 137 - 50.

111 E.g., Testamenta Eboracensia (n. 43) vol. I, pp. 7 - 9 (Richard de la Pole, 1345); Testamenta Vetusta (n. 42) vol. I, p. 73 (Michael de Poynings, 1368); *ibid.*, p. 79 (Thomas Beauchamp, Earl of Warwick, 1369); Testamenta Eboracensia (n. 43) pp. 105 - 06 (John Constable of Frysmersk, 1378); *ibid.*, pp. 128 - 29 (John Bigod, 1388).

112 Beauchamp Cartulary (n. 16) f0.15 - 15v, Calendar of Patent Rolls 1343 - 1345, pp. 517 - 18.

113 E.g., Testamenta Vetusta (n. 42) 118 - 20 (Hugh Earl of Stafford, 1385); B.L. Additional Charter 22213 (John de Seyton, 1383).

champ's feoffment for his daughters was part of his comprehensive estate plan in which he used entails to provide for his heir and his other sons[114]. A father with less land than an Earl of Warwick could not afford to assign parts of his inheritance to different intergenerational purposes. If he was to provide for his soul, have his executor and feoffees pay his debts, and provide for his daughters, his feoffment to uses would have to exclude his heir for a time. And the ideal time during which to exclude his heir was while the heir was underage. With some luck, by the time the heir came of age, the revenues of the inheritance would have supported the feoffor's widow, paid his debts, and accumulated into portions for his daughters. But achieving this goal meant excluding the lord from wardship of the lands, for during wardship the revenues of the inheritance went into the lord's purse.

III. Uses and Wardship

Historians such as *Bean* and *Palmer* who have written about the tension between uses and wardship entertain too simple a picture of the effective right to wardship during the period in which landholders increasingly created uses[115]. Their picture is too simple in three respects. First, they picture a tenant holding land in fee simple or fee tail. If such a tenant creates an intergenerational use and dies leaving an heir underage, his use deprives his lord of wardship. Many tenants, however, did not hold land so simply. When one considers how many tenants in fact held their lands, the effect of uses on wardship becomes problematic. Second, taking the seignorial point of view, *Bean* and *Palmer* suppose that it would have been wrong for a tenant to create a substitute for feudal wardship. But wishing to absolve tenants of wrongdoing, they resort to an argument that resembles the casuistry of double effect. In creating intergenerational uses, tenants, we are told, were not primarily motivated to avoid wardship. Wardships simply got in the way of their making last wills. This argument relies upon the doubtful premise that the legal rules of wardship were so well supported by social norms that substitutes for feudal wardship were thought to be wrong. But the legal rules of wardship did not reflect a social consensus. English society was deeply divided between the official norms reflected in the legal rules and the unofficial norms reflected in the practice of creating substitutes for feudal wardship. On this view, there were both social norms supporting feudal wardship and social norms supporting substitutes for feudal wardship. The one participated in the social ordering too neatly known as feudalism and the other in the social ordering misleadingly known as "bastard" feudalism. The conflict between these two conceptions of wardship, wardship by tenure and wardship by contract, took place case by case, lordship by lordship[116]. In legal

114 *Given-Wilson* (n. 108) 141 - 42.

115 *Bean* (n. 3) 136 - 37, 181 - 97; *Palmer* (n. 38) 116 - 18.

116 I borrow the vocabulary of *S.L. Waugh,* Tenure to Contract: Lordship and Clientage in Thirteenth-Century England, (1986) 101 English Historical Review 829 ff.

terms the conflict over the two conceptions of wardship came down to a fight over the word "collusion" and the application, or extension, of Chapter 6 of the Statute of Marlborough to feoffments to uses[117]. Third, historians have not considered the possibility of seignorial opportunism, the possibility that lords used a tenant's feoffment to uses as the opportunity to claim wardship although they would not have had a claim to wardship if the same or similar settlement had been effectuated at common law.

1. Establishing a Baseline

One cannot speak of feoffments to uses causing lords to lose their wardships unless one has a baseline from which to measure the loss. If the conveyancing practices of the mid-14th century be taken as the baseline, the extent to which lords in fact lost wardships to feoffees to uses is problematic. The simple picture of a tenant who holds land in fee simple or fee tail conveying his land to feoffees is inaccurate in many cases. The sample of final concords in Table I shows that in the decades 1320 - 29 and 1330 - 39 some 61 per cent of final concords resulted in a landholder holding either jointure or under a 'ife estate-remainder settlement. In the decade 1340 - 49 this percentage declined to 55 per cent. In the next two decades, there was a substantial decline in the number and percentage of life estate-remainder settlements, but even in the 1360 - 69 decade a third of final concords created either jointure or life estate-remainder settlements. Where land was held in jointure, the lord did not have wardship until both husband and wife had died[118]. One reason for jointure was to reduce the possibility of wardship[119]. We will shortly see that lords took a feoffment to uses in which the feoffees were to convey to the feoffor's widow for her life as an opportunity to claim wardship even though they could not have claimed wardship if there had been a jointure without a feoffment to uses.

A lord probably did not have wardship if the tenant held a life estate with remainder to his named heir. The question runs along side the murky early history of the Rule in *Shelley's Case* and the Doctrine of Worthier Title, both of which deal with remainders limited to the heirs, as a class, of the life tenant. The difficulty in finding cases in which the question arose is itself a little mysterious. *Sutton*'s *Case* in 1366 involved a settlement on a father for life, remainder to his son and his son's wife in tail, remainder to the right heirs of the father[120]. After the father had died

117 Stat. 52 Hen. III, c.6 (1267).

118 Y.B. (Rolls Series) Hil. 17 Edw. III, p. 86 - 91 (1342 - 43) (decision after consultation with the King's Council); Y.B. Pas. 39 Edw. III f.10 (1364). See Y.B. Mich. 7 Hen. VI, f.14, pl.23, Hil. 7 Hen. VI, f.20, pl.4 (1419 - 1420).

119 *W.M. Ormrod,* The Reign of Edward III, 1990, p. 113.

120 Y.B. Hil. 40 Edw. III, f.9, pl.18 (1366). A portion of the printed report supplemented by manuscript reports is reproduced in *J.H. Baker, S.F.C. Milsom,* Sources of English Legal History, 1986, pp. 65 - 67. See Y.B. Trin. 9 Edw. IV, f.17, pl.19 (1469) (if a father grants life

and his son and his son's wife had died without issue, another son entered. The lord claimed relief. The Justices held that relief was due because the second son entered as heir not as remainderman. *Justice Thorpe* explained that the remainder was not limited to the second son by name but to the right heirs of the father. The implication is that an heir named as remainderman takes by purchase. The conclusion is supported by an earlier case in which a man and his wife had a life estate, remainder in tail to their son[121]. The couple survived their son, who left two daughters underage at the death of their grandparents. *Justice Willoughby* ruled that the lord have wardship of the daughters. The writer of the report commented that the possession of the daughters was adjudged to have been by descent. This decision was favorable to lords, because for other purposes the remainderman first to take possession took by purchase even if the remainder had been limited to his ancestor. If the issue had been whether the daughters ought to use formedon in the remainder or formedon in the descender or whether their nonage would delay litigation, they would have been treated as purchasers, because they were the remaindermen first able to take possession of the land. But they had not been identified by name in the conveyance limiting the remainder. Thus the case is similar to *Sutton's Case*. Most often in both a life estate-remainder settlement and in a feoffment to uses in which the feoffees were ultimately to regrant the lands to the feoffor's son and heir, the conveyances named the heir and provided for his unexpected death by means of alternative remainders to the grantor's other sons and daughters. It is doubtful that the lord had wardship in many of these cases. We will see that lords began to claim that this type of settlement was collusive within the meaning of Chapter 6 of the Statute of Marlborough. Viewed against the background of jointures and life estate-remainder settlements the seignorial loss of wardship because of uses becomes a less clear and distinct idea.

2. Social Practice

The degree to which it was believed to be acceptable to arrange substitutes for feudal wardship raises further difficulties with the received view of uses. As *Ormond* has observed, by the mid-14th century the institution of wardship did not enjoy the degree of social acceptance it had enjoyed in the 13th century[122]. Legal historians lack a study of wardship during the 14th and 15th centuries comparable to *Waugh's* study of wardship during the 13th century[123]. Without such a study it is hard to know how representative are the episodes revealed in bits of evidence which disturb simple pictures. Parliamentary petitions on the subject reveal a poli-

---

estate to son and then dies, the son inheriting the land in fee, the lord does not have wardship because the son had possession by purchase).

121 Y.B. Mich. 24 Edw. III, p. 33, pl. 28 (1350).

122 *W.M. Ormrod* (n. 119) 114; *Saul* (n. 110) 24 - 27.

123 *S.L. Waugh,* The Lordship of England: Royal Wardship and Marriages in England Society and Politics 1217 - 1327, 1988.

tical society divided on the question of wardship. On the one hand, in 1339 the "great men" of the realm complained of "men who when dying make alienations of their lands ... by fraud to deprive the chief lords of the wardship of them"[124]. But also in 1339 a petition in parliament requested that the wardships in the King's hands be given to the friends or kinsmen of the deceased rather than to royal favorites or the highest bidder[125]. The 1339 petition resulted in a statute[126]. It is questionable how well the statute was observed because in 1376 a parliamentary petition repeated the request of 1339[127]. The attitudes toward wardship expressed in the 1339 and 1376 petitions were no doubt shared by mesne tenants. In their testaments landholders frequently made bequests to their widows for the sustenance of their young children[128]. They lacked confidence in the institution of wardship. A feoffment to uses with a last will expanded a landholder's testamentary capacity to assure the well-being of his children. Lest the idea that friends make better guardians than do lords be taken too far down the social scale, a petition in 1404, invoking the Statute of Marlborough, requested a statute to abolish uses which deprived lords of wardship[129]. The King's reply acknowledged "the perils and inconveniences" which would result from the wholesale elimination of intergenerational uses[130]. The King was perhaps aware of the difficulty in specifying exactly which uses impermissibly deprived a lord of wardship. Parliament did not act to resolve the tension between feudal wardship and contract wardship until 1490[131]. The statute in that year, a clarification of the Statute of Marlborough, prohibited uses unless the feoffor had left a last will. The statute thus banned only those intergenerational uses which served no other purpose than to deprive a lord of wardship.

The tension between uses and wardship was handled retail. A lord's effective right to wardship depended very much upon his power and vigilance. When considering a lord's ability to prevent a feoffment to uses we are at a loss because so little is known about the later interpretations of *Quia Emptores* and about how the law on the books operated on the ground. In some early cases over wardship, lords make the argument that a tenant's grantee is not the lord's tenant until he is accepted by the lord[132]. This argument drops out of the legal reports but did not for that cease to be a social reality. Some lords were vigilant and had sufficient power to police against feoffments to uses[133]. The *Black Prince* and *John of Gaunt*, for

---

124 Rotuli Parliamentorum, vol. II, p. 104a.

125 *Ibid.*, p. 104.

126 Stat. 14 Edw. III, st.1, c.13 (1440).

127 Rotuli Parliamentorum, vol. II, p. 341.

128 See *supra* n. 46.

129 Rotuli Parliamentorum, vol. III, pp. 58 - 59.

130 Rotuli Parliamentorum, vol. III, pp. 58 - 59.

131 Stat. 4 Hen. VII, c. 17 (1490).

132 *Fitzherbert,* Abridgement, Garde 33 (1358).

133 *Given-Wilson* (n. 108) 149 - 50.

examples, were vigilant in inquiring into and suppressing attempted feoffments which would deprive them of wardships[134]. A powerful lord could require a license for a feoffment much as the Crown required licenses for alienations. For example, in 1467 Stephen Scrope made a feoffment to uses to secure the marriage of his daughter[135]. He obtained a pardon from his lord, Richard Earl of Warwick, for making the feoffment without a license[136]. The pardon instructed the Earl's seneschals, bailiffs, receivers and reeves not to molest Scrope, which hints at how a powerful lord could resist an unwanted feoffment. Perhaps *Quia Emptores* gave Scrope a right to alienate his land, but perhaps, too, a seignorial license was cheaper than a flurry of trespass actions.

On the other hand, a tenant's ability to pay his debts and honor his obligations to his children, friends, servants, and his own soul required him to avoid wardship. The probability that a tenant would leave an heir underage was substantial. *Rosenthal* has estimated that during the reign of *Henry IV* and *Henry V* as many as 55 per cent of male landholders left underage heirs[137]. Where the heir was male, the percentage rises to 64 per cent[138]. Besides providing for his immediate family, a feoffment to uses enabled a feoffor to assure that fees and annuities granted to his retainers for life were maintained after his death[139]. For the nobility feoffment to uses strengthened their ability to establish military retinues[140]. Lesser lords also had their estate officials, servants, and associates who expected to be remembered in the lord's last will. Feoffments to uses strengthened a network of social relationships that had little to do with feudal tenure.

Landholders also employed uses to maintain the unity of their landed properties. Consider the case of John del Clyf of Dunwich. In December 1341 he demised all his lands to four feoffees[141]. His lands consisted of the manor of Hernetherne in Westelton, Suffolk, held of the Prior of Ely, and five parcels of land also in Suffolk ranging from forty acres to three acres, each held of a different lord. He died the following April leaving an heir under age. If John del Clyf had not created his intergenerational use, each lord would have had wardship over each parcel. During the wardship, the various parcels would not have been maintained as the unit they apparently formed in John del Clyf's mind. His feoffees, two of whom appear to have been brothers or at least kinsmen, could maintain the unity of the inheritance

134 *K. B. McFarlane,* The Nobility of Later Medieval England, 1973, pp. 216 - 220.

135 Scrope Cartulary, B.L. Add. Ms. 28206, f. 42v-45v.

136 Scrope Cartulary, B.L. Add. Ms. 28207, f.31.

137 *J. T. Rosenthal,* 'Heirs' Ages and Family Succession in Yorkshire 1399 - 1422, (1984) 56 Yorkshire Archaeological Journal 88.

138 *Rosenthal,* (1984) 56 Yorkshire Archaeological Journal 88.

139 *Bean* (n. 3) 147 - 48.

140 See Calendar of Patent Rolls 1364 - 1367, pp. 333 - 34 for the use established by *John of Gaunt* to assure payment of his retinue both while he is in France and in the event of his death.

141 Calendar of Inquisitions Post Mortem, vol. 8, no. 424 (1343).

for his heir[142]. In other cases as well one finds lesser landholders collecting parcels held of different lords and conveying them as a unit to feoffees[143]. Lesser landholders who held of various lords could employ uses to maintain the integrity of the inheritance against the threat posed by multiple wardships.

Royal wardships present a complicated picture[144]. The Crown was willing to trade revenues from wardships for other revenues or for services. In *Edward III's* reign, one reason for the Crown's willingness to grant licenses for feoffments which would later deprive the Crown of wardships, besides the price of the licenses, was a shift in royal finances toward taxation[145]. At the same time, by giving licenses for feoffments to those who went with him to fight in France, the King purchased their military service[146]. In the 15th century, royal expeditions to France were the occasion for royal permissions to make feoffments to uses[147]. There is also evidence that the Crown was willing to compromise with its tenants-in-chief. In the 15th century, the Crown frequently took care not to permit tenants-in-chief to enfeoff all of their lands but to insist that the tenant-in-chief remain a tenant of the King with respect to part of his lands[148]. By making a tenant-in-chief remain a tenant for part of his tenant's lands the Crown retained the wardship and marriage of the tenant's heir.

Consequences of these compromises appear among the Chancery petitions. For example, in the 1420s John Fray and Thomas Aleyn in a petition to the Chancellor said that the King had committed to them the wardship of the lands and the heir of John Tyringham[149]. They pointed out that Tyringham had enfeoffed feoffees of his manor of Tyringham in Bukinghamshire with the intent that they pay Tyringham's debts after his death and then convey the manor to his heir. One might expect them to complain that the feoffees are depriving the King of his wardship and that the feoffment was collusive. But that was not their complaint. Rather, they complained that the feoffees were wasting the manor, not paying Tyringham's debts, and were keeping Tyringham's charters and muniments to the disinheritance of the heir. The Chancellor examined the feoffees on the charges of waste, but the result is not known[150]. Similarly, in another case from the 1420s a woman who described herself as fourteen years old and in the King's wardship petitioned the chancellor to

142 Two of the feoffees were Augustine del Clyf, parson of Brampton, and Augustine's brother Peter; Calendar of Inquisitions Post Mortem, vol. 8, no. 424 (1343).

143 E.g., Calendar of Inquisitions Post Mortem, vol. 7, no. 597 (1334).

144 *Bean* has royal efforts, chiefly through escheators and inquisition *post mortem*, to protect royal rights to wardship; *Bean* (n. 3) 197 - 220.

145 *Given-Wilson* (n. 108) 150.

146 *Given-Wilson* (n. 108) 150; *Ormond* (n. 119) 114.

147 *Bean* (n. 3) 146.

148 *Bean* (n. 3) 199 - 200.

149 C1/5/75.

150 C1/5/76, 77.

require her father's feoffees to convey her father's lands to her[151]. Royal wardship coexisted with feoffment to uses.

3. The Cases: Seignorial Opportunism

In legal terms, the conflict over wardship by tenure and wardship by contract came down to a fight over which intergenerational uses were collusive and thus prohibited by Chapter 6 of the Statute of Marlborough[152]. The statute prohibited two devices which would deprive a lord of wardship: an outright grant by the tenant to his underage heir and a lease by the tenant to third parties on terms which became uneconomical at or shortly after the heir came of age. The statute also spoke more generally of false or collusive enfeoffments. It was for the common law courts in the 14th and 15th centuries to determine which conveyances by tenants would be deemed to be collusive within the meaning of the statute. In the 14th century, a lord could not plead that his tenant's conveyance was collusive without showing special matter, which meant he had to describe the terms of the feoffment[153]. By the 15th century, defendants pleaded the term of the feoffment and plaintiff then alleged collusion. In either case, that one of the parties had to plead the terms of the conveyance is certainly a benefit to historians. For we can see the terms of the conveyances and glean some idea why they were or were not thought to be collusive.

There were two fairly clear methods of circumventing the statute. If a tenant conveyed his land to his underage heir jointly with another, although the lord would lose his wardship, the conveyance did not come within the statute[154]. Parents could use a grant-regrant transaction to settle an estate on themselves jointly with their son and the heirs of their son's body with remainder to the son's right heirs[155]. When they died, their son had a fee tail and if he were underage there would be no wardship. That this form of conveyance did not come within the statute was no aid to a tenant who wished to convey to feoffees to uses. And if a tenant conveyed to feoffees who conveyed over to other feoffees, the transaction did not come within the statute, even if the second feoffees were to convey to the underage heir[156]. This curious rule might explain why a feoffor would make his enfeoffment in the form of two successive life estates, the first to one set of feoffees, after whose deaths, another set of feoffees were to have the land for their lives[157].

---

151 C1/5/104.

152 Stat. 52 Hen. III, c.6 (1267).

153 *Fitzherbert,* Abridgement, Garde 33 (1358); *ibid.*, Collusion 29 (1357).

154 *J. H. Baker,* Introduction to English Legal History, 3rd ed., 1990, p. 279.

155 E.g., Calendar of Patent Rolls 1324 - 27, p. 6; *ibid.*, p. 179; *ibid.*, p. 203. A variant was to settle the land on one's wife and son and the heirs of the son's body: *ibid.*, p. 133; *ibid.*, p. 157.

156 *Fitzherbert* (n. 153) Collusion 29 (1357).

An obvious line of attack on a feoffment to feoffees was to attack the effectiveness of the conveyance. In the earlier cases, defendants make a point of the fact that the lord had accepted the feoffees as his tenants[158]. The idea apparently was that if the lord accepted the feoffees as his tenants he could not later complain that the enfeoffment was collusive. In one case, for example, when the defendant answered that the lord was seised of feoffees' service, the lord was forced to answer that the service was for other lands than those he claimed in wardship[159]. Conversely, there could be an issue whether the tenant's tenants attorned to the tenant's feoffees[160]. Whether tenants attorned to the feoffees was an indication whether the enfeoffment had been real. The Justices did not, however, stick at this point. A lord could also attack the validity of an enfeoffment on the grounds that since the tenant held in fee tail the conveyance to feoffees was void and the entail continued[161].

The inquiry into collusion often focused on the technical form of the conveyance. In the cases in *Edward III's* reign defendants believed that a conveyance to feoffees was not collusive if there were no condition in the conveyance that the feoffees grant the land to the heir when he came of age. Defendants produced the charter of conveyance to the feoffees showing that the conveyance was without condition and tried, unsuccessfully. to insist that the plaintiff lord be required to produce a writing showing that the conveyance contained a condition[162]. The lord, of course, would be unlikely to have any such document, which is why defendants demanded that he produce it. In the case before Parliament over *Edward III's* will the Justices stated their opinion that a feoffment was conditional as long as the condition was stated at the time of the conveyance either in the charter of enfeoffment, in another document, or orally[163]. Later instructions to feoffees were not binding, because they could not change the estate of the feoffees.

This doctrine promoted the belief that a feoffment to uses was not collusive if the instructions to the feoffees were not technically conditions on the grant to them. The cautious conveyancer would have the charter of feoffment state that the grant to feoffees was without condition[164]. Feoffors also took care not to state their will in such a way as it could be read as a technical condition of their feoffment. A cautious feoffor might not state his will to his feoffees during his life. In 1393

---

157 Calendar of Patent Rolls, 1374 - 77, pp. 33 - 34.

158 *Fitzherbert* (n. 153) Garde 33 (1358).

159 *Ibid.*

160 *Fitzherbert* (n. 153) Collusion 29 (1357); Lib. Ass., f.258, pl.6 (1368).

161 Y.B. Mich. 4 Hen. IV, f.1, pl.17 (1402).

162 *Fitzherbert* (n. 153) Garde 33 (1358); Lib. Ass., f.258, pl.6 (1368); Y.B. Trin. 45 Edw. III, f.22, pl.25 (1371). See Y.B. Mich. 47 Edw. III, f.16, pl.28 (1373); Y.B. (Ames Society , vol. 4) Mich. 8 Ric. II, p. 99, pl.19 (1384). See Y.B. Hil. 44 Edw. II, f.1, pl.3 (1370).

163 Rotuli Parliamentorum, vol. III, pp. 60 - 61.

164 E.g., Bohun Cartulary (n. 108) f.1d (1375). Henry V also took the trouble to state that his grant to feoffees was without condition: *J. Nichols,* A Collection of All the Wills of the Kings and Queens of England, 1780, p. 236.

Chancery examined John Filioll's feoffees to determine whether his grant to them was collusive[165]. Not surprisingly, they denied any collusion. The reason they gave was that John during his life had not declared "voluntatem suam nec aliquam condicioniem feoffamenti"[166]. He had left his will with another who did not give it to the feoffees until after John's death. When asked, however, whether the grant to them was made with the intent that they re-enfeoff John's heir, two of the feoffees admitted they thought that had been the point.

The attempt by defendants and their lawyers to tie the idea of collusion to the technicalities of a conditional grant failed. As the 1393 examination suggests the main concern was with the intent of feoffor however expressed. In the 15th century Chancery records, when a petitioner speaks of a feoffor's last will as conditions of his feoffment, it is hard to know whether the word is being used in a technical sense[167]. Petitions also spoke of the feoffor's intent[168]. As one petitioner put it, the feoffor granted to his feoffees "touts cours symplement et saunz condicion al entent" to perform his last will[169]. In 15th century wardship case, plaintiffs use the language of condition and the language of intent apparently interchangeably[170].

We can now turn to substantive questions of collusion, that is, what instructions to feoffees counted as collusive within the meaning of the Statute of Marlborough. In a fairly early case (1368), the justices were concerned whether the feoffor's intent was to disinherit his heir[171]. The idea seems to have been that a lord's right to wardship could be no greater than the heir's right to inherit the land. The next step would be that if the heir was temporarily disinherited, the lord's right to wardship was extinguished for the same period. On this view, there would be collusion only if the feoffees were to do no more than collect the profits during the heir's minority and then convey to him when he came of age. That lawyers and justices were indeed thinking along these lines may explain why lords were driven to plead that the conveyance collusive because it was made with the intent that the feoffees collect the profits during the heir's minority and then convey to him when of age.[172] This line of thinking also fits the belief held by some justices that a feoffment to perform the will of the feoffor, that is, to make bequests for the benefit of his soul and to pay his debts, is not a collusive feoffment[173]. This interpretation of collusion was codified in 1490[174].

---

165 C1 / 3 / 16e.

166 *Ibid.*

167 E.g. C1 / 4 / 36; C1 / 4 / 74; C1 / 4 / 105; C1 / 4 / 109; C1 / 4 / 187; C1 / 5 / 11. When the complaint is about a grant on condition that the feoffee regrant, perhaps the word condition was being used in its technical sense. E.g., C1 / 4 / 37; C1 / 4 / 129; C1 / 4 / 146; C1 / 4 / 163.

168 C1 / 3 / 128; C1 / 4 / 79; C1 / 5 / 14; C1 / 5 / 66; C1 / 5 / 75; C1 / 5 / 177; C1 / 6 / 118.

169 C1 / 6 / 152.

170 Compare Y.B. Hil. 14 Hen. IV, f.15, pl.8 (1413) (intent) with Y.B. Hil. 3 Hen. VI, f.32, pl.23 (1425) (condition).

171 Lib. Ass., f.258, pl.6 (1368).

172 Y.B. (Ames Society, vol. 4) Mich. 8 Ric. II, p. 99, pl.19 (1384);

In one line of cases, a lord attacked as collusive feoffments with the intent that the feoffees grant the land to the feoffor's widow for life with remainder to the feoffor's heir[175]. Since in the case of a jointure a lord could not claim wardship until both parents were dead, lords who claimed wardship when the same settlement was achieved by means of a feoffment to uses were acting opportunistically. The justices did not tolerate this seignorial opportunism. In one case, the lord had to plead that the wife was participating in the collusion and that the plan was for her to release her life estate to the heir when he came of age[176]. In another case *Justice Hankford* asked the plaintiff's sergeant whether the tenant's widow was still alive[177]. When the plaintiff said she was, *Hankford* responded: "It is worse for you because if the condition was that the woman is to have an estate for the term of her life, the remainder to the son, if the woman were dead before any estate made to him, then the collusion must take effect in as much as the feoffment cannot be made but immediately to the heir"[178]. In a third case, in which the defendant was the tenant's widow, plaintiff alleged that (a) the feoffment was made while defendant was pregnant on the condition that if she was delivered of a boy the feoffees should enfeoff him, (b) she was delivered of the boy whose wardship he sought, and (c) the enfeoffment was collusive[179]. *Justice Martin* said that the plea was double in that the allegation of the condition was a matter of fact and the allegation of collusion was a matter of law. Plaintiff was forced to the general plea of collusion. This was probably a weak issue for plaintiff. For a tenant's intent to deprive his lord of wardship was not sufficient. The feoffment had in fact to deprive impermissibly the lord of wardship[180]. If the feoffees had enfeoffed the tenant's widow, as they appear to have done, plaintiff had the problem pointed out by *Hankford*. Feoffors thus had incentive to make generous provisions for their widows in their wills. It is not surprising that widows might have received more in this type of jointure than they would have received as common law dower[181].

In at least two cases, one in 1357 and one in 1440, lords claimed that a tenant's grant to feoffees to regrant to the tenant for life remainder to the tenant's heir was collusive. In neither case are the facts of the transaction terribly clear. The 1357 case had to do with a man who entered into religious orders and sought to provide

---

173 Y.B. Pas. 33 Hen. VI, f.14, pl.6 at f.15 (*Danby J.*) (1440).

174 Stat. 4 Hen. VII, c.17 (1490).

175 *Fitzherbert* (n. 153) Collusion 29 (1357); Y.B. Mich. 46 Edw. II, f.31, pl.34 (1372); Y.B. Hil. 12 Hen. IV, f.13, pl.5 (1411); Y.B. Hil. 12 Hen. IV, f.16, pl.11 (1411); Y.B. Hil. 3 Hen. VI, f.32, pl.23 (1425).

176 Y.B. Hil. 12 Hen. IV, f.13, pl.5 (1411).

177 Y.B. Hil. 12 Hen. IV, f.16, pl.11 (1411).

178 *Ibid.*

179 Y.B. Hil. 3 Hen. VI, f.32, pl.23 (1425).

180 Y.B. Mich. 10 Hen. IV, f.4, pl.11 (1408).

181 *Avery*, History of Equitable Jurisdiction of Chancery before 1440, (1969) 42 Bulletin of Historical Research 140; *Bean* (n. 3) 136.

for his wife and child[182]. Before his entry into orders, he enfeoffed feoffees and took back an estate to himself and his wife for life, remainder to his heir in tail, remainder over in tail, remainder in fee to a Prior. As soon as the tenant entered religion, his wife would hold for her life, remainder in the heir. Apparently, this arrangement by itself was not collusive, for the plaintiff alleged that the wife was to release to the heir as soon as he came of age. In the 1440 case, the lord also attacked a life-estate-remainder settlement as collusive but did so after the life estate had ended and the heir was still underage[183]. A woman had conveyed to feoffees who were to reconvey to her for life, remainder to her heir. When she died leaving her heir underage, the lord entered and took beasts on the land. The agents of the heir brought replevin. The lord argued that his entry was lawful because the woman's conveyance had been collusive. A good deal of the discussion, tangential to our main concern, was whether the lord could enter in such a case or whether he had to bring a writ of wardship to try the collusive. The substantive pleading issue was how the lord had to plead collusion in a case like this. The lord had pleaded that the woman's grant to the feoffees was collusion. This pleading started a discussion whether the feoffe's grant back, thought not to be collusive, could cure the collusive nature of the grant out. The justices decided that the lord had to plead that the grant out was collusive and that the grant back of the remainder was also collusive. It was not clear what would make the grant back of the remainder collusive. In the discussion of collusion *Danby* argued that a feoffment to enfeoff the heir at full age would be collusive, but a feoffment to arrange the marriages of the feoffor's daughters or to pay his debts and then to enfeoff the heir would not be collusive. *Moyle* agrees but *Ashton* seems to disagree. He seems to realize that *Danby's* position would mean the end of wardship. Yet *Danby's* position was adopted in the 1490 statute which established that a feoffment to uses was collusive unless the feoffor had left a last will[184].

IV. Uses and Chancery

During the period from the later 14th to the later 15th centuries Chancery, acting as a court, came to enforce the duties accepted by feoffees to uses. The details of this development remain hidden in the records of Chancery and the common law courts and in the law reports of the period. The thread of the story has three strands. First, there is the gradual separation of the Chancellor's judicial work from the work of the King's Council. In the earlier years of the period petitions to the Council might be delegated to the Chancellor for hearing and resolution and petitions to the Chancellor might be heard and decided by the Council. The first sur-

182 *Fitzherbert* (n. 153) Collusion 29 (1357).

183 Y.B. Pas. 33 Hen. VI, f.14, pl.6 (1440).

184 Stat. 4 Hen. VII, c.17 (1490).

viving judgment by the Chancellor alone does not come until 1473[185]. Second, disputes pertaining to feoffments to uses came to dominate the case load of the Chancellor's court. When, if ever in the 15th century, the Chancellor became preoccupied with uses is a matter of debate. *Avery* thought that by the 1450's about 90 per cent of the cases in Chancery involved uses[186]. *Pronay*, on the other hand, surveying a sample of cases the majority of which dated from the years 1480 - 1483, found that only about 10 per cent of the cases involved uses[187]. Third, there is the development of Chancery rules of law created to solve problems and resolve disputes concerning feoffments to uses. This third strand is the focus of this section.

Historians ordinarily take up this third strand by noticing when Chancery first decided cases in favor of persons with an interest in a feoffment to uses – the feoffor, the feoffor's heir, a third party – and when Chancery first held that a feoffee's heir or purchaser of land subject to a use was bound by the use. We will turn to these milestones, more like islands rising from a sea of records, in the development of Chancery in a moment. Before we do so, it is important to put the Chancery's work with uses in context. First, Chancery was not the only institution available to resolve disputes arising out of a feoffment to uses. Second, there is the largely unexplored topic of the relation and interaction between Chancery and the common law courts not only in the matter of uses but in other matters as well. Although this topic would take us well beyond the scope of this essay, it is nevertheless worth suggesting at least that the traditional view might be too simple. The traditional view is that Chancery developed as a court of equity and conscience because common law rules and procedures were so rigid as to work injustice. To some extent, however, it is also true that the common law maintained rigid rules and procedures because Chancery developed as a court of conscience.

1. In Search of a Forum

Chancery and the common law courts were not the only fora for resolving disputes involving uses. *Helmholz* discovered that litigation over uses took place in Church courts, more precisely, in the diocesan courts of Canterbury and Rochester from the last quarter of the 14th century to the 1460s[188]. In all of *Helmholz's* cases, the feoffor was dead and the dispute pertained to the feoffees' performance of the feoffor's last will[189]. As we have seen the distinction between testament and last

185 *Avery*, An Evaluation of the Effectiveness of the Court of Chancery under the Lancastrian Kings, (1970) 84 L.Q.R. 89.

186 *Ibid.* 84.

187 *N. Pronay*, The Chancellor, the Chancery and the Council at the End of the Fifteenth Century, in: H. Herder, H. Loyn (eds.), British Government and Administration: Studies Presented to S.B. Chrimes, 1974, pp. 92 - 93.

188 *R. H. Helmholz*, The Early Enforcement of Uses, (1979) 79 Columbia L.R. 1503 ff.

189 *Helmholz*, (1979) 79 Columbia L.R. 1506.

will and between executor and feoffee were not always clearly drawn by testator-feoffors. In cases of debt, the common law treated feoffees as *de facto* executors. Even where a feoffor kept his testament separate from his last will, as we have noted, he frequently named some of his feoffees his executors. It is understandable that Church courts might also treat feoffees as executors or as *de facto* executors for all provisions of a testament-last will. Church courts had the advantage, shared by Chancery, of being able to order specific performance. After *Helmholz's* discovery, the surprising thing is that other diocesan courts were not also hearing claims against feoffees[190]. The Canterbury and Rochester cases peter out in the 1460s[191]. Why plaintiffs should cease taking their cases to Church court at this time is not clear. It appears that by the 1460s Chancery had a better defined jurisdiction over uses, although this appearance might be a matter of surviving records. A better defined and more active jurisdiction in Chancery over uses might explain why plaintiffs no longer brought their cases to the Church courts.

Disputes involving uses also ended up in arbitration. For example, in 1484 Thomas Norris enfeoffed feoffees of certain lands the profits of which were to be paid to the chantry priest of St. Thomas of Childewell[192]. On the same day his brother John also enfeoffed an overlapping groups of feoffees with 20 shillings rent for the same purpose[193]. 10 years later we learn that there have been "variances" between the chantry priest and the feoffees over which lands had been devoted to the support of the chantry and whether the income was sufficient to support the priest. A panel of arbitrators award that the feoffees pay the chantry priest a lump sum, that certain lands claimed by Richard and John Norris be retained by them for their lives with the profits of those lands to benefit the chantry after their deaths, and that Richard and John yearly provide any additional moneys necessary to sustain the chantry priest[194]. Arbitration became fairly frequent in the later 14th and 15th centuries because it offered the same advantages over the common law usually attributed to Chancery: speedier and more flexible procedures[195]. Perhaps the most important procedural advantage arbitration shared with Chancery was the ability

---

190 As *Helmholz* observes, the absence of evidence of similar litigation in other diocesan courts might well be owing to the paucity of surviving records; *Helmholz,* (1979) 79 Columbia L.R. 1510. See however the results of *Helmholz's* further research in his essay in this volume.

191 *Helmholz,* (1979) 79 Columbia L.R. 1511.

192 *A Calendar of Norris Deeds* (n. 21) p. 167, no. 923 (1484).

193 *Ibid.*, p. 167, no. 924.

194 *Ibid.*, p. 168, no. 927 (1494).

195 For late medieval arbitration, see *C. Rawcliffe,* The Great Lord as Peacekeeper: Arbitration of English Noblemen and their Councils in the Later Middle Ages, in: J. A. Grey, H. G. Beale (eds.), Law and Social Change in British History, 1984; *E. Powell,* Arbitration and the Law in England in the Late Middle Ages, (1983) 33 Transactions of the Royal Historical Society 49 ff.; *I. Rowney,* Arbitration in Gentry Disputes of the Later Middle Ages, (1982) 26 History 367 ff.; *J.T. Rosenthal,* Feuds and Private Peace-Making: A Fifteenth Century Example, (1970) 9 Nottingham Medieval Studies 84 ff.

of arbitrators to order specific performance. Parties to arbitration would enter into penal bonds, with the penalty conditioned on non-performance of the arbitral award[196]. Arbitration also permitted the decision-makers to adjust the conflicting claims of the parties according to norms of fairness. In his study of Nottinghamshire, *Payling* found that the complicated issues of inheritance frequently generated by feoffments to uses was an important reason why landholders used arbitration to settle their disputes[197]. But, as *Payling* observed, arbitration had its shortcomings[198]. Arbitrators were not immune from the influence of powerful lords. The enforcement of agreements to arbitrate and the enforcement of arbitral awards also presented difficulties. Disputes over these issues frequently brought the parties into Common Pleas[199]. In the 15th century, the parties to an arbitration also petitioned the Chancellor[200]. *Pronay* found that a fair number of petitions in Chancery sought the enforcement of decrees by arbitrators[201].

The relation and interaction between Chancery as a court of conscience and the common law courts is a largely unexplored subject. It is unknown, for example, when conscience, conceived as a source of legal norms, come to be the province of Chancery. In the 14th century, appeals to conscience were not uncommon in legal arguments in Common Pleas. Yet recourse to Chancery was not unknown either. In a 1343 case, a creditor sued his debtor's three executors only one of which appeared[202]. The creditor got a jury verdict that the document he had proffered as his debtor's obligation was indeed his debtor's obligation. By statute, his judgment ran against all three executors[203]. The two executors who had not previously appeared showed up with a writ out of Chancery ordering the Justices to execute the judgment in accordance with "law and reason"[204]. They sought to make sure that the judgment went against the goods of their testator and not against their own goods. The serjeants discussed whether a writ from Chancery was necessary. Some argued that the writ was not necessary because the Justices did not need a writ to tell them to supervise the execution of the judgment so that it went according to law and reason. Others thought that a writ was necessary because without a writ the Justices would have no basis for hearing complaints about execution from the executors who had not been parties to the verdict. In this rather early case of Chancery intervention, recourse to Chancery was thought to be necessary, if at all, in order to

196 *E. Powell* (n. 195).

197 *S. Payling*, Political Society in Lancastrian England: The Greater Gentry of Nottinghamshire, 1991, p. 213.

198 *Payling* (n. 197) 213 - 15.

199 *E. Powell* (n. 195).

200 E.g., C1 / 61 / 50; C1 / 54 / 98; C1 / 70 / 12.

201 *Pronay* (n. 187) 92.

202 Y.B. (Rolls Series) Pas. 17 Edw. III, pp. 226 - 31 (1343).

203 Stat. 9 Edw. III, St. 1, c.3 (1335).

204 Y.B. (Rolls Series) Pas. 17 Edw. III, pp. 226 - 31 (1343).

fill a small gap in common law procedures. Chancery was not yet thought to have any special or exclusive access to reason or conscience as a source of legal norms.

2. Uses at Common Law

There is some evidence that in the first decades of the 15th century the Justices of Common Pleas were not insensitive to some of the problems arising from a feoffment to uses. We have seen that a feoffor's creditors could recover their debts against the feoffees as if they were executors. Instructions to feoffees to pay debts were thus enforceable at common law. Indeed, common law protection of creditors did not depend upon whether feoffees had been instructed to pay debts. They were liable as *de facto* executors. In 1400, an heir brought an action of account against his father's feoffee for the revenues he had received while plaintiff had been underage[205]. Plaintiff characterized the feoffee as receiver for plaintiff's benefit. The feoffee admitted that plaintiff's father had enfeoffed him to re-enfeoff plaintiff when he came of age and that the moneys sought were revenues of the land held as the father's feoffee. The issue was whether the action of account could be used in this novel manner. *Rickhill* and *Markham* debated the issue much as they had debated whether a feoffor's creditor could sue the feoffees as *de facto* executors. *Rickhill* thought it would be "marvelous" to allow the action. *Markham* focused on the fact that feoffees were not to receive the revenues to their own use. Defendant argued that as he was not a guardian in socage he did not come within the statute giving wards an action of account[206] and that the father's will said nothing about an accounting. When these arguments failed, defendant was forced to plead that he was not a receiver for plaintiff.

The discussions in later cases suggest that heirs might have been able to hold their ancestors' feoffees accountable until the mid to later 15th century. I have not been able to find another case in which an heir attempted to hold his father's feoffees accountable as receivers. But there is some evidence that heirs were attempting to hold their fathers' feoffees accountable as *de facto* guardians in socage much as creditors held feoffees liable as *de facto* executors. The relevant reports suggest that heirs might have been successful but, if so, their success was short lived. In a 1431 case, plaintiff sought an accounting against defendant as his guardian in socage[207]. Defendant alleged that plaintiff's ancestor held of defendant by military tenure, but defendant was not permitted to plead that he did not occupy the land as guardian in socage. He had to plead that plaintiff's ancestor had not held the land by socage tenure. Unfortunately, at this crucial point the record, though printed, is not clear. *Cotesmore* tells defendant that he must plead the ancestor's tenure because if he

---

205 Y.B. Mich. 2 Hen. IV, f.12, pl.50 (1400).

206 Stat. 52 Hen. III, c. 17.

207 Y.B. Mich. 10 Hen. VI, f.7, pl.21 (1431).

occupies in his own right / wrong he will be charged as a guardian in socage. Where the text has *Cotesmore* speaking of defendant occupying "de son droit demesne" in a 1482 case in which the same pleading point arose the speaker uses the phrase "de son tort demesne"[208] and the abbreviation in the text of the 1431 case seems to combine both words. If the phrase means defendant occupies in his own right, the phrase could awkwardly describe a feoffee. The more likely reading, however, is that the phrase means that defendant occupies on his own wrong. This same phrase was also used to hold feoffees liable as *de facto* executors.

Cotesmore seems to have things backwards. Only if defendant can plead the status of his occupation of the land can he deny the very possibility *Cotesmore* has in mind: liability as a *de facto* guardian in socage. The desire to exclude that possibility might have been the reason why defendant tried to frame his answer as he did. The idea that feoffees were accountable as *de facto* guardians in socage seems to have been alive at least in the minds of lawyers. In the 1482 case, plaintiff objected to defendant only pleading the ancestor's tenure. He argued that defendant had to plead the status of his occupation because if he holds the lands and takes the profits "de son tort demesne" he should be held accountable. *Catesby*, however, holds that by pleading that the ancestor held by military tenure, defendant precluded the possibility that he was guardian in socage. This argument denies the possibility of a *de facto* guardian in socage. By 1482, and probably earlier, the justices turned back the pleading moves which would have enabled feoffees to be held accountable as *de facto* guardians in socage. But a good deal of mystery remains. Petitions to the Chancellor requesting an accounting from defendant were not infrequent. The petitions sought to avoid such defects in the common law as the rules that an action of account died with the obligor and that a written acquittance was necessary to prove that defendant had accounted and had paid what was owed to plaintiff[209]. Accounting in Chancery could also avoid the more cumbersome common law procedure whereby there were, in effect, two proceedings: an action for an account followed by an accounting before auditors[210]. It seems likely, though this is speculation, that the idea of holding feoffees liable to an accounting as *de facto* guardians in socage fizzled out because Chancery began to enforce that liability.

Feoffments to uses were often made on condition that the feoffees regrant the land to the feoffor or his heir or that the feoffees perform the feoffor's last will and then regrant the land to the feoffor's heir. At common law, the feoffor or his heir could re-enter the lands if the feoffees failed to perform their instructions. The condition, as *Barton* observed, was a satisfactory method of compelling performance by feoffees[211]. The heir's entry, for example, could induce litigation in which the legality of his entry would be the issue. Since the legality of his entry depended

208 Y.B. Pas. 22 Edw. IV, f.5, pl.15 (1482).

209 *W. T. Barbour* (n. 103) 13 - 17.

210 *W. T. Barbour* (n. 103) 15 - 16.

211 *Barton*, (1965) 81 L.Q.R. 566.

upon whether the feoffees had broken the condition on their feoffment, the Justices of Common Pleas would be in a position to review the performance of the feoffees. A case of novel disseisin in 1400 illustrates the point[212]. A man granted his lands to feoffees on condition that they re-enfeoff himself and his wife and the heirs of their bodies. The man died without issue and his widow remarried. The feoffees enfeoffed the widow and her second husband for the life of the widow with remainder to the right heirs of the first husband. Believing that the feoffee breached the condition, the heir of the first husband entered, was ousted, and brought novel disseisin. Plaintiff argued that the feoffee had not performed the condition because the woman should have received an entail and the second husband should not have been enfeoffed at all. *Justice Hankford,* however, pointed out that the heir was in a better position than if the widow had been given an entail. The court ruled that the conditions had been well performed and that plaintiff take nothing by his writ. In 1410, *Justice Markham* discussed a similar case[213]. In *Markham's* case, a husband and wife with children grant to feoffees on condition that they re-enfeoff them in fee tail. The wife dies before the re-enfeoffment. In *Markham's* view, the condition cannot be performed in whole but can be performed *cy-près* in that the feoffees can grant the land to the husband and the heirs of his body of his now deceased wife. The entail would be preserved in the right persons. The doctrine of *cy-près* apparently was not exclusive, and perhaps not original, to Chancery. In a third case, in 1428, an heir entered to enforce a condition on an feoffment by his ancestor that the feoffees regrant the land when requested to do so[214]. When the feoffees refused the heir's request, he entered and the feoffees brought an action of trespass. The point of the case was that the heir could plead the condition without written evidence. These cases, and especially the last one, pose the puzzle of why feoffors or the heirs were petitioning the Chancellor that feoffees had failed to regrant land according to the condition in the grant to them[215].

Feoffments on a condition were satisfactory protection only in the simple case of a re-enfeoffment[216]. Where the feoffor's instructions included directions in favor of beneficiaries other than the heir, a right of entry in the heir would not help the beneficiaries. The movement away from making a feoffment to uses in the technical form of a conditional grant removed a common law remedy for the heir. Heirs as well as beneficiaries were thus left without a remedy until Chancery came to their aid. Before Chancery asserted jurisdiction over a feoffee's performance of his duties feoffors experimented with other methods of making the instructions given to feoffees enforceable against them. In 1363, John Pyel, a London merchant, granted lands in Northhampshire to feoffees and had them agree to pay John, his

212 Y.B. Mich. 2 Hen. IV, f.5, pl.20 (1400).

213 Y.B. Mich. 12 Hen. IV, f.1, pl.3 (1410).

214 Y.B. Mich. 7 Hen. VI, f.7, pl.10 (1428).

215 E.g., C1/4/13; C1/4/37; C1/4/129; C1/4/146; C1/4/163; C1/5/80.

216 See *Bean* (n. 3) 160; *Barton,* (1965) 81 L.Q.R. 566 - 68.

heirs and his executors £2,000 should they fail to implement his will[217]. In 1350, when Simon de Drayton granted to feoffees he had them take an oath on the gospels that after his death they would use the revenues of the lands to pay for masses for the benefit of his soul and that of his wife Margaret[218]. In 1383, John de Seyton provided in his will that if any of his feoffees did not wish to perform or obstructed the performance of the conditions in his will, then the offensive feoffee lost his estate in the lands[219]. This measure seems to be an invitation to chaos. And none of these efforts to secure protection against wayward feoffees offered much protection.

The traditional view that the common law courts did not recognize uses is a little too simple, as is the view that Chancery from the outset operated with legal norms distinct from those of the common law courts. The earliest clear evidence that lawyers and judges thought of the common law as different from the law of Chancery is a remark to that effect by *Moyle* in 1464[220]. *Catesby,* however, had just said that the law of Chancery was the common law. The 1464 case was a trespass action brought by feoffees against their *cestui que use.* Defendant sought to answer that plaintiffs held to his use and that he had occupied the land at plaintiff's sufferance and will. *Catesby* thought that "in reason" defendant had a good justification. It is at this point that *Moyle* made his famous statement that defendant's attempted justification would be good matter in Chancery. *Moyle* was not simply making an observation. He was making an argument why defendant's attempted justification should be held to be out of place in Common Pleas. He was in effect arguing that Common Pleas ought to leave the matter to Chancery, that Common Pleas need not recognize the *cestui que use* because Chancery would see that no injustice was done. *Catesby's* line of thinking shows how easy it would have been for the common law to recognize the *cestui que use.* The debate between *Moyle* and *Catesby* could take place because there was not yet any rule or practice which assigned the matter exclusively to Chancery.

The common law courts could enforce the duties of a feoffee only if lawyers could figure out how to get a common law writ to fit the case. Although the ingenuity of medieval lawyers should not be underestimated, they could not surmount one major disadvantage of common law remedies – the lack of specific performance. Even if medieval lawyers could have gotten covenant or trespass on the case in assumpsit to fit the case of a feoffee who breached his duties to beneficiaries, which would have meant expanding both actions to include third-party beneficiaries and to try title to freehold and expanding assumpsit to cases of nonfeasance early than was done, they still would have had to match the specific perfor-

217 The Cartularies of John Pyel and Adam Fraunceys (n. 11) pp. 123 - 24, nos. 59, 62 (1363).

218 *Ibid.*, p. 120, no. 49.

219 B.L. Additional Charter 22214.

220 Y.B. Pas. 4 Edw. IV, f.8, pl.9 (1464).

mance available in Chancery. Specific performance had ceased to be the remedy in covenant in the 14th century[221]. Assumpsit, as a species of trespass, allowed only money damages. The advantage of specific performance brought plaintiffs to Church courts, to arbitration, and to Chancery.

3. Uses in Chancery

We can turn now to the milestones in the development of Chancery's work with uses. Each milestone is evidence showing that the Chancellor protected a person with an interest in a feoffment to uses. They are of uncertain significance because frequently there are many earlier petitions, without recorded judgment, similar to the one for which we have evidence of a judgment. Since it is unlikely that petitioners would persist in a futility, the Chancellor must have been hearing and perhaps even deciding the cases begun by the earlier petitions. This difficulty with the surviving evidence makes it hard to reconstruct a chronology of the Chancellor's developing jurisprudence.

The first known case brought by a living *cestui que use* in which the Chancellor rendered a judgment in his favor occurred in 1409[222]. One Joan Waterfall complained that she had enfeoffed defendant on condition that they re-enfeoff her when she requested them to do so but defendant refused. Defendant answered that the condition was not to re-enfeoff Joan in fee simple but to grant her a life estate with remainders over in fee tail and for failure of issue to sell the property and pay the debts of Joan and the remaindermen. They admitted that they had not fulfilled the condition alleged by Joan, perhaps because they balked at a change of mind on her part which would cut out the entails. As *Hargreaves* noted, the Chancellor dealt with the case in terms of the common law of conditional grants. As have seen, at the time of this case Common Pleas was dealing with feoffees who breached a condition requiring re-enfeoffment. Perhaps the reason the Chancellor heard what appears to be a common law case is that the property lay in the borough of Coventry. The Mayor of Coventry assisted the Chancellor by taking custody of the disputed muniments and delivering them to Chancery. The case seems to be an instance of Chancery reviewing or displacing the work of borough courts[223]. The case is not one in which Chancery was clearly treading on the territory of the common law.

The earliest case in which the Chancellor is clearly known to have enforced the instructions of a deceased feoffor in favor of a beneficiary occurred in 1439[224].

---

221 *Baker* (n. 154) 364.

222 *A.D. Hargreaves*, Equity and the Latin Side of Chancery, (1952) 68 L.Q.R. 487 - 89; *Bean* (n. 3) 168.

223 *N. Pronay* (n. 187) 93, 95 - 96 found a substantial number of Chancery cases coming from boroughs.

Before turning to that case, it is well to note that Chancery received many petitions by beneficiaries before and after 1439. The beneficiaries petitioning Chancery tended to be primarily heirs and widows and, in lesser number, other sons and daughters of the feoffor[225]. Only in cases in which the records include at least an answer by the feoffees it is possible to learn the nature of the dispute. A picture of heirs at the mercy of fraudulent feoffees until the Chancellor intervenes is much too simple. For example, an heir petitioned that his father's feoffees had failed to perform his father's will because they had refused to enfeoff him of the manor of Southall in Raynham, Essex, when he reached 21 years of age[226]. The feoffees answered that under the last will they were not to enfeoff the heir of Southall until its revenues had paid the father's debts but the heir and his mother's second husband had occupied Southall and had taken the revenues without paying any of the father's debts[227]. They were holding the manor for the purpose of performing the last will. In another petition brought by an heir part of the complication was that when the father himself was underage his father's feoffees had been ousted by a lord who was disputing with another lord the right to wardship of the lands[228]. As these two instances illustrate, where we do have an answer, the seemingly straightforward petition often leads quickly to a tangle of transactions. But few of the many early Chancery petitions are accompanied by answers, let alone replications. We are left in the dark.

Returning to the 1439 case, one Elizabeth Burgh sought to have her late husband's feoffees enfeoff her for life of her husbands lands with various remainders in tail in accordance with his directions of 1434. The feoffees, however, also had instructions from her late husband dated 1438. The issue, of course, was which instructions should control the feoffees. The 1434 will was in the form of a tri-partite indenture. The 1438 will was in the form of instructions to the feoffees. The Chancellor enforced the 1434 will. *Bean* viewed the case as important because "although the Chancellor was exercising a jurisdiction outside the bounds of the common law, he was nevertheless employing common law rules in making his decision"[229]. If this statement suggests that the Chancellor was choosing between a common law rule and some other kind of rule, the statement is misleading. In a case in 1414, a sergeant asserted that a second testament makes the first testament void[230]. The argument of counsel proceeded on the truth of that statement. In the

---

224 Calendar of Patent Rolls 1441 - 1446, pp. 112 - 13; *Bean* (n. 3) 170 - 71.

225 E.g., Petitions by heirs: C1 / 4 / 13; C1 / 4 / 45; C1 / 4 / 74; C1 / 4 / 79; C1 / 4 / 109; C1 / 5 / 11; C1 / 6 / 88; C1 / 6 / 306. Petitions by widows: C1 / 4 / 52; C1 / 4 / 67; C1 / 4 / 72; C1 / 4 / 163; C1 / 5 / 115; C1 / 5 / 116; C1 / 5 / 167. Petitions by younger sons: C1 / 4 / 79; C1 / 4 / 184. Petitions by daughters: C1 / 4 / 24; C1 / 4 / 109. See *Bean* (n. 3) 171 - 72.

226 C1 / 31 / 400.

227 C1 / 31 / 399. The will may be found at C1 / 31 / 398.

228 C1 / 55 / 169. Related documents are C1 / 55 / 159 - 170.

229 *Bean* (n. 3) 171.

230 Y.B. Trin. 2 Hen. VI, f.8, pl.13 (1414).

1439 case, the Chancellor was choosing between this common law rule and the significance common lawyers gave to indentures. He enforced an agreement over unilateral instructions.

Yet the association of a last will, as opposed to a testament, with the feoffment which enabled the feoffor to make a last will prevented Chancery from adopting a simple rule. In 1453, *Fortescue* discussed the reasons which would permit a feoffor to change his last will[231]. If a feoffor who had a daughter and no sons granted to feoffees with an instruction to enfeoff his daughter and the feoffor later had a son, the feoffor could change his last will in order to have the feoffees enfeoff his son. In the case *Fortescue* posed, the problem of which will would control the feoffees arose because the first will was part of the original grant to the feoffees. 15th century lawyers might well think of it as a condition on the grant. Once he makes a grant a grantor cannot unilaterally change its terms to the detriment of the grantee. But an indenture or a set of instructions made some time after the grant to feoffees could be almost as separate from the feoffment as would be the feoffor's testament. This case would be governed by the common law rule for testaments[232]. The relative priority of wills was a matter of their connection to the feoffment which made a last will possible.

The Chancellor also had to deal with the situation in which a feoffee died before they had performed the feoffor's last will. The issue was whether the feoffee's heir was bound by the instructions of his ancestor's feoffor. In 1451 it appears that the Chancellor held that the heir was bound[233]. There had been numerous petitions seeking to bind the heir before this decision[234]. Yet in 1468 it was a matter of debate whether a subpoena would issue against the heir if the feoffee had appointed executors[235]. The issue was not whether the use survived the feoffee but whether or not the feoffee's interest should be treated as personal property. In 1482, the Chancellor told the justices that it was the common practice in the Chancery to hold the heir bound by the instructions given his ancestor[236]. *Hussey,* Chief Justice of King's Bench, however, said that this had not been the practice when he had first come to the bar thirty years earlier. He went on to argue that it was a bad practice. *Hussey's* concern was that it was too easy to prove, erroneously, in Chancery that land descended to an heir in trust for a plaintiff. He thought it was better for the feoffor who had allowed his feoffee to die without replacement to lose the land than for an heir wrongly to lose his inheritance. A problem similar to that of the feoffee's heir was posed by a feoffee who sold the land entrusted to him and

---

231 *Fitzherbert* (n. 153); Subpoena 23 (1453); *Barton,* (1965) 81 L.Q.R. 571. See *Baker* (n. 154) 287 with n. 15.

232 Y.B. Mich. 5 Edw. 4, f.8, pl.20 (1465).

233 Calendar of Chancery Proceedings, vol. II, p.xxvii; *Barton,* (1965) 81 L.Q.R. 570.

234 *Avery,* (1969) 42 Bulletin of Historical Research 136.

235 Y.B. Trin. 8 Edw. IV, f.6, pl.1 (1468).

236 Y.B. Pas. 22 Edw. IV, f.6, pl.18 (1482).

pocketed the proceeds. A remark by *Finch* in 1459 suggests that he thought there was no remedy in this case[237]. But in 1465, it was held that a purchaser for value without notice of the use was not bound by the use[238]. The elements of the idea can be traced back at least to 1453[239].

237 Y.B. Trin. 37 Hen. VI, f. 35, pl. 23 (1459).

238 Y.B. Mich. 5 Edw. IV, f.7, pl.16 (1465); Y.B. Trin. 7 Edw. IV, f.14, pl.8 (1467); *Bean* (n. 3) 174 - 75.

239 31 Hen. VI, Statham Abr., Subpoena, pl.[1] reprinted with annotation in *Baker/Milsom* (n. 120) 95.

RICHARD HELMHOLZ

Trusts in the English Ecclesiastical Courts 1300 - 1640

I. Introduction

This contribution has two purposes. The first is to show that trusts – or at least what can legitimately be called trust-like devices – existed and were regularly enforced in the English ecclesiastical courts before 1640[1]. The second is to describe the characteristics of these trusts in as much detail as the sources allow. Dealing with legal practice rather than legal doctrine, this paper is mainly descriptive. It intentionally leaves discussion of the relevant doctrines of the Canon and Roman laws to the contributions by *Shael Herman, David Johnston,* and others. It does, however, take up the question of the relationship between practice in the English ecclesiastical courts and the European *ius commune* in its concluding section.

The material presented here is derived from a continuing exploration of the records of the courts of the English Church. These records survive in significant quantities, even for the medieval period, although they are still in manuscript act books and cause papers kept in record offices spread around England[2]. Despite difficulties in making effective use of them, they are important sources for understanding English legal history[3]. They have been the source of an expanding body of valuable historical scholarship during the past 30 years. However, to date no one has examined them in search of evidence about the history of the trust, and this is a gap this paper attempts to fill[4].

---

1 This terminal date was chosen because the outbreak of the Civil War in that year effectively curtailed ecclesiastical jurisdiction in England. The courts ceased to sit altogether in 1649. They were restored after the return of the monarchy and episcopacy in 1660.

2 These records are discussed and listed in: Charles Donahue, Jr. (ed.), The Records of the Medieval Ecclesiastical Courts, Part II: England (= Comparative Studies in Continental and Anglo-American Legal History, vol. 7), 1994. See also *R. H. Helmholz,* Records and Reports: the English Ecclesiastical Courts, in: Alain Wijffels (ed.), Case Law in the Making (= Comparative Studies in Continental and Anglo-American Legal History, vol. 17/1), 1997, pp. 83 ff.

3 See *G. R. Elton,* England: 1200 - 1640, 1969, pp. 104 ff.

4 See, however, the remarks based upon examination of the wills in the Prerogative Court of Canterbury: *E. F. Jacob,* The Archbishop's Testamentary Jurisdiction, in: Mediaeval Records of the Archbishops of Canterbury, 1962, p. 47: "There are, in the records of the Prerogative, abundant instances of the employment of such trusts".

The broader aim of this paper is to present relevant background to the history of the trust in the English common law and in European legal history more generally. Its assertion is that the evidence presented from the archives of the Church's tribunals is of more than purely antiquarian interest. Three reasons support this assertion. First, ecclesiastical jurisdiction long played an important role in the English legal system. The common law claimed a limited competence, leaving many areas of human life to other courts, including those of the Church. Any account of English legal development that does not take account of ecclesiastical jurisdiction is therefore an incomplete account. Second, the *ius commune* brought into England by the Church influenced the growth of the common law itself at several points and in several ways. Its overall importance did not remain confined within the jurisdictional limits that separated the courts of Crown and Church. Common lawyers knew something of it, and it is entirely legitimate to ask whether what they knew had a connection with the rise of the trust. Third (and of particular relevance to this volume), ecclesiastical jurisdiction in England was one of the bridges between law in England and Continental legal systems[5]. As will be explained at the end of the paper, it would certainly be incautious, and probably quite incorrect, to assert that the ecclesiastical courts developed a law of trusts, to suppose that it was then taken over by the royal courts, even by the Court of Chancery, and to suggest that this proved the existence of ties with Continental law. However, that does not mean that the English trust and its ecclesiastical counterpart existed in two entirely separate worlds. There were connections between them.

II. The Jurisdictional Setting

Description of the ecclesiastical trust requires a preliminary word of introduction for readers unfamiliar with the general history of ecclesiastical jurisdiction in England. During the Middle Ages, the English Church exercised a considerable subject matter jurisdiction over both the laity and the clergy. Among other things the ecclesiastical courts had virtually exclusive competence over matrimonial causes, testamentary matters concerned with personal property, and the violation of oaths. A wide disciplinary jurisdiction over offenses against morality by lay men and women also existed. Defamation, sexual transgressions, and offenses against religion properly speaking fell within the exclusive jurisdiction of the Church in medieval England.

In exercising this jurisdiction the English Church enjoyed relative freedom from conflicts with the courts of the King[6]. Occasional disputes over jurisdiction did of

---

[5] *Knut Wolfgang Nörr*, The European Side of the English Law: a few Comments from a Continental Historian, in: Helmut Coing, Knut Wolfgang Nörr (eds.), Englische und kontinentale Rechtsgeschichte: ein Forschungsprojekt (= Comparative Studies in Continental and Anglo-American Legal History, vol. 1), 1985, p. 15: "Thus the *ius utrumque* as administered by the Church, joined England and the continent together".

course occur. The nature of a legal system in which jurisdiction was divided between spiritual and secular inevitably left room for disputes about the side of the division into which particular matters fell[7]. By and large, however, the conflict was less sharp than in most places on the Continent, and the English Church maintained its jurisdiction over the laity during the medieval period without substantial loss. The jurisdiction of the courts thus never became limited in practice to the regulation of the clergy, and, with some exceptions, the English common lawyers were content that most of the traditional jurisdictional boundaries should remain as they were. Maintenance of the Church's testamentary jurisdiction was particularly important in the context of the development of trusts.

It is also noteworthy that most aspects of the Church's medieval jurisdictional competence were retained over the course of the 16th century. Whatever its effects on the beliefs and habits of the people and whatever the consequences of the abolition of appeals to the Roman court, the English Reformation did not have a substantial impact on the scope of ecclesiastical jurisdiction. A few legal questions, it is true, were moved from one side of the boundary line to the other over the course of these turbulent years. However, apart from jurisdiction over oaths and trusts involving freehold land, both of which had already been lost to the Church by the time the Reformation began, none of the jurisdictional changes affected the trusts discussed in this contribution. This essay therefore omits any treatment of conflicts with the royal courts, except where they were directly relevant to the kind of trust being discussed.

III. Uses and Land

1. The Rise of the Feoffment to Uses in England

The most important early trust-like institution in England was the feoffment to uses. A person who held freehold land (called the feoffor in the English common law) conveyed it to grantees (the feoffees to uses), who would hold the land either for the benefit of the feoffor or that of other beneficiaries he named. Typically, the feoffment instructed the feoffees to hold the land for the benefit, not of any particular new beneficiaries, but of those persons the feoffor would later name in his last will and testament. In the meantime the trustees were to hold title for the feof-

6 See *David Millon*, Ecclesiastical Jurisdiction in Medieval England, 1984 University of Illinois Law Review 621 ff.; *R. L. Storey*, Clergy and common law in the reign of Henry IV, in: R. F. Hunnisett, J. B. Post (eds.), Medieval Legal Records Edited in Memory of C. A. F. Meekings, 1978, pp. 351 ff.; *W. R. Jones*, Relations of the Two Jurisdictions: Conflict and Cooperation in England during the thirteenth and fourteenth centuries, in: William M. Bowsky (ed.), Studies in Medieval and Renaissance History, vol. 7, 1970, pp. 79 ff.

7 For the period after the Reformation, see *Charles M. Gray*, The Writ of Prohibition: Jurisdiction in Early Modern English Law, 2 vols., 1994.

for's benefit. Using the technical terms of the common law, the feoffees were said to hold the land *ad opus*. Their tenancy was said to be for benefit of the *cestui que use*, a general term employed to designate the beneficiary, present or future[8].

In a general sense, the Church has long been associated with such trust-like devices. Indeed the connection has been traced back to the 4th century[9]. In England the connection is old. Perhaps the earliest appearance of such a device in an ecclesiastical setting is associated with the Crusades. Early crusaders sometimes conveyed their land to a trustee, to be held to the use of their wives or children while they were in the Holy Land[10]. It served, as many of the later uses also did, as a protective device, used to preserve the interests in property of men and women who would otherwise be exposed to special risk of loss.

The strongest early connection between the Church and the use in England is not, however, related to the Crusades, but rather to the Franciscans, who arrived in England early in the 13th century. As the contribution by *Karl Otto Scherner* in this volume shows, some of the legal consequences of this development in England were not greatly different from those that occurred in Germany. The rules of their order prohibited the Franciscans from owning income producing property. Apostolic poverty required this act of self-denial. But the friars had to have a place to live and eat and pray. Some means had to be found to reconcile their immediate needs with the rule of apostolic poverty. An added obstacle in England was presented by passage of the Statute of Mortmain in 1279. It prohibited direct gifts of lands and tenements to religious houses without royal assent[11]. There was thus a double problem.

It was the feoffment to uses that provided an answer. It became the means by which the benefactions for the Franciscans could be reconciled with both the letter of the Statute of Mortmain and the requirements of apostolic poverty. Trustees were found, and land meant to sustain the Franciscans was conveyed first to these fiduciaries to be held to the use of the friars[12]. For instance the corporation of the

---

8 *J. H. Baker,* An Introduction to English Legal History, 3rd ed., 1990, pp. 283 - 87.

9 See *Brendon F. Brown,* The Ecclesiastical Origin of the Use, (1935) 10 Notre Dame Lawyer 353 ff.; *Vincent R. Vasey,* Fideicommissa and Uses: the Clerical Connection Revisited, (1982) 42 The Jurist 201 ff.; *Shael Herman,* Utilitas Ecclesiae: the Canonical Conception of the Trust, (1996) 70 Tulane L.R. 2239.

10 *Frederick Pollock, F.W. Maitland,* History of English Law, 2nd ed., 1898, reissued 1968, vol. 2, p. 231.

11 7 Edw. I (*De viris religiosis*), Statutes of the Realm, vol. 1, 1810, p. 51. See *A. G. Little,* The Franciscans and the Statute of Mortmain, (1934) 49 English Historical Review 673 ff. and *Sandra Rabin,* Mortmain Legislation and the English Church, 1279 - 1500, 1982, pp. 29 - 30. That evasion of this statute lay behind the early popularity of the feoffment to uses has long been asserted; e.g. *Charles Viner,* A General Abridgement of Law and Equity, tit. Uses (A)(3), 2 ed., London, 1794, vol. 22, p. 179.

12 See esp. *Stephen W. DeVine,* The Franciscan Friars, the Feoffment to Uses, and Canonical Theories of Property Enjoyment before 1535, (1989) 10 J.L.H. 1 ff.

city of London became such a trustee, receiving land to be held for the benefit of those friars who lived within the city walls. As *Maitland* himself put it, "The nascent corporation was becoming a trustee"[13].

These examples were widely followed. Other ecclesiastical institutions employed uses for their own purposes[14], and they were soon joined by many laymen who had no intention of taking the cross or receiving the tonsure. The feoffment to uses provided English land holders with a way of avoiding some forms of feudal taxation and, more importantly, of evading the common law rule that prohibited testamentary devises of freehold land. Like the *fideicommissum* more broadly, the English use provided a way around inconveniences in the law of succession. By putting legal title into the hands of a third party, but leaving the beneficial use in the grantor and those he would name at a later date, many things could be accomplished that otherwise could not be. As a result, the use became a widespread institution from at least the 14th century[15].

2. The Ecclesiastical Courts and Enforcement

The principal problem with the use lay in its enforcement. At the time when uses were becoming widely adopted, the common law courts supplied a very limited recognition of the right of the beneficiaries to enforce their terms. Prior to the middle of the 15th century, when the Court of Chancery began to provide a remedy to disappointed beneficiaries, the problem was particularly acute. It has long seemed to legal historians, therefore, that the use must have been a purely informal device, dependent for its efficacy on moral suasion and familial influence, and therefore of uncertain reliability[16].

However, the records of the ecclesiastical courts show that, at least in some parts of England, the Church courts were active in enforcing some declarations of uses. They required the feoffees to fulfill the duties imposed by the feoffor, acting either under the Church's testamentary jurisdiction or as a part of its jurisdiction over oaths[17]. For example, in 1375 the feoffees to uses of a man named John Roger

---

13 *Pollock/Maitland* (n. 10) vol. 2, 231.

14 See, e.g., Original Papal Letters in England, 1305 - 1415, ed. P. N. R. Zutshi, 1990, No. 516 (1415), describing lands held for the see of Worcester as "in emphiteosim seu perpetuam firmam in evidentem utilitatem episcopi pro tempore existentis".

15 See generally, *A. W. B. Simpson,* The History of the Land Law, 2nd ed., 1986, pp. 173 - 207; *J. M. W. Bean,* The Decline of English Feudalism, 1215 - 1540, 1968.

16 *Maitland* was an exception. See *Pollock/Maitland* (n. 10) vol. 2, 232: "Some of them may have been enforced by the ecclesiastical courts".

17 A fuller exposition of the evidence is contained in The Early Enforcement of Uses, in: *R. H. Helmholz,* Canon Law and the Law of England, 1987, pp. 341 ff. The present contribution adds evidence discovered in the records since the above article was published. See also *Stephen W. DeVine,* Ecclesiastical Antecedents to Secular Jurisdiction over the Feoffment to

were cited to appear before the judge of the commissary court at Canterbury for allegedly having violated directions contained in Roger's will[18]. The feoffees did appear, confessing that they had been granted several parcels of land under instruction to convey it to Roger's wife after his death, contending moreover that they had not fulfilled his instructions because (they said) another man had compelled them to grant half the land to him. They held legal title to the land, it was admitted, and under the common law as it stood, the intended beneficiary would have been without a remedy. Not so in the spiritual forum. The judge of the ecclesiastical court at Canterbury decided that the compulsion the feoffees claimed was only a subterfuge, and declared that they should be obliged by ecclesiastical sanctions to fulfill the obligation originally imposed upon them by the feoffor. Thus did this ecclesiastical court enforce this trust-like institution. Although freehold land was involved, and therefore under some views beyond the matter fell outside the competence of the Church's courts, a way was found to fill the lacuna left by the royal courts. A testament was the ultimate source of the feoffee's obligation, and the use was enforced under the Church's testamentary jurisdiction.

The great majority of cases involving uses that came before the ecclesiastical courts were like this Canterbury case; they involved disputes about the intentions of a person who had died and left instructions about disposal of the lands in his will. Many of the cases seem to have been particularly difficult to resolve because the use had been declared *inter vivos* and the feoffor's testament had been silent or not entirely clear about the ultimate disposal of the land subject to a use. For instance, in a case from 1397, the three feoffees of Richard Pratt of Sturry in Kent were cited to appear before the commissary court and to be examined about the terms under which they had taken the decedent's lands and tenements[19]. Were they to apply the corpus for the soul of the decedent, or was it to be held as part of the assets of the estate? It was not clear. The feoffees contended that it had been the former, but others said the contrary, and the feoffees were required to verify their contention by canonical compurgation.

Such is the nature of the evidence concerning the Church's role in enforcing uses of land. There are two limitations to be noted in it. First, the only evidence of sustained enforcement of uses comes from two dioceses in the south of England, Canterbury and Rochester. Second, that evidence, which is relatively abundant in these two dioceses from the first half of the 15th century, disappears from the records after the middle of the century.

The second of these limitations is easier to understand than the first. The Court of Chancery began to offer a remedy to beneficiaries from about the middle of the

---

the Uses to be Declared in Testamentary Instructions, (1986) 30 American Journal of Legal History 295 ff.

18 Ex officio c. Smyth and Holynbroke (Canterbury 1375), CCA, Act book Y.1.1, f. 94v.

19 Ex officio c. Proude, Forstall and Forstall (Canterbury 1397), CCA, Act book Y.1.2, f. 27.

15th century. It was a natural consequence of such a change that the role of the spiritual courts in enforcing uses of land withered. There was no need for it. In any case, the Canon law of the Church claimed only a subsidiary competence over disputes over uses, as it did in most areas of law involving secular property[20], and it made sense even from the canonical point of view that the jurisdiction should last no longer than the need. That is in effect what happened.

The apparent geographical limitation to two English dioceses is more difficult to explain. It may be, however, that the accidents of record survival account for it, and that jurisdiction over uses was in fact exercised much more widely than at first appears. From the years before the 1450s, the court records from Canterbury and Rochester are more complete than from anywhere else in England. Since ecclesiastical jurisdiction over uses disappeared in the 1450s, it is natural that no trace of them can be found for other dioceses after that date. It may therefore be that the limitation reflects only the accidents of record survival, and if fuller records had survived before then, we would see more general enforcement elsewhere.

In support of this possibility, it can be said that there are isolated pre-1450 references to enforcement of uses in the fragmentary records that do exist from other dioceses. A 1394 cause from the diocese of York involved an acre of land originally granted to feoffees to the use of Roger Chamberleyn[21]. The question in dispute was whether or not he had directed that the land was to pass after his death in the way the party complaining had alleged. Similarly, an act book of 1442 from the diocese of Hereford records that Walter Harald, rector of a parish church, was cited to appear before the consistory court and to answer "with what intention he had received the feoffment" of the lands and tenements of William Marlowe[22]. He replied that he had received them only to the use of divine service in a chantry, thus refuting, or at least attempting to refute, the claims of the plaintiff who claimed to be the true beneficiary of Marlowe's use[23].

It cannot be contended that such isolated bits of evidence are sufficient to prove that regular enforcement of uses occurred outside of Canterbury and Rochester before 1450. And it is undeniable that once the records become more abundant in the late 15th and 16th centuries, cases involving uses and freehold land disappear from the records of the ecclesiastical courts. Only if the suggestion made by *Joseph Biancalana* in this volume – that testamentary executors were sometimes identical in all but title with feoffees to uses – turns out to be confirmed for post-1450 prac-

---

20 See Decretales Gregorii IX, ad X 2. 2. 11, and DD. ad *idem.*

21 Harpour and Braken (executors of Chamberleyn) c. Teryngton et ux. (York 1394), BIHR, CP.E.214. For more details, see *D. M. Smith,* Ecclesiastical Cause Papers at York: the Court of York 1301 - 1399, 1988, p. 71.

22 Ex officio c. Harald (1442), Herefordshire Record Office, Hereford, HD 4/1, O/2, p. 45: "qua intentione fuerat feoffatus".

23 *Idem* (n. 22): "quod huiusmodi terra et tenementa etc. post decessum suum remanerunt ad usum et opus divini servicii cantarie ecclesie de Layntwardyne".

tice in the spiritual courts, will it be possible to speak of continued enforcement of uses there. This possibility (and it is no more than that) arises because executors were routinely ordered to carry out the last wishes of decedents by the ecclesiastical courts. Sometimes those last wishes concerned land owned by the testator. If these executors were also feoffees to uses in fact, they were in effect being ordered to carry out wishes involving land they held to uses already. Only their formal title would have changed from pre-1450 practice. Perhaps it was an indirect way of avoiding a clash with royal jurisdiction.

Whatever the reality, it is also worth noting that English ecclesiastical lawyers continued to concern themselves with problems involving uses of land even after cases expressly dealing with feoffments to uses disappeared from their court records. In an early 17th century ecclesiastical lawyer's notebook, for example, one finds the following practice point: "Legacies and land given to the Church are to be passed to the feoffees, soe that those feoffees or the large part or a certain number of them, do name other feoffees before they shall die"[24]. Another example dealt with the consequences of a feoffment to uses in the context of a charitable gift made in favor of the poor of the town of Fulbourne[25]. Thinking about the subject of uses and land on the part of English ecclesiastical lawyers thus did not end in the middle of the 15th century, even though the direct enforcement of feoffments to uses in the ecclesiastical tribunals seems to have come to an end.

IV. Uses and Chattels

The English use was never restricted to land. Chattels could be held subject to a use from the earliest dates the institution comes into the historian's view[26]. Examination of the ecclesiastical court records confirms the frequency with which this happened, and it shows that uses of chattels were long subject to the jurisdiction of the church. This most basic point, one that demonstrates that ecclesiastical trusts existed in fact, is readily apparent in the records and is subject to no chronological or geographical limitations such as those found with uses of land. The records commonly stated that personal property was to be held and administered "to the use and for the advantage and benefit" of a named beneficiary. The courts acted to enforce those terms[27].

---

24 Worcestershire Record Office, Worcester, 794.093 BA 2470, Collectanea B, f. 127.

25 BIHR, MS. Prec.Bk.11, f. 14v.

26 E.g., The Cartulary of Blyth Priory, ed. *R. T. Timson,* 1973 - 74, no. 406 (1279), dealing with law books allegedly held by Ingeram Stirap to the use *(ad opus)* of Richard of Mattersay.

27 E.g., an entry from an act book in the diocese of Bath and Wells from 1533, Som. R.O., D/D/Ca 8, f. 43v: "Agnes Powynes ab intestata decessit cuius bona ministrat Johannes Saunders in usum commodum et utilitatem Walthiane filie eius".

Such language and the fiduciary relationship it created would have been familiar to any observer of practice in the ecclesiastical courts before 1640. Both appeared in many legal handbooks of court practice[28]. Indeed, the courts seem to have favored the creation of trusts. In 1623, when a man on his deathbed said to Sir Lewis Pemberton, "All that I have, I had from you, ... and I give it back to you to dispose of to the good of my wife and children as it shall please you only", the consistory court at Peterborough held that the decedent's words amounted to a declaration of a trust of his property "for the use and benefit" of his widow and children.[29] Pemberton was therefore ordered to act as trustee of the estate's assets.

The only thing unusual about this particular entry is the doubt about the decedent's intentions. Entries dealing with trusts like this one reflected established practice in the ecclesiastical courts. Trusts were created and enforced. The records dealing with their terms do not unfortunately answer all questions about which legal historians are rightly curious, but they do provide much useful information about the ways in which trusts were treated in the ecclesiastical forum. The information can be grouped roughly under one of 4 headings.

1. The Subject Matter

The corpus of the trusts mentioned in the court records covered a surprisingly broad spectrum of personal property. Among them are trusts in which books[30], cows[31], spoons[32], and sheep[33] were held to the use of a named beneficiary. In the vast majority of the cases, however, the corpus held in trust consisted of a sum of

28 E.g., *Henry Conset,* The Practice of the Spiritual or Ecclesiastical Courts, London, 1685, 294: property left by will "to the use and behoof of the said Minor".

29 Taken from a manuscript called "Law Precedents" in the catalogue, BL Harl. MS. 6891, fols. 2 - 3: Pemberton was to hold the decedent's property "in usum et commodum relicte et liberorum dicti defuncti disponeneda" (spelling modernized).

30 See *supra* n. 26.

31 Hart c. Pownde (Canterbury 1522), CCA, Act book Y.2.10, f. 126: "quandam vaccam ad custodiendum pro usu Thome Sebrand quousque dictus Thomas pervenerit ad legitimam etatem". In Holmes c. Wakelin (Lichfield, 1595), Lichfield Record Office, B / C / 5 / 1595, a cow was being held in trust for minors. The trustee responded to a charge that he had not fulfilled his duties: that he "dothe employe yt to the best profit of the children".

32 Redrise c. Carswell and Andro (Exeter 1534), Devon Record Office, Exeter, Act book Chanter MS. 778 s.d. 7 August. They were to be held by a Michael Brown, a proctor, "ad usum dicti Redrise".

33 Churchwardens of St. Oswald c. Forster and Sparew (Durham 1497), Department of Palaeography, The University of Durham, Act book CB.Pr.Off., f. 112v: twenty sheep allegedly bequeathed "ad usum invendiendum unam lampidem in choro ecclesie". In a Winchester visitation book of 1516 (Hants. R. O. B1 / 1, f. 59v), there is a reference to appearance by John Edwards who "fatetur quod pater suus legavit v oves ad manutenendum unum cereum coram sancto Tibbald quas voluit remanere in custodia sua tempore vite ipsius et post decessum ipsius remanere in custodia proximioris de sanguine".

money. At least the records stated it that way, although the amounts involved were sometimes large enough to make it unlikely that the money being held in trust was actually handed over in court or counted out in coin.

Some of the trusts were matters of real consequence. Historians commonly say that land was the principal form of wealth in medieval and early modern England, and doubtless this is true. There is, however, good evidence to show that contemporary lawyers regarded chattel interests in property as of legal importance[34]. Certainly some of the trust cases heard by the ecclesiastical courts involved considerable sums of money. The largest so far discovered involved £ 136 held in trust – this from a case heard in the consistory court of Bath and Wells in 1524[35]. £ 136 was a large sum of money in the early 16th century; the average weekly wage of an agricultural laborer at the time was only 2s[36]. It is true that the great majority of the trusts discovered seem to have been declared for smaller sums, ranging from £ 3 to £ 20 during the medieval period, rising slightly afterwards[37], but in a world where £ 1 was ten times the average weekly wage of a farm worker, these were not insignificant sums.

2. The Trustees

So far as can be determined from the act books, any person could lawfully act as a trustee. Doubtless there were more restrictions than were stated in the records, very likely conforming with the Canon law on the subject. Monks and unfree persons, for instance, were ordinarily excluded from such offices by the Canon law, and there are no cases in which one can say for sure that the persons acting as trustees were under the legal control of others, as monks and serfs were. However, women, who might be thought to fall into this category, did act as fiduciaries in at least some cases[38]. In part, their presence as trustees may be explained by the habit

34 *J. H. Baker,* The Reports of Sir John Spelman, vol. II (= Selden Society, vol. 94), 1977, pp. 209 ff.

35 The sum had been left by will to minor children, and was to be held by the testator's widow, "in usum utilitatem et commodum [of the named children]", Bath and Wells (1534), Som. R.O., Act book D/D/Ca 9a, f. 24. In Estate of Hunter (London 1514), Guildhall Library, London, Act book 9064/11, f. 126v, the sum of £ 56 was being held for the use of orphans. The sum of £ 350 was mentioned in Horsey v. Horsey (Ct. of High Commission 1631), CUL, Act book Dd.2.21, f. 23v, but it is not entirely clear that this case fell within ecclesiastical jurisdiction.

36 *James E. Thorold Rogers,* Six Centuries of Work and Wages, 1949, p. 388. Thus the amount in the case was 1,360 times the average wage.

37 E.g., Powell c. Deane (Archdeaconry of Essex 1630), Essex Record Office, Chelmsford, Act book D/AEC 10, f. 34, recording that the defendant "ad evitandas lites" admitted to receiving £ 10 each to the use *(ad usum)* of each of three children. By this time, of course, the value of the amounts involved would have been much less than during the Middle Ages.

38 Estate of Moone (York 1592), BIHR, Exch.AB.5, fols. 105 - 06, a challenge to the administration of Elizabeth Moone on the basis of her actions as trustee, but not against incapa-

of attaching trusteeship to specific offices, such as testamentary executors or sequestrators appointed to collect the revenues of a vacant parish church. Women commonly served as testamentary executors and administrators in England. It was natural, therefore, that the records should sometimes describe them as holding to the use of a third party when they were acting in that capacity. The trusteeship went with the office.

At the same time, women were certainly not named as trustees at anything approaching their proportionate share of the population. Men acted in the overwhelming number of cases. They often acted in concert. As was true with feoffments to uses of land, frequently more than one man was named to administer trusts of chattels. The existence of multiple trustees preserved continuity of administration, or at least made it easier, where one fiduciary died during the life of the trust.

3. Objects of the Trusts

The objects for which uses were created and enforced in the ecclesiastical courts covered a very considerable range of activities. Although the distinction is not one made in the records themselves, some trusts one would class as charitable in purpose. Some were private. A relatively full example may be instructive. In the 1370s, William Sawtre, rector of the parish church of Gransden in the diocese of Ely, found that he could no longer carry out the duties required by his benefice; he was, the act book stated, "old, blind, deaf, and decrepit"[39]. Retiring with a pension was apparently impossible under the circumstances, but so was continued service. In consequence, a portion of the income coming from his church was assigned to two men, Walter Rede and John Sawtre, who were to receive the income "ad utilitatem et commodum dicti rectoris". These two were required to use the assets for the rector's benefit, presumably until he died[40]. Indeed they had previously taken an oath to that effect. At least according to the complaint that had been made against them in the consistory court, Rede and Sawtre had failed to carry out that

city to act because she was a woman. Similar is Howell c. Sabot (Winchester 1524), Hants. R.O., Act book 21 M 65/C1/2, f. 82. The allegation was that the defendant Emmota Sabot had received £ 20 to dispose for the soul's health of her brother. She was cited for violating the terms in her brother's last will and testament, and ultimately £ 15 was awarded to another person to hold to the same uses. Seemingly, she was permitted to keep the £ 5. In a case from the diocese of Exeter in 1629, recorded in Devon Record Office, Act book, Chanter MS. 803, s.d. 11 December, Susanna Southcott was acting as trustee for four named children in a *causa legati*.

39 CUL, Act book EDR D/2/1, fols. 51v and 57 (1376): "senis surdus cecus et valetudinarius".

40 Similar in substance though different in occasion were sequestrations of benefices during vacancies; their revenues were to be held, "ad usum futuris incumbentis". E.g., BIHR, Prec.Bk.12, 10.

oath and their duties as fiduciaries, and an accounting was being demanded of them. How the case came out we do not know, but the dispute well illustrates the kind of trust relationship that commonly came before a spiritual court.

There are many examples. The records produce contested cases of trusts declared in favor of the insane[41], orphans and other minor children[42], women in distress[43], and elderly men and women[44]. Gifts to be held for the benefit of the poor generally[45], for the needs of a specific parish church or other religious organization[46], or even for a London guild[47], were among the purposes of cases found in the court records. Something like a trust declared in favor of creditors occasionally appears among testamentary matters, as could happen when a person died bankrupt

---

41 KAO, DRb O10 (15th century precedent book), f. 30: "ad custodiendum servandum et fideliter administrandum ad usum et utilitatem ipsius [the insane person]".

42 CCA, MS. D 8 (15th century precedent book), f. 47: oath for a tutor "de fideliter convertendo dictam pecuniam in usus et utilitatem dicti minoris". See also Marsh's Library, Dublin, MS. Z.3.1.18, Pt. 2 (16th century precedent book), fols. 71v-72v, where this language was used: "ad ipsius commodum proficuum et utilitatem debite conservandum". In Guildhall Library, London, Act book 9064 / 11, f. 126v (1514), the words were "ad usum dictorum orphanorum usque cum venerunt ad etatem legitimam". The same feature appears to have been found in Scotland; see *A. E. Anton,* Medieval Scottish Executors and the Courts Spiritual, (1955) 67 Juridical Review 145.

43 In 1490 a man who had committed adultery with Elizabeth Medigo was required to pay £ 4 to two named men, who were thereafter to administer that sum "ad usum dicte Elizabethae". See also an example in: *William Hale,* A Series of Precedents and Proceedings in Criminal Causes, 1475 - 1640, 1st ed., 1847, reprint 1973, pp. 18 - 19. Similar is Stevenson al. Bloncke c. Young al. Bloncke (York 1612 - 13), BIHR, CP.H.868: in it Thomas King, a cleric, had been left £ 30 in the testament of Nicholas Bloncke "for and to the use of the said Anne (the plaintiff)". She claimed that this had been "for and in consideration of manifest wronge donne by him the said Nicholas unto her" in selling lands that had belonged to her. More common in the records was a simple devise to a grown child or to another fiduciary of "omnia bona ad sustentationem matris sue". E.g., Estate of Cade (Rochester 1458), KAO, Act book DRb Pa 3, f. 357.

44 Ex officio c. Lambolde (Winchester 1525), Hants. R. O., Act book 21 M 65 / C1 / 2, f. 131v: The allegation was that the defendant had received goods from a woman named Christiana Balsse "ad alimentandum se in senectute sua". Another probable example: Ex officio c. Tiherst (Rochester 1446), KAO, Act book DRb Pa 2, f. 76, dealing with lands to be held by the trustee from Simon Michell "ad inveniendum eidem Simoni durante vita sua victus sui necessaria et post eius mortem tenebatur solvere predictis feoffatis [of Simon]".

45 E.g. a testamentary gift from the diocese of Rochester in 1591: Ex officio c. Pilcher (1591), KAO, Act book DRb Pa 21: "xii d. ad usum pauperum".

46 As, for example, for the benefit of a specific church, but not naming any particular use of the fund. Elmeley c. Lemerch (Bath and Wells 1460), Som. R.O., Act book D / D / Ca 1, pp. 18 - 19: "applicandos ad aliquod opus necessarium eiusdem ecclesie iuxta advisamentum et discretionem eorundem rectoris et custodum". Another example: Worthyngton c. Bucke et al. (Gloucester 1554), Gloucester Record Office, Act book GDR 7B, p. 321, describing the defendants as *custodes* of the revenues of the parish church of Bibury. They were being required to render an accounting.

47 BL, Harl. MS. 2179 (15th century precedent book, f. 81v: "in usus ipsius gilde necessarios".

and a trustee was appointed to administer the remaining assets for the benefit of the decedent's creditors[48].

In sum, the continuing trust of chattels was a frequent feature of ecclesiastical court practice. These trusts were employed in a variety of situations, but most commonly where a legacy to minor children was involved or where property could usefully be administered for the benefit of disadvantaged persons, often persons who would have qualified as *miserabiles personae* under the Canon law. Settling a decedent's estate or administering the revenues of a vacant church also provided frequent occasions for trusts to be established.

4. Remedies and Basis for Liability

It is disappointing that little detailed information about the nature of the law applied in trust cases is forthcoming from examination of the act books. They were formal records, of course, and by their nature they contained little by way of statement about the law being applied. Sometimes legitimate inference is possible, but we cannot know, for example, whether the courts traced the proceeds of an improper sale by the trustee into the hands of a purchaser, *bona fide* or *mala fide.* Whether any formal separation was made between legal title and equitable title – a hallmark of the English common law of trusts – simply cannot be ascertained. There is not a hint in the records. This "basic question" of where title to the property held in trust lies – often an unsettled problem in civil law regimes that have adopted trust-like institutions[49] – seems also to have been unsettled in the pre-1640 English ecclesiastical practice. And whether these trust-like devices were regarded as belonging to the law of contracts or to that of property is quite impossible to determine. Indeed these questions seem not to have been asked.

What one can say with assurance on the basis of the evidence is that the duty of trustees was not simply a matter of choice or moral obligation on their part. A formal accounting could be and often was required of them. In such accountings, which were normally brought before the courts by the beneficiaries themselves[50], questions were raised about the propriety of their actions. Trustees had to satisfy the courts that they had fulfilled their duties. In fact, the demand for an accounting

48 Estate of Symons (Bristol 1565), Bristol Record Office, Act book EP/J/1/6, p. 259: "ad usum dictorum creditorum". It is not clear how long this "trust" was to last, however, and it seems more likely than not that it was to endure no longer than it took to make a ratable distribution to the creditors.

49 *Adair Dyer, Hans van Loon,* Report on Trusts and analogous institutions, in: Conférence de La Haye de droit international privé, Actes et documents de la Quinzième session 8 au 20 octobre 1984, vol. 2: Trust, 1985, p. 30.

50 E.g., Blande c. Oughton (Lincoln 1554), Lincolnshire Archives Office, Act book Cj/7, f. 58: "ad promotionem Willelmi Blande ad reddendum compotum administrationis bonorum Willelmi Blande".

assumed a common name in the act books; it was styled *negotium compoti*[51]. The records speak of a "faithful accounting" being required in such cases, and this was also the language used in the oath fiduciaries commonly took upon assuming their duties in the first place.

Disputes about many individual actions taken by trustees occurred as one part of these accountings. An illustrative example comes from the diocese of Rochester in 1591. William Stayne had received assets from the estate of Alexander Wayman. Wayman's testament charged Stayne "to see the children of the said Alexander well brought up" and to pay over their portions to them when they reached the age of sixteen. The children involved were still under that age at the time the litigation had begun, and it was alleged against Stayne that he had "no regard of their bringing up, but wasteth their portions in so much that it is greatly doubtfull that their portions will be all spent before they shall come to be of age". The remedy sought was to require him to provide a sufficient bond (*cautio)* for payment of the portions.

In other cases, seemingly where more extreme misconduct was alleged, actual removal of the trustee was sought[52]. But whatever the precise remedy invoked against trustees, a failure to comply with the ecclesiastical court's direction meant that they would be excommunicated for disobedience. Refusal to comply amounted to contumacy in the ecclesiastical law, and this could lead quickly to a sentence of excommunication against an "unfaithful" trustee. In England, such a sentence could entail loss of important civil rights, even imprisonment where contumacy continued for a length of time[53]. The Church's legal system, including the law of trusts it administered, did not depend upon voluntary compliance by the laity involved. It had teeth.

V. Was the Trust Transplanted?

At first blush, the cumulation of the evidence suggests that the English trust found its earliest home within the ecclesiastical courts. It is even tempting to think

51 E.g., Knowles c. Jon (Carlisle 1633), Cumbria Record Office, Carlisle, Act book DRC 3/3, p. 51. This was a promoted *ex officio* action brought against Frances John "pro redditione compoti in bonis Roberti Jon". The action was probably brought in connection with her husband's estate and administration in favour of children.

52 Ex officio c. Stayne (Rochester 1591), KAO, Act book DRb Pa 20, f. 51. See also an action begun by the supervisor of a testament to require the guardian of the decedent's children: "ad inveniendum sufficientem securitatem de salvo custodiendo dicta bona remanencia ud usum dictorum orphanorum usque cum venerint ad etatem legitimam". £ 56 was involved. Estate of Hunter (London 1513), Guildhall Library, London, Act book 9064/11, f. 126v.

53 See *F. Donald Logan,* Excommunication and the Secular Arm in Medieval England, 1968. The system lasted into the 19th century, despite widespread sentiment that it was obsolete even among the civilians. See *S. M. Waddams,* Law, Politics and the Church of England: The Career of Stephen Lushington 1782 - 1873, 1993, pp. 13, 258.

of the trust as a transplant, one which had its origins in the Roman law as filtered through the medium of the medieval Canon law. The suggestion does not lack plausibility. The trust entered the English common law primarily through the Court of Chancery, and many of the Chancery officials were trained in the *ius commune*. Canonical models were widely followed in the Chancery's procedural law, for instance. The trust would appear to be another instance of a not uncommon pattern[54]. Indeed the connection between the trust and Roman law was once a commonplace. Prior to the late 19th century and the scholarship of *O.W. Holmes* and *F.W. Maitland*, it was widely assumed that the use or trust had in fact been derived from the Roman law *fideicommissum*.

However, a fuller consideration of the evidence cautions against too ready acceptance of this suggestion. It would certainly go farther than the evidence allows to speak of the trust as an institution imported into the English common law from the *ius commune*, and there is some evidence that points in the opposite direction.

1. The Negative Side

First, there is no direct causal evidence that the trust came from the *ius commune*. Admittedly, the lack of direct evidence is not necessarily determinative. Sometimes there is no clear evidence of borrowing, even in situations where it is recognized by all scholars that civilian influence played a role in the development of the common law. Still, it weakens the case. Moreover, in this instance, a negative answer to the question is suggested by the ecclesiastical records themselves. The trusts described in this paper were never treated by the ecclesiastical lawyers as falling under the same heading. There was not, in other words, "a law of trusts" or a "law of uses" within the jurisdiction of the English ecclesiastical courts.

This is a telling absence. It means that the law of trusts could not have been a transplant because there was no law of trusts to be transplanted. Jurisdiction in the English ecclesiastical courts was divided by subject matter, somewhat along the lines of the famous "forms of action" in the royal courts. Accordingly, there was a *causa matrimonialis* and a *causa testamentaria*, and all litigation involving marriage or testaments was classified accordingly in the court records. But there was no *causa usus*. Still less was there a *causa fiduciaria* or a *causa fideicommissi* in the English ecclesiastical forum. Instead, the cases involving uses of lands and chattels discussed above were recorded, and I think also regarded, as belonging within some other subject matter area, most often the law of last wills and testaments.

---

54 It fulfils the requirement of accessibility that is normal in cases of transplantation; see *Alan Watson*, Legal Transplants: An Approach to Comparative Law, 2nd ed., 1993, p. 113.

It is revealing, I think, that the standard index to the Provinciale of *William Lyndwood* (d. 1446), the most famous medieval English writer on ecclesiastical law, contains no entry for *fideicommissum, fiducia,* or *usus*. In this, he followed not only English customary practice. He also followed the law of the Decretals[55], which likewise had no special title devoted to trusts. Although the fiduciary principle underlay much of the Canon law, as *Shael Herman's* contribution to this volume shows, the trust was not one of the legal categories around which ecclesiastical jurisdiction was organized. No provincial constitutions and no legal headings were devoted to uses or trusts. That fact prevented, or at least seriously hindered, the English civilians from thinking about trusts as forming a distinct area of the law.

It is significant that after the Reformation no English civilian wrote a treatise about trusts. The 16th century witnessed the enactment of statutes that had an impact on practice in the ecclesiastical courts. As a consequence, English ecclesiastical lawyers felt compelled to produce works on virtually all areas of their practice. The changes in law meant that there was a market for such works. The law of procedure, tithes, marriage, testaments, and usury all attracted civilian authors for this reason[56]. Not so the law of trusts. No treatise or tract was written. Even the more general treatises written by English civilians on the ecclesiastical law of England do not contain sections devoted to trusts, uses, or *fideicommissa*[57]. The standard Sweet & Maxwell bibliography of English law contains fourteen separate titles concerning the law of tithes written by the 1640s[58]. It has no entry at all for trusts.

Evidently, the civilians (and most common lawyers for that matter) did not regard the trust as a distinct legal category. At least the civilians did not think of it as a subject that belonged within their jurisdiction, and this meant that there was nothing definite about which they could write. One searches in vain, for example, for any treatment by the civilians of the question that so exercised later and more systematic commentators: whether the beneficiary of a trust held a *ius in rem* or simply a *ius in personam* against the trustee[59].

Indeed, it is fair to say that the 17th century civilians often treated the analogous *fideicommissum* as more properly belonging within the jurisdiction of the Court of

55 The harmonization of English practice with the law of the Western Church was a continuing theme in his work. See *Brian Edwin Ferme,* Canon Law in Late Medieval England: A Study of William Lyndwood's *Provinciale* with particular reference to Testamentary Law, 1996.

56 This literature is described briefly in *R. H. Helmholz,* Roman Canon Law in Reformation England, 1990, pp. 121 - 57.

57 So *John Ayliffe,* Parergon juris canonici Anglicani, 1st ed., London, 1726; *Francis Clerke,* Praxis ... in foro ecclesiastico, 1st ed., Dublin, 1664; *John Godolphin,* Repertorium canonicum: or Abridgment of the Ecclesiastical Laws of this Real consistent with the Temporal, London, 1684.

58 W. H. Maxwell, L. F. Maxwell (eds.), A Legal Bibliography of the British Commonwealth of Nations, vol. 1: English Law to 1800, 1955, pp. 190 - 97.

59 See *Hein Kötz,* Trust und Treuhand, 1963, § 13.

Chancery than within their own[60]. As proved true on the Continent itself, a developed law of trusts considered as a legal category worthy of study in itself was a product of a later period. It was only with the arrival of the 19th century that treatises on the English law of trusts began to be written[61].

2. The Positive Side

This is the negative. It deals with the possibility of a wholesale transplant of the institution of the trust. Things may always look slightly different when examined in detail and from a different angle, however, and in fact they do. Many points of law that became important in the developed English law of trusts seem to have been taken from the *ius commune*. English civilians constantly used the texts of the Roman and Canon laws in stating the rules relevant to the trust-like institutions discussed in this paper. For instance an ecclesiastical formulary now in the Cambridge University Library noted in its margins a law from the Digest's title, *De annuis legatis et fideicommissis,* presumably the foundation for the trust in favor of children recorded next to it[62]. This annotator was dealing with a practical problem of the law of wills and testaments, not a more general law of trusts. And in this he was typical. In more elaborate treatments of the law, the civilians frequently invoked treatises of the Continental commentators in formulating the principles that governed trust-like institutions, but it does not appear that they were alluding to a "law of trusts".

Examples of recourse by the English ecclesiastical lawyers to the *ius commune* in such situations are legion. *William Lyndwood* defined the fiduciary character of the office of the testamentary executor by citing texts from the Digest, the Gregorian Decretals, and the Novels. He made use of the *Commentaria* on the Decretals by *Joannes Andreae* for the same purpose[63]. Similarly, in stating the requirement of consent by beneficiaries and the importance of the principle of utility in the division and uses of the resources of a parish church, the more obscure English canonist, *John Lydford* (d. 1407), cited the works of *Hostiensis* and *Joannes Andreae* in

---

60 See Civilian's notebook (c. 1615), London Guildhall Library, MS. 11448, f. 153: "If a fidecomissarie bee wished to paie a legacie to another the legatarie cannot sue in our law, because hee can sue none but the exequutor, yet in the chauncerie there is reliefe".

61 The earliest listed in the standard bibliography is *F. W. Sanders,* Essay on Uses and Trusts, 1791. It went into five editions. There were five other treatises on trusts published in the first half of the 19th century. See John S. James, L. F. Maxwell (eds.), A Legal Bibliography of the British Commonwealth of Nations: English Law from 1801 to 1954, 2nd ed., 1957, p. 513.

62 CUL, Add. MS. 8866, 46 - 47; the reference is to D. 33, 1, 21, 4.

63 *William Lyndwood,* Provinciale (seu Constitutiones Angliae), Oxford, 1679, 178, s.v. moderatis, and 179, s.v. propriis suis bonis. Many other examples of such usage of Continental commentaries and texts can be found in *Ferme* (n. 55).

addition to several texts from the Decretals and *Gratian's* Decretum[64]. As *Michele Graziadei's* contribution in this volume shows happened with principles of *fiducia* in the works of Continental writers of the *ius commune*, so did it happen with the medieval English ecclesiastical lawyers.

This habit of mind did not die with the 16th century. Although the Protestant Reformation severed the ties between England and the Roman Church for most purposes, it did not break all ties between the English ecclesiastical lawyers and the evolving *ius commune*. The *ius commune* continued to supply the principal source of their jurisprudence. For instance, *Henry Swinburne* (d. 1624), the best of the English civilian writers on testamentary law, cited the treatises of *Bartolus de Saxoferrato, Jason de Mayno* and *Michael Grassus* in stating the rule that one of the privileges of a charitable testamentary trust was that it could exist without specific beneficiaries being named in a decedent's last will and testament[65]. Similarly, the prolific civilian, *John Godolphin* (d. 1678), took the distinction between words that imposed a trust upon a legatee and those which merely expressed the testator's wish that the legatee spend the legacy in a certain way directly from the *glossa ordinaria* to *De legatis II* in the Digest and from *Bartolus'* Commentaries on the same title[66]. Finally, the author of an anonymous treatise on the testamentary executor written around 1600 drew many of his conclusions about the law of scope of the fiduciary obligation from the treatise by *Joannes Jacobus a Canibus* (d. 1490) that was included in the influential *Tractatus universi iuris*[67]. He also made use of (though less frequently) a long list of writers from the Continent, including *Bartolus, Joannes Andreae, William Durantis,* and what he called the "Compendium fidecommissarium" by *Jacobus de Arena*[68].

This kind of "piecemeal" influence derived from the civil and Canon laws in fact outlasted active ecclesiastical jurisdiction over trusts in England. Rules drawn from the learned laws were applied in the temporal courts, and eventually some of

---

64 Dorothy M. Owen (ed.), John Lydford's Book, 1974, p. 183.

65 *Henry Swinburne,* A Brief Treatise of Testaments and Last Willes, 1590, reprint 1978, Part 1 § 16.5, speaking about testamentary gifts for the benefit of the poor. On this author, see *J. Duncan/M. Derrett,* Henry Swinburne (?1551 - 1624) Civil Lawyer of York, 1973.

66 *John Godolphin,* The Orphan's Legacy: or a Testamentary Abridgment, London, 1701, Pt. III, Ch. 22, no. 17. There is no thorough treatment dealing with this civilian and his work, but there is a useful summary: *J. H. Baker,* Famous English Canon Lawyers: VII: John Godolphin and Richard Burn, 1994 Ecclesiastical Law Journal 214 ff.

67 BL, MS. Cleo F 1, f. 359 ff. This manuscript seems to have had some connection with the chief probate court in England, the Prerogative Court of Canterbury in London, but I have not yet been able to trace its authorship.

68 The reference must be to the treatise by this author that appeared in the Tractatus universi iuris and is noted in *Martinus Lipenus,* Bibliotheca realis iuridica, Leipzig, 1757, reprint 1970, vol. 1, p. 278. The treatise contains a list of authors used; the principal authors are *Joannes Oldendorpius* and *Benedictus Capra.* The author did not exclude English common law authors, however, making use *inter alia* of *Brooke's* Abridgement, *Fitzherbert's* Novel Natura Brevium, and *Christopher St. Germain's* Doctor and Student.

them were incorporated within the general English law of trusts. As the contribution by *Michael Macnair* in this volume shows, using Continental sources to shape the emerging law of trusts was a method that some English common lawyers shared with the civilians. Thus, although in this instance it is mistaken to speak in terms of a "reception" of a civilian institution – indeed no such institution had come into being by 1640 – it *is* right to think that some of the elements of trust law in England were shaped by the *ius commune*. The process happened gradually and without much notice being taken of it.

VI. Conclusion

At least if the concept of a trust is defined broadly as a continuing device by which one person holds property and administers it for the benefit of another, trusts were a part of English ecclesiastical court jurisdiction for a very long time. They existed centuries before there came to be a separate concept of "the trust". No such concept had emerged by the mid-seventeenth century, when the coverage of this paper ends, although trusts had long existed in practice before that date. They were an expression of the ideals of the Canon law sketched in this volume by *Professor Herman*, and they made frequent use of rules drawn from the Roman law. In practice, they had become one means of protecting the interests of men and women, most of whom were unfortunates and needed special protection. Trusts in this sense were very much a part of the English legal landscape at the same time, and even before, the Chancery's jurisdiction over uses became established. It may be speculation to attribute any particular legal importance to that fact, but it is a reasonable speculation. The existence of so many trusts seem likely to have played some role in the evolution of the trust in English law.

That the trusts enforced in the ecclesiastical courts served as a bridge between English and Continental law also seems very likely. Certainly it has long been accepted that many of the legal rules applied to their interpretation and implementation came from the literature of the *ius commune*. The English civilians referred constantly to it in discussing the law regulating executors, legacies, and trust-like institutions. Reference to the learned laws was the norm of practice within the spiritual forum in England, at least up to 1640, and it can be no surprise to find that the evidence from the law of trusts conforms to it.

Like the testamentary executors described in *Reinhard Zimmermann's* contribution to this volume, English trusts do not fit a uniform pattern. They were different in several particulars when compared to the institutions found in the *ius commune*. This should not of itself exclude the possibility that substantive connections existed, although it would be easier to assess the possibility if more research had been done on the records of the ecclesiastical courts on the Continent. However, the *ius commune* certainly provided much of the law that applied to trusts in the English courts, and there are interesting parallels with Continental practice visible already[69]. When due allowance has been made for the inevitable variations in jurisdictional competence that existed within the Western Church, the larger pattern of fiduciary law does not seem so very different.

---

69 See, e.g., *Anne Lefebvre-Teillard,* Les Officialités à la veille du Concile de Trente, 1973, pp. 259 ff.

NEIL JONES

Trusts in England after the Statute of Uses: A View from the 16th Century

I. Introduction

The Statute of Uses 1536[1] marks a watershed in the history of trusts in England, forming "the starting point of [the] modern law of uses and trusts"[2]. Yet the period of something over a century immediately after the passage of the statute has long been one of the "dark places" of English legal history[3].

Our approach to the statute has cast its own shadow. Fascinated both by its supposed significance in the defence of the royal feudal revenue, and by the ease with which it might be evaded by the addition, as *Lord Hardwicke* put it, of "at most three words to a conveyance"[4], we have misunderstood or neglected much of importance in the decades after 1536. But understanding has not been easy, for there are shadows in the evidence too. "The object of the report from the very first is science, jurisprudence, the advancement of learning"[5], but in the years after 1536 the gladsome light of jurisprudence has shone but dimly over trusts[6], the relative lack of equity reports and analytical treatment of trusts thrown all the more into relief by the beacon of *Lord Nottingham's* work in the later 17th century[7]. The his-

1 27 Hen. VIII, c. 10. Unless otherwise indicated, all manuscripts are in the Public Record Office. Dates are given in new style. Quotations from manuscripts in English have been rendered into modern orthography. Brief explanations of technical terms of English property law are given in the notes where appropriate; for a more detailed introductory treatment see *F. H. Lawson, B. Rudden,* The Law of Property, 2nd ed., Oxford, 1982.

2 *W. S. Holdsworth,* History of English Law, vol. IV, London, 1924, p. 409. The Romans, said *Lord Nottingham,* "made a law much like our statute of 27 Hen. 8 [of Uses] called *senatusconsultum Trebellianum et Pegasianum* by which they made cestui que use to be heir in substance": D.E.C. Yale (ed.), Lord Nottingham's "Manual of Chancery Practice" and "Prolegomena of Chancery and Equity", Cambridge, 1965, p. 252.

3 D.E.C. Yale (ed.), Lord Nottingham's Chancery Cases, vol. II, London, 1961, p. *88.*

4 *Hopkins v. Hopkins* (1738) 1 Atk. 581 at 591.

5 F. W. Maitland (ed.), Yearbooks of 1 and 2 Edward II, London, 1903, Selden Society vol. 17, p. x.

6 "My lord Coke's pretty phrase about the gladsome light of jurisprudence", as *Maitland* put it, is from the epilogue to Coke Upon Littleton: C. H. S. Fifoot (ed.), The Letters of Frederic William Maitland, London, 1965, p. 17 and note.

tory of trusts in England in the 16th century must be written without treatise literature of the type which begins to be available from the later 17th century.

But though some lights will never come on again, and much remains to be done, we may now say more about trusts in England between the Statute of Uses and the time of *Lord Nottingham* than has previously been possible. Study of the Chancery record between 1536 and 1660, together with examination of manuscript reports, Inns of Court readings, and conveyancing precedents and muniments has begun to shed new light upon this dark place in English legal history, and in particular upon the years before 1600 which are the subject of this paper[8].

II. The Difficulty of Definition

"No doubt we should like to begin our discussion with a definition of a 'trust'. But I know not where to find an authoritative definition"[9]. *Maitland's* difficulty remains. "Many attempts have been made to define a trust, but none of them has been wholly successful"[10]. *Maitland* himself defined a trust as follows: "When a person has rights which he is bound to exercise on behalf of another or for the accomplishment of some particular purpose he is said to have those rights in trust for that other or for that purpose and he is called a trustee"[11]. *Maitland* then sought to comment upon this "wide vague definition" by "distinguishing cases of trust from some other cases". This in some measure we shall do also[12]. But a consideration of the trust itself will come first. It will be helpful to begin with an illustration, before proceeding to consider trust property, and the nature of the beneficiary's interest.

The litigation in Chancery in *Bertie v. Herenden* (1560) has been well known since *J. H. Baker's* publication of a report of it made in 1572 by *Nicholas Barham,* serjeant at law[13]. Richard Bertie sued on behalf of his wife Katharine, dowager Duchess of Suffolk[14]. Lady Katharine, clearly a protestant by 1547[15], left England

---

7 D.E.C. Yale (ed.), Lord Nottingham's Chancery Cases, 2 vols., London, 1957 and 1961, Selden Society vols. 73 and 79. Nottingham's reports cover the period 1673 - 1682. The lack of reports of Chancery cases before Nottingham's time is not complete: see *M. Macnair,* The Nature and Function of the Early Chancery Reports, in: C. Stebbings (ed.), Law Reporting in Britain, London and Rio Grande, 1995, pp. 123 ff. Printed reports, and those in manuscript Chancery collections may be examined with ease. More difficult are isolated cases outside Chancery collections.

8 A fuller account of this stage of the work will be found in *N. G. Jones,* Trusts, Practice and Doctrine: 1536 - 1660, unpublished University of Cambridge Ph.D. dissertation, 1994.

9 *F. W. Maitland,* Equity, 3rd ed. J. Brunyate, Cambridge, 1936, p. 43.

10 *J.E. Martin,* Hanbury and Martin, Modern Equity, 14th ed., London, 1993, p. 46.

11 *Maitland* (n. 9) 44.

12 Section VI. *infra.*

13 *J. H. Baker,* The Use upon a Use in Equity 1558 - 1625, (1977) 93 L.Q.R. 33 ff.

early in 1555 in the face of the Marian persecution to join her husband on the continent. The accession of Elizabeth allowed the fugitives to return, and litigation was begun both at common law and in Chancery. The action at common law concerned the restoration of forfeited lands without a fine for contempt in disobeying a command to return[16]. The Chancery suit considered certain transfers of property which had been made by Lady Katharine and her husband before leaving England.

Firstly, various chattels personal[17] had been delivered to the defendant, Walter Herenden, a member of Gray's Inn[18], and steward of Lady Katharine's Lincolnshire manors. Secondly, a lease[19] had been granted of all Bertie and Lady Katharine's Lincolnshire manors, lands, tenements and hereditaments, to Herenden, and to Thomas and Alice Bertie, Richard's parents. The third transfer, which pre-dated the lease, was a conveyance "to the only use and behoof of the said Walter Herenden and of his heirs"[20], of freehold land[21] in Lincolnshire, Norfolk and Warwickshire.

Title at law was very firmly in Walter Herenden, but that was not the end of the matter: the aim of the Chancery litigation was to demonstrate that the personalty, the lease, and the realty were all held upon trust for Bertie and his wife. A decree was made in favour of the plaintiffs, it being found proved by the evidence of witnesses and by "divers notes of account, letters and other notes in writing" that the lease had been made, and that the lands in Lincolnshire, Norfolk and Warwickshire had been conveyed, to Herenden and his heirs "upon special, faithful and secret trust and confidence, and to have been employed to the use and behoof of [Bertie]

---

14 For biographical detail, see *Lady Georgina Bertie,* Five Generations of a Loyal House, London, 1845, pp. 1 - 56; *Lady Cecilie Goff,* A Woman of the Tudor Age, London, 1930; *E. Read,* Catherine, Duchess of Suffolk, London, 1962. For the exile see *C. H. Garrett,* The Marian Exiles, Cambridge, 1938, pp. 87 - 89.

15 *S. J. Gunn,* Charles Brandon, Duke of Suffolk, Oxford, 1988, p. 199.

16 Dyer 176.

17 English law distinguishes between real property and personal property, real property being interests in land other than leasehold interests, and personal property being leases and interests in moveables. Moveables are called chattels personal, while leases are called chattels real.

18 *J. Foster,* Register of Admissions to Gray's Inn 1521 - 1889, London, 1889, col. 14.

19 In this context a lease is a grant of land to be held of the grantor for a fixed term of years.

20 *Bertie* (n. 14) 500 - 502 (indenture, dated 30 March 1554, enrolled at Maidstone 9 June 1563); Common Pleas Feet of Fines (CP 25): CP 25 / 2 / 73 / 618 (the foot of the Lincolnshire fine, number 58 in the file).

21 Freehold land is distinguished both from leasehold land, and from copyhold land. Freehold land might be held (of a feudal lord) in fee simple, in fee tail, or for life. The fee simple was the largest possible freehold interest, and the closest English law came to absolute ownership of land. The fee tail was a cut down fee simple: it was heritable not by heirs general, but only by heirs of the body of the donee. Persons holding land by freehold tenure had the protection of those ancient remedies known as the real actions. Leaseholders and copyholders did not have access to the real actions.

and Lady Katharine, and the other intents and meanings aforesaid, and not meant to be to the profit or benefit of the said defendant". It was decreed that the lease be cancelled and the land be reconveyed in fee simple. The question of the personalty was left open.

Here there was "trust and confidence", but that alone is insufficient. "Trust", like "nuisance", is a chameleon word[22]: English lawyers have never appropriated it entirely to themselves[23]. In *Siddenham v. Harrison* (1579 - 1580)[24] the plaintiff complained that he had "put one in trust" to enrol a recognisance and deed of bargain and sale, which had not been done, while in 1583 Henry Skelton complained that "he whom the plaintiff put in trust to follow his cause nominated two commissioners on the plaintiff's part which are but yeomen, and but of little or no experience"[25]. These cases illustrate, as *Roger Cotterrell* has put it, a "social relationship of trust"[26]. But they do not illustrate the "legal structure of the trust, as between trustees and beneficiaries", for beyond "trust and confidence" there must be trust property in the hands of the trustee[27], which point emerges especially clearly from *Bertie v. Herenden* where the conveyance in question was expressed to be "to the only use and behoof of ... Walter Herenden and of his heirs". Lady Katharine had good reason to cover her tracks; "[n]othing more could have been done at common law to vest the fee simple beneficially in Herenden"[28]. But though title at common law was in Walter Herenden, nevertheless the land had been transferred "upon special, faithful and secret trust and confidence, and to have been employed to the use and behoof of [Bertie] and Lady Katharine, and the other intents and meanings aforesaid, and not meant to be to the profit or benefit of the said defendant". Without trust property Herenden could not have been a trustee. But since he was a trustee he was not to be permitted to exploit the property for his own benefit. Instead he must employ it to the use and behoof of the beneficiaries, which obligation was enforced not in a court of common law but by the equitable jurisdiction of the court of Chancery[29].

---

22 *J. R. Spencer,* Public Nuisance – A Critical Examination, (1989) Cambridge Law Journal 55, 56.

23 *T. F. T. Plucknett,* A Concise History of the Common Law, 5th ed., London, 1956, pp. 598 - 599.

24 Cary 97.

25 *Skelton v. Hacon* (1583) Chancery Entry Books of Decrees and Orders (C 33): C 33/67 f. 196v.

26 *R. Cotterrell,* Trusting in Law: Legal and Moral Concepts of Trust, (1993) 46 Current Legal Problems 75, 77.

27 Cf. modern controversy over the imposition of the obligations of trusteeship upon persons who have dishonestly assisted in a breach of trust but have never received or controlled trust property. See *A. J. Oakley,* Constructive Trusts, 3rd ed., London, 1997, pp. 188 - 190.

28 *Baker,* (1977) 93 L.Q.R. 33, 34.

29 The English side of the court of Chancery was the archetypal equity jurisdiction, but there were others, including the equity side of the court of Exchequer which after about 1590 was handling a considerable number of cases (*W. H. Bryson,* The Equity Side of the Ex-

These are the essentials of a trust: a trustee has been compelled in equity to hold property for the benefit of some persons called beneficiaries (or *cestuis que trust),* so that the real benefit of the property accrues not to the trustee but to the beneficiaries. But *Bertie v. Herenden* will not stand for all kinds of trust. The English lawyer may speak of "the trust", but knows that such monolithic usage can only be shorthand, for trusts are various. *Bertie's Case* illustrates an express private trust created by the transfer of trust property from a settlor to a trustee. It does not illustrate an express private trust created by one declaring himself a trustee of his own property. It does not illustrate trusts of equitable interests. It does not illustrate resulting or constructive trusts, those private trusts which are not express but arise, as *Lord Nottingham* put it, "by act or construction of law"[30]. And it does not illustrate trusts which are not private at all, or created for an individual beneficiary or beneficiaries, but public and created for some charitable purpose[31]. We shall return to charitable trusts below, but it will first be helpful to consider the property which may be the subject matter of a trust.

III. Trust Property

The question of what might be the subject matter of a trust was not of inherent difficulty, and the potential variety of trust property is well illustrated by cases within the period[32]. But the Statute of Uses added its own complications: whether it would operate to transfer legal title from the feoffee to uses to the beneficiary, so executing and putting an end to the use, depended in part upon the nature of the property in question[33].

---

chequer, Cambridge, 1975), the chancery courts of the palatinates of Durham and Lancaster, and the court of Duchy Chamber.

30 *Cook v. Fountain* (1676) 3 Swanston App. 585, 586. The sixteenth-century evidence reveals little of trusts created by declaration of oneself as trustee, or of constructive or resulting trusts, though some indication of resulting trust doctrine is found in cases in which the proof of a trust for the transferor turns upon the absence of consideration moving from the transferee: *Savery v. Archer* (1585) C 33 / 69 f. 495; *Clerke v. Spachhurst* (1595) C 33 / 89 f. 9v; *University College, Oxford v. Nuttall* (1596) C 33 / 89 f. 907.

31 It also does not illustrate the operation of trusts or trust-like devices at common law, for a discussion of some aspects of which see section VI. *infra.*

32 Though the illustration is not exhaustive. We do not, for example, at this time find discussion of trusts of beneficial interests under trusts.

33 Feoffees to uses were, in broad terms, medieval trustees, that is persons to whom land had been conveyed by the solemn mechanism of a feoffment with livery of seisin to hold that land to the use of another. For more detail see *Professor Biancalana's* paper in this volume. After the Statute of Uses situations within the scope of the statute continued to be called uses. Situations outside the scope of the statute were now usually called trusts (with trustees rather than feoffees to uses) but such situations might also be called uses. See *N. G. Jones,* Uses, Trusts, and a Path to Privity, (1997) Cambridge Law Journal 175, 181 f.

1. The Operation of the Statute of Uses

Where trustees had active duties there was no difficulty: the statute had no application. The same was true of trusts of pure personalty, trusts of copyhold land, and trusts in the form of a use upon a use. These exceptions are well known and require no further discussion[34]. The question of the application of the statute to trusts of leases has recently been clarified and merits further attention.

A well-known question to the judges by the Lord Chancellor in 1580, now identified as *Dacre v. Musgrave*[35], has usually been taken to concern the application of the Statute of Uses to a trust of a term of years, the judges responding that trusts of terms of years were outside the scope of the statute[36]. Manuscript reports and the Chancery record make it clear that the case concerned the application to leases, not of the Statute of Uses, but of the statute 1 Richard III, c. 1 (1484). The decision turned upon a provision in the statute of Richard, rendering feoffments by *cestui que use* good against the feoffor and his heirs, the reference to heirs showing that "uses of inheritance were principally intended and not use [*sic*] of a chattel". Leases were chattels, albeit chattels real, and uses of leases were therefore outside the scope of the statute of Richard. The Statute of Uses was not in issue.

The orthodox position that a passive trust of a term of years was un-executed had been reached by the last decade of the 16th century: in the time of *Egerton L.K.*[37] it could be said that "If I convey a lease for years to A to the use of B ... by the statute of 27 H 8 this use be not transferred"[38], and the supposed doubt on the point in 1580 has been shown to be illusory. There is evidence to carry the orthodox position back before 1580, but it seems that the non-execution of passive trusts of terms of years was not established without some doubt. The general opinion in the 1550s, and perhaps also in the late 1540s, was that a passive trust of a term of years was not executed, but as late as 1563 it was possible to think otherwise[39], and that this had at some time been the view of the Middle Temple is sufficient to

34 For standard accounts see *J. H. Baker,* An Introduction to English Legal History, 3rd ed., London, 1990, pp. 328 - 329; *A. W. B. Simpson,* A History of the Land Law, 2nd ed., Oxford, 1986, pp. 194 - 196.

35 Dyer 369a; *R. Crompton,* L'Authoritie et Iurisdiction des Courts de la Maiestie de la Royne, London, 1594, fo. 65. BL MS. Harg. 281, fo. 187, BL MS. Harg. 373, fo. 205, BL MS. Lans. 640, fo. 53. C 33/60 ff. 21, 40, 153v, 188v, 238, 249v, 321v, 336v, 423, 440; C 33/61 ff. 42v, 46, 63v, 417v, 438,454; Chancery and Supreme Court of Judicature, Chancery Division: Six Clerks' Office and successors: Decree Rolls (C 78): C 78/56/7.

36 For example, *Simpson* (n. 34) 194; *S.F.C. Milsom,* Historical Foundations of the Common Law, 2nd ed., London, 1981, p. 234.

37 Thomas Egerton, Lord Keeper of the Great Seal 1596 - 1603, Lord Chancellor 1603 - 1617.

38 Cambridge University Library (CUL) MS. Gg.2.31, fo. 463 pl. 200. This is undated, but in a collection of decisions of *Egerton L. K.*

39 See *Elton v. Denton* (1598) at C 33/96 f. 324.

show that it had not always been obvious that passive trusts of terms of years were outside the scope of the Statute of Uses[40].

2. Chattels Personal

The earliest examples of trusts of chattels personal in the Chancery record arose in the late 1540s. *Hodges v. Payne* (1561)[41] concerned a delivery of money in about 1547 by a father to his son "upon trust and confidence" which the father had in his son, to the intent that the son should use the money to buy certain land from the king for the father. The son employed two intermediaries to obtain the land, and procured from them a deed of "feoffment, bargain and sale" for himself, forging a deed of conveyance to his father to hide the fraud. The father discovered the fraud upon the son's death, and title still being in the intermediaries, the survivor of them was ordered to convey to thé father[42].

Josselyn v. Luson (1548 / 49)[43] concerned a trust of plate created before the Statute of Uses. In 1525 Phylyp Josselyn had delivered pieces of gold and silver plate to Nicholas Luson "upon especial trust and confidence", safely to be kept to her use and to be redelivered upon request[44]. Phylyp Josselyn having died, the plaintiff took administration of her estate. The court found that the plate had come to the hands of an executor of Nicholas Luson, who had delivered it to Lord Audley L. C. upon a bill for the saving harmless of Nicholas Luson, his executors and administrators, against all men concerning the plate. But nevertheless the defendants, Luson's executors, were ordered to pay the value of the plate to the plaintiff. The court clearly had no difficulty with the idea of a trust of chattels personal, and was indeed prepared to enforce it against the executors of the trustee, despite their having delivered the trust property to a former Lord Chancellor[45]. There are many further examples of 16th century trusts of personalty, including money[46], money bonds[47], statutes staple[48], and a patent for the production of playing cards[49].

---

40 See a note of 1573 recording the view of the Middle Temple, printed in *J.H. Baker, S. F. C. Milsom,* Sources of English Legal History, London, 1986, p. 124.

41 C 78 / 18 / 6.

42 It is not clear why title was still in the intermediaries. It may be that the deed of bargain and sale had not been enrolled in accordance with the Statute of Enrolments, 27 Hen. VIII, c. 16 (1536).

43 C 78 / 5 / 17.

44 The relationship with bailment is close here. See section VI. *infra.*

45 There is no indication that Audley decreed the case, which may explain why a delivery to him was insufficient to discharge the executors.

46 E.g., *Burdytt v. Potter* C 33 / 87 f. 433v (1594).

47 E.g., *Hurley v. Tredell* C 33 / 91 f. 245 (1596) (a money bond being a sealed writing acknowledging an indebtedness).

48 E.g., *Mathewe v. Weste* C 33 / 87 ff. 502, 736v, 841, C 33 / 89 ff. 73, 171, 811 (1594 - 1596) (a statute staple being a publicly enrolled acknowledgement of indebtedness).

3. Copyhold Land

The first trust of copyhold land decreed after the Statute of Uses was that in *Byllyngesley v. Barons* (1548 / 49)[50]. The plaintiff had asked the defendant to buy certain copyhold land from two executors, the defendant claiming that since he had greater "acquittance" with them he could save £ 40 on the purchase price. And "for the great trust and confidence" which he had in the defendant, the plaintiff asked him to take the conveyance in the defendant's name, to the intent that he would then release his interest to the plaintiff. The defendant's claim that he had bought the land to his own use did not convince the court: it had been proved to have been bought only to the use of the plaintiff, and was decreed for him[51].

Chancery never had any difficulty with trusts of copyhold in principle, though such trusts were not to be allowed to prejudice the lord of whom the land was held. Thus in *Gobe v. Dore* (1604)[52] the plaintiff gave the defendant £ 100 to buy copyhold in the defendant's name to the plaintiff's use, because differences between the lord and the plaintiff led the plaintiff to believe that he would not succeed for himself. Having bought the land the defendant refused to surrender according to the trust, and the plaintiff was refused relief, *Lord Ellesmere L. C.* declaring that he would not base a decree upon a falsity, as it seemed to him that the aim had been to impose upon the lord a tenant to whom he objected.

4. Leases

Trusts of leases have caused more difficulty. It has been shown above that doubt was possible as to whether a use of a lease was within the scope of the Statute of Uses. At a more fundamental level it has been said that it was a question as late as the 1590s "whether a use of a [lease] was possible at all"[53]: only after debate did the judges in the decision in Serjeants' Inn known as *Sir Francis Inglefield's Case* (1593 - 1598)[54] conclude "que le use de Lease poit estre". But the question must be correctly understood. The judges were considering "le use de Lease" in a narrow sense: could there be a use of a lease in the sense in which there had been uses of freehold land before the advent of the Statute of Uses[55]? So it was said that if A

49 *Wendover v. Higgens* C 33 / 77 f. 125 (1588).

50 C 78 / 5 / 24.

51 For a reason unexplained it was decreed that the defendant should have one piece of the land, which was to be taken out by the Chancellor or those appointed by him, upon payment to the plaintiff of a sum to be taxed by the Chancellor.

52 Hertfordshire Record Office MS. Verulam XII.A.50.

53 *Simpson* (n. 34) 194.

54 1 Anderson 293. The point arose out of discussion of a question by the attorney general as to the position of *cestui que use* of a lease who committed treason.

55 See the discussion of the pre-statute use in section V *infra*.

made a feoffment of freehold land to B to the use of C for years, then the Statute of Uses would take effect, and C would acquire not merely the profits of the land for the term of years but the possession of the land as well, which showed that there might be a use of a lease just as much as of anything else. In this sense only was there doubt as to whether a use of a lease could be. Whether a trust (or a use in a broader sense) of a lease could be was not in issue. Ewens B., probably present at the discussion of the case, had himself been a trustee for Sir Francis Hastings of a term for 500 years, and upon acquiring the freehold reversion had assigned the term to his own trustees to keep it on foot to protect the freehold from incumbrances[56]. There is little evidence of Chancery involvement with trusts of terms of years before the 1550s[57], but thereafter such trusts were frequent.

5. Freehold Land

Trusts of freehold land, either in fee simple or for life gave rise to no inherent difficulty. Trusts of estates tail faced the old rule which suggested that a tenant in tail could not stand seised to a use[58], but while it is not clear that trusts of estates tail were ever very common the old rule was never applied to trusts.

IV. The Purposes of Trusts

The purposes for which trusts were created after 1536 were many and various; only an indication of the flexibility and pervasiveness of trusts can be given here.

1. Evasion of the Royal Feudal Revenue

We must begin with the use of trusts to evade the royal feudal revenue. Such evasion had been a feature of the old practice of making feoffments to uses, and much attention has been given to the question of how trusts might have been used to achieve the same end after 1536. Consideration has centred upon the possibility of creating a passive trust of freehold land, in which the trustees had no active duties but merely held legal title for the benefit of an otherwise absolutely entitled

56 *Haskett v. Hastings* (1600/01) C 78/113/24. Matthew Ewens, created serjeant 1594, baron of the Exchequer 1594 - 98. Richard Branthwaite, who died in 1594 shortly after being created serjeant, was a joint trustee for Sir Francis of a second term for 500 years.

57 *Hopton v. Mompesson* (1546) C 78/3/7, *Meryk v. Togwell* (1548) C 78/5/18, and *Preste v. Blakwall* (1548) C 78/5/13 may involve trusts of terms, but none is a clear case.

58 *J. Gilbert,* The Law of Uses and Trusts, 3rd ed. E.B. Sugden, London, 1811, pp. 19 - 20; *P. Bordwell,* The Conversion of the Use into a Legal Interest, (1935) 21 Iowa Law Review 1, 13 - 14. The effect of tenure upon the limiting of uses requires further study.

cestui que trust. The Statute of Uses would usually prevent the existence of a passive trust of freehold, but such a trust could be created, and the old passive use be revived, by limiting a trust in the form of a use upon a use. Trusts in such a form might be created in several ways, a simple example being a conveyance of freehold land by X to A to the use of B to the use of (or in trust for) C. It had been established shortly after the Statute of Uses that a use upon a use was void[59], and the effect of that rule in the above example was to prevent the operation of the Statute of Uses upon the second use in favour of C, so that B, by force of the statute, would end up seised of the land upon a passive trust for C.

Around this device much misleading history has gathered. If the Statute of Uses was the principal defence of the royal feudal revenue, then here was a means whereby both the statute and that revenue might be circumvented. "[T]he old use might still be effected, despite the Statute of Uses, by a use on a use"[60]. And if such would be the effect of creating a trust in the form of a use upon a use, then clearly the chancellor cannot have acted to enforce such a trust until the importance of the feudal revenue had disappeared[61].

But the chancellor did so act, and well before the disappearance of the feudal revenue. *Bertie v. Herenden* (1560) with which we began was itself an example of such a trust. By 1623 trusts in the form of a use upon a use were common[62], and the Chancery record reveals five further examples between 1584 and 1600[63]. It is not clear that entirely passive trusts in the form of a use upon a use were ever common[64], but the question is less important than has been supposed. In intervening in use upon use cases, and in other trust cases not involving uses upon uses, the chancellor posed no threat to the revenue, for, as has been shown elsewhere[65], the Sta-

---

59 *Jane Tyrrel's Case* (1557), see *N.G. Jones, Tyrrel's Case* (1557) and the Use upon a Use, (1993) 14 J.L.H. 75.

60 *P. Bordwell,* The Repeal of the Statute of Uses, (1926) 39 Harvard L.R., 466, 471.

61 For example, *A. W. Scott,* The Trust as an Instrument of Law Reform, (1922) 31 Yale L.J. 457, 464.

62 *Henry Sherfield's* reading on 32 Hen. VIII, c. 1, in Lincoln's Inn 1623, BL MS. Harg. 402, fo. 34v, printed in *Baker/Milsom* (n. 40) 125 f.

63 *Dymocke v. Alcocke* (1584) C 33/67 f. 503v; *Rushebrooke v. Payne* (1585) C 33/71 ff. 126, 208; *Society of the Staple of England v. Fayrefaxe* (1589) C 33/77 f. 694v; *Sydney v. Atye* (1592) C 33/83 f. 461v; *Burghe v. Williams* (1600) C 78/109/7. It is possible that there were other cases of this type, the form of which is not apparent from the record. Further indications of lack of objection to trusts in the form of a use upon a use are provided by *Killio v. Tavener* (1595) C 33/89 f. 646, Bod. Lib. MS. Rawl. C.647, fo. 138, and *Sir Moyle Finch's Case* (1600) E. Coke, Fourth Part of the Institutes of the Laws of England, London, 1644, p. 85, where in both cases the sole difficulty perceived is evidential.

64 The trust in *Bertie's Case* was active, as were the trusts in all the other use upon use cases in Chancery in the 16th century, except that in *Society of the Staple of England v. Fayrefaxe* (1589) C 33/77 f. 694v.

65 *N.G. Jones,* The Influence of Revenue Considerations upon the Remedial Practice of Chancery in Trust Cases, 1536 - 1660, in: M. Lobban, C. W. Brooks (eds.), Communities and Courts in Britain, 1150 - 1900, 1997, pp. 99 ff.

tute of Wills 1540[66], and not the Statute of Uses, was the revenue's prime defence. If the execution of uses was the means to protect the revenue, then all trusts, being of necessity unexecuted uses, were potential revenue evasion mechanisms. But since after 1540 the scope of the revenue was defined by the Statute of Wills, not all trusts had the potential to defeat the revenue, and the practice of the Chancellor in trust cases was formed around the identification and neutralisation only of those trusts which did pose a financial threat. This was so of trusts enabling land to be bought in the name of another, and of trusts of long terms of years. Such devices may have been employed with the aim of evading the revenue, and required careful remedial handling. But other trusts, including passive trusts in the form of a use upon a use, fell within the normal working of the Statute of Wills, serving no revenue avoiding purpose and subject to no revenue protecting action by the chancellor.

2. Charitable Trusts

Though there have been doubts as to the willingness of the courts to enforce private trusts in the period, it has never been doubted that public or charitable trusts were enforced willingly[67]: the tenderness of Chancery towards trusts for charitable purposes is well known[68], and may be illustrated by a number of cases from the record. Prominent among them are cases in which a charitable trust was upheld despite a lack of capacity in the trustees to take legal title to the trust property, a difficulty which afflicted churchwardens in particular. Thus in *Churchwardens of Ibberton v. Crooke* (1580)[69] it was held sufficient that the churchwardens, though not incorporate, had the personalty of the parish vested in them and so "may be capable for some purposes". In other cases a spirit of compromise prevailed. Thus in *Dister v. Lane* (1585)[70] Robert Franckham had devised a house to his wife for

66 32 Hen. VIII, c. 1 (together with its explanatory statute 34 & 35 Hen. VIII, c. 5 (1542)).

67 Considerable work has been done on charitable trusts in the period. See *G.H. Jones*, History of the Law of Charity 1532 - 1827, Cambridge, 1969; *W. K. Jordan*, Philanthropy in England 1480 - 1660, London, 1958; *idem*, The Charities of London, 1480 - 1660, London, 1960; *idem*, The Charities of Rural England, 1480 - 1660, London, 1961.

68 *Maitland* regarded the "extreme liberality" of English law about charitable trusts as "a matter of great historical importance". "It seems to me that our people slid unconsciously from the enforcement of the rights of [*cestui que trust*] to the establishment of trusts without a [*cestui que trust*] – the so-called charitable trusts: and I think that continental law shows that this was a step that would not and could not be taken by men whose heads were full of Roman law. *Practically* the private man who creates a charitable trust does something that is very like the creation of an artifical person, and does it without asking leave of the State". Fifoot (n. 6) 242, letter to John Chipman Gray, 19 April 1902. See also H. A. L. Fisher (ed.), The Collected Papers of F. W. Maitland, vol. III, Cambridge, 1911, pp. 271 ff., and 321 ff.

69 C 33/61 ff. 220, 351v, 353, 371v, 455v, 485v, 524, 546v; C 33/67 f. 696v; C 33/74 ff. 193v, 307; C 33/79 f. 806v.

70 C 33/69 ff. 172v, 679v; C 33/74 f. 288v.

term of her life, with remainder to his daughter in tail, with remainder over to the churchwardens of West Barfold in Essex. The wife being dead, and the daughter being dead without issue, the churchwardens claimed the house upon trust for the poor. "But for that the defendant's wife claims the ... house as next heir to the said Franckham, and the ... will seemed in extremity of law no good gift to the churchwardens for that they are no corporation enabled to take such a gift, and for that the defendants are, as it is informed, very poor", it was ordered that the defendants should have and enjoy the possession of the house to them and their heirs, but that they should also grant a rent charge of 10 shillings a year out of the house to trustees for the use of the poor.

3. Private Trusts for the Vulnerable

Non-charitable private trusts were created for the relief or protection of specific individuals. So a widow contemplating re-marriage might provide for the children of her first marriage by means of a trust, which would keep property destined for the children of the first marriage from the hands of a potential second husband. Thus in *Lacye v. Brimesmeade* (1561)[71] the court concluded that the female plaintiff had before remarriage delivered £ 365 to her father, the defendant, upon trust to buy land to the use of her son and his heirs. The father used the money to buy certain copyhold land, which the court ordered him to convey to the son at his full age.

Provision was made by means of trusts not only for children, but also for adults incapable of managing their own affairs. In *Loddenden v. Danyell* (1585)[72] the defendant, having persuaded the plaintiff "a very simple fellow and of little understanding", to sell land to a third party, kept the purchase price and gave the plaintiff two bonds, each for half the price, payable at the end of 10 and 20 years respectively. The court was not prepared to allow the defendant to keep the price on these terms, but it was not to be paid directly to the plaintiff either. Instead the defendant, having received back his bonds, was ordered to transfer the money to four trustees who were "with the use thereof" to see the plaintiff "kept and maintained", the capital sum being preserved.

Lack of capacity to manage affairs arose not only from simpleness of mind, but also from spendthrift habits. So Nicholas Halghe in about 1558 "for the relief of his wife and children" assigned a term of years to three trustees "upon consideration that if he ... should fortune to waste or consume his inheritance, as in truth he did, that yet the same lease should be to them in trust for the relief of his wife and children"[73]. Others, less prudent, required outside intervention. We are told in a

71 C 78/22/29.

72 C 33/75 ff. 316v, 801v.

73 *Halghe v. Howson* (1583) C 33/67 ff. 177v, 210, 219, 344v, 486, 572v, 593; C 78/65/6.

late Elizabethan note that "the way to prevent an unthrifty son is to make a feoffment in fee, and to reserve an estate for life the remainder to feoffees in trust during the life of the son the remainder to the heirs of the son"[74].

The same effect could be obtained by means of bonds or recognisances[75]. So in *Poope v. Tytchborne* it was said in 1588 that a recognisance of £ 2000 had been entered into about 30 years earlier by one Francis Tytchborne to "John White, sometime Bishop of Lincoln ... and to Stephen Gardyner late Bishop of Winchester, of trust without consideration, to the intent only to bridle or retain the said Frauncis Tytchborne from wasting or impairing his living"[76].

4. Trusts and Persecution

Trust beneficiaries might be vulnerable not only through infancy, simplicity, or wastefulness, but also through persecution and political opposition. *Bertie v. Herenden* is a well-known example of this type of case, and shortly followed the litigation in *Dudley v. Ellis* (1559)[77] concerning a trust created by John Dudley, Duke of Northumberland, of leases late the property of his executed rival, Edward Seymour, Duke of Somerset. Northumberland took the leases in trust in a servant's name, for if he should take them in his own name "he knew that such as were his enemies and friends to the ... Duke of Somerset would say that he had helped the said Duke to his death for the lucre and desire of his good[s] and lands".

Richard Bertie and his wife were not alone in resorting to trusts as a means of protecting their property to maintain a source of revenue in the face of the Marian persecution[78]. And as the accession of Elizabeth returned England to Protestantism, Roman Catholics found succour in the same device[79]. So, for example, Christopher Lockwood, secretary to Charles Nevill, the Catholic Earl of Westmorland, was attainted for his part in the northern rising of 1569, but his estate was saved, at least in part, by the Lascelles family convincing the judges that "even what he seemed to own was the property of Lascelles trustees"[80]. A trust for the benefit of "the sect of Jesuits and seminary priests" was found "superstitious and illegal" in

---

74 BL MS. Lans. 1074, fo. 312.

75 A recognisance being an enrolled acknowledgement of indebtedness made before a court.

76 C 33 / 75 f. 473v. John White, bishop of Lincoln 1554 - 56, subsequently bishop of Winchester, Stephen Gardiner, bishop of Winchester 1531 - 52, Lord Chancellor 1553 - 56.

77 C 78 / 17 / 10. See *N. G. Jones*, Trusts for Secrecy: The Case of John Dudley, Duke of Northumberland, (1995) Cambridge Law Journal 545 ff.

78 See also *Wield v. Wield* (1560) C 78 / 17 / 36; *Jeffrey v. Tyrrell* (1561) C 78 / 18 / 36; *Magnus v. Snell* (1561) C 78 / 18 / 41.

79 Though in the case of Catholics the evidence is less plentiful: unlike the Marian regime Elizabeth's protestantism was lasting.

80 *H. Aveling*, Northern Catholics, London, 1966, p. 87.

Croft v. Evett (1605)[81], but charitable trusts to maintain members of the "seminary of Wisbech" were permissible, *Egerton L. K.* upholding Mr. Throckmorton's devise to Catholic prisoners in Wisbech gaol, who were, as he said "obstinate papists yet they were men and ought to be pitied and relieved"[82].

5. Trusts for Married Women

Married women were vulnerable too: at common law a wife's property vested in her husband during the marriage. But the creation of trusts enabled married women to dispose of property held to their separate use independently of their husbands. The point was clearly made in 1635 in relation to wills: "A woman that hath a husband cannot devise lands by the Statute of 32.H.8[83]. But if lands be settled in others in trust for her use and to be at her disposing, then she may dispose as she will in equity, and in Chancery the trustees must execute the estate according to the disposition"[84].

The idea of a separate use had at least been discussed before the Statute of Uses[85]. For the period after the statute *A. L. Erikson* has recently concluded, on the basis of the printed reports, that the "earliest date currently ascribed to separate estate is the 1580s and 1590s", while suggesting that it may have pre-dated the 1580s[86]. In her study of the separate use[87], *M. L. Cioni* took the decisions in *Sanky alias Walgrave v. Golding* (1579 - 1581)[88] to be "the foundation stone upon which evolved the concept of a married woman's separate estate", while drawing attention to the earlier litigation in *Lady Anne Bourchier v. Walgrave and Butler* (1560)[89].

Lady Anne's case arose from the attainder in 1553 of her husband, William Parr, Marquess of Northampton, and is complicated by Parr's "most unfortunate matrimonial history"[90]. The plaintiff, daughter and heir of Henry Bourchier, Earl of Es-

---

81 Moore K.B. 784, Tothill 61; CUL MS. Gg.2.5, fo. 335, BL MS. Lans. 640, fo. 14.

82 CUL MS. Gg.2.31, fo. 454v pl. 150.

83 32 Hen. VIII, c. 1 (of wills).

84 CUL MS. Add. 23, fo. 44.

85 *Baker* (n. 34) 553, and 553 n. 39.

86 *A. L. Erikson,* Women and Property in Early Modern England, London and New York, 1993, pp. 106 - 107.

87 *M. L. Cioni,* Women and the Law in Elizabethan England with Particular Reference to the Court of Chancery, University of Cambridge Ph.D. dissertation, 1974, pp. 169 - 171 (published in the Garland Economic History series, New York, 1985).

88 Cary 87, Tothill 95, BL MS. Harg. 281, fo. 90, BL MS. Lans. 599, fo. 54, BL MS. Lans. 1110, fo. 95v, CUL MS. Dd.9.22, fo. 72, CUL MS. Gg.2.26, fo. 130v; C 33/60 f. 158v, C 33/61 f. 32v, 603v. The litigation consisted of two separate suits between the same parties.

89 C 78/15/12, C 78/15/15.

90 Dictionary of National Biography, vol. XLIII, p. 368.

sex[91], brought her father's lands to her husband upon marriage. Parr's attainder left the plaintiff "destitute of living": by reason of the attainder, manors, lands and other premises worth 2,500 marks per annum which had belonged to the Earl of Essex "in effect came to the hands and possession" of the queen[92]. Upon petition to Queen Mary, Lady Anne was granted part of the land which had fallen into the hands of the crown upon the attainder. But because "for divers causes well known she could by no means have ... good assurance to receive and enjoy the benefits and commodities of the ... grant by the order of the laws of this realm, but only by having the assurance of the same to be made to such as were trusty and assured friends to the said Lady Anne", the land was granted by letters patent to Sir Robert Rochester and Sir Edward Walgrave for term of 40 years, if William Parr should so long live, "to perform the same trust".

This appears to be a clear example of a trust created to keep title out of the hands of the husband of a married woman, an interpretation which is strengthened by the provision for a term of 40 years in the trustees only if the husband should so long live. The position was complicated by doubts as to whether, following the Reformation, a divorce *a mensa et thoro* might permit re-marriage. William Parr had divorced the plaintiff *a mensa et thoro* in 1548 and had married Elizabeth Brooke, daughter of Lord Cobham. In 1552 he procured an act of parliament declaring the legality of this second marriage, but it appears that early in Mary's reign this act was repealed, leaving the position of his second wife uncertain[93]. It seems that at the date of the plaintiff's petition for relief to Queen Mary her status as a *feme sole*[94] was by no means clear, and that therefore a trust was employed.

Litigation arose because after Sir Robert Rochester's death, Sir Edward Walgrave the other trustee, had leased part of the trust property to Sir John Butler. The court made two decrees. As against Sir John Butler the rents and profits of the manor were decreed for the plaintiff, while to Sir John was reserved the possibility of exhibiting a bill against Sir Edward Walgrave. No mention was made in this decree of the question of whether Sir John Butler had had notice of the trust, though he claimed to have paid the rent due to the crown.

Sir Edward Walgrave, the other defendant, based his answer upon the plaintiff's married status. The Marquess of Northampton was yet "in full life in the city of London, without whom the ... complainant is not able to maintain any suit against

---

91 Died without male issue 13 March 1540.

92 The words "in effect" may have had some import since Staunford was clear in 1557 that by the statute 5 & 6 Ed. VI, c. 11 a man would not forfeit any lands which he had "in the right of another, as in the right of his wife", *W. Staunford,* Les Plees del Coron, London, 1557, fo. 187v (translated). In the time of Elizabeth "the queen's majesty had of her special favour and grace to many women whose husbands had been attainted yielded to some reasonable portion for their jointure or dower": *Delahye v. Somerfyeld* C 33/77 f. 470v (1589).

93 On the marriages see Dictionary of National Biography (n. 90) 368, and *Baker* (n. 34) 564.

94 That is, an unmarried woman.

the ... defendant or against any other". Lady Anne replied, relying upon the divorce, and upon the fact that the lease had been made to the trustees towards her maintenance, and asserting that by the order of the common law she "may take and use her living in divers respects as a *feme sole*"[95]. The court concluded that Sir Edward Walgrave had showed nothing to prevent a decree for the plaintiff, who was to enjoy the rents and profits of the premises without interference from the defendant.

Cioni has suggested that this latter decree shows an acceptance by the court of the "validity" of the divorce. But it does not appear that at the time of the decree the plaintiff was treated simply as a *feme sole.* The plaintiff herself did not assert that since she was a *feme sole* there was no question but that she might sue in her own name. Instead she took a number of points. One of these was the divorce, but from this she argued no more than that she had had a "stipend to her appointed for her living" and that she "by the order of the common law may take and use her living in divers respects as a *feme sole*". Beyond that she relied upon the existence of the trust. The reasoning behind the court's decision is not clear, but from the plaintiff's replication it seems unlikely that it was simply that because of the divorce she was a *feme sole.*

This case thus shows the creation in the reign of Mary of a married woman's separate use, and also a readiness in the Chancery to allow a woman, not clearly a *feme sole,* to sue to protect her interest under a trust for her separate use. The case was decided in the same year as *Bertie v. Herenden,* and may likewise be suspected of political overtones. William Parr, attainted early in the reign of Mary, was restored to the Marquessate early in the reign of Elizabeth. Mary had granted maintenance to his wife, and *Bacon L. K.* may have needed little encouragement to be at least as generous. But if to begin with, as *Holdsworth* suggested[96], either the consent of the husband or some facts such as a separation or the husband's wasteful habits would be necessary to persuade the court to intervene, then the case may accurately reflect the early origins of the married woman's separate use. Upon that basis Lady Anne Bourchier had a strong case.

Beyond the separate use, trusts were involved in two further aspects of women's property. It seems to have become a common practice to prevent dower by the creation of joint tenancies, one of the joint tenants being a trustee of his interest for the other. In *Whalley v. Castlon* (1583)[97] it was found that the land in question had been mortgaged long before the time of the suit to Sir Roger Marten, late alderman of London, and to his brother-in-law, the defendant. The mortgage having been re-

95 The meaning of this assertion is unclear, but clearly she did not claim that she *was* a *feme sole. Cf.* the claim in *Middleton v. Hamner* that John Hamner "and his wife lived separately, and that she dealt as a sole person in all things concerning herself", C 33/79 f. 583v (1590).

96 *W. S. Holdsworth,* A History of English Law, vol. 5, London, 1924, pp. 312 - 313.

97 C 33/65 f. 429, C 33/65 f. 632v; BL MS. Harl. 736, fo. 95/195, *Crompton* (n. 35) 54v.

deemed, and the defendant having been "only named as a friend in trust, for that the wife of the ... alderman should not claim any dower of or in the ... lands", he was ordered to release all his interest to the plaintiff.

And if trusts were used to avoid dower, they might be used also to ensure the making of jointure provision for a wife by means of a trust of an obligation. Thus it was said in *Johnson v. Smythe* in 1586 that the defendants had been "only named as friends in trust to take a bond of £ 1000 for the assurance of a jointure" to be made to the plaintiff's wife[98].

6. The Attendancy of Satisfied Terms

Trusts played a further role in family provision in cases where it was desired to prevent a merger of lease and reversion[99]. At law, if lease and reversion were vested in the same person, in the same right, with no intervening vested estate, the lease merged with the reversion and ceased to have any independent existence[100]. This result could be avoided by vesting the lease in a trustee, and such a trust of a term was a constituent element in the settlement practice of attaching satisfied terms to attend the inheritance[101].

Leases, which did not disturb the remainders in tail, were used in strict settlements as a means of raising money for portions and other incidental purposes[102]. Such leases were vested in trustees, upon trust to use the lease to raise money. Once the required sum had been raised the lease was satisfied. But it was common to provide for such satisfied terms to remain in existence and to "attend the inheritance", passing as though they were realty, and operating to protect the freehold from incumbrances. It is said that though there are examples from before 1660, the practice of attaching satisfied terms to attend the inheritance "never really got on its feet till after the Restoration"[103]. But the use of trusts to prevent merger of lease and reversion, and to protect the freehold estate from incumbrances, was known in the time of Elizabeth.

98 C 33 / 71 ff. 472, 563.

99 The reversion being the interest in the land retained by the lessor after granting the lease.

100 *R. E. Megarry, H. W. R. Wade,* The Law of Real Property, 5th ed., London, 1984, pp. 685 - 686.

101 See the discussion in Yale (n. 3) *150 - 160.*

102 Strict settlements were based upon a life estate in a father followed by a fee tail in his eldest son. While the father was alive the son's interest was in remainder, not in possession: the son had an alienable interest, but no present entitlement to enjoy the land.

103 Yale (n. 3) *151,* n. 1. *Huddleston v. Lamplugh* (1630) BL MS. Harg. 281, fo. 185v, BL MS. Lans. 640, fo. 35v, "concerning a lease attending upon an inheritance" seems to be an early example.

So in *Glascocke v. Savell* (1598)[104] it was found that "the plaintiff having the inheritance of the said lands, and minding to purchase the said lease and to keep the same on foot for the defence of the inheritance, procured the conveyance of the said lease to be made in his ... son's name, he then being but a child, in trust to be disposed of at the plaintiff's will". And in *Haskett v. Hastinges* (1601)[105] it was found that Sir Francis Hastings, who had redeemed two terms for 500 years which the late Earl of Huntingdon had mortgaged, had assigned the terms in trust "to keep the ... leases unextinguished and by them to defend ... the manors from statutes and other incumbrances made by the ... late Earl of Huntingdon mean between the time of the said leases and the conveyance of the inheritance ... to ... Sir Francis". These cases do not represent the fully developed device of the satisfied term limited to attend the inheritance in the context of a strict settlement, but they do show that an essential element of the device was current in the time of Elizabeth.

V. The Interest of the Beneficiary[106]

1. The "Engrafting Principle"

In considering the beneficiary's interest we must begin with that of the trustee. "It's of no use", said *Maitland,* "for Equity to say that A is a trustee of Blackacre for B, unless there be some court that can say that A is the owner of Blackacre. Equity without common law would have been a castle in the air, an impossibility"[107]. The interest of *cestui que trust* depends upon the interest of the trustee: the creation of a trust is a process of cumulation, and not of division. "[T]he notion", said *McLelland J.* in the Supreme Court of New South Wales in *Re Transphere Pty Ltd* (1986)[108], "that absolute ownership of property can properly be divided up into a legal estate and an equitable estate" is imprecise. "An absolute owner holds only the legal estate, with all the rights and incidents that attach to that estate. Where a legal owner holds property on trust for another, he has at law all the rights of an absolute owner but the beneficiary has the right to compel him to hold and use those rights which the law gives him in accordance with the obligations which equity has imposed on him by virtue of the existence of the trust. Although this right of the beneficiary constitutes an equitable estate in the property, it is engrafted onto, not carved out of, the legal estate".

104 C 33/96 f. 81.

105 C 78/113/24.

106 For discussion of this topic in the late 17th century and 18th century see *Dr. Macnair's* paper in this volume.

107 *Maitland* (n. 9) 19.

108 5 N.S.W.L.R. 309, at 311.

Discussing the interest of *cestui que trust* in terms of the carving out of equitable interests is possible and not unknown[109]. But the engrafting principle is necessary to an understanding of the historical development of trusts[110], and its operation is apparent in the structure of equitable interests at the time of the Statute of Uses. The old use had been rendered "thinglike" in lawyers' minds[111]. It had "originated as a personal confidence or trust placed by one person in the other", and though the marks of its origin remained always visible, it "became a species of property"[112]: "[w]e might say that 'the use' is turned into an incorporeal thing"[113]. As *Christopher St German's* student of the laws of England said in 1530 "every man that has lands has thereby two things in him, that is to say, the possession of the land which after the law of England is called the frank tenement or the free hold, and the other is authority to take thereby the profits of the land ... And so when a man makes a feoffment to another and intends that he himself shall take the profits then that feoffee is said [to be] seised to his use that so enfeoffed him"[114].

Upon this analysis possession and use are always distinct; absolute ownership is indeed "divided up into a legal estate and an equitable estate". And, as *St German* said, "when a man makes a feoffment to another and intends that he himself shall take the profits", the use remains in the feoffor's hands, while the possession passes to the feoffee to uses. This was the situation to which the Statute of Uses was addressed. It was "the statute made ... for the uniting of possession to uses" or "for the transferring of possessions to [or "into"] uses"[115]. And where possession and use remained united in the hands of one person, albeit a trustee, the statute had no operation. The point is apparent, for example, in the case of an active use or trust, where the trustee might hold property to raise money to pay debts. The use, being "the authority to take ... the profits of the land"[116], must necessarily remain united with the possession in the hands of the trustee: without the use the trustee

109 See, for example, *B. Green*, Grey, Oughtred and Vandervell – A Contextual Reappraisal, (1984) 47 Modern Law Review 385 ff.

110 It is helpful also to an understanding of some aspects of modern English trust law. Thus it has been suggested that a specifically enforceable contract of sale will give rise to a constructive trust only where the subject matter of the contract is a legal interest: "the constructive trust, assuming as it does a division of legal and equitable interests, is irreconcilable with the sale of an equitable interest": *D. W. M. Waters*, The Constructive Trust, London, 1964, p. 116. Thinking in terms of division has here led to error. See *Oakley* (n. 27) 278 - 280.

111 For *Maitland's* envy of those possessed of the word Dinglichkeit see *F. Pollock, F. W. Maitland*, The History of English Law, vol. II, 2nd ed., Cambridge, 1898, p. 125.

112 *Simpson* (n. 34) 181.

113 *Fisher* (n. 68) 343.

114 *C. St German*, Doctor and Student, ed. T. F. T. Plucknett, J. L. Barton, London, 1974, Selden Society vol. 91, p. 222 (spelling and punctuation modernised).

115 C 78/30/23 (1566); C 78/35/28 (1566); C 78/36/8 (1566); C 78/32/6 (1566/67); C 78/99/10 (1584). The statute was also referred to as the statute for the transferring of uses into possession. See *Jones*, (1993) 14 J.L.H. 75 (82).

116 *St German* (n. 114) 222.

could not perform the trust. But while the trustee has both use and possession he may not in conscience exploit them for his own benefit, but rather must do so for *cestui que trust,* whose interest is engrafted onto the rights of an absolute owner, both possession and use, vested in the trustee.

2. Trust and Promise

The trustee's obligation to exploit the trust property only for the benefit of *cestui que use* may be traced to more than one source. The simplest case is that in which the settlor has transferred property to a trustee upon trust for himself. Were the trustee permitted to keep the trust property for his own benefit he would be unjustly enriched. In transferring the trust property the settlor has relied upon the trustee to his detriment. And "[f]requently, of course, a trustee will expressly agree, or promise to observe the terms of a trust"[117]. The importance of this contractual element in a trustee's liability has recently been re-emphasised[118], and there is some support for it within the period.

Maitland found it seemingly impossible "to frame any definition of a contract which shall not include the acts by which ninety-nine out of every hundred trusts are created", without escaping the difficulty by defining contract to exclude trusts[119]. And the possibility of bracing a claim with contractual language was not lost upon 16th century Chancery litigants, or rather upon their counsel, trained in the Inns of Court: the common law language of *assumpsit*[120] was familiar and slipped easily into equity pleadings. So in *Sharpe v. Hill* (1568)[121] the complainant alleged that the land in variance had been assured by William Newcombe to the defendant "upon special trust and confidence" which the complainant reposed in the defendant, that the defendant should make assurance of it to the complainant and his heirs. This the defendant "faithfully promised" to do, "in consideration" that the complainant had paid Newcombe for the land[122]. Such *assumpsit* language

---

117 *P. S. Atiyah,* The Rise and Fall of Freedom of Contract, Oxford, 1979, p. 156.

118 *J. H. Langbein,* The Contractarian Basis of the Law of Trusts, (1995) 105 Yale L.J. 625. See also, for a later period, the discussion in *Dr. Macnair's* paper in this volume.

119 *Maitland* (n. 9) 111. The hundredth case was that of the settlor who constituted himself a trustee. See also *ibid.* pp. 28 - 29, where *Maitland* found consideration for the trustee's promise in the detriment to the promisee in parting "with legal rights, with property and with possession". *Maitland* saw the use "accomplishing its manifest destiny" in appearing as "equitable ownership" but had the 13th century common law courts "come to a comprehensive doctrine of contract", and had they been ready to distinguish real and personal rights, they might have assigned the use a place in their scheme of actions and "might have given the feoffor a personal, a contractual, action against the feoffee": *Pollock/Maitland* (n. 111) 232.

120 The action called *assumpsit* came to replace the old actions of covenant and debt in contract cases.

121 C 33/37 f. 198.

need not be taken to have any technical meaning, but the acts by which trusts are created may well be phrased in contractual terms.

Not only was promissory language used, but some of the obligations of a trustee might be cast in the form of an obligation in a technical sense. In *Houghton v. Sheppard* (1584)[123] it was said that land had been conveyed "but upon trust" that it should be reconveyed as directed, and that the trustee had given a bond in £ 2000 for the reconveyance. John Wield the elder, of Writtle in Essex, fleeing for religion in the time of Mary, conveyed land to third parties "of very trust and upon their promise" that he, his wife and children, should be relieved with the profits. Here again is a mixture of trust and promissory language, and here again the trustee entered into a bond, in this case to perform a covenant to pay £ 12 monthly out of the land for the maintenance of Wield, his wife and children[124].

But trust and contract would not always behave in the same fashion. In *Hopkins v. Hedloe* (1591)[125] it was said that an infant heir would not be bound by his father's promise to assure land, as he would have been had the father had the land in trust, and "Periam chief baron put a diversity between a trust and [a] promise concerning land, for the trust is united and one with the land, and [a] promise is collateral". Trusts and contracts might behave differently, and trusts depended not simply upon agreement, but quite literally upon trust and confidence affecting the conscience of the trustee[126]: the plaintiff's assertion in *Jones v. Mustyn* (1566)[127] that one Hughe Whitforde had assigned a lease, not simply "upon trust", but "upon the great trust and confidence which the said Hughe had" in the assignees, is not atypical of 16th century trust pleadings, and the commonplace that a use is a trust or confidence need not necessarily be circular.

In comparing trust and promise *Periam C. B.* had seen the former as united with the land, and the latter as collateral. But the matter was relative. "[T]he use", it was said in *Delamere v. Barnard* (1567) "is not like a rent out of the land, but it is a thing collateral annexed to the person touching the land, and is no more than a confidence for the use of the land"[128]. Trust was personal, "for in common sense a

---

122 For "faithfully promised" see *R. H. Helmholz,* Assumpsit and Fidei Laesio, (1975) 91 L.Q.R 406, 425; for "consideration" see *J. H. Baker,* Origins of the Doctrine of Consideration, 1535 - 1585 in: M. S. Arnold, T. A. Green, S. A. Scully, S. D. White (eds.), On the Laws and Customs of England, Chapel Hill, 1981, pp. 336 - 358, reprinted in The Legal Profession and the Common Law, London, 1986, pp. 369 - 391.

123 C 33 / 67 f. 635.

124 *Wield v. Wield* (1560).

125 *Hopkins v. Hedloe* (1591) Bodleian Library (Bod. Lib.) MS. Rawl. C.647, fo. 131v; BL MS. Add. 40897, fo. 44; BL MS. Lans. 640, fo. 9v; BL MS. Stowe 572, fo. 73. C 33 / 84 f. 214. The defendant's name appears in the record as Hedylo or Hodylo.

126 For a recent re-affirmation of the central role of conscience in trust law see *Westdeutsche Landesbank Girozentrale v. Islington London Borough Council* [1996] A.C. 669, at 705 (*Lord Browne-Wilkinson).*

127 C 78 / 36 / 12.

man cannot trust one whom he does not know"[129], and, as *Coke* said, "[it] is absurd to say that confidence and trust can be reposed in land, which wants sense ... it would be less absurd to say that beasts may be trusted, who have sense and want reason, than land, which wants sense and reason also should be trusted"[130]. It followed from the personal nature of trust that a corporation aggregate could not be a trustee, "because it is a dead body, although it consist of natural persons: and in this dead body a confidence cannot be put, but in bodies natural"[131]. It followed too that breach of trust was not so much a failure to comply with abstract standards laid upon a trustee by equity, as a breach of a personal relationship of confidence. No doubt the chancellor would decree a trust in favour of a third party beneficiary, but if that beneficiary were ignorant of the trust the trustee would commit no breach of trust in re-transferring the trust property to the settlor. As *Egerton L. K.* said in *Yelverton v. Yelverton* (1599) "it is no breach of trust if any man of his own accord, minding to do good to another, do put one in trust with assurance and the party trusted do redeliver it at the request of him which did trust him without the privity of him to whom the good was meant, for the party to whom the good was meant did not trust him, but the party which did mean to do good"[132].

Coke glossed the "comparatively clear definition"[133] in *Plowden's* report of *Delamere's Case* saying that a "use is a trust or confidence, which is not issuing out of land, but as a thing collateral annexed in privity to the estate, and to the person touching the land ... So that, he who hath a use hath not *jus neque in re neque in rem,* but only a confidence and trust"[134]. And if a use did not issue out of land, and

128 1 Plowd. 346, at 352.

129 Huntingdon Library MS. EL 482, fo. 59v (in a collection of *Egerton L.K.'s* briefs and cause papers). I am grateful to *Professor J.H. Baker* for this reference.

130 *Chudleigh's Case* (1594) 1 Co. Rep. 120 (127a).

131 *Chudleigh's Case* (1594) (*sub nom. Dillon v. Fraine)* Poph. 70, at 71, *per Ewens B.*, *Owen* and *Fenner JJ.*, and "Bateman" (perhaps *Beaumont J.*). See also *Croft v. Howell* (1578) 2 Plowd. 530, at 538, *arguendo.* This was not the sole ground upon which it was said that a corporation could not be seised to a use: see *Gilbert* (n. 58) 6 ff. and note. Despite *Egerton L.K.'s* assertion that he would not trust "a corporation of all persons in the world" with a charitable act for a testator's soul because "bodies politic had no soul to lose but private men had" (CUL MS. Gg.2.31, fo. 450v), in the case of charitable trusts the corporate nature of the trustee posed no difficulty. See, for example, *Warden and Commonalty of the Weavers of New Sarum v. Grafton* where in 1595 the defendant was ordered to assure the land in question to the plaintiff corporation upon trust for the poor. C 33 / 87 ff. 122v, 208v, 349v, 734v, C 33 / 89 f. 76v, C 33 / 91 ff. 101, 231.

132 BL MS. Add. 48097, fo. 57; C 33 / 96 ff. 30, 856. In outline, the assurance was an indenture of covenant to stand seised of after-acquired property to the plaintiff's use. The plaintiff claimed the land or recompense therefore, or to be permitted to bring an action on the covenant in the covenantee's name without showing the indenture, since the covenantee, "for that he was but only trusted therewith", had returned the indenture "in discharge of the said trust". I am grateful to *Professor W. H. Bryson* for bringing this case to my attention.

133 *V. V. Palmer,* The Paths to Privity, San Francisco, 1992, p. 121.

134 *Chudleigh's Case* (1594) 1 Co. Rep. 120, at 121a-121b; Coke upon Littleton, f 272b.

he who had a use had neither *ius in re* nor *ius in rem,* then the interest of *cestui que trust* was no more than a chose in action. So, in *Lord Nottingham's* words, it was held in *Wytham v. Waterhowse* (1596) by all the judges in Serjeants' Inn that "if the wife be cestui que trust of a term ... if the husband survives he shall not have this trust by survivorship, but the administrator of the wife shall have it; for it consists in privity and is a thing in action"; "the confidence was", as a contemporary report of the same case put it, "a quasi chose in action"[135]. The same point was made in *Sir Moyle Finch's Case* (1600)[136], with the addition of the inevitable corollary that a trust, being a chose in action, could not be assigned: "it was resolved by all the justices, that admitting that Sir Thomas Heneage had a trust, yet [he] could not ... assign the same over to the plaintiff, because it was a matter in privity between them, and was in nature of a *chose* in action, for he had no power of the land, but only to seek remedy by *subpoena*"[137].

The definition in *Delamere v. Barnard* and *Coke's* gloss upon it, arising in actions at common law, were both couched in terms of the pre-statute use. But their applicability to the trust is apparent in the distinction drawn between use and trust in *Sir Moyle Finch's Case* (1600)[138]: the beneficiary of a trust, it was said, was "not like to *cestui que use,* for thereof there should be *possessio fratris*[139], and he should be sworn on juries in respect of the use, and he had power over the land by the statute of 1 R. 3. cap. [1] and if a bare trust and confidence might be assigned over great inconvenience might thereof follow by granting of the same to great men etc.". Of the pre-statute use it might be said that it "was but a trust at the first, and no remedy for it but a subpoena", but "time made it descendible as the land was"[140]. The same process of time and the establishment of a regular course of the

---

135 Inner Temple MS. Misc. 46, fo. 60v (translated). I owe this reference to *Professor W.H. Bryson.*

136 *E. Coke,* Fourth Part of the Institutes of the Laws of England, London, 1644, p. 85. This case originated in Chancery.

137 And if at this date the trust could not be assigned, it could not be devised by will either: "this trust is but [a] chose in action which he cannot devise and so the subpoena descends to the heir of the feoffee as the land should have done", *per Coke A.-G.*, CUL MS. Gg.2.31, fo. 465 (partly translated) (1596 - 1603). But compare *Kedeward v. Baker* (1597) C 33/93 ff. 404, 457, C 33/96 f. 517, where it was said that though "the assignment made by John Tyler and his wife to the plaintiff's father of the moiety of the lands in question is void in law, ... yet ... the trust and equity for that moiety was in the said Tyler and his wife and ought in true meaning as it seemed to pass by their assignment to the plaintiff's father and so from him to the plaintiffs".

138 *E. Coke,* Fourth Part of Institutes of the Laws of England, London, 1644, p. 85.

139 For *possessio fratris* see Coke upon Littleton, f. 14a ff. *Possessio fratris de feodo simplici,* it was said, *facit sororem esse hæredem.* So if a tenant of land in fee simple had a son and a daughter by his first wife, and a son by his second, and after his father's death the elder son entered upon the land and died without children, the daughter would have the land and not the younger son. That there might be *possessio fratris* of a use was not universally accepted. See J. Spedding, R. L. Ellis, D. D. Heath (eds.), The Works of Francis Bacon, vol. VII, London, 1859, p. 402.

Chancery in enforcing trusts, was to alter the nature of the trust in the same way. But time was required, and "to regard the trust before *Lord Nottingham's* time as conferring an interest in land would be an anachronism"[141].

3. Privity and the Doctrine of Notice

Not only did the trust require confidence, but it required privity also, "which is nothing else but a continuance of the confidence without interruption"[142]. It was early established that the effect of the pre-statute use was not limited to the original feoffee to uses, the subpoena becoming available against the heir of a deceased feoffee to uses perhaps in the 1450s during the chief justiceship of *Sir John Fortescue*[143]. Perhaps at about the same time it was established that the subpoena would lie also against a grantee of a feoffee to uses[144]. The doctrine is stated clearly in a year book note, perhaps of 1465: "If J. enfeoffs A. to [J's] use and A. enfeoffs R., even though [A.] sells to [R.], if A. gives notice to R. of the intent of the first feoffment, [R.] is bound by writ of *subpoena* to carry out [J.'s] will"[145].

Here are the seeds of the doctrine of notice, which has passed down to modern times as definitive (statute apart) of the effect of equitable interests on third party purchasers: "*Cestui que trust* has rights enforceable against all save a *bona fide* purchaser ... who for value has obtained a legal right in the thing without notice actual or constructive"[146]. But the requirement of privity for some time imposed a significant limitation upon the doctrine of notice: those who did not come in through the feoffee to uses but who simply came after him by a paramount and extraneous title, for example a disseisor or a feudal lord taking by escheat[147], were unaffected by the use even if they had notice of it[148]. This doctrine continued to be

---

140 Bod. Lib. MS Rawl. C. 647 f. 143. A note, probably of 1596, in a set of reports in Chancery 1579 - 1580 and 1588 - 1598 collected by Richard Powle.

141 Yale (n. 3) 91. And as *Dr. Macnair* shows in his paper in this volume, even after *Lord Nottingham's* time a proprietary explanation of trusts was by no means universal.

142 Spedding (n. 139) 401. *Bacon* here quotes a *dictum* by *Fenner J.* in 1593 - 94.

143 See *Palmer* (n. 133) 118 n. 161 and references there.

144 *Baker* (n. 34) 287.

145 Y.B. Mich. 5 Edw. IV, fo. 7v, pl. 16, printed in *Baker/Milsom* (n. 40) 97.

146 *Maitland* (n. 9) 115. Third parties who gave no consideration were affected by the trust even though they had no notice for the law implied notice. See *Chudleigh's Case* (1594) 1 Co. Rep. 120, at 122b; Yale (n. 2) 253; and *Dr. Macnair's* paper in this volume.

147 Freehold land would escheat to the feudal lord if its tenant died without heirs or was convicted of felony.

148 Though it was said that *cestui que use* might in Chancery compel his feoffees to enter upon the disseisor, or recover the land against him at common law, "and then the chancery may compel the feoffees to execute the estate according to the use". BL MS. Harg. 227, fo. 66; BL MS. Harley 736, fo. 251v.

applied to trusts in the 16th century and beyond[149], but, unlike the doctrine of notice, has not survived in the modern law.

The doctrine of notice is found again shortly after the Statute of Uses. In a note of 1538/39 in *Brooke's Abridgment* is a distinction between a case where a use does not arise until after the relevant conveyance, in which case the purchaser will be bound even if he has no notice of the use, and a "case where a feoffee in use sells the land to someone who has no notice of the first use"[150]. The earliest clear consideration of notice in the Chancery record is in *Rooke v. Staples* (1577)[151], where "it appeared ... that the ... plaintiff had sufficiently proved that the lease mentioned in his bill of complaint was by him made to the defendant only in trust and confidence to the use of the ... plaintiff". It was therefore decreed that the plaintiff, his heirs and assigns, should quietly and peaceably "have, hold, occupy, and enjoy" all the lands demised by the lease without interruption by the defendant, his executors or assigns, "or any other person or persons whatsoever claiming from by or under the ... defendant (since the plaintiff's bill exhibited) and having notice or understanding of the said trust and confidence at such time as he or they did obtain the ... lease of the ... defendant". And it was further decreed that if the defendant had made over his interest in the lease or any part of it "to any person or persons not having notice of the ... trust and confidence ... since the ... plaintiff's bill exhibited", then the defendant should pay to the plaintiff such money as the plaintiff should show the interest so made over to have been worth: once the trust property had reached the hands of persons not having notice of the trust the beneficiary's sole recourse was against the trustee himself.

Rooke v. Staples only refers expressly to the question of notice. Other cases illustrate the requirement of consideration. In *Ford v. Pomery*[152] a decree had been made against the defendant, who was found to have been granted a lease in trust

---

149 In *Lord Nottingham's* day "he who comes in in the *post,* as lord by escheat, disseisor, etc., is never subject to the former uses. And this is the standing rule for trusts ... as appears by common experience". Yale (n. 2) 244. For further discussion of this point see *Dr. Macnair's* paper in this volume.

150 *R. Brooke,* La Graunde Abridgement, London, 1573, *Feoffments al uses,* pl. 50, printed in *Baker/Milsom* (n. 40) 120.

151 Cary 76, BL MS. Harg. 281, fo. 84, BL MS. Lans. 599, fo. 51, BL MS. Lans. 1110, fo. 81v, BL MS. Stowe 415, fo. 116, CUL MS. Dd.9.22, fo. 65; C 33/53 f. 259, C 33/60 ff. 36v, 43v, 232. There is mention of privity and knowledge in the plaintiff's pleadings in *Ailyff v. Wrenne* (1560) C 78/16/26, but the case was dismissed for lack of proof, and stands at the border of trust and bailment.

152 C 33/67 ff. 61v, 70v; C 33/69 ff. 37v, 522, 557v; C 33/71 ff. 131, 260v, 341, 518v, 555; C 33/74 ff. 152v, 271, 316, 362, 398, 404v, 470, 476, 483, 518, 524v, 611, 632v; C 33/75 ff. 74v, 123v, 273, 357, 434v, 468, 496v, 529v, 546, 593, 626v, 666, 713, 744v, 755v; C 33/77 ff. 34v, 39v, 132v, 154, 226, 305v, 790; C 33/79 ff. 19, 257, 476, 772v; C 33/83 ff. 91, 184v, 197, 211, 364v; C 33/85 ff. 158v, 217v, 395, 415, 632v; C 33/87 ff. 347v, 429v, 623v, 743; C 33/89 ff. 229, 245, 446, 853v; C 33/91 ff. 155, 206; C 33/93 f. 723v; C 33/97 f. 74v; C 78/85/15B

by the plaintiff's father, the decree to bind all claiming under the defendant with certain exceptions. In 1589 information was made to the court on behalf of Christopher Mecombe and Lawrence Baron, not falling within the exceptions, who "trust that it was not meant by this court to overthrow their estates if they came unto them ... bona fide for good consideration and knew not of the trust which hath been adjudged against the defendant"[153].

The 16th century cases are discussed in terms of "notice", "knowledge", or "privity"; the terms appear to be interchangeable and might be used in conjunction[154]. Consideration of the meaning of notice was as yet undeveloped, though a little detail was added in the late 16th century, not entirely conducive to a widening of the trust jurisdiction. In *Cornwallis's Case* (1594 - 96)[155] *Egerton L. K.* held that if there were a "conveyance absolute in words" and yet "a bruit[156] of a trust but doubtful whether there be a trust or not", one who bought the land hearing the bruit would not be concluded by it, neither was a buyer to believe "one which would not have him to buy it if he tell him there is a trust". A similar sentiment was expressed with characteristic forcefulness in *Ragland v. Wilegosse* (1601)[157]. It was asked whether if A was seised in trust to the use of B, and sold the land to C, would C have notice if someone came to him before the sale and said "take heed how you buy such land for A hath nothing in it but in trust to the use of B", and another came and said "it is not as he is informed, for A is seized of this land absolutely"? By analogy with the law concerning publishers of forged deeds and receivers of felons *Popham C. J.* argued that C in this case would have notice. But "Egerton lord keeper said he would not draw blood upon such an opinion, and in the principal case he said that the caveat given was no notice, for flying reports are many times fables, and not truth, and if it should be admitted for a sufficient notice then the inheritance of every man might easily be slandered"[158].

---

153 C 33/79 f. 19.

154 For example, C 33/69 f. 282v (1584/85, *Metcalfe v. Fletcher*) "had notice of and were privy to the trust and confidence"; C 33/79 f. 812v (1590, *Drewrye v. Danyell*) "privy or knowing of that trust"; C 33/91 f. 116 (1596, *Poole v. Gauntlet*) "not ignorant but made privy and acquainted with the former proceedings".

155 Tothill 186, BL MS. Harg. 281, fo. 225v, BL MS. Harl. 1576, fo. 149v, BL MS. Lans. 640, fo. 12, BL MS. Stowe 572, fo. 74v, CUL MS. Gg.2.31, fos. 225v, 408v.

156 That is, a noise or a rumour.

157 Gouldsb. 147, pl. 67 (*sub nom. Wildgoose v. Wayland*), CUL MS. Gg.2.31, fo. 410, CUL MS Gg.3.25, fo. 92v, BL MS. Harl. 1576, fo. 151, BL MS. Lans. 640, fo. 73v; C 78/93/10.

158 See Yale (n. 2) 254. *Cf.* Bod. Lib. MS Rawl. C.647, fo. 141v where the analogous question arose in the case of an assertion by a third party that one being in another's house had committed felony. *Egerton L. K.* and the chief baron held that the householder would not commit felony in letting the alleged felon go unless he knew the allegation to be true or "in some sort [took] notice" that it was true. Similarly, it was said, in the case of one who published a deed which a stranger alleged to be forged. I owe this reference to *Professor W. H. Bryson*.

But even *Egerton L. K.* was prepared to accept that "a suit depending for a trust which upon hearing is proved shall be sufficient notice of trust to any man that shall buy it (hanging that suit)"[159], a doctrine which appears to extend beyond actual notice into the territory of constructive notice[160], and which may be reflected in the difficulties of the defendant in *Heddon v. Chawnor* in 1597[161], faced with a dilatory plaintiff in a trust case, and "greatly prejudiced for that so long as the same suit dependeth he cannot sell the same lands".

VI. Trusts in Context

Having considered trust property, the purposes for which trusts were employed within the period, and the nature of the beneficiary's interest, it remains to return to *Maitland's* definition of a trust, and his commentary upon it "by distinguishing cases of trust from some other cases"[162]. The relationship between trust and account has been considered elsewhere[163], and that between trust and contract has been discussed above. It is proposed here to address two further situations in which trusts displayed a close relationship with other legal concepts: grants upon condition, and bailments.

1. Trusts and Conditions[164]

The effects of a transfer of property by A to B upon trust for C, and a transfer of property by A to B upon condition that B do something for C, are clearly distinct[165]. Two types of condition must be distinguished. A transfer subject to a condition precedent is ineffective unless and until the condition is performed. A transfer subject to a condition subsequent is immediately effective, but liable to terminate upon the happening of a contingency[166]. It is with the latter that we are concerned. In the case of such a transfer B's title is liable to be divested upon a contingency, but C has neither an interest in the property transferred, nor the benefit of an obligation binding B. Indeed, B is under no obligation at all, but merely

159 *Diggs v. Boys* (1598) Tothill 186, BL MS. Harl. 1576, fo. 154v, BL MS. Lans. 640, fo. 13v, BL MS. Stowe 572, fo. 75v, CUL MS. Gg.2.31, fo. 230v.

160 *Lord Nottingham* called such notice "legal" as opposed to "actual", Yale (n. 2) 253.

161 C 33/91 f. 823, C 33/93 f. 713, C 33/96 f. 646.

162 *Maitland* (n. 9) 44. See *Dr. Macnair's* paper in this volume for 17th and 18th century discussion of the relationship between trust and other legal concepts.

163 *Jones,* (1997) Cambridge Law Journal 175, 189 ff.

164 For discussion of conditions and the medieval use see *Professor Biancalana's* paper in this volume.

165 It is possible for A and C to be the same person.

166 The contingency must necessarily be an event the happening of which is not certain.

vulnerable to the loss of his title should the condition not be performed[167]. Subject to the condition, B's title to the property is absolute. In contrast, in the case of a transfer upon trust C has at least the benefit of an obligation binding B, and B is not entitled to retain any surplus remaining after C's interest has been satisfied[168].

But despite the clarity of the theoretical distinction between trust and condition, the effect of a transfer of property "upon condition" is a matter of interpretation of A's words[169]. Because of the disadvantages of the common law condition, most notably the rule that no-one might re-enter for breach of condition other than the grantor or his heirs[170], the tendency in English law has been towards an analysis in terms of trust: "much better for the legatees to have the lands liable upon a trust than upon a condition, and to send them to equity against the devisee than against the heir"[171]. Such flexibility of interpretation indicates the difficulty of separating trust and condition. A transferor making a transfer of property upon a condition in the strict sense may also in a loose sense trust the transferee. And a condition ineffective at law for want of formality may nevertheless be effective in conscience.

"[W]hat", asked *Christopher St German's* Doctor of Divinity, "do you think of a feoffment made without a writing, under a condition permitted in law; is the condition binding in conscience?"[172]. It was clear that at common law a condition could not be pleaded to defeat a freehold without the production of a writing under seal[173], but *St German's* student of the laws of England was of opinion that a condition without writing "binds in conscience; for it may even be binding in law if,

167 Cf. the "topsy-turvy" functioning of the conditioned bond as a contractual device. The bond functioned to procure performance of the condition, but the obligation was not to perform the condition but rather to pay the sum acknowledged to be owed. See *A. W. B. Simpson,* A History of the Common Law of Contract, Oxford, 1975, p. 112.

168 *Hill v. Bishop of London* (1738) 1 Atk. 618; *King v. Denison* (1813) 1 V. & B. 260; *Croome v. Croome* (1888) 59 L.T. 582. The surplus may be retained by B if it is possible to find an intention to give him a beneficial interest.

169 For modern discussion see *T. C. Thomas,* Conditions in Favour of Third Parties (1952) Cambridge Law Journal 240.

170 The other principal disadvantage being that if a condition subsequent attached to real or personal property, or a condition precedent attached to personal property, became impossible of performance, the interest to which the condition was attached became absolute in the hands of the grantee. See *Thomas* (n. 169) 242 - 246. The difficulty of the rule mentioned in the text is absent if the condition is in favour of the initial grantor.

171 *Per Scroggs C. J.* in *Freak v. Lee* (1679) 2 Show. K.B. 36. Similarly, it was said that the words "on condition that" could support a charitable trust, since "all words of trust are words of limitation and appointment and thus within the letter of the statute [of charitable uses]": *Jones* (n. 67) 63 - 64, quoting from Francis Moore's reading in the Middle Temple in 1607 on the Statute of Charitable Uses, 43 Eliz., c. 4. The initial folio references to CUL MS. Hh.3.2 at p. 63 nn. 9 and 10 are transposed: "on condition that" appears on fo. 28v, "in confidence that" on fo. 136.

172 *St German* (n. 114) 145.

173 YB P 11 Hen VII, f. 22, pl. 12; Coke upon Littleton 225a. In the case of chattels real and personal no deed was required.

for example, the condition were found by a jury; for the law of England is not that every condition made without a writing is void, but that it cannot be pleaded without a writing. And because the condition in this case may be valid even in law ... therefore it is valid and binding in conscience".

A similar point arose in Chancery in *Betty v. Betty* (1565)[174]. One Henry Betty had become bound as surety for the debts of his brother John, whereupon John conveyed freehold land to Henry "absolutely without any condition", though the true meaning of the conveyance was that Henry be saved harmless upon his suretyship, and that if he were so saved then the conveyance should be void. This arrangement was made "by word without writing before divers witnesses". The lack of formality prevented a remedy at law, but a remedy was available in Chancery: the land in question was to be conveyed to four named individuals "to the use of the ... plaintiff and his heirs upon condition" that the plaintiff pay to the defendant a specified sum, and if the sum was not paid "to the use of the ... defendant and his heirs for ever without any manner of condition". A condition without formality might be binding in conscience; and the role of conscience was not lost upon John Betty: his conveyance had, he said, been made "upon a very special confidence and trust" that he had in his brother.

Trust and condition might be run together even more closely. Thus the plaintiff in *Hayes v. Holwell* (1584)[175], "alleged that he hath assured and conveyed an advowson ... unto the defendant and his heirs upon trust and upon condition agreed between them"[176], while in *Hydden alias Clyddisdale v. Clyfford* (1562)[177] the plaintiff asserted that a lease had been granted both "upon trust and confidence and to the use" of the plaintiff when he should attain the age of 23, and "upon condition" that the premises should be regranted to the plaintiff when he reached 23. These expressions may represent simply a loose use of language, but trust and condition might literally be combined. In *Blunt v. Sawnders* (1584)[178] Richard Blunt had granted a lease of a manor to his brother Thomas "upon condition and confidence" that when Richard or his executors should pay five shillings to Thomas at a certain place the grant should be void, and in the meantime Richard took the profits of the manor and granted estates to the tenants "as if he had been still lawful and proper owner of the said manor": the conditional interest was itself the subject matter of a trust in favour of its grantor.

---

174 C 78/26/25.

175 C 33/67 f. 492v.

176 The terms of the trust and condition are not apparent from the record.

177 C 78/21/1.

178 C 33/67 f. 570.

2. Trusts and Bailment

It has proved difficult to speak of bailment without using trust language. *Blackstone's* explanation that a bailment is "a delivery of goods in trust upon a contract expressed or implied, that the trust shall be faithfully executed on the part of the bailee"[179], though condemned as "a fruitful source of confusion"[180], has been in the minds of English judges in modern times[181]. And *Blackstone* was drawing upon earlier usage. In the declaration in *Hayden v. Raggelond* (1510)[182], the plaintiff said that he had bailed a deed to the defendant, in whom he had placed great trust (*magna confidencia*), while it was said in *Southcote v. Bennet* (1601)[183], that "if A. bails to B. a locked coffer to keep, and he takes away the key himself, in this case if the goods are stolen B. shall not be charged, for A. did not trust B. with them".

In modern cases a definition in terms of trust may not be entirely misplaced; bailees have been treated as fiduciaries liable to account for the proceeds or subject matter of the bailment[184]. But a fiduciary duty does not render a bailee a trustee, and whether the parties have created a bailment or a trust is a question of intention. It is true that the legal consequences of bailment are radically different from those of trust: and though it may not be helpful to say that bailment is a matter at common law, while trust is a matter in equity[185], clearly enough the bailee obtains no title to the goods bailed, and has not that prospect which a trustee has of giving good title to a third party. But however clear the theoretical distinction, it can only come into play once it has been decided whether the situation amounts to a bailment or a trust. And in taking the decision as to how to present a case plaintiffs within the period may have had an eye upon the remedies available at common law and in Chancery.

In *Churchan v. Radney* (1581)[186] the plaintiff claimed evidences and writings. The defendant confessed that he had them, and said that they were "to him deliv-

---

179 *W. Blackstone,* Commentaries on the Laws of England, vol. II, 17th ed., London, 1830, p. 451.

180 *Martin* (n. 10) 47.

181 "To constitute a bailment chattels must be delivered in trust, on a contract express or implied, that the trust shall be duly executed, and the chattels re-delivered as soon as the time or use for, or conditions on, which they were bailed shall have elapsed or been performed", *per Evershed J.*, giving the judgment of the Court of Appeal in *Rosenthal v. Alderton and Sons Ltd.* [1946] 1 All E.R. 583 at 584. See generally *N. E. Palmer,* Bailment, 2nd ed., London, 1991, pp. 189 - 192.

182 Court of Common Pleas De Banco Rolls (CP 40): CP 40/992 m 451; *Baker/Milsom* (n. 40) 528.

183 4 Co. Rep. 83.

184 *Palmer* (n. 181) 190 and references there.

185 *Maitland* (n. 9) 45.

186 C 33/61 f. 481.

ered in trust, to keep safely until the controversy were decided for certain lands that the same do concern". The court concluded that unless cause was shown to the contrary, the evidences should be delivered to the plaintiff to enable her to defend an action at law for land which she had. In *Townsende v. Windham* (1583)[187] the plaintiff and one Thomas Drewry entered into a bond in 1000 marks conditioned for payment of £ 320. By agreement between the parties to the bond it was "committed in trust to the custody" of the defendant, *Wyndham J.*, "he safely to keep the same" as an escrow[188]. The delivery of the bond as the plaintiff's deed was conditional upon Drewry's procurement of a committal by the Lord Treasurer of the custody of a named lunatic to Sir Rowlande Haywarde or his nominee[189]. Upon the death of the lunatic the plaintiff alleged that custody had not been procured and demanded his bond back. The defendant was ordered to deliver the bond into court, it to be delivered to the plaintiff unless Drewry showed cause, or the Lord Treasurer showed that custody had been granted. Both of these cases might have been presented as cases of bailment leading to a common law remedy. But the unique nature of the deeds in question rendered a Chancery decree for specific performance more attractive, and led to an analysis of the situation in terms of trust.

VII. Conclusion

In the decades after the Statute of Uses trusts in England were in a state of transition. "[T]hough the trust turned out to be a different product and was put to very different ends from those of the use, it was of the same raw material from the same source"[190]. And so the influence of pre-statute learning is apparent in the 16th century. The requirement of privity and the concept of the trust as a chose in action, both corollaries of the trust's basis in personal confidence, imposed serious limitations upon trusts. The influence of personal confidence was in due course reduced: "[a]s the influence of the use recedes, so does the dominance of the notion of confidence reposed in the feoffee by the beneficiary, and the emphasis shifts rather to the beneficiary's interest with its increasingly proprietary tinge"[191]. But that story does not belong to the 16th century.

There was both within the period and after it a certain hostility to trusts, pervasive though they were. The dichotomy in the court's summary of the plaintiff's as-

187 C 33/65 f. 486.

188 An escrow is a deed the delivery of which is conditional, the deed taking effect only upon fulfilment of the condition.

189 At common law it was impossible to create an escrow without the intervention of a third party between the grantor and the potential grantee. See *D.E.C. Yale,* The Delivery of a Deed, (1970) Cambridge Law Journal 52 (where the discussion is quite naturally in terms of bailment of the deed).

190 Yale (n. 3) *88.*

191 Yale (n. 3) *90.*

sertion in *Johanes v. Pryce* (1587) as being that a lease had been "made to the ... defendant only upon trust and confidence and not otherwise bona fide" was not atypical[192]: trusts had about them a flavour of *mala fides. Egerton L. K.* was reluctant to enforce trusts against third parties without clear evidence of notice[193]. Even without the intervention of a third party strict proof of a trust might be required, though a certain flexibility was possible. Finding in *Mynne v. Cobb* (1604)[194] that "the trust was not so fully proved as [he] would make a full decree thereupon, so as it should be a precedent for other causes; and yet so far forth proved as it satisfied him as a private man" *Lord Ellesmere L. C.* "thought fit to write his letters to the defendant to conform himself to reason"[195].

Henry Sherfield, reading on the Statute of Wills in Lincoln's Inn in 1623, was less ready to be generous: "For now a man may pass his lands by fine or feoffment, etc., to the use of John Style in fee, and yet upon trust and confidence for the feoffee or any other: which is now an use upon a use ... And this upstart hath as great a place in the Court of Chancery as ever uses had; and it will be no doubt as perilous to the common laws. And I did then, and still do, think that it were most happy to this state if uses and trusts of that kind were extirpated totally"[196].

But for all his hostility towards trusts, *Sherfield* had seen a point which has largely escaped the notice of legal historians. The Statute of Wills, he said, "does not respect the estate conveyed to enforce of any necessity that the same should attach in the person advanced by way of interest, but that it did suffice if it were made to strangers upon trust for the benefit of the wife or children or to pay debts"[197]. Such hostility as there was towards trusts was not a consequence of their potential to evade the royal feudal revenue. "[W]e can be sure that [the chancellor] would not feel himself automatically unable to prevent unconscientious conduct just because of the Statute of Uses"[198]: the Statute of Wills had seen to that.

The absence of any general revenue difficulty renders the frequency of trust cases in the 16th century Chancery more readily explicable. Trusts were as yet in

192 C 33/75 f. 38v.

193 *Ragland v. Wilegosse* (n. 157).

194 Cary 25, BL MS. Lans. 599, fo. 5v, BL MS. Stowe 415, fo. 98, BL MS. Harg. 281, fo. 44v, CUL MS. Dd.9.22, fo. 23v; C 33/105 ff. 219v, 901, 946, 979, 1020, C 33/106 f. 212v, C 78/450/17.

195 It appears from the record that counsel were agreed that a surrender of copyhold had been made in trust, but that it appeared doubtful to the court "what the meaning of the ... [settlor] was touching the same lands".

196 Reading on 32 Hen. VIII, c. 1, BL MS. Harg. 402, fo. 34v, printed in *Baker/Milsom* (n. 40) 125 - 126. The point was not new: Thomas Audley had argued a century before that: "to a great extent [uses] have been pursued by collusion for the evil purpose of destroying the good laws of the realm", reading on 4 Hen. VII, c. 17, Inner Temple, 1526. Printed in *Baker/Milsom* (n. 40) 103 ff.

197 BL MS. Harg. 402, fo. 40v.

198 *Milsom* (n. 36) 239.

general simple, express, and intended only for a short term of operation, and a decree that the trustees reconvey to the settlor might frequently be the most apt remedial solution: the employment of trusts in the family settlement or in the management of floating funds of investments was yet to come. And they were frequently active: the search for the passive trust of freehold in the form of a use upon a use has been misleading. The use upon use indeed became common form, but this was not true of the 16th century. Such trusts as there were in this form in the 16th century were almost always active, and there is no reason to suppose that entirely passive trusts were ever very common after the Statute of Uses.

But though trusts in the period were as yet less than fully developed, and analytical treatment of them was yet to come, the seeds of future development may nevertheless be seen. Trust property was wide-ranging. The separate use of married women, and the practice of keeping terms on foot to protect the inheritance both had their origins in this period. Charitable trusts flourished, doubts over the execution of trusts of leases were resolved, and the doctrine of notice was finding its post-statute feet[199] .

This paper has concentrated upon the Chancery, but trusts were not the sole preserve of that court, or even of equity. In Chancery pleadings are trustees who have "faithfully promised" in the approved *assumpsit* fashion, and at common law there are occasional actions on the case for breach of trust, represented in the 16th century by *Megod's Case* (1586)[200]. Bailees and others[201], though creatures of the common law, may at times bear a close likeness to trustees. The internal divisions of legal thinking were less clear than one might suppose.

In some cases the imprint of political events is very strong. Trusts provided a means of support and a cover of secrecy for those threatened by religious persecution or by political danger: changes of regime in the immediate aftermath of the Statute of Uses may have had a very significant effect upon the development of the trust by enabling litigation, such as that in *Bertie v. Herenden,* over trusts created by those at risk under a former regime. And such cases indicate the limitations of the evidence: trusts for secrecy may leave no trace unless they come to litigation. That they should come to litigation was unthinkable when they were created: they were trusts in the fundamental sense that they depended upon trust reposed in the trustees. Should the trustees fail, unless the circumstances were changed which had given rise to the need for the trust in the first place, nothing could be done. The cases which came to litigation were the exception and not the norm. Not only was trust not confined to the Chancery or even to equity, it was not confined to the law as a whole.

---

199 English lawyers may note in particular that it has by no means always been clear that the plea of *bona fide* purchase for value without notice should be restricted to purchasers of legal interests: Yale (n. 3) 162 - 164.

200 See *Jones,* (1997) Cambridge Law Journal 175.

201 Including executors, accountants, mortgagees, and guardians in socage.

MICHAEL MACNAIR

The Conceptual Basis of Trusts in the Later 17th and Early 18th Centuries

I. Introductory

The standard modern explanation of the trust concept, found in the textbooks on equity and trusts, is inextricably linked with the general explanation of the English equity jurisdiction. This link is historical in one direction: the equity jurisdiction arose, it is argued, because of the development in the later medieval period of the practice of creating trusts (uses) and the absence of any remedy for breach of trust at common law. In juridical analysis, on the other hand, the argument proceeds in the other direction. The beneficiary of a trust (if there is more than one beneficiary, all of them together) is seen as having a proprietary interest in the subject-matter of the trust. The separation of this proprietary interest from the legal ownership which is vested in the trustee falls to be explained by the existence of the equity jurisdiction, which enables the separation of legal *dominium*, in the trustee, from equitable *dominium*, in the beneficiary[1].

This explanation is dependent on certain assumptions both about the history of the equity jurisdiction (that the enforcement of trusts is central to its origin and hence at its conceptual core), and about the attitude of courts of equity to trusts (that the beneficiary is to be seen as having an equitable proprietary interest, an interest in some sense at least *in rem)*. Both assumptions are actually or potentially controversial[2]. In the early 18th century they could not be taken for granted.

---

1 See, for example, *J. E. Martin*, Hanbury & Martin, Modern Equity, 1993, pp. 5 ff.; *P. H. Pettitt*, Equity and the Law of Trusts, 1993, pp. 3 ("the central institution of equity jurisdiction, the trust") and 11 ff.; *D. J. Hayton*, Hayton & Marshall, Cases and Commentary on the Law of Trusts, 1991, pp. 6 ff.

2 The nature of the early English bill jurisdiction of Chancery is the subject of an extensive literature, which has been recently reviewed in *Timothy S. Haskett*, The Medieval English Court of Chancery, (1996) 14 Law and History Review 245 ff. Much of this literature "decentres" uses / trusts in the jurisdiction. However, the traditional view has been reasserted by *R. C. Palmer*, English Law in the Age of the Black Death, 1993, pp. 104 ff. For the question whether the beneficiary has an interest *in rem* see *F. W. Maitland*, Equity, 1909, pp. 110 ff., and subsequent discussion summarised in *Martin* (n. 1) 18 ff.; *Hayton* (n. 1) 10 ff. The issue has been recently aired in the European Court of Justice: *Webb v. Webb* [1994] 2 All E.R. 911. In addition, *J. H. Langbein* has recently argued that a contractual analysis of trusts offers superior solutions to a range of problems: The Contractarian Basis of Trusts, (1995) 105 Yale

Though some lawyers held views close to the modern standard explanation, the most systematic treatise, that attributed to *Henry Ballow*, explains both equity in general and trusts in particular by contract theory; and both explanations of equity, and some of the details of trusts law discussed by *Ballow* and other writers, further complicate the picture. In this paper I aim to explore this question to a limited extent through a study of four analytical treatments of trusts in the period: those of *Nottingham, Gilbert, Ballow* and the anonymous "General Abridgement of Cases in Equity" (1 Equity Cases Abridged). I will consider first the explanations of the trust offered by treatise writers in this period; second, the extent to which these affected their analytical organisation of their material; thirdly, what, if anything, the detail of their accounts and the case-law they rely on can tell us about equity lawyers' understanding of the trust; and finally, what the relative weight of "trusts" in the texts, their uses, and the wider uses of the expression "trust" in these and some other sources, can tell us.

I do not offer a full survey of either rules governing trusts, or the case-law relating to them. *D.E.C. Yale* has provided a fairly extensive study of the detail of trusts law in the period, focused on the work of *Lord Nottingham*[3], and *M. R. Chesterman* has offered a general socio-economic explanation of the transition, between the late 17th and early 19th century, from the passive trust of land to the actively managed trust of a fund of investments[4]. My concern is more narrowly with conceptual frameworks: hence the focus on general analytical texts, and within these on a limited range of questions.

II. Explaining Equity, Explaining Trusts

1. Background

The early 18th century saw a new development of analytical treatise literature on the equity jurisdiction (particularly that of Chancery). *Sir Jeffrey Gilbert's* "Forum Romanum", on the procedure of the Court, and "Lex Praetoria", on its substantive doctrine, were written (in their final form) in the early 1720s, though not published until 1756[5]. (*Gilbert's* "The Law of Uses and Trusts", published in 1734 but prob-

L.J. 625 ff. (*inter alia* discussing the American literature on the question whether the beneficiary's right is *in rem* or *in personam).*

3 Introduction to Lord Nottingham's Reports of Chancery Cases, vol. II, Selden Society, vol. 79, 1961 - 62, pp. 87 ff.

4 Family Settlements on Trust: Landowners and the Rising Bourgeoisie, in: G. R. Rubin and David Sugarman (eds.), Law, Economy and Society, 1984, pp. 124 ff.

5 Two Treatises on the Proceedings in Equity and the Jurisdiction of that Court ... by a late learned Judge, Dublin, 1756, has a poor version of the Forum Romanum, and a good version of the Lex Praetoria, separately paginated. The History and Practice of the High Court of Chancery, London, 1758, has a much better version of the Forum Romanum, but a weaker version of the Lex Praetoria. For the present paper I have primarily used the Dublin edition,

ably based on work done in the 1690s, mainly concerns common law, not equity[6].) *Richard Francis* published in 1728 his "Maxims of Equity", whose form follows

---

from Research Publications Microfilm series "The 18th Century", Reel 2342 No. 1. The book originated as part of a larger work written in the reign of Queen Anne dividing the law into *Persons* (probably; none of this survives), *Property, Personal* and *Real,* and *Actions.* For this general structure and the background see *M. Macnair,* Sir Jeffrey Gilbert and his Treatises, (1994) 15 J.L.H. 252, 258 ff. The outline of *Actions* is extant in Columbia Law School Singleton MS. 26 ff. 35 - 6 and 57 ff. 1 - 2. The topic is divided into a general part and treatment of particular actions; the general part contains discussion of the jurisdiction of courts, and the general features of process. The Chancery is discussed in outline notes at ff. 37 - 40 of this. The next stage was a fuller text called The Originall of the Chancery which appears in Col. LS MS. Singleton 34 (1), item (ii); this contains no material later than 1714, and was still not intended as an independent book, since it is without chapter divisions. In the 17-teens someone, presumably *Gilbert,* extracted the disorganised procedural material from this text and reorganised it on the basis of civilian procedural sources under the title Forum Romanum. Early versions of this, containing no material later than 1720, are in Harvard Law School MSS. 1064 item (iii) and 5141 item (ii). In around 1722 - 3, both texts were updated using MS. reports and the writer's personal memory. Versions in this form are (The Originall) Col. LS MSS. Singleton 28 and 27 (a fair copy from 28); (Forum Romanum) Col. LS MSS. 33 and 34(1) item (i). Finally, the Forum Romanum version of procedure was substituted for the procedural material in The Originall; the work takes this form in HLS MS. 1163. In this form the work was printed.

The Lex Praetoria exists in manuscript in (at least) Columbia Law School MS. Singleton 33 and Harvard Law School MS. 1064 item vi, and imperfect later copies in Col. LS MSS. Singleton 34(2) (datable to after 1733), and 34(3) (datable to after 1756). From the text as in Col. LS MS. Singleton 33 and HLS MS. 1064 and the cases used, the work appears to date to the early 1720s; the latest printed reports cited are *Salkeld's* (1721), and in the text as printed what appears to be part of *Gilbert's* preparatory work for his own judgment in *Whitchurch v. Whitchurch* (H1724/5) Gilb. Rep. 168, 9 Mod. 124, 1 Stra. 619, has been added to the end of the text. (In *Macnair* (above in this footnote) at 267 n. 107, I suggested that *Matthew Bacon* might have been the author of the Lex Praetoria. This view was based on study of the London, 1758, printed text, and is superseded by my study of the Dublin text and the MSS.)

It seems likely that the revised version of the Forum Romanum dating to this period, the Lex Praetoria (which appears to be new) and the updating of the Exchequer to 1725, for which see *Macnair* (above in this footnote) at 267, n. 107, represent *Gilbert's* preparation for his new responsibilities as one of the Commissioners of the Great Seal in 1725 and as Chief Baron of the Exchequer from June 1725.

6 The Law of Uses and Trusts, London, 1734. The title is the publisher's. The book contains (1) pp. 1 - 166, *Of Uses,* a highly structured discussion of uses at common law and under the Statute of Uses, belonging to *Gilbert's* treatment of *Real Property* (n. 5 *supra)*; (2) pp. 166 - 312, the same material in a disorganised form, beginning in the form of a forensic argument but lapsing into a disorganised general treatment; (3) pp. 313 - 353, late 17th and early 18th century case reports on matters of equity added by the editor; and (4) pp. 354-end, "A short and accurate treatise of Dower", belonging to *Gilbert's* Actions, Particular Actions. The dating of the substance of the work on uses to the 1690s is given by the presence in the main body of the argument of *Burchet v. Durdant* (1690) 2 Vent. 512, Ex. Ch. (it is the most recent authority used), but not of the rejection of this decision in *Broughton v. Langley* (1703) below n. 120; while the very important case on the creation of uses, *Jones d. Bellingham v. Morley* (1694) 4 Mod. 261, (1697) Comyns 29, Comb. 429, Carth. 410, Holt K.B. 321, (1698) Comyns 47, 12 Mod. 159, 1 Ld. Raym. 287, Salk. 677, K.B., aff'd in error in H. L. *Morley v. Jones* (1698) Show. P.C. 140, is absent, which strongly implies a date before 1698 at the

Francis Bacon's "Maxims of the Law" (1630) or the "Regulae Iuris" literature[7]. In 1732 there appeared the "General Abridgment of Cases in Equity" which is printed in the English Reports reprint as "1 Equity Cases Abridged", and which has been attributed to various authors[8]. And in 1737 there was published "A Treatise of Equity", which is usually attributed to *Henry Ballow*[9].

---

latest. It is possible that the work done in the 1690s was the disorganised version at pp. 166 - 313 and that the analytic version of pp. 1 - 166 was a subsequent reorganisation without substantive revision. Uses not exceuted by the Statute (i.e. trusts) are briefly discussed at pp. 161 - 166. I will refer later to *Gilbert's* account at pp. 1 - 3 of this book of the origin of uses, but there is little else in it relevant to my present concerns.

7 For the *Regulae Iuris* literature and its influence in England see *P. Stein,* Regulae Iuris, 1966. I have made no further use of *Francis'* Maxims in this paper, since its methodology makes it uninformative for my present concerns.

8 According to *Sir William Holdsworth,* A History of English Law, 1903 - 1966, vol.XII, p. 172, the contemporary *Charles Viner* attributed the text to a *Mr. Pooley,* to whom various reports were attributed; but *Holdsworth* prefers an attribution of both 1 and 2 Equity Cases Abridged to *Matthew Bacon,* and this is followed by *P. R. Glazebrook,* Bacon, Matthew, in: A. W. B. Simpson (ed.), Biographical Dictionary of the Common Law, 1984, p. 27. *A. W. B. Simpson,* The Rise and Fall of the Legal Treatise, (1981) 48 University of Chicago L.R. 632, 655, suggests an attribution of 1 Equity Cases Abridged to *Gilbert.* The British Library Catalogue, *sub* title, offers the alternatives of *Gilbert, Pooley,* or *Foley.* Stylistic and organisational evidence implies that 1 and 2 Equity Cases Abridged are not by the same author; the author of 2 Equity Cases Abridged shows, for example, a cruder organisation of the section on trusts, and less confidence in his ability to summarise cases in his own words, as opposed to quoting from the reports *in extenso.* Both the attributions of 1 Equity Cases Abridged to *Gilbert,* and to *Bacon,* are inconsistent with the style, and though from a stylistic point of view *Bacon* could have been responsible for 2 Equity Cases Abridged, any possible motivation is weak, since *Bacon* was engaged at the same time in a larger Abridgment project which covered some of the same material. The argument in favour, the use of identical MS. reports in both texts, is weakened by the fact that a body of MS. Chancery reports was clearly in circulation in the early 18th century, as can be seen from *Gilbert's* citations in the Lex Praetoria and from overlaps between the equity reports attributed to *Gilbert* and Precedents in Chancery, some involving reports which cannot have been made by *Gilbert.* The form of equity abridgments may have been partially continuous, as was the case with the earlier form of index to precedents printed as *Tothill,* The Transactions of the High Court of Chancery, London, 1649 (for this point see *M. Macnair,* The Nature and Function of the Early Chancery Reports, in: C. Stebbings (ed.), Law Reporting in Britain, 1995, pp. 123 ff., 127); there are earlier MS. equity abridgments, though simpler and shorter than Equity Cases Abridged, in Lincoln's Inn MS. Miscellaneous 576, dating from the 1650s, and British Library MS. Lansdowne 1125, dating from 1702 and bound under the title Equity Cases Abridged. An attribution of either of the volumes printed as 1 and 2 Equity Cases Abridged to a single hand might therefore be inappropriate. All citations to this text in this paper are to the English Reports reprint.

9 The book was published anonymously. The attribution was already in existence when it was questioned by *Fonblanque,* who edited the treatise in the 1790s, on the ground that *Ballow* was too junior at the time to have written the book, but *Holdsworth* (n. 8) vol. XII, 191 - 2, considered it established by circumstantial evidence. I am slightly more hesitant, as from working on it for the present paper, the analytic method of the book appears to be informed to a considerable extent by a civilian academic training, while the *Corpus iuris* is quoted as "the law", unqualified (which is unusual in writers primarily trained in the common law), and we have no evidence that *Ballow* had a background of this type (the only plausible *Henry*

To some extent this development was part of a more general growth of legal treatise literature in this period[10]. In the equity literature, however, there were some particular dynamics involved. In the early to mid 17th century accounts of equity in print or MS. circulation tended either to be based on the early 16th century "Diversitie de Courtz" and *Christopher St German's* "Doctor and Student", or to take the form of practice books based on the decisions of *Sir Thomas Egerton (Lord Ellesmere)*, as Master of the Rolls and later Lord Keeper and Lord Chancellor, between 1597 and 1616, primarily concerned with procedure and treating substantive rules of equity either under the heading of demurrers, or that of relief[11]. At the same period the dominant forms of case-reporting were extracts from the records of the court, and indexes to these records[12]. Substantive analytical treatments of equity doctrine therefore represented more of an innovation than the equivalent development of treatise literature at common law. The process of change began in the later 17th century. An early example of the analytical treatment of equity doctrine only put into print in modern times is the "Prolegomena of Chancery and Equity" by *Heneage Finch (Lord Nottingham)*, Lord Keeper and then Chancellor 1673 - 82, written by *Nottingham* soon after his appointment[13]. At the same period, in the Restoration, the dominant form of case reporting in equity shifted to the form normal in common law reports of the period, of reports of what was said in court[14].

These changes reflected fundamental changes worked by the events of 1640 - 60 in the place of the equity courts in the English legal system. Before 1640 the Chancery and the equity side of the Exchequer were two among a range of prerogative courts answerable to the Crown; a commonly held explanation of the jurisdiction of these courts was as an appeal from the regulated power of the prince *(potestas ordinata)* to his absolute power *(potestas absoluta)*; and in Chancery civil lawyers played an important role among the court's judicial officers, though the bar were common lawyers. After 1660 the other prerogative courts, abolished in the 1640s,

---

Ballow in the *Alumni* of the two English Universities was admitted at Magdalene College, Cambridge, in 1720, and departed for Lincoln's Inn the following year without taking a degree: *John Venn, J. A. Venn,* Alumni Cantabridgienses, Part I: From the earliest times to 1751, reprint 1974 - 6, vol. I, *sub nomine).* In addition, the Dictionary of National Biography, vol. I, *sub nomine,* tells us that *Ballow* was an intimate of *Dr. Johnson* and that he was party to an absurd incident involving a challenge to a duel, never fought, arising out of his *opponent's* republican opinions, both of which suggest Toryism; but the author of the treatise uses an explicitly contractarian theory of the foundations of legal authority, which strongly suggests Whiggism. I will nonetheless continue, for convenience, to refer to the author as *Ballow.*

10 See *Simpson,* (1981) 48 University of Chicago L.R. 632

11 I discuss the changing patterns of equity literature more extensively in *M. Macnair,* The Law of Proof in Early Modern Equity (forthcoming), Ch. 1 § 3.

12 On this point see *Macnair,* Chancery Reports (n. 8) 126 - 8.

13 D.E.C. Yale (ed.), Lord Nottingham's Manual of Chancery Practice and Prolegomena of Chancery and Equity, 1965; the dating is at p. 76, though *Yale* notes that *Nottingham* continued to add to the text thereafter.

14 See *Macnair* (n. 8) 127.

were not re-established; the remaining equity courts became subject to Parliament, in the form of appeals to the House of Lords[15]; and the civilians were marginalised, though the idea that equity procedure was civilian in character persisted[16]. These developments brought the Chancery at least partly "into line" with the courts of common law, as an ordinary part of the legal system, run by common lawyers who produced literature of a "common law" type. They also meant that new explanations both of the equity jurisdiction in general, and of the specific aspects of this jurisdiction, were required; the idea of the equity jurisdiction as the practical expression of the idea that the prince is above the law, though *Nottingham* still used it in his "Prolegomena"[17], did not fit well with Restoration ideas about law and the constitution and still less with early 18th century ideas[18].

Conversely, if in the early 17th century some common lawyers had perceived the Chancery as a growing threat to the common law jurisdictions, by the late 17th and early 18th century a commoner view was that at least some of the "routine" elements of the equity jurisdiction could be incorporated into the common law; and from the reign of Queen Anne we begin to see evidence of Chancellors resisting changes at common law which threaten to render redundant elements of the equity jurisdiction of Chancery[19]. From either side of these discussions both the equity jurisdiction as a whole, and its component elements, were in need of juridical explanation on the basis that they were part of a unitary legal system, not processes of extra-legal intervention. Trusts were clearly going to play a key role in any such explanation, for three reasons: because they involved a persisting relationship, rather than a mere remedy; because they were integral to a widely used conveyancing device, the strict settlement; and because even some authors who argued

15 I discuss some of the general points made here in more detail in *M. Macnair,* Juge et jugement dans les juridictions anglaises d'*equity* au début des temps modernes, in: R. Jacob (ed.), Le juge et le jugement dans les traditions juridiques européennes, 1996, pp. 137 ff. The rise of the appellate jurisdiction of the House of Lords is discussed in *James S. Hart,* Justice upon Petition, the House of Lords and the Reformation of Justice 1621 - 1675, 1991.

16 The idea that equity procedure was civilian in character can still be found, for example, in *Gilbert,* Forum Romanum (n. 5) *passim.*

17 Yale (n. 13) c 3 §§ 10 - 21, pp. 189 ff.

18 For the idea of law as a fundamental source of authority in the Restoration, see generally *Howard Nenner,* By Color of Law: Legal Culture and Constitutional Politics in England 1660 - 1689, 1977; for the Whig party *Richard Ashcraft,* Revolutionary Politics and Locke's Two Treatises of Government, 1986, pp. 181 ff.; for the Tory party, *Tim Harris,* Tories and the Rule of Law in the Reign of Charles II, (1993) 8 The Seventeenth Century 9 ff., though more ambiguity is seen in the attitudes of literary Tories by *Susan J. Owen,* Restoration Theatre and Crisis, 1996, pp. 120 f.

19 I discuss this point further in *M. Macnair,* Common Law and Statutory Imitations of Equitable Relief under the Later Stuarts, in: C.W. Brooks, M. Lobban (eds.), Communities and Courts, 1997, pp. 115 ff. For Chancellors' resistance to changes in the common law in the reign of *Queen Anne,* see C. Jones, G. Holmes (eds.), The London Diaries of William Nicolson, Bishop of Carlisle, 1985, pp. 351, 361; and for later in the 18th century see, e.g., *Holdsworth* (n. 8), vol. XII, 600 *(Hardwicke L.C.),* 596 - 7 (*Eldon L.C.).*

strongly for the scope of the equity jurisdiction to be cut down or replaced by changes at law accepted that it should still deal with trusts[20].

2. *Fideicommissum*

The standard starting point for the explanation of trusts in this period was that a trust was merely a use not executed by the Statute of Uses (either because it concerned leasehold, copyhold or personalty; or because the trustee had active duties to perform; or because it was a use on a use)[21]. This, however true it may be as a historical explanation, in juridical terms begs the question: what is a use? And the standard answer to this question begins: "A use is a trust or confidence ..."[22].

Explaining the trust in conceptual terms needed to go further, therefore, than reference to uses. Strategically, there were two alternatives available. The first was to identify the trust in terms of proprietary interests and relations, focusing on the interest of *cestui que trust;* if so, it was essential to distinguish the trust from common law proprietary interests, since otherwise the trust would collapse into whichever of these was closest[23]. The second was to identify the trust as a species of contract, focusing on the relationship between settlor and trustee; in this case overlap with common law contracts was not a problem, but it was necessary to explain the availability of specific relief to *cestui que trust*[24]. For both purposes, the authors studied in this essay used Roman law analogies.

---

20 *David Jenkins,* Eight Centuries of Reports, trans. *T. Barlow,* 4th ed., London, 1885, "Abuses of the Law", p. XXI. Similarly, *Francis North,* who argued for extensive changes to the common law to reproduce equitable relief (*Macnair* (n. 19) *passim)* thought that trusts belonged exclusively to courts of equity (see n. 108 *infra* and the text there). *Contra, Sir Robert Atkyns,* An Enquiry into the Jurisdiction of the Court of Chancery, London, 1695, argues at pp. 25 - 6 and 38 - 9 that all trusts should be treated as executed uses.

21 See, e.g., Yale, Prolegomena (n. 13) 236 - 7, nos. 1 - 7; *Gilbert,* Lex Praetoria (n. 5) 46 - 48; *Thomas Wood, LL.D.,* An Institute of the Laws of England, or, the Laws of England in their Natural Order, according to common use, 5th ed., London, 1734, p. 257; *Ballow* (n. 9) 54.

22 E.g. *Ballow* (n. 9) 53; *Matthew Bacon,* The New Abridgment, 3rd ed., London, 1770, vol. V, p. 342 (this section is by *J. Sayer:* see *Glazebrook* (n. 8); it draws heavily on *Gilbert,* Uses); *Wood* (n. 21) 254.

23 Thus *Francis Bacon,* The Learned Reading of Sir Francis Bacon ... on the Statute of Uses, London, 1735, pp. 2 ff., started his argument by way of exclusion: a use is not an interest in property, and hence is neither tenancy at will nor pernency of profits; conversely, a use cannot be defined as a fraud or collusion, though particular uses may be fraudulent or collusive.

24 The issues of privity of contract, and priority over the trustee's general creditors, which drive modern lawyers towards a proprietary explanation of the trust, were less problematic for lawyers in this period, since the doctrine of privity had not attained its modern rigidity (see *Vernon R. Palmer,* The Paths to Privity, 1992, pp. 26 ff.; *A. W. B. Simpson,* A History of the Common Law of Contract, 1975, pp. 475 ff.; and compare *Langbein,* (1995) 105 Yale L.J. 646 - 7; *N. G. Jones,* Uses, Trusts and a Path to Privity, (1997) 56 Cambridge Law Journal

Lord Nottingham, as already indicated, follows the earlier explanation of equity as an appeal to the absolute power of the prince. When he comes to explain trusts, he follows *Francis Bacon's* "Reading on the Statute of Uses", which was printed in 1642 and reprinted several times in the 18th century[25]. *Bacon* quotes an unidentified civilian as saying that "usus est dominium fiduciarium" and as defining *fides,* in turn, as "obligatio conscientiae unius ad intentione alterius"[26]. He proceeds to draw an analogy between the development of uses and that of *fideicommissa* in Roman law: initially created without any means of legal enforcement, then under *Augustus* enforced on an individual basis by direct appeal to the emperor, then their enforcement routinised, and finally incorporated by statute (*SC Trebellianum* and *SC Pegasianum*) into the general body of the law. It should be noted that neither *Bacon* nor *Nottingham* is directly saying that a trust *is* a *fideicommissum* (though they come close to doing so). The function of the analogy is primarily to stress the point that trusts (uses before the Statute) were unenforceable at law. *Bacon* (but not followed here by *Nottingham*) reinforces the argument with an analogy with copyhold tenure: originally unenforcable and merely at the will of the lord of the manor, then enforceable only in the manor court, but not at law, finally enforceable at law[27]. For *Bacon,* this view provides a context for the decision in *Sharington v. Strotton* (1565) that a covenant to stand seised to uses requires consideration (because consideration was required in equity before the Statute) though a covenant at law did not require consideration[28]. For *Nottingham,* it is more generally connected to the necessity of the equity jurisdiction and the survival of trusts after the Statute. The analogy could be used, though it was not by either of these authors, to support a narrow view of the equity jurisdiction: the Chancellor could be seen as a *praetor fideicommissarius* with a jurisdiction limited to trusts and closely related matters. In either use, the analogy with *fideicommissa* focuses on the proprietary character of the trust[29].

---

175 ff.) and the rules of priority were complex ones in which the existence of a trust did not automatically give *cestui que trust* priority over all creditors, though this was the trend of development (see Yale (n. 3) 62 ff.). The problem of proprietary or contractual approaches was not new; *Neil Jones'* essay in this volume indicates that an approach which was close to, if not exactly being, contractual – certainly one based on personal obligations – was dominant around 1600.

25 *Francis Bacon* (n. 23). 18th century editions are listed in *J. N. Adams, G. Averley,* A Bibliography of Eighteenth Century Legal Literature, 1982, p. 301.

26 *Francis Bacon* (n. 23) 9; quoted in Yale, Prolegomena (n. 13) 236 § 1.

27 *Francis Bacon* (n. 23) 18 - 19 (*fideicommissum*) (quoted in Yale, Prolegomena (n. 13) 252 §§ 15 - 18), 19 - 20 (copyhold).

28 1 Plowd. 298. *Bacon's* interpretation is possibly questionable: see *Simpson* (n. 24), 348 ff.

29 It should be added that *Sir William Blackstone,* Commentaries on the Laws of England, 16th ed., London, 1825, vol. 2, pp. 337 ff., follows *Bacon* on this point, treating uses/trusts primarily as a mode of conveyance of property and deploying the *fideicommissum* analogy; here there is no link with the general theory of equity, which Blackstone explains in other ways.

The limit of this analogy was that the *fideicommissum* was in some respects unlike the English trust. It was primarily a testamentary arrangement[30]. Moreover, the civilian *Thomas Wood* in his "New Institute of the Imperial or Civil Law" (1704), though he explained *fideicommissa* in the first instance as trusts, pointed out that the contemporary use of fideicommissary substitutions in France was closer to the English entail[31]. It is possibly for this reason that *Jeffrey Gilbert*, though he makes use of the *fideicommissum* concept in the context of executorship[32], when he seeks to explain the trust uses a different analogy: that of the usufruct.

3. Usufruct

Gilbert's explanation of trusts is that the original impetus for the practice of feoffments to uses came from clerical attempts to evade the Statute of Mortmain. "The Original of Uses was from a Title under the Civil Law, which allows of an usufructuary possession, distinct from the Substance of the Thing itself; and it was brought over to us from thence by the Clergy, who were Masters of the Civil Law"[33], drawing on the separation of *dominium* and beneficial enjoyment in usufructs to create a way round the statute. The context of evasion of statutory provisions explained the absence of enforcement at common law; the clerical origin, the willingness of (clerical) Chancellors to enforce uses. Then in the 15th century, according to this account, the practice spread to lay landowners seeking to avoid forfeiture for treason in the uncertain conditions of the Wars of the Roses. The Statute of Uses attempted to get rid of the practice, but it was reintroduced because of the need for trustees to support contingent remainders in strict settlements[34].

This argument, like the *fideicommissum* analogy, is proprietary in focus, and similarly historical in starting from absence of enforcement at common law. It differs in two respects. The first is that the origins story is anticlerical in cast and to

---

30 Though, for its wider potential, see *David Johnston*'s essay in the present volume.

31 London, 1704; 4th ed. London, 1730; citing *Jean Domat*, Les Loix Civiles en leur Ordre Naturel, "Tom 3. Lib. 5. tit. 3".

32 *Gilbert*, Lex Praetoria (n. 5) 60: "the personal Estate is a *fideicommissum*, and the Executor a *fideicommissarius*, and therefore he is only a Trustee to dispose of the personal Estate as the Testator has appointed"; p. 62: "the stranger is but *fidei commissarius quoad* the profits of that part of the real estate which are devised from him". Compare *Durantis'* characterization of the executor as "minister legatarius vel fideicommissarius", cited in *Reinhard Zimmermann*'s essay in this collection.

33 *Gilbert* (n. 6) 3, quoted by *Matthew Bacon* (n. 22) vol. V, 344. In *Gilbert's* Forum Romanum (n. 5) 28 - 9, and Lex Praetoria (n. 5) 43 - 5, the explanation in terms of the activity of the clergy is used, but without the reference to usufructs; since the *Uses and Trusts* is considerably earlier, it is possible that *Gilbert* thought better of the analogy. Compare *Shael Herman*'s discussion of *usus* in his essay in this book and in Utilitas Ecclesiae: the Canonical Conception of Trust, (1996) 70 Tulane L.R. 2239 ff., esp. at 2245 - 6, 2252 - 3.

34 *Gilbert*, Lex Praetoria (n. 5) 45 - 6.

some extent hostile to the use / trust concept, since it is presented as primarily a means of evading legal obligations. This feature reflects *Gilbert's* Whig party commitments[35]. The story does not in itself imply anything about the equity jurisdiction as a whole. The title of *Gilbert's* book, "Lex Praetoria", implies an analogy with another bit of Roman law, later developed more fully by *Blackstone:* the common law can be seen as analogous to the law of the XII Tables and the *legis actiones,* Chancery to the praetorian jurisdiction[36]. This analogy implies a view of equity as an engine for the reform of the law, but one whose content should in principle become part of the ordinary law.

The second difference is that the usufruct analogy has slightly different consequences from that with *fideicommissa.* Though it is commonly said (and was said by *Francis Bacon* and following him *Nottingham)* that the similarity of name between use and usufruct is misleading[37], in some respects the usufruct analogy captures some features of the later 17th and early 18th century trust which are not caught by the *fideicommissum* analogy. One of these is that the relationship is as likely to be created *inter vivos* as by will, and that it involves a continuing relationship between legal owner and beneficiary, rather than a mere duty to transmit the property in question. The other is that the usufructuary / beneficiary has (at least to some extent) the right to enjoy the proceeds of the property, without possessing the power of disposition. This is more helpful to the analysis of, for example, trusts for the payment of debts, or portions terms in settlements – both common uses of the trust at this period – than is *fideicommissum.* Like the *fideicommissum* analogy, however, the usufruct analogy remains focused on property concepts and on the use of land. *Henry Ballow's* account, which characterises the trust as a contract of the species *depositum,* represents a radical departure in the theorisation both of equity and of trusts.

4. *Depositum*

Ballow's argument starts with the general nature of law and equity. Law, he argues, is a moral science, which is particularly concerned with distributive justice (Book I, c 1, § 1). In distributive justice all claims arise from obligations (which *Ballow* calls "contracts"); these are either involuntary (delictual) or voluntary (contractual in the modern sense) (I.1.2). It will be noted that this argument assumes, without fully expressing it, a social contract theory: "all civil Rights must arise from Obligations, and these Obligations are founded on Compacts" (*ibid.*)[38]. Since

35 For *Gilbert's* Whiggism, see *Macnair,* (1994) 15 J.L.H. 252 ff.

36 *Blackstone* (n. 29) vol. 3, 49 f.

37 *Francis Bacon* (n. 23) 15, quoted by Yale (n. 13) 252 § 15.

38 Also, "Neither do we at present intend to treat of those universal Pacts, by which the Propriety and Dominion of Things was at first established" (I.1.4).

the equity jurisdiction of Chancery does not include torts and crimes these can be put on one side (*ibid.*). Equity "therefore, as it stands for the whole of natural Justice, is more excellent than any human Institution" (I.1.3). "As the Rules of the municipal Law are finite, and the subject of it infinite, there will often fall out Cases, which cannot be determined by them; ... So that there will be a Necessity of having Recourse to the natural Principles ... And this is what is properly called Equity in opposition to strict Law ..." (*ibid.*). This is a modernised variant of the Aristotelian "leaden rule" idea, but with the more or less clear idea of an appeal from rules to principles; there follows some general discussion of the relation of equity to common law rules, statute and precedent.

The critical move is taken in §§ 4 - 5. In § 4 *Ballow* tells us that he is at present concerned with "particular Contracts, which are limited to the Benefit of certain Persons, and presuppose Property and Price. These saith the Praetor ... if they are not gain'd by ill Practice, nor made against the Laws, I will see kept; for what can be so agreeable to human Faith, as the Observance of those Things, which they themselves have approv'd of, and made a Law amongst one another"[39]. § 5 begins, "But the Law of *England* was very defective in this Point, and fell short of natural Justice ... for executory Agreements were there look'd upon but as a personal security, and Damages only to be recover'd fcr the Breach of them ...". Equity therefore stepped in to compel specific performance; and §§ 6 - 7 offer a defence of this practice against common law objections, and some elaboration of its range.

For *Ballow,* then, the core of equity is the specific enforcement of contracts; and the remainder of Book I of the treatise is "Of Agreements in general", covering agreement, evidence of agreement, the subject matter of contracts (here called covenants), consideration, and "the execution of the agreement" covering what would now be called express and implied terms, performance and breach. Book II, c. 1, § 1 begins:

> "We will now proceed to some of the particular kinds of agreements, which occur most usually in Chancery. And 1st, of a *Depositum* or Trust, to which this Court owes its Original, and which, if well consider'd, will still be found to make the principal business here. For whoever has the Possession of Goods or Lands, either hath the absolute Property or Estate in them, by a sufficient Title; or, so far as this is wanting, is consider'd as a Trustee for the true Owner. ..."

The theoretical link with the Roman law real contracts, and hence contractual concept of equity, is continued in Book III, on Mortgages, which is titled "Of Mortgages and Pledges" (pledges appear to be introduced only to link mortgages to *vadium),* but breaks down in Book IV, "Of Last Wills and Testaments"[40].

---

39 The first part of this passage paraphrases D. 14, 7, 7: "Ait praetor: pacta conventa, quae neque dolo malo, neque adversus leges plebis scita senatus consulta decreta edicta principum, neque quo fraus cui eorum fiat facta erunt, servabo".

40 Since, as *Reinhard Zimmermann* shows in his essay in this volume, executors were conceptualized by *usus modernus* writers as mandataries, it is possible that *Ballow* intended to

This approach is sharply divergent from both the *fideicommissum* analogy, and that with usufructs. In the first place we have a general theory of equity which is explicitly linked to a contractarian Natural law concept, and focused to the actual jurisdiction by way of the specific performance of contracts. Secondly, this approach removes the necessity to explain trusts in proprietary terms. Treating the trust as a *depositum* in principle allows trusts of chattels and money – common law bailment and receipt to the use of another – to come easily under the same head[41]; neither would fit particularly well with either *fideicommissum* or usufruct. The proprietary / *in rem* consequences of trusts become merely another case of specific enforcement; a trust is a kind of contract; but it is perfectly general that equity allows contracts to have proprietary consequences.

II. Analytic Organisation of the Material

1. *Nottingham*

Nottingham devotes seven chapters of his "Prolegomena" to the discussion of trusts[42]. The analytic ordering of these is relatively weak. Ch. 12 is "Of Trusts in general, quid sint"; Ch. 13, "Where Trust shall be raised by construction and implication of law, and where not"; Ch. 14, "Where Uses at Common Law and Trusts at this day may be said to agree, and where not"; Ch. 15, "What Notice shall be sufficient to affect or charge another with a Trust, and what not"; Ch. 16, "What shall be said to be a breach of Trust, and who chargeable with it"; Ch. 17, "Of Trustees"; and Ch. 18, "What shall be a sufficient declaration of trust". Within these heads, some groups of sections contain continuous argument (for example, Ch. 12 §§ 1 - 9; Ch. 14 §§ 1 - 12), but the method is generally that of a common law Abridgment, of collecting cases within the headings more or less in chronological order, but with some grouping of cases with similar subject matter, albeit not drawn out into a subhead[43].

---

treat executorship as mandate. But Book IV gets entangled in issues of jurisdictional conflict between Chancery and the Church courts before it begins to consider issues of principle, and the nearest approach to a principled explanation is *Ballow's* justification of the liability of executors to account by analogy with "Stewards, Receivers, Bailiffs, Guardians, Factors and such as have to deal for other persons" (IV, Part II, c 3 § 1, p. 115), which refers primarily to the common law action of account.

41 Thus, e.g., payment of money by mistake is explained as a trust enforceable at law, at II.1.1., p. 52. Compare also *Lord Hollis' Case* (*infra* at n. 111 and text there), debt payable to creditor's order "a *depositum* and trust thereon", and *Neil Jones'* discussion of the overlap between bailment and trust in his essay in this volume.

42 Yale (n. 13) 236 - 269.

43 Thus, for example, Ch. 13 on constructive / implied trusts is nearly completely disorderly; Ch. 15 on notice starts by distinguishing purchase from conveyance without consideration, then legal and actual notice; then (at §§ 4 - 11) come a range of cases on "actual notice", which includes what in the modern law would be treated as constructive notice; followed

In this context it is doubtful how much can be inferred from the organisation of the materials considered as an analysis. I think three inferences *are* possible. First, the analogy with *fideicommissa* has no operative effects. Second, *Nottingham* was more concerned than the other writers studied here to explore the relationship (similarities and distinctions) between trusts and uses. Third, his primary interest appears to be in conveyancing implications, starting from the standpoint of the purchaser of land which may be affected by a trust; hence the early treatment of implied trusts, the distinct chapter on notice, and the late placement of both trustees and express declarations of trust.

2. *Gilbert*

Gilbert in "The Law of Uses and Trusts" after giving an explanation of the origin of trusts (discussed above) proceeds directly to a treatment of the common law rules affecting uses and their modification by the Statute of Uses[44]. This is also, for practical purposes, the approach of *Wood* in his "Institute of the Laws of England"[45]. In the "Lex Praetoria", *Gilbert* after the initial explanation of origins gives no explicit analysis[46]. Groupings of particular matters can, however, be detected, as follows: (1) Merger of trust terms in the fee (pp. 48 - 58); (2) When portions terms on early death of the principal beneficiaries fail and sink in the personal estate or for the benefit of the heir or remaindermen (58 - 63); (3) Resulting trusts and advancements (63 - 66); (4) Where the beneficiaries of a portions term can claim early payment or intermediate interest (66 - 72); (5) Married women's separate property issues (72 - 83); and (6) Breach of trust, third party liability, and trustees' powers (83 - 89).

As in *Nottingham's* account, this is Abridgment methodology and few inferences can be made as to analysis. The analogy of usufruct has no operative effect either in the "Law of Uses" or in the "Lex Praetoria" (where it is in any case not repeated). On the other hand, the focus of *Gilbert's* treatment is not the same as *Nottingham's*. The relationship between uses and trusts bulks much less large in the

---

(at §§ 12 - 16) by a group of cases on purchase *pendente lite;* with, finally, a *dictum* by *Egerton* distinguishing *notum et notorium* (possibly to be equated to legal notice) from *notum et privatum*, and a case of equitable relief against fraud on a marriage, relevant presumably as showing that in some cases a purchaser without notice will be positively relieved against a legal title.

44 Summaries of the headings are at n. 6 *supra*, at 4 (rules at common law) and 73 - 4 (consequences of the Statute).

45 See n. 20, 254 - 8.

46 Apart from two cross-heads, at pp. 48 and 78, which may have originated as running heads in the MS used by the printer (cf. the relationship between Harvard Law School MS. 2107, *Gilbert's* Evidence, and the text as printed, *Sir Geoffrey Gilbert*, The Law of Evidence, Dublin, 1754, reprint, NY, 1979: running heads in the MS. appear as cross-heads in the printed text, with some consequent displacement).

"Lex Praetoria", and the main focus of interest is on trusts of terms in settlements and their workings as between the beneficiaries *inter se* and the beneficiaries and the trustees. Indeed, *Gilbert* clearly had some uncertainty as to the proper title of the section. At p. 1 in the Dublin printed edition, the relevant one of the "proper heads of relief" in Chancery is listed as "2ly Portions"; the Harvard MS. has "2ly Trusts / 3ly Portions"[47]. The section begins, however, "2ly Trusts and Portions. / Trusts are the original Creatures of the Court of Equity ..." (p. 43). This uncertainty whether "Portions" or "Trusts" is the appropriate heading emphasises the importance of portions terms for *Gilbert's* account; as does the fact that he uses these to explain the revival of trusts after the Statute of Uses (p. 45).

3. *Ballow*

Ballow offers a much more explicit and systematic analysis; and here, the underlying theorisation of trust as a sort of contract has clear consequences, though they do not completely determine the treatment. After Book 2 c 1 on the nature of uses and trusts, c 2 deals with the creation of uses, following the common law rules in relation to transmutation of possession or agreement and consideration (the latter rather more fully treated) and adding consideration of the effect of the Statute of Frauds and the parol evidence rule; c 3, "Of the Limitation of Uses by the Party", with the construction of the terms of expressly created uses *inter vivos* or by will; c 4, "Of the Limitation of Uses where the Intent does not appear", with equity following the law in relation to the devolution of trusts of terms attendant on the inheritance, explained as cases where the party has not fully expressed the terms of the trust; c 5, "Of Uses raised by operation of Law", with resulting uses and trusts, explained in the first instance as following the person from whom consideration moved; c 6, "Of the Extinguishment of Uses" deals with conveyance to a purchaser without notice as destroying the trust, powers of revocation, and merger of portions terms; c 7, "Of the Office and Duty of a Trustee", with the powers and duties of trustees and the scope of their liability to account; and c 8, "Of the Execution of the Trust", with reconversion, executory and executed trusts, the raising of portions and rights to intermediate interest.

Ballow's Part I on contracts in general followed the structure agreement, consideration, execution; the (inevitably rather more complex) account of trusts follows the same underlying pattern: intention and consideration in c. 2, intention and its limits in cc. 3 - 4, consideration and intention in c. 5, execution in cc. 6 - 8. The homology cannot, in fact, be made complete, but the theorisation has been useful to the analysis. It has, in fact, provided *Ballow* with a structural framework on which he can hang a considerably broader treatment than *Gilbert's* (or, for that matter, *Wood's* in the "Institute of the Laws of England") with a much greater degree of analytical coherence than is found either in *Gilbert*, or in *Nottingham*.

---

[47] HLS MS. 1064 fo. 42.

4. Equity Cases Abridged

For the sake of completeness it is worth noticing the analysis of "1 Equity Cases Abridged", though this is a simple Abridgement. The title Trust and Trustees is divided into eight subtitles:

(A) When a Trust shall be said to be raised.

(B) Of resulting Trusts, or Trusts by Implication.

(C) What shall be a Trust, and not a Use executed by the Statute.

(D) What Act of the Trustee shall defeat the Trust, or be a Breach of the Trust in him.

(E) What Acts of the Trustee jointly with *Cestui que* Trust, or by *Cestui que* Trust, shall defeat the Trust, or destroy contingent Remainders.

(F) When a Trust is to be executed, what Estate or Interest is to be conveyed, and to whom.

(G) Trustees how to account, and what Allowances to have.

(H) How far Trustees are answerable for each other[48].

This is a fairly logical analysis, without being obviously informed by any particular theory: the first three subtitles relate to the creation of trusts, the next three to the termination of the trust by breach, joint act of trustee and beneficiary, or execution by court order, and the last two to the personal liability of trustees. The main focus is fairly clearly on trusts to preserve contingent remainders in settlements, though some other types of trust are treated. The treatment is thus more coherent than those of *Nottingham* and *Gilbert,* which implies that the proprietary focus which "1 Equity Cases Abridged" shares with these authors does not in itself force analytic incoherence; but, on the other hand, it is less comprehensive than *Ballow's* analysis.

III. Trust as Property or Contract? Some Details

1. The Beneficiary's Rights

Perhaps the most direct indication of a proprietary concept of a trust is the *dictum* of *Hale C.B.* in *Roscarrock v Barton* (1672), reported by *Lord Nottingham* in the "Prolegomena", that the equity of redemption "is become a distinct kind of inheritance quite different from an estate in land or a trust"[49]; a statement which strongly implies that a trust has already become recognised as a "kind of inheritance", that is, a property interest. Less direct, but still indicative, are rules requiring the trust to follow rules affecting property at law, or giving the beneficiary a

48 1 Equity Cases Abridged at p. 379.

49 1 Ch. Cas. 17; Prolegomena (n 13) c 21 §§ 22 - 3.

power of disposing of the trust *res* even in the absence of an express power to do so.

The first of these two kinds of rules are clearly evidenced in *Nottingham's* account: uses and trusts of land descend as the land should, including following local custom of the land where the trust property is located[50]. The general principle involved was clear law throughout this period, with the exception of the rule, generally accepted to be anomalous, that the widow could not claim dower of land held in trust for her husband[51]. These rules and in particular the rule about local customary descent clearly imply that the beneficiary's interest is *in rem.* However, two caveats must be made. The first is that the trusts in question were normally not of freehold, but of long terms (leases) held in trust to "attend the inheritance"[52]. Treating them as realty for the purposes of descent, etc., depended on the doctrine that equity treats as done what ought to be done[53]; and it was neither general common ground that such trust leases should in all respects behave like freeholds[54], nor automatic that they should do so, since this was dependent in part on an analysis of the purpose and hence scope of the trust[55]. In some respects the converse of this point is that *Ballow* was able without too much difficulty to treat the application of those rules that were applied simply as terms implied in trusts in the absence of express terms[56].

---

50 Yale, Prolegomena (n. 13) c 4 §§ 3 - 4; c 14 § 4, citing *Jones & Reasby's Case* (1634) *Henry Rolle,* Un Abridgment des plusieurs Cases et resolutions del Common Ley, London, 1668, p. 780 No. (D) 7.

51 *Sutton v. Sutton* (1732) 2 P. Wms. 645, 2 Equity Cases Abridged 738(a), applying it also to *possessio fratris* (which *Nottingham* doubted, Yale, Prolegomena (n. 13) c 14 § 11), to the legality of limitations, and to the means of barring entails. On curtesy and dower of trusts, see the discussions in *Susan Staves,* Married Women's Separate Property in England 1660 - 1800, 1990, pp. 27 ff., and *Eileen Spring,* Women, Land and Family, 1994, pp. 42 ff., 121.

52 For the earlier development of this practice see *Neil Jones'* essay in this collection.

53 It is possibly interesting that *Gilbert* derives this rule from the civil law, quoting the *regula iuris* that *qui remedium ad rem habet ipsam rem habere videtur* (D. 50, 17, 15: "Is, qui actionem habet ad rem reciperandam ipsam rem habere videtur"): Lex Praetoria (n. 5), 62 - 3, in the context of treating portions due to be raised as raised.

54 See, e.g., *Turner v. Bromfield* (1678) 1 Ch. Cas. 307, (*Turner v. Turner*) Selden Society vol. 79, 1961 - 62, p. 711 no. 893, where *Lord Nottingham* held that on alienation of a jointure term by a second husband, the wife should be separately examined, by analogy with a jointure in fee, but the House of Lords disagreed; discussed by *Gilbert,* Lex Praetoria (n. 5) 78 - 9. (*Jacob v. Thatcher* (1675) 1 Ch. Cas. 247, cited there, is probably an error for *Doily v. Pershall* (1674) 1 Ch. Cas. 225, 2 Freem. 138, Selden Society, vol. 73, 1954, p. 29 no. 64, an earlier case on the same point.) *Nottingham's* reasoning, however, as can be seen from his own report, is that a trust is at law a *chose in action* i.e. a contract, (which the husband could not dispose of without previously converting,) so that the assistance of equity was needed to allow him to dispose of it at all. On this last point cf. *Neil Jones*' discussion of the late 16th century law in his essay in this book.

55 See the discussions of merger and husband and wife in *Gilbert,* Lex Praetoria (n. 5) 48 - 58 and 78 - 83, and of this topic generally by *Ballow* (n. 9) Book 2 c 4.

56 *Ballow* (n. 9) 2.4.1.

The second group of rules is if anything more ambiguous. *Francis Bacon* said that *cestui que use* had neither *jus in re,* nor *jus ad rem;* but in *Smith v. Wheeler* (1668) it was said by counsel for the plaintiff that *"cestui que* trust hath *jus habendi, et jus disponendi.* And though he that hath a trust, hath in law neither *jus in re,* nor *jus ad rem,* yet in equity he hath both"[57]. The reality was more complex. It was clear that the beneficiary of a bare trust was entitled to a conveyance of the legal estate from the trustee, and hence could require the trustee to convey to a third party; but the same was true of a purchaser entitled to specific performance.

Where the trust terms were more complex, the extent of the rights given to the beneficary or beneficiaries was a matter of the interpretation of these terms and of the intention of the settlor; not simply of what legal estate the trust interest corresponded to (though this was also important). Thus in some cases the primary concern was that the trustees should be adequately indemnified for participating in a transaction which was not strictly consistent with the terms of the trust[58]. The court retained discretion: in *Saunders v. Nevil* (1701) *Trevor M. R.* said that in some cases the court would refuse to decree conveyance to a *cestui que trust* who was apparently entitled to a legal estate in tail, "sometimes for a Politick Reason, as if it were to enable a Nobleman to suffer a Recovery, and leave the Honour bare, without Estate; or if the Party were a notorious Spendthrift ..."[59]; and executory trusts, where a settlement had been covenanted or willed to be made, could be reshaped according to what was considered to be the underlying intention of the set-

---

57 1 Mod. 38, *Jones* for the plaintiff; cited by *Matthew Bacon* (n. 22) 407 (M). Same point more briefly reported 2 Keb. 644. Similarly, *Pemberton* for the plaintiff at 1 Mod. 17 argued that "a trust ... was a right to receive the profits of the land, and to dispose of the land in equity". *Contra, Winnington* for the defendant, 1 Mod. 39, 2 Keb. 644, argued that "a trust is a confidence reposed in the person ...". The circumstances of the case were that Sir Simon Mayne assigned a term in trust for himself for life with remainders over, with a power if he had issue to revoke the trusts and resettle; was attainted of treason as a regicide in 1660; and died, having issue, but without exercising the power. The Act of Attainder gave the Crown *inter alia* "trusts" for the benefit of those convicted, and the question was whether the unexercised power had the consequence that the whole term was in trust for Mayne, so as to forfeit to the Crown: hence the plaintiff's counsel's insistence that a trust involves a power of disposition, so as to conclude that an power of disposition implies a trust. The Exchequer Chamber eventually upheld the Common Pleas' judgment for the defendant, on the basis that only Mayne's life interest was forfeited: (1671) 1 Mod. 40, 2 Keb. 772, most fully 1 Vent. 128; other reports, at different stages, 1 Freem. 9, 1 Lev. 279, 2 Keb. 564, 608, 763.

58 E.g. *Duke of Buckingham v. Lord Chancellor (Shaftesbury) & others* (1673), Yale, Prolegomena (n. 13) 17.16, trustee for payment of debts compellable to release to the other trustees who would execute a lease granted by the settlor; the creditors were not required to be parties; *Needham v. Leicester & o'rs* (1673) Yale, Prolegomena (n. 13) 30.76, (1674) Lord Nottingham's Chancery Cases, Selden Society, vol. 73, 1954 no. 77, Rep. t. Finch 62, daughters who had attained 30 without marrying could compel the payment of portions due on marriage on giving security not to marry without consent; and a similar point discussed in *Ballow* (n. 9) 2.7.2.

59 1 Equity Cases Abridged 392.3 at 393, (more briefly 2 Vern. 428); *Ballow* (n. 9) 2.8.1 reproduces this passage.

tlor[60]. Conversely, trustees to raise portions and / or preserve contingent remainders under *executed* settlements would be decreed to join in conveyances to destroy contingent remainders, not only where there was a person presently entitled to be tenant in tail in possession, but also where the primary purposes of the settlement to benefit descendants had failed and the only opposition was from collaterals, or where the descendants supported the conveyance[61]. In *Tipping v. Pigot,* in 1713, *Harcourt C.* said that the collaterals were not protected because they were volunteers, where the descendants were purchasers; an idea which has a somewhat contractual flavour[62].

2. The Liabilities of Trustees

Modern trustee liability points in the direction of a proprietary conception of the trust in three ways. The first is that the express trustee is not merely obliged to give to the beneficiaries what the settlor has said they should get, but to manage the trust assets for the benefit of the beneficiaries; thus, the trustee who fails to invest properly may be liable to account for income he has not received, and conversely he *is* liable to account for incidental profits arising from or in connection with the trust *res*[63]. The second is the law of priorities affecting the trustee's insolvency, which generally puts trust assets out of the reach of the trustee's general creditors[64]. The third is the possibility of enforcing the trust against persons other than the original express trustee who have received trust assets[65]. The law of priorities can be put on one side, since the rules at this period operated generally so far *in personam* as to be capable of affecting the priorities of holders of legal estates *inter se* and in relation to creditors, as well as the beneficiaries of trusts[66].

In relation to the idea of the trustee as a manager of the trust property, the key is the extent of the liability to account. In the first place in relation to income of the assets, it was clear that a trustee of land was in general accountable for the rents and profits received from the land[67]. How far was he obliged to produce income?

---

60 *Ballow* (n. 9) Book 2 c 8; 1 Equity Cases Abridged 392 - 397. Cf. also the discussion by Yale (n. 3) 120 ff.

61 1 Equity Cases Abridged 384 - 391.

62 1 Equity Cases Abridged 385 (E) 2, Gilb. Rep. 34. In the modern law the voluntary character of an interest is only a bar to relief where the trust is incompletely constituted and the matter hence rests in contract. Yale (n. 3) 88 ff. argues that *Nottingham's* policy was to push the trust towards a proprietary conception, "modelling equitable interests upon their legal counterparts" (88). It will be apparent from the present discussion that movement in this direction had, in my view, by no means produced a settled result before the mid-18th century.

63 See, e.g., *Martin* (n. 1) Chs. 17, 10.

64 *Martin* (n. 1) 641.

65 *Martin* (n. 1) 300 ff.

66 Yale (n. 3) 62 ff.

Nottingham states the general rule as that accountants are charged with what they would have received without their wilful default; but proceeds to argue that this rule originated in the civil law and should, following that law, be limited to *mala fide* possessors, and hence, as far as trustees are concerned, to those who either deny a trust which is then proved, or are guilty of "wilful neglect in the managing"[68]. In *Palmer v. Jones* (1678) he applied this rule to a trustee for payment of debts who had covenanted to let at the best value, but had not let and had left the management of the property to a shepherd. In 1683, however, *Francis North L. K.* on rehearing the case was disposed to reverse it, saying that "he would never charge a trustee with imaginary values; but that he should be charged as a bailiff only", i.e. with what he had received; on being pressed by counsel that the wilful default rule was established law, *North* said that "very supine negligence indeed might in some cases charge a trustee with more than he had received ... but then the proof must be very strong"; in the end the case was settled[69]. In *Brown v. Litton* (1712)[70] *Harcourt C.* said, *obiter*, that a trustee who had express power to lend money at interest was liable to pay the interest even if he had not lent; but in *Howard v. Webster* (1725)[71] *North's* rule was followed; and since it appeared in a printed report, it found its way into Equity Cases Abridged and into *Ballow's* account[72].

In relation to portions and trusts to pay legacies, this issue was interlinked with the question whether the beneficiary was entitled to interest. The clearest account is *Gilbert's*. The prototype, as it were, was the legacy, in which it was clear that an adult legatee of an immediate legacy was only entitled to interest from the time of demanding the legacy and then only after a year had elapsed since the executor was entitled to a year to get in assets[73]. The background to this rule was that the common law gave the executor the residue, and though equity would presume a resulting trust for the next of kin, this was merely a presumption which could be displaced by contrary evidence[74]. The executor was not, therefore, a manager for

---

67 This rule is so obvious as to be nowhere explicitly stated; the accounts of the subject by our authors and the case-law they cite concern the operation and limits of the rule.

68 See n. 12, *Practice* pp. 166 - 7, *Prolegomena* 4.2 p. 196 and 4.19 p. 200.

69 (1678) Selden Society, vol. 79, 1961 - 62, no. 824; (1683) 1 Vern. 144.

70 10 Mod. 20, at 21, 2 Equity Cases Abridged 5 (A) 5 - 8, 739 (A) 3. (1 P. Wms. 140 not same point.).

71 2 Equity Cases Abridged 746 (F) 4, Cas. t. King 53.

72 1 Equity Cases Abridged 397 (G) 2; *Ballow* (n. 9) 2.7.4, p. 74. See further the discussion of the topic by Yale (n. 3) 141 ff.

73 *Gilbert*, Lex Praetoria (n. 5) 163 - 4; sidenote cites *Smell v. Dee* (1707) 2 Salk. 415, 1 Equity Cases Abridged 205.5. The notes to that case indicate that the law was actually a good deal more complex.

74 For this presumption see *Foster v. Munt* (M1687) 1 Vern. 473, *Cordell v. Noden* (T1690) 2 Vern. 148, Pre. Ch. 12, 1 Equity Cases Abridged 144.5, *Cunningham v. Mellish* (M1691) 2 Vern. 247, Pre. Ch. 31, 1 Equity Cases Abridged 273, *Lady Bellasis v. Crompton* (T1693) 2 Vern. 294, 1 Equity Cases Abridged 381.5, *Petit v. Smith* (P1696) 1 P. Wms. 7

the legatee(s); the obligation to answer interest after the year and demand was a matter of default on a personal obligation. Even though, for some other purposes, *Gilbert* describes the executor as *fideicommissarius*[75], here he says that after the year "it is a Deposit in the hands of the hands of the Executors for the benefit of the Legatee, and that Deposit must be answered on demand".

The rule was different where the legatee was an infant. According to *Gilbert,* in this case "the Executor is to be considered as a Trustee, who ought to act for the benefit of the Infant, and to put out his Legacy under the Decree of the Court"[76]. *Ballow,* on the other hand, explains all obligations to pay interest as due to delay by the payor; the obligation to account for interest to an infant therefore arises because the infant cannot be guilty of *laches.* However, if the legacy was postponed, it did not carry interest until the due date for payment, unless it was a devise of portions to children otherwise unprovided for[77].

Even where it arose, the obligation to answer interest was not an obligation to manage a fund for the best interest of the beneficiary. The starting point was a rule that the legatee was entitled to *ordinary interest;* if the executor or trustee invested the fund to better advantage, the profits over ordinary interest were his to keep[78]. *Macclesfield C.,* however, explained the primary rule by the proposition that the trustee had borne the risk of failure of the investments, since he would still have to account if the fund was lost; hence he took the profit associated with this risk. Accordingly, where the trustee was insolvent at the time of making the investment, the beneficiary was entitled to the profit, since only the beneficiary was at risk of loss of the capital[79]. There were further issues in relation to authorised and unauthorised investments[80] and assets which were, or were not, normally employed

((M1695) 1 P. Wms. 7, 5 Mod. *Powell & Mead* (M1698) 2 Vern. 361, 2 Freem. 225, Pre. Ch. 92, 1 Equity Cases Abridged 224.1, 1 Bro. CC 333, HLS MS. 1105 202, *Dormer v. Bertie* (1699) Pre. Ch. 94, 2 Equity Cases Abridged 430, 434, Colles. 128, *Pawlett v. Lady Morley* (M1702) 2 Freem. 263, 2 Equity Cases Abridged 436, Harv. 1105 237, *Griffith v. Rogers* (T1704) Pre. Ch. 231, 1 Equity Cases Abridged 245, *Cooke v. Walter* (?M1704) 2 Freem. 276, 1 Equity Cases Abridged 44, Harv. 1105 250, *City of London v. Garway* (H1706/7) 2 Vern. 571, 1 Equity Cases Abridged 272.5, *Smith v. Goodman* (P1707) 2 Vern. 586, *Wingfield v. Atkinson & Myres* (M1711) 2 Vern. 673, *Ball v. Smith* (H1711/12) 2 Vern. 675, 1 Equity Cases Abridged 245, *Colesworth v. Brangwin* (H1711/12) Pre. Ch. 323, Gilb. R. 72, 2 Equity Cases Abridged 438, *Wych v. Packington* (1712) 3 Bro. P.C. 44.

75 *Supra* n. 32.

76 *Loc. cit., supra* n. 73.

77 *Gilbert,* Lex Praetoria (n. 5) 164 - 5; SN cites *A.G. v. Thompson* (1712) Pre. Ch. 337, 1 Equity Cases Abridged 301.2; *Ballow* (n. 9) 119.

78 *Gilbert,* Lex Praetoria (n. 5) 165. On the topic covered in this paragraph generally see the discussion by Yale (n. 3) 143 ff.

79 *Gilbert,* Lex Praetoria (n. 5) 185 - 6; *Bromfield v. Wytherley* (1718) Pre. Ch. 505, 1 Equity Cases Abridged 398 (G) 8.

80 *Terry v. Terry* (1708) *Gilbert,* Lex Praetoria (n. 5) 184, Gilb. Rep. 10, Pre. Ch. 273; *Lee v. Lee* (1706) 2 Vern. 548, 1 Equity Cases Abridged 398 (G) 7; *Le Croy v. Eastman* (1722) 10 Mod. 498, 2 Equity Cases Abridged 6 (A) 12.

for trading profit[81]; but enough has been said to indicate that whatever the underlying concept of the trust, the trustee had more than a bare legal title to be managed for the beneficiary, the beneficiary less than an equitable *dominium* (or even a usufruct).

In relation to "proprietary" remedies for the beneficiary, four points deserve notice. The first concerns the availability of the tracing of assets against the trustee. In *Kirk v. Webb* (1699)[82] the trustee had employed the profits of the land (for which he would have been accountable) to purchase land in his own name. The House of Lords held that the beneficiaries were barred by the Statute of Frauds from claiming this land, and hence restricted to their remedy against the trustee's personal estate. The decision was controversial at the time, but in the end made settled law[83]. Secondly, it was a matter of uncertainty how far the trustee's purchase of titles connected with the trust brought the titles in question within the scope of the trust (in modern terms: created a constructive trust); the point does not appear to have been definitely settled until the 1720s[84].

The other two matters concern the explanation or classification of rules rather than their existence. It seems to have been clear that a volunteer recipient of trust property was in general bound by the trust and accountable, at least to the extent of the property received. One important exception was the rule, stated by *Nottingham,* following *Hale C. B.* in *Pawlett v A. G.* (1667)[85], that a subsequent owner of land

81 *Brown v. Litton* (1712) 10 Mod. 20, 1 P. Wms. 140, 2 Equity Cases Abridged 5 (A) 5 - 8, 739 (A) 3.

82 Pre. Ch. 84, 2 Equity Cases Abridged 743 (E) 1.

83 *Heron v. Heron* (1701) Pre. Ch. 163, 2 Equity Cases Abridged 744 (E) 2; *Halcott v. Markant* (1701) Pre. Ch. 168, 2 Equity Cases Abridged 744 (E) 3; *Kinder v. Miller* (1701) Pre. Ch. 171, 2 Equity Cases Abridged 744 (E) 4, (*Kendar v. Milward)* 2 Vern. 440, *Hooper v. Eyles* (1704) 2 Vern. 480. Distinguished, rather than rejected, in *Anon.* (1725) Cas. t. King 57, 2 Equity Cases Abridged 749 (E) 3; followed, *Deg v. Deg* (1727) 2 P. Wms. 414.

84 See the discussion by Yale (n. 3) 124 ff. *Gilbert,* Lex Praetoria (n. 5) 183, limits liability to cases where the trustee purchased at an undervalue. *Ballow* (n. 9) 2.5.1, p. 65, has the case of renewal as an instance of trust by operation of law, and 2.7.7, p. 75 - 6 has, like *Gilbert,* buying in titles at an undervalue. The cases cited by our authors are divided:

No trust: Darrel v. Whitchcott (1672), Yale (n. 13) c 13 § 2, renewal of mining lease (though this was later compromised when the House of Lords seemed about to reverse it: Yale (n. 3) 126 - 7); *Combes v. Dawson* (1678) Selden Society, vol. 79, 1961 - 62, p. 712 - 3, purchase of equity of redemption after paying interest with beneficiaries' money; *Lesley's Case* (1680) 2 Freem. 52, 2 Equity Cases Abridged 738 (A) 1, 742 (D) 1, purchase of title paramount.

Trust: Palmer v. Young (1684) 1 Vern. 276, 1 Equity Cases Abridged 380 (B) 2, renewal; *Walley v. Walley* (1687) 1 Vern. 484, 1 Equity Cases Abridged 384 (D) 2, renewal; *Whitacre v. Whitacre* (1725) Cas. t. King 13, 2 Equity Cases Abridged 740 (B) 2, agent for trustee buys and sub-sells at a profit; *Pugh v. Ryall* (1725) Cas t. King 40, 2 Equity Cases Abridged 741 (B) 6, letting to trustee's relative at an undervalue; *Keech v. Sandford* (1726) Cas t. King 61, 2 Equity Cases Abridged 741 (B) 7 is the *locus classicus.*

85 *Yale* (n. 13) c 12 § 12, c 14 § 3; Hardres 465. *Contra,* Yale (n. 13) c 14 § 1; 1 Equity Cases Abridged 384 (D) 1, note to *Eales v. England* (1702) Pre. Ch. 200 (on appeal (1704) 2

who was in the *per* (by conveyance under the trustee) was bound, but one who was in the *post* (by escheat or forfeiture of the trustee's interest) was not. On the face of it, this rule seems to treat trusts as analogous to conditions attached to the fee and hence as proprietary; though an alternative possible explanation, given that the person most likely to take in the *post* was the Crown, was that the Crown could not be bound by trusts. *Hale's* explanation followed by *Nottingham,* however, distinguishes trusts (where the taker in the *post* is not bound) from equities, i.e. the equity of redemption, where he is; and does so on the basis that "Trust is a kind of contract, wherein the cestui que trust must take care to provide for himself ... and regularly a trust *non egreditur personam,* and therefore the diversities of notice and consideration came in. But now an equity is an interest fixed on the land ..."[86].

The general liability of volunteer recipients was approached in two ways: either (in particular in relation to money, chattels, and profits arising from land) as an aspect of trusteeship, or (in particular in relation to conveyances of land held in trust) as an aspect of the doctrine of notice. *Nottingham* provides a good example of the first approach; he characterises a father who received profits from land held in trust for his son as "trustee of his own wrong", making an analogy with common law (more exactly statutory) executorship *de son tort*[87]; and several cases on related matters are collected by "1 Equity Cases Abridged" under the sub-title "Trustees, how to account" and the main title *Account* – not under the sub-title "When a trust shall be said to be raised".

A *bona fide* purchaser for value and without notice was free of trusts and other equities; and would be protected against claims for ancillary relief, such as discovery of documents and examination of witnesses; and might be protected by injunction against some legal titles[88]. None of this applied to either a purchaser with notice, or a volunteer. *Ballow* explains the case of the purchaser with notice as proceeding on the basis that he is a participant in the trustee's wrongdoing, and is bound as *particeps criminis*[89]. Conversely, *Gilbert* in his "Law of Uses" explains this case as a presumption of good faith, i.e. that the purchaser intended to accept the trust, because to infer he intended not to be bound would involve inferring dishonesty[90].

The case of the volunteer might be explained, on a proprietary concept of the trust, as an instance of *nemo dat quod non habet:* the trustee only had the property

---

Vern. 466) (where it was held that where a trustee of a legacy pre-deceases the testator, the legacy does not lapse). See generally the discussion by *Yale* (n. 3) 94 - 5, 99 - 100.

86 *Yale* (n. 13) 238 - 9. Compare *Neil Jones*' discussion of the topics of privity and notice in his essay in this volume.

87 *Yale* (n. 13) 260 no. 3, *Sir George Heneage's case* (1670). For the common law of executorship *de son tort* see *Holdsworth* (n. 8) vol. III, pp. 571 f.; the statute is 43 Eliz. I c 18.

88 For a general discussion of the plea of purchase see Yale (n. 3) 160 ff.; *Neil Jones,* in this volume, discusses the earlier history.

89 *Ballow* (n. 9) Book 2 c 6 § 3, p. 69.

90 *Gilbert* (n. 6) 7.

sub modo, and therefore passed it to his donee subject to the same limits. The case of the purchaser without notice then falls to be explained as the exception (*Nottingham* justifies it as an instance of equity following the common law, which contained various rules designed to protect purchasers[91]. *Nottingham* says that "he who comes in the *per* without consideration is either presumed to have notice, or bound without it, for the old use cannot be changed without a consideration"[92], and later "On conveyance without consideration notice of a trust is presumed and implied; or, which is all one, the party is as much bound as if he had notice of the trust"[93]. *Ballow* starts from the case of the purchaser with notice as *particeps criminis,* and then extends this case to that of the volunteer by explaining that the volunteer is presumed (by inference, conclusively presumed) to have notice. The consideration functions to purge the *prima facie* fraud[94]. *Gilbert* uses a similar approach in discussing executorship *de son tort* by receiving assets of the estate: "such disposition is fraudulent; and therefore it is as if they were in the hands of the Executor; and he in whose hands they are being *particeps criminis,* the creditor has a Demand against him"[95]. There may be a relationship involved with the explanation of the fraudulent conveyances legislation of Elizabeth I, which protected *subsequent* purchasers and creditors from prior voluntary conveyances, which were presumed fraudulent[96]. But it seems that both bases of third party liability, either as a trustee *de son tort,* or as having imputed notice and thus being a *particeps criminis,* focus on the personal character of the trustee's obligations.

IV. The Importance of Trusts

1. Express Trusts are more Important in Concept than in Practice

Modern textbooks which characterise themselves as being on equity are mostly about trusts[97]. One might suppose, from *Ballow's* comment quoted earlier that the trust "if well consider'd, will still be found to make the principal business here"[98], that the same would hold true of equity in this period. In fact, this is not the case[99].

---

91 Yale (n. 13) c 6 § 13.

92 Yale (n. 13) 14.1, p. 244.

93 Yale (n. 13) 15.1, p. 253.

94 *Ballow* (n. 9) 2.6.3, p. 69.

95 *Gilbert,* Lex Praetoria (n. 5) 147 - 8 (sidenote cites *Paget v. Haskins* (1716) Gilb. Rep. 111, Pre. Ch. 431).

96 13 Eliz. I c 5 and 27 Eliz. I c 4; cf. *Holdsworth* (n. 8) vol. IV, p. 481 f.

97 E.g., *Martin* (n. 1); *Pettitt* (n. 1).

98 2.1.1.

99 *Ballow's* point is in fact an analytical one: if I need to have recourse to Chancery, the legal title must be with someone else, *ergo* all forms of Chancery relief (including contracts, mortgages, etc.) involve trusts.

Henry Horwitz' recent study of the subject matter of Chancery suits between 1627 and 1818-19 found *inter vivos* trusts accounting for 2.4 per cent of the sample in 1685, and 3.0 per cent in 1735. Of course, a significant number of the suits classified by *Horwitz* as "Estate", which accounted for 27.9 per cent of the sample in 1685 and 31.4 per cent in 1735, will have involved *inter alia* testamentary trusts[100]. However, even though *Horwitz* remarks that estate and trust cases are significantly overrepresented in cases which reached a decree and in reported cases[101], this relative marginality in practice is also reflected in the content of "1 Equity Cases Abridged": the title "Trust and Trustee" forms just over 20 pages of the book's 417 pages (4.8 per cent).

It is therefore possibly significant that trusts are relatively overrepresented in the treatise literature discussed so far. In *Nottingham's* "Prolegomena" trusts occupy 44 pages of a total of 180 in *Yale's* edition (24.4 per cent); in *Gilbert's* "Lex Praetoria" they occupy 46 of a total of 195 (23.6 per cent); in *Ballow*, 32 of a total of 132 (24.2 per cent). Trusts were perhaps more of a conceptual problem than a practical one. Even so, trusts form less than a quarter of these accounts; the remainder being accounted for in *Nottingham's* account by a wide variety of substantive and procedural matters, in *Gilbert's* by Agreements, Frauds, Powers, and Wills, etc. and in *Ballow's* by Agreements, Mortgages, Wills, etc. Interest, and Evidence.

In part this divergence from modern treatment reflects the disappearance or incorporation into the general body of the law, since the 19th century, of numerous elements of the equity jurisdiction. In part, however, it also reflects the fact that some matters now dealt with as species of trust fell, for our authors, under other heads. For example, the expression "constructive trusts" in our period includes what would now be called implied and resulting trusts; the phenomena now characterised as constructive trusts are variously distributed among the heads agreement, fraud, and trustee liability.

A particularly important example of this is the "core instance" of the modern express trust-arrangements whereby a fund of money invested in various securities is held for the benefit of persons in succession. The nearest thing to an example of this practice shown in our authors is the trust term to raise portions or preserve contingent remainders, which is, however, a trust specifically of land. This seems in some respects anomalous, since securities markets were developing strongly in England from the 1690s, and one might expect persons who had invested capital in interest or dividend bearing securities to seek ways of creating settlements of these assets[102].

The evidence of the Chancery reports suggests that the apparent anomaly is a matter of legal mechanisms. Commonly litigated in this period was a practice

---

100 *Henry Horwitz*, Chancery Equity Records and Proceedings 1600 - 1800, 1995, p. 32.

101 *Horwitz* (n. 100) 32, n. 13.

102 A general account of the transition to the modern trust of investments is offered by *Chesterman* (n. 4) though this does not consider the alternative legal form discussed below.

whereby rather than a *settlement of land* being made on marriage (or in addition to it), the intending husband entered into a contract under seal (*marriage articles)* in which he *covenanted* to lay out a specific cash sum in a paurchase of land and settle it on certain terms. The beneficiaries of the settlement, or at least the wife and the children of the marriage, had a right to specific performance of this covenant; as a result of which, money or other assets in the hands of the husband could be treated in equity as *converted* into land and settled on the terms of the marriage articles. It is clear that the fund was deliberately left invested in securities for substantial periods of time[103].

Here contract, by virtue of the quasi-proprietary effects of the right to specific performance, is playing the role which was later to be played by trusts. Contract can also be found playing a role which was *previously* played by uses and trusts (and was to be again later). In *Bosvil v. Brander* (1718)[104] the issue was whether, on the bankruptcy of a husband, his wife had any claim on personalty which had been hers before the marriage, or whether it went to the husband's creditors' committee. *Sir Joseph Jekyll M.R.* said that if there had been any *agreement* before the marriage that the assets should remain in the wife's control, this would create a lien on the property in question, but given that the actual marriage agreement gave the wife a different security, which failed by the bankruptcy, "the court could not better it against her own agreement". Previously a fully created trust had been required to oust the husband of his common law right to the wife's property[105]; now an ante-nuptial contract was sufficient to have proprietary effects. These proprietary or quasi-proprietary effects of contract in early 18th century equity may help to explain not only the (relatively) low level of prominence of trusts litigation, but also the centrality of contract in *Ballow's* account of equity.

---

103 There is a brief discussion of the practice, citing a few of the relevant authorities, in *M. Macnair,* Equity and Volunteers, (1988) 8 Legal Studies 172, 175. An early case which shows the practice already fully developed, since the articles contained a clause excluding the covenantor from liability for the risk of leaving the fund out on securities, is *Lambell & Ux' v. Bower* (1644) BL MS. Hargrave 174 fo. 12r. A spectacular instance of delayed enforcement is *Trevor v. Trevor* (1719) 1 Equity Cases Abridged 387 (E) 7, 1 P. Wms. 622, 9 Mod. 161, 10 Mod. 436, where a covenant to settle contained in marriage articles executed in 1669 was specifically enforced fifty years later.

104 1 P. Wms. 458. Cf. also *Acton v. Pierce* (1704) 2 Vern. 480, (*Acton v Acton)* Pre. Ch. 237, and note at 2 Vern. 480.

105 *Earl of Suffolk v. Greenvill* (1631) BL MS. Hargrave 174 fo. 18r, and slightly variant versions HLS MS. 1105 p. 126, 3 Chan. Rep. 89, Nels. 15, 2 Freem. 146. (Cf. *Lady Greenvill v. late Earl of Suffolk* (1654) *G.W. Sanders,* Orders of the High Court of Chancery, London, 1845, vol. I, p. 251); *Lady Dacre v. Chute* (1663) 2 Freem. 148, 1 Chan. Cas. 21, BL MS. Hargrave 174 fo. 19.

2. Implied Trusts are Pervasive: Common Law Trusts

The reverse of this coin is that the expression "trust" is used, with a clear intention that it should have a legal meaning, in a wide range of cases which would not now be called trusts. We have already seen that *Ballow* incorporated the common law action for money had and received on the grounds that it had been paid by mistake into his discussion of trusts in general. A considerably earlier example, which also carries the implication that trust is a concept recognised at common law, is *William Shepherd's* book, "Actions upon the Case for Deeds" (1663). Chapter 7 of this book is entitled "Of an Action on the Case for breach of Trust, and where it will lye for this, or not". The method is that of an Abridgment, and there are no subheads. The content covered by the cases listed is (1) negligence or misconduct by employees; (2) the action will not lie against trustees of land; (3) carriers; (4) bailees generally (5) agents for the delivery of money or the purchase of lands; (6) lawyers; (7) negligence by farriers or ferrymen; (8) innkeepers[106].

The idea that trusts were recognised at law can also be found in *Nottingham's* account; he cites three cases for the view that an action would lie at common law for breach of trust, of which one (*Megod's Case* (1586)) concerned a conveyance of land for the feoffee to convey over, and two (*Coleman v. Stoddell* (1656) and *Butler v. Butler* (1657)) testamentary trusts for the payment of debts and legacies out of land[107]. The idea that an action would lie at law was denied by *Francis North* when Chief Justice of Common Pleas in 1674, though in questionable circumstances, but reaffirmed in *dicta* by *Jeffreys C.* in 1685 and by "1 Equity Cases Abridged"[108]. *Nottingham* refers to a trust as existing at law in one other area. This was the case of concurrent interests (joint tenancy or tenancy in common) of land or chattels, where he follows *Master v. Boley* (1620) to conclude that the common law "raised a trust" between co-owners; so that there was a liability to account in equity, which, in turn, being a trust, was outside the Statute of Limitations[109].

It is evident from *Joseph Biancalana's* and *Neil Jones'* essays in this volume that the idea that trusts could in principle be enforced at law was not new, though it is obvious that the remedies offered by Chancery were superior. From the late 16th

106 *William Shepherd,* Actions on the Case for Deeds, viz. Contracts, Assumpsits, Deceipts, Nusances, Trover and Conversion, Delivery of Goods, and for other Male-feasance and Mis-feasance, London, 1663, pp. 135 ff.

107 Yale (n. 13) 262, nos. 1 - 3. *Yale* gives further references to these and other relevant cases in the footnotes; for *Megod's Case* see also *David J. Ibbetson,* Consideration and the Theory of Contract, in: John Barton (ed.), Towards a General Law of Contract, 1990, pp. 67 ff., 96 - 7 and 116, and *Jones,* (1997) 56 Cambridge Law Journal 192 - 8.

108 *North C. J.* in *Barnardiston v. Soame* (1674) 6 St. Tr. 1064, at 1098, 1107 - 8, discussed more fully in *Macnair* (n. 19) n. 61; *Jeffreys C.* in: *Jevon v. Bush* (1685) 1 Vern. 342, 343 (& also *Holt arg.* in *Earl of Kildare v. Eustace* (1686) 1 Vern. 419, expressly arguing that a trust is a kind of contract, and hence that the English Chancery had jurisdiction over a trust of lands in Ireland); 1 Equity Cases Abridged 384 (D) n. 1, note to *Eales v. England* (1702).

109 *Yale* (n. 13) cc. 7 § 3, 13 § 15, 20 § 16, 30 § 69.

century there was clearly a strand of legal opinion – not yet dominant – which held that trusts (at least of land) were of purely equitable jurisdiction. The rise to ascendancy of this opinion appears, from the evidence considered here, to date to later than the mid-18th century. This rise may well be associated with lawyers beginning to feel a need to draw sharp distinctions between trusts and contractual relationships; a need they seem not to have felt at this period.

Nottingham, and "1 Equity Cases Abridged", contain a number of other instances in which a relationship which is, in its essence, one of contract is said to be in nature of or implied to be a trust. *Nottingham* reports *Moss v. Browne* (1641), in which a promise to pay the residue of an outstanding debt, in consideration of the creditor giving a general release on payment of a lesser sum, was said to be relievable in equity, as proceeding on the basis that the transaction was "in the nature of a trust reposed in the defendant"[110]; and *Burgh v. Francis* (1672) as deciding that a defective mortgage created not merely a contractual right to further assurance, but a trust for the benefit of the mortgagee[111]. "1 Equity Cases Abridged" includes at least three cases of this type. In *Lord Hollis' Case* (1674), Lady Hollis lent the defendant £ 100, and the note of the debt mentioned that it was to be disposed of as she should direct; this was held to be "a *depositum,* and a trust thereupon to the Lady", so outside the Statute of Limitations[112]. In *Carter v. Horne* (1728) A and B bought an estate in equal shares, the incumbrances to be discharged out of the purchase price. B received a discount from the incumbrancers, and was held by *Jekyll M. R.* to be liable to account to A, "The purchase being made for their equal benefit, and upon a mutual trust between them"[113]. In *Meliorucchi v. Royal Exchange Assurance* (1728) it was held that a partner's debts to a partnership could be set off against his share, "for this was a transaction between them as private persons, and on a mutual credit and trust", contrasting the case of a loan by a corporation to one of its shareholders[114].

"2 Equity Cases Abridged" has five cases which date to our period. In *Dutton v. Dutton* (1715) the son took a conveyance of the father's land and covenanted to indemnify the father against maintenance of his separated wife; *Cowper C.* "took [the son] in this case to be in nature of a trustee for the wife, so far as a reasonable allowance for her maintenance"[115]. In *Philpot v. Herbert* (1721) the plaintiff borrowed from B *via* the defendant, a broker, on the security of South Sea Stock which was transferred to the defendant. B directed sale of the stock before the legal date for redemption of the loan, and then broke. *Macclesfield C.* held that the de-

---

110 *Yale* (n. 13) c 30 § 18; March N.R. 151, pl. 220.

111 *Yale* (n. 13) c 13 § 14.

112 2 Vent. 345, 1 Equity Cases Abridged 380 (A) 4.

113 1 Equity Cases Abridged 7, pl. 13.

114 1 Equity Cases Abridged 9, pl. 8, at 9 - 10.

115 2 Equity Cases Abridged 739 (A) 4 cites *Charles Viner,* A General Abridgement of Law and Equity, Aldershot, 1756, 23 vols., vol. 21, p. 511, pl. 9.

fendant "was a trustee for both parties, and was guilty of a breach of trust in selling before the time"[116]. In *Parks v. Wilson (Allison's Case)* (1723) a mother gave her son a bond conditioned to surrender to him a copyhold of which she was heir. She was decreed to be a trustee for the son[117]. In *Hawkins v. Freeman* (1723) set-off and account was said to be available after verdict and judgment in a partnership case because "though Lane was the Acting partner and agreed for the paper, yet he is but in the nature of a trustee for the other partners"[118]. In *Skirne v. Myrick,* a case right at the end of the period, in 1739, the equity side of the Exchequer held that a person who took an estate with notice of a covenant to settle it was a trustee; this gives the proprietary effect of the covenant to settle, already seen above, the name of trust[119].

What these cases show is that the boundary between trust and contract (and, in *Shepherd,* assumption of responsibility leading to a duty of care) was fluid at this time. Our authors, following *Bacon,* generally carefully marked uses off from common law proprietary rights, and they were equally careful to mark off trusts from uses executed by the statute (perhaps because there was some risk that an incautiously drawn trust would be held to be an executed use)[120]. There is no such care in marking trust off from contract, agency, bailment, etc.; and in the cases cited, contracts are construed as creating trusts with a good deal of ease.

V. Conclusions

From the material considered we can draw a number of conclusions. In the first place are two points about the general treatments. First, all the authors studied were concerned to incorporate both the conception of the equity jurisdiction, and the concept of the trust, within a single legal order, rather than seeing law and equity as distinct legal orders. Secondly (as is perhaps unsurprising) the resources of the medieval common law literature did not provide a satisfactory basis for conceptualising the trust, leading at most to historical or negative conclusions (what

116 2 Equity Cases Abridged 746 (F) 2 cites *Viner* (n. 115) vol. 21, 511, pl. 10.

117 10 Mod. 515, 9 Mod. 62, 2 Equity Cases Abridged 739 (A) 7.

118 2 Equity Cases Abridged 10 (B) 10 cites *Viner* (n. 115) vol. 8, 560, pl. 26.

119 Comyn 700, 2 Equity Cases Abridged 740 (A) 9. In *Moorecroft v. Dowding* (1725) 2 P. Wms. 314, 2 Equity Cases Abridged 746 (F) 3, A bought a copyhold in the name of B, who gave a bond conditioned to surrender to such persons or uses as A or his personal representatives should direct. *King C* said that A was "a plain trustee" and must account. Here there would obviously be a resulting trust to A, but for the fact that the executors had sued the bond at law and recovered the penalty, which was (unsuccessfully) argued to be an election to rely on the contractual remedy.

120 *Gilbert,* Lex Praetoria (n. 5) 46 - 7; sidenote cites *Broughton v. Langley* (1703) 2 Salk. 679, Holt K.B. 708, 2 Ld. Raym. 873, Lutw. 823, K.B. rejecting the ruling in *Burchet v. Durdant* (1690) 2 Vent. 512, Ex. Ch.

the trust was *not)*. In this situation *Nottingham* (following *Francis Bacon)*, *Gilbert*, and *Ballow*, all made significant use of concepts drawn from the civil law.

The second area of conclusions concerns the concrete explanations and analyses themselves. Of these the first is that explanations of the trust fell broadly into two camps: proprietary (as in *Nottingham* and *Gilbert)* and contractual (as in *Ballow)*. We can, moreover, infer that the contractual analysis was somewhat more productive of integration of the trust concept both into the general body of the law, and into a general concept of equity; and of means for analysing and classifying the case-law on trusts. Secondly, the focus of the analyses shifts over time, possibly following the balance of the recent case-law, with *Nottingham* focusing primarily on conveyancing from the purchaser's point of view, *Gilbert* on portions terms, and "1 Equity Cases Abridged" on trusts to preserve contingent remainders. In this context the main focus on the trust of *land* is noteworthy, and is shared by *Ballow*, though his concepts are better adapted than the other writers' are to dealing with trusts of other property.

None of the explanations of the trust discussed in Section I of this essay have "stuck"; modern lawyers don't tend to use civilian analogies to explain the trust concept, and English law schools, at least, teach trusts as a branch of property law, not a branch of obligations. However, the more detailed discussion in Sections III and IV – though it is by no means a full discussion of any of the subjects covered – may provide some indication as to why it was that the most successful of the theorisations of the trust concept was *Ballow's* explanation of trust as a species of contract. It seems clear that the binding effects of contract were at the forefront of equity lawyers' thought in this period – not only at a theoretical level, but also as providing mechanisms for tasks performed at other times by trusts; that there was a good deal of overlap between trust and contract; and that *in some ways* the rights of the beneficiary, and the liabilities of the trustee, could be more usefully conceived as contractual rights and liabilities than as a proprietary relationship. No doubt there is, as there is explicitly in *Ballow's* underlying account of equity, a relationship between these ideas and the more general contractarian natural law approach to legal and political obligation which had wide currency at this time[121].

In relation to our common concerns in this book, the effect is to place the late 17th and early 18th century trust concept at less distance from the contractually based analyses of fiduciary relationships found in the civilian literature by *Reinhard Zimmermann* (executor as mandatary) and *Michele Graziadei* (testamentary *fiducia* as mandate, *fiducia* as deposit or contract). It also perhaps reinforces *John*

121 Certainly a traditional view: see e.g. *Basil Williams*, The Whig Supremacy, 2nd ed. C. H. Stuart, 1960, pp. 3 ff., on the influence of *John Locke's* ideas. *J. C. D. Clark*, English Society 1688 - 1832, 1985, and The Language of Liberty, 1994, has argued that the ideas of *Locke* (and other contract theorists) were relatively marginal in 18th century England. The strength of contractual ideas in the authors and cases discussed here suggests that *Clark's* argument is at least overstated, and that the approach of *H.T. Dickinson*, Liberty and Property, 1977, which links these issues to party commitments, is preferable.

H. Langbein's recent argument that the contractarian approach can be deployed to achieve a better understanding of modern trusts law[122]; and, as such, feeds back in to *Stefan Grundmann's* argument that today's "contractual" *Treuhand* and "proprietary" trust are less distant than they might immediately appear.

122 *Langbein*, (1995) 105 Yale L.J. 625 ff., though *Langbein* dates the contractarian evolution to the post-1850 development of U.S. law.

KARL OTTO SCHERNER

Formen der Treuhand im alten deutschen Recht

I. Definitionsfragen, Forschungsschwerpunkte, Strategie

Wenn ein Rechtshistoriker von der Treuhand spricht, in diesem Fall von der Treuhand im alten deutschen Recht, so ist er versucht, dem Gesprächspartner zunächst in etwa zu umreißen, worum es geht. Mit anderen Worten: am Anfang steht eine Definition, die man, weil alle Definitionen ungenau sind, sogleich mit salvatorischen Klauseln versehen sollte. Daß bei aller Vorsicht unterschiedliche Definitionen möglich sind, zeigen zwei von ihnen, die ich herausgreife. Die eine stammt von *Franz Beyerle* (1932) und lautet: Der Grundgedanke aller Treuhandfälle sei, fremde Belange an Personen, Sachen, Vermögen oder Rechtsbeziehungen wahrzunehmen[1]. Die andere stammt von *Helmut Coing* (1973): Es werden jemandem Vermögenswerte im Rahmen eines besonderen Treue- und Vertrauensverhältnisse übertragen, damit der Erwerber die ihm anvertrauten Rechte zwar rechtlich und nach außen hin als eigene halten und verwalten soll, aber seine Rechtsstellung im Interesse von anderen Personen oder für objektive Zwecke ausüben soll, die jenseits seiner persönlichen Eigeninteressen liegen[2].

Da die Treuhand im alten deutschen Recht – ich verstehe darunter das mittelalterliche Recht, von den Quellen her gesehen das Recht zwischen dem 8. und 15. Jahrhundert – seit rund 250 Jahren Gegenstand der rechtshistorischen Forschung ist, könnten dem noch weitere Definitionen hinzugefügt werden. Es würde sich zeigen, daß sie sich alle weitgehend ähneln, aber in Details unterscheiden. Da jeder Definition die Nachteile einer Generalisierung und der möglicherweise falschen Optik des Definierenden anhängen, soll dieser Punkt zunächst zurückgestellt werden und an seine Stelle ein weniger zweifelhafter Ansatz treten, über den mehr Konsens besteht: die Anwendungsfälle, man kann auch sagen, die *Erscheinungsformen der Treuhand.* Um hier ein möglichst breites Spektrum zu erhalten, sollen die Zuordnungen auch der älteren rechtsgeschichtlichen Literatur berücksichtigt werden. Dabei wird sich zeigen, daß eine erstaunlich große Übereinstimmung darin besteht, was zusammengehört und wo die Trennungslinien zu ziehen sind, ganz gleich, wie man den Gesamtkomplex definiert. Das gilt auch im Hinblick auf interne Gruppierungen. Die folgende Auflistung der Anwendungsfälle orientiert sich

---

1 *F. Beyerle,* Die Treuhand im Grundriß des deutschen Privatrechts, 1932, S. 7.

2 *H. Coing,* Die Treuhand kraft privaten Rechtsgeschäfts, 1973, S. 1.

in der Abfolge zunächst an der neuesten, einen beträchtlichen Komplex der Treuhand erfassenden Darstellung, der Habilitationsschrift von *Clausdieter Schott* mit dem Titel „Der Träger als Treuhandform" (1975). Da dieses Werk besonderes Gewicht auf die Lehnsträgerschaft legt, werden im folgenden anhand anderer, meist älterer Untersuchungen vor allem die Fallgruppen erweitert, die sich nicht auf lehnrechtliche Tatbestände beziehen.

In diesem Zusammenhang erscheint noch eine Bemerkung zu den *Quellen* und zur *Forschungssituation* notwendig. Die ältere Forschung, besonders seit der Mitte des 19. Jahrhunderts, immer aber diejenige, die sich mit dem Treuhandkomplex im rein *privatrechtlichen* Bereich befaßt, also in Fällen der Letztwillenstreuhand oder im Hinblick auf Grundstücksgeschäfte außerhalb des Lehnrechts, stützt sich fast ausschließlich auf Urkunden und Traditionsbücher, die oft den Bestellungsakt näher wiedergeben. Anders als in England spielen hier Gesetze oder gar Gerichtsentscheidungen als Quellen kaum eine Rolle. Die Forschung beschäftigte sich in Deutschland, weniger in Frankreich, außerdem – zumindest eine gewisse Zeit oft zu einseitig – mit einzelnen Konstruktionsfragen. Die hervorstechendste ist die Behauptung, der Treuhänder sei mehr oder weniger Eigentümer des Treuguts, oder er habe die Gewere inne. Andere Aspekte sind dabei meist vernachlässigt worden. Auf diesen Punkt ist noch zurückzukommen. Anders ist es im *Lehnrecht*. Lehnrechtliche Anwendungsfälle der Treuhand sind zwar von Anfang an, seit dem 18. Jahrhundert, von der rechtshistorischen Forschung wahrgenommen worden; später standen sie weniger im Mittelpunkt des Interesses der historischen Treuhandforschung, wurden jedoch innerhalb der historischen Darstellung des Lehnrechts als Treuhandfälle mitbehandelt; hier ist noch Forschungsbedarf. Mit *Schotts* Arbeit zum Träger sind hier jedenfalls für Süddeutschland die meisten Lücken geschlossen worden. Im Gegensatz zur privatrechtlichen Treuhand gibt es bei der lehnrechtlichen außer dem Urkundenmaterial auch normative Aussagen. Kaum oder nur in Einzelaspekten untersucht ist das Weiterleben der Treuhand in der Neuzeit. Hier ist nicht nur die Behandlung des Lehnsträgers (*provasallus*) durch die Literatur zum neuzeitlichen *Ius publicum* ein Desiderat[3], sondern auch die Erforschung des Fortlebens des Treuhänders außerhalb des Lehnrechts, die Umstände und Stationen der Weiterentwicklung einer Fallgruppe zur Testamentsvollstreckung[4], oder der Übergang von der Treuhand zur Stellvertretung. Allerdings ist auch die mittelalterliche Treuhand in Deutschland nur in Bruchstücken behandelt. Die neueren Arbeiten haben die vielen Lücken – in zeitlicher, regionaler und perspektivischer Hinsicht – nur zum Teil schließen können. Unter diesen Vorbehalten ist die vorliegende Darstellung zu verstehen.

Diese schließt sich auch insofern an die bisherigen an, als sie die lehnrechtlichen und nicht lehnrechtlichen Komplexe getrennt betrachtet. Auch wenn man von der

---

3 Wertvolle Hinweise bei *C. Schott*, Der Träger als Treuhandform, 1975, S. 70 f., *passim*.

4 Eine beachtliche Basis für weitere Untersuchungen bei *G. Otten*, Die Entwicklung der Treuhand im 19. Jahrhundert, 1975, S. 24 ff.

Vorstellung einer „Einheit" des mittelalterlichen Rechts ausgeht – dies wäre näher zu definieren – läßt sich nicht übersehen, daß schon die Rechtsbücher zwischen Lehnrecht und Landrecht unterscheiden. Dies trägt der Tatsache Rechnung, daß unterschiedliche Aufgaben zu divergierenden Institutionenbildungen führen. Das Beispiel des in den Quellen auch terminologisch hervorstechenden und schon früh zu einem Rechtsbegriff verdichteten Lehnsträgers, dem außerhalb des Lehnrechts nichts Vergleichbares entspricht, ist der beste Beweis dafür. Schließlich spricht auch das hier verfolgte Ziel, konkrete Erscheinungsformen zu betrachten, für die Respektierung gewachsener, differenzierender Institutionen. Schon deshalb empfiehlt es sich, anstelle der vielleicht naheliegenden Unterscheidung Lehnrecht – Privatrecht die mittelalterliche Unterscheidung Lehnrecht – Landrecht zu setzen. *Konrad Beyerle* hat sogar die – wie er sagt – landrechtliche Treuhand von der stadtrechtlichen noch einmal unterschieden. Darauf ist noch zurückzukommen.

Im folgenden soll, nachdem die Anwendungsfälle der Treuhand – zunächst die der Lehnsträgerschaft, dann die der übrigen Treuhandverhältnisse – vorgestellt worden sind, ein Gesamtbild versucht werden. Dabei stütze ich mich – wie schon angedeutet – auf die wichtigsten rechtshistorischen Arbeiten des 19. und 20. Jahrhunderts zur Treuhand im deutschsprachigen Raum. Bei der Fülle der Fallgruppen und des Quellenmaterials mußte auf die Anführung von Quellenbeispielen verzichtet werden. Das daraus gewonnene Gesamtbild wird zunächst auf gemeinsame Strukturen achten und dann auf die Definitionsfrage zurückkommen. In diesem Zusammenhang ist darauf einzugehen, ob und inwieweit die Institution, die mit „Treuhand" oder auch anders umschrieben wird, auch von den Zeitgenossen als eigenartiges Phänomen verstanden worden ist. Am Schluß ist zu überlegen, inwieweit eine Gesamtbetrachtung Treuhand – Trust weiterhelfen kann.

II. Die einzelnen Fallgruppen

1. Lehnrecht

Den ersten großen Komplex der Treuhandfälle kann man unter dem Stichwort „Lehnsträgerschaft" zusammenfassen. „Der Lehnsträger (*provasallus)* trat anstelle des eigentlichen Lehnsinhabers in die Rechte und Pflichten des Lehnsverhältnisses ein. Gerade die selbständige Übernahme der Lehnspflichten unterscheidet den Lehnsträger vom Lehnsbevollmächtigten oder Gesandten, der nur im Auftrag des Lehnsinhabers handeln konnte. Das Rechtsinstitut des Lehnsträgers konnte bei den verschiedenen Treuhandverhältnissen auftreten und dementsprechend modifiziert werden" (*K. H. Spieß* 1978)[5]. Schon die ältesten rechtsgeschichtlichen Versuche über die (mittelalterliche) *fiducia Germanorum* (*Johannes Heumann* 1740, kurz

[5] *K. H. Spieß,* Art. Lehnsträgerschaft, in: A. Erler, E. Kaufmann (Hrsg.), Handwörterbuch zur deutschen Rechtsgeschichte (HRG), II, Sp. 1747.

vor ihm *Franz Karl Conradi* 1733) haben den Lehnsträger einbezogen. So heißt es bei *Heumann:* „de feudo fidelibus manibus provasalli tradito loquuntur non pauca documenta". Ein von ihm herangezogenes Quellenbeispiel spricht vom „tragen zu treuer hand"[6]. Den Lehnsträger noch stärker berücksichtigt hat *Wilhelm Eduard Albrecht* in seiner Arbeit über die Gewere (1828)[7]. Auch *Albrecht* grenzt ihn schon vom *„Procurator"* ab und ordnet innerhalb der Lehnsträgerschaft deren Anwendungsfälle. *Clausdieter Schott* hat nun vor einigen Jahren die Zusammenhänge auf der Grundlage der neueren lehnrechtlichen Forschung[8] und eigener Quellenstudien vortrefflich dargelegt. Die Lehnsträgerschaft ist ohne die Verdinglichung des Lehnswesens nicht denkbar, im Sinn einer „Gewichtsverlagerung von der Mannschaftsleistung auf das Lehengut" (*Schott*)[9] mit der Herausbildung der Vererblichkeit und Veräußerlichkeit. Während die Möglichkeit der Unterverleihung mit der im 12. Jahrhundert entstandenen und sich ursprünglich auf die militärische Befehlsgewalt im Reichsheer beziehenden Heerschildordnung mit dem König an der Spitze gleichsam Verfassungsbestandteil wurde, durch die der exklusive Kreis der Lehnsfähigen, man kann auch sagen: der feudalen Gesellschaft[10], bestimmt wurde, konnten Vererblichkeit und Veräußerlichkeit des Lehnguts zu einer Trennung von Lehnspflicht und Nutzung des Lehnguts führen. Da sich im Reich die Vererblichkeit früh durchgesetzt hatte, blieb die Frage, wie die Veräußerung des Lehnguts durch den Vasallen bewerkstelligt werden konnte. Eine solche war im Ergebnis dann unproblematisch, wenn der Lehnsherr mitspielte: das Lehen wurde vom „Veräußerer" an den Lehnsherrn zurückgegeben und dieser belehnte den „Erwerber". Schwierigkeiten entstanden dann, wenn die Belehnung für den „Erwerber" eine Schildniederung bedeutete[11]. Das war der Fall, wenn der Belehnte dem gleichen oder gar einem höheren Heerschild angehörte als der Belehnende. Der Sachsenspiegel sagte das unmißverständlich: „Wirt ein nach sines genozen man, sine gebort noch sin lantrecht en hat er da mete nicht gekrenkit, sinen herschilt hat her abir da mete genederet"[12]. Das Bestreben, die Heerschildordnung als ständi-

6 Hierzu *K. O. Scherner,* Fiducia Germanorum. Johannes Heumann und die Erfindung der Treuhand in der deutschen Rechtsgeschichte, in: Wirkungen europäischer Rechtskultur: Festschrift für Karl Kroeschell, München, 1997, S. 973 ff.; es geht hier um *Johannes Heumann,* Commentatio academica de Salmannis, 1740; die im Text zitierten Quellenbeispiele finden sich im Cap. XIII, S. 25.

7 *W. E. Albrecht,* Die Gewere als Grundlage des älteren deutschen Sachenrechts, 1828, Nachdruck 1967, S. 233 ff.

8 Hier sind vor allem die Arbeiten von *S. Bovet,* Die Stellung der Frau im deutschen und langobardischen Lehnrecht, Diss. Basel, 1927, und *B. Diestelkamp,* Das Lehnrecht der Grafschaft Katzenelnbogen, 1969, zu nennen.

9 *Schott* (Fn. 3) 87.

10 Mit dem vierten Schild wurde allerdings die Heerschildordnung des Sachsenspiegels und Schwabenspiegels ungewisser. Auch ist von einer tatsächlichen Vielfalt auszugehen, vgl. *Schott* (Fn. 3) 89.

11 *Schott* (Fn. 3) 89 f.

12 Sachsenspiegel Landrecht III 65 § 2; Text nach der Ausgabe Sachsenspiegel (Landrecht), hrsg. v. Cl. Frhr. von Schwerin, eingeleitet von Hans Thieme, 1987.

sche Gliederung und die Position des einzelnen darin zu erhalten einerseits, und das Bedürfnis, über das Lehngut als Vermögensstück verfügen zu können andererseits, konnten miteinander nur durch eine „konstruktive Umgehung der Heerschildordnung" (*Schott*)[13] im Sinn der eingangs umschriebenen Lehnsträgerschaft in Einklang gebracht werden. Dies war aber nur möglich, wenn es nicht als unzulässige Umgehung betrachtet wurde, sondern als Fortbildung des Lehnrechts.

Es gab zwei Konstellationen, in denen diese Problematik auftauchen konnte. In der ersten ging es darum, daß die Veräußerung vom Lehngut beabsichtigt war, aber der Erwerber nicht lehnspflichtig werden sollte, weil damit eine Heerschildniederung verbunden gewesen wäre. Die zweite Konstellation besteht darin, daß der zu Belehnende nicht lehnsfähig ist, insbesondere dann, wenn er nicht in der Heerschildordnung vorgesehen ist. Daneben gibt es noch eine dritte, die nichts mit lehnrechtlichen Umständen zu tun hat. Die im folgenden dargestellten Fallgruppen lehnen sich an die *Schotts* an, wenn auch nicht in der dortigen Reihenfolge.

(a) Die Veräußerung von Lehngut unter Umgehung der Heerschildordnung

(aa) Behalten zu treuer Hand

Um ständische Hindernisse bei der Veräußerung von Lehen zu vermeiden, die sich aus der Heerschildordnung ergaben, blieb der „Veräußerer" Lehnsmann, räumte dem Erwerber Nutzungsrecht und Weisungsbefugnis ein. So mußte das Lehen nicht auf dem Umweg über den Lehnsherrn an den Erwerber verliehen werden, was insbesondere bei längeren Lehnsketten teilweise schwierig oder aufgrund der Heerschildordnung gar unmöglich war. Seit dem 13. Jahrhundert sind solche Vereinbarungen üblich, in denen der Lehnsmann dem Erwerber gegenüber verspricht, daß er dessen *getrwer trager* ist[14]. Man kann mit *Schott* diese Lösung als „Behalten zu treuer Hand"[15] bezeichnen.

(bb) Treuleihe

Für den Erwerber sicherer, lehnrechtlich jedoch anstößiger war, wenn, wiederum um eine Heerschildniederung des Erwerbers zu vermeiden, der „Veräußerer" zwar Lehnsmann blieb, aber das Lehen an einen Vertrauensmann des „Erwerbers" als Träger verlieh. Schon die ältere Germanistik hat auf diese Fallkonstellation hingewiesen: „Auch für diesen Fall ist es klar, daß, wenn überhaupt Vertretung des Vasallen zugelassen wurde (wozu der Lehnsherr schwerlich gezwungen werden konnte), sie nur durch einen Lehnträger, der im Heerschilde unter dem Lehnsherrn

[13] *Schott* (Fn. 3) 90.

[14] *Schott* (Fn. 3) 90 f.

[15] *Schott* (Fn. 3) 90.

stand, geschehen konnte. Denn der Zweck, den man dabey im Auge hatte, war offenbar der, dem abnormen Lehnsverhältnisse die Gestalt eines regelmäßigen zu geben, zu welchem die Stellung des Lehnsherrn über dem Vasallen im Heerschilde gehörte, und dieses wurde nur erreicht, wenn der Vertreter selbst als Vasall erschien und den eigentlichen Lehnsmann gleichsam gänzlich verdeckte"[16]. Auch hier war der Lehnsträger nur nach außen berechtigt; Nutzen und Weisungsrecht standen dem Treugeber (also dem „Erwerber") zu. Diese Konstruktion wurde zusätzlich zum „Behalten zu treuer Hand" eingesetzt, so daß der „Erwerber" durch eine doppelte Trägerschaft gesichert war[17].

Obwohl mit der Möglichkeit der Unterverleihung ohne Zustimmung des Oberlehnsherren im 13. Jahrhundert die Treuleihe nicht zu beanstanden war, wurde diese bekämpft. Im 12. Jahrhundert wurden solche rechtlichen Konstruktionen als Umgehungen bei Strafe des Lehnsverlusts verboten; Friedrich Barbarossa hatte sie in den Konstitutionen von 1154 und 1158 mißbilligt[18]. Auch noch in den Rechtsbüchern war die Treuhandleihe verpönt[19]. Trotz allem setzte sie sich am Ende durch. Der Lehnsherr konnte von vornherein für den Erwerber einen Träger belehnen. Gegen Ende des 13. Jahrhunderts, noch zur Entstehungszeit des Schwabenspiegels, gehörte die Treuleihe (ein älterer Autor bezeichnet die Unterleihe an den Träger noch als „Scheinleihe") zum festen Bestandteil des jüngeren Lehnrechts. Nun findet sich in den Quellen auch der Begriff des Trägers, der zu Beginn des Jahrhunderts dort noch nicht vorkommt[20].

(b) Umgehung der Lehnsunfähigkeit

Einer Reihe von Personen kam weder aktive noch passive Lehnsfähigkeit zu. Schon ein Rechtshistoriker des frühen 19. Jahrhunderts wie *Albrecht* hatte die Lehnsunfähigen als „die wichtigste Gattung" unter denjenigen bezeichnet, die eines Lehnsträgers bedurften[21]. *Clausdieter Schott* behandelt die Überwindung der Lehnsunfähigkeit der verschiedenen Personengruppen durch Trägerschaft zu Recht getrennt, da der Ausschluß aus der ritterlichen Feudalgesellschaft verschiedene Ursachen hatte und auch zum Teil recht unterschiedlich ausfiel.

---

16 *Albrecht* (Fn. 7) 244, Anmerkung 670a, unter Hinweis auf einen Autor aus dem 18. Jahrhundert.

17 *Schott* (Fn. 3) 92 f. mit weiteren Einzelheiten.

18 Monumenta Germaniae Historica, Legum Sectio IV, Tomus I, Hannoverae, 1893, S. 208, 248.

19 *Schott* (Fn. 3) 93 mit Hinweis auf *C. G. Homeyer,* System des Lehnrechts der sächsischen Rechtsbücher, 2. Teil, Der Sachsenspiegel, 1844, S. 430, 507.

20 *Schott* (Fn. 3) 93 f.

21 *Albrecht* (Fn. 7) 235.

(aa) Frauen

Ein praktisch wichtiger und auch in den mittelalterlichen Rechtsbüchern wie dem Sachsenspiegel und Schwabenspiegel besonders eingehend behandelter Fall der Lehnsträgerschaft ist die für Frauen[22]. Frauen als Heerschildlose standen grundsätzlich außerhalb des Lehnsrechts (Sachsenspiegel Lehnrecht 2 § 1: „Papen unde wif, dorpere, koplude, unde alle de rechtes darvet oder unecht geboren sint, unde alle de nicht ne sin van ridderes art van vader un van eldervader, de scolen lenrechtes darven"[23]. Das bedeutete jedoch nicht, daß in der Praxis Frauen nicht belehnt werden konnten. Jedem Lehnsherrn blieb es überlassen, ob er sich mit einer Heersteuer begnügen oder an eine Frau Lehngut unter Verzicht auf die Mannschaft vergeben wollte[24]. Dadurch wurden die Frauen jedoch nicht heerschildfähig mit der Folge, daß ihnen mit dem Tod des Lehnsherrn ein Folgerecht dessen Nachfolger gegenüber zustand[25]. Mit anderen Worten: die lehnrechtlichen Wirkungen blieben auf das Verhältnis der Frau zum Lehnsherrn beschränkt. Ausnahmen waren Leiblehen und unmittelbare Reichslehen, die die Frau auch nach einem Herrenwechsel behalten durfte[26]. Insbesondere konnte die Frau auch nicht ihr Lehen weiter vererben. Hinter dieser Tendenz zur lehnrechtlichen Besserstellung der Frau stand der wachsende Modernisierungsdruck des langobardischen Lehnrechts mit seinem *feudum femineum.*

Ein Weg, der hier nicht näher zu erörtern ist, ist die Privilegierung der Frau, wie ein Mann behandelt zu werden. *Schott* spricht hier von der „Mannrechtsfiktion"[27]. Der andere, praktisch bedeutendere Weg, der auch in den Rechtsbüchern behandelt wird, ist der des Lehnsträgers. Dieser Weg war überall dort ohnehin der einzige, wo es das Mannrechtsprivileg nicht gab. Darüber hinaus war dieses für den Lehnsherrn nachteilig, weil er seiner Dienste verlustig ging. Deshalb ist die Lehnsträgerschaft für Frauen auch dort – sozusagen ergänzend – anzutreffen, wo ihnen das Privileg der Mannrechtsfiktion erteilt worden war. Mit der Einsetzung eines Lehnsträgers vermied man die Nachteile einer bloßen Belehnung der Frau. Insbesondere entstanden ihr keine Nachteile durch den Herrenwechsel. Die ältere Erscheinungsform – sie ist auch als ältere Lehnsträgerschaft bezeichnet worden[28] – erscheint noch im Schwabenspiegel. Art. 122 erwähnt in einem anderen Zusammenhang, daß der Ehefrau eines Vasallen das Lehen zur Nutzung überlassen werden kann. Es

---

22 Hierzu *Albrecht* (Fn. 7) 237 f., der sich vor allem auf den Sachsenspiegel bezieht; *Schott* (Fn. 3) 174 ff.

23 Text nach der Ausgabe Das Lehnrecht des Sachsenspiegels ed. tertia cur. *Karl August Eckhardt,* 1975 (Sachsenspiegel Lehnrecht).

24 Sachsenspiegel Lehnrecht (Fn. 23) 2, 36; hierzu auch *Albrecht* (Fn. 7) 235, 236, Anmerkung 637, auch unter Hinweis auf den *Vetus auctor de beneficiis* I § 5; S. 238.

25 In diesem Sinn etwa Schwabenspiegel Lehnrecht 4.

26 Dazu *Schott* (Fn. 3) 175 mit weiteren Angaben in Anmerkung 6.

27 Hierzu *Schott* (Fn. 3) 175 f.

28 So *Bovet* (Fn. 8) 16, 56 ff.

ist davon auszugehen, daß diese Treuhänder der Zustimmung des Lehnsherrn bedurften.

Die Rechtsbücher selbst bilden schon die jüngere Form der Lehnsträgerschaft ab. Im Gegensatz zur älteren wird hier die Frau selbst belehnt, allerdings zusammen mit einem Lehnsträger (Sachsenspiegel Lehnrecht 56 § 5: „he heve de lenunge unde den herscilt, unde se hevet de selven lenunge unde de gewere")[29]. Das bedeutete alles in allem, daß der Lehnsträger die Lehnsdienste verrichtete und damit auch den Vasallen der Frau vorstand, während der Frau die Nutzung des Lehens zukam. Allerdings spricht der Sachsenspiegel von Vormundschaft[30]. Die süddeutsche Urkundenpraxis des 13. Jahrhunderts kennt zahlreiche einschlägige Beispiele für die Einschaltung eines Trägers.

Auf die reiche Entfaltung der Lehnsträgerschaft für Frauen, der auch eine große Zahl von überlieferten Fällen entspricht, soll hier nicht näher eingegangen werden. Es sei nur so viel gesagt, daß mit diesem Institut die Rechtsstellung der Frauen, soweit sie überhaupt dem Lehnrecht zugänglich waren, entscheidend verbessert worden ist. Die in jenen Kreisen zentrale Vermögensform, das Lehngut, war damit für die rechtliche Ausstattung der Frau in jener Hinsicht zugänglich. Das galt für den Bereich der güterrechtlichen Ausstattung der Ehefrau, aber auch für die Trägerschaft etwa eines Sohnes für seine verwitwete Mutter, oder für Frauen, die in ein Kloster eintraten und so mit Lehngut ausgestattet werden konnten[31].

Die Vorteile der Lehnsträgerschaft für die Frau zeigten sich vor allem im Erbrecht. Es galt zwar der Satz, daß, ebenso wie im langobardischen Lehnrecht, die Frauen grundsätzlich von der Nachfolge im Lehen ausgeschlossen waren – auch wieder eine Konsequenz aus der Lehnsunfähigkeit der Frau[32]. Hier hatte aber schon das langobardische Lehnrecht eine Ausnahme in Gestalt des *feudum femineum* gemacht, das dadurch begründet werden konnte, daß schon der erste Lehnsempfänger eine Frau war, oder daß dem ersten Erwerber die Folgefähigkeit der Frauen zugesichert war. Was südlich der Alpen seit dem 12. Jahrhundert entwickelt war, fand sich nördlich der Alpen im 13. Jahrhundert. Die Frauenerbfolge in dieser Form setzte allerdings immer die Einschaltung eines Lehnsträgers voraus, da die Zulässigkeit einer Vererbung an der Lehnsunfähigkeit nichts geändert hatte. Das Auftreten des Lehnsträgers ist seit dem 13. Jahrhundert zu verzeichnen und verstärkt sich noch im 14. und 15. Jahrhundert.

Neben diesen schon existentiellen Bedürfnissen für eine Besserstellung der Frauen dehnte sich die Liberalisierung des Lehnrechts der Frau auch insoweit aus,

---

29 Das ist insofern mißverständlich, als der Lehnsträger auch die Lehnsgewere hat, allerdings *van der frowen halven*, Sachsenspiegel Lehnrecht (Fn. 23) 56 § 1.

30 Sachsenspiegel Lehnrecht (Fn. 23) 56 § 2.

31 Zu allem vgl. *Schott* (Fn. 3) 180 ff.

32 Sachsenspiegel Lehnrecht (Fn. 23) 21, Libri feudorum 1 F, § 2, zu alledem eingehend u. a. Schott (Fn. 3) 192 ff.

daß von Frauen überhaupt Lehngut rechtsgeschäftlich erworben werden konnte, allerdings nicht vor dem 15. Jahrhundert[33].

(bb) Minderjährige

Daß ein Kind keine Lehnsdienste leisten konnte, überbrückte man dadurch, daß der Herr unter Verzicht auf die Dienste die Einkünfte für sich behalten konnte. Im Hinblick auf das Lehngut sah man den Herrn insoweit als Vormund an (Herrenvormundschaft)[34]. Damit trug das Lehnrecht dem mittelalterlichen Minderjährigenrecht Rechnung, nach dem jedes Kind einen Vormund hatte (Sachsenspiegel Landrecht 42 § 1). War ein Vormund zugleich Lehnsmann des Herrn, dann entfiel die Herrenvormundschaft. Die auch schon außerhalb des Lehnrechts auftauchende Vorstellung, daß der Vormund ein *salmannus* sei, also jemand, ein Recht für einen andern wahrnimmt, wurde schon früh mit dem Lehnsvormund verbunden. Dem entsprach dann auch hier die Sprache der Quellen, besonders breit seit dem 14. Jahrhundert, wie *Schott* gezeigt hat[35]: „fidelis portator, er treit in zu getrewer hant, er ist ein getrewer trager". In Schwaben, Bayern und Österreich gab es Gegenden, in denen Träger sinngleich mit Vormund verwendet wurde, auch außerhalb des Lehnrechts[36].

(cc) Geistliche, Klöster, Ritterorden und Spitäler

Die Aufzählung der Personengruppen im Lehnrecht des Sachsenspiegels 2 § 1 „de scolen lenrechtes darven" beginnt mit den *papen,* also den Pfaffen; sie haben keinen Heerschild. Dem folgt auch der Schwabenspiegel[37]. Damit haben die Rechtsbücher des 13. Jahrhunderts etwas in ihr Lehnssystem aufgenommen, was sich bereits zu Anfang des 12. Jahrhunderts als eines der Ergebnisse des Investiturstreits durchgesetzt hatte. Die päpstlichen Erlasse, Synodal- und Konzilsbeschlüsse seit der Mitte des 11. Jahrhunderts, die das Verbot von Mannschaft und Treueid für Kleriker aussprachen, fanden im Wormser Konkordat vom 23. September 1122, dem *Pactum Calixtinum,* ihren Abschluß. Danach konnten nur Reichsbischöfe und Reichsäbte Temporalien erhalten. Nur sie sind neben den Laien in der Heerschildordnung berücksichtigt[38]. Eine Ausnahme galt nur für ritterbürtige Kleriker, die al-

---

33 Hierzu *Schott* (Fn. 3) 202 f.

34 Zu alledem *Schott* (Fn. 3) 204 ff.; zur Entwicklung der Lehnsvormundschaft *H. Mitteis,* Zur Geschichte der Lehnsvormundschaft, in: Festschrift für Alfred Schultze, 1934, S. 129 ff.

35 *Schott* (Fn. 3) 206 ff.

36 *Schott* (Fn. 3) 214 ff. mit weiteren Nachweisen; zu dem umgekehrten Fall, daß der Träger auch als Vormund bezeichnet wird, vgl. *Johannes Heumann* (Fn. 6) Cap. XIII, S. 25.

37 Schwabenspiegel Lehnrecht I.

38 Zu alledem *Schott* (Fn. 3) 111 f.; *Albrecht* (Fn. 7) 239, nennt die „Geistlichen" als weiteren Anwendungsfall und beschränkt sich auf den Hinweis auf das Lehnrecht des Sachsenspiegel und eine Urkunde aus dem 13. Jahrhundert.

lerdings auf ein Leiblehen (persönliches, nicht vererbbares Lehn) beschränkt waren (Schwabenspiegel Lehnrecht 4). Alle anderen Geistlichen, vor allem die hier besonders betroffenen Klöster, konnten zwar Eigentum erwerben oder Zinsleihen übernehmen[39], nicht jedoch Lehngut, es sei denn nach Rückgabe an den Lehnsherrn durch diesen als Eigentum oder gegen Zins. Oder der Lehnsherr – häufig waren dies Bischöfe oder Reichsäbte – erlaubte seinem Lehnsmann, einem Kloster Lehngut zu Eigentum zu übertragen[40]. Wie beim Erwerb von Lehngut durch Frauen griff man auch hier gelegentlich nach Privilegien oder der Fiktion, *als ob er weltlich und niht priester wäri* (1405)[41]. Auch hier blieben genug Fälle, in denen ein Lehnsträger gebraucht wurde, sei es, daß ein Eigentumserwerb überhaupt oder vorläufig ausgeschlossen war; Trägerschaft wurde also auch als Erwerbssicherung eingesetzt. Das galt für Priester, Kollegiatstifter und Klöster. Träger waren Adlige oder lehnsfähige Bürger. In den von Schott angeführten Quellen aus dem 13. bis zum 15. Jahrhundert wurden sie als *(getriuwe) tragere, pfleger* oder *portitores*[42] bezeichnet. *Albrecht* weist auf einen „lehenträger" hin[43].

Das gleiche ist mit der folgenden (seltenen) Formulierung gemeint, wenn den Freiburger Franziskanern ein halbes Haus, *in manus quorundam civium videlicet Werneri dicti de Rinvelden, Nicholai dicti Rethig et Cunradi dicti Wollebe ad usum fratrum Minorum* übertragen wird. *Schott,* der diese Stelle mitteilt, weist unter Bezugnahme auf *Hans Würdinger*[44] darauf hin, daß auch von den Franziskanern in England reicher Gebrauch von der „Treuhand ad usum, ad opus" gemacht worden sei.

Ähnlich verhält es sich bei den Ritterorden[45], die trotz der Herkunft und des militärischen Dienstes ihrer Mitglieder keinen Heerschild besaßen, auch nicht die einzelnen Ordensritter, weil auch sie dem kirchlichen Verbot der Treuleistung unterlagen. Die Privilegien des Templerordens (1163), der Johanniter (1192) und des Deutschen Ordens (1220) sprechen das klar aus. Da man sich daran hielt, war beim Erwerb von Lehngut auch hier die Trägerschaft notwendig[46].

Spitäler und Siechenhäuser unterlagen nicht nur als dem kirchlichen Schutz unterstehende Institutionen dem Treueidverbot, und sie blieben es auch trotz ihrer Kommunalisierung in den Städten seit dem 13. Jahrhundert, sondern sie waren als nicht natürliche Personen nicht passiv lehnsfähig. Deshalb waren auch sie für den

---

39 Zu dieser Frage unten II. 2 (b) (aa).

40 Beispiele aus dem 13. und 14. Jahrhundert bei *Schott* (Fn. 3) 112 f.

41 *Schott* (Fn. 3) 114 mit weiteren Nachweisen.

42 Zu alledem ausführlich *Schott* (Fn. 3) 114 ff., 117 ff., 126 ff.

43 *Albrecht* (Fn. 7) 239.

44 *H. Würdinger,* Geschichte der Stellvertretung (agency) in England, zugleich ein Beitrag zur Entwicklung des englischen Privatrechts, 1933, S. 313 ff.

45 Zu diesem Komplex *Edmund E. Stengel,* Hochmeister und Reich: Die Grundlagen der staatsrechtlichen Stellung des Deutschordenslandes, ZSS (GA) 58 (1938) 195 ff.

46 Zu allem mit Quellenbeispielen *Schott* (Fn. 3) 122 ff.

Aufbau, die Erweiterung und Erhaltung ihrer wirtschaftlichen Grundlage auf die gleichen Mittel wie die Orden, u. a. den Träger angewiesen. Treuhänderisches Behalten und Treuleihe sind die Formen, derer man sich bediente, soweit es nicht zum Eigentumserwerb der Güter kam[47].

(dd) Städte, Gemeinden und Stiftungen

Wilhelm Eduard Albrecht hat 1828 als dritte Gruppe der Lehnsunfähigen die „juristischen Personen" angeführt[48]. Seine Begründung ist ebenso schlicht wie unwiderlegbar: weil in den älteren Quellen niemals der „Vorstand", wohl aber dritte Personen Lehnsträger gewesen seien[49]. *Schott* differenziert schon nach der Bezeichnung und liefert auch eine Begründung[50]: Im Gegensatz zu den italienischen, französischen und englischen Städten, die als Seigneurien auch lehnsfähig waren[51], habe die deutsche Lehre keine Kollektiv-Vasallität entwickelt. Man kann ergänzen: wozu die mittelalterliche Rechtswirklichkeit auch keinen Anlaß gegeben hat. Hinzu kam, daß bei juristischen Personen kein Heimfall zu erwarten war. Die ältere Lehnrechtsdogmatik hat sich intensiv mit dieser Frage befaßt[52]. Ohne den Lehnsträger ging es also auch hier nicht.

(ee) Juden, Bürger und Bauern

Während die ältere Germanistik noch eine Gruppe der nicht Lehnsfähigen unter den „Nicht-Ritterbürtigen" zusammenfaßte und sich auf das Lehnrecht des Sachsenspiegels bezog[53], unterscheidet hier *Schott* richtiger zwischen Juden, Bürgern und Bauern, denn die Behandlung war unterschiedlich.

Die Juden, denen zur Zeit der Rechtsspiegel keine Waffenfähigkeit zukam, waren, zusammen mit Geächteten und Gebannten absolut lehnsunfähig[54] und damit von der Feudalgesellschaft ausgeschlossen. Deshalb findet sich Güterbesitz der hö-

---

47 Zu allem *Schott* (Fn. 3) 147 ff.

48 *Albrecht* (Fn. 7) 239.

49 *Albrecht* (Fn. 7) 139, 255 ff.

50 *Schott* (Fn. 3) 162 ff.

51 *Schott* (Fn. 3) 162, unter Hinweis auf *H. Mitteis,* Lehnrecht und Staatsgewalt, 1933, Nachdruck 1958, S. 384.

52 Hierzu *Schott* (Fn. 3) 162 f.

53 *Albrecht* (Fn. 7) 240; er sieht nach dem Lehnrecht des Schwabenspiegels eine gewisse Sonderstellung dergestalt, „daß sie gewisse aus der Lehnsfähigkeit herfließende Rechte hatten, die übrigen Lehnsunfähigen nicht theilhaftig waren; namentlich wissen wir dieses von der Schöffelbarkeit und allgemeinen Zeugnißfähigkeit in dem Lehngericht ihres Herrn und dem Rechte der Vererbung des Lehens auf ihre Nachkommen", unter Verweisung auf Schwabenspiegel Lehnrecht I, § 5.

54 *K. H. Spieß* (Fn. 5) 1710 f.

heren Leihformen in ihrer Hand nur ganz selten. Ausnahmen gab es nur im späten Mittelalter zum Zweck der Sicherheitsleistung. Soweit Juden wirklich Lehngut innehatten, war dies nur über Vermittlung durch einen Träger möglich. *Schott* verweist hier auf ein bekanntes Konstanzer Beispiel aus dem Jahr 1328, wo der *portitor* ein lehnsfähiger, der Oberschicht angehöriger Bürger war[55].

Anders war es bei Bürgern und Bauern. Zwar stellt der Sachsenspiegel *koplude* und *dorpere* außerhalb des Lehnrechts und läßt nur eine gnadenweise Belehnung zu. Die Rechtswirklichkeit sah jedoch anders aus[56]. Die Belehnung ganzer Städte und Bürgerschaften, in Italien schon im 12. Jahrhundert überliefert, findet sich in Deutschland seit dem 13. Jahrhundert. Daß bei der Belehnung von Städten, Bürgerschaften oder dem Rat Lehnsträger nötig waren, wurde schon erwähnt. In den späteren Rechtsbüchern fällt deshalb zu Recht die Einschränkung weg, daß Kaufleute, also Bürger, der Lehnsfähigkeit ermangeln. Die ausdrückliche Zuerkennung der Lehnsfähigkeit durch königliche Stadtprivilegien seit dem 13. Jahrhundert rechtfertigt, von Bürgerlehen zu sprechen, deren Zahl später infolge des Widerstands des Adels zurückging. Die Bürgerlehen waren meist Passivlehen; Vasallen von Bürgern sind sehr selten. Der Einsatz eines Trägers war nach alledem hier nicht notwendig[57]. *Schott,* der nur eine Ausnahme nennt, mahnt hier Forschungsbedarf an[58].

(c) Überwindung der Unteilbarkeit des Lehens

Schon *Albrecht* trennt die Anwendungsfälle der Trägerschaft wegen Lehnsunfähigkeit von denen, die „auf anderen Gründen" beruhen. Die erste Fallgruppe, die er hier anführt, ist die Bestellung eines Provasallen bei „Gesammtbelehnten"[59]. Nach deutschem Recht waren durch die Beschränkung der Erbfolge auf die männlichen Nachkommen des Lehnsmannes die Seitenverwandten grundsätzlich von der Erbfolge ausgeschlossen. Auch war der Lehnsherr nur verpflichtet, das Gut im Todesfall an einen einzigen Leibeserben zu vergeben. Allerdings war es auch möglich, mehrere Nachkommen zusammen zu belehnen (Gesamtlehen), die dieses ohne Zustimmung des Lehnsherrn in einzelne Teillehen auflösen konnten. Voraussetzung war jedoch die Mündigkeit aller Erben. Um die unmündigen Erben nicht leer ausgehen zu lassen, wurde der (volljährige) Erstgeborene als Träger eingesetzt, der für seine unmündigen Geschwister das Gesamtlehen bis zu ihrer Volljährigkeit trug. Dies fand auch Eingang in den Sachsenspiegel, den Schwabenspiegel, das Kleine Kaiserrecht und das Rechtsbuch Ruprechts von Freising[60]. Fälle dieser

55 *Schott* (Fn. 3) 229 mit weiteren Nachweisen.

56 *W. Goez,* Art. Bürgerlehen, in: HRG (Fn. 5) I, 553 ff.

57 Zu alledem *Goez* (Fn. 56) 553 ff.

58 *Schott* (Fn. 3) 230 f.

59 *Albrecht* (Fn. 7) 241.

60 Näheres bei *Schott* (Fn. 3) 219 f.

Gesamthandsträgerschaft sind durch zahlreiche Urkunden aus dem 13. bis zum 16. Jahrhundert belegt.

(d) Erwerbssicherung

Einen Lehnsträger hat man gelegentlich auch dann eingesetzt, wenn keiner der bisher angeführten Umstände vorlag, also weder eine Heerschildniederung zu befürchten war oder eine Gesamtbelehnung anstand, noch der Erwerber lehnsunfähig war.

Treuleihe und Behalten zu treuer Hand wurden auch seit dem Ende des 13. Jahrhunderts dann eingesetzt, wenn eine ordnungsgemäße Belehnung des Erwerbers durch den Lehnsherrn zwar vorgesehen, aber noch nicht vollzogen war. Bis dahin gab es nur das Versprechen des Veräußerers, das Lehen zurückzugeben und für eine Belehnung des Erwerbers zu sorgen. Hier half man sich mit der zeitweiligen Unterbelehnung eines Trägers für den Erwerber. Eine solche Konstruktion wählte man auch, wenn eine Belehnung des Erwerbers durch den Lehnsherrn zwar möglich gewesen wäre, eine solche jedoch politisch untunlich war. Unter Umständen konnte auch das „Behalten zu treuer Hand“ ausreichen, den Erwerber zu sichern. Insbesondere war das dann der Fall, wenn der Lehnsherr abwesend war und etwa noch weitere Mittel vorhanden waren, die Veräußerer – Träger zur Erfüllung seiner Pflichten anzuhalten[61]. Hierher gehörte auch die Einschaltung eines Lehnsträgers als Zwischenmann bei Abwesenheit des Lehnsempfängers. Diese Anwendungsform der Treuhand spielte im Lehnrecht jedoch nur eine geringe Rolle. Die Belege datieren spät und sind nicht zahlreich: der Erklärung Schotts, die im Lehnrecht verhältnismäßig früh ausgebildete Stellvertretung habe hier schneller zum Erfolg geführt[62], kann man nur beipflichten.

2. Früh- und hochmittelalterliches Stadt- und Landrecht

Auch hier sollen die einzelnen Unterfälle näher betrachtet werden. Dabei folge ich neben der Schott'schen Darstellung vor allem den Abhandlungen von *Otto Stobbe*[63] und *Konrad Beyerle*[64], die allerdings noch ergänzt werden.

---

61 *Schott* (Fn. 3) 106 ff.

62 *Schott* (Fn. 3) 109 f.

63 O. Stobbe, Ueber die Salmannen, ZRG 7 (1868) 405 ff.

64 *K. Beyerle,* Grundeigentumsverhältnisse und Bürgerrecht im mittelalterlichen Konstanz, Bd. 1, 1. Teil, Das Salmannenrecht, 1900.

(a) Letztwillenstreuhand

Seit dem 8., spätestens dem 9. Jahrhundert, wurden Mittelsleute bei der Grundstücksübertragung eingeschaltet. In den weitaus überwiegenden Fällen handelt es sich um letztwillige Verfügungen, *donationes post obitum,* fromme Schenkungen an einen Heiligen (also ein Kloster) um des Seelenheils willen. Da die Rechtsform des Testaments nicht bekannt war, half man sich mit der Einschaltung eines Mittelsmannes. Nach den Urkunden war das Geschäft zweigliedrig, einmal zwischen dem Schenker und dem Mittelsmann, zum andern zwischen diesen und dem Schenkungsempfänger nach dem Tod des Schenkers. In der einfachsten Version der Urkunden finden sich immer wieder die Formeln *trado ut tradas* oder *trado per manum* oder *cum manu,* bezogen auf das Schenkungsgut. Die ältere Forschung hat hier zunächst einen Fall der Salmannschaft, später der Treuhand gesehen und sich dabei unter anderem auf die erwähnten Formeln gestützt. Dabei ist immer mehr die Frage in den Mittelpunkt gerückt, ob der Bestellungsakt eine Eigentumsübertragung war. Während die ältere Lehre, vor allem seit der Arbeit von *Alfred Schultze* zur langobardischen Treuhand dazu neigte[65], ist diese Betrachtungsweise später in Zweifel gezogen worden[66].

Die Verwendung von Letztwillenstreuhändern hat sich auch in den folgenden Jahrhunderten fortgesetzt. Spezifische Bezeichnungen dieser Personen findet sich frühestens in den Urkunden des 13. Jahrhunderts, seitdem aber reichlich. Oft werden sie als *Salmann* bezeichnet, auch als *Träger* oder *manufidelis, delegator, mediator* usw.[67] Auch den Testamentsvollstrecker bezeichnete man, wie die Nürnberger Reformation von 1479, in XVIII, 1,1 noch als „vollzieher und treushender der verlassen gescheft"[68].

Mit dem Testamentsvollstrecker[69] ist auch die Rechtsfigur bezeichnet, die den Letztwillenstreuhänder schließlich abgelöst hat. Mit der Durchsetzung des Testaments als letztwilliger Verfügung und dem Vermögensübergang ipso iure gab es für eine Zwischenhand keine Verwendung mehr.

---

65 *A. Schultze,* Die langobardische Treuhand und ihre Umbildung zur Testamentsvollstrekkung, 1895, Nachdruck 1973.

66 *K. O. Scherner,* Salmannschaft, venditio iusta und Servusgeschäft, 1971, S. 16 ff., 93 ff. Zu dieser Streitfrage auch *Otten* (Fn. 4) 36 ff.

67 Eine Zusammenstellung dieser Quellenausdrücke schon bei *Heumann* (Fn. 6); neuerdings hierzu die außerordentlich förderlichen Ausführungen von *Schott* (Fn. 3) 56 ff.

68 Hier benutzt der Abdruck der Reformation von 1479 bei W. Kunkel, H. Thieme, F. Beyerle (Hrsg.), Quellen zur Neueren Deutschen Privatrechtsgeschichte Deutschlands, 1936, Bd. 1, S. 25 f., 26.

69 Vgl. u. a. *W. Schönfeld,* Die Vollstreckung der Verfügungen von Todes wegen im Mittelalter nach sächsischen Quellen, ZSS (GA) 42 (1921) 240 f., *G. Hückstädt,* Der Testamentsvollstrecker im deutschen Recht des Mittelalters, Diss. Kiel, 1971, weitere Hinweise bei *Otten* (Fn. 4) 25, zu den Einflüssen der Rezeption S. 28 ff., *W. Ogris,* s.v. Testament, HRG (Fn. 5) 33. Lieferung, S. 154 ff. sowie nunmehr *Reinhard Zimmermanns* Beitrag zum vorliegenden Band.

(b) Einschaltung eines Treuhänders zur Überwindung der Erwerbsunfähigkeit im mittelalterlichen Stadtrecht

Die zweite in sich geschlossene Gruppe von Anwendungsfällen der privatrechtlichen Treuhand führt uns in die mittelalterliche Stadt. *Konrad Beyerle,* der sich in der Erschließung dieses Treuhandphänomens große Verdienste erworben hat, hat diesen Komplex – im Gegensatz zu den Fällen, die im wesentlichen unter a) behandelt worden sind und die er als die „ältere Treuhand" bezeichnet – als die jüngere Form der Treuhand verstanden[70]. Er nennt es das „jüngere Salmannenrecht" und weist damit zugleich auf ein jedenfalls in Süddeutschland und insbesondere in Konstanz zentrales Quellenwort für den Treuhänder hin: *Salmann.* Es ist im Bayerischen, Fränkischen und Alemannischen anzutreffen. Die jüngeren Formen des Salmannenrechts hätten nicht (wie die ältere Treuhand, d. Verf.) „die Vermittlung des Gutes durch den Salmann an einen Dritten zum Gegenstand", sondern stellten sich „als reine Schutz- und Gewaltverhältnisse für den Berechtigten ohne jede unmittelbare Veräußerungsabsicht" dar. Auf diese Weise, so *Beyerle,* „tritt der Pflichtenkreis des Salmannes gegen früher viel mehr hervor, um alsbald die Rechtsmachtseite zu überwiegen. Der Wunsch nach möglichster Sicherheit ihrer Rechtsstellung veranlaßte vielfach Kirchen und Klöster, mächtige Männer als Salleute über ihre Güter beizuziehen, die schon durch ihr Ansehen chikanöse Personen vor ungerechtfertigten Prozessen zurückschreckten. Wenn aber auch das Schutzverhältnis ein allen Formen des neueren Salmannenrechts gemeinsames Moment ist, so scheidet sich dasselbe doch wesentlich in zwei Richtungen. Davon dient die eine, wie *Heusler,* und vor ihm *Stobbe,* richtig bemerkt haben, lediglich dem Zwekke der erhöhten Gewährschaft. Die andere Gattung ist außerdem dazu bestimmt, bei Vorliegen irgend eines rechtlichen Mangels in der Person des Berechtigten einen den gesetzlichen Erfordernissen genügenden Vertreter ihm zur Seite zu stellen"[71].

Da die erstgenannte „Gattung", die der „erhöhten Gewährschaft" diente, besser an einer anderen Stelle einzuordnen ist[72], soll hier nur auf die zweite „Gattung" eingegangen werden. Schon *Otto Stobbe* hatte das Problem treffend umrissen: „Aehnlich wie bei dem römischen in bonis esse im Gegensatz zum quiritarischen Eigenthum, oder beim Eigenthum dessen, der im Hypothekenbuch eingetragen ist, während ein Anderer von ihm das Eigenthum ohne Umschreibung erworben hat, übt der Eine das Eigenthum selbst aus und vertritt der Andere nur nach außen hin das Gut wie ein Eigenthümer. In dieser Anwendung ist die Salmannschaft eine Species des Treuhänderverhältnisses und der Lehnsträgerschaft verwandt. So wie im Gebiet des Lehnrechts der Lehnsträger nach außen hin als Vasall erscheint, nach innen hin aber, d. h. was Nutzungen, Verfügungen, Erbrecht u.s.w. betrifft,

---

70 *K. Beyerle* (Fn. 64) 22 f.

71 *K. Beyerle* (Fn. 64) 23.

72 Vgl. hierzu unten II. 2 (d).

eine ganz andere Person das Lehnrecht ausübt, findet bei der Salmannschaft ganz dasselbe im Gebiete des Landrechts statt“[73]. *Konrad Beyerle* sagt kurz und bündig: „Nur Bürger dürfen freien Grundbesitz zu eigener Hand in [sc.: der Stadt] Konstanz besitzen“[74].

Daß diejenigen Personen, die für ihre Verteidigung einer Stadt verantwortlich waren, auch über den Boden *intra muros* verfügen wollten, hat zu diesem Satz geführt, der in vielen Städten galt. Er war auch als Schutzmittel gegen den Verlust städtischer Steuerobjekte durch Übergabe in geistliche Hand geschaffen worden. Um von diesen Grundsätzen Ausnahmen machen zu können, war die Einschaltung eines in Konstanz so genannten Salmanns oder mehrerer Salleute notwendig, wobei zu beachten ist, daß diese Salleute eigentumsberechtigte Bürger waren, die dadurch eine Kontrolle ausüben konnten.

Im folgenden sollen hier einige Anwendungsfälle angeführt werden.

(aa) Geistliche, Klöster und Kirchen

Sollte ein Geistlicher persönlich Eigentümer eines Konstanzer Grundstücks werden, bedurfte es dazu eines Salmanns[75]. Auch in Lübeck wurden hinsichtlich solcher Grundstücke, die Geistlichen gehörten, Bürger in die Stadtbücher als Eigentümer eingetragen. Sie erklärten bei der Eintragung, daß ihnen das Grundstück nur „ad fideles manus“ gehöre. Damit behielt die Stadt ihr Recht auf Abgaben und die weltliche Jurisdiktion[76].

Das Franziskanerkloster in Konstanz konnte städtisches freies Grundeigentum mit Hilfe von Salleuten erwerben. In den älteren Urkunden des 13. Jahrhunderts wird noch vom *procurator*[77] gesprochen. Auch Beghinenhäuser wurden auf diesem Wege geduldet[78].

(bb) Spitäler

Das Heilig-Geist-Spital wurde ähnlich behandelt. Als Anstalt hatte es keine Bürgerqualität. Also hat man Spitalpfleger eingesetzt, die ebenfalls salmannfähige Bürger waren[79].

---

73 *Stobbe* (Fn. 63) 431 f.

74 *K. Beyerle* (Fn. 64) 67.

75 Hierzu *K. Beyerle* (Fn. 64) 68 für Konstanz.

76 *Stobbe* (Fn. 63) 432 f.

77 Zum procurator auch *Heumann* (n. 6) Cap. XII, S. 22; vgl. zum Umfeld *Scherner* (Fn. 6) 982.

78 *K. Beyerle* (Fn. 64) 69 f., zu Übertragungen an die Kirche S. 70 ff.

79 *K. Beyerle* (Fn. 64) 72 ff.

(cc) Auswärtige

Auswärtige als gleichsam „natürliche Stadtfremde" waren grundsätzlich vom Grundstückserwerb ausgeschlossen. Wo eine Vertretung durch Bürger nicht völlig ausgeschlossen war, wie es eine Nürnberger Polizeiordnung einmal angeordnet hatte, konnten, wie etwa in Hamburg, Bürger als „Besitzer zur treuen Hand" ins Stadtbuch eingetragen werden[80]. Dies war allerdings nicht notwendig, wenn, insbesondere beim Erwerb durch Erbgang, dem Erben das Bürgerrecht verliehen wurde, wie in Konstanz[81].

(dd) Juristische Personen

Schon die ältere Literatur hat darauf hingewiesen, daß – wie der Lehnsträger im Lehnrecht – beim Eigentumserwerb durch juristische Personen natürliche Personen eingeschaltet werden müssen. So hat im Jahr 1288 die *universitas iudeorum colonensium* ein Grundstück erworben *in manus episcopi*[82].

(ee) Eingesessene Nichtbürger

Hatte ein zugewanderter Nichtbürger Vermögen angesammelt und wollte er ein Haus in der Stadt erwerben, bedurfte er eines Salmanns. Der Besitz zu Salmanneigen war für ihn bis 1372 in Konstanz die einzige Möglichkeit, das Bürgerrecht zu erwerben, und wurde deshalb oftmals angestrebt[83].

(ff) Juden

Anders als im Lehnrecht war die Erwerbsfähigkeit der Juden auf dem Gebiet des städtischen Grundbesitzes nicht völlig ausgeschlossen. Die Verhältnisse waren von Stadt zu Stadt verschieden, wie die Untersuchung von *A. Kober* (1907) gezeigt hat. In Städten, wo Grundbesitzerwerb durch Juden zulässig ist, wurde dieser mit Hilfe von Salleuten abgewickelt[84]. Daß christliche Bürger für die jüdischen Hausbesitzer in den Büchern eingetragen waren, ist bis in das 17. Jahrhundert nachgewiesen.

---

80 *Stobbe* (Fn. 63) 433 f.

81 *K. Beyerle* (Fn. 64) 74 ff.

82 *Stobbe* (Fn. 63) 435.

83 *K. Beyerle* (Fn. 64) 77.

84 *A. Kober*, Das Salmannenrecht und die Juden, 1907, S. 153 ff.

(gg) Frauen und Minderjährige

Soweit Frauen und Minderjährige aus Gründen, die in der Sprache des Bürgerlichen Gesetzbuchs als fehlende oder eingeschränkte Geschäftsfähigkeit umschrieben worden wäre, nicht rechtsgeschäftlich tätig werden konnten, ist dies Problem im Mittelalter unterschiedlich gelöst worden, unter anderem auch über das Institut der Vormundschaft, der man – wiederum in moderner Rechtssprache – in vielen Fällen Stellvertretungsfunktion zuschreiben kann.

Ungeachtet dessen gab es auch außerhalb des Lehnrechts Fälle, in denen die Salmannen auch für Frauen und Minderjährige auftraten, so wenn der verstorbene Ehemann als Nichtbürger unter Zuhilfenahme eines Salmanns ein Haus besessen hatte und dieser sein Amt für Witwe und Kinder weiterführte[85].

Ein weiterer Fall ist der, daß die rechtliche Stellung der Frau in einem Ehevertrag nach einem Salmann verlangt, was im Leibzuchts- oder Leibgedingerecht als Witwenversorgung bzw. bei der Widerlegung als Sicherstellung der Heimsteuer durch Liegenschaftsverpfändung gegeben ist[86]. Die Leibzuchtbestellung ist hier der Einräumung eines vollen dinglichen Rechts angenähert, das nur durch die Bedingung des Todes des Berechtigten beschränkt ist[87]. Bei der bestellten Widerlegung als dingliches Recht am verpfändeten Grundstück war der Ehemann auf die Zustimmung der Frau und ihres Salmannes angewiesen, wenn er etwa in bezug auf dieses Grundstück einen Rentenkauf eingehen wollte[88].

(c) Treuhänder im bäuerlichen Recht

Den Einsatz eines Treuhänders gab es auch im mittelalterlichen bäuerlichen Recht. Schon *Stobbe* hat Fälle angeführt, in denen bei Personen, die für den Erwerb von Grundstücken nicht „die erforderlichen Eigenschaften besitzen, eine qualificirte Person als getreue Hand an das Gut zu setzen“ sei; so konnte nach einem Hildesheimer Weistum ein „freyman“ „eigenbehörige Meyerdingsgüther“ nur über eine „getreue handt“ besitzen, wenn er frei bleiben wollte. Auch hier geht es um die Verhinderung einer Standesniederung; für *Stobbe* war das ein Fall einer „Umgehung“[89]. *Clausdieter Schott* hat, auch unter Verwendung landesgeschichtlicher Forschungen, erstmals einen zusammenfassenden und strukturierten Überblick über die Treuhand im mittelalterlichen und frühneuzeitlichen Bauernrecht gegeben und damit das Gesamtbild der Treuhand wesentlich erweitert[90]. Hier fin-

85 *K. Beyerle* (Fn. 64) 80.

86 *K. Beyerle* (Fn. 64) 81.

87 *K. Beyerle* (Fn. 64) 81.

88 *K. Beyerle* (Fn. 64) 83.

89 *Stobbe* (Fn. 63) 434 f.

90 *Schott* (Fn. 3) 239 ff.

den wir nicht nur den von *Stobbe* angeführten Fall der zu verhindernden Standesniederung[91], sondern auch andere, uns schon vom Lehnrecht und Stadtrecht her bekannten Konstellationen. Denn die Interessen waren in gewisser Weise vergleichbar: Der Grundherr war interessiert, daß ihm die aus den Grundleihen zugewiesenen Einkünfte nicht verlorengehen. So hätten Teilungen der verliehenen Güter seine Ansprüche gefährdet; wie im Lehnrecht gab es auch hier Teilungsverbote[92]. Ihnen konnte man nur durch Einsetzungen von Trägern entsprechen, die für die Abführung der Einkünfte verantwortlich waren, obwohl der Nutzen im Sinn der Teilungen mehreren zukam. Es handelt sich hier um Anwendungsfälle des Trägers, die noch bis in die Neuzeit hinein vorkommen. Sollte eine Hausgemeinschaft Leihgut erhalten, wurde der Älteste als Träger, also als alleinverantwortlich bestimmt – also eine Trägerschaft für eine Gesamthand. *Schott* nennt hier Belege, die bis in die Neuzeit hineinreichen[93]. Entsprechendes galt bei Höfeteilungen[94]. Da weder Frauen noch Minderjährige als vollwertige Hofhuber galten, wurde für die Trägerschaft oftmals ausdrücklich verlangt[95].

(d) Einschaltung eines Mittelsmanns zur Erwerbssicherung

Wesentlich häufiger als im Lehnrecht ist ansonsten ein Treuhänder zur Erwerbssicherung im weitesten Sinn eingesetzt worden. Dazu gehört das Auftreten eines Konstanzer Salmanns für einen Abwesenden; *Konrad Beyerle* spricht hier, allerdings untechnisch, von der „Stellvertretung“[96]. Ähnlich war es, wenn der endgültige Erwerber noch nicht bestimmt war[97], oder wenn er zwar feststand, nicht jedoch, ob das Ereignis eintreten würde, an das die Vergabung geknüpft ist, etwa, daß der Schenker auf einer Reise oder im Krieg umkommen sollte[98]. Das ist aber schon eine der oben behandelten, seit dem 8. Jahrhundert nachweisbaren letztwilligen Verfügungen unter Hinzuziehung eines Mittlers: Auch hier geht es um die Sicherung des Erwerbs. Der Bedachte hatte, jedenfalls nach vereinzelten Quellen, eine Klage gegen den Letztwillenstreuhänder[99].

Ist hier noch die Einsetzung einer Mittelsperson das Vehikel, schon im vorhinein „vollendete Tatsachen“ zu schaffen, so gilt das nicht mehr für jene Fälle, in denen

---

91 *Schott* (Fn. 3) 258 ff.

92 *Schott* (Fn. 3) 241.

93 *Schott* (Fn. 3) 244 ff.

94 *Schott* (Fn. 3) 250 ff.

95 *Schott* (Fn. 3) 265 ff.

96 *K. Beyerle* (Fn. 64) 43 ff.; *Stobbe* (Fn. 63) 424. Vgl. dazu auch *Otten* (Fn. 4) 24 mit weiteren Nachweisen.

97 *G. Beseler*, Die Lehre von den Erbverträgen. 1. Teil, Die Vergabungen von Todes wegen im älteren deutschen Rechte, 1835, S. 267.

98 So *Beseler* (Fn. 97) 268; *Stobbe* (Fn. 63) 423 f.

99 *Stobbe* (Fn. 63) 426.

das nicht nötig war, sondern die besondere Sicherung eines an sich schon perfekten Geschäfts darin bestand, sich einer angesehenen Persönlichkeit als Garanten der Beständigkeit des Geschäfts zu bedienen. In allen maßgeblichen Untersuchungen zur Treuhand seit dem 18. Jahrhundert finden wir einschlägige Urkunden erwähnt, angefangen bei *Johannes Heumann*, ferner *Georg Beseler*[100] oder *Otto Stobbe*, der auf die Fälle hinweist, in denen der Erwerber einen „Salmann" eingeschaltet hat, um damit die Sicherheit seines Erwerbes zu erhöhen[101]. In der Tat dürfte die Heranziehung eines hochgeachteten, vielleicht auch gefürchteten „Garanten" in noch größerem Maße im Interesse des Erwerbers als des Veräußerers gelegen haben. Deshalb gehört hierher auch jene Urkunde, in der betont wird, daß *dictam villam ad usus ecclesiae beatae virginis tamquam verus salman conservabit simul et defendet*[102], also der Salmann wie ein Gewähre die Interessen des Erwerbers gegenüber Ansprüchen Dritter im Prozeß verteidigen muß.

Solche Fälle meinte *Konrad Beyerle*, als er von der einen Richtung des neueren Salmannenrechts sprach, die „lediglich dem Zwecke der erhöhten Gewährschaft" gedient habe. Er verweist hier auf den „vorwiegend bayerische(n) Gebrauch"[103], für alle Güter Salleute zu bestellen, daß jeder Grundeigentümer seinen Salmann gehabt habe, der das Gut vor Gericht vertreten und der selbstverständlich auch bei Veräußerungen mitgewirkt habe. Auf dieses besondere Phänomen hat bereits die ältere Forschung, wie *Heumann*[104], *Beseler*[105] und *Stobbe*[106] hingewiesen; in der Regel sind die gleichen bayerischen Urkunden aus dem 12. und 13. Jahrhundert gemeint. In Nürnberg mußten die Salleute bei allen Veräußerungen und sonstigen Übertragungen hinzugezogen werden[107]. Nach *Stobbe* kam den Salleuten die gleiche Funktion zu wie den Hypothekenbüchern des 19. Jahrhunderts[108]. Sie waren, wie man heute sagen kann, wie ein „lebendes Grundbuch"[109].

---

100 *Beseler* (Fn. 97) 271.

101 *Stobbe* (Fn. 63) 428 ff.

102 So eine bayerische Urkunde aus dem Jahr 1244, zitiert bei *Beseler* (Fn. 97) 276 mit weiteren Nachweisen.

103 *K. Beyerle* (Fn. 64) 23 ff.

104 *Heumann* (Fn. 6) Cap. X, S. 13 ff.; vgl. hierzu *Scherner* (Fn. 6) 973 ff.

105 *Beseler* (Fn. 97) 272 f.

106 *Stobbe* (Fn. 63) 428 ff.

107 Vgl. die Beispiele bei *Stobbe* (Fn. 63) 435 ff., der sich seinerseits auf *Heumann* (Fn. 6) beruft.

108 *Stobbe* (Fn. 63) 438.

109 *Otten* (Fn. 4) 22.

III. Auswertung

1. Die verschiedenen Funktionen der Treuhand

In der Darstellung ist mehrfach deutlich geworden, daß das Phänomen Treuhand in der deutschen Rechtsgeschichte von den hier angeführten Autoren in der Regel aufgegliedert wurde. Dabei haben sich überraschende Übereinstimmungen gefunden. Diese Übereinstimmungen beziehen sich nicht unbedingt bloß auf jeweils dieselbe Gruppe der Treuhandfälle, auf der einen Seite also die lehnrechtlichen, auf der anderen Seite die landrechtlichen Fälle, sondern beziehen sich vor allem auch auf Gemeinsamkeiten beider Gruppen.

(a) Die Umgehungsfälle

Besonders augenfällig ist in beiden Bereichen der Einsatz des Treuhänders beim Fehlen der persönlichen Voraussetzungen eines der an einem rechtlichen Vorgang Beteiligten. Im Lehnrecht ist diese Gruppe mit „Umgehung der Lehnsunfähigkeit" umschrieben worden, im Bereich des Stadtrechts mit „Einschaltung eines Treuhänders zur Überwindung der Erwerbsunfähigkeit im mittelalterlichen Stadtrecht", und sie kehrt auch wieder im bäuerlichen Rechtskreis. Die Treuhand wird hier eingesetzt, um ein von der jeweiligen Rechtsordnung (Lehnrecht oder Stadtrecht) vorgegebenes Rechtshindernis zu vermeiden, um damit Rechtsvorteile für den Personenkreis zu erreichen, der von der Rechtsordnung für diese gerade nicht vorgesehen ist (eine Frau soll ein Lehngut nutzen können, einem Nichtbürger sollen die Erträge eines städtischen Grundstücks zufließen). Man könnte es auch anders ausdrücken: Die Rechtsvorteile, die einem „privilegierten" Personenkreis vorbehalten sind, kommen auf dem Umweg über die Treuhand ökonomisch einem nichtprivilegierten Personenkreis zu. Da im allgemeinen Privileg als Umschreibung eines Sonderrechts verwendet wird, sollte man diesen Begriff jedoch besser vermeiden. Der Träger eines bestimmten Heerschilds ist nicht privilegiert, sondern er nimmt innerhalb der Lehnsverfassung einen bestimmten Platz ein.

Die Treuhand kann deshalb als planmäßig eingesetztes Instrument angesehen werden, bestimmte rechtliche Folgen, die sich aus der ständischen Ordnung ergeben, faktisch, d. h. im Ergebnis, außer Kraft zu setzen. Dies ist dadurch möglich, daß eine solche Umgehung dem Interesse aller Beteiligten entsprochen hat, oder dem Interesse einzelner Beteiligter, das jedoch von den anderen toleriert worden ist, weil andere Lösungen erwünscht waren: Man will Juden den Erwerb von Grundstücken ermöglichen, weil ihr Zuzug in eine Stadt erwünscht ist oder die Versorgung einer Witwe mit Lehngut, wenn eine andere Form der Versorgung nicht vorhanden ist oder nicht ausreicht. Allgemeiner umschrieben: Die Treuhand ist ein Instrument gewesen, um ständerechtliche Beschränkungen im Interesse eines erweiterten Rechts- und Wirtschaftsverkehrs zu überwinden[110]. Mit Recht hat *Kon-*

rad Beyerle von einer „verfassungsrechtlichen Funktion“ des Salmanns gesprochen[111]. Die „Treuhandlösung“ ist ein Musterbeispiel dafür, eine Staats- und Gesellschaftsverfassung zu respektieren und gleichzeitig deren Inhalte punktuell zu verändern. Deshalb ist es auch vor allem im Lehnrecht zu Widerständen gekommen, die in Deutschland jedenfalls schnell überwunden waren. Nur in ganz wenigen Fällen gab es nahezu unüberwindliche Schranken, wie etwa an manchen Orten der Erwerb städtischer Grundstücke durch Juden.

Da der jeweils „privilegierte“ Personenkreis, der den Träger im Lehnrecht und den „Salmann“ im Stadtrecht stellte, ja mitwirken mußte, konnte er, soweit das gewollt war, diese Vorgänge auch kontrollieren. Das Salmannenrecht in Konstanz ist nach Ansicht *Konrad Beyerles* gerade mit dem Ziel einer solchen Kontrolle aufgebaut worden. Eine gewisse Abmilderung dieses Umgehungseffektes ergab sich in allen Fällen daraus, daß sich die Umgehung nur vermögensrechtlich ausgewirkt hat. Ob diese Treuhandpraxis den Zusammenbruch der ständischen Gesellschaft beschleunigt hat, ist eine andere Frage. Man könnte allerdings auch umgekehrt fragen, ob sie dadurch nicht länger überlebt hat.

Zu den Umgehungsfällen gehört im Lehnrecht auch noch der erste Anwendungsbereich „Veräußerung von Lehngut unter Umgehung der Heerschildordnung“ in beiden Anwendungsfällen. Ähnliches gab es allerdings auch im bäuerlichen Recht.

(b) Die Erwerbssicherung

Im Lehnrecht geht es bei dieser Gruppe um die Überbrückung tatsächlicher vorübergehender Hindernisse, insbesondere, wenn einer der Beteiligten bei der Begründung eines Lehens abwesend war. In diesen Fällen war auch eine andere Überwindung des Hindernisses möglich, etwa auf dem Weg der Stellvertretung, die sich im Lehnrecht früh herausgebildet hat.

Von viel größerer Bedeutung ist diese Gruppe der Treuhandfälle im mittelalterlichen Stadtrecht, wo es dafür noch keine Stellvertretung gab. Von der Funktion her gehören hierher auch die Fälle, in denen ein Dritter hinzugezogen wurde, um spätere Einwirkungen anderer auszuschließen wie die Sicherung des Erbenlaubs oder eine Garantenstellung. Auch der echte Salmann als grundbuchähnliche Einrichtung, wo also alle Eigentumsübertragungen über Salleute abgewickelt werden mußten, gehört hierher.

Schließlich gehört hierher auch die älteste mittelalterliche Treuhandform, der Letztwillenstreuhänder. Seine Einschaltung beruht darauf, daß es Rechtsordnungen

---

110 *K. O. Scherner*, Art. Treuhand, in: Lexikon des Mittelalters, Bd. VIII (noch nicht erschienen), Sp. 978 f.

111 *K. Beyerle* (Fn. 64) 49. Hierzu auch *Schott* (Fn. 3) 234.

gibt, bei denen eine letztwillige Verfügung gar nicht anders durchgeführt werden kann. Sobald ein anderes geeignetes oder gar besseres Instrument, wie das Testament, anerkannt war, ist der Treuhänder zum Testamentsvollstrecker degradiert worden, falls man einen solchen überhaupt für notwendig gehalten hat.

(c) Das zeitliche Auftreten der Gruppen

Während die Lehnsträgerschaft wie auch die nicht lehnrechtliche, vor allem städtische Treuhand im Grundstücksverkehr erst dann aufgetreten sind, als diese Verfassungs- und Gesellschaftsordnungen gefestigt waren, also seit dem 13. und 14. Jahrhundert, gilt das nicht für die Gruppe der Erwerbssicherungstreuhand. Da die tatsächliche Verhinderung einzelner Beteiligter bei Rechtsgeschäften zu allen Zeiten eine rechtliche Lösung erfordert und nicht jede Epoche über ein flexibles Instrumentarium an Rechtsfiguren verfügt, gab es die Treuhand dieser Art während des ganzen Mittelalters. Das gilt insbesondere für die Letztwillenstreuhand. Hierher gehören allerdings auch Fallgruppen, insbesondere aus dem Frühmittelalter, die im allgemeinen nicht zu den Treuhandfällen gezählt werden, die aber von der Funktion her hier einzuordnen sind. Das gilt insbesondere für die Rechtsverhältnisse, die mit spätantiken Rechtswörtern wie *commendare, commendatio* umschrieben wurden und die auch außerhalb der Letztwillensgeschäfte anzutreffen sind, wie z. B. das Anvertrauen einer Sache zur Aufbewahrung oder zum Verkauf[112].

2. Definitionsfragen

Angesichts dieser doch recht unterschiedlichen Funktionen tritt die Frage eines einheitlichen Begriffs, also einer allgemeinen Definition der Treuhand in den Hintergrund. Wichtiger erscheint, die hier vorgestellte Gruppierung zu überprüfen und gegebenenfalls zu ergänzen. Der Wandel und auch die modische Bevorzugung bestimmter Begriffe, wie „Salmann“, „Treuhand“ oder „Träger“ oder der Begriff, der sich in den ältesten Untersuchungen deutscher Germanisten findet, nämlich „fiducia“ (*Heumann,* 1740) beruhen auf unterschiedlichen Anknüpfungen, so Salmann und Träger auf Quellenausdrücken, während *fiducia* und Treuhand eher juristische Bewertungen sind. Von den alten Streitfragen bleiben zwei wichtige Dinge im Blick, einmal die Umschreibung des „Treuhänders“ durch die Quellen selbst, auf die noch zurückzukommen ist, und zum andern der Versuch der systematischen Einordnung der Treuhandfunktionen in die jeweilige Rechtsordnung.

Hierher gehört die in der deutschen Rechtsgeschichte alte Kontroverse um die dingliche oder nichtdingliche Stellung des Treuhänders. Abgesehen davon, daß es

---

112 *Scherner* (Fn. 110) Sp. 978 f.; *idem* (Fn. 66) 137 ff.

hier um Auslegungsfragen geht und eine allgemein gültige Antwort mit Sicherheit falsch wäre, kann aufgrund der vorliegenden Zusammenstellung in diesem Punkt in einer Hinsicht eine klare Antwort gegeben werden. Eine Eigentümerstellung des Treuhänders in den Fällen der stadtrechtlichen Erwerbsunfähigkeit bzw. die Frage der Inhaberschaft in den Lehnsträgerfällen ist eindeutig zu bejahen. Denn die Funktion dieser „Umgehung" besteht ja gerade darin, an der ständerechtlichen Zuordnung nichts zu ändern. Der Lehnsträger ist also der Lehnsinhaber, und der *Salmann,* der ein städtisches Grundstück für einen Nichtbürger hält, ist nach städtischem Grundstücksrecht der Eigentümer.

Umgekehrt ist der Treuhänder in der Gruppe Erwerbssicherung nicht zwingend Eigentümer. Nur hier läßt sich über seine Rechtsstellung streiten.

3. Die Vorstellungen der Beteiligten: Treuhand als Institut des mittelalterlichen Rechts

Viel wichtiger als Zuordnungen durch die rechtshistorische Nachwelt ist im Interesse einer möglichst objektiven Geschichtsschreibung die Frage, ob, und wenn ja, wie die Treuhand oder wie immer man das Gebilde nennt, von den Zeitgenossen als besonderes Institut überhaupt gesehen worden ist, mit anderen Worten, ob die Treuhand bloß ein wissenschaftliches Konstrukt oder auch eine „wirkliche" mittelalterliche Rechtsfigur ist. Da diese Frage auf eine Rechtsordnung bezogen ist, die nicht das Produkt einer Rechtswissenschaft ist, welche in Definitionen denkt, ist sie schwierig zu beantworten. Einzig zuverlässiges Kriterium ist die Rechtssprache der Beteiligten, unter Umständen auch die verwendete Symbolik. Was die Rechtssprache angeht, so ist zunächst auf die Verwendung volkssprachlicher Ausdrücke zu achten. Hier ist gerade der *Träger,* wie *Schott* vor einigen Jahren gezeigt hat, der beste Beweis dafür, daß im süddeutsch-schwäbisch-schweizerischen Bereich ein der Volkssprache angehöriger Begriff, der des Trägers, existierte. Diesem standen festumrissene Aufgaben zu, die in der Vielfalt der unter II. angeführten Anwendungsfälle zum Vorschein kommen. Ähnliches gilt für den *Salmann.* Mit Recht hat *Schott* darauf hingewiesen, daß der Träger nahezu überall, wo er „für Eigentum bestellt" wird, mit dem Salmann zusammentrifft. Alle diese Begriffe tauchen erst im 13. Jahrhundert auf. Wie *Schott* nachgewiesen hat, gibt es sogar Quellen, so eine Urkunde aus dem Jahr 1282, in der *tragen* und *Sal* gleichgesetzt werden, andere, in denen Träger und Salmannen in einem Atemzug genannt werden, andere, in denen man von „zainem getruwen Salman" oder dem „getruwe trager" spricht[113]. Die Beispiele zeigen, daß auch der dritte Begriff, die „Treue" in der Treuhand, mit dem gleichen Institut verbunden wird. Die „trieuwe" Hand, wie sie noch in Quellen des 15. Jahrhunderts vorkommt, taucht in älteren Quellen seltener auf, dafür aber der lateinische Begriff *manus fidei* und *fidelis manus.*

---

113 *Schott* (Fn. 3) 232 ff.

Bei der Massierung weniger Begriffe, teilweise sogar deren Gleichsetzung, innerhalb eines doch recht festumrissenen Kanons von Anwendungsfällen, die zudem verschiedenen Bereichen des mittelalterlichen Rechtslebens zuzuordnen sind, wie Lehnrecht und Stadtrecht, ist man berechtigt, von einem Institut des mittelalterlichen Rechts zu sprechen.

Zur Analyse dessen, was sich die Beteiligten unter dem Rechtsverhältnis vorgestellt haben, das volkssprachlich „Träger", „Salmann" oder „Treuhand", genannt wird, sollte man allerdings auch die dort verwandten Bezeichnungen in lateinischer Sprache heranziehen. Sie sind leider nur in der älteren Literatur zur Treuhand beachtet worden[114], auch etwa in der neueren spanischen, portugiesischen und französischen Literatur[115]. Es handelt sich um folgende Bezeichnungen: *delegator, mediator, advocatus, defensor, conservator, executor* und *fideiussor.* Alle diese Quellenausdrücke finden sich in Fällen, die zu den oben angeführten Fallgruppen gehören, allerdings auch erst in großer Breite seit dem Hochmittelalter. Eine noch ausstehende gründliche Analyse des gesamten Urkundenmaterials dürfte dann auch Aufschluß über lokale Konzentrationen geben; die hier angeführten Ausdrükke finden sich jedenfalls in bayerischen und fränkischen Urkunden. Sie stellen, da hier spätantike Urkundenformeln keine Vorbilder sein dürften, den Versuch eines Urkundenschreibers dar, den Vorgang inhaltlich zu erfassen und zu umschreiben. Oft befinden sich in diesen Urkunden auch Gleichsetzungen mit „*Salmann*"[116]. Inhaltlich sind diese Ausdrücke, wie man sieht, genauer, spezifischer als Träger, Treuhand und Treuhänder oder Salmann, insoweit, als sie auf die jeweilige Pflicht des Treuhänders abheben, die etwa im Übermitteln oder im Aufbewahren bestehen kann. Insgesamt kann gerade auch angesichts der überlieferten Wortgleichungen davon ausgegangen werden, daß das, was die Rechtsgeschichte als Treuhandgeschäfte umschreibt, durchaus einer institutionellen Vorstellung der jeweiligen an den Rechtsvorgängen Beteiligten entspricht, und, daß diese Vorstellung mit Sicherheit nicht vor dem 13. Jahrhundert nachgewiesen werden kann, aber dann in weiten Kreisen geteilt worden ist.

Das 13. Jahrhundert ist auch der Zeitraum, in denen die Umgehungsfälle entstanden sind. Ältere Phänomene, wie die Letztwillenstreuhand, mögen unter dem Eindruck dieser hochmittelalterlichen Hauptgruppe als gleichgeartet assimiliert, vielleicht auch mißverstanden worden sein.

---

114 Das gilt vor allem für *Johannes Heumann* (Fn. 6), besonders Cap. X ff.

115 Dazu *Scherner,* Salmannschaft (Fn. 112) 16 ff.

116 Vgl. dazu *Heumann* (Fn. 6) Cap. X ff.; zur lateinischen Rechtssprache jetzt *Schott* (Fn. 3) 56 ff.

IV. Ergebnis

Als vorläufiges Ergebnis dieses Überblicks über das Bild der Treuhand im alten deutschen Recht kann man festhalten, daß es nicht nur in der Germanistik einen weitgehenden Konsens darüber gibt, was Treuhand ist und was zu ihr gehört, sondern auch, daß die Treuhand ein mittelalterliches Rechtsinstitut ist, also von den beteiligten Zeitgenossen durch spezifische Benennung mit einem bestimmten inhaltlichen Profil verbunden worden ist, das bei unterschiedlichen Fallkonstellationen als das gleiche angesehen worden ist. Zum andern hat sich gezeigt, daß der ganze Umfang des Instituts am besten dadurch verdeutlicht wird, daß man die mit diesem Institut auch von Zeitgenossen in Verbindung gebrachten Fälle anführt: Die mittelalterliche Treuhand war in den verschiedenen Treuhandformen lebendig.

V. Trust und Treuhand

Trust und Treuhand, zwei Phänomene der europäischen Rechtsgeschichte, die teilweise gleichzeitig existiert haben, werfen die Frage nach ihrem Verhältnis zueinander auf. Meines Erachtens gibt es drei Perspektiven, sich diesem zu nähern.

1. Vergleich der Fallgruppen

Wenn das Symposium „Trust und Treuhand" auch nach der möglichen gemeinsamen Wurzel fragt, dann bedeutete dies in der engsten Auslegung der *common roots* genetische Verwandtschaft im Sinn einer mehr oder weniger auseinanderlaufenden Abstammung aus gemeinsamen Wurzeln. Denkbar wären allerdings auch heterogene Parallelentwicklungen. Bevor man eine solche schwierige Frage stellt, liegt ein einfacheres Verfahren im Rahmen einer Gegenüberstellung Treuhand – Trust näher: der Vergleich von Fallgruppen. Je größer die Ähnlichkeit ist, umso berechtigter wäre die Annahme eines gleichen oder vergleichbaren Hintergrunds.

Da einer Auswertung der Ergebnisse dieses Symposiums nicht vorgegriffen werden soll, will ich das Trust-Bild, wie es im 13. Kapitel in „Introduction to English Legal History" von *J.H. Baker*[117] erscheint, meinen Ergebnissen gegenüberstellen. Dabei soll weniger von der Deckungsgleichheit oder Ähnlichkeit rechtlicher oder rechtshistorischer Erklärungsversuche oder -muster ausgegangen werden, sondern in erster Linie von der Deckungsgleichheit oder Ähnlichkeit der äußeren Fallkonstellation.

---

117 *J.H. Baker,* An Introduction to English Legal History, London, 1971, S. 120 ff., 129 ff.

(a) Übertragung eines Lehnsgutes durch den Lehnsmann

Der Pächter *(tenant)* will das Land veräußern. Zwischen der Aufgabe *(surrender)* an den Herrn und der Überlassung an den Erwerber hält der Herr das Land *ad opus* für den Erwerber.

Das hier eingeschlagene Verfahren der Veräußerung von Lehnsgut durch den *tenant* entspricht genau dem Verfahren, das im deutschen Lehnrecht bei der Veräußerung von Lehnsgut durch den Lehnsmann an einen Dritten beachtet wurde. Allerdings wird dieses Verfahren als Konsequenz aus dem Lehnrecht und nicht als Treuhandfall angesehen[118].

(b) Einsatz eines Treuhänders bei „unmöglichen" Geschäften

Ein Ehemann will sein Gut auf seinen Namen und zugleich den Namen seiner Frau oder die Namen anderer übertragen. Er überläßt zu diesem Zweck das Gut einem Freund oder mehreren Freunden *on trust,* um es in der gewünschten Weise zurückzuübertragen. *Baker* nennt als Grund die Unmöglichkeit, daß jemand sich selbst gegenüber verfügen kann[119].

Im mittelalterlichen deutschen Recht ist mir dieser Anwendungsfall nicht bekannt, dafür aber andere Fälle, in denen ein Treuhänder wegen diverser, nicht rechtlicher Hinderungsgründe eingeschaltet worden ist. Hierher gehören alle die Fälle der Erwerbssicherung, in denen der Erwerber abwesend war oder noch nicht bestimmt[120].

(c) Letztwillenstreuhand

Ein Mann gewährt einer Gruppe von Freunden ein Gut *on trust,* um es nach seinem Tod seinem Erben oder einem anderen Bedachten, den er benennt, zu gewähren. Dadurch konnte er das feudalrechtliche Verbot letztwilliger Verfügungen über Grundstücke umgehen *(avoid).*

Es liegt nahe, hier an die kontinentale Letztwillenstreuhand bei Grundstücksübertragungen, vor allem fromme Schenkungen, zu denken, wie sie seit dem 8. Jahrhundert in Urkunden überliefert sind[121].

In beiden Fällen wird ein Rechtsgeschäft von Todes wegen durch Einschaltung eines Mittelsmanns vorgenommen, dem der Verfügende vertraut, und der nach

---

118 Vgl. oben II. 1; *Schott* (Fn. 3) 89.

119 *Baker* (Fn. 117) 129 f.

120 Vgl. oben II. 1 (d); II. 2 (d).

121 Vgl. oben II. 2 (a), II. 2 (d).

dem Tod die Verfügung durchführt. Der Unterschied liegt im rechtlichen Grund. Während in den von *Baker* umschriebenen Fällen die Umgehung einer Verbotsnorm Grund für den Trust war, hat sich die kontinentale Rechtsgeschichte die Letztwillenstreuhand in der Regel anders erklärt: in der einfachen, aber auch sehr praktischen Vorstellung, daß man über seinen Tod hinaus keine Macht hat. Die Einschaltung eines Mittelsmanns ist hier die Umgehung eines „Naturgesetzes".

(d) Grunderwerb durch Kleriker

Die Gewährung von Gütern an den Franziskanerorden, dem Landbesitz verboten war, war in der Weise erlaubt, daß die Mönche das Eigentum, das ein anderer innehatte *(vested)*, nutzen *(enjoy the use)* konnten; wer dem Orden eine Wohltätigkeit erweisen wollte, gewährt das Land an eine Gruppe von Lehnsleuten *(feoffee)*, die diese zum Nutzen der Ordensbrüder hielten.

Hier liegt eine völlige Identität bei beiden Fallgruppen vor, nicht nur im äußeren Ablauf. Das Verbot für den über ganz Europa verbreiteten Franziskanerorden, Grundbesitz zu erwerben, galt auch im alten Reich. Dort bedeutete es zunächst, daß Kleriker und damit auch Klöster grundsätzlich kein Lehnsgut erhalten durften[122]. Das Verbot, städtisches Grundeigentum zu erwerben, war nicht päpstlich, sondern ein städtisches, um keinen Steuerschuldner zu verlieren[123].

(e) Grunderwerb durch „Juristische Personen"

Nach dem gleichen Prinzip konnten die Statuten über die *Tote Hand* umgangen werden. Diese verboten die Veräußerung von Land an eine Körperschaft, die als ein toter Eigentümer keine Erbschaftssteuer *(death duties)* schuldete. Eine Veräußerung war nur mit Genehmigung der Krone möglich. Bis zur Genehmigung konnte der Schenker oder ein von ihm Benannter das Land zu Nutzen der Körperschaft halten.

Im Prinzip war es im Reich genauso. Der Anwendungsbereich der Vermeidung der *Toten Hand* war sogar noch weiter. Da Städte nicht lehnsfähig waren, war hier ein Träger nicht nur vorübergehend, sondern ständig notwendig. Die frühneuzeitliche juristische Literatur hat hier zusätzlich noch auf die Tote Hand und die damit wegfallenden lehnrechtlichen Leistungen hingewiesen[124]. Auch die Städte verlangten für den Erwerb städtischer Grundstücke durch „juristische Personen" – in dem von mir herangezogenen Beispiel war es die *universitas iudeorum colonensium* – die Einschaltung einer natürlichen Person[125]. Schließlich drohte auch im

122 Vgl. oben II. 1 (b) (cc); *Schott* (Fn. 3) 111 ff.

123 Vgl. oben II. 2 (b) (aa); dazu *K. Beyerle* (Fn. 64) 68.

124 Vgl. oben II. 1 (b) (dd); *Schott* (Fn. 3) 162 ff.

bäuerlichen Recht der Wegfall der mit dem Tod einer Person anfallenden Abgaben. Deshalb wurde beim Verbleiben ländlicher Grundstücke an Spitäler und andere Gemeinschaften die Einschaltung eines Trägers verlangt[126].

(f) Lehnsvormundschaft

Zum Bild der mittelalterlichen (im übrigen auch noch neuzeitlichen) Treuhand gehört die Lehnsvormundschaft, die deshalb notwendig war, weil ein Kind keine Lehnsdienste leisten konnte. Sie stand dem Herrn bis zur Mündigkeit unter Einbehaltung der Einkünfte zu[127]. Dem entsprach im äußeren Tatbestand und von dem rechtlichen Grund her voll und ganz die englische *wardship*[128].

Diese sicher nicht vollständige Zusammenstellung zeigt, daß mindestens sechs wichtige Fallgruppen sowohl im mittelalterlichen angelsächsischen als auch im deutschen Recht vorkommen, wobei sie einerseits dem Trust-Komplex, auf der anderen Seite dem Treuhandkomplex zugeordnet werden. Übereinstimmung besteht nicht nur in der Einschaltung von Zwischenpersonen, sondern – das erscheint mir noch wichtiger – in der Identität oder Vergleichbarkeit der rechtlichen Gründe, wie die Lehnsunfähigkeit eines Kindes, das *main-mort*-Problem, Erwerbsverbote für Kleriker oder die mit letztwilligen Verfügungen verbundenen Schwierigkeiten.

2. Unmittelbare Beeinflussung und die gemeinsame mittelalterliche Welt

Einflüsse rechtlicher Institutionen auf Gebiete, in denen sie nicht entstanden sind, bis hin zu bewußten Rezeptionen, sind immer genau nachzuweisen, sonst bleibt es bei bloßen Hypothesen. Während solche Nachweise im Bereich des gelehrten Rechts verhältnismäßig einfach sind, sind sie dort, wo das Recht vorwiegend in Urkunden, Urteilen oder Rechtsaufzeichnungen wie Spiegeln erscheint, außerordentlich schwierig, wenn nicht sogar aussichtslos. Ein Weg wäre beispielsweise die Tradierung bestimmter Inhalte über „wandernde", um nicht zu sagen „vagabundierende" Formulare von Geschäftsurkunden, etwa in Gestalt der fränkischen Formelsammlungen, die spätantike Geschäftsformen tradiert haben.

Solche Beeinflussungen liegen dort allerdings nicht nur näher, sondern sind geradezu zwingend – die Bezeichnung „Beeinflussung" ist dann eigentlich auch nicht mehr angemessen –, wo sich überhaupt keine unterschiedlichen, eigenständigen Rechtskulturen oder Rechtskreise gegenüberstehen. Ein schönes Beispiel dafür fin-

125 Vgl. oben II. 2 (b) (dd).

126 Vgl. oben II. 2 (c); hierzu näher *Schott* (Fn. 3) 261 ff.

127 Vgl. oben II. 1 (b) (bb).

128 *Baker* (Fn. 117) 126.

det sich auch im Komplex Trust – Treuhand, wenn in einer Konstanzer Urkunde aus dem Jahrhundert ein Grundstück *ad opus* der dortigen Franziskaner gehalten wird.

Dieses *ad opus* ist aus deutschen Urkunden des Mittelalters nicht bekannt und kann nur auf der Verwendung einer Vorlage beruhen, die aus England, genauer: von dortigen Franziskanern stammt.

Noch deutlicher ist die gemeinsame Welt des mittelalterlichen Lehnswesens. Bei allen sich später herausbildenden nationalen Sonderbildungen handelt es sich um eine homogene Rechtsordnung europäischen Formats, wie schon *Heinrich Mitteis* hervorgehoben hat. Daß hier weitgehend die gleichen Fragen aufgeworfen werden, bedarf keiner näheren Darlegung.

3. *Vestigia fiduciae?*

Ein deutscher Autor aus dem 18. Jahrhundert hat bei der Betrachtung über den mittelalterlichen Salmann davon gesprochen, daß es sich hier zwar nicht um *vestigia fiduciae* im Sinn der antiken *fiducia*, aber immerhin um *conventiones fiduciae Romanorum similes* handelt[129]. Anlaß für ihn war die humanistische Wiederentdeckung der römischen *fiducia*. Er und andere Autoren haben diese *fiducia* nicht nur im mittelalterlichen (in Gestalt des Salmanns), sondern auch im neuzeitlichen Recht wiedergefunden. Hier wurde mit Hilfe der antiken *fiducia* eine überzeitlich geltende Struktur behauptet und nachzuweisen versucht, die im übrigen auch für das Aufkommen des Treuhandgedankens in der deutschen Rechtsgeschichte verantwortlich zu machen ist. Kommt hinzu, daß *fiducia* ein mittelalterliches und neuzeitliches Quellenwort ist, dann bietet sich hier ein weiterer gemeinsamer Nenner an, der in etwa in der eingangs zitierten Definition *Franz Beyerles* formuliert worden ist.

---

129 Hierzu und zum folgenden *Scherner* (Fn. 6) 973 ff., 992.

REINHARD ZIMMERMANN

Heres fiduciarius?

Rise and Fall of the Testamentary Executor

I. Introduction

A testamentary executor is an independent person appointed by the testator to carry out his dispositions *mortis causa.* By appointing an executor, the testator may pursue a number of different aims. He may want to make sure that dispositions which do not benefit the heirs are properly executed. He may wish to provide for a situation where there is no heir, or where the appointed heir is still too young or inexperienced to take care of the property. Or he may simply have it in mind to save his heirs the trouble of having to administer the estate. The appointment of an executor may be an act of distrust against, or of care for, the heirs. But it may also be based on a desire on the part of the testator to dominate his successors from his grave. The institution of executorship appears to be an indispensable part of a modern law of succession and is known to all modern European legal systems. It constitutes part of a contemporary European *ius commune.* But there are significant differences between a modern French, German or English executor[1]. This paper aims at explaining how the modern institution of executorship has evolved and how its various national modifications may be understood and intellectually related to each other[2]. We will start our investigation in Roman law even though we are

1 For an overview of executorship in modern European legal systems, see *Alexander Beck,* Historisches und Rechtsvergleichendes zur Stellung des Willensvollstreckers, in: Itinera Iuris, Arbeiten zum römischen Recht und seinem Fortleben, 1980, pp. 300 ff.; *Carsten Thomas Ebenroth,* Erbrecht, 1992, nos. 711 ff. The general theme underlying the present contribution is that of a considerable diversity of modern legal regimes within an overarching intellectual unity based on common roots in medieval law. It has been developed particularly clearly by *Robert Caillemer,* Origines et développement de l'exécution testamentaire, thèse pour le doctorat, Lyon, 1901, who summarizes as follows (p. 682): "Et c'est ainsi que l'exécution testamentaire, après avoir présenté, dans les premiers siècles du moyen âge, une si remarquable unité, s'est diversifiée à dater du XIIIe siècle, et commence à présenter, au moment où notre étude s'arrête, dans les divers pays de l'Europe occidentale, une physionomie assez variée". Arguably, this is generally one of the essential characteristics of the civilian tradition; cf. my essay in David Carey Miller, Reinhard Zimmermann (eds.), The Civilian Tradition and Scots Law: Aberdeen Quincentenary Essays, 1997, pp. 259 ff.

2 For an attempt at explaining why this is important, see *Reinhard Zimmermann,* Savigny's Legacy, (1996) 112 L.Q.R. 576 ff.; *Alfred Cockrell,* Studying Legal History in South Africa: The Lesson of Lot's Wife, ZEuP 5 (1997) 436 ff.

warned by *Fritz Schulz* that within "the rich store of the classical law of succession" the institution of the executor "was completely missing" – a "fateful omission", as *Schulz* ominously adds[3].

II. Roman Law

1. Early and Classical Roman Law

As in other ancient legal systems, intestate succession probably preceded testamentary succession in Roman law[4]; and when the earliest form of *testamentum* came to be recognized, it was designed to constitute an imitation of what was regarded as right and natural: a childless testator was allowed to provide himself with a *suus heres* who would inherit his property and continue to conduct the religious rites of the family[5]. The *testamentum calatis comitiis*[6], a solemn act before the popular assembly, was a kind of adoption which, however, took effect only upon the testator's death. But it was a cumbersome way of appointing an heir and thus the need was felt to make available a relatively simple private act that could be executed at any time. Also, testators who had not only one but several sons required the means of determining one of them to take over their undivided estate. The *testamentum per aes et libram,* or mancipatory will, could be resorted to to satisfy these needs[7]. It was a creation of pontifical jurisprudence which ingeniously adapted an existing transaction to the new purpose. A man, as *Gaius* relates[8], who has not made a will in the *comitia calata,* would mancipate his *familia,* i.e. his entire estate, to a friend whom he would request to distribute it after his death to such

---

3 *Fritz Schulz,* Classical Roman Law, 1951 (reprint 1992), no. 576.

4 *Ernst Rabel,* Grundzüge des römischen Privatrechts, 2nd ed., 1955, p. 203; *Max Kaser,* Das römische Privatrecht, Erster Abschnitt, 2nd ed., 1971, pp. 91 ff.; *Heinrich Honsell, Theo Mayer-Maly, Walter Selb,* Römisches Recht (= *Paul Jörs, Wolfgang Kunkel, Leopold Wenger,* Römisches Recht, 4th ed.), 1987, pp. 434 ff.

5 *Eberhard Friedrich Bruck,* Zur Entwicklungsgeschichte des Testamentsvollstreckers im römischen Recht, Grünhuts Zeitschrift für das Privat- und öffentliche Recht der Gegenwart 40 (1914) 546 ff. (with comparative references to other ancient legal systems); *idem,* Über römisches Recht im Rahmen der Kulturgeschichte, 1954, pp. 32 ff.

6 On which see *Gai.* Inst. II, 101 sqq.; *Biondo Biondi,* Successione testamentaria e donazioni, 2nd ed., 1955, pp. 33 ff.; *Kaser* (n. 4) 105 f.; *Honsell/Mayer-Maly/Selb* (n. 4) 447 f.

7 On the historical development of which see *Gai.* II, 102 ff.; *Hermann Deutsch,* Die Vorläufer der heutigen Testamentsvollstrecker im Römischen Recht, Dr. iur. thesis, Göttingen, 1899, pp. 3 ff.; *Otto Lenel,* Zur Geschichte der "heredis institutio", as reprinted in Labeo 12 (1966) 358 ff., 368 ff.; *Beck* (n. 1) 290 ff.; *Francis de Zulueta,* The Institutes of Gaius, Part II (Commentary), 1953 (reprint 1975), pp. 88 ff.; *Bruck* (n. 5) 35 ff.; *Biondi* (n. 6) 35 ff.; *Pasquale Voci,* Diritto ereditario romano, vol. I, 2nd ed., 1967, pp. 86 ff.; *Kaser* (n. 4) 107 ff.

8 *Gai.* Inst. II, 102 ("qui neque calatis comitiis ... testamentum fecerat, is si subita morte urguebatur, amico familiam suam, id est patrimonium suum, mancipio dabat, eumque rogabat quid cuique post mortem suam dari vellet").

person or persons as he indicated. The transfer of the property occurred *nummo uno,* i.e. for a symbolic price. As in every other *mancipatio,* there had to be (at least) five Roman citizens as witnesses and a man who held a scale *(libripens).* The seventh person, apart from the testator, who had to be present (and who had to pronounce the mancipatory formula) was the "purchaser" of the estate, the *familiae emptor.*

Interestingly, therefore, the Roman jurists used a transaction *inter vivos* as a model for what was to become the normal civil law will of the classical period. Or rather: *familiae mancipatio* began as a makeshift – "it was not a *testamentum,* but a device for doing without one"[9]. It entailed the transfer of the estate to a third party who had to distribute the estate, after the testator's death, in accordance with what the latter had declared in his *nuncupatio*[10]. It is likely that this kind of transaction was originally resorted to when death was imminent and when it was not therefore advisable to wait for the next *comitia curiata* to meet. Since *mancipatio* was designed to transfer ownership, it may be assumed that *mancipatio familiae,* too, had the effect of transferring ownership to the *familiae emptor.* This was inconvenient in cases where the testator managed to recover. Thus, the transfer of the full right was probably deemed to be postponed until the death of the testator. In the meantime, there was a situation of split ownership: the testator retained his right to dispose of his property, a right which superseded the *familiae emptor's* dormant title[11]. *Mancipatio familiae* was thus, indeed, "a *mancipatio* with a difference"[12]. This is brought out by the formula which, according to *Gaius,* the *familiae emptor* had to utter: "Familiam pecuniamque tuam endo mandatela tua custodelaque mea esse aio ..." – I declare your estate to be subject to your directions and in my custody[13]. In a normal mancipation, he would merely have asserted "hanc rem meam esse aio"[14].

With some justification, therefore, the *familiae emptor* is usually described as a fiduciary[15]. He might have provided the perfect starting point for the institution of executorship. For when, in due course, *mancipatio familiae* was transformed into a (unilateral) will, he could easily have become the key figure in the administration and winding up of the estate: an independent third party whose task it was to carry out the dispositions of the testator. Alternatively, of course, the *familiae emptor*

9 *De Zulueta* (n. 7) 88.

10 The *nuncupatio* was the oral declaration, in front of the witnesses, which contained the dispositions to be executed by the *familiae emptor.*

11 *Max Kaser,* Das altrömische ius, 1949, pp. 150 ff.; *idem* (n. 4) 108; *Beck* (n. 1) 292 f.

12 *Barry Nicholas,* An Introduction to Roman Law, 1962, p. 254.

13 *Gai.* Inst. II, 104.

14 Cf. *Gai.* Inst. I, 119.

15 See *Bruck* (n. 5) 554 ff.; *Beck* (n. 1) 290 f.; *Schulz* (n. 3) no. 432; *Rabel* (n. 4) 203 f.; *Voci* (n. 7) 89; *Kaser* (n. 4) 118; *Honsell/Mayer-Maly/Selb* (n. 4) 448 f.; *Peter Apathy,* Die Treuhandschaft aus rechtshistorischer Sicht, in: Peter Apathy (ed.), Die Treuhandschaft, 1995, pp. 4 f.; cf. also *Lenel* (n. 7) 369 ff.

could have developed into the *heres*[16] – "heredis locum obtinebat", after all, is how *Gaius,* somewhat ambiguously, describes his position when he relates the ancient law[17]. But none of this happened. Mancipation became a mere formality which served to give validity to the *nuncupatio* which, in principle, continued to contain the testator's dispositions. However, in order to facilitate proof and to keep these dispositions secret, they were normally written down elsewhere, and the *nuncupatio* merely contained a declaration to the witnesses that the testator wished to dispose of his property "ita ut in his tabulis cerisque scripta sunt"[18]. There were now, as a rule, seven witnesses, who sealed the document, and one of them was the *familiae emptor.* His presence no longer had any substantive significance – he had become a relic of the past and only remained part of the ceremony "propter veteris iuris imitationem"[19].

It was the heir who had taken over the key role in the Roman law of testate succession. No will was valid without the appointment of an heir: "testamenta vim ex institutione heredis accipiunt, et ob id velut caput et fundamentum intellegitur totius testamenti heredis institutio"[20]. The heir took the place of the deceased testator in that he succeeded to his rights and duties in their entirety *(successio in locum/in universum ius defuncti)*[21]. This was the principle of universal succession[22]. It was of central importance historically, because of the need to continue the *sacra familiaria*[23] and thus to secure the spriritual as well as material continuity of the family. Two well-known and important rules were closely related to this principle: nobody could die partly testate and partly intestate *(nemo pro parte testatus pro parte intestatus decedere potest)*[24]; and a person who became the heir of a deceased person remained his heir forever *(semel heres semper heres)*[25]. Against this background there simply was no place for an executor. The heir succeeded into the position of the testator and thus it appeared only natural to let him carry out the testator's dispositions. An executor would have curtailed the heir's position unduly[26].

---

16 *De Zulueta* (n. 7) 88.

17 *Gai.* Inst. II, 103.

18 *Gai.* Inst. II, 104; cf. *Kaser* (n. 4) 679.

19 *Gai.* Inst. II, 103.

20 *Gai.* Inst. II, 229.

21 Cf., e.g., *Gai.* Inst. II, 156; *Gai.* Inst. III, 7 f.; *Iul.* D. 50, 17, 62.

22 On which, see *Bruck* (n. 5) 561 ff.; *Schulz* (n. 3) nos. 367 ff.; *Rabel* (n. 4) 202 f.; *Voci* (n. 7) 163 ff.; *Nicholas* (n. 12) 235 ff.; *Kaser* (n. 4) 672 f.

23 On which, see *Adolf Berger,* Encyclopedic Dictionary of Roman Law, 1953, p. 688; *Bruck* (n. 5) 24 ff., 32 ff.

24 Cf. Inst. II, 14, 5; *Voci* (n. 7) 496 ff.; *Kaser* (n. 4) 677; and see *Zimmermann,* ZSS (RA) 101 (1984) 238 f. (with references).

25 Cf. *Kaser* (n. 4) 688.

26 Cf., in particular, *Bruck* (n. 5) 561 ff., 565.

2. Developments in Legal Practice and Surrogate Devices

This does not, of course, mean that individual testators would not occasionally have found it convenient, or desirable, to name an executor. The *testatrix* of D. 36, 1, 80, 1, for instance, specifically regretted not having been able to appoint two friends as administrators of her estate: "... quos etiam, si licuisset, curatores substantiae meae dedissem". There were others who did not have these inhibitions, most notoriously perhaps the veteran *C. Longinus Castor.* In his will, drawn up in A.D. 189 in Egypt, he made "M. Sempronium Heraclianum, amicum fide dignum, procuratorem ex ipsius fide". (The Greek translation of this will, significantly, has the word *epitropos* for *procurator*[27]). Also from Egypt, and also from the second century A.D., is the will of *Antonius Silvanus* who made a person other than the heir "procurator bonorum meorum castrensium ad bona colligenda et restituenda"[28]. It is uncertain how the law dealt with such dispositions and it may well be that their implementation depended merely "on loyalty, good faith, and goodwill"[29]: that is, on the characteristically Roman concept of *fides*[30]. But in evaluating the Roman position, account must also be taken of the many devices available to a testator to ensure that his wishes were implemented after his death[31]. He could rely on the initiative of co-heirs, legatees and, eventually, *fideicommissarii* to claim what was due to them. He could make his disposition dependent upon the occurrence or non-occurrence of a specific act or event by means of a condition, or he could impose a duty on any of the beneficiaries by way of *modus*[32]. If a legacy was subjected to a *modus,* the heir saw to it that the legatee complied with its requirements by asking him to provide security[33]. The testator could also, of course, choose a reliable person and institute him as a kind of pseudo-heir: as long as he was prepared to sacrifice the *quarta Falcidia,* and as long as that person was not frightened by the prospect of personal liability for the testator's debts, he could serve as a *de facto* executor[34]. A person facing death could make a *donatio mortis*

---

27 Fontes Iuris Romani Antejustiniani (FIRA), vol. III, 2nd ed., 1972, no. 50 (p. 152). The will was, apparently, drawn up in Latin, but it is a Greek translation which has been preserved.

28 FIRA III (n. 27) no. 47 (pp. 130 f.).

29 *Schulz* (n. 3) no. 577; cf. also *Biondi* (n. 6) 609.

30 On which, see *Fritz Schulz,* Principles of Roman Law, 1936, pp. 223 ff.; *Harald Fuchs* and *Ernst Meyer,* in: Hans Oppermann (ed.), Römische Wertbegriffe, 1983, pp. 23 ff., 529 ff.; *Franz Wieacker,* Römische Rechtsgeschichte, Erster Abschnitt, 1988, pp. 506, 643 f.

31 Cf. *Deutsch* (n. 7) 14 ff.; *Ludwig Mitteis,* Römisches Privatrecht bis auf die Zeit Diokletians, vol. I, 1908, pp. 105 ff., n. 30; *Bruck* (n. 5) 566 ff.; *Bernhard Kübler,* Testamentsvollstreckung, in: Paulys Realencyclopädie der classischen Altertumswissenschaft, 2nd series, 9th half-volume, 1934, cols. 1013 ff.; *Biondi* (n. 6) 606 ff.; *Beck* (n. 1) 292 ff.; *Rabel* (n. 4) 240 f. Cf. also *infra* n. 107.

32 On the latter device, see *Max Kaser,* Das römische Privatrecht, Zweiter Abschnitt, 2nd ed., 1975, pp. 98, 582 f.

33 *Valens* D. 32, 19.

34 *Deutsch* (n. 7) 14 ff.; *Bruck* (n. 5) 567 f.

causa and postpone its execution until after his death[35]. By way of a contract of mandate he could also request another person to take care of matters after his death. Such *mandata post mortem* were not legally recognized in classical law[36]; nevertheless, they created a strong moral obligation[37]. *Justinian* provided also legal recognition "pro communi hominum utilitate", as he put it[38]. "Mando autem cura funeris mei et exequiarum et rerum omnium et aedificiorum monumentorumque meorum Sex. Iulio Aquiliae nepoti meo ..." we read in the will of a *civis Romani Gallicae nationis* from the turn of the first to the second century A.D.[39]. *Ulp.* D. 11, 7, 14, 2 also deals with the case of a testator who asked someone to take care of his funeral ("Si cui funeris sui curam testator mandaverit").

The terminology used by testators as well as lawyers when they wished to designate the person who was to carry out the testator's instructions was often vague and inconsistent. In *Marcell.* D. 31, 17 pr. we read of a *minister* whom the testator could appoint[40]. *Scaev.* D. 26, 3, 11 refers to a *curator.* The presbyter instituted as co-heir in *Nov. Marc.* 5 and vested with additional powers of administration is cautiously referred to as "paene etiam dispensatoris fungatur officio". *S. Ambrose* relates that one of his brethren in Christ "dispensatores non heredes reliquit"[41]. C. 1, 3, 28, 1 mentions a "specialiter designatus" whom the testator had charged with the redemption of captives. Sometimes the public authorities intervened to secure implementation of the testator's dispositions. *Pap.* D. 5, 3, 50 deals with a case where the testator had asked for a monument to be erected; it states that "quamvis enim stricto iure nulla teneantur actione heredes ad monumentum faciendam, tamen principali vel pontificali auctoritate compelluntur ad obsequium supremae voluntatis". (In other cases we find a private person being appointed in the will in order to supervise the erection of a monument[42]). According to *Ulp.* D. 11, 7, 12, 6 the praetor or the municipal magistrate had to see to it that the expenses of the funeral were met from the estate. *Marc.* D. 30, 113, 1 presupposes intervention on the part of the magistrate when an heir was obliged by the testator's instructions to feed the testator's slave. And if the testator had not specifically designated anyone to use part of his estate for the redemption of captives, the local bishop ("vir reverentissimus episcopus illius civitatis, ex qua testator oritur") had to step in to execute the good deed[43].

35 Cf. *Kaser* (n. 4) 763 f.

36 *Reinhard Zimmermann,* The Law of Obligations: Roman Foundations of the Civilian Tradition, 1990 (paperback edition 1996), pp. 425 f.

37 *Kaser* (n. 4) 693.

38 C. 4, 11, 1; cf. also C. 8, 37, 11.

39 FIRA III (n. 27) n. 49 (p. 146).

40 Cf. also *Deutsch* (n. 7) 19 ff.

41 *Biondi* (n. 6) 606, n. 3.

42 Cf., e.g., *Pomp.* D. 35, 1, 6 and *Mitteis* (n. 31) 107. Cf. also *Biondi* (n. 6) 606 f. (concerning the carrying out of other tasks).

43 C. 1, 3, 28, 1.

All in all, therefore, the Roman lawyers appear never to have recognized an executor who would have been in charge of the entire estate. But they provided testators with a wealth of surrogate devices and they also occasionally endorsed the institution of third parties, or the intervention of a magistrate or bishop, for the purposes of carrying out, or supervising, the execution of specific tasks. Such tasks tended to be of a charitable nature or to lie in the public interest. Testamentary dispositions *ad pias causas,* in particular, had become very common by *Justinian's* time. Testators were increasingly inclined to leave part of their estate to the poor, to Jesus Christ, to the Angels and martyrs, or to the Church[44]. This was the Christianized version of the dead man's part of pagan times[45], designed to redeem the testator's soul *(pro animae redemptione). Justinian* sought to promote these charities in many different ways. For instance, he did everything he could to save testamentary dispositions *ad pias causas* from invalidity[46] and he set up mechanisms to ensure that they were duly carried out[47]. Once again, the local bishop played a central role in this respect: whether the testator himself had instituted him as executor ("curam iniunxerit")[48], or whether the testator had just left parts of his estate to the poor, to Christ, or for the benefit of the captives: "In omnibus enim talibus piis voluntatibus sanctissimos locorum episcopos volumus providere, ut secundum defuncti voluntatem universa procedant"[49].

3. Greek and Byzantine Law

In the subsequent history of Byzantine law, this inchoate institution of executorship quickly began to be more fully developed. In an enactment of *Emperor Leo VI*

---

44 The Greek Fathers of the Church of the 4th century A.D. claimed that part of every estate should be given to Christ (on behalf of the poor): for all details, see *Eberhard Friedrich Bruck,* Kirchenväter und soziales Erbrecht, 1956, pp. 1 ff., 41 ff., 55 ff. An essential characteristic of the *portio Christi* was that it had to be given voluntarily (for the origin and migration of the idea of the "cheerful giver" – whom God loveth: 2 Cor. 9, 7 – see *Eberhard Friedrich Bruck,* Über römisches Recht im Rahmen der Kulturgeschichte, 1954, pp. 101 ff.). A fixed quota was therefore not prescribed at first: "optima mensura est donatarum [sanctissimis ecclesiis] rerum immensitas" (*Justinian,* Nov. 7, 2, 1). On the practice in Justinian's time ("Quoniam in multis testamentis invenimus tales institutiones ...") see C. 1, 2, 25 and *Bruck,* Kirchenväter, pp. 120 ff.

45 For details, see *Bruck,* Kirchenväter (n. 44) 31 ff., 37 ff. But cf. also *Alfred Schultze,* Augustin und der Seelteil des germanischen Erbrechts, 1928, pp. 66 ff. and, mainly following *Heinrich Brunner,* Der Totenteil in germanischen Rechten, ZSS (GA) 19 (1898) 107 ff., *Adalbert Erler,* Totenteil, in: Handwörterbuch zur deutschen Rechtsgeschichte, 34th part, 1992, cols. 282 ff. On foundations for the dead in Rome, see *Bruck,* Über römisches Recht (n. 5) 46 ff.

46 Cf. *Kaser* (n. 32) 488; *Reinhard Zimmermann,* "Cy-Près", in: Festgabe für Max Kaser, 1986, pp. 395 ff., 403 f.

47 C. 1, 3, 45 pr. – 8; Nov. 131, 12 pr. – 1.

48 C. 1, 3, 45 pr.

49 Nov. 131, 11; cf. also, e.g., C. 1, 2, 25; C. 1, 3, 24; C. 1, 3, 28; C. 1, 3, 45; C. 1, 3, 48.

(886 - 912) a distinction is drawn between two kinds of *epitropoi:* the one acting as guardian of a minor, the other administering the estate of a deceased person. Monks and clergymen may only be charged with an *epitropä* in the second sense[50]. The contours of this kind of executorship become reasonably clear from the decisions of the supreme tribunal, as collected in the *Peira*[51]: the *epitropos* could be instituted to carry out individual tasks or to administer the entire estate; he had to draw up an inventory of the estate in the presence of the heirs; if he died before having discharged his duties, he was succeeded by his co-executors, his heirs, or whomever he designated; before he distributed the estate as intended by the testator he had to retain the assets for long enough (but not more than four years) to allow creditors to come forward and to obtain satisfaction; if he wanted to bring an action on behalf of the estate, he could avail himself of (but was also exposed to) a special summary procedure; and he could be removed from office if he neglected his duties.

The appointment of an executor can be found in testaments drawn up by Byzantine monks, like that of abbot *Athanasios* of Mount Athos (around 990 A.D.)[52]. The main task of the *epitropos* in this testament was to hold the monastery together and to ensure the continuity of the monastic life until such time when the new abbot could be elected. *Athanasios*' will displays notable parallels[53] with the wills of the peripathetic philosophers of the third century B.C., particularly those of *Strato, Lykon* and *Theophrastos*[54]. They, too, wished to preserve the continuity of their philosophic school by appointing (in their case) several *epitropoi;* apart from that, they also wanted to ensure proper performance of the funeral and of the periodic rituals in memory of the dead. It is not unlikely that the practice of the ancient Greeks, well known also outside of philosophic circles[55], survived in the Hellenistic East and facilitated the emergence of the *epitropos* of Christian Byzantium[56]. We may thus be dealing here with an example of the resilience of what *Ludwig Mitteis* termed *Volksrecht* as opposed to the Imperial (i.e. Roman) law[57]. This conjecture is confirmed by the existence of wills like that of *C. Longinus Castor* in Roman Egypt[58]; and also, for instance, by the recognition of executorship in the

50 *Kübler* (n. 31) cols. 1015 f.

51 For what follows, see *Karl Eduard Zachariä von Lingenthal,* Geschichte des griechisch-römischen Rechts, 3rd ed., 1892 (reprint 1955), pp. 163 ff.

52 See *Phillip Meyer,* Die Haupturkunden für die Geschichte der Athosklöster, 1894, pp. 123 ff.; on which, see *Kübler* (n. 31) col. 1015; *Eberhard Friedrich Bruck,* Totenteil und Seelgerät im griechischen Recht, 1926, pp. 320 f.

53 *Bruck* (n. 52) 320; *Kübler* (n. 31) col. 1015.

54 On which see *Bruck* (n. 52) 256 ff., 260 ff.

55 For details, see *Kübler* (n. 31) cols. 1010 ff.; *Egon Weiß,* Griechisches Privatrecht auf rechtsvergleichender Grundlage, 1923 (reprint 1965), pp. 211 ff.

56 Cf., in particular, *Bruck* (n. 5) 569 ff.; *Biondi* (n. 6) 608.

57 *Ludwig Mitteis,* Reichsrecht und Volksrecht in den östlichen Provinzen des römischen Weltreichs, 1891.

Syrian-Roman Law Book dating from the late 5th century A.D.[59]. Once again, the term *epitropos* is used to designate the person whom the testator wanted to take charge of his estate[60].

III. Medieval Law

1. The "Nature" of Medieval Germanic Law

Research into the Germanic origins of executorship has been bedevilled for a long time, at least in Germany, by the unfortunate split between legal history of the *romanistische, germanistische* and *kanonistische* variety. This split was bound to lead to rivalry, exaggeration and ideological blinkers[61]. The hubris of the pandectist school, which tended to regard the legal system as a closed system of rules and concepts derived from the higher and purer world of Roman law, was countered by scholars of Germanic legal sources who endeavoured to demonstrate the contribution of Germanic law to modern legal doctrine. They even tried to devise a set of concepts and categories in order to construe a system of exclusively Germanic private law[62]. *Treuhand* (trust) appeared to be a paradigmatic example of a concept, unknown to Roman law, which had an impeccably Germanic pedigree[63]. This was all the more important in view of the great interest of contemporary lawyers in a theory of *Treuhand*[64]. The medieval *Salmann* (the term is etymologically related to "sale") was presented both as a model and as an historical ancestor to support this theory[65] and it was argued that the historical investigation could be "exploited"[66]

58 Cf. *supra* n. 27.

59 London manuscript 30; see *Karl Georg Bruns, Eduard Sachau,* Syrisch-römisches Rechtsbuch, 1880, translation p. 49.

60 See *Bruck* (n. 5) 572 f.; *Kübler* (n. 31) col. 1013; *Walter Selb,* Zur Bedeutung des syrisch-römischen Rechtsbuches, 1964, p. 175; on the law of succession in the Syrian-Roman Law Book generally, see *Mitteis* (n. 31) 318 ff.

61 Cf., e.g., in the present context, *Walther Schönfeld* who emphazises, "daß dieses aus germanischem Geiste geborene Institut die Sintflut der Römerey siegreich überstanden hat": ZSS (GA) 42 (1921) 378. On the ideology involved in the creation, and the use, of a "Germanic" concept of faith, see *Ekkehard Kaufmann,* Treue, in: Handwörterbuch zur deutschen Rechtsgeschichte, 34th part, 1992, cols. 324 ff.

62 On the history of the concept of a Germanic private law (*Deutsches Privatrecht),* see *Hans Thieme,* in: Handwörterbuch zur deutschen Rechtsgeschichte, vol. I, 1971, cols. 702 ff.

63 *Franz Beyerle,* Die Treuhand im Grundriß des deutschen Privatrechts, 1932, for instance, attempted to analyse *Treuhand* as one of the three basic types of "personal concatenation" (*persönlicher Verkettung)* of Germanic private law.

64 *Helmut Coing,* Die Treuhand kraft privaten Rechtsgeschäfts, 1973, pp. 28 ff.; *idem,* Europäisches Privatrecht, vol. II, 1989, pp. 423 ff.; and see the paper by *Sibylle Hofer* in the present volume.

65 See the account in *Karl Otto Scherner,* Salmannschaft, Servusgeschäft und venditio iusta, 1971, pp. 6 ff.

for modern doctrinal purposes. The *Salmann* or *Treuhänder* was thus streamlined. It became an institution with fixed contours and specific doctrinal characteristics[67]; over *Treuhand* was regarded as a substitute for "agency"[68], a concept which, it was claimed, had been entirely alien to the Germanic world of thinking[69]. It had been an enormously fertile concept which could be put to many different uses. One of these was the execution of the last will of a deceased person. And so it was long claimed that the executor was actually of Germanic origin[70].

Today, however, a more cautious approach prevails. It is widely recognized that medieval law was "open-ended" law[71]. It was characterized by the complete absence of systematic integrity and conceptual lucidity. It lacked a rational structure. And it constituted a rich and flexible, but also infinitely complex mélange of individual customs. Very widely, therefore, one has lost confidence in being able to discover a system of Germanic private law that is something more than a pale and artificial abstraction[72]. The same is true of the notion of *Treuhand* (which, over the last few decades, seems to have replaced the term *Salmann)*[73]. It cannot be taken as a general concept with an essentially uniform structure. Thus, for instance, it cannot be realistically analysed in terms of an obligations / property divide, or even according to a doctrinal distinction between agency and fiduciary transactions. There appear to have been many different forms of *Treuhand* in the customary laws of the various Germanic tribes[74]. Not all developed in the same manner. Moreover, it becomes increasingly clear today that early medieval law cannot properly be understood from either a purely "Germanic" or a purely "Roman" point of view characteristic of modern historiography[75]. Recent studies have revealed the many com-

66 *Alfred Schultze*, Die langobardische Treuhand und ihre Umbildung zur Testamentsvollstreckung, 1895, p. 1; cf. also the remarks *sub* II. by *Joachim Rückert* in his contribution to the present volume.

67 See, in particular, *Schultze* (n. 66) 52 ff.

68 See *Heinrich Mitteis, Heinz Lieberich*, Deutsches Privatrecht, 9th ed., 1981, p. 32.

69 Cf., e.g., *Andreas Heusler*, Institutionen des Deutschen Privatrechts, vol. I, 1885, pp. 203 ff.; *Schultze* (n. 66) 62 ff.; *Hans Planitz*, Grundzüge des Deutschen Privatrechts, 1925, pp. 14 f.; but see *Scherner* (n. 65) 1 ff.; *W. Ogris*, Stellvertretung, in: Handwörterbuch zur deutschen Rechtsgeschichte, vol. IV, 1990, cols. 1956 ff.

70 Cf., e.g., *Otto Stobbe*, Handbuch des Deutschen Privatrechts, vol. V, 1st and 2nd ed., 1885, p. 260; *Planitz* (n. 69) 152; *Mitteis / Lieberich* (n. 68) 180 f.; *W. Ogris*, Testament, in: Handwörterbuch zur deutschen Rechtsgeschichte, 33rd part, 1991, col. 163.

71 Cf. the summary of the results of modern research by *Hans Schlosser*, Grundzüge der Neueren Privatrechtsgeschichte, 8th ed., 1996, pp. 14 ff.

72 See, e.g., the references provided by *Joachim Rückert* in n. 6 of his contribution to the present volume, or the skeptical analysis by *Karl Otto Scherner*, Das "Deutsche Privatrecht" und seine Darstellbarkeit, ZEuP 7 (1999), forthcoming.

73 See *Scherner* (n. 65) *passim* and in his contribution to the present volume; *idem*, Treuhand, in: Handwörterbuch zur deutschen Rechtsgeschichte, 34th part, 1992, cols. 341 ff.; cf. also *R. W. H. Pitlo*, De ontwikkeling der executeele, 1941, pp. 86 f.

74 One of them, the *Träger*, has been the subject of a detailed study by *Clausdieter Schott*, Der "Träger" als Treuhandform, 1975.

plex interactions between the Roman "vulgar" law of late antiquity and the customary laws of Visigoths and Ostrogoths, or of the Lombard and Franconian tribes that have led to a mixed legal culture of many different shades and nuances[76]. All this makes it very difficult, if not impossible, to trace the history of "the institution" of executorship. In broad outlines, however, the following picture emerges from the sources.

2. Succession in the Germanic Laws

As in Rome, intestate succession preceded testate succession in Germanic legal systems. Real property did not belong to the individual but was inseparately connected with the family. The family, moreover, constituted a "community of collective hand", and thus it was neither possible nor necessary for any individual member of the family to dispose of the estate *mortis causa:* God rather than man created the heir[77]. "Heredem tamen successoremque sui cuique liberi, et nullum testamentum", as the position is put in *Tacitus*' "Germania"[78]. As in Roman law, however, a problem arose in cases where God had failed to provide an heir; and as in Rome, this problem was solved, at first, by way of *imitatio naturae* – by providing a transaction by means of which an artificial family tie could be created. Whoever was to become the heir had first to be adopted by the family. This transaction was called *Affatomie* among the Franconians (derived from *ad fatmire* = to receive into the bosom [of the family])[79] and *Gairethinx* among the Lombards[80]. It was somewhat cumbersome to perform, but it achieved the purpose of providing for the succession of property. Less inconvenient were two other transactions which, however, did not affect the entire estate but only individual parts. These were the *donationes reservato usufructu* and *post obitum*[81]. The former left the donor (in modern par-

75 Cf., e.g., *Theo Mayer-Maly,* Pactum, Tausch und laesio enormis in den sog. leges barbarorum, ZSS (RA) 108 (1991) 213 ff., 232.

76 See, in particular, *Harald Siems,* Handel und Wucher im Spiegel frühmittelalterlicher Rechtsquellen, 1992; *Ennio Cortese,* Il diritto nella storia medievale, vol. I, 1995.

77 Cf., e.g., *Henri Auffroy,* Évolution du testament en France des origines au XIIIe siècle, thèse pour le doctorat, Paris, 1899, pp. 133 ff.; *Walther Schönfeld,* Die Vollstreckung der Verfügungen von Todes wegen im Mittelalter, ZSS (GA) 42 (1921) 240 ff.; *Gerhard Hückstädt,* Der Testamentsvollstrecker im deutschen Recht des Mittelalters, Dr. iur. thesis, Kiel, 1971, pp. 13 ff.; *H.-R. Hagemann,* Erbrecht, in: Handwörterbuch zur deutschen Rechtsgeschichte, vol. I, 1971, cols. 971 ff.; *Ogris* (n. 70) cols. 153 f.

78 Cap. XX.

79 All details concerning *Affatomie,* however (in particular, to what extent it was, or resembled, an adoption), are very much disputed; see, e.g., *Richard Schmidt,* Die Affatomie der lex Salica, 1891; *Auffroy* (n. 77) 147 ff.; *Caillemer* (n. 1) 29 ff.; *Pitlo* (n. 73) 54 ff.; *W. D. Wackernagel,* Adoption, in: Handwörterbuch zur deutschen Rechtsgeschichte, vol. I, 1971, cols. 57 ff.; *Scherner* (n. 65) 21 ff. (questioning the continuity between *Salmann* and *Affatomie).*

80 *Schultze* (n. 66) 6 ff.; *Auffroy* (n. 77) 159 ff.; and see now *Cortese* (n. 76) 120 ff., 137 ff.

lance) without title but with the right to the emoluments. The latter postponed the effects of the donation until after the death of the donor. Sometimes, apparently, the donor even added another condition, reserving the right to revoke the donation and to make a new disposition[82]. Interestingly, all of these were transactions *inter vivos,* even if their main aim was to bring about a regulation for the time after the donor's death[83]. The same is true of yet another transaction that took the place of a testament: the *Treuhand mortis causa*[84]. A specific part of the estate, or even the entire estate, was transferred to a person or an institution in whom the transferor had confidence, under certain instructions about the final disposition of the property. It is at this point, therefore, that the *Salmann* enters into the picture, and we find him in a position very similar to that of the *familiae emptor* under the Roman *mancipatio familiae.*

3. The Influence of the Church

(a) Dispositions ad pias causas

There is an important distinction that must be drawn between parallel development, intellectual stimulation, and the reception of ideas. The Lombards and Franconians cannot have known about the *testamentum calatis comitiis,* or about *mancipatio familiae.* All developments pointed out so far appear to have been nothing more than parallels. But on a much more subtle level, Roman law seems to have stimulated repeatedly the evolution at least of Lombard law. The distinction between ownership and usufruct, the donation in which the effect is postponed until after the death of the transferor, the use of Roman testamentary phraseology: however rudimentary these distinctions, devices and phrases may have been and in whatever way they may have worked in Lombard practice, they do betray some acquaintance with the world of Roman law[85].

---

81 For details, see *Rudolf Hübner,* Die donationes post obitum und die Schenkungen mit Vorbehalt des Nießbrauchs im älteren deutschen Recht, 1888; *Schultze* (n. 66) 6 ff.; *Caillemer* (n. 1) 268 ff.; *Schönfeld,* ZSS (GA) 42 (1921) 252 ff.; *Pitlo* (n. 73) 74 ff.; *Planitz* (n. 69) 149; *Hückstädt* (n. 77) 19 ff.; *W. Ogris,* Freiteil, in: Handwörterbuch zur deutschen Rechtsgeschichte, vol. I, 1971, cols. 1249 ff.; *idem,* Nutzungsvorbehalt, in: Handwörterbuch zur deutschen Rechtsgeschichte, vol. III, 1984, cols. 1126 f.; *idem* (n. 70) col. 154.

82 *Schultze* (n. 66) 12.

83 For cases where death was imminent, (the Lombard) *King Liutprand* seems to have gone a significant step further, however: a unilateral, formless declaration on the part of the testator was regarded as sufficient: see *Schultze* (n. 66) 14 ff. ("... potestatem habeat ... pro anima sua iudicandi vel dispensandi de rebus suis, quid aut qualiter cui voluerit").

84 *C. F. Rosshirt,* Ueber Testamentsexecutoren, (Rosshirt's) Zeitschrift für Civil- und Criminalrecht 1 (1831) 223 f.; *Auffroy* (n. 77) 209 ff.; *Schultze* (n. 66) 37 ff.; *Schönfeld,* ZSS (GA) 42 (1921) 316 ff.; *Pitlo* (n. 73) 83 ff.; *Hückstädt* (n. 77) 29 ff.

85 This is specifically acknowledged by *Schultze* (n. 66) 5, 12, 14, 16, 34, and *passim.* Cf. also, in particular, *Cortese* (n. 76) 120 ff., 137 ff. on the relationship between *mancipatio familiae* and *gairethinx.*

But there was an even more potent force moulding the way in which the law developed; and since it had also left its traces in the Roman legal sources, it provided a common denominator of great potential: the Church[86]. Wealthy Lombards were as much influenced by religion as were their Roman counterparts. In particular, they were equally anxious to save their souls by donation of their estates, or at least parts of them, *ad pias causas*[87]. The *donatio pro anima,* of course, was encouraged by the Church and also received privileged treatment by the Lombard kings. *Liutprand,* for instance, removed the requirement of *launegild* (consideration) wherever "in ecclesiam aut in loca sanctorum aut in exenodochio pro anima sua aliquit quiscumque donaverit"[88]. Obviously, the Church regarded itself as the ideal recipient of the property in question: not, of course, in order to use it simply for its own benefit but to employ it in the interest of the redemption of the transferor's soul. Thus, the Church was bound to favour the idea of trusteeship[89] – the very idea it had managed to implant, if only just, into the somewhat less receptive soil of Roman law[90]. The ancient Roman *familiae emptor* had withered away without giving birth to the institution of executorship. If the medieval *Treuhand* of Germanic origin did not suffer a similar fate, it was largely due to the sustained interest of the Church.

One final step remained to be taken in order to establish the modern concept of a testamentary executor. It was, of course, also taken by the Church in combining the *Treuhand* concept with the Roman notion of the testament as a unilateral disposition *mortis causa.* The Church was keen to encourage dispositions *ad pias causas,* and therefore equally eager to promote the last will as a convenient means of effecting that goal[91]. The Church itself lived according to Roman law *(ecclesia vivit lege Romana)*[92] and so it could have simply accepted the Roman testament for

---

86 See generally *Rosshirt* (n. 84) 221 ff.; *Auffroy* (n. 77) 365 ff.; *Alfred Schultze,* Der Einfluß der Kirche auf die Entwicklung des germanischen Erbrechts, ZSS (GA) 35 (1914) 75 ff.; *Jean Engelmann,* Les testaments coutumiers en XVe siècle, 1903, pp. 1 ff.; *Pitlo* (n. 73) 57 ff.

87 See *Schultze* (n. 66) 8 f. For the development in the Netherlands, see *Pitlo* (n. 73) 57 ff. Generally, see *Auffroy* (n. 77) 182 ff., 347 ff.; *Caillemer* (n. 1) 47 ff.

88 *Schultze* (n. 66) 9.

89 For details of the development, see *Schultze* (n. 66) 46 ff.; cf. also *Victor Wolf von Glanvell,* Die letztwilligen Verfügungen nach gemeinem kirchlichen Recht, 1900, pp. 199 ff.; *Hückstädt* (n. 77) 69 ff.

90 Cf. *supra* II. 2.

91 For what follows, see *Georg Beseler,* Von den Testamentsvollziehern, ZDR 9 (1845) 146 ff.; *Auffroy* (n. 77) 371 ff.; *Engelmann* (n. 86) 13 ff.; *Schultze* (n. 66) 151 ff.; *von Glanvell* (n. 89) 105 ff.; *Schönfeld,* ZSS (GA) 42 (1921) 295 ff.; *Pitlo* (n. 73) 89 ff.; *Michael M. Sheehan,* The Will in Medieval England, 1963, pp. 119 ff.; *Hückstädt* (n. 77) 53 ff.; *Emilio Bussi,* La formazione dei dogmi di diritto privato nel diritto comune (contratti, successioni, diritti di famiglia), 1971, nos. 102 ff., 106 ff.; *Ogris* (n. 70) cols. 154 ff.; *Helmut Coing,* Europäisches Privatrecht, vol. I, 1985, pp. 564 ff.

92 See *A. Erler,* Ecclesia vivit lege Romana, in: Handwörterbuch zur deutschen Rechtsgeschichte, vol. I, 1971, cols. 798 f.

all Christians. But it even went one significant step further, relaxing the formal requirements for the validity of the Roman testament. Thus, for instance, the Church no longer required seven witnesses but recognized as valid a testament made before the local priest and two or three "suitable" witnesses[93]. This was based on *St. Matthew* 18, 16 ("in ore duorum vel trium testium stet omne verbum"). Dispositions *ad pias causas* were even recognized, if two witnesses could testify to the will of the testator[94]. The "caput et fundamentum testamenti"[95] or, as it now tended to be put, the "domina testamenti" was no longer the institution of an heir but the bequest *pro animae remedio*[96]. Such a bequest had to be saved – in the interest of the testator! – from invalidity at all costs. Hence the dispensation from even the modest formal requirements found in X 2, 26, 10[97]. Hence also the notion that the institution of an heir was not required. Nor, of course, did the Church embrace the Roman rule that no one could die partly testate and partly intestate[98].

(b) Executor ultimae voluntatis

In a way, therefore, the disposition *ad pias causas* had ousted the heir; and the testament had become an essentially spiritual instrument *(Seelgerät)*. The decline in importance of the heir had opened up a gap as far as the winding up of the estate, and in particular the implementation of the dispositions *ad pias causas,* was concerned; and it was this gap which could conveniently be filled by the appointment of some person or institution acting in the best interests of the testator, i.e. as a fiduciary. This was the executor. He was referred to as *executor testamenti,* or *executor ultimae voluntatis,* and features prominently in Title XXVI (*De Testamentis et ultimis voluntatibus)* of the *Decretales Gregorii IX.* The Popes emphatically insisted that *in omnibus piis voluntatibus* everything had to be carried out in accordance with the wishes of the testator ("ut secundum defuncti voluntatem universa procedant")[99] and they therefore made it their business to see to it that the executor

93 Decretales Gregorii IX, Lib. III, Tit. XXVI, Cap. X.

94 Decretales Gregorii IX, Lib. III, Tit. XXVI, Cap. XI; for a commentary, see *von Glanvell* (n. 89) 124 ff. It was disputed, however, whether these two witnesses had to have been present at the time the will was made *(Solemnitätszeugen)* or whether they were merely ordinary witnesses for what the testator had wanted *(Beweiszeugen)*: see *Heimbach sen.*, Testamentum ad pias causas, in: Julius Weiske (ed.), Rechtslexikon für Juristen aller teutschen Staaten, vol. X, 1856, pp. 868 ff.; *Bernhard Windscheid, Theodor Kipp,* Lehrbuch des Pandektenrechts, 9th ed., 1906, § 545, 5; *Udo Wolter,* Ius canonicum in iure civili, 1975, p. 17.

95 *Gai.* Inst. II, 229.

96 Cf., e.g., *Philippe Ariès,* Geschichte des Todes, 1980, pp. 233 ff., 242 ff.; *Bruck* (n. 44) 257 ff.; *Beck* (n. 1) 297 f.; and cf. *supra* n. 44.

97 Cf. *supra* n. 93.

98 Cf., e.g., *Beck* (n. 1) 299; *Ogris* (n. 70) cols. 155 f.; *Coing* (n. 91) 563, 571 ff. Cf. also *Bussi* (n. 91) nos. 107 ff.

99 Decretales Gregorii IX, Lib. III, Tit. XXVI, Cap. XVII.

did not neglect his duties. Generally speaking, the Church could be involved on two different levels. The testator might have appointed a cleric as executor[100]; but even if he had not, the Church sought to ensure that the person appointed properly distributed the bequests *ad pias causas*[101]. Moreover, it stepped into the breach when the testator had merely left his property to Christ, or to the poor, without naming any specific person to implement these instructions.

In view of this level of involvement and of the spiritual character of the testament, it is not surprising that the Church took testamentary affairs to be part and parcel of its sphere of competence and influence, and indeed subject to the jurisdiction of its own courts. It was a jurisdiction *ratione rerum,* not merely *ratione personarum,* and thus the ecclesiastical principles concerning last wills, and their execution, not only affected clerics (and, possibly, crusaders, students and other special groups of persons) but everyone. Not everywhere in Europe was the Church as successful as in England where it managed to establish exclusive jurisdiction in probate matters[102]. But even where it was not, ecclesiastical principles in this area of the law were so convenient and convincing that they tended to be followed by secular courts and legislators. There were, of course, considerable variations from city to city and from country to country. But the general pattern of the development was characterized by (i) recognition of the institution of a last will, (ii) proliferation of different types of wills combined with a general relaxation of the formal requirements of Roman law, and (iii) adoption of the executor[103]. In Germany, he was referred to as *salemanne, totestere, vormunder, selgereter, manufidelis, testamenti executor, provisor, procurator, distributor, dispensator* and by a number of other terms[104]. Originally, even the word *testator* was used[105]. The executor's legal position is impossible to summarize in general terms. His powers and his duties were often described, in the testament, in great and somewhat clumsy detail. He could be called upon to carry out specific tasks or he could be placed in charge of the entire estate[106]. In the latter case, he has often, in the past, been regarded as *succes-*

100 Cf., e.g., *Pitlo* (n. 73) 142 ff.

101 See Decretales Gregorii IX, Lib. III, Tit. XXVI, Cap. XVII and Cap. XIX; and see *Schultze* (n. 66) 151 ff.; *von Glanvell* (n. 89) 199 ff.; *Hückstädt* (n. 77) 69 ff.

102 Cf. the overview in *Winfried Trusen,* Die gelehrte Gerichtsbarkeit der Kirche, in: Helmut Coing (ed.), Handbuch der Quellen und Literatur der neueren europäischen Privatrechtsgeschichte, vol. I, 1973, pp. 488 ff.; *Coing* (n. 91) 565; for details, see *Auffroy* (n. 77) 355 ff., 384 ff., 560 ff.; *Caillemer* (n. 1) 637 ff.; also *Engelmann* (n. 86) 124 ff.; *Pitlo* (n. 73) 137 ff.

103 See the references above, n. 91. And see *Engelmann* (n. 86) 39 ff., 224 ff.

104 Cf., e.g., *Stobbe* (n. 70) 262; *Schönfeld,* ZSS (GA) 42 (1921) 314 f.; *Pitlo* (n. 73) 110 ff.; *Henning Piper,* Testament und Vergabung von Todes wegen im braunschweigischen Stadtrecht des 13. bis 17. Jahrhunderts, 1960, p. 88. Generally on the terms used for a testamentary executor, see *Caillemer* (n. 1) 112 ff.

105 See the discussion by *Christian Friedrich Glück,* Ausführliche Erläuterung der Pandekten nach Hellfeld, fortgesetzt von Christian Friedrich Mühlenbruch, vol. 43, 1843, p. 403; *Schönfeld,* ZSS (GA) 42 (1921) 334 ff.; and see, in this context, the following note on the delegation of the power to make the will.

sor in universum ius defuncti – as *heres fiduciarius* who acquired full title[107]. Any such clear-cut and rational analysis does, however, run the danger of imposing anachronistic conceptions on medieval practice. It must thus remain an open question whether the executor's position, in actual practice, might not be better described as that of a fiduciary with a limited real right of disposition over the estate[108].

4. The *executor* in the Learned Literature

It is hardly surprising that contemporary learned authors also found it difficult to conceptualize the new institution that had developed at the intersection between Roman law, Canon law and medieval customary law of Germanic derivation[109]. The Roman legal sources did not provide a clear doctrinal framework; they contained only a few scattered texts from the postclassical era. The *Corpus iuris canonici,* too, offered no more than a handful of authoritative provisions

---

106 For details, see *Beseler* (n. 91) 150 ff.; *Schultze* (n. 66) 173 ff.; *Schönfeld,* ZSS (GA) 42 (1921) 351 ff.; *Pitlo* (n. 73) 93 ff.; *Louis de Charrin,* Les testaments dans la région de Montpellier au Moyen Age, thèse pour le doctorat, Montpellier, 1961, pp. 128 ff.; *Hückstädt* (n. 77) 101 ff. The testator could also, inciaentally, leave it to the unrestricted discretion of a third party to dispose of the estate; even the institution of an heir could be delegated. Of central importance, in this respect, was a rescript by *Pope Innocent III* who wrote in general terms (Decretales Gregorii IX, Lib. III, Tit. XXVI, Cap. XIII): "... qui extremam voluntatem in alterius dispositionem committit, non videtur decedere intestatus". On its interpretation, see *Gerhard Immel,* Die höchstpersönliche Willensentscheidung des Erblassers, 1965, pp. 42 ff.; *Windscheid/Kipp* (n. 94) § 547, n. 3; *Christian Friedrich Glück,* Ausführliche Erläuterung der Pandekten nach Hellfeld, vol. 33, 1842, pp. 447 f. and vol. 34, 1842, pp. 1 ff.; *Beseler* (n. 91) 193 ff.; *von Glanvell* (n. 89) 147 ff.; *Schultze* (n. 66) 153 f.; *Pitlo* (n. 73) 106; *Hückstädt* (n. 77) 106 ff.; and see generally *Reinhard Zimmermann,* "Quos Titius voluerit" – Höchstpersönliche Willensentscheidung des Erblassers oder "power of appointment"?, 1991, pp. 16 ff.

107 *Erbe zu treuer Hand; Schultze* (n. 66) 173 ff.; *Schönfeld,* ZSS (GA) 42 (1921) 377; *Planitz* (n. 69) 152; *Pitlo* (n. 73) 93 ff., 96 ff.; *Piper* (n. 104) 91; cf. also the detailed discussion by *Caillemer* (n. 1) 336 ff. *Helmut Coing* (Die Treuhand kraft privaten Rechtsgeschäfts, 1973, pp. 13 f.) has drawn attention to the fact that the term *heres fiduciarius* occurs in the Digest: cf. *Iav.* D. 36, 1, 48 and *Valens* D. 36, 1, 69, 3. It is used there to describe an heir who was charged with making over the entire inheritance, or part of it (*fideicommissum hereditatis).* This was one of the devices available to Roman testators (and mentioned above, text after n. 31) to substitute for testamentary executorship. It was to become the historical root of the modern institution of "reversionary heirship" (*Nacherbschaft);* cf., e.g, § 2100 BGB: "The testator may appoint an heir in such manner that the latter becomes heir only after another person has previously been an heir". This also was not possible in Roman law (*semel heres semper heres!*). On *fideicommissum hereditatis,* see *Kaser* (n. 4) 761 ff.; *idem* (n. 32) 761 ff.; *Peter Apathy,* Fideikommissarische Substitution und Treuhand, in: Gedächtnisschrift Herbert Hofmeister, 1996, pp. 17 ff.; and the paper by *David Johnston* in the present volume.

108 *Hückstädt* (n. 77) 141 ff.; *Gunter Wesener,* Geschichte des Erbrechts in Österreich seit der Rezeption, 1957, p. 187; *Ogris* (n. 70) col. 164.

109 For a general overview, see *Rosshirt* (n. 84) 226 ff.; *Beseler* (n. 91) 157 ff.; *Caillemer* (n. 1) 186 ff. and *passim; Schultze* (n. 66) 151 ff.; *Pitlo* (n. 73) 108 ff.; *Beck* (n. 1) 298 ff.; *Coing* (n. 91) 597 ff.

dealing with special issues. And the medieval *Salmann* was not a product of anything approaching legal science and had never been subjected to close doctrinal analysis. Legists and canonists alike used whatever sources they could find: no matter whether they were contained in the texts of Canon law or Roman law. *Durantis*' "Speculum Judiciale" provides a first great synthesis: a lengthy treatise *De ultimarum voluntatum executoribus,* hidden away in Lib. II, Partic. II *De Instrumentorum editione*[110]. *Johannes Andreae* in his introductory notes described it as "generalissimus, et utrique iuri et foro communis". In it, we are informed about a number of different terms used for the executor, among them *divisor, dispensator* and *minister*[111] – terms that could all be, and were in fact, traced back to the Roman sources. The canonists preferred *executor,* as did *Accursius*[112]. The executor's function is to carry out the will of the testator ("... qui testatoris voluntatem exequi, seu adimplere debet")[113]. He could either be instituted in the testament itself *(executor testamentarius)*, or he could be appointed by order of the court or of a public authority *(executor dativus)*, or he could hold his office by force of law *(executor legitimus,* or statutory executor)[114]. *Executor legitimus* was usually the bishop of the place where the deceased was domiciled. He had to take charge of the estate, where the *executor testamentarius* declined to act as executor or where a bequest *ad pias causas* had been made without an executor having been appointed in the will to implement it[115].

Of greater significance, however, was another distinction underlying *Durantis*' discussion: the distinction between an *executor universalis* who, in the absence of an heir, was put in charge of the entire estate, and an *executor specialis* who had to carry out specific dispositions and whose position had to be coordinated with that of the testate or intestate heirs[116]. The place of the *executor generalis* was equated to that of an heir: "nullo herede instituto, executor loco heredis est"[117]. More complex was the determination of the legal position of the *executor specialis*[118]. Indisputably, he did not hold the place of an heir[119]. Nevertheless, he occupied a place

---

110 *Guilelmus Durantis,* Speculum Iudiciale, vol. I, Basileae, 1574, Lib. II, Partic. II, § 13. Cf. also *Bussi* (n. 91) 178 ff.

111 *Durantis* (n. 110) no. 3.

112 *Durantis* (n. 110) no. 3.

113 *Durantis* (n. 110) no. 1.

114 *Durantis* (n. 110) nos. 1 f.; cf. also *Caillemer* (n. 1) 620 ff.

115 *Durantis* (n. 110) no. 1. Concerning legal practice, see *Pitlo* (n. 73) 135 ("Men kan aannemen dat in een opengevallen nalatenschap in de middeleeuwen altijd eenige uitvoerders aanwezig waren").

116 Cf. *Durantis* (n. 110) nos. 26 ff., 29.

117 *Durantis* (n. 110) nos. 26 f. For a detailed analysis, see *Schultze* (n. 66) 173 ff.

118 For a detailed analysis, see *Schultze* (n. 66) 184 ff.; cf. also *Pitlo* (n. 73) 114.

119 "Porro si sit executor non ad omnia, sive non universalis, sed aliquorum bonorum tantum, et in testamento sit haeres institutus, tunc indubitate talis non habetur loco haeredis": *Durantis* (n. 110) n. 29.

in his own right, one quite independent from that of the heir. Thus, for instance, he could not be regarded as *procurator:* for then it could hardly be maintained that he could sue the heir (as undoubtedly executors did) – heir and decedent, after all, being regarded as one and the same person, it would be absurd "*quod contra dominum procurator agere posset*"[120]. Nor, in view of his institution in the last will or his statutory entitlement, could he be taken to be a *negotiorum gestor*[121]. In the end, *Durantis* emphasized the structural parallels between executor and legatee, or fideicommissary, and concluded his analysis by describing him as "minister legatarius vel fideicommissarius"[122].

The *executor testamentarius,* no matter whether *generalis* or *specialis,* could not normally be forced to accept his *ministerium,* unless he had either previously undertaken to do so, or unless he had received a benefit under the will: "qui non est honoratus, non debet onerari"[123]. The matter was different, *favore religionis,* where dispositions *ad pias causas* were concerned[124]. The executor had to draw up an inventory of the estate, at least where he was an *executor generalis*[125]. Once he had embarked on the execution of the will, he had to act diligently. He was subject to far-ranging episcopal supervision[126]. If his administration of the decedent's affairs left something to be desired, the bishop had to issue an admonition, and if this failed he could either invoke disciplinary measures of a spiritual nature (*suspensio* or *excommunicatio)* or require the secular authorities to intervene by imposing a *mulcta* or by resorting to *pignoris capio* or *personae detentio*[127]. After the estate had been distributed, the bishop could require the executor to render an account[128].

120 *Durantis* (n. 110) no. 67. Moreover: if one were dealing with a mandate, the contractual relationship would have to be considered to have come to an end with the death of the mandator (*mandatum solvitur morte mandatoris)*; and finally: if the executor were to be considered a *procurator,* and the heir the *dominus,* the latter would have the power, *re integra,* to revoke the mandate and thus to frustrate the intentions of the testator.

121 *Durantis* (n. 110) no. 66.

122 *Durantis* (n. 110) no. 68. The edition Basileae, 1574, has "minister, legatarius, vel fideicommissarius"; but cf. *Schultze* (n. 66) 195.

123 *Durantis* (n. 110) nos. 27, 55. There were, however, a number of Canonists who were not prepared to grant the *executor* the discretion to refuse to undertake the execution: executorship, so they argued, was a *munus publicum* (see *Pitlo* (n. 73) 1125 f.). But they were probably thinking of the will *ad pias causas.* Cf. also *Durantis* (n. 110) no. 55 ("Sed et favore religionis de canonica aequitate videtur cogendus et suscipere et exequi: puta cum relictum est ad pios usus"). *Pitlo,* however, draws attention to the fact that this question was of a purely theoretical nature. Cf. also *Caillemer* (n. 1) 573 ff.

124 *Durantis* (n. 110) no. 55.

125 *Durantis* (n. 110) no. 44; cf. also *Caillemer* (n. 1) 580 ff.; *Pitlo* (n. 73) 130 f.

126 For details, see *Schultze* (n. 66) 156 ff.; *Pitlo* (n. 73) 126 ff.; *Bussi* (n. 91) no. 125.

127 *Durantis* (n. 110) no. 56. The executor who did not carry out bequests *ad pias causas* could also be sued "a legatariis, vel ab episcopo, vel ab ecclesia, vel a pauperibus, vel a quocumque, cui legatum sit, ut exequatur piam defuncti voluntatem": *Durantis* (n. 110) no. 58; cf. also *Caillemer* (n. 1) 612 ff.

128 *Durantis* (n. 110) no. 45; and see *Caillemer* (n. 1) 614 ff.; *Pitlo* (n. 73) 131 ff.

If, as was usually the case[129], several executors had been instituted and if they could not agree upon how to proceed, the bishop had to be approached for a decision[130]. Episcopal intervention was also called for where the instructions in the will were unclear[131]. There was some concern that the executor should carry out his tasks within a reasonable time: in view of C. 1, 3, 28 he was taken by many to have a year "a die, qua res distribuendas accepit". However, "in piis voluntatibus" everything even had ordinarily to be distributed within six months "ab insinuatione testamenti"[132]. How these periods were to be calculated was discussed in great detail[133], as were a variety of other, not always practically very useful, questions[134]. "One reason more", summarizes *Pitlo*[135], "not to pay too much attention to the learned lawyers is that in their attempts to squeeze the execution into the much too narrow rules of the *Corpus iuris* they created insoluble problems by always drawing finer distinctions and thus piling up more and more difficulties". In spite of all these intellectual efforts, already in the 14th century we find complaints about executors abusing their position ("perfidia manufidelium")[136], and in England it was even maintained that three executors made three thieves[137].

It is obvious that the material compiled in *Durantis*' treatise related to the medieval will – a will dominated by legacies, and dispositions that were similar to legacies, rather than by the institution of an heir, and that aimed, above all, at the redemption of the testator's soul. "In primis quid pro anima sua dari iusserit proponat, quia anima est plus quam corpus, et quibus locis et personis legari voluerit nominet, quid et quantum; deinde instituat commissarios qui sint solliciti circa funus et sepulturam et disponant ea quae designaverit pro anima", as it was put in a contemporary work on notarial practice[138]. Somewhat dimly, however, the person of the heir had by now appeared on the horizon, and his position in some way had to be coordinated with that of the executor. The heir had not yet challenged the

---

129 Cf., e.g., *Caillemer* (n. 1) 386 ff.; *Pitlo* (n. 73) 123.

130 *Durantis* (n. 110) nos. 13, 50.

131 *Durantis* (n. 110) no. 63.

132 *Durantis* (n. 110) no. 82.

133 Cf., e.g., *Didacus Covarruvias à Leyva,* Opera Omnia, Madriti, 1610, Tomus I de Testament. cap. 3 (the first of four lengthy chapters in this treatise dealing with the executor). In actual practice, execution often seems to have taken much longer; according to *Pitlo* (n. 73) 107, it was not exceptional for the winding up of the estate to take six years or more (cf. also p. 132).

134 Cf., e.g., the lively discussion as to the specific form of action available to the *executor specialis:* cf. *Schultze* (n. 66) 195. And see the general discussion by *Caillemer* (n. 1) 418 ff.; *Pitlo* (n. 73) 115 ff.

135 *Pitlo* (n. 73) 109 (my translation from the Dutch original).

136 *Pitlo* (n. 73) 107 f.

137 *Caillemer* (n. 1) 111.

138 Cf. the reference in *Schultze* (n. 66) 170 f. Cf. also *Pitlo* (n. 73) 99 f. and, concerning specifically the appointment of an executor, p. 135 ("nominatio executoris indicat perfectionem testamenti").

place of the *executor generalis*[139]. But in the case of the *executor specialis* coordination was already proving difficult. Under which circumstances could he bring an action against the heir?[140] Could he sue the testator's debtors?[141] And could he dispose of property belonging to the estate?[142] The answer to these questions was far from straightforward and did not, in any event, flow easily from the analogies drawn with *legatarii* or *curatores*[143].

IV. *Usus Modernus* in Germany and in the Netherlands

With the increasing influence of the Roman law of succession in countries like Germany and the Netherlands[144], the position of the heir was bound to be strengthened. By the days of the *usus modernus pandectarum* the heir had re-acquired his central position within the law relating to testamentary succession. He succeeded *in locum defuncti*[145] which entailed, *inter alia,* that he acquired ownership of the testator's property, became responsible for discharging the debts, satisfied the *legatarii,* and administered the estate. If testators continued to appoint executors – as they frequently did[146] – the latter could no longer be regarded as being *in loco her-*

139 But see the tentative discussion by *Schultze* (n. 66) 198 ff.

140 In principle, he could not sue; but the exceptions were interpreted so liberally that the principle appears, for all practical purposes, to have been reversed; see *Schultze* (n. 66) 186 ff.; *Caillemer* (n. 1) 600 ff.; *Pitlo* (n. 73) 116 ff.

141 *Durantis* answered in the affirmative: (n. 110) no. 33; on the other hand, however, he maintained that the debtors could only discharge their obligations by paying the heir: (n. 110) no. 36. Others did not find this convincing: see *Pitlo* (n. 73) 120 f.

142 Only if the testator had specifically empowered him to do so: *Durantis* (n. 110) no. 32. Again, however, the question was controversial, particularly in view of the more liberal practice: see *Pitlo* (n. 73) 121 f.; cf. also *Caillemer* (n. 1) 603 ff.; *Coing* (n. 91) 600.

143 For the historical roots of the latter analogy, see *Beseler* (n. 91) 149 ff.; *Heimbach sen.* (n. 94) 1017 f.; *Caillemer* (n. 1) 104 ff., 356 ff.; *Schönfeld,* ZSS (GA) 42 (1921) 328 ff.; *Hückstädt* (n. 77) 45 ff.; *Karlheinz Muscheler,* Die Haftungsordnung der Testamentsvollstreckung, 1994, pp. 29 f. For the 17th and 18th centuries, see *Pitlo* (n. 73) 168 ff.

144 For the Netherlands see, e.g., *R. W. Lee,* An Introduction to Roman-Dutch Law, 5th ed., 1953, p. 352 ("No department of the Roman-Dutch Law is more thoroughly penetrated by the Roman tradition than that of testamentary succession"); *F. J. van Zyl,* Universele opvolging in die Suid-Afrikaanse Erfreg, LL.D. thesis, University of Stellenbosch, 1981, pp. 27 ff.; for Austria, see *Gunter Wesener,* Geschichte des Erbrechts in Österreich seit der Rezeption, 1957, pp. 119 ff.; for Germany, *Heimbach sen.* (n. 94) 1022; generally, see *Coing* (n. 91) 564 ff.; *H.-R. Hagemann,* Erbrecht, in: Handwörterbuch zur deutschen Rechtsgeschichte, vol. I, 1971, cols. 975 ff.; *W. Ogris,* Testament, in: Handwörterbuch zur deutschen Rechtsgeschichte, 33rd part, 1991, cols. 157 ff. (Roman principles were "eagerly" absorbed).

145 Cf., e.g., *Hugo Grotius,* Inleiding tot de Hollandsche Rechtsgeleertheyd, ed. *R. W. Lee,* vol. I, 1926, II, XIV, 7 ("An heir is one who enters upon the deceased's estate as universal successor to his rights and burdens", tr. R. W. Lee).

146 Cf., e.g., *Georg Adam Struve,* Syntagma Juris Civilis, cum additionibus Petri Mülleri, vol. II, 3rd ed., Francofurti et Lipsiae, 1738, Exerc. XXIV, Lib. XXIX, Tit. II, XXXI (α):

edis: no matter whether they had been put in charge of the entire estate or entrusted with a specific task. The term *executor generalis* thus acquired an extended meaning[147]. It meant simply the person to whom "universa defuncti voluntas ad exequendum est commissa"[148], and it was no longer true that he had no rival in the person of the heir. At the time of *Durantis, executor specialis* and *generalis* had really been two rather different institutions; and if anything, one had sought to mould the former to fit the image of the latter[149]. In the 17th century, however, the position was reversed. The *executor generalis* became little more than an *executor specialis* with a comprehensive range of tasks. No longer did any structural difference exist. *Christian Friedrich Mühlenbruch,* two hundred years later, was even to reject any such distinction as unfounded[150]; the institution of an *executor heredis loco,* though still conceivable, was regarded as too anomalous to provide a foundation for conceptual analysis.

As a result of these developments, all the old doctrinal difficulties concerning the *executor specialis* now bedevilled any discussion of the executor in general. Such discussion was conducted, predominantly, in books on notarial practice and collections of legal opinions, in special treatises or disputations, rather than in the standard textbooks[151]. Writers like *Voet* ("Commentarius ad Pandectas") and *Vinnius* ("Commentarius in Institutiones"), *Stryk* ("Usus modernus pandectarum") and *Struve* ("Syntagma Jurisprudentiae") hardly mention the executor[152]. He was, and continued to be, essentially a creation of legal practice. The range of the executor's rights and duties largely depended on what the testator had specified in his will[153]. *Wolfgang Adam Lauterbach* in a much quoted "Commentatio de ex-

---

"Moribus nostris nullam fere testamentum sit, in quo non aliqui constituantur Executores ... unus pluresque pro arbitrio Testatoris, quibus ea cura a testatore demandatur, ut omnia, quae disposuit, impleantur"; *Samuel Stryk,* Usus modernus pandectarum, vol. II, 4th ed., Halae Magdeburgicae, 1722, Lib. XXX. XXXI. XXXII, § XXXVI ("Haec de executoribus ultimarum voluntatum materia hodie est in praxi longe frequentior ..."); *Glück/Mühlenbruch* (n. 105) 404 f.; *Pitlo* (n. 73) 18 ("In de 17de en 18de eeuw is er bijna geen testament zonder executeur"), 157 ff.

147 This comes out very well in *Wolfgang Adam Lauterbach,* Commentatio de executoribus voluntatum ultimarum (resp. Johannes Ulricus Zeller), 1668, Cap. III, nos. 11 ff.

148 *Lauterbach* (n. 147) Cap. III, no. 13.

149 Cf. also *Pitlo* (n. 73) 118.

150 *Christian Friedrich Glück,* Ausführliche Erläuterung der Pandekten nach Hellfeld, fortgesetzt von Christian Friedrich Mühlenbruch, vol. 43, 1843, pp. 410 ff.

151 Cf. also the observation by *Pitlo* (n. 73) 16 f.; *Beinart,* Heir and Executor, 1960 Acta Juridica 228, n. 42.

152 *Stryk* only has one comparatively brief paragraph in *op. cit.* (n. 146) Lib. XXX. XXXI. XXXII, § XXXVI (summarized in the following words "Quod assignatur executori pro legato haud habendum"), and in *Struve's* Syntagma Juris Civilis (n. 146) there is only a lengthy note by *Petrus Müller.*

153 "Potestas eorum dependet ex testamento, cujus tenor ante omnia inspiciendus est": *David Mevius,* Commentarii in Ius Lubecense Libri Quinque, Francofurti ad Moenum, 1646, Pars II, Tit. I, Artic. XV, 7; "[q]uam potestatem executores habeant, ex verbis testamenti col-

ecutoribus voluntatum ultimarum" (published in 1668) attempted to summarize the contemporary discussion, emphasizing the variety and perplexity inherent in the subject[154]. And he stressed that one could not rely on a firm set of rules but had to argue "ex analogia Juris" or simply to follow "juris et aequitatis rationem"[155]. He defined executors as persons "principaliter ad id constitutae, ut legitimam testatoris voluntatem adimpleant"[156] but drew attention to the fact that this definition confined him to a discussion of the *executor merus* as opposed to the *executor mixtus* who also had the task of administering the estate[157]. An analogy was often drawn with the office of a *tutor* or *curator*[158], but in the course of the 18th century the executor came to be regarded, predominantly and despite all the doctrinal problems raised by earlier authors[159], as a kind of mandatary: "Executoris testamentarii officium procuratio quaedam est"[160]. He had thus ceased to have a real right and was clearly regarded as subordinate to the heir[161]. The executor could not be forced to accept his position[162], but if he did he had to carry out his tasks with due diligence. He was normally required to take an inventory and to render an account of what he had done. He could not usually wind up the estate against the wishes of the heir. Under exactly what circumstances he could alienate property belonging to the estate remained disputed. What was his position in legal disputes concerning the estate? Could he sue debtors in his own right? And could he bring an action against the heir? These and many other ques-

---

ligendum est ante omnia. Nam eorum potestas tota descendit ex concessione testatoris": *Johann Oldendorp,* Tractatus et doctus et compendiosus de executoribus ultimarum voluntatum, 1549, quoted by *Coing* (n. 91) 599; *Pitlo* (n. 73) 18 ("... dat zijn positie vrijwel uitsluitend afhing van de bepalingen in het testament").

154 *Lauterbach* (n. 147) Praefatio ("Nam summa iis inest varietas et perplexitas"; it is not quite clear, however, whether "iis" refers to the executors or to the treatises written about them).

155 *Lauterbach* (n. 147) Praefatio.

156 *Lauterbach* (n. 147) Cap. II, no. 9.

157 On this distinction see *Lauterbach* (n. 147) Cap. III, nos. 22 ff.; *Glück/Mühlenbruch* (n. 105) 426 f.

158 *Mevius* (n. 153) Pars II, Tit. I, Artic. XV, 7; cf. also *Lauterbach* (n. 147) Cap. IX, no. 17 ("Executores nostri Tutoribus et Curatoribus in multis sunt similes"); *Struve/Müller* (n. 146) (α), XIX ("Quamvis Executores ultimae voluntatis Tutoribus et Curatoribus in multis sunt similes ..."); and see *Beseler* (n. 91) 159 ff.

159 Cf. *supra* n. 120.

160 *Lauterbach* (n. 147) Cap. IV, no. 48; *Glück/Mühlenbruch* (n. 105) 416; *Heimbach sen.* (n. 94) 1024; *Dionysius Godefridus van der Keessel,* Praelectiones iuris hodierni ad Hugonis Grotii Introductionem ad Iurisprudentiam Hollandicam, ed. and trans. *Paul van Warmelo et al.*, 1963, Th. 323 ("Ex eo autem quod exsecutor sit mandatarius, consequitur, ..."); cf. also *Beseler* (n. 91) 162 ff.

161 Cf., e.g., *Pitlo* (n. 73) 153 ff.

162 As to what follows, see *Mevius* (n. 153) Pars II, Tit. I, Artic. XV, 4 ff.; *Lauterbach* (n. 147) Cap. IV ff.; *Van der Keessel* (n. 160) Th. 323; *Rosshirt* (n. 84) 231 ff.; *Glück/Mühlenbruch* (n. 105) 390 ff., 415 ff.; *Heimbach sen.* (n. 94) 1024 ff.; *Pitlo* (n. 73) 158 ff.; *Beinart,* 1960 Acta Juridica 226 ff.; *Wesener* (n. 108) 188 ff.; *Coing* (n. 91) 598 ff.

tions continued to be discussed in much the same way, and similarly inconclusively, as they had been by the medieval writers[163].

One thing had changed, however: the bishop had been replaced by secular authorities in supervising the executor[164]. The magistrate, rather than the Church, was regarded as *supremus executor testamenti.* But this came to little in practice. There was a tendency to regard the administration of estates as an essentially private matter between the various parties named in the will. In 17th and 18th century Roman-Dutch law "there was hardly any official estate supervision"[165]; the same may be said for 19th century Germany[166].

V. Austrian Law

Austria, however, has retained a system of comprehensive and obligatory official estate supervision[167]. It even made its way into the General Civil Code (*Allgemeines Bürgerliches Gesetzbuch,* ABGB) for it was bound to appeal to the enlightened paternalism of 18th century Habsburg vintage that permeated the Austrian state[168]. According to § 797 ABGB, the heir may not, under his own authority, take possession of the deceased person's property. His right to succeed must first be for-

---

163 The same conclusion is drawn by *Pitlo* (n. 73) 158.

164 *Mevius* (n. 153) Pars II, Tit. I, Artic. XV, 16 ("in terris Evangelicae religioni addictis"); *Augustin Leyser,* Meditationes ad Pandectas, vols. V and VI, 3rd ed., Lipsiae et Guelpherbyti, 1744, Spec. CCCLXXIV, IX and X; *Pitlo* (n. 73) 146 sq.; *Hückstädt* (n. 77) 126 ff.; *Coing* (n. 91) 601.

165 *Beinart,* 1960 Acta Juridica 228.

166 *Glück/Mühlenbruch* (n. 105) 428 ff.; *Beseler* (n. 91) 178; *Heimbach sen.* (n. 94) 1038. *Heinrich Dernburg,* Pandekten, vol. III, 5th ed., 1897, §§ 124 f. does not refer to the public authority in the present context. According to *Bernhard Windscheid, Theodor Kipp,* Lehrbuch des Pandektenrechts, vol. III, 9th ed., 1906, § 567, the execution of a last will is not, exceptional cases apart, the object of state supervision. They do, however, draw attention to the fact that such state supervision is recognized, to a greater or lesser extent, in the laws of the individual German territories. The exceptional cases are those where nobody has been designated who could implement the will of the testator. Cf. also the detailed comparative discussion by *Gottfried von Schmitt,* in: Werner Schubert (ed.), Die Vorlagen der Redaktoren für die erste Kommission zur Ausarbeitung des Entwurfs eines Bürgerlichen Gesetzbuches, Erbrecht, Teil 1, 1984, pp. 332 ff.

167 For comparative and historical discussions of the somewhat reduced function of the Austrian executor in view of the official estate supervision, see *Wolfgang Siebert,* Testamentsvollstrecker, in: Franz Schlegelberger (ed.), Rechtsvergleichendes Handwörterbuch, vol. VI, 1938, p. 563 and *passim; Beck* (n. 1) 300 f.; *Erich Lang,* Der Testamentsvollstrecker in den ausländischen Rechten und seine Stellung im deutschen Rechtsgebiet, Dr. iur. thesis, Frankfurt/M., 1959, pp. 74 ff.; *Coing* (n. 64) 617, 640, 646; *Muscheler* (n. 143) 21 f. The historical background of official state supervision is traced in *Wesener* (n. 144) 23 ff.; and see pp. 187 ff. on the history of the executor in Austrian law before codification.

168 See generally *Konrad Zweigert, Hein Kötz,* Einführung in die Rechtsvergleichung auf dem Gebiete des Privatrechts, 3. Aufl., 1996, pp. 156 ff.; *Reinhard Zimmermann,* Codifica-

mally established by the probate court (*Verlassenschaftsgericht*). The heir therefore has to demonstrate his legal title to the satisfaction of the court and also declare his readiness to accept the inheritance (*Erbserklärung*)[169]. Thereupon the court issues a decree investing him with the estate (*Einantwortung*)[170]. For the period between the testator's death and the *Einantwortungs*-decree the estate is without an owner; it constitutes *hereditas iacens* in the hands of the probate court[171]. The probate court determines who has to administer the estate during this state of pendency. After the *Erbserklärung* has been given, the court will normally appoint the presumptive heir[172]. Alternatively, it may nominate a curator[173].

This curator (appointed by the court) is not to be confused with an executor nominated by the testator. The latter does not receive a great deal of attention in the Austrian Code: he is dealt with in a single section. According to § 816 ABGB the executor is free to decide whether he wants to take on the office ("... dieses Geschäft auf sich nehmen"); if, however, he accepts, he has either to undertake the execution of the testator's dispositions himself or see to it that the dawdling heir ("der saumselige Erbe") carries out the execution. The exact range of his rights and duties is disputed[174]. This does not, however, appear to have led to much inconvenience and uncertainty, because the institution of the executor is not of great practical significance in Austrian law[175]: very largely, it has been rendered redundant by the obligatory intervention of the probate court[176]. Also, of course, the testator is free to specify the executor's sphere of activity. He may even charge him with the administration of the entire estate[177], in which case the probate court ap-

---

tion: history and present significance of an idea, (1995) 3 European Review of Private Law 98 ff.

169 § 799 ABGB.

170 § 819 ABGB.

171 The legal nature of the *hereditas iacens* is disputed. For details, see *Winfried Kralik*, Das Erbrecht, 1983 (= Ehrenzweig / Ehrenzweig, System des österreichischen allgemeinen Privatrechts, 3rd ed.), pp. 26 ff. According to § 547, 3 ABGB, the estate is deemed to be still in the possession of the deceased person. If the *hereditas iacens* needs to be represented, the court appoints a curator (see *Kralik*, p. 28).

172 § 810 ABGB.

173 Cf. *Rudolf Welser*, in: Peter Rummel (ed.), Kommentar zum Allgemeinen bürgerlichen Gesetzbuch, vol. I, 2nd ed., 1980, § 810, nos. 27 ff.; *Helmut Koziol, Rudolf Welser*, Grundriß des bürgerlichen Rechts, vol. II, 10th ed., 1996, p. 402.

174 This is emphasized by *Rummel / Welser* (n. 173) § 816, no. 5 and *Koziol / Welser* (n. 173) 347.

175 See, e.g., the comparative evaluation by *Siebert, Beck and Lang*, all n. 167; *Andreas Wacke*, Die Testamentsvollstreckung im deutschen und europäischen Recht, Jura 1989, 578; *Ebenroth* (n. 1) no. 714; *Muscheler* (n. 143) 21.

176 The probate court may therefore still be described as the supreme statutory executor of the last will; see *Siebert* (n. 167) 563.

177 *Rummel / Welser* (n. 173) § 816, nos. 10 ff.; *Koziol / Welser* (n. 173) 347. This is disputed by *Kralik* (n. 171) 273.

points him as *curator hereditatis*. But he remains under the supervision of the court in any case. § 816 ABGB refers to the executor as a mandatary (*Machthaber*). Whether this is doctrinally correct[178] or whether the execution is an institution *sui generis*[179] remains disputed but does not appear to be practically significant. A number of modern textbooks and commentaries do not even discuss the question[180].

VI. French Law

1. Medieval Customary Law

One cannot say that in its modern Austrian incarnation the executorship has reached the apogee of its career. Of marginally more substantial stature is its French counterpart, for it has not been overshadowed by the intervention of the state authorities[181]. As in the Netherlands and Germany[182], estate regulation was regarded as an essentially private matter, even before the French revolution. Thus, for instance, already in the 15th century it was established that the executor had to render his account before the heir rather than the bishop or a state official[183]. *Pothier* in his discussion of the testamentary executor[184] does not mention any public supervision concerning the way in which he managed his affairs[185]; nor is there any indication that the magistrate would have been regarded as *executor legitimus*[186]. As in the other European countries, the testamentary executor in France was originally an *elemosinarius:* he had to carry out bequests *ad pias causas*[187]. After the 12th century, however, dispositions not inspired by religious motives began to appear in testaments, and the last will ceased to be an

178 *Franz Gschnitzer*, Österreichisches Erbrecht, 2nd ed. by *Christoph Faistenberger*, 1984, p. 65.

179 *Kralik* (n. 171) 271.

180 Cf. *Rummel/Welser* (n. 173) § 816; *Koziol/Welser* (n. 173) 346 ff. According to *Bernhard Eccher*, in: Michael Schwimann (ed.), Praxiskommentar zum Allgemeinen Bürgerlichen Gesetzbuch, vol. III, 1989, § 816, no. 8, the rules relating to mandate (concerning remuneration) apply "in principle"; cf. also *Kralik* (n. 171) 275.

181 For a comparative overview, see *Siebert* (n. 167) 562; *Beck* (n. 1) 301 ff.; *Lang* (n. 167) 19 ff.; *Ebenroth* (n. 1) no. 711; *Muscheler* (n. 143) 24 f.; *Astrid Offergeld*, Die Rechtsstellung des Testamentsvollstreckers, 1995, pp. 194 ff.

182 Cf. *supra*, text before n. 166.

183 *Engelmann* (n. 86) 243.

184 *Robert-Joseph Pothier*, Oeuvres, ed. M. Dupin, vol. VII, Paris, 1825, Traité des donations testamentaires, Chapitre V, Section I.

185 Contrary to the position under the ABGB, for example, *Pothier* states "que l'exécuteur peut se mettre *de lui-même* en possession des biens de la succession" (Chapitre V, Section I, Article II, § IV).

186 As he was according to *Leyser* (n. 164) Spec. CCCLXXIV, IX.

187 *Auffroy* (n. 77) 347 ff.; *Caillemer* (n. 1) 113 ff.; *Engelmann* (n. 86) 39 ff.

exclusively spiritual instrument[188]. As a result, jurisdiction over testamentary causes became a matter of contention between ecclesiastical and secular courts[189]. The latter eventually managed to assert exclusive jurisdiction, in Burgundy and Hainault by the middle of the 15th century[190]. As everywhere else, of course, the concept of testament as a unilateral disposition *mortis causa*, revocable at any time before death, derived from Roman law. But in the *pays du droit coutumier* it developed its own characteristic features. Thus, for instance, the advent of the holograph will[191] constituted a relaxation of the testamentary formalities beyond even what had already been accepted by the Church[192]. Even more importantly, we find significant variations in the substantive requirements for a valid will. Contrary to Roman law, it had become accepted in some parts of medieval and early modern Europe[193] that a testament no longer required the institution of an heir[194]. French customary law went one step further in that it refused to accept the testamentary institution of an heir: "Institution d'heritier n'a lieu", as the matter was put succinctly by *Antoine Loisel* in his "Institutes Coutumières"[195]. This was a survival of the old idea that only God could create an heir, not man ("Solus Deus heredem facere potest, non homo")[196]. Thus, the heir was always the intestate heir, *l'héritier légitime*. The testator could only appoint legatees, be it for specific objects, be it for a share of the estate. However, a legacy could comprise the entire estate over which the testator had power to dispose (*legatum universale, legs universel*); and this was indeed how the institution of an outsider as heir was usually understood and thus, effectively, upheld[197].

---

188 *Engelmann* (n. 86) 14 ff.

189 *Auffroy* (n. 77) 560 ff.; *Caillemer* (n. 1) 648 ff.; *Engelmann* (n. 86) 16 ff., 115 ff.; and see *Philippe de Beaumanoir,* Coutumes de Beauvaisis, ed. A. Salmon, 1899 - 1900 (reprint 1970), Ch. 11, nos. 320 f.

190 *Engelmann* (n. 86) 127. *Engelmann,* however, also draws attention to the fact that usually the testator himself appended a clause to his testament determining the proper kind of court for any dispute arising under his will.

191 See *Engelmann* (n. 86) 64 ff.; *Paul Viollet,* Histoire du droit civil français, 3rd ed., 1905, p. 954; and cf. the references in *R. H. Helmholz,* Der Usus Modernus Pandectarum und die Ursprünge des eigenhändigen Testaments in England, ZEuP 3 (1995) 770 f. *Pothier* (n. 184) Chapitre I, Article II, § I says: "Le testament olographe est admis dans tout le pays coutumier".

192 Cf. *supra* nn. 93 f.

193 Though not in the French *pays de droit écrit;* cf. *Viollet* (n. 191) 961. Generally on medieval wills in the *pays du droit écrit,* see *Auffroy* (n. 77) 481 ff., 630 ff.; *Louis de Charrin,* Les testaments dans la région de Montpellier au moyen age, thèse pour le doctorat, Montpellier, 1961.

194 Cf. *supra* III. 3. a); and see *Coing* (n. 91) 573.

195 See *Viollet* (n. 191) 962; *Auffroy* (n. 77) 566 ff.; *Caillemer* (n. 1) *passim;* and see *Pothier* (n. 184) Chapitre II, Section I, § I.

196 Cf. *supra* n. 77.

197 For details, see *Engelmann* (n. 86) 158 ff. and the authors quoted in n. 195.

These peculiarities of French customary law hardly affected the practice of instituting persons charged with the execution of the decedent's last will. The "Coutumes de Beauvaisis" (around 1238) contain a substantial discussion on testamentary executors[198]; we are informed that in the 15th, as in the 13th century, one very rarely finds a will in which an executor (or, more precisely, several executors)[199] were not appointed[200]; and for the 18th century we have the statement by *Pothier* that "il est assez d'usage que les testateurs, pour procurer une plus sûre, plus exacte et plus diligente exécution de leurs dernières volontés, nomment ... des ... exécuteurs testamentaires"[201]. The executor has to distribute the *legata ad pias causas* as well as all other legacies; he has to collect the debts due to the deceased and to pay his debts; and he has to take an inventory[202].

Once again, it is obvious that the executor's exact legal position is not easy to conceptualize. *Philippe de Beaumanoir* described him as representing the person of the deceased[203]. He probably did not mean thereby to equate the executor to a contractual mandatary but rather saw in him the deceased's successor, the person who acted in his place[204]. It is in this spirit that testators in the 15th century usually transferred to their executors "la saisine" of all their movable and immovable property. "Les exécuteurs de nos testaments" writes *Jean Engelmann* on the basis of his research into contemporary wills[205], "sont toujours investis des pouvoirs les plus larges et la saisine qui leur est attribuée a pour effet de leur donner ... un droit d'administration parfois extérieurement semblable à un véritable droit de propriété". The exact range of their powers depended, of course, on the way in which the will was drafted. In France, as in the rest of continental Europe, the executor was a creation of legal practice; and practice could differ from *coutume* to *coutume*. Also, it must be kept in mind that *saisine*, the French equivalent of the German *Gewere*, was an extremely elusive concept – elusive, at least, for a modern observer accustomed to drawing a clear-cut distinction between a right to possession and possession itself. A person who was *ensaisiné* not only exercised actual control over the estate but was taken to have a kind of real right in it[206].

---

198 *Philippe de Beaumanoir* (n. 189) Ch. 12, nos. 391 ff.

199 For details, see *Engelmann* (n. 86) 225 ff.; for the previous period see *Auffroy* (n. 77) 569 ff.

200 *Engelmann* (n. 86) 224. The institution of an executor was the soul of the last will (*l'âme du testament*); cf. *Yves Jeanclos*, La pratique de l'execution testamentaire à Troyes, T.R. 59 (1991) 68.

201 *Pothier* (n. 184) Chapitre V, Section I, *initio*. Concerning the executor in the *pays du droit écrit*, see *de Charrin* (n. 106) 123 ff., 128 ff.

202 For details, see *Engelmann* (n. 86) 224 ff.; *Pothier* (n. 184) Chapitre V, Section I, Articles II and III; *Jeanclos*, T.R. 59 (1991) 67 ff.

203 *Philippe de Beaumanoir* (n. 189) Ch. 12, n. 391.

204 Cf. *Auffroy* (n. 77) 569 ff.; *Engelmann* (n. 86) 235; *Beck* (n. 1) 302.

205 *Engelmann* (n. 86) 235. Cf. also *Jeanclos*, T.R. 59 (1991) 74 ff. (*plenariam potestatem*).

2. *Dumoulin, Pothier* and the *code civil*

The learned authors of the later *ius commune,* however, tended to equate *saisine* with possession[207]. This was true, for instance, of *Pothier*[208]; and when he therefore stated, in his "Traité des donations testamentaires," that the power of the executor consisted, principally, in the *saisine* with which he was invested under the *coutumes*[209], he can hardly have had in mind a real right. But there was also considerable difficulty in attributing possession to the executor in view of the fact that with the death of the testator the heir had become possessor according to the rule "le mort saisit le vif"[210]. *Dumoulin* had tried to wriggle his way out of this difficulty by stating: "Haec consuetudo non negat, nec facit quin haeres sit saisitus, ut dominus: sed operatur quod executor potest ipse manum ponere, et apprehendere, non autem vendere sine haerede, et usque ad concurrentiam tantum. Et etiam executor non est verus possessor et nisi ut procurator tantum"[211]. *Pothier* put it more elegantly, and in French, but hardly more clearly[212]. The heir is the real possessor of the estate and if the executor is also possessor, he can only have that position vicariously, in the name of the heir. No longer does he succeed the deceased, he merely acts as the heir's representative. Hence, for instance, he can only sell property belonging to the estate, if the heir agrees[213]. The status of the executor was further reduced according to the *Coutume de Paris* (and a variety of other *coutumes).* They confined the executor's *saisine* to movable property. Moreover, it lasted only a year and a day from the death of the testator[214].

The draftsmen of the French civil code, ill disposed towards any interference with the rights of the intestate heirs and apprehensive of the dangers inherent in allowing a person's assets to be tied up for a long time, went even further[215]. They

206 *Werner Ogris,* Gewere, in: Handwörterbuch zur deutschen Rechtsgeschichte, vol. I, 1971, cols. 1658 ff. Cf. also, in the present context, *Engelmann* (n. 86) 47 ("La saisine était une sorte de possession juridique qui permettait aux exécuteurs testamentaires de se comporter en maîtres à l'égard des biens du de cujus sur lesquels elle portait"); and see, for the earlier period, the comprehensive analysis by *Caillemer* (n. 1) 183 ff., 317 ff., 336 ff. For Germany see, e.g., *Beseler* (n. 91) 148 f.

207 *Coing* (n. 91) 279 ff.

208 Traité de la possession, in: Oeuvres, ed. M. Dupin, vol. VIII, Paris, 1825, no. 85.

209 Chapitre V, Section I, Article II, § I.

210 Cf. *Coutume de Paris,* Art. 318; and see *Robert-Joseph Pothier,* Traité des successions, in: Oeuvres, ed. M. Dupin, vol. VII, Paris, 1825, Chapitre III, Section II for a detailed exposition.

211 *Carolus Molinaeus,* Commentarii in Consuetudines Parisienses, in: Opera quae extant omnia, vol. I, Parisiis, 1681, § XCV, nos. 10 f.

212 *Pothier* (n. 184) Chapitre V, Section I, Article II, § I.

213 *Pothier* (n. 184) Chapitre V, Section I, Article II, § IV.

214 *Pothier* (n. 184) Chapitre V, Section I, Article II, § II.

215 The French code civil maintained the rule that the testator may not appoint an heir. He may, however, institute a *légataire universel;* for details, see art. 1003 code civil; *Philippe*

were only prepared to attribute *saisine* to the executor on the strength of a specific provision to that effect in the will[216]. It covered only movables and was still restricted to a year and a day[217]. In addition, the heir might terminate the executor's *saisine* by offering him a sum sufficient to pay all legacies of movables or by proving that these legacies had already been paid[218]. Even the executor invested with *saisine*, incidentally, requires the consent of the heir, if he wishes to sell movables belonging to the estate in order to satisfy the legatees, unless the testator has specifically conferred the power of sale upon him[219]. If the testator has merely instituted an executor, without further specification, the latter is not taken to enjoy *saisine* but rather has the task of seeing to it that the testamentary dispositions are properly carried out by the heir. Apart from that, he is obliged to seal the estate if the heirs are either minors or not present and he has, in the presence of the heirs, to make an inventory of the estate[220]. Doctrinally, the French executor is traditionally regarded as a special kind of mandatary ("Les fonctions d'exécuteur ... constituent ... un mandat privé d'une nature particulière"[221]) from which it follows that no one can be forced to accept the position. The French courts have, over the past two hundred years, cautiously extended the powers of the executor[222], without however having rendered his position substantially more attractive to potential executors. Reform proposals have been submitted but not yet been implemented[223]. At present, therefore, many French testators prefer to institute a *légataire universel* to whom nothing but a small portion of the estate is left as *honorarium*[224], for then he is vested with the comprehensive *saisine* of an heir[225]. Such a *légataire universel* in effect

---

Malaurie, Cours de droit civil: Les successions, les libéralités, 1989, pp. 268 ff.; *Murad Ferid,* Frankreich, in: Murad Ferid, Karl Firsching, Peter Lichtenberger (eds.), Internationales Erbrecht, vol. II, nos. 177 ff.

216 Art. 1026; and see, e.g., *Karl Salomo Zachariä von Lingenthal,* Handbuch des Französischen Zivilrechts, vol. IV, 3rd ed., 1828, pp. 311 f.

217 Art. 1026 code civil.

218 Art. 1027 code civil. This provision also has its roots in the *droit coutumier;* see *Pothier* (n. 184) Chapitre V, Section I, Article II, § II.

219 Cf., e.g., *Malaurie* (n. 215) 256; *Ebenroth* (n. 1) no. 711.

220 Art. 1031 code civil. For further details, see *Aubry* and *Rau,* Cours de droit civil français, 5th ed., vol. XI, 1919, § 711 (pp. 422 ff.); *Malaurie* (n. 215) 255 f.

221 *Aubry/Rau* (n. 220) § 711 (p. 421); cf. also, e.g., *Zachariä* (n. 216) § 715 (pp. 308 f.); *Siebert* (n. 167) 562, 566; *Beck* (n. 1) 303; *Ferid* (n. 215) no. 195. For more modern views, see *Malaurie* (n. 215) 254.

222 For details, see *Aubry/Rau* (n. 220) § 711; *Lang* (n. 167) 22 ff., 28 ff.; *Malaurie* (n. 215) 255 ff.; *Ebenroth* (n. 1) no. 711. Most importantly, perhaps, the courts have accepted that the testator may invest the executor with *saisine* over immovable property and allow him to sell the same, provided there are no *héritiers réservatoires* (i.e. persons who may claim a legitimate portion (*légitime*)); for the historical development of which, see *John P. Dawson,* Gifts and Promises, 1980, pp. 29 ff.

223 See *Muscheler* (n. 143) 25.

224 *Muscheler* (n. 143) 25; cf. also *Beck* (n. 1) 303.

225 Unless there are *héritiers réservatoires;* see artt. 1004 ff. code civil.

has the position of an executor. Thus, it has been argued that the rules relating to executorship have to be applied *per analogiam*[226].

VII. Developments in 19th Century German Law

1. Bringing Clarity into an Obscure Institution?

In Germany, 19th century authors of the Romanist persuasion continued to deplore the lack of (Roman) sources concerning executorship[227] and they went on, predominantly, to mould the office in the image of a *procurator*/mandatary[228]. By and large, they did not devote much attention to the subject; the discussion in *Windscheid/Kipp*, for example, comprises only fifteen lines of text[229]. The *Germanisten*, on the other hand, attempted to breathe new life into the old Germanic concept of the *Salmann*[230]. But there was a fairly general agreement that the institution of executorship suffered from "a certain instability"[231]; or, as *Heimbach* put it more strongly, everything was so undeveloped, confused and disputed that one could not possibly speak of consistent and logical legal development[232]. The draftsmen of the German Civil Code were therefore faced with a challenging task: they had, as they themselves perceived it, "to bring clarity into an obscure institution"[233]. The first draft contained no fewer than twenty sections, but it was still cautious and conservative[234]. It was based on the idea of treating the executor as a legal representative of the heir[235]. Thus, for instance, the executor even had to sus-

226 See *Muscheler* (n. 143) 25.

227 Cf., e.g., *Glück/Mühlenbruch* (n. 105) 405; *Rosshirt* (n. 84) 217.

228 Cf., e.g., *Glück/Mühlenbruch* (n. 105) 416. But there were also other views; cf. *Beseler* (n. 91) 165 ff.; the overviews by *Schmitt* (n. 166) 335 ff. and in Motive, in: Benno Mugdan, Die gesammten Materialien zum Bürgerlichen Gesetzbuch für das Deutsche Reich, vol. V, 1899, p. 114; *Alfred Scholtissek*, Die letztwillige Treuhand des älteren deutschen Rechts. Die gemeinrechtlichen Theorien über die Testamentsvollstreckung. Die Rechtsstellung des Testamentsvollstreckers im BGB. – Die geschichtliche Entwicklung und ein Vergleich, Dr. iur. thesis, Breslau, 1911, pp. 19 ff.; Offergeld (n. 181) 51 ff.; cf. also the somewhat equivocal statement by *Windscheid/Kipp* (n. 94) 307 f.

229 *Windscheid/Kipp* (n. 94) § 567 (pp. 307 ff.).

230 Cf., in particular, *Beseler* (n. 91) 165 ff.; *Johann Caspar Bluntschli*, Deutsches Privatrecht, vol. II, 1854, § 201.

231 *Stobbe* (n. 70) § 308 (p. 260) ("... leidet an einer gewissen Haltlosigkeit").

232 *Heimbach sen.* (n. 94) 1027. Cf. also *Schmitt* (n. 166) 330 who commences his discussion with the words: "Kein Institut zeigt weitere Verbreitung – und größere Unklarheit im Rechtsgedanken als das des Testamentsvollstreckers" (There is no legal institution which is more widely spread, and, at the same time, more unclear in its basic legal idea, than the testamentary executor).

233 Motive, in: Mugdan (n. 228) 124.

234 §§ 1889 ff. E I

235 Cf., e.g., § 1903 I E I.

pend payment of legacies and implementation of other directions contained in the will if the heir raised an objection[236].

Not surprisingly, these provisions were harshly criticized. *Otto von Gierke*, undisputed leader of the Germanic school of legal thinking, maintained that the whole perception of the essence of testamentary executorship was misguided and that therefore the entire institution had been crippled[237]. The matter was discussed at great length in 1891 at the 21st German Lawyers Congress (*Deutscher Juristentag*). In an opinion prepared for that occasion, *Gustav Hartmann* explained that of the three elements contained in the phrase "legal representative of the heir" none was actually applicable to the executor[238]. One of the main speakers was *Otto von Gierke* who caused some amusement in the audience by pointing out, apropos the draftsmen's claim to have achieved doctrinal clarity by depriving the executor of his alien character, that in the language of the draftsmen of the first draft "legal system" always stood for "pandectist system", that "generally recognized" or "normal" meant "of Roman origin", and that the words "dark", "alien" or "abnormal" suggested "of Germanic legal origin" or "modern"[239]. There appears to have been fairly general agreement at the time that the executor had to be given an independent position in his own right[240].

These sentiments impressed the Second Commission[241]. Their members were also animated by a desire to pick up the thread of historical development. They referred, in this context, to the Germanic *Salmann* and criticized the much restricted position of the executor in the recent German territorial laws[242]. In the end, they provided the executor with the most detailed regulation, by far, found in any of the great codes (32 sections)[243] and they strengthened his role very considerably. One thing, however, they very wisely refrained from doing: they did not determine the exact "legal nature" of the executor but considered this to be a task of legal science[244].

236 § 1897 E I.

237 *Otto von Gierke*, Der Entwurf eines bürgerlichen Gesetzbuchs und das deutsche Recht, 1889, pp. 520 ff.; cf. also *idem*, in: Verhandlungen des 21. Deutschen Juristentages, vol. III, 1892, p. 224.

238 *Gustav Hartmann*, in: Verhandlungen des 21. Deutschen Juristentages, vol. I, 1890, pp. 6 ff.

239 Verhandlungen (n. 237) 227; cf. also *idem*, Der Entwurf (n. 237) 520.

240 See the discussion by *Offergeld* (n. 181) 43 ff.

241 *Offergeld* (n. 181) 45 ff.

242 Protokolle, in: Mugdan (n. 228) 659.

243 Even the Prussian Code of 1794, famous for its obsession with exhaustive regulation, down to the finest detail, for every imaginable set of facts (see generally *Franz Wieacker*, A History of Private Law in Europe, trans. *Tony Weir*, 1995, pp. 260 ff.) only has six sections dealing with the executor (§§ 557 - 562 I 12 PrALR).

244 Motive, in: Mugdan (n. 228) 114.

German legal science, of course, eagerly took up the challenge and produced a large body of literature dealing with the question[245]. The practical significance of all the theories proposed since then has turned out to be very low[246]. Predominantly, today, the executor is seen to be the holder of a private office (*Amtstheorie)*[247] conferred upon him by the testator. He exercises his functions in his own right, i.e. independently of the heir, but in the latter's interest[248]. In order fully to evaluate the position of the executor in modern German law[249], it has to be kept in mind that the law of succession is based upon the principle of universal succession[250]. Moreover, with the death of the testator, the heir acquires both ownership and possession[251]. There is no state of pendency. Nor does the heir have to declare his preparedness to enter upon the estate. Thus, German law does not recognize the necessary executor, nor any kind of *executor legitimus.* Only the testator may institute an executor[252]. The latter is not, of course, bound to accept the office[253]. If he decides to do so, however, he is bound to administer the estate and to carry out all testamentary dispositions of the testator[254]. Thus, *inter alia,* he has to distribute the legacies, to satisfy the testator's creditors and to collect the debts due to the deceased, he is entitled to take possession of the assets of the estate[255] and to dispose of them[256], and he may incur obligations on behalf of the estate in so far as

245 Cf. the references in *Heinrich Lange, Kurt Kuchinke,* Lehrbuch des Erbrechts, 4th ed., 1995, pp. 629 ff. and the discussion by *Offergeld* (n. 181) 53 ff.; cf. also the comparative discussion by *Siebert* (n. 167) 565 ff.

246 *Hans Erich Brandner,* in: Münchener Kommentar zum Bürgerlichen Gesetzbuch, vol. VI, 2nd ed., 1989, Vor § 2197, n. 5 ("The question has no practical significance"); *Lange/Kuchinke* (n. 245) 630.

247 BGHZ 25, 275 (279); BGH, NJW 1983, 40.

248 Thus, he is in the position of a fiduciary; cf. specifically BGH, *loc. cit.* (testamentary executor has "die Stellung eines Treuhänders und ist Inhaber eines privaten Amtes").

249 Concerning his (considerable!) significance in practical life, see the interesting remarks in HansOLG Hamburg, Juristische Wochenschrift 1934, 2247 and the study by *Hans G. Blechner,* Die Testamentsvollstreckung in der Praxis, Dr. iur. thesis, Marburg, 1981. The institution of executorship is generally regarded as an indispensable part of the modern German law of succession; cf. Münchener Kommentar/*Brandner* (n. 246) Vor § 2197, no. 2; *Lange/Kuchinke* (n. 245) 628 f.

250 *Theodor Kipp, Helmut Coing,* Erbrecht, 14th ed., 1990, pp. 4 ff.; *Lange/Kuchinke* (n. 245) 82 ff.

251 §§ 1922, 857 BGB.

252 For details as to what follows, see *Kipp/Coing* (n. 250) 371 ff.; *Lange/Kuchinke* (n. 245) 634 ff.; *Ebenroth* (n. 1) nos. 619 ff.; *Offergeld* (n. 181) 74 ff. The amount of legal literature devoted to the executor is enormous: cf. the references in Münchener Kommentar/*Brandner* (n. 246) Introduction; *Lange/Kuchinke* (n. 245) 680 ff.; this demonstrates the great practical importance of the executor in Germany.

253 Cf. § 2202 BGB.

254 §§ 2205, 2203 BGB.

255 § 2205, 2 BGB.

256 § 2205, 2 BGB.

this is necessary for its proper administration[257]. If there are several heirs, he has to effect a settlement and division of the estate among them[258]. He is also authorized to litigate on behalf of the estate[259]. The estate regulation by an executor is not subject to a time limit. The probate court (*Nachlaßgericht)* may, however, dismiss him from office upon application of an interested party, if a serious reason exists[260]. Concerning the relationship between executor and heir, the code refers to certain rules relating to the contract of mandate[261] without, however, entitling the heir to give directions to the executor. The executor becomes liable to the heir if, as a result of fault, he commits a breach of any of the duties imposed upon him[262]. On the other hand, he is entitled to a reasonable remuneration[263]. The code presumes that the executor is placed in charge of the entire estate. The testator is, of course, free to appoint an *executor specialis.* He may also limit the range of rights and duties in other respects[264].

2. The Long-term Administrator / Executor

All these provisions are topped, however, by another fairly sweeping innovation contained in § 2209 BGB: "The testator may give to an executor the administration of the estate without imposing upon him any other duties than the administration; he may also direct that the executor shall continue the administration after the performance of any other duties imposed upon him"[265]. This long-term administrator of the estate[266] can hardly be referred to any longer as an "executor" in any literal sense of the word. He dates from the 19th century when testators started to insert clauses in their wills by virtue of which they excluded the heir for a certain period of time (for instance, until reaching the age of majority) from any control over the estate[267]. These clauses were at first interpreted as *nuda praecepta:* as burdens (*modus)* which were primarily in the interest of the heir and as such unenforceable[268]. In the course of the second half of the 19th century, however, this attitude

257 § 2206 BGB.

258 § 2204 BGB.

259 For details, see §§ 2212 f. BGB.

260 § 2227 BGB.

261 § 2218 BGB.

262 § 2219 BGB.

263 § 2221 BGB.

264 § 2208 BGB.

265 The translation is taken from *Ian S. Forrester, Simon L. Goren and Hans-Michael Ilgen,* The German Civil Code, 1975.

266 He is the object of the monograph by *Karlheinz Muscheler,* Die Haftungsordnung der Testamentsvollstreckung, 1994.

267 *Muscheler* (n. 143) 32 ff.

268 *Muscheler* (n. 143) 33 f. (with references).

changed[269]; and it was, once again, under the influence of Germanistic doctrine[270] that the courts started to regard such dispositions as binding.

The draftsmen of the First Commission, naturally, did not welcome these developments[271] and adopted an attitude which *Otto von Gierke*, in turn, attacked as overly cautious: an idea that had fought its way through in actual practice and which the Imperial Supreme Court had solemnly recognized as conforming to the requirements of life, he argued, could not be denied entry into the new code[272]. The Second Commission took these words to heart and even went beyond what had been endorsed by the courts[273]. The testator was granted the power directly to transfer the administration to the executor rather than having to impose a burden upon the heir. Also, the executor's administrative function had now acquired a more active, wide-ranging and independent character. Only a time limit was imposed upon the administrative executor: any direction given under § 2209 BGB becomes ineffective if thirty years have elapsed from accrual of the inheritance. The testator may, however, direct that the administration shall continue until the death of the heir or of the executor[274].

All in all, therefore, the institution of a long-term administrative executor left the heir with hardly more than a *nudum ius*[275]. The "marionette of the heir"[276] had emancipated itself; it had become the "formal representative"[277] of the testator. This was about as far as one could go within a legal system which recognized the institution of an heir and the principle of universal succession, and rejected the notion of split ownership. It was a triumph for the 19th century Germanicists[278]. There is no continental legal system that recognizes a more powerful executor[279].

---

269 For details, see *Muscheler* (n. 143) 36 ff.

270 Cf., particularly, *Beseler* (n. 91) 173 (and see also 152 ff.) describing the heir as the substantive, and the executor as the formal, representative of the testator. The executor, he argued, takes over the position, as far as his range of activities is concerned, which was allotted in Roman law to the heir.

271 Cf. the discussion by *Muscheler* (n. 143) 45 ff.

272 Verhandlungen (n. 237) 229.

273 Cf. the analysis by *Muscheler* (n. 143) 47 ff., 53 ff.

274 § 2210 BGB.

275 Cf. also the evaluation by *Muscheler* (n. 143) 3, 56 f.

276 Cf. Levy, in: Verhandlungen des 21. Deutschen Juristentages, vol. III, 1892, p. 236.

277 Cf. *supra* n. 270.

278 "Der germanistische Vollstreckermythos des 19. Jahrhunderts war bis in seine extremen Konsequenzen getrieben worden": *Muscheler* (n. 143) 56.

279 The Greek executor (artt. 2017 ff. ZGB) is closely modelled on the German *Testamentsvollstrecker.* The Swiss *Willensvollstrecker,* even though only dealt with in two provisions (artt. 517 f. ZGB) also largely corresponds to the German model; he is, however, subject to a relatively strict official supervision. The Dutch *bewindvoerder* (art. 1066 BW) offers another parallel; but he may not, for example, dispose of objects belonging to the estate without the consent of the heir. Dutch law also recognizes another type of executor, the *uitvoerder van de uiterste wilsbeschikking* (artt. 1052 ff. BW) who is very closely modelled on

Nevertheless, structurally the office remains something of a *corpus alienum*[280]. This is particularly apparent if one considers the great difficulties of harmonizing the long-term administrative executorship concerning commercial enterprises, originally run by the deceased, or by a partnership of which he was a member, with the liability regime for obligations of the estate, as laid down in §§ 1967 ff. and 2058 ff. and focusing on the heir rather than the executor[281].

VIII. English Common Law

The only European country, therefore, where a congenial environment has been retained for the executor is England[282]. "The last will of English common law provides an interesting example of a legal instrument born of the meeting of the three great cultural strains of medieval Europe"[283]. England formed part of the world of a medieval common law that antedated the intellectual rediscovery of the Digest[284]. It was based on Germanic custom, Christian teaching and Roman law. It is not, therefore, surprising that we should find a pattern of development concerning dispositions *mortis causa* very similar to that in continental countries[285]. Thus, we

---

the French *executeur.* The provisions in the Belgian (artt. 1025 ff. code civil) and Spanish (art. 892 codigo civil) codes are also based on French law. The Italian *executore testamentario* (artt. 700 ff. codice civile) has emancipated himself in a number of respects from the French example; thus, he is normally entitled to *saisine* (*possessio*). The Nordic countries appear to have a system of official estate regulation which in some respects resembles the Austrian model. Cf. the comparative overviews in *Siebert* (n. 167) 561 ff.; *Lang* (n. 167) 37 ff., 82 ff., 85 ff.; *Ebenroth* (n. 1) nos. 711 ff.; *Muscheler* (n. 143) 17 ff., 68 ff.; *Offergeld* (n. 181) 194 ff.

280 Cf., e.g., Münchener Kommentar / *Brandner* (n. 246) Vor § 2197, no. 1; *Muscheler* (n. 143) 2.

281 Cf., e.g., the discussion in Münchener Kommentar / *Brandner* (n. 246) § 2205, nos. 14 ff.; *Lange / Kuchinke* (n. 245) 647 ff.; *Wolfgang Edenhofer,* in: Palandt, Bürgerliches Gesetzbuch, 55th ed., 1996, § 2205, nos. 6 ff.; and the analysis by *Muscheler* (n. 143) 285 ff.

282 For comparative discussions, see *Siebert* (n. 167) 561; *Beck* (n. 1) 304 ff.; *Lang* (n. 167) 55 ff.

283 See the conclusion in *Michael M. Sheehan's* splendid book The Will in Medieval England, 1963, p. 303.

284 On which see generally *Siems* (n. 76) *passim; Maurizio Lupoi,* Alle radici del mondo giuridico europeo, 1994.

285 For all details see, in the first place, the book by *Michael Sheehan* (n. 91) *passim.* Cf. also *Oliver Wendell Holmes,* Executors, (1895 / 96) 9 Harvard L.R. 42 ff.; *Sir Frederick Pollock, Frederic William Maitland,* The History of English Law before the Time of Edward I, 2nd ed., 1898, pp. 314 ff.; *Robert Caillemer,* The Executor in England and on the Continent, in: Select Essays in Anglo-American Legal History, vol. III, 1909, pp. 746 ff.; *Melville Madison Bigelow,* The Rise of the English Will, in: Select Essays in Anglo-American Legal History, vol. III, 1909, pp. 770 ff.; *Theodore F. T. Plucknett,* A Concise History of the Common Law, 5th ed., 1956, pp. 732 ff.; *Sir William Holdsworth,* A History of English Law, vol. III, 5th ed., 1942, pp. 534 ff.

have at first, in Anglo-Saxon times, certain irrevocable transactions *inter vivos* – among them the *donatio post obitum* (post obit gift) – by means of which these dispositions were effected[286]. We also occasionally find that use was made of a third party: the Anglo-Saxon version of the *Salmann*[287]. In the wake of the Norman conquest, the Roman will came to England in its canonical garb[288]. As on the continent, it was at first a purely spiritual instrument and was used to effect bequests *ad pias causas*. A will was not only valid without the institution of an heir, such institution was even frowned upon as an unwarranted interference with the family bonds established by God: "Solus Deus heredem facere potest, non homo" was the adage quoted by *Glanvill*[289]. As in many French coutumes, the principle came to be established that immovable property (heritage or realty) and movables (chattels) should devolve in different ways[290]. Only chattels could be disposed of in a testament[291]. We find the Church establishing jurisdiction over testamentary matters[292] and developing a requirement of probate as a prelude to any distribution of property according to the terms of the will[293]. In spite of some competition with the Royal courts[294], the Church managed to acquire, and maintain, a more extensive jurisdiction in this area than in any of the continental countries[295].

As a result, of course, the testamentary executor – "who was in so many ways the creature and darling of the ecclesiastical courts"[296] – was bound to flourish[297].

---

286 *Sheehan* (n. 91) 19 ff.; *Pollock and Maitland* (n. 285) 316 ff.

287 *Sheehan* (n. 91) 41 ff., 149; *Pollock and Maitland* (n. 285) 319; *Holdsworth* (n. 285) 564.

288 *Sheehan* (n. 91) 138 ff.; *Pollock and Maitland* (n. 285) 331 ff.; *Holdsworth* (n. 285) 535 ff.

289 The treatise on the laws and customs of England commonly called *Glanvill*, ed. G. D. G. Hall, 1965, VII, 1 (p. 71); and see *supra*, text before n. 196. Cf. also *Sheehan* (n. 91) 183 ("There was no English equivalent to the institution of an heir required by Roman civil law"); *Pollock and Maitland* (n. 285) 327 f. ("... of any institution of an heir in the Roman sense there had never been any talk in England").

290 *Sheehan* (n. 91) 266 ff.; *Pollock and Maitland* (n. 285) 325 ff.

291 For details, see *Sheehan* (n. 91) 282 ff.

292 *Sheehan* (n. 91) 163 ff.; *Pollock and Maitland* (n. 285) 332 ff.; *Caillemer* (n. 1) 673 ff.

293 *Sheehan* (n. 91) 196 ff.; *Pollock and Maitland* (n. 285) 341 ff., intimating that possibly "some slender thread of texts traversing the dark ages connects [probate] directly with the Roman process of insinuation, aperture and publication".

294 This concerned the question who was to represent the deceased in pleas of debt; cf. *Sheehan* (n. 91) 220 ff.; *Pollock and Maitland* (n. 285) 343 ff.; but see now the re-evaluation by *R. H. Helmholz*, Debt Claims and Probate Jurisdiction in Historical Perspective, (1979) 23 American Journal of Legal History 68 ff.

295 Cf., e.g., *Plucknett* (n. 285) 740; *Sheehan* (n. 91) 163 ("... it extended to lengths unknown on the Continent"); *Coing* (n. 91) 599; and see generally *Sir William Holdsworth*, A History of English Law, vol. I, 7th ed., 1956, pp. 580 ff., 625 ff.

296 *Sheehan* (n. 91) 230.

297 For details, see *Sheehan* (n. 91) 148 ff., 195 ff.; *Pollock and Maitland* (n. 285) 334 ff.; *Holdsworth* (n. 285) 563 ff.

In the course of the 13th century, he came to be seen as a representative of the deceased and was, eventually, equated with the Roman *heres*[298]. Thus, for instance, he could even keep what was left of the estate after the debts had been paid and the legacies had been carried out[299]. It was only in 1830 that this rule was abolished[300]. It was even later (in 1857) that the ecclesiastical courts finally surrendered their jurisdiction over grants of probate to the Royal courts[301]. And as a result of the Land Transfer Act of 1897 and the Administration of Estates Act of 1925 the old dualism between land and chattels was abolished, with the result that the executor was now in charge both of the testator's realty and personal property. Apart from that, however, the legal position of the executor has changed remarkably little over the centuries. Most importantly perhaps, in matters of personal property he did not have to give way to the heir. Even today[302], the person who receives the remainder of the estate is formally only a residuary legatee. It is the executor who acts as the personal representative of the deceased and upon whom, therefore, the estate devolves[303]. The executor thus succeeds to the position of the testator, although he must act in the interests of the beneficiaries. He is generally

298 "It was the executor who made the English will the flexible and effective instrument it was. The testator's desire, as revealed in surviving documents, and the obvious intention of the ecclesiastical courts, was to make the executor's powers as much as possible like those of the person for whom he acted. ... [Thus,] the executor tended more and more to become a projection after death of the legal personality of the deceased": *Sheehan* (n. 91) 215. See also *Caillemer* (n. 1) 763; *Pollock and Maitland* (n. 285) 348; *Holdsworth* (n. 285) referring to *Lyndwood's* treatise ("Executores universales, qui loco haeredis sunt") and to *Christopher St. German's* Doctor and Student ("The heir which in the laws of England is called an executor"). For the historical development, see *Holdsworth* 572 ff.

299 Cf. *Caillemer* (n. 1) 764 ff.; see also, generally, *idem* (n. 1) 478 ff.

300 Cf., e.g., *Beck* (n. 1) 307.

301 See *Holdsworth* (n. 295) 629 f. Their powers over the administration of estates of deceased persons had already been absorbed by the court of Chancery at a much earlier stage.

302 For all details, see Williams, Mortimer and Sunnucks on Executors, Administrators and Probate by *J. H. G. Sunnucks, J. G. Ross Martyn, K. M. Garnett,* 1993; *Roger Kerridge,* The Law of Succession, 10th ed., 1996, pp. 294 ff.; *Dieter Henrich,* Großbritannien, in: Murad Ferid, Karl Firsching, Peter Lichtenberger (eds.), Internationales Erbrecht, vol. III, nos. 97 sqq. On the testamentary trust as the English equivalent to the German long-term administrator / executor, see *Muscheler* (n. 143) 60 ff.

303 The English model of estate regulation has been successful throughout the common law world. The English executor has even supplanted the Roman-Dutch system (revolving around the heir) in South Africa. But the South African legislation has "in what seems to be excessive beaurocratic zeal ... gone much further in the control and surveillance of the executor (or personal representative) than has the English law": *Ben Beinart,* The English Legal Contribution in South Africa: The Interaction of Civil Law and Common Law, 1981 Acta Juridica 20; and see the more detailed historical exposition in *Beinart,* 1960 Acta Juridica 223 ff.; *Van Zyl* (n. 144) 59 ff. Closely related is the reception of the English law of trusts; on which see *Tony Honoré,* Trust, in: Reinhard Zimmermann, Daniel Visser (eds.), Southern Cross: Civil Law and Common Law in South Africa, 1996, pp. 849 ff. Scots law has developed independently from English law but, as far as the administration of estates and the position of the executor is concerned, it has arrived at very similar principles; cf., for an historical

regarded as a trustee[304]. Or, in the learned language of the Middle Ages: he is considered to be *heres fiduciarius.*

analysis, *A. E. Anton,* Medieval Scottish Executors and the Courts Spriritual, (1955) 67 Juridical Review 129 ff.; and see *W. M. Gloag, R. Candlish Henderson,* The Law of Scotland, 10th ed., 1995, pp. 803 ff.; *Henrich* (n. 302) 266 ff.

304 The law of trusts started to be applied to executors when the jurisdiction over the administration of estates shifted to the court of Chancery; see *Sir William Holdsworth,* A History of English Law, vol. IV, 3rd ed., 1945, p. 476; *idem,* vol. V, 3rd ed., 1945, pp. 316 ff. On the compatibility of the trust-concept with last wills of the continental type, see *Maurizio Lupoi,* Trusts, 1997, pp. 581 ff.; for the similarities between executors and trustees, see the list on pp. 588 - 590.

ROBERT FEENSTRA

Foundations in Continental Law since the 12th Century: The Legal Person Concept and Trust-like Devices

In a volume of comparative studies on the history of the concepts of trust and *Treuhand* some attention should be paid to other concepts by which the purposes of trust and *Treuhand* can and have been achieved. Among these an important part is played by the foundation concept. It is generally agreed that in civil law countries foundations are broadly equivalent to at least public or charitable trusts of the common law. The foundation concept is common to most of the civil law countries; one might therefore suppose that it stems from Roman law. In a certain sense it does, but it seems that modern writers do not fully agree as to the extent and the character of the influence of Roman law on the concept of the foundation; there is, moreover, some confusion as to the definition of the foundation concept and to its history both in the Middle Ages and in modern times. In discussing some of these questions I would like to show to what extent the foundation concept – or perhaps better: *a* foundation concept – has been employed from the twelfth to the twentieth century[1].

---

[1] The starting point of this contribution is an article by the author, L'histoire des fondations, à propos de quelques études récentes (review article on *H. R. Hagemann,* Die Stellung der piae causae nach justinianischem Recht [1953], *C. P. Joubert,* Die Stigting in die Romeins-Hollandse Reg en in die Suid-Afrikaanse Reg [1951] and *D. Pleimes,* Irrwege der Dogmatik im Stiftungsrecht [1954]), T.R. 24 (1956) 381 ff. Pages 381 - 382 and 408 - 433 of this article, concerning the Middle Ages, have been reprinted (with addenda) in my Le droit savant au moyen âge et sa vulgarisation, London, 1986, as Nr. I. This article gives full documentation up to 1956; for a much shorter preliminary study see *infra* n. 9. An English survey was given in a paper read at various universities and finally published (without documentation) under the title, The development of the concept of foundation in Continental law, 1971 Acta Juridica 123 ff.; the text of this paper has been used for parts of the present contribution.

Since 1956 many studies have appeared on the history of foundations after 1100 and on the origins of the legal person concept. Part of them deal with special aspects of my 1956 article and will be mentioned in the course of the present contribution; I refer in particular to n. 33 *infra* for studies which take the doctrines of *Innocent IV* as their starting point. Among the remaining studies of a more general character I can mention here: *H. Liermann,* Handbuch des Stiftungsrechts, I: Geschichte, 1963; *P. C. Timbal,* La vie juridique des personnes morales ecclésiastiques en France aux XIIIe et XIVe siècles, in: Etudes d'histoire du droit canonique dédiées à Gabriel Le Bras II, Paris, 1965, pp. 1425 ff.; *P. Michaud-Quantin,* Universitas: Expressions du mouvement communautaire dans le moyen âge latin (L'Eglise et l'Etat au moyen âge, 13), Paris, 1970; *H. Coing,* Europäisches Privatrecht I, 1985, pp. 267 f., 596 f.; II, 1989, pp. 349 ff., 612 (cited as *Coing,* EP I and II); *idem,* § 5 (Geschichte) in: W. Seifart (ed.),

I. Different Foundation Concepts

In fact there is not one foundation concept in the history of Continental law. The predominant concept today – which some authors call the concept of a "real" or "proper" foundation – is that a foundation is a species of the legal or juristic person. A "legal person" is the antithesis of a "natural person", defined as a human being having capacity to bear rights and duties. The "legal person" is an "artificial person" on which the law confers a capacity to bear rights and duties. The extension is necessary because not all human affairs can be satisfactorily handled in terms of the rights and duties of individual human beings. This is particularly true when these rights and duties belong to a group of human beings, as to a corporation. Corporations as legal persons are of course known to the common law as well as to the civil law. But this seems to be the only type of legal person which the common law recognizes, whereas most civil law systems admit, alongside the corporation, another type of legal person, namely the foundation. In the foundation there is no well-defined group of human beings to which rights and duties belong; it is an aggregate of assets devoted to a particular purpose and provided with an organization of administrators to give effect to this purpose. In this arrangement some human beings are administrators and others are beneficiaries of the assets, but it is not they who form the corporation (not even two distinct corporations).

Since legal personality is created by law in the case of corporations, there is no reason – it is argued – why the law should not also confer legal personality in cases where there is no corporation but only an aggregate of funds devoted to a particular purpose. The property which has been set aside belongs neither to the administrators nor to the persons who benefit from the foundation; it belongs to the foundation itself, seen as an artificial, a juristic person.

Apart from this concept of a "real" or "proper" foundation there are situations in which the term foundation (German: *Stiftung,* French: *fondation)* is used in a much looser sense, viz. in cases where an aggregate of assets has been set aside and ear-

---

Handbuch des Stiftungsrechts, 1987, pp. 51 ff. (cited as *Coing,* Geschichte); *R. Schulze,* Historischer Hintergrund des Stiftungsrechts, in: Entwicklungstendenzen im Stiftungsrecht, Bericht über ein Symposion vom 12. bis 14. 2. 1987, no year, pp. 8 ff. (cited as *Schulze,* Hintergrund); *idem,* Stiftungsrecht, in: Handwörterbuch zur deutschen Rechtsgeschichte IV, 1990, cols. 1980 ff. (cited as *Schulze,* Stiftungsrecht); *M. Borgolte,* Die Stiftungen des Mittelalters in rechts- und sozialhistorischer Sicht, ZSS (KA) 74 (1988) 71 ff.; *I. Birocchi,* Persona giuridica nel diritto medioevale e moderno, in: Digesto, IV Edizione, vol. XIII, Sezione civile, 1996, pp. 407 ff.

Two studies which have not been accessible to me would seem of some general interest. One dates already from before my 1956 article: *A. d'Emilia,* Per una comparazione fra le "Piae Causae" nel diritto canonico, il "Charitable Trust" nel diritto inglese e il "Waqf-Khairi" nel diritto musulmano, in: Atti del primo convegno nazionale di studi giuridico-comparativi (Istituto italiano di studi legislativi), Roma, 1953, pp. 187 ff.. The other study is: *P. G. Caron,* Persona giuridica, ufficio ed organo nel diritto canonico, Annali della Facoltà giuridica dell'Università degli studi di Camerino 27 (1961) 221 ff.

marked for definite purposes, irrespective of the question "who owns that property?"[2]. In this way there can be a foundation not only where the law uses the legal person device, but also where other methods are employed to handle the question of ownership of the funds. These methods generally do not differ in essence from the English trust: title to the property is attributed to administrators or to a corporation whose agents the administrators are. These individuals or the corporation are only fiduciary owners: they are bound to administer the property on behalf of other persons or for the purposes of the foundation. In comparison with the English trust there is only one difference, namely that in the English trust there is dual ownership, the administrator is legal owner, the beneficiary is equitable owner of the trust property; in the continental fiduciary relationship the beneficiary has no ownership but only a personal right. This difference is not essential from a historical point of view: the exclusion of dual ownership has not always been a part of Continental law[3]. The essential point is that in both systems the administrators or the corporation own the assets merely *qua* administrators; theirs is a fettered ownership, as some authors put it. As to this looser foundation concept in Continental countries one could legitimately say that it is based on a "trust-like device"[4]. The general predominance of the "legal person concept", however, has led some Continental jurists to speak of "improper" or "dependent" foundations (German: *unselbständige Stiftungen).*

This discussion of modern terminology should help us in studying the history of foundations in Continental law[5]. We shall have to see whether the distinction between "proper" and "improper" foundations is as deeply rooted in Continental law as it might seem after our examination of the modern terminology. We must trace not simply the development of the foundation concept in its predominant modern meaning as a distinct species of the juristic person, but also look for other juridical devices resembling "improper" foundations.

II. Some Remarks on Developments before the 12th Century

Our starting point will be the twelfth century. We cannot, however, completely neglect some earlier developments[6], although in the present volume they will be discussed mainly by other members of our group[7]. Modern civil law is based on

---

2 See the citations and references in *Feenstra* (n. 1) 388, nn. 16 and 17.

3 See *infra*, at n. 71.

4 In my 1956 article I have used the terms "l'idée du trust" and "la construction du trust"; see the explanations in *Feenstra* (n. 1) 389, nn. 19 and 20.

5 For some further remarks on the importance of the distinction between "trust-like device" and "legal person concept" see *Feenstra* (n. 1) 389, n. 20.

6 In 1956 I paid some attention to the pre-1100 period because it was dealt with by *Joubert;* see *Feenstra* (n. 1) 401 - 407.

7 See, in particular, the contributions by *David Johnston* and *Harald Siems* in this volume.

Roman law and the texts of the Justinianic codification were largely used by the medieval jurists, civilists as well as canonists. The latter may also have been inspired by developments in the ecclesiastical institutions before the twelfth century[8].

Classical texts in the Digest dealing with foundations are not numerous[9]. Much more is to be found in the inscriptions of this period. They have been examined by many scholars, but most of these scholars, at least of the older generation, held some prejudices as to the legal forms which were employed in these inscriptions. *Eberhard Bruck*[10], however, has rightly emphasized that we should speak of foundations not only where corporations like *collegia* or *municipia* are appointed as administrators of funds devoted to particular purposes, but also where human beings are chosen as administrators and / or beneficiaries. The devices may seem very rudimentary to modern eyes, but they are nevertheless not essentially different from the trust-like device of "improper foundations". It is true that the classical Roman jurists did not pay much attention to these foundations, which were often devoted to very personal purposes such as, for instance, the worship of the dead by holding an annual repast on his grave. But there are in fact some cases of major importance discussed in the Digest: in them, the Roman jurists did not use the concept of *fiducia* – as some modern Continental writers would perhaps expect – but they generally kept the discussion within the limits of legacy and *fideicommissum.* In many of these cases a charge is laid on a corporation, usually a town. In one text, D. 33, 1, 20, 1, *Scaevola* seems to imply that a *templum* could be the subject of rights, but these words should perhaps be considered as a gloss[11].

---

8 Cf. *Feenstra* (n. 1) 406 - 407, where I relied probably too much on S. *Reicke,* Stiftungsbegriff and Stiftungsrecht im Mittelalter, ZSS (GA) 53 (1933) 247 ff.; see *Schulze,* Hintergrund (n. 1) 12 *contra* the theories of *Stutz, Reicke* and *Liermann,* and cf. *Landau* (*infra* n. 32) 87 f.

9 For foundations in the Roman law see *Feenstra* (n. 1) 392 ff., mainly based on *H. R. Hagemann* (n. 1), *P. Duff,* Personality in Roman Private law, Cambridge, 1938, and *B. Eliachevitz,* La personnalité juridique en droit privé romain, Paris, 1942. Cf., also, *Feenstra,* Le concept de fondation du droit romain classique jusqu'à nos jours: théorie et pratique, Revue internationale des droits de l'Antiquité, 3e série, 3 (1956) 245 ff., a preliminary study for my 1956 article. For more recent studies on the subject see, in particular, *D. Johnston,* The Roman Law of Trusts, Oxford, 1988, with further references. Not accessible to me was: *F. Fabbrini,* La personalità giuridica degli enti di assistenza (detti "piae causae") in diritto romano, in: La persona giuridica collegiale in diritto romano e canonico, Atti del III Colloquio (Roma 24 - 26 aprile 1980) "Diritto romano – diritto canonico" (collectio "Utrumque ius"), Città del Vaticano, 1990, pp. 57 ff.

10 *E. F. Bruck,* Die Stiftungen für die Toten in Recht, Religion und politischem Denken der Römer, in: *idem,* Über römisches Recht im Rahmen der Kulturgeschichte, 1954, 72 ff., in particular 76.

11 See *Feenstra* (n. 1) 396 and n. 33 (= Feenstra [n. 9] 253 - 254) where I was more explicit in saying that it was a post-classical gloss. Cf., however, my forthcoming article, D. 33, 1, 20, 1 (*Scaevola* 18 dig.) revisited, in a Festschrift for Alan Watson (title as yet unknown).

In post-classical times there are signs of important changes as a result of the recognition of Christianity by Constantine. These changes have two aspects which might bear on our discussion of the foundation concept. In the first place there is the question of the Church's legal position. Before Constantine the Church was organized, for practical purposes, in a number of congregations which from the official point of view would be considered as *collegia illicita.* These *collegia,* these corporations, owned the church buildings, etc. By the Edict of Milan of 313, all this property, as far as it had fallen into the hands of the persecutors, was restored to the *corpus Christianorum,* itself a very obscure legal term[12]. It may be that after Constantine and even in the time of Justinian local churches were spoken of as *collegia,* or *corpora,* but the vague terminology of the Edict of Milan foreshadowed a changing conception of Church organisation. In actual practice church property was not administered by all the members of a local church, as it would have been in the case of an ordinary corporation; it was the bishop who exercised effective control, and each diocese was modelled not on the old colleges but on the Empire. Generally the texts do not go so far as to recognize the bishops as fiduciary owners of the Church property; they prefer to speak of this property as belonging to an *ecclesia,* to a *monasterium,* etc., using more or less abstract notions. In doing so they can be said to have paved the way for the concept of a legal person which is not a corporation, i.e. for the modern concept of the "proper foundation". There must be no misunderstanding of this formula, however: the Romans did not know the abstract concept "legal person". *Patrick Duff* has put this in an excellent way[13]: "They knew several kinds of what we call juristic persons. They allowed them to exercise all the rights which make up what we call personality. But they never theorised about them, they never discussed the nature and origin of a right-and-duty-bearing unit." If this is true, the "paving the way for the foundation concept" must be seen as a very modest beginning. But in my opinion *Duff* has rather underestimated this aspect, not only where he is discussing the Church's legal position – our first point – but especially where he is dealing with the charitable foundations – the second point which we now must examine.

By charitable foundations *Duff* understands establishments and funds "devoted to the eternal welfare of the founder and the temporal good of the sick and needy"[14]. Most of them fall under the generic name of *venerabiles domus;* they include the *xenodochium,* the house for the stranger, the *ptochotrophium,* for the poor, the *nosocomium,* for the sick, the *orphanotrophium,* for the orphans, etc. For these "houses" the problems are not fundamentally different from those of churches, monasteries, etc., with which they are often put on the same level. But besides these "houses" other charities are found in Byzantium: special funds are devoted to the relief of the poor in general and to the redemption of captives. In

---

12 *Feenstra* (n. 1) 397 f., mainly based on *Eliachevitz* (n. 9) 339.

13 *Duff* (n. 9) 203.

14 *Duff* (n. 9) 177.

modern books they are often called *piae causae;* this term occurs in the *Corpus iuris civilis,* but as *Duff* has rightly pointed out[15], it can always be translated as "pious motives" or something similar. For those types of charitable foundations where there is no visible substratum like a "house", the texts certainly do not give any support to the concept of a foundation as a legal person; when reading the not very clear terminology of the *Corpus iuris civilis* one is reminded much more of what I have called the trust-like device, the continental fiduciary ownership. So far *Duff* is certainly right and the reluctance of some Continental Romanists to recognize this simple fact certainly has to be explained as doctrinal prejudice. But is it not a similar prejudice when *Duff* sees in the texts on foundations where there is a visible substratum, the *venerabiles domus,* only a trust-like device and is reluctant to draw any legal deductions at all from Justinian's language where property is given to such a *venerabilis domus?* It may be that German scholars have been wrong in saying that the position of these *venerabiles domus* was essentially that of a German *Stiftung;* it may also be that the personification of such a building "fits the language of laymen in every age and clime"[16]. But this does not mean that Justinian's text speaks simply the language of a layman and that in these cases the modern foundation concept was any further away from its mind than the modern trust concept. There is a definite contrast between the terminology used for funds devoted to the relief of the poor or for the redemption of captives and the words used in the case of *venerabiles domus.*

III. Medieval Romanists and Canonists

This brings us to the main part of this paper, which has first to deal with the medieval interpreters of the *Corpus iuris civilis.* They gradually developed the idea of personification of buildings and the like into a juristic concept. Such a development would have been impossible had the Justinian texts not given some support to these views. These interpreters generally had an excellent grasp of the implications of the texts. Their thought was not poisoned by modern German ideas about *Stiftungen.* It may be that they also had some practical reasons for thinking this way, but expediency alone cannot account for the stress they laid on the *persona* concept.

We may start with a famous controversy mentioned in the Accursian Gloss, which leads back to a very early and not well-known representative of the School of the Glossators, in whose opinion some modern authors have seen a prefiguration of the distinction between foundations and corporations: *Moses,* Archbishop of Ravenna, who died in 1154[17]. He probably taught in Bologna[18] before becoming

---

15 *Duff* (n. 9) 179.

16 *Duff* (n. 9) 197.

17 Before becoming Archbishop of Ravenna he had been a canon and archdeacon of Vercelli, see *Cortese* (*infra* n. 18) 118.

archbishop in 1144. We have reports of an opinion of his – which may have been presented in a disputation – on the following question. A monastery had been abandoned by all the monks: is the property belonging to this monastery *res nullius* which could be claimed by the papal fiscus? *Moses* answered in the negative: the property is not *res nullius* but is possessed by the walls of the monastery. This opinion of *Moses* has been transmitted to us in various forms[19], the most accessible being the Accursian Gloss on the *lex Sicut municipium* (D. 3, 4, 7)[20]. In this text, which has mainly been taken from *Azo*[21], *Accursius* has added that according to *Moses* the walls could be said to possess even when the *collegium* – i.e. the monastery – is still functioning (*durante collegio)*[22]. *Azo* and *Accursius* at first seem to reject completely *Moses*' idea and to prefer the opinion of *Johannes Bassianus,* that if others install themselves in the buildings they should be considered by a fiction to have been the owners since the departure of the old monks. But at the conclusion of their gloss *Azo* and *Accursius* make concessions to *Moses*: various texts use the term *ecclesia* for a *locus* surrounded by walls and elsewhere an *ecclesia* is

18 This has been established by various authors. The most recent survey, with many valuable new elements, is by *E. Cortese,* Per la storia di una teoria dell'arcivescovo Mosé di Ravenna (m. 1154) sulla proprietà ecclesiastica, in: Proceedings of the Fifth International Congress of Medieval Canon Law, Salamanca, 21 - 25 September 1976 (Monumenta iuris canonici, Series C: Subsidia, 6), Città del Vaticano, 1980, pp. 117 ff., 119; cf. the addenda to my 1956 article in Le droit savant (n. 1) 1 - 2. What *Michaud-Quantin* (n. 1) 214 and 289 says on *Moses* is criticized by *Cortese* 123.

19 Apart from the Accursian Gloss (*infra* n. 20) and a passage in *Azo's* Summa Codicis (see *Feenstra* (n. 1) 409 n. 76) *Moses'* opinion is reported in a *quaestio* of *Johannes Bassianus;* see *E. Seckel,* ed. *E. Genzmer,* Die Quaestiones Vindobonenses des Johannes Bassianus, ZSS (RA) 55 (1935) 338 ff., 340 - 341, 343; cf., also, *Cortese* (n. 18) 119, mentioning verifications in two other manuscripts by *G. Fransen.* This text reveals the name of *Moses'* opponent, *Gualfredus,* to whose opinion *Johannes Bassianus* subscribes.

20 I quote the gloss *Nomen universitatis* on D. 3, 4, 7, 2 from the Venice 1488 edition, reprinted in Corpus glossatorum iuris civilis VII, Augustae Taurinorum 1969: "... Item quid si nullus omnino remansit? Respondit Ioannes solutum esse collegium et res in nullius bonis sint, sicut et hereditarie. Sed tamen si postea auctoritate domini pape, vel eius ad quem spectat cura eiusdem collegii, instituatur aliquis in eodem collegio, iuris artificio fingitur istius fuisse ut [D. 1, 8, 1 pr., D. 50, 17, 193 et D. 50, 17, 138], licet quidam archiepiscopus Moyses ipsos parietes possidere dixerit etiam durante collegio, quod durissimum est dicere et contra legem videtur ut [D. 47, 4, 1, 15]. Verum tamen id esse videtur ut nullo modo dicantur esse ullius, scilicet ab eo tempore quo solutum est collegium, sed ipso iure sint fisco vel pape quesita ut [D. 39, 4, 14, D. 49, 14, 1, 1 et D. 49, 14, 34]. Et hoc quantum ad dominium; secus quantum ad possessionem, ut [D. 41, 2, 23]. Posset tamen pro Moyse allegari quod plerumque dicitur ecclesia ipse locus parietibus circumdatus et consecratus; et alias dicitur ecclesia ius habere et possidere et vendicare ut [C. 1, 2, 14, 2 et 9]. Unde videtur quod talis locus sive parietes possideant etiam durante collegio et vendicent per prelatos, tanquam quivis privatus per procuratorem vel colonum".

21 *Feenstra* (n. 1) 409, n. 76 has to be corrected as indicated in Le droit savant (n. 1), addenda 2: the whole text appears already in the *apparatus* of *Azo,* except for "etiam durante collegio" (twice), added by *Accursius.* The whole passage in *Feenstra* (n. 1) 410 - 411 has also to be adapted as to the negative judgment on *Moses.*

22 See *supra* n. 21.

said to have rights; such a *locus* or its walls can exercise these rights through the clerks as *procuratores*. This opinion as well as the original opinion of *Moses* could, although in an anachronistic way, be seen as a prefiguration of the foundation concept. Apparently this was done explicitly[23] for the first time in 1907 by an Italian legal historian, *Francesco Schupfer*[24]. A South African author, *C. P. Joubert,* went much further. In his Leyden doctoral thesis of 1951 he wrote that *Archbishop Moses* "ploughed a lonely furrow in the dim twilight of the twelfth century by endeavouring to attribute legal personality to the *ecclesia materialis*" and "in all fairness, might justly be styled the father of the notion of the foundation"[25].

I am still inclined – as I was fourty years ago – to reject such anachronistic interpretations, but I would refrain from adding – as I did in 1971 – that archbishop *Moses*' effort was not undeservedly ignored by later interpreters. In 1980 *Ennio Cortese* showed that several authors lent credence to *Moses*' opinion, in the twelfth century as well as in later times[26]. It was even still cited in the opinion of a Neapolitan court in 1810, but this was not in any connection with churches or monasteries: it concerned the so-called *usi civici* for inhabitants of villages who had been forced to abandon their homes by war or other calamities[27].

Apart from this famous *locus* in the Accursian Gloss referring to *Archbishop Moses,* there are other passages to be found in the works of the Glossators in which one might see a prefiguration of the foundation conceived as legal person[28]. It would, however, seem that it was in fact the Canonists who took the decisive steps in what a Belgian author, *Pierre Gillet,* in 1927 called "la marche vers la personnification"[29]. It is in an also famous and much discussed passage in the work of a canonist that, for the first time[30], the term *persona* appears as keyword in a discus-

23 Implicitly it had already been done by *F. Ruffini,* La classificazione delle persone giuridiche in Sinibaldo dei Fieschi (Innocenzo IV) ed in Federico Carlo di Savigny, in: Studi[i] in onore di Francesco Schupfer II, Torino, 1898, pp. 313 ff. (reprinted in: *idem,* Scritti giuridici minori, II: Scritti giuridici varii, Milano, 1936, pp. 3 ff.), 321 (=11).

24 *F. Schupfer,* Il diritto privato dei popoli germanici con speciale riguardo all'Italia, I: Le persone, la famiglia, Città di Castello etc., 1907, p. 164.

25 *Joubert* (n. 1) 228 (in the English summary of his book, which is written in Afrikaans).

26 *Cortese* (n. 18) 122 - 130; he mentions *inter alios* the names of *Aldricus* and *Guillaume de Cunh. Aldricus* is cited in this context by *Huguccio;* see *W. P. Müller,* Huguccio, The life, works, and thought of a twelfth-century jurist (Studies in medieval and early modern canon law, 3), Washington D.C., 1994, p. 132, n. 39. *Huguccio* himself did not follow *Moses,* see a quotation from *Gillet* (*infra* n. 29) in *Feenstra* (n. 1) 411, n. 78a.

27 *Cortese* (n. 18) 133 - 136; in this context he also mentions (pp. 136 ff.) a decision of the Corte di Cassazione of 13 October 1953.

28 See *Feenstra* (n. 1) 411, n. 78.

29 *P. Gillet,* La personnalité juridique en droit canonique (Universitas Catholica Lovaniensis, Dissertationes ad gradum in facultate theologica, series II, tom. 18), Malines, 1927, p. 103. On the importance of *Gillet's* work, which "in der deutschen Forschung kaum die gebührende Beachtung gefunden hat", see *Landau* (*infra* n. 33) 87 f.; cf., also, *Feenstra* (n. 1) 411, n. 78a and 414 f.

sion of the juridical character of what we now call corporations and foundations: *Sinibaldus Fliscus,* more generally known as *Pope Innocent IV* (1243 - 1254), in his commentary on the Decretals, used the argument "cum collegium in causa universitatis fingatur una persona" ("where a *collegium* in matters concerning the *universitas* is treated as one person")[31].

Otto Gierke[32], and many others after him, have seen in these words an adumbration of the so-called "fiction theory" of the legal person: they interpret the text as if *Innocent* had spoken of the *collegium* as a *persona ficta,* a fictitious person, a person who did not exist in reality but did exist only in the contemplation of the law. Now this is certainly a misinterpretation of the text[33]. *Innocent* is stressing the word *una: una persona fingatur* is something quite different from *persona fingatur.* These words *una persona* have been taken from a constitution in Justinian's Code to which *Innocent* refers immediately after the passage cited. In this constitution *una persona* means "one human being" and is opposed to *corpus vel vicus vel alia universitas. Innocent* says this in the special case he is dealing with: the oath of an

30 Another interesting text in which the term *persona* appears as a keyword is a gloss on Brachylogus 2, 11, 1, but this text cannot be dated with certainty as earlier than the commentary of *Innocentius IV.* The text of this gloss is given in *Feenstra* (n. 1) 402: "Id est venerabiles domus vel fiscus personae dicuntur quia vicem personae in acquisitionibus tenent, sicut de hereditate dictum est". See, for commentary, *Feenstra* 402 ff., 412 n. 79 (cf. Le droit savant (n. 1), addenda 2) and 428: the gloss could have had its origins at the Orléans Law School in the middle of the 13th century.

31 *Innocentius* on X 2, 20, 57 (= VI 2, 10, 2), *verbis "in animas".* For a full quotation of the text and for commentary, see *Feenstra* (n. 1) 415 ff.

32 *O. Gierke,* Das deutsche Genossenschaftsrecht III, 1881 (reprint 1954), especially pp. 279 f.; cf. *Feenstra* (n. 1) 412 f. For *Gierke* and his theories, see the recent study of *P. Landau,* Otto Gierke und das kanonische Recht, in: J. Rückert und D. Willoweit (eds.), Die Deutsche Rechtsgeschichte in der NS-Zeit, ihre Vorgeschichte und ihre Nachwirkungen (Beiträge zur Rechtsgeschichte des 20. Jahrhunderts 12), 1995, pp. 77 f., with many references to earlier literature.

33 See *Feenstra* (n. 1) 414 ff., with references to literature up to 1956. Among more recent studies I may mention in particular *M. J. Rodriguez,* Innocent IV and the element of fiction in juristic personalities, (1962) 22 The Jurist 287 ff. (with some criticism of my 1956 study at 312); *S. Panizo Orallo,* Persona jurídica y ficción, Estudio de la obra de Sinibaldo Fieschi (Inocencio IV), Pamplona, 1975 (referring often to my 1956 study, also for the opinions of the professors of the Orléans Law School); *F. Todescan,* Diritto e realtà, Storia e teoria della *fictio iuris* (Pubblicazioni della Facoltà di giurisprudenza dell'Università di Padova, 81) Padova, 1979, pp. 89 - 102 (summarized in § 2 of his article, Dalla "persona ficta" alla "persona moralis": Individualismo e matematismo nelle teorie della persona giuridica del sec. XVII, Quaderni fiorentini per la storia del pensiero giuridico moderno 11 / 12 (1982 / 1983) 59 ff., 62 - 65); *Vera Bolgár,* The fiction of the corporate fiction, from Pope Innocent IV to the Pinto Case, in: R.H. Graveson *et al.* (eds.), Festschrift für Imre Zajtay, Tübingen, 1982, pp. 67 ff.; *Birocchi* (n. 1) 411 ff. (with further references, *inter alia,* to studies by *Adriana Campitelli* (1988) and *F. Belvisi* (1993). Not very helpful is a new study by *A. Rota,* La persona giuridica collettiva nella concezione di Sinibaldo de' Fieschi (Papa Innocenzo IV), Archivio storico sardo di Sassari 3, 1977, 5 ff. (For an earlier study by Rota on the subject, see *Feenstra* (n. 1) 381, n. 1.). I have not been able to check whether the study of *Caron* (n. 1) contains new material on *Innocent.*

abbot and of a prior on behalf of all the monks. The *collegium* (viz. the monastery) is not to be treated as *corpus vel vicus vel alia universitas* but should be considered by fiction as *una persona,* one human being. This of course is a very special and limited ruling, one which should not be generalized. In this respect *Gierke* has been rightly criticized by more recent authors, although these authors do not seem to have fully understood the meaning of *una persona* in connection with the constitution in Justinian's Code. However, the fact remains that *Innocent* used the words *persona* and *fingere*[34] in a situation where modern Continental scholars would have applied the legal person concept.

There is another passage in *Innocent's* commentary[35] in which he seems to be very near to the concept of the legal *persona:* for the statement that excommunication cannot be used as a sanction against a *universitas* because such a *universitas* is incapable of doing wrong *(delinquere) Innocent* argues that *universitates* such as a chapter or a people and the like are *nomina iuris et non personarum*[36]. Here again *Gierke* and others have seen an adumbration of the "fiction theory". However, *Gierke* was forced to concede that in practice most Canonists treated a *universitas* as capable of doing wrong and that *Innocent* himself in an immediately following passage – beginning with *Fatemur tamen* – considered the possibility of *maleficium* being committed by the *rectores universitatis* or other representatives, for which the *universitas* was to be punished by the spiritual[37] censures of suspension and interdict as well as by the temporal censure of a pecuniary fine; only the *pena capitalis vel mortis vel relegationis* could not[38] be inflicted when criminal procedure was instituted against the *universitas,* but this capital punishment was to be commuted into a pecuniary fine. It would seem that the argument of the fictitious character of a *universitas* was only invented by *Innocent* to justify *a posteriori* a concrete decision in a decretal he had issued himself shortly before. Nevertheless the use of this argument proves that *Innocent* had a tendency towards the legal person device.

---

34 Cf. *Todescan* (n. 33) 97 f., who says that the "interpretazione 'finzionalistica' della persona giuridica" by *Sinibaldo dei Fieschi* was taken over by *Pope John XXII* in the controversy about the poverty of the Franciscan Order and that this point was heavily criticized by *Ockham.*

35 *Innocentius* on X 5, 39, 53, *verbis "in consiliarios".* For a full quotation of the text and for commentary, see *Feenstra* (n. 1) 417 ff.

36 Cf. *Rodriguez* (n. 33) 300. It is curious that very little about *Innocent's* opinion is to be found in *M. A. Zurowski,* Die Haftung der Korporation für Delikte ihrer Vorgesetzten nach der Lehre der Dekretalisten, ZSS (KA) 68 (1982) 470 ff.

37 Not "special" as is found in some 16th century editions of *Innocent's* commentary; see *Feenstra* (n. 1) 421, n. 139. This error seems to occur also in the Venice 1570 edition, which is quoted by *Rodriguez* (n. 33) 299 (cf. 292, n. 15).

38 For the omission of "non" in a number of 16th century editions of *Innocent's* commentary, see *Feenstra* (n. 1) 421, n. 137 (cf. also Le droit savant (n. 1), addenda 3, and p. 418, n. 20). Here also the Venice 1570 edition (cf. *supra* n. 37) is wrong; *Rodriguez* (n. 33) 301 would seem to have paid no attention to my 1956 article on this point when he neglects the insertion of "non" and says that *Innocent* contradicted himself.

The two texts of *Innocent* hitherto cited deal mainly with *collegia,* corporations; the problems raised by these texts rather concern the legal person concept in general than the foundation concept. But there is another text of *Innocent*[39] which directly concerns the foundation: speaking of prebends and other church offices (*prebendae, dignitates, administrationes), Innocent* puts them on the same level as *abbatia, hospitale vel quaecumque alia domus;* they can have rights in the same way as an abbey, a hospital or other charitable foundations can. This is a very important step forward from *Justinian's* way of looking at charitable foundations. *Justinian* did not deal with the case of *prebendae* and *dignitates,* but neither did he equate the *venerabiles domus* with the funds devoted to the relief of the poor or the redemption of captives; therefore still less could he have done so in the case of prebends, where funds are devoted to a few individuals in succession only. Again *Innocent* did not clearly say that these *dignitates* were to be regarded as legal persons, but he put the theory that dignitaries *finguntur... eaedem personae cum predecessoribus,* they are regarded as the same persons as their predecessors. This comes close to legal personality (cf. the famous concept of the corporation sole which is special to English law, but which has its roots in Canon law).

Summarizing, we may say that *Innocent* made important contributions to the development of the concepts of the legal person and the foundation, but he did not take the final step of speaking simply of a *persona ficta* or *repraesentata.* This step was taken not by *Cinus* and *Bartolus* – as was commonly held until 1956[40] – but by two French jurists of the University of Orléans, where they taught in the second half of the thirteenth century, namely *Jacques de Révigny* and *Pierre de Belleperche*[41]. The main part of their works has not been printed; it exists only in manuscript, which accounts for the fact that in later times it was not known that *Cinus* and *Bartolus* had taken the essence of their ideas on the *persona repraesentata* or *ficta* from the French jurists, whom they used very often, not always mentioning it.

The main text is one of *Jacques de Révigny* in his commentary on the *Digestum vetus,* to be found in manuscripts of the libraries of Leiden and Naples. When discussing the well-known case already dealt with by *Archbishop Moses* and the Accursian Gloss, that of the monastery abandoned by all the monks, he does not reject *Moses'* opinion completely[42]. He agrees that the goods are the

---

39 *Innocentius* on X 2, 19, 3 *verbo "fundi"*. For a full quotation of the text and for commentary see *Feenstra* (n. 1) 430 f.; cf. *Rodriguez* (n. 33) 306 f.

40 I.e. before the publication of my article cited above, n. 1. This opinion is still to be found, however, in *Todescan* (n. 33) 99 f., although he cites my article on other points.

41 This was one of the main points I made in my 1956 article; see *Feenstra* (n. 1) 423 ff., to which I may refer for all details not mentioned in the following footnotes; see also Le droit savant (n. 1), addenda 3 - 4. *Panizo Orallo* (n. 33) 126 ff. has paid much attention to my remarks on the Orléans Law School; he had photographs made of the manuscripts cited and reproduces them in his "Apendice documental" (447 ff.).

42 *Révigny* on the paragraph *In decurionibus* of the *lex Sicut municipium* (D. 3, 4, 7, 2): "... Pone quod omnes de universitate moriantur. In monasterio sunt multi monachi. Omnes

property of the monastery itself but apparently rejects *Moses'* line of argument that the *locus edificatus* – the walls, as the Accursian Gloss has it – is the owner. According to *Révigny* the goods remain the property of the *collegium* – even if there are no monks left – because he understands by *collegium* a *persona repraesentata;* he refers to the *lex Mortuo,* D. 46, 1, 22, where it is said that an inheritance can play the role of a person (*persona)* just as a *collegium* or a *municipium* can. He thus changes the idea of 'playing the role of a *persona*' into 'being a *persona repraesentata*', that is 'a person which is represented'[43]. With this motivation he tries to explain *Moses' sententia*[44]. He acknowledges however that the *sententia doctorum* is different, i.e. that the *fiscus clericorum, scilicet papa,* owns the goods, although no one has possession of them[45]. He then returns to the idea that the *collegium* is a *persona repraesentata,* referring to the opinion of his own teacher who limits it to the case where there is a *spes restaurandi*[46]. This case is akin to that of the *hereditas* left by the *de cujus*[47]. In both there is a hope, a *spes,* that another physical person will come to take over the task which provisionally is performed by the *persona repraesentata.* A comparison is even drawn with a prebend in a cathedral chapter: when the dignitary dies, the prebend does not fall to the chapter, but is considered a *persona repraesentata* until a new dignitary appears[48].

---

moriuntur. Cuius erunt bona universitatis? Vel sic: Civitas est destructa, ut curia nulla remansit. Cuius erunt bona universitatis? Dicunt quidam quod ecclesie vel civitatis. Dixit quidam archiepiscopus Moyses quod, licet moriatur civitas vel ecclesia, bona remanent in dominio ecclesie vel civitatis. Unde credebat quod essent in dominio loci edificati. Verum est quod res sunt in dominio ecclesie, id est in dominio personarum constitutarum in ecclesia, ut [C. 1, 2, 14, 8 *et s.*]. Et sic dico quod bona collegii sunt in dominio collegii, quia per collegium intelligo personam representatam, argumento [D. 46, 1, 22]. Unde scripta sententia illius archiepiscopi ..." (this passage is taken from lines 5 - 19 of the edition in *Feenstra* [n. 1] 426, where the full text is to be found, with references to the manuscripts used; cf. Le droit savant [n. 1], addenda 3 - 4, and *Panizo Orallo* (n. 33) 135, n. 43). I would not say, as *Cortese* (n. 18) 129 does, that *Révigny* and other Orléans professors "si occupano dell'idea dell arcivescovo solo per respingerla". Cf. *infra* n. 44.

43 On the concept of "representation" in the Middle Ages, cf. *W. Brückner,* Bildnis und Brauch: Studien zur Bildfunktion der Effigies, Berlin, 1966, pp. 90 f.

44 "Unde scripta sententia illius archiepiscopi", see *supra* n. 42; *Révigny* would not seem to reject *Moses'* opinion completely.

45 See the continuation of the passage cited *supra* n. 42 in *Feenstra* (n. 1) 426 ll. 19 - 28.

46 It is to be noted that *Révigny* also refers to this opinion of his teacher in his commentary on D. 1, 3, 9: this passage is edited by *E. Cortese,* La norma giuridica II, Milano, 1964, p. 188, n. 50; cf. *Cortese,* Per la storia (n. 18) 129, n. 44. For an interpolated (?) mention of *Moses* in *Révigny's lectura* on the Authenticum see *ibid.* 130, n. 45.

47 "Dicebat dominus domini mei quod si collegium destruebatur, cuius erunt bona omnibus mortuis? Dicebat quod collegii. Dicebat enim sic. Domino mortuo bona sunt hereditatis que representat personam defuncti; sic omnibus de collegio mortuis durat collegium que [lire 'quia' ou 'quod'?] est persona representata sicut hereditas que representat personam. Et hoc est verum ubi collegium dissolvitur et est spes restaurandi collegii' (ll. 29 - 35 of the edition in *Feenstra* [n. 1] 426).

These ideas are all very important; they remind one in some respects of the ideas of *Innocent* but they do not seem to have been inspired directly by him or by other Canonists. *Révigny*, in referring to his own teacher, his *dominus*, probably meant an older Orléans professor, *Jean de Monchy*, but unfortunately we know very little about this man and we cannot therefore trace the source of this theory any further. Until further proof appears, the main credit should be given to *Révigny*, who certainly formulated it in a very clear way. It would seem that *Révigny* himself was followed[49] not only by *Belleperche* but also by a French Canonist, *Jean Lemoine (Johannes Monachus)*, through whom it came down to one of the most influential Canonists of the end of the thirteenth century, *Johannes Andreae*. *Bartolus*[50] probably took the idea from *Cinus*, who cites *Pierre de Belleperche*. *Bartolus* did add something of his own, but the essential work had been done by either *Révigny* or *Jean de Monchy*.

From *Bartolus* onwards the writings of the Medieval and later Romanists[51] contain an endless repetition of the ideas which we have tried to trace to their oldest sources. We may note, however, that though the concept of the legal person was born, this did not necessarily mean that the concept of the foundation also was given its definitive form. What we now call foundations were then called by the learned jurists *personae fictae*, but no fundamental distinction was made between the corporation and the foundation; simply all the phenomena were called *personae fictae*.

In this context it should be noted that the word *fundatio* is not used in the discussions of the Medieval Romanists and Canonists on *universitates*. The verb *fundare* in the sense of the creation of an entity consisting of an aggregate of assets distinct from the material act of building a monastery or the like, occurs, however, in medieval documents[52]. The noun *fundatio* is mainly used for the "act of founding"; it is only at the end of the Middle Ages that it occurs in the acceptation of "what has

---

48 For the remarks on *spes* and the comparison with the prebend, see *Feenstra* (n. 1) 426 - 427, where a full edition of the continuation of the text is given (30 lines, with many other interesting details).

49 For details and references concerning the influence of *Révigny's* opinion on later authors, see *Feenstra* (n. 1) 423 ff., 428 f., 431 ff., as well as Le droit savant (n. 1), addenda 3 - 4.

50 For *Bartolus'* opinions on the subject, cf. *U. Navarrete*, La posesión de las "universitates" especialmente en caso de extinción de todos sus miembros, según Bartolo, in: Bartolo da Sassoferrato, Studi e documenti per il VI centenario II, Milano, 1962, pp. 347 ff.

51 Mention may be made of the first monograph on what we now call legal persons, published at the beginning of the 17th century: *Nicolaus Losaeus*, De iure universitatum tractatus, Augustae Taurinorum, 1601 (many later editions). On this treatise see *E. Ruffini Avondo*, Il trattato "De iure universitatum" del torinese Nicolò Losa (1601), Rivista di storia del diritto italiano 4 (1931) 5 ff. *Losaeus* does not deal, however, with what we now call foundations.

52 See *Feenstra* (n. 1) 440 f. See, in addition, *J. F. Niermeijer*, Mediae latinitatis lexicon minus, Leiden, 1976, s.v.; *Olga Weijers* and *Marijke Gumbert-Hepp*, Lexicon latinitatis neerlandicae medii aevi IV, Leiden, 1990, s.v.

been founded"[53]. The same applies for the German *stiften* and *Stiftung*[54] or the Dutch *stichten* and *stichting*[55].

IV. Customary Law in the Middle Ages and Early Modern Times

This terminology (*fundare* etc.) would seem to belong in particular to the customary law, which we now have to deal with not only for the medieval period, but also for early modern times. The customary law in the different Continental countries treated what we now call foundations in a quite different way than the *droit savant* (Romanists and Canonists) did; it applied to a greater extent what I have called the "trust-like device"[56]. This customary law was not set down in municipal statutes or the like, but appears mainly in the terminology of documents concerning foundations of purely secular origin, like town hospitals[57]. Documents on foundations relating to the Church sometimes also exhibit traces of concepts drawn from customary law, but in general these foundations were more likely to be treated as *personae fictae* on the basis of Roman-Canonical law. It must be said, however, that from the sixteenth century onwards changes occurred. This happened mainly in countries where the Reformation prevailed but not only there: in France, for example, an Ordonnance of 1543 brought foundations under the control of the parliaments[58]. In Protestant countries special solutions had to be found for institu-

53 See *Feenstra* (n. 1) 441. Cf. the Lexicon of *Weijers* and *Gumbert-Hepp* (n. 52) s.v.

54 Cf. *Schulze*, Hintergrund (n. 1) 9 - 11.

55 *Feenstra* (n. 1) 441, n. 247; cf. *P. Gerbenzon*, Opmerkingen over rechten ten aanzien van kerkelijke goederen ten tijde van de hervorming, in: Vrijheid en Recht ('s Jacobbundel), Zwolle, 1975, pp. 47 ff., 56 ff.

56 Mention should also be made of concepts other than the trust-like device. I may quote here a passage from *R. Schulze*, Hintergrund (n. 1) 13, who mentions "[für] das ältere Stiftungsdenken ... zwei wesentliche Aspekte ... die auf archaische Vorstellungen zurückführen und es von dem modernen, seit *Mühlenbruch* und *Savigny* die Rechtswissenschaft beherrschenden Stiftungsbegriff unterscheiden: die Vorstellung einer *metaphysischen Fortexistenz* des Stifters innerhalb der durch die Stiftung konstituierten Gemeinschaft sowie auf dieser Grundlage eine *korporative* Auffassung der Stiftung als eines vom Stifterwillen geleiteten (metaphysisch den Stifter selbst einschliessenden) *Personenverbandes*". *Schulze* refers *inter alios* to the fundamental study of *Borgolte* (n. 1), where further references are given; cf. also *Schulze*, Stiftungsrecht (n. 1), col. 1982. For the purpose of my present contribution I abstain from other details concerning these two "archaic" ideas; it is interesting to note, however, that the "korporative Auffassung der Stiftung als eines vom Stifterwillen geleiteten ... Personenverbandes" is still to be found in passages from *Grotius* and *Huber* to be dealt with below in section V.

57 See *Coing*, Geschichte (n. 1) 58, with further references to *Liermann* (n. 1) and *D. Pleimes*, Weltliches Stiftungsrecht, Geschichte der Rechtsformen (Forschungen zum deutschen Recht, Band III, Heft 3), 1938.

58 See *Coing*, EP I (n. 1) 268. For the developments in France since the 14th century in general see *A. Geouffre de Lapradelle*, Des fondations (Histoire – jurisprudence, vues théoriques et législatives), thèse, Paris, 1894; cf. *Feenstra* (n. 1) 438 - 443.

tions that could no longer be accepted after the breach with the Roman-Catholic church, like monasteries, chapters and prebends.

For the property belonging to monasteries and chapters a simple solution was possible: confiscation by the secular authorities, resulting in disappearance of the original institutions as such. This is what occurred, for example, in most of the Dutch provinces[59] (a notable exception is the continued existence of the five Utrecht chapters); the secular authorities administered the property of the institutions for different purposes, ecclesiastical and non-ecclesiastical (e.g., in favour of a newly-erected university).

More complicated was the solution for prebends. Some of them were destined for bursaries; in these cases there was no reason to make changes. Members of families from which the candidates had to be chosen could continue to receive stipends. The problem was the juridical device to be used where the Canon law was no longer applied. The Roman law, which after the Reformation was largely "received" in most Protestant countries, offered some solutions: the *legata ad pios usus* of the Christian period as well as the *legata annua* of the classical law[60]. Many Protestant jurists went in this direction, which I will not deal with in this contribution. I may refer only to the fundamental study of *Dieter Pleimes*, "Irrwege der Dogmatik im Stiftungsrecht" (1954)[61], where he deals with *selbständige Hauptgeldstiftungen* in the period before 1800[62]. One might add only that besides the German authors cited by *Pleimes*, a number of Dutch authors of the seventeenth and eighteenth centuries also deserve attention for their efforts, "das gesamte Hauptgeldstiftungsrecht im Rahmen des überlieferten Testamentsrechts und der Vorstellung einer ewigen unentgeltlichen Zuwendung zu erfassen"[63].

V. Special Developments in the Dutch Provinces

Interesting concepts relating to bursaries dating back to the pre-Reformation period are found in *Grotius* and *Huber*. They attribute the ownership[64] of the assets of such foundations to the families from which the candidates for the stipends had to be chosen.

---

59 See *Joubert* (n. 1) 144 ff.

60 See *Feenstra* (n. 1) 436 and n. 227, where the use of the *fideicommissum* device is also discussed.

61 Published as no. 1 of the series Forschungen zur neueren Privatrechtsgeschichte; it was one of the three books discussed in my 1956 article; see *supra* n. 1.

62 *Pleimes* (n. 61) 21 ff., 42 ff. and 51 ff.

63 *Pleimes* (n. 61) 51.

64 On the use of the ownership concept, in this context, see *Gerbenzon* (n. 55) 59 ff., who holds that for the Middle Ages and even for the 16th century we should not interpret the foundations in terms of ownership but rather in those of the old customary *gewere*.

Hugo Grotius deals with the subject in his "Inleidinge tot de Hollandsche Rechtsgeleerdheid" (Introduction to the Jurisprudence of Holland)[65], a work remarkable for its systematics. The passage on bursaries occurs in the chapter on 'the legal condition of things and their classification' (Inleidinge II, 1). *Grotius* follows the Roman law scheme of D. 1, 8, 2 and Inst. 2, 1 pr., stating that "all things belong either to all men in common, or to some great community of men, or to individuals, or to no one" (II, 1, 16). "Things belonging to a great community of men belong either to a whole civil community or to a smaller community" (II, 1, 24). The Latin equivalents of the Dutch terms are given by *Grotius* himself in the margin: *res publicae* and *res universitatis.* Among the *universitates* he mentions, *inter alia,* towns, corporations and *gheslachten,* "families" (II, 1, 31). The third of these categories – families in the sense of lineages – is not found in the Roman law scheme. *Grotius* gives two examples of ownership by "families": "burial places" (II, 1, 37) and "property destined by members of a family for the maintenance of young students belonging to the family" (II, 1, 38). About these bursaries he adds that they are "to be granted by – and for the benefit of – such persons as the foundations[66] import"; in cases where nothing is said with regard to this matter he provides some rules as to who has the right of nomination and to whom the appointment may go. The context makes it clear that *Grotius* does not use the term foundation in the sense of "what has been founded" but rather in that of "[the document rendering] the act of founding". He does not say that the "foundation" belongs to the category of *universitates;* it is rather the "family" which is mentioned in that capacity. *Grotius* does not specify the way in which this "ownership", vested in a "family", has to be conceived. It would seem that he is thinking only of rights exercised by certain individuals belonging to the family, who may be either administrators or beneficiaries; in this way he is nearer to the trust-like device than to the legal person concept for the foundation[67].

---

65 Written during his imprisonment at Loevestein (1619 - 1621) but published only in 1631. The best and most recent critical edition is by F. Dovring, H. F. W. D. Fischer and E. M. Meijers, Leiden, 1952; there is a useful English translation by *R. W. Lee:* The Jurisprudence of Holland by Hugo Grotius, I: Text, Oxford, 1926; 2nd ed., 1953 (reprint Aalen, 1977). In my quotations below I have followed this translation with only a few exceptions.

66 In all editions of the Inleidinge "stichtinge" is interpreted as a plural: it is followed by "medebrengen". However, a manuscript of the Inleidinge, dating from circa 1626 - 1627, has the singular "medebrengt", which would seem to be a better reading; "stichtinge" means "[the document rendering] the act of founding" (cf. below in the text). For this manuscript see *Feenstra,* Een handschrift van de Inleidinge van Hugo de Groot, T.R. 35 (1967) 444 ff., in particular 473.

67 For some references, see *Feenstra* (n. 1) 437 - 438 and notes 231 - 234. (In the citation of *Bijnkershoek,* Observationes tumultuariae, in note 232, a printing error has to be amended: for "873" read "879"). I have some doubts, however, whether I was right in mentioning a "perpetual legacy" or a *fideicommissum familiae relictum* as the only devices *Grotius* could have had in mind. *Bijnkershoek,* in Observationes tumultuariae, nr. 1996, ed. Harlemi, 1934, vol. II, pp. 692 - 693, accuses *Grotius* of having followed the *successio feudalis* in his description of the rules as to who has the right of nomination and to whom the appointment may go; he should have followed the *doctrina juris canonici.* Indeed among the commenta-

Ulricus Huber deals with bursaries in his "Heedendaegse Rechtsgeleertheyt, soo elders als in Frieslandt gebruikelijk" (Contemporary Jurisprudence, in use in Friesland and elsewhere)[68]. Although he certainly was inspired by *Grotius'* "Inleidinge", he does not deal with the subject in the same context. In Book II, Chapter 1, where he follows the Roman law scheme of D. 1, 8, 2 and Inst. 2, 1 pr. he does not mention "families" among the (smaller) communities[69] . The bursaries occur in a quite different context: in chapter 36 of the second book, dealing with *leen-recht* ("feudal right") as a specimen of *halve of nutlijke eygendom* (= *dominium utile*). According to *Huber* this *leen-recht* is twofold. "Firstly, it is the right by which one holds the possession and profits of any property under condition of rendering service to another: in Latin these rights are called *feuda*" (§ 4); in Friesland they have no great importance because there are only two feuds in the whole province, but *Huber* nevertheless gives an exposition of feuds "in order to obtain a general sketch of a thing which is so common among all the peoples of Europe" (§ 7). In § 25 only does he come to speak of the second category of *leen-recht:* "There are still other *leenen*[70] more in use, of which our Ordinance speaks in Book 4, Title 2. They consist of fixed property directed by their former owners, generally by will, to remain always in a certain family, with the object that some person may be at his studies upon it, or some other good use made of it to the advantage of Church or State" (§ 25). In using the term *leenen* not only for feuds but also for ecclesiastical *beneficia*[71] he follows an Ordinance of the Estates of Friesland of

tors of the Inleidinge there has been much discussion on this paragraph. For further details I may refer to *Johannes Voet,* Commentarius ad Pandectas, ad D. 37, 14, nr. 12, ed. Hagae Comitum, 1731, II, p. 571, *Gerlach Scheltinga,* Dictata [on the Inleidinge, in the edition of W. de Vos and G. G. Visagie, Johannesburg, 1986], ad Inl. II, 1, 38, pp. 93 f., and *D. G. van der Keessel,* Praelectiones iuris hodierni ad Hugonis Grotii Introductionem ad iurisprudentiam hollandicam, ed. P. van Warmelo et al., vol. II, Amsterdam / Kaapstad, 1963, ad Inl. II, 1, 38, pp. 24 f.

68 The first edition was published in Leeuwarden in 1686 (many later editions up to 1768). There is an English translation by *Percival Gane,* under the title, The Jurisprudence of my Time, by Ulrich Huber, 2 vols., Durban, 1939. In my quotations below I have followed this translation, with a few exceptions; the quoted passages are found in vol. I, at 298 and 301 (in the *editio princeps* in vol. I, at 327 and 331).

69 In II, 1, 20 he even explicitly excludes from "communities" *huis-gezinnen,* which is translated by "households". Cf. his Praelectiones iuris civilis, ad Inst. 2, 1, nr. 7 (nr. 8 in the Lipsiae, 1735, edition): "Videtur negative definienda universitas, Civilis hominum societas, quae nec familia nec libera sit Respublica, ut ...". It is clear that in this text "familia" means a "family" living in the same house. For "family" in the sense of lineage *Huber* uses the term *geslacht,* just as *Grotius* did in the "Inleidinge", cf. above.

70 *Gane* translates "feuds", which does not account for the different meanings of the Dutch word. If it must be translated, it should be "loans" (in an obsolete sense of this English word); but it is better not to translate it at all because readers will not easily see the reason for dealing with feuds and "loans" in one chapter.

71 The term *le[e]nen* is still used today for the surviving institutions of that kind. A recent article on the subject, with further references, is *F.C.J. Ketelaar,* Friese lenen, in: Liber amicorum Jhr. Mr. C. C. van Valkenburg, 's-Gravenhage, 1985, pp. 161 ff.

10 December 1590, incorporated in the *Statuten van Friesland* (1602 edition), Book 4 Title 2. After giving some rules concerning the right to bestow and the capacity to receive such *leenen* (§§ 26 - 28) *Huber* says: "The *opper eygendom* [= *dominium directum*] then of these *leen-goederen* is in the family of the founder, and the *nutlijke eygendom* [= *dominium utile*] in those who possess the property from time to time" (§ 29). The parallel with feudal law is obvious: in continental legal science the dual ownership originated in interpreting the *Libri Feudorum* and remained in use mainly for feudal property. Its use for foundations reminds us of the trust-like device.

In relation to foundations in the Dutch provinces after their independence we should emphasize that it is not only the surviving pre-Reformation institutions which merit our attention. Many new, secular charitable foundations, *Anstaltstiftungen* as well as *Hauptgeldstiftungen,* were created after the Reformation. One of their most notable features was that they required no control by the public authorities. This is a striking difference with the surrounding countries, not only those which remained in the Roman-Catholic tradition, such as France, but also other Protestant countries, especially in the German Empire[72]. This certainly led to the existence of a very great number of such foundations in the Netherlands, an aspect which also may be responsible fcr their survival into the nineteenth century[73] in spite of the fact that the Netherlands then lived under a codification inspired by the French *Code civil,* which did not acknowledge foundations at all[74].

As for the law applicable to such new foundations, the Dutch jurists did not develop new theories. In general the rules governing them were fixed to a large extent in the act of foundation itself; for the rest the Roman law texts on *collegia, piae causae, legata, fideicommissa* were applied in much the same way as with the pre-Reformation foundations.

VI. Foundations in the 18th and 19th Centuries

From this excursus to the Dutch provinces we have to return to more general European developments. It has been stated by various authors[75] that the Enlightenment was not much in favour of foundations: what was to be done for *publica utilitas* was regarded as a task of the state, not a function of private institutions like foundations.

---

72 See *Coing,* Geschichte (n. 1) 59.

73 And for their flourishing in the XXth century.

74 For efforts to divert from the *Code civil* on this point, see *infra* n. 96.

75 See, e.g., *Schulze,* Hintergrund (n. 1) 15; *Coing,* Geschichte (n. 1) 59 f. and EP I (n. 1) 268, where he refers, *inter alia,* to the article "Fondation" in *Diderot's* Encyclopédie; this article, which is anonymous in the editions I could consult, would have been written by *Turgot.*

This point of view can be found very clearly in the Prussian *Allgemeines Landrecht* (PrALR) of 1794[76]. It states that charitable foundations[77] need a charter of erection and are under *Oberaufsicht*, of the State; they are classified as *moralische Person,* a concept created by *Samuel Pufendorf,* who seems to have first used the term *persona moralis*[78] (the term has been rather successful in eighteenth century Europe). The *Landrecht* also contains rules on "improper" or "dependent" foundations which are attached to corporations. Finally it acknowledges *Familienstiftungen,* which can be created by contract or by will[79] without a license from the State[80]; these *Stiftungen* are defined as *Anordnungen* and are not classified as *moralische Personen.*

The Austrian *Allgemeines Bürgerliches Gesetzbuch* (ABGB) of 1811 has no special rules on foundations[81]. It gives a short definition of *Stiftungen* and adds simply that the rules about them are to be found "in den politischen Verordnungen" ("in the political ordinances")[82]. The ABGB uses the concept *moralische Person* but seems not to consider foundations as belonging to this category[83].

The two codifications, PrALR and ABGB, do not show the influence of the concept "legal person", *juristische Person,* which was probably created by *Gustav Hugo* in 1798[84]. A clear link between foundation and legal person was only established by another German professor of the beginning of the nineteenth century, *Alfred Heise*[85]. In the second edition[86] of his draft for a (new) system of the Common Civil Law, "Grundriss eines Systems des gemeinen Civilrechts", published in

---

76 *Coing,* Geschichte (n. 1) 60 and *Pleimes* (n. 61) 67 ff.

77 The word *Stiftung* is not used here; it occurs, however, in *Familienstiftungen,* see *infra.*

78 In fact the concept *persona moralis* has known various developments since *Pufendorf,* see *M. Lipp,* "Persona moralis", "Juristische Person" und "Personenrecht", Eine Studie zur Dogmengeschichte der "juristischen Person" im Naturrecht und frühen 19. Jahrhundert, Quaderni fiorentini per la storia del pensiero giuridico moderno 11 / 12 (1982 / 1983) 217 ff., 254 f. *Persona moralis* is not the predecessor of the legal person (*Lipp* 250).

79 And by "einseitige Verfügungen unter Lebenden".

80 Cf. *Schulze,* Hintergrund (n. 1) 23.

81 See *H. Schnizer,* Die juristische Person in der Kodifikationsgeschichte des ABGB, in: Festschrift zum 60. Geburtstag von Walter Wilburg, 1965, pp. 143 ff., 154 f., and *W. Brauneder,* Von der moralischen Person des ABGB zur juristischen Person der Privatrechtswissenschaft, Quaderni fiorentini per la storia del pensiero giuridico moderno 11 / 12 (1982 / 1983) 263 ff., 272.

82 This does not mean that the *Stiftungen* belonged within public law, see *Brauneder* (n. 81) 272, n. 27 against *Schnizer* (n. 81) 154 f.; cf. also *Brauneder* 276 on the opinion of *Zeiller.*

83 *Brauneder* (n. 81) 271 (*contra Schnizer* (n. 81) 154 f.).

84 *Schnizer* (n. 81) 144.

85 For *Alfred Heise* and his influence see, in particular, *Pleimes* (n. 61) 72 ff.

86 In the first edition, which was published in 1807, *Heise* had limited himself to mentioning some examples of the new concept "juristische Person", cf. *Pleimes* (n. 61) 73 and *Feenstra* (n. 1) 443, n. 253a.

1816, he added a substantial footnote[87] in which various kinds of legal persons were distinguished[88]. Among them an important place is given to legal persons whose "Substrat" consists of "irgendeiner Masse von Gütern, welche zu einem gemeinnützigen Zweck gewidmet und unter eine besondere Verwaltung gestellt ist (venerabiles domus, legata pro redemptione captivorum, Witwenkassen, Stipendien)". In the text of his "Grundriss" he then refers to this category of legal persons as "gemeinnützige Stiftungen" and he puts them on the same level as *fiscus* and *universitates*. *Friedrich Carl von Savigny*, in his "System des heutigen Römischen Rechts" of 1840, was no doubt influenced by *Heise* when he formulated the remarkable theory that the foundation was one of the two types of legal person[89]. In *Heise's* as well as in *Savigny's* conception[90] *all* foundations, even bursaries, were considered legal persons. This had important consequences in practice. Even before *Savigny's* "System" was published there was the famous *Städelfall*[91], concerning a foundation created by will for the erection of a museum in Frankfurt: in this case it was argued *inter alia* that a foundation could not receive a legacy in the same will that established it, because it had no existence as a legal person at the death of the testator. According to older conceptions the municipal authorities of Frankfurt could have played a role as recipients of the legacy and supervisors for the erection of the museum.

The new theory also exercised its influence on nineteenth century legislation in Germany[92], as, after *Landesgesetze* in, e.g., Sachsen and Baden, the *Bürgerliches Gesetzbuch* of 1896 clearly shows[93].

---

87 The full text of this footnote is given by *Pleimes* (n. 61) 73.

88 He distinguishes the legal persons according to their "Substrat ... welches die juristische Person bildet oder vorstellt". When the "Substrat" consists of "Menschen", he makes a subdistinction between "einem einzelnen zur Zeit (bey öffentlichen Beamten)" – cf. the "corporation sole" – and "einer gleichzeitigen Vereinigung mehrerer (universitates)". The "Substrat" can also consist of "Sachen"; there he makes another subdistinction, of which the main categories are "das ganze Vermögen einer Person (fiscus, hereditas)" and "irgendeine Masse von Gütern ... zu einem gemeinnützigen Zweck gewidmet" (for this last category see what follows below).

89 *Savigny*, System des heutigen Römischen Rechts, II, 1840, pp. 243 f. For *Savigny's* theories on legal persons in general, see *W. Flume*, Savigny und die Lehre von der juristischen Person, in: O. Behrends *et al.* (eds.), Festschrift für Franz Wieacker zum 70. Geburtstag, 1978, pp. 340 ff., and *M. Diesselhorst*, Zur Theorie der juristischen Person bei Carl Friedrich [*sic*] von Savigny, Quaderni fiorentini per la storia del pensiero giuridico moderno 11 / 12 (1982 / 1983) 319 ff.

90 For differences between *Heise's* and *Savigny's* concepts of the legal person, see *Flume* (n. 89) 341.

91 On the *Städelfall* see, in particular, *H. Kiefner*, Das Städel'sche Kunstinstitut: Zugleich zu C. F. Mühlenbruchs Beurteilung eines berühmten Rechtsfalls, Quaderni fiorentini per la storia del pensiero giuridico moderno 11 / 12 (1982 / 1983) 339 ff., and *H.-J. Becker*, Der Städel-Paragraph, in: G. Baumgärtel *et al.* (eds.), Festschrift für Heinz Hübner zum 70. Geburtstag, 1984, pp. 21 ff. For a short survey see *Schulze* , Hintergrund (n. 1) 10 f.

92 Also in Switzerland, in Bluntschli's *Privatrechtliches Gesetzbuch für den Kanton Zürich* (1854 - 1856); see *Coing*, Geschichte (n. 1) 60 f., and *idem*, EP II (n. 1) 353.

Nineteenth century codifications in other parts of Europe, which took the French *Code civil* of 1804 as their example, mostly abstained from giving rules about foundations, just as their model had[94]. This was true, for example, of the Netherlands' *Burgerlijk Wetboek* of 1838, although in drafts of 1816 and 1820 an effort had been made to diverge from the *Code civil* on this point[95]. This effort was quite understandable in a country where, as we have seen, charitable foundations and family bursaries had played such an important role in the seventeenth and eighteenth centuries. In the absence of codified law many of these institutions survived under rules created by legal science (in particular of German origin) and court decisions; legal personality was mostly attributed to these old foundations. The creation of new foundations as legal persons could therefore be accepted rather easily; no license from the State was required. In the twentieth century, foundations have often been erected also for purposes other than charity or culture. Finally, in 1956, a Foundations Statute was passed which gave statutory sanction to most of the principles already in use[96]; and in 1976 the rules of this Statute were incorporated in the *Burgerlijk Wetboek*[97].

VII. Epilogue

The introduction stated that at least public or charitable trusts of the common law were the equivalent to the foundations in civil law countries. Most of the foundations mentioned above indeed had (or have) a religious, charitable or cultural purpose. I do not consider it my task to discuss in the present context the use of the foundation concept for other purposes, in particular by industry or government. Developments of this kind started in Germany for industries at the end of the nineteenth century (*Carl-Zeiss-Stiftung* 1889); they have reached enormous proportions

---

93 See *Coing*, Geschichte (n. 1) 60 f., and *idem*, EP II (n. 1) 353; cf. also *Huussen-de Groot* (cited *infra* n. 95) 165 ff.

94 This did not prevent the French courts from the middle of the 19th century from accepting the validity of some foundations by way of a legacy to one or several individuals (*legs à charge de fonder)*, see *Vera Bolgár,* Why no trusts in the civil law?, (1953) 2 American Journal of Comparative Law 204 ff., 215 f. This is what I have called the trust-like device.

95 For details see *Feenstra* (n. 1) 446 f.; also *F. M. Huussen-de Groot,* Rechtspersonen in de negentiende eeuw: Een studie van privaatrechtelijke rechtspersonen in de negentiende-eeuwse wetgeving van Frankrijk, Nederland en Duitsland (Rechtshistorische studies, 2), Zwolle, 1976 (also published as thesis, Leyden, 1976), in particular 84 ff. (cf. the German *Zusammenfassung* 211 ff.).

96 See *Feenstra* (n. 1) 448, n. 267; for an earlier attempt to include rules on foundations in the *Burgerlijk Wetboek* – in a draft revision of 1886, which did not succeed – see *Huussen-de Groot* (n. 95) 112 ff. (cf. 213).

97 Book II, title 5; a number of modifications in the 1956 text was, however, made. Another recent legal regulation of foundations is to be found in the Austrian *Privatstiftungsgesetz* of 1993.

there since the Second World War[98]. In the Netherlands new developments appeared rather suddenly just after the First World War: quite apart from industrial uses, many social and governmental organisations then began to be established as foundations[99]. Since the Foundations Statute (1956) and the new chapter in the *Burgerlijk Wetboek* (1976) their number has continued to increase.

However this may be, the dominating foundation concept in the law of these and other civil law countries would not seem to have changed much since the nineteenth century. In any case, a return to trust-like devices, as used in the course of earlier centuries, has not taken place.

98 See *Schulze*, Hintergrund (n. 1) 30 f. and *idem*, Stiftungsrecht (n. 1) col. 1989. For a comparative survey of the present situation, see *Herbert Kronke*, Stiftungstypus und Unternehmensträgerstiftung: Eine rechtsvergleichende Untersuchung (Beiträge zum ausländischen und internationalen Privatrecht, 52), Tübingen, 1988.

99 It was extremely easy to establish foundations, not only because no license of the State was required but also because the setting aside of capital became purely symbolic (even ten guilders could suffice). Since 1956 no setting aside is required at all.

MICHELE GRAZIADEI

The Development of *Fiducia* in Italian and French Law from the 14th Century to the End of the *Ancien Régime*

I. Introduction

The purpose of this contribution is to outline the history of *fiducia* from the time of *Bartolus* and *Baldus* to the enactment of the *Code Napoléon* and of the Italian civil code of 1865. In general terms, *fiducia* emerged during the epoch of the *ius commune* in the context of testamentary practices, and out of a process of differentiation from the law of *fideicommissa. Fiducia* involved the institution of an heir (or the appointment of a legatee) who could not benefit from the disposition, but had to deal with the property according to the instructions left by the testator. Sometimes the testament hinted at the existence of those instructions, sometimes it was completely silent about them.

Over the centuries, arrangements of this kind served various purposes, both licit and illicit, in many respects familiar to modern students of trust law. Fiduciary dispositions sprang, for example, from the desire to find a convenient way of making restitution of property which testators deemed necessary to save their souls. They were also used as a surrogate of *tutela,* where the legatee was under age, in order to avoid wardship or the formalities linked with *tutela.* Such dispositions enhanced the position of the surviving spouse who could be instituted fiduciary heir for the children. Fiduciary dispositions were also employed to pursue less commendable ends. They were among the techniques by which property could be left to persons lacking capacity to acquire property *mortis causa,* such as children born out of wedlock, outlaws, or certain collective bodies. Testamentary *fiducia* also protected property from the danger of confiscation, or from the reach of the beneficiary's creditors.

In the course of history, fiduciary dispositions apart, other devices performed some of the functions just mentioned. We will briefly consider one neglected instance of such devices, the *confidentia beneficialis,* which seems more strictly related to our main theme[1].

---

1 The neighbouring subject of testamentary execution is covered by *Reinhard Zimmermann's* paper in this volume. As the title of his contribution suggests, there is some overlapping between his theme and mine.

II. Scope of Enquiry

Any treatment of the topic outlined above must face preliminary difficulties. First, it is undeniable that to speak of Italian or French law with reference to the age of the *ius commune* cannot be wholly accurate. Until codification the territories which are now France and Italy hosted a variety of legal systems[2]. Nevertheless, the Italian peninsula and the *pays de droit écrit* of Southern France show more similarities than differences in their approaches to *fiducia*. The same does not hold true for the *pays de droit coutumier* of Northern France. They fall outside the scope of this study, which is dedicated to the area most closely connected with Roman law.

A second problem arises from the attempt to cover so vast a timespan. The danger in making this choice is obvious, since every epoch shapes its own law by reinterpreting the legacy of the past. The decision to explore the *longue durée* none the less, instead of dealing with a fragment of the larger picture, does not imply that throughout the period considered there was a single doctrine of *fiducia* recognized as such. Still less does it mean that such doctrine, when recognized, satisfied identical needs. From this perspective, the approach adopted is selective rather than analytical, as clearly there is space for further investigation.

A final difficulty stems from the noiion of *fiducia* itself. If "trust" is a "protean word"[3] *fiducia* is similarly elusive. Today Italian and French law feature a doctrine of *fiducia*, or *fiducie*. In a nutshell, this doctrine provides a way of organizing *inter vivos* transactions, whereby one party holds property on behalf of another, or by way of security[4]. This legal technique is, however, a comparatively recent addition to the stock of conceptual tools at the disposal of French or Italian lawyers. One looks in vain for it in the law of these two countries during the greatest part of the 19th century. This absence should not provoke surprise. It is well known that the

2 In France, however, some pieces of legislation such as the Ordonnance sur les Donations (1731) and the Ordonnance sur les Substitutions fidéicommissaires (1747) reflect the early tendency towards the unification of law, which culminated in the enactment of the codes. For the context in which such legislation took shape see *Jacques Poumarède*, Le testament en France dans les pays de droit écrit du Moyen Age à l'époque moderne, in: Recueils de la Societé Jean Bodin pour l'histoire comparative des institutions, LX, Actes à cause de mort, Deuxième partie, Europe médiévale et moderne, 1993, pp. 129 ff., 134 f.

3 *Tito v. Wadell* (No. 2) [1977] 3 All E.R. 129, 230, per *Megarry V.-C.*

4 For analysis of the shortcomings of this institution in comparison with common law trusts, see *Antonio Gambaro*, Trust in Continental Europe, in: Alfredo Mordechai Rabello (ed.), Aequitas and Equity: Equity in Civil Law and Mixed Jurisdictions, 1997, pp. 777 ff.; *Maurizio Lupoi*, Trusts, 1997, pp. 461 ff., especially 543 ff. Recently, France was on the verge of codifying *la fiducie* (cf. *Michel Grimaldi*, La fiducie: réflexions sur l'institution et sur l'avant-projet de la loi qui la consacre, Répertoire du notariat defrénois, 1991, I, pp. 897, 961; *Madeleine Cantin-Cumyn*, L'avant-projet de loi relatif à la fiducie, un point de vue civiliste d'outre-atlantique, Dalloz Chronique, 1992, p. 117). The failure of this project is bringing about piece-meal legislative innovation. For criticism of this approach: *Pierre Decheix*, La fiducie ou du sens des mots, Dalloz Chronique, 1997, p. 33.

contemporary notion of *fiducia* first blossomed in the hands of 19th century German legal science, which succeeded in giving new life to the Roman and German legal heritage[5].

From the last years of the 19th century the German experience in this field provided a source of inspiration for scholars active in other countries. They soon began to study the German approach to fiduciary operations, thus opening the door to a circulation of models which would delight any student of comparative law.

All these considerations explain why it would be anachronistic to choose today's notions of *fiducia* as a starting point for the present essay[6]. To have a picture of *fiducia* before the 19th century one must look in another direction instead, i.e. to testamentary practices. By the end of the *ancien régime* Italian and French lawyers were familiar with a testamentary device that was known by the name of *fiducia*, or fiduciary disposition. It is still possible to catch a glimpse of this fossil by reading art. 627 of the Italian civil code:

> "No action can be brought to establish that dispositions made in favour of a person mentioned in the will are only apparent and that in reality they concern another person, even if the expressions in the will can indicate or raise the assumption that an intermediary [*persona interposta*] is involved.
>
> However, the person mentioned in the will, if he has spontaneously performed the *fiduciary disposition* by transferring the property to the person intended by the testator, cannot sue to recover it, unless he is a person lacking legal capacity.
>
> The provisions of this article do not apply to the case in which the institution [of an heir] or the legacy are impugned as having been made through an intermediary [*persona interposta*] for persons lacking legal capacity"[7].

---

5 The German contribution on *fiduziarische* and *deutschrechtliche Treuhand* is reviewed by *Karl Otto Scherner,* Salmannschaft, Servusgeschäft und venditio iusta: Frühformen gewillkürter Mittlerschaft im altdeuschen Privatrecht, 1971, pp. 1 ff.; *Helmut Coing,* Die Treuhand kraft privaten Rechtsgeschäfts, 1973, pp. 11 ff.; *idem,* Europäisches Privatrecht, II, 1989, pp. 426 f.; *Giseltraud Otten,* Die Entwicklung der Treuhand im 19. Jahrhundert – Die Ausbildung des Treuhandbegriffs des modernen Rechts, 1975, pp. 49 ff. (*der deutschrechtliche Treuhandbegriff*), 143 ff. (*der fiduziarische Treuhandbegriff*); *Clausdieter Schott,* Der Träger als Treuhandform, 1975; *Wolfgang Asmus,* Dogmengeschichtliche Grundlagen der Treuhand: Eine Untersuchung zur romanistischen und germanistischen Treuhandlehre, 1977; and *Sibylle Hofer's* and *Karl Otto Scherner's* chapters in this volume. See also *Karl Otto Scherner,* Fiducia Germanorum – Johannes Heumann und die Erfindung der Treuhand in der deutschen Rechtsgeschichte, in: Wirkungen europäischer Rechtskultur, Festschrift für Karl Kroeschell, 1997, pp. 973 ff.

6 See, further, *infra* III. To be sure, this is not an invitation to overlook the Humanists' efforts to recover the notion of *fiducia* familiar to *Gaius* and his contemporaries (*infra* VI.).

7 The translation is mine; emphasis and brackets added. The Italian civil code entered into force in 1942. The provision cited in the text re-enacts with minor changes art. 829 of the first Italian civil code (1865). Its antecedent was art. 809 of the civil code for the Kingdom of Piedmont and Sardinia (1837). The current Italian debate on *fiducia* is so distant from any reflection on previous schemes bearing such name that the best and most complete treatment of the Italian law of property dedicates a chapter to *la proprietà fiduciaria,* but omits any

Apart from the exception carved out in its last phrase, this provision mandates that claims based on the allegation that the testator did not intend to benefit the person named in the testament as heir or legatee, but rather meant to benefit someone else, should be disregarded.

It is noteworthy that the code does not state the precise legal position of the intermediary to whom the testator communicated the name of the final recipient. There is a hint that the fiduciary disposition is only apparent. Yet, at least in Italy, it is frequently argued that the person named in the testament is not a simulated heir or legatee[8]. One should also keep in mind that the Italian civil code has separate rules for *fideicommissa* (artt. 692 - 697) as well as for executorship (artt. 700 - 712). In other words, according to contemporary doctrine, the fiduciary disposition of art. 627 is different from both.

As we will see in a moment, the French civil code contains no similar provision concerning testamentary *fiducia*. Apart from this, French and Italian law converge on the issue, however. They share similar notions of testamentary *fiducia*, keeping it distinct both from *fideicommissa* and from testamentary execution[9].

These preliminary remarks may seem obscure to any common lawyer. Yet, those who are familiar with the law of trusts will at least recognize the factual situation. In common law jurisdictions the same pattern of facts falls under the familiar heading: "secret and half secret trusts". The Italian rule on this matter, however, is dif-

---

reference to the old doctrine of testamentary *fiducia*, as well as to art. 627 c.c. (cp. *Antonio Gambaro*, Il diritto di proprietà, in: Trattato di diritto civile e commerciale già diretto da Cicu e Messineo, continuato da Mengoni, VIII, t. 2, 1995, pp. 609 ff.). The important work by *Claude Witz*, La fiducie en droit privé français, 1981, shows a similar inclination with respect to French law.

8 *Lycia Gardani Contursi-Lisi*, Dell'istituzione di erede e dei legati – Disposizioni generali, Art. 624 - 632, in: Commentario del codice Civile Scialoja-Branca, 1983, pp. 88 ff. Cf. *Nicolò Lipari*, Il negozio fiduciario, 1964, pp. 182 - 184, 359 - 380. According to *Witz* (n. 7) 48 - 49 "... cette institution semble belle et bien reposer sur la theorie de la simulation", because the *fiduciaire* is an "interposé fictif". Yet, for the same author the doctrine of simulation does not fully apply here. The fact that the *fiduciaire* should manage the property without being authorized by its actual owner – i.e. the beneficiary designated by the testator – speaks against a true case of simulation.

9 The French civil code, art. 896, prohibits substitutions and declares them null and void to all purposes, with the exceptions listed in artt. 897 - 899, artt. 1048 - 1050. These norms are silent on the *fiducie*, but French interpreters hold that the general prohibition of substitutions does not apply to the testamentary *fiducie*. See *Witz* (n. 7) 43 ff., who thinks that the survival of the *fiducie* under the code "fut assurée par la doctrine et la jurisprudence avec une déconcertante facilité". Louisiana legal writers are perfectly aware of this point: *John H. Tucker Jr.*, Substitutions, Fideicommissa and Trusts in Louisiana Law: A Semantical Reappraisal, (1964) 24 Louisiana Law Review 439, 483 - 487. Testamentary execution is regulated by the French civil code in artt. 1025 - 1034. According to *Witz* (n. 7) 49 - 50, there has never been an outright assimilation of the *fiduciaire* to the executor, though some nineteenth century writers speak of this intermediary as a special kind of executor, thus confirming the "profonde identité de nature qui existe entre les pouvoirs du fiduciaire, simple administrateur des biens légués et ceux de l'exécuteur testamentaire".

ferent from the English one. English law enforces secret and half-secret trusts in favour of their beneficiaries on the basis of one theory or another, even though they do not satisfy the formal requirements applicable to testamentary dispositions[10].

In Italy the beneficiaries of these arrangements cannot enforce them. Under Italian law, the beneficiaries will get the testator's bounty only if the person named in the testament as heir or legatee voluntarily decides to give effect to the testator's wishes[11]. For our purposes it is important to remark, however, that the current status of Italian law on this issue does not reflect the approach to it that prevailed before codification.

Even today, the French civil code does not deny effect to the *fiducie.* As a matter of fact, in the first half of 19th century French courts regularly enforced secret testamentary dispositions made by testators[12]. To be sure, French legal writers now consider the old *fiducie* obsolete: those 19th century cases on *la fiducie* play a swan-song of the fiduciary device as it existed before the *Code Napoléon*[13]. Yet, this is in fact the main topic that needs to be investigated: the institution which flourished during the era of the *ius commune.*

III. The Place of the Roman Law of *fiducia* in the Age of the *ius commune*

The doctrine of *fiducia* which gradually developed from the 14th century onwards was built upon Roman law sources, but actually owed little to the original Roman law of *fiducia.*

This paradox helps to dispel the impression of continuity between the notion of *fiducia* in classical and post-classical Roman law and the conception of *fiducia* that emerged in the context of testamentary dispositions during the age of the *ius commune.*

It is well-known that all the references to the original sources on *fiducia cum creditore* or *cum amico* were removed by interpolation from the *Corpus iuris*[14].

---

10 For a lucid introduction to the English law of secret and half-secret trusts, see Hanbury and Martin, Modern Equity, 14th ed. by *Jill E. Martin,* 1993, pp. 152 ff.; for in-depth treatment, see *A. J. Oakley,* Constructive Trusts, 3rd ed., 1997, pp. 243 ff. Some of the early precedents on these trusts are: *Chamberlaine v. Chamberlaine* (1678) Free. Ch. 34; *Thynn v. Thynn* (1684) 1 Vern. 296; *Crook v. Brooking* (1688) 2 Vern. 50. The legal basis of these decisions are discussed by *Gareth Jones,* The Role of Equity in the English Law of Restitution, in: Eltjo J. H. Schrage (ed.), The Comparative Legal History of the Law of Restitution, 1995, pp. 149 ff., 155 ff.

11 See the comparative discussion in *Lupoi* (n. 4) 146 f.

12 *Witz* (n. 7) 43 ff.

13 *Witz* (n. 7) 47 ff.

14 See the paper by *David Johnston* in this volume.

This is not to say, however, that what was left outside the *Corpus iuris* was altogether lost after *Justinian.* The memory of the legal technique that the Roman jurists named *fiducia* was preserved in a few texts which survived the fall of the Western Empire[15].

Furthermore, the legislation of some of the Germanic peoples who settled within the borders of the empire, as well as a number of private documents dating back to the High Middle Ages, suggest that the Roman heritage with respect to *fiducia* may have been a conscious or unconscious source of inspiration for the later practice of the law[16].

The history of *fiducia* during the centuries of the *ius commune* is, however, the story of doctrines which initially developed by reference to the Roman laws on *fideicommissa* that had entered into the Justinianic compilation.

Not until the time of the Humanists do we find a serious attempt to grasp the original features of the Roman *fiducia.* Yet, when the Humanists exercised their philological capacities in this field, the Commentators had already engrafted their conception of *fiducia* onto the Roman law sources. Thus, the humanistic critique prepared the way for the 19th century study of the interpolations of the Digest, but did not displace the notion of testamentary *fiducia* which had already emerged.

15 See, e.g., C. Th. 5, 1, 3; 15, 14, 9. One well known description of *fiducia cum amico* was given by *Boetius,* Ad Ciceronis topica, 4, 10, 41: "Fiduciam accipit cuicumque res aliqua mancipatur, ut eam mancipanti remancipet; velut si quis tempus dubium timens amico potentiori fundum mancipet, ut ei, cum tempus quod suspectum est praeterierit, reddat. Haec mancipatio fiduciaria nominabatur, id circo quod restituendi fides interponitur". For references to other literary sources see *infra* VI.

16 See, e.g., *Ennio Cortese,* Il diritto nella storia medioevale, I, L'alto medioevo, 1995, p. 144: "... la riapparizione [of the word *fiducia*] nel mondo longobardo è quella di una semplice parola: ma è anche vero che il perpetuarsi di un nome, seppur con significati diversi da quelli originari, potrebbe indicare occulte – magari oggi inafferabili – vicende volgari d'istituti pregiustineanei". One may compare on this point *Paolo Frezza,* L'influsso del diritto romano giustineaneo nelle formule e nella prassi in Italia, in: Ius Romanum Medii Aevi, I, 2, c, ee, Milano, 1974, with *Giovanni Diurni,* Fiducia e negozio fiduciario nel diritto intermedio, in: Digesto, 4th ed., Discipline privatistiche: Sezione civile, VIII, 1991, pp. 288, 292 ff.; *idem,* Fiducia – Tecniche e principi negoziali nell'alto medioevo, I, Torino, 1992, pp. 74 ff.; *Adriana Campitelli,* Pegno (dir. interm.), in: Enciclopedia del diritto, XXXII, 1982, p. 675 (these studies concentrate on Langobardian law). It is certain, in any case, that the jurists contributing to the renaissance of the Roman law during the formative epoch of the *ius commune* ignored the materials on fiduciary arrangements that belonged to the High Middle Ages. The pathbreaking study by *Maurizio Lupoi,* Alle radici del mondo giuridico europeo: Saggio storico-comparativo, 1994, demonstrates how this attitude led to the demise of an earlier European common law which left a permanent mark only in England. See also *idem,* Il diritto comune europeo in Inghilterra: Profili terminologici, in: Scintillae Iuris – Studi in memoria di Gino Gorla, II, 1994, pp. 1065 ff., 1075 - 1076 (with specific regard to trusts). From the 18th century onwards, scholars began to pay more and more attention to institutions that were considered to have Germanic origins, like the *Salmann.* Eventually, the *Germanisten* used them to contrast the *deutschrechtliche Treuhandbegriff* with the Romanistic *fiducia.*

IV. The Birth of the Doctrine of Testamentary *fiducia*

Testamentary *fiducia* became a recognized legal category only after the time of the early Commentators.

The path of its development can be traced with some certainty to *Bartolus* and *Baldus*. They did not codify the notion of testamentary *fiducia*, but established the conceptual framework and the rules which would later give substance to this notion in their interpretation of the Roman texts on *fideicommissa*. Before them we have only the seeds of this institution.

To be sure, the Roman law sources did not distinguish between *fideicommissa* and testamentary dispositions of a fiduciary nature[17]. The *Corpus iuris civilis* contains, however, several fragments of the Digest dealing with problems raised by some *fideicommissa* created for the exclusive benefit of the person to whom the instituted heir or legatee was to restore the testator's property[18]. Other passages of the Digest dealt with testamentary dispositions which raised *fideicommissa* in favour of persons whose identity was not disclosed by the testator[19]. Furthermore, the Justinianic *Codex* admitted (by way of exception) an unattested *fideicommissum*, provided that the plaintiff swore an oath *de calumnia*[20].

For the Roman jurists all the cases that would later be classified as fiduciary dispositions were examples of *fideicommissa*. The same attitude was shared by the Glossators, when they began to revive the Roman doctrine of *fideicommissa*[21]. The *Glossa ordinaria* by *Accursius* (1259 - 1263?) does not mark a departure from this approach. *Accursius* does not give any special meaning to the expression *fiduciaria (hereditas)*[22]. Even the fragment of the Digest which features the *heres fiduciarius* attracts only a plain exegesis of the opinion that *Iavolenus* had given on the case put to him, although the words *testamentum fiduciarium* are glossed with the laconic (if suggestive) statement: "quia de eo multum confidebat testator"[23].

---

17 On the Roman law of *fideicommissa* see the enlightening study by *David Johnston*, The Roman Law of Trusts, 1988.

18 D. 22, 1, 3, 3; D. 28, 5, 47; D. 31, 17 pr.; D. 36, 1, 48.

19 D. 28, 5, 47; D. 34, 5, 25. It will be seen that these texts should be distinguished from those allowing the operation of powers of appointment (e.g., D. 34, 5, 25).

20 C. 6, 42, 32 (A.D. 531). See *Johnston* (n. 17) 150.

21 On the Glossators' adherence to the Roman sources in this field, see generally: *Romualdo Trifone*, Il fedecommesso – Storia dell'istituto in Italia (dal diritto romano agli inizi del secolo XVI), Roma, 1914, pp. 62 ff.; *Mario Caravale*, s.v. Fedecommesso (diritto intermedio), Enciclopedia del diritto, XVII, 1968, pp. 109 ff.

22 Gloss *Fiduciaria* to D. 12, 1, 9 pr.: "Fiduciaria hereditas, id est fideicommissaria ...". I have consulted the following edition: Pandectarum seu Digestum Vetus Iuris Civilis ... Commentarii *Accursii*, t. 1, Venetiis, 1691, p. 826.

23 Gloss *Fiduciarium* to D. 36, 1, 48, 46 in *Accursius* (n. 22), t. 2, p. 1127.

The Glossators did, however, debate some questions related to our topic, such as the validity of an oral *fideicommissum* created without the presence of witnesses[24].

Furthermore, *Accursius'* comments on D. 31, 17 pr.[25] tell us something about the ambience in which the Glossators were immersed. By the 13th century the appointment of executors had become a standard feature of last wills[26]. This development needed to be reconciled with the Roman doctrines that reserved to the heir the pivotal role in the transmission of property on death. From it arose a tendency favouring testamentary execution only in securing enforcement of dispositions *pro anima* or *ad pias causas*[27].

In this context, *Accursius* argued that the intermediary appointed *legatarius* who was under a duty to transfer the object of the legacy to the beneficiary of the arrangement (the *fideicommissarius)* did not act simply in a ministerial capacity, i.e. as an executor. Such an intermediary "nec fuit minister tantum. Voluit enim testator in hunc transire dominium et de eo in fideicommissarium"[28]. As will be seen, the legal problem addressed by *Accursius* would be handled in a more sophisticated way by the successive generation of jurists.

The fact that the Glossators did not distinguish between *fideicommissa* and fiduciary dispositions made by testament does not mean that the practice of leaving property to somebody in order to have it transferred to a secret beneficiary did not exist. On the contrary, the practice was well known. Perhaps this aspect is best illustrated by the most influential guide to notarial practice on of testaments for the

24 These debates concerned the interpretation of C. 6, 32, 42. See the controversy referred to by Codicis Chisiani Collectio, § 163, de remedio l. ult. c. de fideic., in: Dissensiones dominorum sive controversiae veterum juris romani interpretum qui Glossatores vocantur, edidit et illustravit *Gustav Haenel,* Lipsiae, 1834, p. 243; see also, on the same issue: Hugolini dissensiones dominorum super toto corpore iuris civilis, § 455, *ibid.,* 546 - 547. On the civil and Canon law doctrines concerning testamentary formalities in general, see *Giovanni Chiodi,* L'interpretazione del testamento nel pensiero dei glossatori, 1997, pp. 516 - 556.

25 D. 31, 17 pr.: "Si quis Titio decem legaverit et rogaverit, ut ea restituat Maevio, Maeviusque fuerit mortus, Titii commodo cedit, non heredis, nisi dumtaxat ut ministrum Titium elegit. idem est et si ponas usum fructus legatum". This excerpt of the Justinianic compilation, belonging originally to *Marcellus*' Digest, 10th book, speaks of a bequest of ten to Titius who is asked (by the testator) to restore them to Maevius. Maevius has died. According to the jurist, the benefit then accrues to Titius (the legatee), not to the heir, unless the testator chose Titius merely "ut ministrum".

26 See the chapter by *Reinhard Zimmermann* in this volume.

27 There is a growing body of literature on these dispositions. The most important and recent studies relating to them are cited by *Chiodi* (n. 24) 144, n. 97. With reference to the bishop's powers over legacies *ad pias causas,* see *Robert Trexler,* The Bishop's Portion: Generic Pious Legacies in the Late Middle Ages in Italy, Traditio 28 (1972) 397.

28 Gloss *Ministrum* to D. 31, 17 pr. The premise to this reasoning is disclosed in the following passage: "Cum alicui sic relinquitur ut ministro, sicut fit quotidie commissari, petere non potest relictum ... nisi relictum sit pro anima seu ad pias causas in alimenta ... *vel nisi aliquod commodum ipse habiturus, quod debet sibi remanere vel aliis restituere. Sed tunc non relinquitur ut ministro*" (emphasis added).

period, i.e. the *Flos testamentorum* by the Bolognese notary *Rolandino Passeggeri* (1234 - 1300)[29]. Under the rubric "De legatis factis pro restitutione illicite acquisitorum"[30] this essential tool of the notarial profession considers the case of a testator who wants to make restitution *ad plenam animae liberationem* of property he had wrongfully acquired, but without disclosing the ultimate recipient of the disposition for fear of incurring *infamia. Rolandino* suggests using the following precaution. The testator should first declare his secret *voluntas* in writing; the *cedula* in question (sealed to preserve the secret) should then be handed over to the testator's confessor, or some other trusted person, in the presence of two witnesses. The testament need in such case recite only that the person who receives property under the testament must convert it into money in order to implement the testator's secret instructions[31].

V. *Bartolus, Baldus* and the *consiliatores* on Testamentary *fiducia*

1. The Protection Granted to the Beneficiary of the Secret Testamentary Disposition According to *Bartolus*

Bartolus a Saxoferrato (1314 - 1357) deals in depth with some problems posed by secret dispositions of a fiduciary nature lacking testamentary formalities. Commenting on C. 6, 42, 32, which addressed the case of a *fideicommissum* created *sine scriptura et presentia testium*[32], *Bartolus* holds it possible to defer an oath to the heir to establish the *fideicommissum,* not simply in cases where the heir initially denied it. In other words, according to *Bartolus,* the heir to whom the testator communicated his wishes is bound *civiliter et naturaliter* towards the secret beneficiary of the arrangement[33].

29 For the biographical profile and an evaluation of the importance of his work see *Giorgio Cencetti,* Rolandino Passeggeri dal mito alla storia, Rivista del notariato 1950, 373 ff.; *Roberto Ferrara,* Introduction to Rolandini Passagerii Contractus, 1993; *Giovanni Rossi,* "Duplex est usufructus", Ricerche sulla natura dell'usufrutto nel diritto comune, I, 1996, pp. 341 ff.

30 *Rolandini Rodulphi Bononiensis* Flos Testamentorum, pars II, cap. VIII, in: *idem,* Summa totius artis notariae, Venetiis, 1546, fo. 260v.-261.

31 *Rolandini Rodulphi Bononiensis* Flos Testamentorum (n. 30), on the second of four cases concerning *restitutiones usurarum, et aliarum quae indebitae acquisita sunt:* "Secundus est quando testator personas, quantitates, res et causas illicitorum propter timorem infamiae in testamento exprimi non vult forte: quia a communi suo sive ab aliis personis ea ex turpis causis extorsit. Et tunc solet habere ea notata, vel manus sua, vel alterius secreto scripta in aliqua cedula quam confessori suo, vel alteri personae fideli sigillatam exibet coram duobus testibus, licet ignorantibus quid contineatur in ea, quo facto in testamento dicetur: 'item relinquit de bonis suis tali sacerdoti vel tali priori centum libras solvendas et convertendas in his, et circa ea quae ei secreto commisit'."

32 The substance of this Constitution of the year 531 is reproduced in Inst. 2, 23, 12.

33 *Bartolus a Saxoferrato* on C. 6, 42, 32: "Nota multum istam lecturam quod quoniam testator noluit solemniter testari, sed confidit de fide haeredis, haeres tenetur ad prestationem

Bartolus argues in favour of the secret beneficiary also on the ground that legacies declared in writing lacking testamentary formalities are nevertheless valid when incorporated by reference in a valid testament[34], unless "non apparet schedulam esse testatoris ex legitima literarum comparatione, vel aliis legitimis indiciis"[35]. The analogy between the treatment of secret or half-secret dispositions which rest on the word of the instituted heir and testamentary dispositions incorporated by reference in a valid testament is thus established. The situation of the instituted heir who must transfer the inheritance to the person secretly communicated to him by the testator is assimilated by *Bartolus* to a *schedula* declaring the testator's will.

This interpretation is further illustrated by a question upon which *Bartolus* had been consulted[36]. The *consilium* deals with the case of a testator who wanted to give up all that he had wrongfully received[37]. The will appointed the testator's brother ("Titius") tutor of the son who was instituted heir. The testator also provided that the brother was to make restitution "secundum quod ipsi Titi placuerit", and added that his declaration was final in the matter. The legal point on which *Bartolus'* opinion was sought was (*inter alia)* whether such a provision was valid. His answer was that the testator's intention expressed by the verb "placuerit" gave

---

illius legati civiliter and naturaliter". I have used the following edition: *Bartoli* Commentaria in Secundam Codicis Partem, Lugduni, 1550, fo. 50v.

34 As in the case discussed by *Bartolus* himself, Commentaria in Secundam Infortiati Partem, Augustae Taurinorum, 1589, on D. 35, 1, 38, fo. 148v.: "testator dixit, volo quod haeres meus det illud quod scriptum est in schedula, quam relinqui apud guardianum fratrum Minorum".

35 *Ibid.* This opinion is supported by citations of the following texts: D. 34, 5, 25, D. 33, 14, C. 6, 42, 32, which should be interpreted: "secundum illam lecturam, secundum quam testator posuit in fide haeredis, et non scripsit". *Richard H. Helmholz,* The Origin of Holographic Wills in English Law, (1994) 15 J. L. H. 97, 100 ff., remarks that, at the time, the doctrine of *comparatio literarum* did not allow probate of a holographic will, except in cases like that discussed by *Bartolus.*

36 Cf. *Bartoli de Saxoferrato* Consilia, Augustae Taurinorum, 1589, Cons. 168, fo. 48.

37 This is the typical disposition *pro exoneratione conscientiae,* or *pro male ablatis,* or *pro illecita adquisita* by which the testator wanted to save his soul, in obedience to the precept of the Church "non remittitur peccatum nisi restituatur ablatum" (Liber Sextus of *Boniface VIII,* reg. 4). The concept of *male ablatum* was very wide. Besides usurious interests on loans, it included anything unjustly acquired or retained by the testator, like payments due to creditors, or compensation due to victims of wrongful damage. Sometime the will declared to whom restitution was due. More often, it featured generic expressions, where the testator ordered restitution of *male ablata* without saying more. The task entrusted to the heir or executor in the latter case was rather troublesome, hence the development of a procedure which should have ensured proper distribution of the things belonging to the deaceased. See *Robert Caillemer,* Origines et développement de l'exécution testamentaire, thèse, Lyon, 1901, pp. 82, n. 1, 440, n. 2. For a typical disposition *pro male ablatis* see the will of Petrus Thomaxini (A.D. 1300), reproduced in *Martin Bertram,* Bologneser Testamente. Zweiter Teil: Sondierungen in den *Libri Memoriali,* Quellen und Forschungen aus italienischen Archiven und Bibliotheken, 1991, LXXXI, pp. 195, 226.

the brother limited discretion *(arbitrium boni viri)* to decide what property was subject to restitution. Such discretion did not violate the prohibition against testamentary dispositions that depended upon the mere *arbitrium* of another person. On the other hand, the instruction to consider the simple declaration of the brother final in the matter could not stand, because it left up to the brother any question "an debeatur, et cui debeatur ... et sic talis dispositio est ipso iure nulla ut d. l. captatorias et l. captatoriae in quibus est casus"[38].

An important corollary to this approach is the following. The declaration of the person who received the testator's instructions is "quodam testimonium voluntatis defuncti". This person must be examined under oath, as a witness would be. Such a witness, though, is not an ordinary witness. When an ordinary witness is called upon to render his deposition the parties must be present and given the opportunity to object. But here the *persona testis* is already *approbata* by the testator: "... unde non potest opponere, nec contra dictum, nec contra iuramentum, nam non posset eius poenitentia trahere in contrariam sententiam. Nihil enim de proprio sensu iudicat sed solum voluntatem testatoris declarat"[39]. The argument leads to the conclusion that the declaration of the testator's *voluntas* by this kind of "witness" is irrevocable, whether it was done before the judge or out of court, in presence of the party which would be advantaged by it.

Bartolus also developed a significant treatment of promises extracted by the testator from the heir to secure the fulfillment of the testor's wishes regarding the payment of legacies lacking testamentary form. According to *Bartolus,* the testator could obtain from the heir the promise to pay the legatee. Such a promise "sapit natura contractus". The legatee could then sue the heir for breach of the promise made to the testator[40]. On the basis of this doctrine the legatee may prove his right against the heir by two witnesses – such is the general rule with respect to contracts – rather than by five or seven witnesses, as it would be where a testament is involved[41].

---

38 The legal background to this solution is discussed in comparative perspective by *Reinhard Zimmermann,* "Quos Titius voluerit" – Höchstpersönliche Willensentscheidung des Erblassers oder "power of appointment"?, 1991, *passim,* esp. pp. 16 ff.

39 *Bartolus a Saxoferrato,* on D. 33, 4, 14, n. 7 - 10. I have consulted the following edition: Commentaria in Primam Infortiati Partem, Augustae Taurinorum, 1589, fo. 93v.

40 *Bartolus* overcomes the problem posed by the absence of privity between the promisor and the beneficiary by supposing that the testator obtained the promise from the heir as the beneficiary's agent.

41 *Bartolus a Saxoferrato,* Commentaria (n. 34) on D. 30, 55, n. 1, fo. 19 v.: "Contra hoc opponit glossa Cod. de fideic. l. fin. [C. 6, 42, 32] ubi sufficit quod in fide haeredis ponatur absque aliqua solemnitatem secundum unam lectura. Solutio: ibi est casus specialis: vel aliter, ponere in fide haeredis: ita quod haeres promittat hoc defuncto, sapit naturam contractus, et ita haeres quia hoc promisit ad hoc convenitur".

2. Of Form and Substance: *Baldus'* Approach to Testamentary *fiducia*

Baldus de Ubaldiis (1320 - 27?-1400), the greatest among *Bartolus'* pupils, deals with the position of the person who is instituted heir or appointed legatee for the exclusive benefit of another in several places of his *Commentaria.* The issue is first tackled in the comment to D. 22, 1, 3, 3. Here *Papinianus* put the case of a certain Pollidius who was made heir by a woman relative and asked to convey to the woman's daughter whatever he obtained from the estate when the daughter reached a certain age. Pollidius was also to have certain land from the same estate for his own benefit. The mother had explained in her will that she did this in order to entrust her daughter's affairs to relatives, rather than to tutors. *Papinianus* then mentions that he persuaded the praetorian prefects that the fruits taken by Pollidius in good faith from the estate of the deceased should be handed over to the daughter, either because only the land was prelegated[42] to him or because the mother had chosen the remedy of *fideicommissum* to avoid the danger of tutelage.

Commenting upon this, *Baldus* holds that the heir instituted *in favorem honorati* cannot subtract the *quarta trebellianica*[43]: "Nam licet nomen, et jus heredis, habeat tamen tamquam minister videtur". This heir is therefore *only a minister,* despite the fact that he is instituted heir and has the corresponding right. The meaning of the word "minister" in this context needs further explanation, which is provided in the comment to another passage of the Digest[44]. It is clear, in any case, that an heir like Pollidius can neither withhold the products of the *res* that should go to the daughter, nor subtract the *quarta trebellianica* from it[45]. The peculiar nature of the disposition emerges "ex causa et verbis testamenti": to establish the true legal position of the heir one has to consider both the precise words employed by the testator and the reason why the disposition was made.

Baldus' views on this matter are further developed in his commentary to D. 28, 5, 47 (46)[46]. This passage from *Africanus'* Questions, Book 2, deals with the case of a man who wanted to institute a son-in-power as his heir in such a way that the head of the household would inherit nothing. To avoid embarrassing the son-in-

---

42 *Praelegatio* was a legacy in favour of one of joint heirs, made *per vindicationem* or *damnationem.* Such a legacy was a burden on all the heirs according to their respective shares, including the legatee.

43 This was the share which the heir accepting the inheritance charged with a *fideicommissum* could withhold. It was named after the *senatus consultus Trebellianum* (A.D. 56), to which *Justinian* engrafted the provision on the *quarta* originally introduced by the *s.c. Pegasianum* (A.D. 73). For the debate among the Glossators and the Post-Glossators concerning the *quarta trebellianica,* see *Trifone* (n. 21) 95 ff.

44 See *infra,* text at n. 50.

45 Commentaria in Secundam Digesti Veteris Partem, Venetiis, 1572, fo. 192v.

46 *Baldus,* Commentaria in Primam et Secundam Infortiati Partem, Venetiis, 1572, fo. 80 - 80v.

power, the testator eventually instituted as heir a friend of the son-in-power, whom he did not know. The question was whether the friend could be sued on a *fideicommissum* or in any other way (and if so whether the action should be brought by the father or the son) if the friend either refused to accept the inheritance or refused to hand it over after acceptance. The reply (by *Julian)* was that, although the friend had accepted a trust *(fidem suam interposuisse)*, no action on the *fideicommissum* lay unless it was proved that the testator himself had also relied on the trust. Nevertheless, the son had an action of mandate (*sub specie actio utilis)* against the friend. The father, however, could not bring this action because it would have been contrary to good faith to restore to him what the testator specified should not. *Baldus* remarks upon this passage that the heir instituted *in favorem alterius* is liable *ex fideicommisso* when the testator relied on him *(accomodat fidem testatori)*, while liability arises *ex mandato* if the person who relied on him was the would-be beneficiary. The reference to the *actio utilis* is translated by *Baldus* into the distinction between *ius utile* and *ius directum*[47]. According to *Baldus,* the heir instituted for the benefit of another acquires the *ius directum,* while the person to whom the inheritance should be restored has the *ius utile.*

Baldus does not consider the testament mentioned by *Africanus* simulated[48]. A simulated transaction is made only in pretence; it is a sham devoid of any effect[49]. Keeping in mind this remark, we can understand the importance of the point. According to *Baldus,* the person who is charged with the duty to convey the inheritance to the designated beneficiary gets title. Even though the intermediary derives no benefit from it, the transfer to him is not fictitious.

What meaning *Baldus* gave to the noun *minister* becomes clearer in his comment to D. 31, 17 pr.[50]. This fragment concerns a bequest to Titius who is asked (by the testator) to restore it to Maevius. Maevius has died. According to *Marcellus,* the benefit then accrues to Titius (the legatee), not to the heir, unless the testator chose Titius merely "ut ministrum". *Baldus'* discussion of the expression "min-

---

47 On the origin and meaning of this distinction, see *Robert Feenstra,* Dominium and ius in re aliena: the Origins of a Civil Law Distinction, in: Peter Birks (ed.), New Perspectives in the Roman Law of Property – Essays for Barry Nicholas, 1989, pp. 111, 112 - 113; *idem,* Les origines du dominium utile chez les Glossateurs (avec une appendice concernant l'opinion des Ultramontani), in: Flores legum H.J. Scheltema oblati, 1971, p. 49, reprinted with further literature in: *idem,* Fata iuris romani, 1974, p. 215. *Rossi* (n. 29) I, 365 ff., II, 10 ff. highlights the development of the categories *ius directum-ius utile* in *Bartolus* and *Baldus.*

48 *Baldus* (n. 46) fo. 80v., n. 4: "licet unus sit scriptus, et alius debet effectum institutionis reportare: quia si esset simulatum, esset nullum sed hic dicit textus aperte quod est aliquod, et quod ex eo potest hereditas adiri quod est notabilis".

49 On the Roman law concerning *simulatio* and the related *ius commune* developments, see *Reinhard Zimmermann,* The Law of Obligations: Roman Foundations of the Civilian Tradition, 1990 (paperback edition 1996), pp. 646 ff. With specific regard to *Baldus,* though without discussion of the question examined in the text, see *Helmut Coing,* Simulatio und Fraus in der Lehre des Bartolus und Baldus, in: Festschrift Koschaker, III, 1939, p. 402.

50 *Baldus* (n. 46) fo. 140 - 140v. For the text of D. 31, 17 pr., see *supra* n. 25.

ister" in this context aims to outline the powers and the rights of the person charged with this kind of *fideicommissum*. The technique deployed for this purpose leads *Baldus* to distinguish whether or not this *minister* is *nudus*, and in which sense he can be so called. According to *Baldus* the *minister* may be *nudus* "a jure agendi"; such a legatee can never be "nudus minister", however, because he has "actionem et titulum legatarii". In this respect the legatee differs from executors who may bring actions but are *nudi executores*, like executors *ad pias causas*, who do not have title (*titulus*) nor actions *nomine suo*, but only *nomine pauperum*.

Then *Baldus* discusses another meaning of "nudus minister". The term also denotes the *minister* who is *nudus* "a commodo", that is to say who cannot benefit from the disposition. The intermediary may be *nudus a commodo* in two senses: *potentialiter*, in which case he is not a *nudus minister*, because if the *fideicommissum* fails he will benefit from the disposition; or *actualiter*, when the legatee never benefits from the disposition, as in the case of an executor. The elegant conclusion of this reasoning is captured in a few lines: "Alias simplicius et conclusio stat in hoc, quod nudum dicitur, vel abstractum a commodo et titulo, vel abstractum a commodo, sed non a titulo". With respect to the case under discussion, *Baldus* concludes that the intermediary who is not allowed to benefit from the disposition would be *nudus a commodo sed non a titulo*.

Commenting on C. 6, 42, 32, *Baldus* is more cautious than *Bartolus* about the possibility of deferring an oath to the heir in order to establish the existence of the *fideicommissum*[51]. On the other hand, according to *Baldus*, the testator's *nuda voluntas* is enforceable where the beneficiary of the informal disposition is confronted with an heir guilty of fraud, just as the *nudum pactum* can be enforced by an *actio doli*[52]. Apart from this, *Baldus* considers whether the testator's informal *voluntas* can generate an *actio ex testamento*, or a *condictio*. His answer is that such *voluntas* creates a natural obligation, "quia deficit solennitas extrinseca, et non deficit consensus"[53]. Eventually, at the end of his comment, *Baldus* strongly hints at a canonical way of looking at the same *quaestio:* "Adde huic legi, quod ubi est electa mera fides, ibi non est opus testibus, plus enim peccat ille de quo testator plus confidit"[54]. Here we have an echo of the canonical doctrine which enforces an informal disposition through the *denunciatio evangelica sive judicialis*[55].

---

51 *Baldi Ubaldi Perusini* Commentaria in vi., vii., viii., ix., x., et xi. Codicis libri, Venetiis, 1572, ad C. 6, 42, 32, n. 1, fo. 165.

52 *Baldus* (n. 51) ad C. 6, 42, 32, n. 8, fo. 165v.: "ultima voluntas nuda vestitur legis auxilio proper dolum et mendacium adversarii. Similiter ff. de dolo l. eleganter servus pactionis". On the enforcement of naked pacts through the *actio doli*, see *Michele Graziadei*, Il patto e il dolo, in: Scritti in onore di Rodolfo Sacco, I, 1994, p. 589.

53 *Baldus* (n. 51) ad C. 6, 42, 32, n. 11, fo. 165v.

54 *Baldus* (n. 51) ad C. 6, 42, 32, n. 26, fo. 166.

55 See, in general, *Helmut Coing*, English Equity and the Denunciatio Evangelica of the Canon Law, (1955) 71 L.Q.R. 233; *Paolo Bellini*, L'obbligazione da promessa con oggetto temporale nel sistema canonistico classico, 1964; *Richard H. Helmholz*, Assumpsit and Fidei

In any case, the testamentary disposition informally communicated to the fiduciary can be upheld because the fiduciary declares the testator's own *voluntas*. Otherwise the disposition would be invalid: "nemo enim potest testari per alium nec committere alii supremum suum iudicium componendum, sed distribuendum et declarandum sic ut ff. de hered. inst. l. illa institutio et ff. de dote prael. l. Theopompus [D. 33, 4, 14]"[56].

3. *Bartolus'* and *Baldus'* Legacy to the *consiliatores*

The works of *Bartolus* and *Baldus* taken together contain the principal ingredients that later jurists would use to fashion a full-blown doctrine of *fiducia* or, rather, of the *heres fiduciarius*. First, the two commentators explain that the person who is instituted heir or legatee for the benefit of another is (in most instances) charged with a *fideicommissum*, but they make clear that the relationship between the *fiduciarius* and the person entitled to the benefit of the disposition may also have a different nature (i.e. *mandatum)*. In any case, even when the relation between the various parties is a *fideicommissum*, it is clear that at least some of the general rules concerning this institution (like those about the *quarta trebellianica)* do not apply where the person charged with the *fideicommissum* cannot benefit from it.

Second, *Baldus* discusses the delicate conceptual issues involved. Fiduciary dispositions vest title in the fiduciary, but because title does not give him any *commodum* he is still considered a mere intermediary. Nevertheless, such dispositions cannot be considered void because they are not simulated.

Thirdly, most dispositions purporting to take effect in favour of persons not named in the testament pose serious problems of enforceability. This happens because they usually fall outside the framework of solemn testaments. None the less, we witness a consistent effort to find reasons and means to enforce them which goes beyond the letter of the Roman law: a) if written, the disposition is held valid when incorporated by reference in the solemn testament; b) the declaration of the person to whom the testator's *voluntas* was communicated may be considered valid on the same basis; c) the beneficiary of the disposition may

---

Laesio, (1976) 91 L.Q.R. 406; *idem*, Contracts and the Canon Law, in: John Barton (ed.), Towards a General Law of Contract, 1990, p. 49. The possibility of resorting to this procedure to enforce an informal disposition *mortis causa* is expressly mentioned by *Alciatus*, Consilia, Basileae, 1582, Consilium 195, lib. 9, n. 3. In this context, one should also be mindful of the doctrine favouring the application of canonical *aequitas* to avoid danger to Christian souls. On the relationship between the *denunciatio evangelica* and such doctrine, see the fundamental contribution by *John L. Barton*, Equity in the Medieval Common Law, in: Ralph A. Newman (ed.), Equity in the World's Legal Systems – A Comparative Study, 1973, pp. 139, 154 - 155. Further bibliography on the role played by canonical equity is cited *infra*, n. 58.

56 *Baldus*, Codex 6, 21, 11, fo. 58v.- 59, at n. 2, fo. 59.

have an action *vi contractus* against the person who promised to perform the testator's *voluntas*[57]; d) he can also enforce the *naturalis obligatio* springing from the testator's informal declaration of his will; e) failure to implement the testator's informal *voluntas* can be interpreted as a form of fraud, sanctioned by an *actio doli* in favour of the victim of the fraud; and f) the beneficiary of the disposition may resort to Canon law and allege a breach of faith by the fiduciary heir, triggering enforcement in his favour through the *imploratio officii iudicis in modum denunciationis evangelicae.*

Finally, according to both *Bartolus* and *Baldus,* one should distinguish between whether or not the intermediary charged with transferring property to specific persons merely declared the will of the testator or applied his own will. In the former case the disposition is valid; in the latter it is void.

Upon these foundations rest the later contributions of other jurists.

Thus, for example, *Baldus*' brother, *Angelus de Perusio,* gives the beneficiary an *actio utilis negotiorum gestorum* which is "ex aequitate introducta vel saltem officio iudicis"[58]. *Angelus* also discusses the problem posed by the case of the heir instituted *in favorem alterius* who refuses to accept the *hereditas.* This heir can be compelled *officio iudicis* to accept the *hereditas* and to tranfer it to the beneficiary[59].

Paulus de Castro's contribution is also noteworthy. Writing in the first half of the fifteenth century, *Paulus* admits the validity of secret dispositions only if they are partially disclosed in the testament[60]. He also suggests the possibility of sanctioning the testator's secret instructions by resorting to Canon law. Thus, referring to a case in which the testator had appointed his son as heir with the secret instruction to make over to his brother one half of what he received, *Paulus* argues that the brother should have either an action of mandate, an action *negotiorum gestorum,* or an: "utilis actio ex testamento quasi [heres] fidem suam tacite accomodaverit testatori de hoc faciendo: Cod. de fideic. l. fin. [C. 6, 42, 32]". He then adds another consideration touching the canonical side of the same question. The heir

---

57 As we have seen, the theory is that a contract between the testator and the heir was concluded for the transmission of the property to the beneficiary. The beneficiary should have an action on this contract by virtue of the (fictitious) premise that the testator acted as the beneficiary's agent in its formation.

58 *Angelus de Perusio,* Super Primam Infortiati (s.l., s.d.) ad D. 28, 5, 46, fo. 34v. The opening remark of his commentary upon this *lex* is: "Guarda de chi tu te fidi". *Baldus* had already interpreted *aequitas canonica* as a factor modifying the rules of the civil law: see *Norbert Horn,* Aequitas in den Lehren des Baldus, 1968. On canonical *aequitas* see, in general, *Paolo Grossi,* L'ordine giuridico medioevale, 1995, pp. 210 ff.; *Peter Landau,* "Aequitas" in the "Corpus Iuris Canonici" in: Rabello (n. 4) 129, 138 - 139.

59 On D. 7, 1, 21.

60 *Pauli Castrensis* in: Secundam Infortiati Partem Commentaria, Venetiis, 1593, ad D. 34, 5, 25, 26, fo. 75v.-76. See also *Consilium* 177, in: Consiliorum sive Responsorum *Pauli Castrensis,* lib. II, Augustae Taurinorum, 1580, fo. 78.

who swears that nothing is due to the brother "impudenter frangit fidem Deo, quem invocavit, et per quem iurasse videtur denegando fratri suo dictam partem [hereditatis], fratrem suum fraudat contra jus naturale et divinum"[61].

Finally, *Alexander Tartagnus* (1424 - 1477) summarized in a short passage what had by then become the conventional wisdom about the *heres fiduciarius:* "... fiduciarius heres, qui censetur esse custos, et non habet sentire commodum. Unde videmus quod non lucratur fructus perceptos, quos alii heredes lucrantur. ... Nec quarta trebellianicam detrahit ... Et ... sic videtur quod iste heres censeatur esse quodammodo nudus minister"[62]. With this last author we come closer to the epoch which saw a new approach to the Roman law.

VI. Humanistic Scholarship and the Rediscovery of *fiducia* in the Ante-Justinianic Sources

In the 16th century humanistic scholarship reached its maturity. The Humanists' programme was to retrieve the original meaning of the texts of the Roman law which had long been obscured by the Glossators and the Commentators.

That programme moves *Guillaume Budé, Annotationes in Pandectas*[63], where the French scholar approaches the institution of *fiducia* through the discussion of a variety of ante-Justinianic sources.

Budé first touches upon the subject of *fiducia* by revealing *Accursius'* false etymology of the word *vindiciae,* which he corrects with the help of *Cicero's* oration against Verre and the commentary upon it traditionally ascribed to *Asconius Pedianus*[64]. In the light of those texts, *Budé* established the role of the *lis vindiciarum* in

---

61 Consiliorum sive responsorum *Pauli Castrensis* (n. 60) Consilium 395, fo. 182, at 182v. n. 2.

62 *Alexander de Imola,* In Secundam Infortiati Secunda Pars Commentariorum, Venetiis, 1541, ad D. 36, 1, 48, 46, fo. 141v.; cf. De Fideicommissis Praesertim Universalibus, Tractatus Frequentissimus *M. Antonii Peregrini,* 10th ed., 1644, art. 3, n. 19, p. 32.

63 *Guillaume Budé* (1468 - 1540) published the first edition of the Annotationes in Pandectas from book I to XXIV in Paris, 1508. These were followed by the Annotationes posteriores, 1st ed., Paris, 1515. I have used the following edition: Annotationes Gulielmi Budaei Parisiensis, Secretarii Regii, in quattuor et viginti Pandectarum libros, Paris, 1542. On *G. Budé's* contribution to the development of modern historical scholarship: *Donald. R. Kelley,* Guillaume Budé and the First Historical School of Law, (1976) 72 American Historical Review 807; *idem,* Foundations of Modern Historical Scholarship: Language, Law and History in the French Renaissance, New York, 1970. For an enlightening assessment of *Budé's* position towards Anti-Tribonianism, Bartolism, and the research of the interpolations, see *Douglas J. Osler,* Budaeus and Roman Law, Ius Commune 13 (1985) 195.

64 *Budaeus* (n. 63) 42 - 44. Cf. *M.T. Cicero,* Actionis in C. Verrem Secundae, Lib. I, 1, cap. 45, 115. *Budé's* reference to *Pedianus* relates to the (spurious) commentary on *Cicero's* Actionis in C. Verrem discovered at St. Gall in 1416. This work was at first ascribed to *Quintus Asconius Pedianus* (9 B.C.-76 A.D.). Later research showed that it was composed in the

the ancient Roman process. It referred to the proceeding whereby the *praetor* granted to one party interim possession of the thing claimed, provided that party gave security (through the intervention of another person called *praes)* to restore the thing and the interim profits if the party lost the principal case. That decision of the *praetor* put one party into temporary possession of the thing; for *Budé* such possession was neither regular (*iusta)* nor absolute, but of a fiduciary nature, akin to that of the *depositarius,* or that found in the contemporary practice of *recredentia*[65]. Just as in the case of *recredentia* familiar to *Budé,* this possession obliged the person who received the property to account for it, and to restore its fruits[66]. Another example of fiduciary possession is extracted from *Titus Livius*[67]. According to *Budé, Livius* writes that *King Philip* of Macedonia consigned the city of Corinth[68] to the Spartan tyrant *Nabis* before going to war. The great historian narrates that *Philip* thought it was an excellent idea to leave *Nabis* in fiduciary possession of the city, so that *Nabis* had to return it to *Philip* if he won the war, or else have it for himself, in case something happened to *Philip. Budé's* survey of the various contexts where the word *fiducia* and its derivatives appear also includes *Caius Julius Caesar's De bello civili* on the *fiduciaria opera* entrusted to ambassadors[69], as well the fragment of the Digest dealing with the *heres fiduciarius*[70].

The examination of all these sources revealed that *fiducia* was a term of art. Yet, *Budé* also noticed that the Pandects ignored it, because *Tribonianus* and his collaborators "... accisas nobis Pandectas verius quam compendiosas dederunt". These remarks urged a return to the technical meaning of *fiducia. Budé* accomplished the feat by reading other passages of *Cicero's* works, where the orator mentions *fiducia* among the relationships and contracts which impose the duty to *fidem praestare*[71], or else makes a facetious reproach to his friend *Trebatius,* reminding him of the words of the *formula fiduciae*[72]. The evidence collected needed only to be supplemented with *Boetius'* description of the *mancipatio fiduciaria* in the Commentary

---

5th century. See *Pseudo-Asconius in M. Tullii Ciceronis* Actionis Secundae in C. Verrem, Lib. I, in: Io. Casp. Orellius (ed.), M. Tullii Ciceronis opera quae supersunt omnia ac disperditorum fragmenta, V, 2, Turici, 1833, pp. 154 ff., at 191.

65 *Budaeus* (n. 63) 43: "Vindiciae hodie recredentiam vocamus ...". *Du Cange,* Glossarium mediae et infimae latinitatis, V, Paris, 1845, p. 632, s.v. *Recredentia,* gives this as a "vox praticorum nostrorum" and briefly discusses the differences and the similarities between the Roman *vindiciae* and the practitioners' notion(s) of *recredentia.*

66 *Budaeus* (n. 63) 44: "Huiusmodi enim possessio, quam Pedianus intelligi ex Cicerone voluit, non iusta et absoluta est possessio, sed fiduciaria, et veluti depositaria, ut haec nostra recredentia rationibus reddendis et fructibus est obnoxia".

67 *Budaeus* (n. 63) 44. Cf. *Titus Livius,* Ab urbe condita libri, lib. XXXII, cap. 38, par. 1 - 2.

68 *Livius* is speaking of Argos, not of Corinth.

69 Cf. *Caius Iulius Caesar,* De bello civili, lib. II, cap. 17, par. 1,2,3.

70 D. 36, 1, 48, 46.

71 Cf. *Marcus Tullius Cicero,* Topica, 10, 42.

72 *Marcus Tullius Cicero,* Epistulae ad familiares, lib. VII, epist. XII, par. 2.

to *Cicero's* Topic[73]. Thus, eventually, *Budé* reached the conclusion that *fiducia* was one of the *bonae fidei* contracts[74]. Such a contract supported an *actio fiduciae,* which another text by *Cicero* mentions in connection with the enforcement of a security transaction based on *fiducia*[75].

John Baker has observed that "... humanist jurisprudence removed Roman law from the land of the living and rendered it as useful to practising lawyers as the study of Greek coins would have been to bankers"[76]. This assessment of the impact of Humanist legal scholarship on the everyday life of the law is confirmed at first by taking a look at the work of a contemporary of *Budé,* the Milanese jurist *Andrea Alciato* (1492 - 1550), another founding father of Legal Humanism.

Alciato deals with *fiducia* in his *Parergon juris*[77], starting from the question "quid sit fiducia in iure nostro" and going on to consider Roman legal antiquities[78]. This treatment clearly does not speak of contemporary practice[79].

Yet, in the end, the *ius commune* was able to weave the humanist contribution into its fabric. Thus, we find practitioners' works citing *Budé* side by side with traditional authorities of the *ius commune* on testamentary *fiducia*[80]. The same approach is evident in printed editions of *Accursius' Glossa ordinaria,* which incorporated a reference to *Budé's Annotationes* on *fiducia* to explain the position of the *heres fiduciarius*[81].

---

73 *Supra,* n. 15.

74 *Budaeus* (n. 63) 46: "Conferantur haec verba Boethii cum exemplis praecedentibus, et facile intelligetur fiduciam bonae fidei contractum, at quae etiam optimae fidei fuisse".

75 *Budaeus* (n. 63) 46 - 47. Cf. *Marcus Tullius Cicero,* Pro L. Flacco oratio, cap. XXI, § 51. On the *actio fiduciae, Budé* cites a passage from *Cicero,* De natura Deorum, lib. III, cap. XXX, 74. Here again *Budé* points to the similitude between the practice of *recredentia* and the fiduciary alienation for security purposes. References to *fiducia* in other sources seemed to the great Humanist more obscure and difficult to clarify. Later Humanists offer a full treatment of *fiducia* as a security device; see, e.g., Codex Theodosianus cum perpetuis commentariis *Jacobi Gothofredi,* § I, Mantuae, 1740, comment on C. Th. 3, 1, 1, pp. 277 ff. The first edition of this work was published in 1655.

76 *John H. Baker,* The Reports of Sir John Spelman, II, Selden Society vol. 94, London, 1978, p. 27. This evaluation is not peculiar to English legal historiography: see, e.g., *Helmut Coing,* Europäisches Privatrecht, I, 1985, p. 68.

77 The first edition of the "Parergon iuris civilis" was published in Basel, 1538.

78 Parergon iuris civilis libri tres, Lugduni, 1548, cap. XXVI, p. 51.

79 Note that *Alciato* was certainly aware of contemporary practice. See *Alciatus* (n. 55) Consilium 175, lib. 9 (the last will of the testator must be respected, though it was not expressed in a solemn form. Therefore, the heir charged with restoring the inheritance to the person secretly designated by testator cannot withold the assets *salva conscientia).*

80 See, e.g., Disceptationum forensium judiciorum *Stephani Gratiani,* IV, Genevae, 1664, cap. 150, p. 113, n. 34; *Iohannis Torre* De pactis futurae successionis tractatus tripartitus, Venetiis, 1679, lib. III, cap. VII, p. 456, n. 1.

81 Cf. *Accursius* (n. 23) t. 2, p. 1127, marginal gloss to D. 36, 1, 48, 46: "Fiduciarius haeres dicitur qui non justus et absolutus est haeres, sed velut depositarius: hoc est, cui fidei credita est haereditas alteri restituenda: quod et fideicommissari dicitur qua forma dicit, et possessio

All in all, therefore, one is tempted to qualify the view of Legal Humanism which sees it as wholly irrelevant to the living law of the time[82]. Its influence on practice becomes even more evident if we take into account some Canon law developments related to our subject.

VII. A Canon Law Detour: *fiducia* and the Canonical Prohibition of *confidentia beneficialis*

Though the Humanists' efforts to unearth the original features of the Roman *fiducia* did not disturb the contemporary conceptions of testamentary *fiducia,* they may well have influenced the drafters of the ecclesiastical legislation against *confidentia beneficialis*[83].

During the Middle Ages (and beyond), ecclesiastical benefices were important forms of wealth. They easily fell prey to wordly appetites. A common device to reap the profits of an ecclesiastical benefice was to hold it *in commendam*[84], but this scheme did not exhaust the ways of tapping this source of income. By means of another device, the benefice was transferred to a person who undertook to hold it on behalf of the transferor, or for the benefit of a third person designated by him. In both cases the transferee, as the holder of the benefice, could not himself profit from it: the income produced by the office was reserved for the beneficiary of the scheme. Eventually, the benefice returned to its original owner, or to the designated beneficiary. This was the basic scheme of the *confidentia beneficialis.*

---

quaedam fiduciaria de qua Budaeus super de originis iuris l. § initium fuisse". In the same spirit, some authors and court decisions simply refer to this gloss as if it were part of *Accursius*' work.

82 See now, for a more accurate assessment of the impact of legal humanism, *Klaus Luig,* Humanismus und Privatrecht, in: Festschrift für Gunther Wesener, 1992, pp. 285 ff., *Robert Feenstra,* The Development of European Private Law: A Romanist Watershed?, in: David L. Carey Miller, Reinhard Zimmermann (eds.), The Civilian Tradition and Scots Law: Aberdeen Quincentenary Essays, 1997, pp. 103 ff., 113.

83 To my knowledge, the best modern study on the subject is still *J. Deshusses,* Confidence, in: R. Naz (ed.), Dictionnaire de droit canonique, IV, Paris, 1949, p. 67. When the papal bulls on *confidentia beneficialis* were drafted, the Roman *curia* was staffed with lawyers belonging to humanistic circles. *Pope Pius IV,* who launched the battle against *confidentia beneficialis,* promoted *Franciscus Alciatus,* nephew of *Andrea Alciatus* and successor to his chair, to be one of the highest officials of the *Curia.* The same Pontifex granted to the *Collegium* of the Jurisconsults of Milan the perpetual right to choose the *Auditor* of the *Sacra Rota* and the Advocate of the Consitory. In this epoch, Milan was one of the centers of legal humanism.

84 On which see *Shael Herman,* Utilitas Ecclesiae: The Canonical Conception of the Trust, (1996) 70 Tulane L.R. 2239, 2249; *idem,* Trusts Sacred and Profane: Clerical, Secular, and Commercial Uses of the Medieval Commendatio, (1997) 71 Tulane L. R. 869; with specific regard to the Italian scenario, see *Gaetano Greco,* I giuspatronati laicali nell'età moderna, in: Giorgio Chittolini and Giovanni Miccoli (eds.), Storia d' Italia – Annali, vol. 9, 1986, pp. 354 ff.

The confidence reposed in the person holding the benefice for another was an essential factor for the smooth working of this secret arrangement: hence the expression *confidentia beneficialis.* Undoubtedly, the canon law at first found it difficult to charge the parties involved in this transaction with simony, because each separate act done in execution of the confidential scheme was not *simoniacum per se*[85]. Therefore, ecclesiastical tribunals (with the possible exception of the *Rota Romana)* traditionally enforced them, compelling the *confidentiarii* to honour their undertakings[86].

It should be observed that the grounds upon which the *confidentiae* were enforced were in many respects identical with the reasons alleged for granting enforcement of similar arrangements in civil matters[87].

The reaction against this practice grew up in the atmosphere of the Council of Trent. *Pope Pius IV* began his battle against the *confidentia beneficialis* in the consistory of 4 May 1562. He raised the same point again during consistories held on 30 June 1563 and on 23 March 1564[88]. Eventually, the papal bull *Romanum Ponteficem* of 17 October 1564 issued the first general prohibition against these arrangements[89]. Apparently, the Pope seized upon the occasion of the death of *Cardinal*

---

85 Cf. *J. Deshusses* (n. 83) 67.

86 *Flaminius Parisius,* De confidentia beneficiali prohibita Tractatus, Venetiis, 1619 (1st ed. published in 1598), Quaestio V, nn. 11, 12, p. 13: "Et ita haec prava consuetudo fuit recepta, ut inceperit paulatim ius in supremis tribunalibus pro fide prestanda reddi, et compelli non reddentes beneficia in custodiam, et confidentiam recepta .... Ab hac tamen labe sacrum Auditorium Rotae semper se abstinuit, et uti rei absurdae semper confidentiis obstitit, et numquam pro eis iudicare voluit, cum interim penes aliorum Iudicum tribunalia male feriati homines perfugium invenirent ... et sic Rota habuit pro absurdo canonizare confidentia, quare vel mandabat, cum casus occurreret, partes concordare ..., vel remittebat ad Auditorem Camerae ...".

87 Cf. *Parisius* (n. 86) 14, Questio VI, Quare tolerabatur antiquitus confidentia? According to Parisius these arrangements were enforced "tum ex utilitate quae resultabat pluribus Curialibus ex hoc, quorum favore id fuit prava consuetudine, seu potius corruptela toleratum". The author gives a short account of the technical grounds which justified the enforcement of *confidentia beneficialis:* "tum etiam, quia quemadmodum antiquis temporibus, antequam fideicommissa essent permissa, grave admodum reputabatur, ea non reddere, seu restituere et per consequens hac forsan ratione fuit per multos annos tolerata: pacta enim servare, est iuris naturae ... nam fides est fundamentum Iustitiae. Considerat ideo censetur proxima iuramento, eius que naturam sapit hinc fidei prestatio parit naturalem obligationem ... Hinc ob fidem non observatam defertum iuramentum in litem .... Et datur actio ad interesse .... Et deceptus sub confidentia, agit de dolo ...".

88 *Ludwig von Pastor,* Storia dei Papi dalla fine del medioevo, § VII, trans. *Angelo Mercati,* Roma, 1928, p. 316.

89 Bullarum Diplomatum et Privilegiorum Sanctorum Romanorum Ponteficum Taurinensis Editio, t. VIII, Neapoli, 1882, pp. 305 - 308. *Shael Herman's* contribution to this volume shows how the Church employed various trust-like devices to promote its activities. My research confirms his findings as far as testamentary *fiducia* is concerned. Considering this general picture, one may wonder why the Pope banned the *confidentia beneficialis,* considering it a form of simony. The answer to this question probably lies in the fact that such an arrange-

Guido Ascanio Sforza (b. 1518) for this move. The cardinal died on 7 October 1564 holding more than twenty *beneficia* in trust for third parties[90].

This first papal bull which condemned *confidentia* as a form of simony met with stubborn opposition. To be sure of its application, the successor of *Pius IV* reserved for himself the decision of the cases in this matter[91]. *Pius V* found it difficult to do justice on the controversial issue, however. Therefore, the bull *Intolerabilis*[92] of 1569, once more directed "ad tollendam fiduciariae mancipationis beneficiorum ecclesiasticorum corruptelam", established some presumptions that made finding a *confidentia beneficialis* easier. The consistory of 14 November 1569 completed the enactment, declaring "ad tollendum ... omne dubium" that the bull applied without exception to cardinals[93].

The French side of the same story was animated by the confrontation between Papal authority and the freedoms of the Gallic Church. The French church, however, did not wait long to take a stand on the issue, along the same lines as the papal legislation. Between 1583 and 1584 several provincial councils adopted sanctions to fight fiduciary alienations of ecclesiastical benefices[94]. Apparently,

---

ment effectively evaded Church control over private transactions concerning ecclesiastical offices. The same was not true for schemes like the *commenda* (similar in other respects to the *confidentia)*, that were instrumental to the organization of the Church.

90 *Ludwig von Pastor* (n. 88) 316. For general accounts of the sale of offices in this period, see the comparative work by *Koenraad Wolter Swart*, Sale of Offices in the Seventeenth Century, 's-Gravenhave, 1949, pp. 82 ff. (sale of offices in the Roman *curia)*; see also the studies collected in I. Mieck (ed.), Ämterhandel im Spätmittelalter und im 16. Jahrhundert, 1984.

91 Motu proprio Licet, in: Bullarum (n. 89) VII, p. 509. In 1586, *Sixtus V 's* bull Divina dei providentia, *ibid.*, VIII, 794 - 800, created a special jurisdiction which was competent to decide those controversies. For the subsequent history of this judicature see *J. Deshusses*, Confidences (Auditeur des), in: Naz (n. 83) IV, 74 - 75.

92 Bullarum (n. 89) VII, 754. The complete title of this bull is: De confidentiis beneficialibus, earum casibus, presumptionibus et probationibus.

93 Bullarum (n. 89) VII, 758. For an early discussion of several cases concerning the application of these bulls, see *Nicolaus Garcia Hispano,* De Beneficiis ecclesiaticis amplissimus et doctissimus tractatus, t. I, 1618, pars XI, cap. 3, pp. 244 ff., n. 164 ff.; the express prohibition of *confidentia beneficialis* remained in force up to the codification of the Canon law: *Deshusses* (n. 83) 72.

94 For the year 1583 see the Acts of the Provincial Councils of Reims and Tours. The following year the council of Bourges intervened on the same issue. These sources are remarkable because they use the legal category "fiducia" in the context of *inter vivos* transactions. Thus, the Council of Reims enacts:

"Quisquis acceptat beneficium, ut ei postea cedat in favorem cujuscumque personae capacis, vel incapacis, secularis vel regularis, laicorum, vel alicuius ex clericis, fiduciarius esse censeatur. Idemque esto judicium de eo, qui per resignationem ejus beneficium recipit, cuijus prius erat illi facta promissio.

Qui eadem confidentiam verbo vel facto juraverit vel procuraverit, ejusdem criminis particeps habeatur. Qui beneficium acceptat, non ut non cedat, sed ut alius fructibus, vel eorum portione, sub ipsius nomine gaudeat, fiduciarius esse judicetur.

those steps were largely ineffective. *Sixtus V's* bull *Pastoralis officii*[95] therefore reaffirmed the legislation of his predecessors in this field. To soothe the potential conflict with the French church the Holy See delegated its powers with respect to *confidentia* (above all, the power of nomination to vacant benefices) to the French bishops. The apostolic *nuncius* and the vice-legate of the Pope in Avignon were authorized to absolve those who had committed simony by confidence. This papal intervention could not have any effect on the Gallican church as a matter of principle, according to the rules of that church. Nevertheless, it spurred the French episcopate to ask the King to fight the "crime de confidence". This happened with an edict of *Louis XIII* registered on the 30 May 1612. It declared vacant all the benefices tainted by simony or confidence[96].

The importance of the Canon law developments in the field of *confidentia beneficialis* should not be underrated in any study dedicated to the history of fiduciary operations. The papal intervention shows that by the end of the 16th century the practice of holding benefices on behalf of others was quite widespread. The Canon law prohibition enacted by the Pope invalidated (among other kinds of arrangements) an *inter vivos* transaction intended to separate title (*titulus*) to the benefice from the profits (*utilitas*) which were to be derived from it[97]. From the point of view of legal doctrine this transaction was explicitly considered a kind of *fiducia*, while the underlying agreement between the holder of the benefice and the person who set up the fiduciary scheme was usually classified as a pact or *conventio*. Leaving aside special reasons that prompted the papal prohibition of *confidentia beneficialis*, it is worth noting that the binding force of the *confidentia* was justified by the arguments jurists deployed to maintain the enforceability of fiduciary arrangements in the civil law. This point may be further investigated by taking a closer look at the growing 17th century literature and case law on the position of the *heres fiduciarius*.

Patroni etiam seu ecclesiastici seu laici, qui clericorum personas interponunt, ut ex pacto vel expresso vel tacito, fructus beneficiorum, ad quae presentant vel eorum partem aliquam in proprios usus convertant, vel qui aliquo supposito, vel etiam nullo titulo existente, fructus beneficiorum occupant, non solum hujus criminis rei, sed etiam injustissimi raptores censeantur, et jure patronatus ipso facto privati existant."

(This is the text reproduced by *Zegeri Bernardi Van Espen*, Jus ecclesiasticum universum, t. V, editio recentissima, annot. Gibert, 1781, p. 173.).

95 Bullarum (n. 89) VIII, 895 - 897. Cf. *Parisius* (n. 86) 27, Quaestio XI, An omni loco Confidentia sit prohibita, et quid in Francia.

96 For citations of cases in this matter see *J. B. Denisart*, Collection des décisions nouvelles et de notions relatives a la jurisprudence actuelle, 7th ed., I, Paris, 1771, s.v. Confidence, p. 603.

97 Cf. *Durand de Maillane*, s.v. Confidence, in: *idem*, Dictionnaire de droit canonique et de pratique béneficiale, I, Paris, 1761, p. 367. To the eight cases listed as common instances of *confidentia beneficialis* the author adds the following general clause: "Enfin, de quelque manière qu'une tierce personne soit interposée au Titre ou aux revenues d'un bénéfice, ce bénéfice est estimé en dépôt et en confidence".

VIII. The 17th Century Elaboration of the Doctrine of Testamentary *fiducia*

During the 17th century the doctrine of the *heres fiduciarius* was consolidated. We may approach this development by examining three cases on the subject that are frequently cited by later commentators and judges. They come from the *Sacra Romana Rota,* the most authoritative of the ancient courts of pre-unitary Italy, one which played a prominent role in the life of the law from the 16th to the 18th century[98].

The first of the three cases was decided in 1612[99]. Here the *Rota* characterizes as *nudus minister* (in the sense that *Baldus* had made clear) the person who had to put into effect the testator's intention. However, the same person is never labelled *fiduciarius* in the decision.

Only four years later, however, the same Tribunal openly applied the doctrine of the *heres fiduciarius*[100]. In a first testament Alexius de Alexijs had instituted as universal heir his nephew Iulius Ursinus. In a second testament he had instituted as universal heir Pietro Alli, his brother-in-law, using the following words: "Nomino mio herede universale il Sig. Pietro Alli, del quale mi confido, et sò esseguirà [sic], secondo lui sà la mente mia".

After the testator's death, the nephew (who was in possession of the assets belonging to the deceased) refused to turn them over to Pietro Alli, claiming that Pietro was actually "... haeredem fiduciarium, seu confidentialem et sic potius custodem, et ministrum, seu depositarium, quam verum haeredem, et propterea te-

98 *Gino Gorla,* I tribunali supremi degli stati italiani fra i secoli XVI e XiX quali fattori della unificazione del diritto nello Stato e della sua uniformazione tra Stati, in: La formazione storica del diritto moderno in Europa, I, 1977, p. 447, now also in *idem,* Diritto comparato e diritto comune europeo, 1981, p. 543; *Mario Ascheri,* Italien, in: Helmut Coing (ed.) Handbuch der Quellen und Literatur der neueren europäischen Privatrechtsgeschichte, II, 2, 1976, p. 1115; Antonella Bettoni, Mario Sbriccoli (eds.), Grandi tribunali e Rote nell'Italia dell'antico regime, 1993. The most recent contribution on the *decisiones* of the *Rota Romana* is provided by *Gero Dolezalek,* Litigation at the Rota Romana, particularly around 1700, in: Alain Wijffels (ed.), Case Law in the Making: The Techniques and Methods of Judicial Records and Law Reports, vol. 1: Essays, 1997, pp. 339 ff., esp. at 345, 355 - 357, where the author makes clear to what extent it is possible to speak of decisions made by a "bench" rather than by individual judges.

99 Decisiones Sacrae Rotae Romanae coram *Alexandro Ludovisio,* nunc Gregorio XV Pontefice (s.d., s.l.), decisio 544, Romana Census 20 millium, pp. 614 - 618. This was confirmed by the decision rendered in the same matter on 3 March 1617, reported in Sacrae Rotae Romanae Decisionum Recentiorum a *Prospero Farinaccio* Selectarum, Venetiis, 1697, pars IV, 1, p. 387. Both decisions overturn the previous decision dated 20 October 1595, decisio 25, reported by *Farinaccio,* pars III, p. 142.

100 Decisiones Sacrae Rotae Romanae coram *Iacobo Cavalerio,* Roma, 1629, Romana Haereditatis de Alexiis, 24 Februarii 1616, decisio 381, pp. 338 - 341. This is also reported in *Farinaccio* (n. 99) pars I, decisio 557, 496 - 497; see also the previous decision in the same matter, pars II, 24 Ianuarii 1614, decisio 765, 587.

neri sibi restituere totam haereditatem, unam cum fructibus non retenta pro se aliqua quarta ...".

The *Rota* ruled in favour of the nephew, dismissing Alli's claim to recover the assets. According to the *Rota* all the requisites necessary to reach such a result existed. Both the *verba testamenti* and its *causa* explained why the instituted heir was an *heres fiduciarius*. The words of the testament were indeed sufficiently clear: "... illud enim verbum *mi confido* et illa verba *sò che esseguirà secondo lui sà la mente mia,* denotant, testatorem, voluisse aliquid committere fidei Petri, quod noluit in testamentum exprimere ...".

The *causa* which had induced the testator to appoint a fiduciary heir was also apparent in the light of the surrounding circumstances. Having been convicted of a crime and then rehabilitated *(remissio),* the nephew risked confiscation of all his assets. Therefore the testator "cogitavit facere alium haeredem fiduciarium, qui bona sua illi servaret, ac tempore, quo tutus esset, restitueret ..."[101]. To undermine the defendant's position the plaintiff objected that the fiduciary disposition should have been proved by seven witnesses, i.e. the number of witnesses the law required to establish a solemn testament. But the Court held otherwise: "... quia hic non agitur de probanda substantia testamenti, sed tantummodo de declaratione voluntatis testoris circa institutionem haeredis, et de declaratione huius confidentiae ..." . For this reason, one witness, or two at most, was sufficient to prove the nephew's claim.

The third relevant decision of the *Sacra Romana Rota* was pronounced in 1640[102]. In it, the testator had instituted as heir his wife, with the provision that fifteen years after his death his son was to receive the advowson *(iuspatronatum)* the testator had left her. The question was whether or not the woman had been instituted heir merely as a fiduciary for the son.

In this case, the testament did not give a hint of secret instructions passed by the testator to his wife[103]. Nor could it be said that the wife had been appointed heir only because the son was a minor. There was nothing to rebut the presumption that the bequest to the wife was in consideration of love and affection[104]. Even the fact that the wife had to collect the fruits of the *hereditas* and to reinvest them at the end of each year *ad commodum hereditatis* did not mean that she was appointed heir in a strictly fiduciary capacity. Indeed, since she was entitled to enjoy the

---

101 This was confirmed by several witnesses: e.g. the one that suggested this expedient, the one who had the notary prepare a draft of the testament; and the notary himself.

102 Decisiones Sacrae Rotae Romanae coram *Coelio Bichio,* § I, Roma, 1671, Bononiensis Iuspatronatum, 4 Iulii 1640, decisio 35, pp. 66 - 67.

103 "Nam in testamento non legitur fidei Ludovicae [i.e. the wife] quidpiam secreto commisum seu verbum aliquod confidentiale pro ut in casu decis. 381 bon. mem. Card. Cavaler" (cp. n. 100).

104 "... potius causa finalis tribuenda est maximo amori testatori erga uxorem quam dilectissimam in ipso actu institutionis enunciavit".

fruits from the moment they were collected until they were brought together she had the *commoditatem medii temporis*, which "repugnat qualitati fiduciariae, seu nudi ministerii, quia nudus minister dicitur qui nihil emolumenti ex haereditate consequitur aut consequi potest". Therefore, the wife was a true heir, charged with a *fideicommissum* in favour of the testator's son, rather than a minister, clothed with the *titulus hereditarii*, but not entitled to the corresponding *commodum*.

These decisions show that by the 17th century the position of the heir or legatee appointed solely for the benefit of another was analyzed and understood on its own terms. The words *heres fiduciarius*, *fiduciarius* and *fiducia* were consciously being used by practitioners and judges to denote a distinctive concept that related to legal rules and a recurrent set of facts.

The number of 17th century reported cases of the *Rota Romana* dealing with problems raised by fiduciary dispositions is significant in this respect, especially if one considers the relatively narrow subject-matter that fell under the above-mentioned headings[105]. The practical interest of the topic is also demonstrated by the collection of 200 questions which *Carlo Antonio De Luca* published on the same subject at the end of the century[106]. Indeed, the growth of the institution was such that *Giovan Battista de Luca*[107], one of the greatest lawyers of this age, noted that fiduciary dispositions had almost supplanted the *fideicommissum purum*, which had formerly been used to charge the heir with the task of transferring the testator's property immediately to the person he had designated[108].

105 Besides the three cases mentioned in the text, the collection by *Prospero Farinaccio* (n. 99) contains the following decisions in this matter: pars IV, 2, Romana pecuniaria, seu legati, 21 Februarii 1622, dec. 351, pp. 334 - 335; pars X, Carpentoratensis haereditatis, 28 Junii 1647, dec. 103, pp. 181 - 183; in the same matter, 5 Junii 1648, dec. 195, pp. 323 - 324; pars XII, Avenionensis Bonorum, 14 Juni 1658, dec. 362, pp. 490 - 491, on appeal: pars XIII, 29 Januarii 1660, dec. 155, pp. 190 - 191; pars XVI, Romana Census, 16 Junii 1670, dec. 258, pp. 314 - 315; pars XIV, Romana incamerationis, 16 Novembris 1672, dec. 536, pp. 568 - 584; pars XVIII, 1, Romana Census, 23 Januarii 1671, dec. XXIII, pars XVII, 27 - 28; in the same matter, 23 Febrarii 1674, dec. 238, pars XVIII, 1, pp. 287 - 288; pars XVIII, 2, Faventina haereditatis, 20 Aprilis 1676, dec. 692, pp. 340 - 342; pars XIX, 2, Romana haereditatis, 12 Decembris 1681, dec. 599, pp. 318 - 320. I have made no attempt to trace decisions concerning the same topic in other collections.

106 *Carolo Antonio De Luca*, De confidentiali haeredis institutione et substitutione tractatus coesareus, Neapoli, 1697, pp. 334, with indexes. On the life and work of this jurist, see *P. L. Rovito*, s.v. *De Luca, Carolo Antonio*, in: Dizionario biografico degli italiani, vol. 38, 1990, p. 330.

107 On the life and works of this jurist, see *Agostino Lauro*, Il cardinale Giovan Battista de Luca, 1991.

108 *Giovan Battista De Luca*, Il dottor volgare ovvero il compendio di tutta la legge civile, canonica, feudale, e municipale nelle cose più ricevute in pratica, t. III, Colonia, 1740, lib. IX, cap. VI, n. 5 (1st ed. 1674). In his major work, the Theatrum veritatis et justitiae, first published in 1679 - 1689, *De Luca* treats in depth our subject. See *idem*, Theatrum veritatis et justitiae, Venetiis, 1726, lib. IX, discursus 45, p. 76; discursus 46, p. 77; 47, p. 79, n. 4; discursus 48, p. 81, n. 2; discursus 79, p. 131; discursus 80, p. 134; discursus 81, p. 135; lib. X, discursus 182, p. 321; discursus 183, p. 323.

During the period under consideration some of the most interesting refinements of this doctrine concern the use of the concept of simulation to approach the position of the *fiduciarius*. While *Baldus* held that testamentary dispositions which disguised the name of the person to whom the testator intended to give did not amount to simulation[109], later authors such as *C. A. De Luca* thought otherwise. The interposition of the *fiduciarius* is now conceived as a *simulatio personae veri haeredi*[110]. Therefore, because truth prevails over simulation, the right which is the object of the fiduciary disposition is acquired directly by the true heir, not by the fiduciary: "et huius persona non attendetur, sed eius, cuius commodo, et contemplatione instituitur fiduciarius"[111].

This use of the doctrine of simulation offers a novel perspective on the subject, which tries to reconcile the legal positions of the fiduciary and the beneficiary by contrasting truth with fiction, rather than by splitting *titulus* and *commodum*. The change of language does not, however, imply any change in the traditional rules governing *fiducia*, but rather shows the gradual demise of the conceptual framework that the Post-Glossators had developed to discuss fiduciary dispositions[112].

IX. Testamentary *fiducia* in the *Pays de droit écrit* of Southern France

The general pattern of development of testamentary *fiducia* so far described was common to French law in the area which lived under the *droit écrit*. This is hardly surprising, given the fact that Southern France participated in the renaissance of Roman law from the 12th century onwards[113].

Rather than looking for the emergence of the *fiducia* in the sources of this early period we may more profitably therefore concentrate on its later manifestations,

109 See *supra*, text at nn. 48 - 49.

110 See *C. A. De Luca* (n. 106) cap. I, pp. 1 - 2, n. 4. In support the author cites Seraphin. decis. 1210, n. 6.

111 *Ibid. G. B. De Luca's* approach to the same topic is more rigorous and lucid. He keeps separate the *fiducia redolente veram simulationem* from the *fiducia redolente verum fideicommissum non fraudolentum*, which is distinguished also from the *fiducia criminosa et fraudolenta*. See *idem*, Theatrum veritatis et justitiae (n. 108) lib. IX, discursus 79, p. 131, 132, nn. 8 - 11. For an application, see discursus 80, p. 134.

112 It would be wrong, however, to read too much into this linguistic shift. Reference to the doctrine of simulation is made to explain why in principle the *fiduciarius* cannot derive any benefit from the disposition, not to argue that the Post-Glossator's doctrines relating to property were untenable.

113 With specific regard to the law of *fideicommissa*, see *Michel Petitjean*, Essai sur l'histoire des substitutions du IXème au XVème siècle dans la pratique et la doctrine spécialement en France méridionale, 1975. On the resurrection of the Roman testament: *Poumarède* (n. 2) 129.

starting from the 17th century[114]. It is true, however, that even in this epoch some French authors of the *Pays de droit écrit* expressly acknowledged their intellectual debt to contemporary Italian jurists, as well as to other authors of the *ius commune*[115].

Legal writing concerning our institution in the 17th century originates mainly from practical questions submitted to courts of law.

A typical example of this literature is *Claude Henrys'* analysis of the *institution fiduciarie,* which discusses a judgment of the *Parlement* of Paris dated 14 August 1634. The issue was whether or not the *demi-lod* – one of the seignoral rights due on the transmission of property at death – was owed by the fiduciary heir[116]. According to *Henrys,* the negative answer to the question followed from the fact that the fiduciary heir: "n'est que le gardien et dépositaire, et comme il ne faut que prêter son ministère, aussi la propriété des biens ne lui est pas acquise, et il est censé le posséder plutôt pour un autre que par lui"[117].

When *Henrys* wrote, the legal position of the heir with respect to the property entrusted to him was indeed perceived as one of the features distinguishing *l'institution fiduciaire* from a fideicommissary substitution, or from a *fideicommissum.* Legal writers and judges shared the opinion that the heir charged with the fideicommissary substitution, or with the *fideicommissum,* owned the assets in his possession, subject to the duties imposed upon him. On the contrary, under the newer conception of *fiducia,* the fiduciary heir does not own the property that he holds for the designated beneficiary[118].

As *Furgole*[119] pointed out, a consequence of this reasoning was that the beneficiary of the fiduciary disposition "est vrai héritier *jure directo,* tout comme s'il

---

114 See, in general, *Witz* (n. 7) 36 - 40; *Jean-Marie Augustin,* Famille et societé – Les substitutions fidéicommissaires à Toulose et en Haut-Languedoc au XVIIIe siècle, 1980, pp. 145, 168 - 170.

115 See, e.g., *Gerauld de Maynard,* Notables et singulieres questions du droict escrit decidées et jugées par arrests memorables de la Cour souverain du Parlament de Toulouse, Paris, 1638, pp. 1018 - 1019; *Claude Henrys,* Oeuvres de Claude Henrys ... contenant son recueil d'arrêts, 6th ed. par B.J. Bretonnier, t. 1, Paris, 1772, lib. III, chap. III, quest. 22, pp. 736 - 738 (an early edition of this work was published in 1708). None of these authors cites *Budé's* Annotationes ad Pandectas.

116 See *Henrys* (n. 115) quest. 23, 740. The *arrêt* of the Parlement de Paris was given on appeal from a judgment of the *sénéchaussée* of Lyon, dated 25 June 1632.

117 *Henrys* (n. 115) 736. In the same vein: *Jean-Marie Ricard,* Traité des donations entre vifs et testamentaires, par *Michel du Chemin,* t. II, Paris, 1754, pp. 540 - 541.

118 The interpretation of the intention of the testator was crucial in this respect. Thus, if the heir instituted in the testament may wait until the end of his life to restore the property to the designated beneficiary it seems that there is no *institution fiduciaire,* but a true *fideicommissum.* See on this point Maynard (n. 115).

119 *Furgole,* Commentaire de l'ordonnance de Louis XV sur le substitutions du mois d'Août 1747, Paris, 1767, sub tit. I, art. XX, pp. 101 ff., 103. The author, who was *avocat au*

avoit été institué en premier rang". This approach conveniently excluded the fiduciary institution from the problems created by the limited number of substitutions allowed by the law, but it posed some problems of its own. Thus, one could argue that the fiduciary heir instituted for the benefit of a minor was essentially a tutor. Yet, the frequent analogy drawn between the fiduciary heir and the tutor was in part misleading because the fiduciary heir, unlike the tutor, did not need to give security to deal faithfully with the property he managed for the minor[120].

The overall picture which emerges from this brief survey is captured by *Philippe-Antoine Merlin,* who experienced as protagonist the transition from the *ancien regime* to the civil code[121]. *Merlin* remarked that the words *héritier fiduciaire* "designent la personne que le testateur a chargée, en l'instituant héritier pour la forme, d'administrer la succession et de la tenir en dépôt jusqu'au moment où elle doit la remettre au véritable héritier". Thus, the fiduciary heir "n'est héritier que de nom; il n'est pas saisi de la succession; ce n'est pas sur sa tête que repose la propriété des biens du défunt; il n'en est que l'administrateur"[122].

X. Towards the Civil Codes

In France, the clash between the revolutionary ideas and the institutions of the old regime left a permanent mark on the law of succession. To be sure, the drafting of the French civil code took place after the most radical proposals of reform in this field had been abandoned[123]. Nevertheless, the general prohibition of substitutions enacted by the code, together with other rules banning unequal treatment of descendants, were certainly inspired by a political desire to break away from the patterns of succession of pre-revolutionary law[124].

parlement de Toulouse, adds the following remark: "C'est l'idée que le Parlement de Toulose a de l'institution fiduciaire ...".

120 *Abraham Lapeyrere,* Décisions sommaires du Palais, par ordre alphabétique, illustrées de notes et de plusieurs arrêts de la Cour de Parlement de Bordeaux, 5th ed., Bordeaux, 1725, sub letter H, no. 20, p. 158, cites on these points two judgments of the Court of Bordeaux dated 21 January 1657 and 21 February 1658.

121 On the life and work of this jurist, see *Hervé Leuwers,* Merlin de Douai (1754 - 1838): un juriste en politique, 1996.

122 *Merlin,* Répertoire universel et raisonné de jurisprudence, 3rd ed., t. V, Paris, 1808, s.v. Fiduciaire (héritier), p. 209.

123 Cf. *R. Villers,* Les primières lois successorales de la Révolution (1790 - 1792), in: La Révolution et l'ordre juridique privé: rationalité ou scandale ?, Actes du Colloque d' Orléans 11 - 13 Septembre 1986, t. 1, 1988, p. 333; *Jacques Poumarède,* La législation successorale de la Révolution entre l'idéologie et la pratique, in: La famille, la loi, l'Etat: de la Révolution au Code Civil, 1989, p. 167; *Augustin* (n. 114) 478 ff.

124 *Napoleon* was conscious of the impact of the reform on the great families of the kingdom of France. Writing to his brother *Joseph,* he suggested that he adopt the same reform in

The winds of change which brought about the code did not, however, involve the *fiducie*. Even before the completion of the codification process it appeared certain that the institution was to be preserved for the future. It is likely that the *fiducie* was spared the fate which befell other devices of the old regime simply because it did not serve the same interest of perpetuating control over family property[125].

Before the enactment of the civil code for the Kingdom of Piedmont and Sardinia in 1837, the approach to *fiducia* in most of pre-unification Italy did not differ from that prevailing in Southern France[126]. Nevertheless, at least in Piedmont, the concept of the fiduciary device as a kind of simulation gained ground between the 17th century and the first decades of the 18th century[127]. Before the Piedmontese civil code in 1837 that idea did not disturb the traditional rules applicable to the institution. Eventually, however, it paved the way for the hostile attitude of the Piedmontese codificators towards *fiducia*. That attitude shaped the code rule against the introduction of evidence to show who the real beneficiary of the testator's bounty was (art. 609)[128]. The change was a watershed, since on this issue the Piedmontese civil code became the model for later codifications.

Thus, the wheel had come full circle. Once more, the intended beneficiary of the testator's bounty whose name was not disclosed in the will was left without a remedy to enforce a secret provision in his favour.

XI. Conclusions

The investigation conducted so far leads to several conclusions. The law of *fiducia* which took shape in the age of the *ius commune* resulted from a variety of sources. First, it was created by the interpreters of the Justinianic compilation, who examined the law of *fideicommissa* without knowing the classical Roman law of

---

the kingdom of Naples so as to accelerate the fall of the local nobility. On the other hand, wishing to promote the stability of his regime, *Napoleon* allowed members of his *entourage* to set up perpetual substitutions, in derogation of the newly enacted civil code. On both episodes see *Augustin* (n. 114) 492 ff.

125 *Merlin* (n. 122) 211.

126 Cf. *Maria Carla Zorzoli*, Note in tema di fedecommesso nei lavori preparatori del codice civile, in: I cinquant'anni del codice civile – Atti del convegno di Milano 4 - 5 giugno 1992, II, 1993, p. 623. An early ban of testamentary *fiducia* had been enacted with the Code of 1771 for the Dukedom of Este, book II, title 21, § 22.

127 See *Giuseppe Maria Regis*, Dizionario legale teorico-pratico ossia corso di giurisprudenza civile e criminale, IV, Torino, 1819, 157, s.v. Fiducie o fiduciarie disposizioni, with abundant references to the case law of the Senate of Piedmont.

128 On the legislative history of this provision, see Codice civile per gli Stati Sardi – Motivi dei Codici per gli Stati Sardi, II, Genova, 1856, pp. 125 ff.; *Torquato Cuturi*, Dei fedecommessi e delle sostituzioni nel diritto civile italiano, Città di Castello, 1889, pp. 132 ff.

fiducia. The direction and the pace of development of the institution were influenced by the Canon law, which stressed the binding force of the *fiduciarius'* undertaking, as well as the necessity to respect the testator's will. Eventually, the Humanists' critique opened the door to an understanding of an original features of *fiducia* as it was known in classical Roman law.

The institution emerging from this process was thus a new means of holding property, by which assets of any kind were put in the name of a person who was obligated to deal with them solely in the interest of another. Across the centuries, this phenomenon was first analyzed in terms of the separation between *titulus* and *commodum,* then as a case of contrast between fiction and reality, or one between form and substance. This conceptual shift did not disturb the rules applied in concrete cases, however. This occurred only where testamentary *fiducia* was abrogated by the legislature.

Concentrating on the central period of our enquiry, we may now turn to the possibility of interchange between civilian doctrines and ideas relating to *fiducia* and the English law of trusts.

It is not necessary to reopen here the long-standing debate in favour of or against such possibility[129]. We are content to summarize the new evidence elicited from the sources that is relevant in comparative perspective[130]. On a general level, the linguistic evidence is impressive: for the laywers studied here, "trust and confidence" gradually turned into terms of art, available to substantiate the claims brought by a disappointed beneficiary against the *fiduciarius.* This usage neatly matches the English usage in the period that witnessed the transition from uses to trusts [131].

The linguistic evidence also points to a common stock of concepts, shared to a certain extent by lawyers on both sides of The Channel. When the English lawyers in the 17th century tried to explain what a trust was they resorted to the same concepts used by contemporary civilians to explain what *fiducia* was: i.e. *fideicommissum* and deposit[132]. By today's learning these notions seem far apart from each

129 For an introduction to this debate, see *H. Patrick Glenn,* The Historical Origins of the Trust, in: Alfredo Mordechai Rabello (n. 4) 748 ff. The author argues that the trust was part of a pan-European law of property, rather than an original product of the English law.

130 The fact that new evidence has been collected is, perhaps, interesting *per se.* Cf. *H. Patrick Glenn* (n. 129): "It is unlikely that any new historical evidence can be added to this long-standing debate". As far as I can tell, the evidence presented in this paper is not wholly unrelated to the continental side of the history of uses (on which see *Shael Herman's* contribution in this collection).

131 See the chapter by Neil Jones in this volume. Note that the word "trust" here does not transpose into English *fideicommissum* but, literally, *fiducia,* just as "confidence" renders exactly the Latin word *confidentia.*

132 See the paper by *Michael Macnair* in this volume. The earlier evidence concerning *fideicommissum* in English ecclesiatical practice is presented and analyzed by *Richard H. Helmholz,* The English Law of Wills and the ius commune, 1450 - 1640, in: Lloyd Bonfield

other. Yet, they were not so distant according to the *doctores legum* who, at the time, discussed fiduciary dispositions. Indeed, jurists talking of *fideicommissum* and deposit with respect to *fiducia* were using different concepts without meaning different things. They did so to capture the various aspects of fiduciary arrangements: *fiducia* stemmed from the law of *fideicommissa,* but it was also understood as a kind of deposit, since the principal task entrusted to the *fiduciarius* was to hold the property for the intended beneficiary[133].

In this context the civilians also recognized that such arrangements separated *titulus* from *commodum,* a distinction that became a foundation of the law of trusts.

The types of dispositions most frequently discussed in this study were linked to succession *mortis causa.*

There are, however, reasons to think that similar devices could have been created *inter vivos* too. The whole history of *confidentia beneficialis* proves that *inter vivos* fiduciary arrangements concerning ecclesiastical property were binding until the Popacy prohibited them for special reasons.

Today, the contribution of equity to the creation of the English law of trusts is frequently considered the hallmark of the English experience regarding trusts[134]. Yet, equity also played a role in the history of *fiducia,* being invoked to sanction fiduciary dispositions where no remedy was available to enforce them. The materials examined above reveal the real impact of concepts of equity upon the growth of *fiducia,* as well as the interplay between civil and ecclesiastical jurisdictions. In particular, they illustrate that the very existence of an alternative jurisdiction moved the jurists to overcome technical objections against the enforcement of fiduciary arrangements.

(ed.), Marriage, Property, and Succession, 1992, pp. 308, 318 ff. For the whole picture see also *Richard Helmholz's* chapter in this volume, as well as his previous article: The Early Enforcement of Uses, in: *idem,* Canon Law and the Law of England, 1987, p. 341.

133 *Macnair* notes that at times the English use was also considered analogous to usufruct, though both *Francis Bacon* and *Lord Nottingham* regarded this analogy to be misleading. The English use might indeed owe something to the medieval transformations of the Roman institution (see on this evolution *Paolo Grossi,* Usus facti: La nozione di proprietà privata nell'inaugurazione dell'età nuova, in: *idem,* Il dominio e le cose, 1992; *Rossi* (n. 29); *Maximiliane Kriechbaum,* Actio, ius und dominium in den Rechtslehren des 13. und 14. Jahrhundert, 1996; and *Shael Herman's* paper in this volume). Leaving aside pseudo-etymology as a key to understanding why use and usufruct were discussed together, it may be observed that civilians trying to explain the position of the heir charged with a *fideicommissum* sometimes also resorted to the notion of usufruct. *David Johnston,* Successive Rights and Successful Remedies: Life Interests in Roman Law, in: Birks (n. 47) 152, shows that the distinction between the two institutions posed interesting problems in Roman law as well.

134 Whether it really still needs to be viewed in this way is another question: *Bernard Rudden,* Equity as Alibi, in Stephen Goldstein (ed.), Equity and Contemporary Legal Developments, 1992, pp. 31, 38 - 39.

Last, we should keep in mind that *fiducia* performed various functions that in common law countries are largely associated with trusts, except that of making possible intra-family transfers of wealth over several generations. That remained the preserve of fully-fledged *fideicommissa*[135,136].

135 *Gérard Delille,* Famiglia e proprietà nel regno di Napoli, XV-XIX secolo, 1988; *Enrico Genta,* Fedecommessi e primogeniture in Piemonte dal diritto comune al diritto del principe, in: Percorsi storici – Studi sulla città di Cavallermaggiore, 1990, p. 355; *Maria Carla Zorzoli,* Della famiglia e del suo patrimonio: riflessioni sull'uso del fedecommesso in Lombardia tra cinque e seicento, in: Lloyd Bonfield (n. 132) 155; *Zorzoli* (n. 126); *Roberta Ago,* La feudalità in età moderna, 1994, pp. 29 ff.; *Andrea Romano,* Famiglia successioni e patrimonio familiare nell'Italia medievale e moderna, 1994; cf. also the contribution by *Klaus Luig* to the present volume.

136 I wish to thank *Richard Helmholz, Shael Herman, David Johnston, Lionel Smith* and *Mauro Bussani* for their valuable comments on a previous draft of this article. The responsibility for any error is mine.

KLAUS LUIG

Philipp Knipschildt und das Familienfideikommiß im Zeitalter des *Usus modernus*

I. Grundsätze

1. Begriff und Funktion des Familienfideikommisses

Das Familienfideikommiß war ein in Deutschland zwischen dem 11. und dem 18. Jahrhundert gebräuchliches Mittel der Bindung des Familiengutes im Mannesstamm durch Rechtsgeschäft. Dieses Mittels konnten sich adelige Familien geringeren Ranges bedienen, denen es etwa verwehrt war, durch ein Hausgesetz die Primogenitur einzuführen. Das Familienfideikommiß verschwand seit Mitte des 18. Jahrhunderts nach und nach als Handelshindernis aus den europäischen Rechtsordnungen. Viel zitiert wurde während des Prozesses zunehmender Ablehnung der Familienfideikommisse der Ausspruch von *Montesquieu:* „Les substitutions gènent le commerce"[1].

Die Geschichte des Familienfideikommisses steht in engem Zusammenhang mit der Geschichte des Erbrechts überhaupt und insbesondere der Testierfreiheit. Vor aller Entwicklung eines Erbrechts steht die Bindung allen Grundeigentums und aller Vermögensstücke von großem Wert an die Familie. Im Anfang war vermutlich nach fränkisch-germanischem Recht das Grundvermögen zwingend an die Familie gebunden. Das ist wohl das, was man als altes deutsches Stammgutsystem bezeichnen kann[2]. Die Freiheit (des Hauptes der Familie?), von Todes wegen über das Vermögen bestimmen zu können, hat sich erst unter dem Einfluß

---

1 *Bernhard Bayer,* Sukzession und Freiheit: Historische Voraussetzungen der rechtstheoretischen und rechtsphilosophischen Auseinandersetzungen um das Institut der Familienfideikomisse im 18. und 19. Jahrhundert, Diss. iur., Köln, 1996, S. 76. Neben *Bayer* generell zum Familienfideikommiß: *Jörn Eckert,* Der Kampf um die Familienfideikommisse in Deutschland: Studien zum Absterben eines Rechtsinstituts, Frankfurt/Main, Bern, 1992. Grundlegend zum Thema des Familienvermögens: Lloyd Bonfield (Hg.), Marriage, Property and Succession, Berlin, 1992. Nach Abschluß des Manuskripts erschien: *Jörn Eckert,* Use, Trust, Strict Settlement – Fideikommißähnliche Bindungen des Grundbesitzes in England, in: Wirkungen europäischer Rechtskultur: Festschrift für Karl Kroeschell, 1997, S. 187 - 201.

2 *Carl von Salza,* „Familienfideicommisse", in: Julius Weiske, Rechtslexikon für Juristen aller teutschen Staaten, Band IV, Leipzig, 1844, S. 237 - 255.

des römischen Rechts und der christlichen Kirche in Westeuropa herausgebildet. Eigentlich handelte es sich dabei um die Freiheit, das nächste Familienoberhaupt zu bestimmen (durch das einer Adoption verwandte Einsetzen eines Erben). Die Entstehung von Familienfideikommissen ist dann erklärlich durch das Bestreben einzelner Familienoberhäupter, die entstandene Verfügungsfreiheit gleichsam im Interesse der Familie wieder auszuschließen[3]. Nicht ganz leicht einzusehen war, daß bei Gründung eines Familienfideikommisses die Testierfreiheit dessen, der das Familienfideikommiß einsetzte, verwendet wurde, um die Freiheit für alle weiteren Generationen auszuschließen – um für die eigene Familie ein „Gesetz" zu erlassen, nach der sich die Erbfolge in der Zukunft zwingend abspielen sollte. Ist der einzelne Herr seines Vermögens oder Sachwalter des Familienbesitzes – das war die Frage[4]. Wenn der Verbleib der Güter in der Familie das richtige Prinzip ist, dann war das Familienfideikommiß nach der Einführung der Testierfreiheit die Wiederherstellung der richtigen Ordnung. Wenn jedoch die Freiheit des einzelnen Eigentümers das Prinzip ist, dann war das Familienfideikommiß eine nur schlecht zu rechtfertigende Einschränkung der Freiheit eines jeden Eigentümers. Am Anfang stand die Einschärfung des Prinzips „Die Familie stirbt nicht" gegen die als nachteilig empfundene Testierfreiheit des römisch-kanonischen Rechts. Seit dem 19. Jahrhundert jedoch herrschte die Freiheit des Eigentümers vor.

2. Parallelen zum englischen Recht

Die Aufnahme eines Beitrages über die Familienfideikommisse im Bereiche des civil law in den vorliegenden Band ist deswegen gerechtfertigt, weil englische und schottische Juristen seit eh und je die Verwandtschaft zwischen dem Familienfideikommiß und den nach Aufgaben und Funktion ähnlichen Erscheinungen des englischen und schottischen Rechts beobachtet haben. In erster Linie hat man stets dem „entail" des englischen Rechts eine solche Ähnlichkeit zugeschrieben. Zumindest eine Anspielung darauf findet sich in *John Cowell's* „Institutiones Juris Anglicani ad methodum et seriem Institutionum Imperialium"[5]. Speziell auf die Verwandtschaft zum „entail" wies *Lord Nottingham* hin, der von 1673 bis 1675 das Amt des Lord Keepers ausgeübt hat[6]. Und in ausführlicherer Form diskutierte *Adam Smith,* der gleichzeitig aber auch als Kritiker des Familienfideikommisses

3 Niklas Luhmann, Das Recht der Gesellschaft, Frankfurt/Main, 1993, S. 292. Gegen *Luhmanns* Deutung: *Bayer* (Fn. 1) 75.

4 *Bayer* (Fn. 1) 25.

5 Zuerst 1605, dann englisch als The Institutes of the Law of the English, Digested into the Method of the Civil or Imperial Institutions, London, 1651, 2nd Book, Title XXIII.

6 *Lord Nottingham's* Manual of Chancery Practice, and his Prolegomena of Chancery and Equity, ed., and with an Introduction by *D.E.C. Yale,* Cambridge, 1965, Prolegomena, S. 252 - 253.

auftrat[7], in seinen 1762 - 1763 und 1766 gehaltenen „Lectures on Jurisprudence" die Zusammenhänge von Familienfideikommiß und „entail"[8].

Smith ging aus von der ursprünglichen Existenz eines zwingenden gesetzlichen Erbrechts, sei es mit Erbteilung oder auch mit Primogenitur. Für letztere diskutierte er die Rechtsstellung der jüngeren Brüder im Verhältnis zu den Söhnen des Ältesten für den Fall des Todes des Ältesten[9].

Dann ging *Smith* über zur gewillkürten Erbfolge und erörterte zunächst die Schwierigkeiten, die überhaupt bei der Zulassung einer gewillkürten Erbfolge an Stelle der gesetzlichen deswegen entstehen, weil ein Toter eigentlich keinen zu respektierenden Willen haben könnte[10]. Dabei zitierte *Smith,* daß *Pufendorf* zur Begründung der Zulässigkeit von Verfügungen von Todes wegen die Unsterblichkeit der Seele bemüht habe. Er selbst begnügte sich aber mit der „natürlichen" Neigung („piety"), die jeder habe, den Willen eines Sterbenden zu erfüllen. Diese Bereitschaft, auf den Willen des Verstorbenen einzugehen, war aber nach *Smith* nichts für „barbarische Nationen", sondern tauchte erst bei Völkern auf, die „civilized manners" hatten. Das Ergebnis war immerhin, daß das Eigentumsrecht über den Tod hinaus ausgedehnt wurde[11].

Das galt aber nur für den unmittelbaren Nachfolger des Verstorbenen. *Smith* schildert dann jedoch eine Ausdehung des Prinzips in zwei schon vom antiken römischen Recht anerkannten Richtungen. Erstens sollte der Erblasser für den Fall, daß der benannte Erbe nicht annahm, einen Ersatzerben bestimmen können und zweitens sollte der Erblasser auch einen Ersatzerben für den Fall bestimmen können, daß der eingesetzte Erbe seinerseits vor Erreichung der Volljährigkeit oder genauer der Fähigkeit, selbst ein Testament zu machen, verstarb.

In allen anderen Fällen hatte nach *Smith* derjenige, der gemäß dem Willen des Erblassers die Nachfolge angetreten hatte, seinerseits für den Fall seines Todes die gleiche Verfügungsbefugnis wie der erste Erblasser[12]. Deswegen hätten, so fährt *Smith* fort, die Römer lange Zeit „no such things as entails" gehabt. Doch später „entails were introduced" in Rom mit Hilfe des Instruments des Fideikommisses, kraft dessen der eingesetzte Erbe verpflichtet wurde, die Erbschaft an einen Dritten herauszugeben. Diese Familienfideikommisse hätten ursprünglich zur Umgehung des Verbots der Erbeinsetzung von Frauen durch die *lex Voconia*[13] gedient, wären

---

7 *Adam Smith,* Lectures on Jurisprudence, ed. *R. L. Meek, D. D. Raphael and P. G. Stein,* Oxford, 1978, S. 465 - 469. Dazu *Bayer* (Fn. 1) 77.

8 *Blackstone* schildert die Entstehung des „entail", jedoch ohne Bezugnahme auf das Familienfideikommiß: *William Blackstone,* Commentaries on the Laws of England, zuerst 1765 - 1770, Band II, 21. Auflage, London, 1844, S. 111 - 112.

9 *Smith* (Fn. 7) 62 - 63, 465 - 466.

10 *Smith* (Fn. 7) 65 ff., 466. Dazu gründlich *Bayer* (Fn. 1) 169.

11 *Smith* (Fn. 7) 467.

12 *Smith* (Fn. 7) 65.

13 *Smith* (Fn. 7) 67, 468.

dann aber generell zulässig geworden und hätten so Schritt für Schritt dazu geführt, die Wirkung des Eigentums über die Person des ersten Nachfolgers von Todes wegen hinaus auf immer weitere Personen zu erstrecken und auf diese Weise in der praktischen Wirkung „entails" zu begründen.

In den Germanenreichen hätte, so berichtet *Smith*, die Kirche nicht ohne Anlehnung an das römische Recht die gewillkürte Erbfolge eingeführt. Und daran hatte sich in der Sicht von *Smith* offensichtlich ohne weiteres die Ausbildung von „entails" angeschlossen: „When once the notion of the will of the deceased directing his succession for one step[14] it was no difficult matter to suppose that it should extend farther"[15]. Das „statute de donis" von 1285[16] brachte schließlich die endgültige Regelung. Derartige „entails" beobachtete *Smith* in ganz Europa[17]. So war also nach *Smith* die Einführung von „entails" im Grunde die Beseitigung der Testierfreiheit und die Wiederherstellung einer gleichsam gesetzlich zwingenden Erbfolge in einer Familie.

Doch *Adam Smith* hielt diese Einrichtung für schädlich. Er meinte, es sei sinnvoll, den Willen des Verstorbenen bei der Verteilung seines Vermögens zu erfüllen, aber das binde nur die beim Erbfall lebenden Personen. Eine Festlegung der Vermögensnachfolge „in infinitum" sei die absurdeste Sache der Welt[18], denn es gelte das Prinzip, daß die Erde Eigentum einer jeden lebenden Generation sei, die sich nicht durch frühere Generationen binden lassen könne. Außerdem sprach nach *Smith* gegen „entails", daß dadurch das Land vom Handel ausgeschlossen werde[19].

Wichtig an *Smith* ist für das Leitthema dieses Bandes das Bewußtsein der europäischen Einheit in Bezug auf „entails" und Familienfideikommiß. Der entscheidende Unterschied zwischen Familienfideikommiß und „entail" lag jedoch darin, daß das „entail" ein Element des Lehnssystems darstellte, wohingegen ein Familienfideikommiß grundsätzlich in Bezug auf ein Allod begründet wurde. Beiden gemeinsam ist die Beseitigung der gesetzlichen Erbfolge nach dem Willen eines bestimmten Erblassers mit Wirkung für alle folgenden Generationen.

Der Schotte *Adam Smith* war vermutlich in dieser Frage nicht ganz unbeeinflußt von der Tradition seines Landes. Die älteste schottische Urkunde, durch die ein „entail", in Schottland bis 1685 meist als „tailzie" bezeichnet, begründet wurde,

---

14 An dieser Stelle ist eine Lücke im Text der Mitschrift von *Smith* (Fn. 7). Zu ergänzen ist etwa „was acknowledged".

15 Smith (Fn. 7) 69, 468: „Thus property was extended beyond the first successor, and when this step was gained they easily advanced further and introduced entails."

16 Statute of Westminster (Statute „de donis") II, 13 Edward I, c. 1. *Hector L. MacQueen*, Common Law and Feudal Society in Medieval Scotland, Edinburgh, 1993, S. 23, 24.

17 *Smith* (Fn. 7) 70.

18 *Smith* (Fn. 7) 467: „To give a man power over his property after his death is very considerable, but it is nothing to an extension of this power to the end of the world". S. 468: „... nothing can be more absurd than perpetual entails".

19 *Smith* (Fn. 7) 70, 468, 469.

stammt aus dem Jahre 1341[20]. Die Bezeichnung „entail" oder „tailzie" beruhte auf der Vorstellung, daß durch dieses Institut etwas abweichend von der normalen lehnsrechtlichen oder gesetzlichen Erbfolge („simple infeftment") aus dem Vermögen des Begründers herausgeschnitten wurde[21]. Im 16. Jahrhundert bedurfte die Errichtung eines „entails" in Schottland der Genehmigung durch den König[22]. In dieser Zeit zeigte sich auch, daß die Einbindung des „entails" in das Lehnssystem im Detail zu vielen vom kontinentalen Familienfideikommiß durchaus verschiedenen Regeln führte[23]. Eine gesetzliche Regelung für Schottland erfolgte durch den „Entail Act" von 1685[24].

In der Reihe der schon seit 1566 auftretenden Kritiker[25] von Familienfideikommiß und „entails" war der schottische Jurist *Stair*, dessen „Institutions of the Law of Scotland" von 1681 *Adam Smith* wohlbekannt waren, nicht ganz unbedeutend. *Stair* gab zu bedenken, daß „entails" den Verkehr, der im gemeinsamen Interesse der Menschheit liege, behinderten, daß sie verhinderten, daß der Erblasser in ordentlicher Weise für Weib und Kinder sorge, und daß es nur vernünftig sei, daß man den eigenen Nachkommen dieselbe Freiheit bei der Verfügung über das Vermögen einräume, die man selbst von den eigenen Vorfahren übernommen habe[26].

3. Der Sonderfall Deutschland

Das für seine Zeit exemplarische Compendium des bayerischen Zivilrechts von *Kreittmayr*[27] definierte im Jahre 1768 die verschiedenen Arten von Fideikommissen wie folgt: „Was der Erbe nur cum onere restitutionis und damit es in weitere Hand durch ihn gebracht werde, überkommt, das heißt ein fideicommiss, und ... zwar universale, wann die ganze Erbschaft oder ein Theil derselben also restituirt werden solle, particulare, wann die Restitution nur ein besonders Stück oder Gut betrifft, conventionale, wann es nicht ex ultima voluntate, sondern ex pacto geschiehet, familiae, wann es einem gewissen Geschlecht zum Besten angeordnet ist ..."[28].

---

20 *David M. Walker*, A Legal History of Scotland, Band II, Edinburgh, 1990, S. 634; *MacQueen* (Fn. 16) 111, 14, 180.

21 *Walker* (Fn. 20) Band IV, 1996, S. 764; *James Viscount Stair*, The Institutions of the Law of Scotland, 1693, ed. *D. M. Walker*, Glasgow, 1981, Buch II, Tit. 3, § 43.

22 *Walker* (Fn. 20) Band III, 1995, S. 759.

23 *Walker* (Fn. 20) Band III, S. 759.

24 Walker (Fn. 20) Band IV, S. 764, unter Hinweis auf Acts of the Parliament of Scotland (A.P.S.), VIII, 477, c. 26. Zum Inhalt dieses Acts näher: *Stair* (Fn. 21) II, 3, 58; *MacQueen* (Fn. 16) 24.

25 *Eckert* (Fn. 1) 131 ff. nennt als ersten den Spanier *Jacobo de Simancas*.

26 *Stair* (Fn. 21) II, 3, 58, S. 382.

27 *W. X. A. Freiherr von Kreittmayr*, Compendium Codicis Bavarici Civilis ... oder Grundriß der gemein- und bayrischen Privat-Rechtsgelehrsamkeit, München, 1768.

Caput X war dann speziell den „Familie-Fideicommissen" gewidmet. Dort heißt es, das „fideicommissum familiae", das auch Stammgut genannt werde, stamme ursprünglich von den alten deutschen, d. h. schon vor der Rezeption des römischen Rechts gebräuchlichen Erbgütern (*bona avita* oder *haereditaria)* ab und sei heutzutage eine Mischung („Miscellanz") dieser Erbgüter und des römischen Fideicommisses.

Das ist wie folgt zu verstehen:

(a) Das römische *fideicommissum,* der erste Bestandteil der von Kreittmayr erwähnten Mischung, war eine Methode der Übertragung von Eigentum auf den Todesfall. Es bestand darin, daß einer Person, in der Regel dem Erben, die Auflage gemacht wurde, den Nachlaß ganz oder zum Teil an eine dritte Person zu übertragen, die der Erblasser bedenken wollte, obwohl sie weder zum Erben eingesetzt noch mit einem Vermächtnis bedacht werden konnte, wie etwa Frauen oder Fremde[29]. Die mit der Weitergabe beauftragte Person (der Beschwerte oder der Treuhänder = *fiduciarius)* mußte aber nicht unbedingt der Erbe sein. Vielmehr kam jeder als *fiduciarius* in Betracht, der etwas von dem Verstorbenen erhalten hatte, auch wenn er nicht selbst der Erbe war, sondern – wie zu zeigen sein wird – vielleicht erst der Erbe des Erben.

Mit dieser Übertragung war das *fideicommissum* im Prinzip erfüllt. Dem Treuhänder konnte aber auch die spezielle Auflage gemacht werden, den Nachlaß erst nach Ablauf einer bestimmten Zeit, etwa erst mit seinem eigenen Tode auf den Dritten, den Bedachten, zu übertragen („cum morieris"). Eine solche Auflage wurde beispielsweise dem Sohne zu Gunsten des Enkels gemacht. In diesem Fall blieb der Treuhänder (Sohn) zu seinen Lebzeiten Eigentümer der zum Nachlaß gehörenden Gegenstände und war somit Begünstigter. Erst bei seinem Tode erschien er zugleich als Beschwerter, der den Nachlaß auf den Bedachten (Enkel) übertragen mußte.

Der Begünstigte, im gewählten Beispiel der Enkel, konnte jedoch seinerseits vom ursprünglichen Erblasser mit der Verpflichtung belastet werden, das Vermögen wiederum seinem Sohne zu übergeben. Hier kam das Prinzip zum Tragen, daß der Treuhänder nicht der Erbe des das *fideicommissum* anordnenden Erblassers sein mußte.

Schließlich konnte diese Art der Vererbung weiterhin auch für viele Generationen angeordnet werden. Dabei war also jeder für die Zeit seines Lebens Begünstigte zugleich für den Fall seines Todes mit der Pflicht zur Weitergabe belastet, oder jeder Begünstigte hatte bereits von Anfang an einen „Substitut"[30]. *Johnston*[31]

[28] *Kreittmayr* (Fn. 27) Part. III, Cap. IX, §§ 1,2,3.

[29] Dazu *David Johnston,* in diesem Band.

[30] *Peter Weimar,* Fideikommiß (Römisches Recht), in: Lexikon des Mittelalters, Band IV, München und Zürich, 1989, S. 431.

[31] *David Johnston,* The Roman Law of Trusts, Oxford, 1988, S. 77 ff.

bemerkt, daß diese Anordnung dazu dienen konnte, späteren Generationen die freie Verfügung über ererbtes Eigentum zu verbieten.

In der klassischen Zeit des römischen Rechts war die Möglichkeit einer solchen Anordnung zeitlich nicht begrenzt. *Justinian* ordnete aber ein Begrenzung auf vier Generationen an[32]. Diese Beschränkung sollte im Mittelalter und in der frühen Neuzeit eine große Rolle spielen[33].

(b) Den zweite Bestandteil dessen, was *Kreittmayr* als „Miscellanz" bezeichnet hat, bildeten die alten deutschen Erbgüter. Die Erbgüter des alten deutschen Rechts wurden im hohen Adel durch Hausgesetze und im niederen Adel, der keine Satzungsgewalt hatte, durch Rechtsgeschäft, nämlich durch eine Stiftung, begründet. Sie bewirkten eine Bindung des Familiengutes im Mannesstamm in der Weise, daß immer der älteste Sohn in das Erbgut nachfolgte.

In der Sicht von *Knipschildt* waren Familienfideikommiß und Stammgut identisch. Andere Autoren verstanden aber unter Stammgut eine gesetzliche Einrichtung des Erbrechts (der jeweilige Inhaber erbt das Recht) und unter Familienfideikommiß das durch Erklärung eingerichtete Institut, bei dem der jeweilige Inhaber in das Recht des Begründers eintritt.

(c) Nach *Erler*[34] kam die Mischung dadurch zustande, daß sich die Stiftungen des germanischen Rechts nach der Rezeption des römischen Rechts im 16. und 17. Jahrhundert nur dadurch „sichern", d. h. als legitime Rechtseinrichtung erhalten ließen, daß „man sie einer Rechtsfigur des römischen Rechts unterstellte", also mit einer im römischen Recht anerkannten Institution identifizierte. Und diese anerkannte Rechtsfigur war eben das „fidei commissum quod familiae relinquitur" der justinianischen Rechtstexte. Dabei nahm man die von *Justinian* in seiner Novelle 159 angeordnete Begrenzung auf vier Generationen zunächst in Kauf, versuchte sich aber später davon zu befreien[35].

Diese Sicherung durch Unterstellung unter das römische Recht ist eine im Zeitalter der Rezeption im deutschen Recht häufige Erscheinung. Weitere Beispiele dafür sind etwa die Unterstellung der Leibeigenen unter das römische Sklavenrecht, die Behandlung der Vormundschaft als Tutela sowie Bezeichnung der Rechtsstellung des Lehnsnehmers oder Vasallen als „dominium" (wenn auch nur als „dominium utile")[36].

---

[32] *Johnston* in diesem Band (Text bei Fn. 22, mit Hinweis auf Nov. 159 (555)); *idem* (Fn. 31) 111 ff.

[33] *Alfred Söllner*, Zur Rechtsgeschichte des Familienfideikommisses, in: Festschrift für Max Kaser zum 70. Geburtstag, München, 1976, S. 657 - 669.

[34] *Adalbert Erler*, Familienfideikommiß, in: Handwörterbuch zur Deutschen Rechtsgeschichte (HRG), Band I, Berlin, 1971, Sp. 1071 ff.

[35] *Söllner* (Fn. 33).

[36] *Maximiliane Kriechbaum*, Actio, ius und dominium in den Rechtslehren des 13. und 14. Jahrhunderts, Ebelsbach, 1996, S. 328 ff.

4. Die anderen europäischen Länder

Wichtig für ein Unternehmen der „Comparative Studies in Continental and Anglo-American Legal History" ist die Beobachtung, daß die „vorrömischen" oder auch germanischen Erscheinungsformen der späteren gemeinrechtlichen Familienfideikommisse im 8. Jahrhundert zuerst in England bezeugt sind, und dann erst seit dem 11. Jahrhundert auch in Deutschland vorkamen[37]. Die ältesten Spuren einer Bindung des Grundbesitzes an die Familie verbunden mit einer Nachfolge des ältesten Sohnes sah *Frommhold*[38] allerdings in den Rechten der Sachsen und Thüringer – belegt durch die *Lex Saxonum* und die *Lex Thuringionum* –, die die Angelsachsen mit in ihre neuen Wohnsitze genommen haben sollen[39]. Die Belege, die *Frommhold* beibringt, deuten aber alle auf eine gesetzliche, im Sinne von gesetzlich zwingend vorgeschriebene Einzelnachfolge des ältesten Sohnes in den Grundbesitz schon vor der Einführung des normannischen Lehnsrechts hin[40].

In Italien wurde das Familienfideikommiß erst in der Schule von Bologna, also von vornherein in romanisierter Form, zu einer Rechtseinrichtung entwickelt[41], deren Prinzipien, wie zu zeigen sein wird, noch in der Theorie von *Knipschildt* erhalten geblieben sind.

Im Recht der iberischen Halbinsel gab es in Gestalt der Majorate eine vergleichbare Erscheinung[42]. Der Einfluß der spanischen Majorate wurde im 17. Jahrhundert in Deutschland wirksam, und zwar auf dem Wege über Österreich und Flandern[43]. Dieser Umweg ist aber meines Erachtens nicht unbedingt notwendig. Denn der höchst einflußreiche Spanier *Ludovicus de Molina*[44] war seinerseits der meistzitierte Autor bei dem hier vorzustellenden deutschen Leitautor *Knipschildt*. Die Majorate wiederum gingen auf arabische Vorbilder zurück[45]. Ursprünglich handelte es sich um fromme Stiftungen, die dazu dienten, das Vermögen zunächst der

---

37 So jedenfalls *Erler* (Fn. 34) 1071.

38 *Georg Frommhold*, Grundzüge der Entwicklung der Einzelerbfolge in Familiengüter im englischen und schottischen Recht, ZSS (GA) 33 (1912) 86 - 126.

39 *Frommhold* (Fn. 38) 87.

40 *Frommhold* (Fn. 38) 91.

41 *Giulio Vismara*, Familienfideikommiß (Italienisches Recht), in: Lexikon des Mittelalters, Band IV, München und Zürich, 1989, S. 431.

42 *Lalinde Abadia*, Fideikommiß (Recht der iberischen Halbinsel), in: Lexikon des Mittelalters, Band IV, München und Zürich, 1989, S. 432.

43 *Eckert* (Fn. 28) 65.

44 *Ludovicus de Molina Morales* (1510/30 - 1573/78), De primogenitorum hispanorum origine ac natura libri quattuor, Compluti, 1573; zahlreiche weitere Ausgaben u. a. Coloniae, 1601 und 1650, Venedig, 1757. Dazu: *Ernst Holthöfer*, Literatur in Italien, Frankreich, Spanien und Portugal, in: Helmut Coing (Hg.), Handbuch der Quellen und Literatur der neueren europäischen Privatrechtsgeschichte, Band II 1, München, 1977, S. 394; *Bartolomé Clavero*, Mayorazgo, Madrid, 1974.

45 So *Bayer* (Fn. 1) 64, unter Berufung auf *Max Weber*.

Araber, dann aber auch der Christen der Konfiskation durch die Kalifen zu entziehen. Aber hier gab es auch gegenläufige Entwicklungen. Teils zwang der König dem Adel im Lehnssystem die Majorate auf, teils errichteten die Adeligen auf zurückerobertem Land eigene Majorate, um ihren Besitz gegen den König zu sichern.

II. *Philipp Knipschildt* und die wissenschaftliche Grundlegung des Familienfideikommisses in Deutschland

Die Begründung einer eigenen Lehre vom Familienfideikommiß im deutschen Rechtskreis wird generell als das Verdienst des Eßlinger Syndicus *Philipp Knipschildt* angesehen, dessen „Tractatus de Fideicommissis Familiarum Nobilium, von Stamm-Gütern" zuerst 1626 in Straßburg als Dissertation und dann in erweiterter Form im Jahre 1641 in Ulm erschienen ist[46]. Ausweislich des Untertitels dienten die Familienfideikommisse, die auf deutsch als „Stamm-Güter" bezeichnet werden, der Erhaltung der adeligen Familien. Weitere Auflagen des Werkes erschienen 1654, 1657, 1661 und 1687 in Ulm, weiter in Köln 1693 und 1696, in Augsburg 1710, 1735 und 1750[47]. Hier wurde die als „Editio nova et emendata" bezeichnete Ausgabe Augsburg 1750 benutzt. Noch 1868 bezeichnete *William Lewis Knipschildts* Buch als unangefochtenes Standardwerk von aktueller Bedeutung[48].

Knipschildt hat das Familienfideikommiß hinsichtlich der gesamten Einzelausgestaltung des Instituts in das theoretische Gerüst des gemeinen römisch-kanonischen Rechts eingefügt. Alle Einzelregelungen hat er, soweit eben möglich, mit Zitaten aus dem *Corpus iuris* und den entsprechenden Kommentierungen belegt. Das gilt insbesondere für die Grundsätze der Rechtsgeschäftslehre und die Theorie der Willenserklärungen, die Wirkung von Veräußerungsverboten, die Grundbegriffe des Sachenrechts und auch des Familienrechts. Ganz konkret konnten sich etwa Legitimität und Illegitimität von Kindern im Bereiche des Familienfideikommisses nicht anders darstellen als im allgemeinen Familienrecht. Dazu kam die Verwendung der gesamten einschlägigen Literatur an Traktaten, sowie Sammlungen von *Decisiones* und *Consilia* aus allen europäischen Ländern, jedoch mit Ausnahme Englands. Die Liste der von *Knipschildt* zitierten Autoren ist höchst umfangreich. Eine Auszählung ergibt etwa folgendes Bild: Meistzitierter Autor ist der Spanier

46 *Eisenhart*, Knipschildt, in: Allgemeine deutsche Biographie (ADB), Band 16, Leipzig, 1882, S. 297 - 298. *R. Stintzing, E. Landsberg*, Geschichte der deutschen Rechtswissenschaft, Band II, München und Leipzig, 1884, S. 15 und 24.

47 Nachweise bei: *Eisenhart* (Fn. 46); *Stintzing / Landsberg* (Fn. 46) 15; *Ernst Holthöfer* (Fn. 44) 606. Die Zahl der Auflagen ist nicht gesichert. *Otto von Gierke*, Grundzüge des deutschen Privatrechts, in: Enzyklopädie der Rechtswissenschaft, begründet von Franz von Holtzendorff und Josef Kohler, Band I, 7. Auflage, München, Leipzig, Berlin, 1915, S. 250, zitiert zusätzlich noch eine Auflage aus dem Jahre 1694.

48 *William Lewis*, Das Recht des Familienfideicommisses, Berlin, 1868.

Ludovicus de Molina Morales mit seinem Werk „De primogenitorum Hispanorum origine et natura libri quattuor“[49]. Daneben fehlt keiner der großen Namen des Mittelalters und des 16. und der ersten Hälfte des 17. Jahrhunderts von *Accursius* bis *Carpzov.* In der Überzahl sind Zitate italienischer Autoren, doch fehlen auch die französischen Praktiker wie *Tiraquellus* und Theoretiker wie *Cuiacius* keineswegs. Das Gleiche gilt für die deutschen Autoren.

Knipschildt stellt das Ganze als generell in Deutschland und sogar in ganz Europa geltendes Recht dar. Eine besondere Rechtsquellenlehre gibt es in dem Werk nicht. Viele Argumente stammen aus dem Lehnrecht, zu dem eine enge Verwandtschaft besteht.

In 16 Kapiteln behandelt *Knipschildt* Begründung, Ausgestaltungen und Wirkungen, Nachfolgeregelung, sowie Beendigung der Familienfideikommisse. Die einzelnen Kapitelüberschriften lauten ins Deutsche übertragen: 1. Ursprung, Bezeichnung und Definition, 2. Einteilung und Arten, 3. *Causa efficiens:* Mögliche Begründer, 4. Mögliche Begünstigte, 5. Einem Familienfideikommiß zugängliche Güter, 6. Art und Weise nebst Form der Errichtung, 7. Zweck, 8. Wirkung der Familienfideikommisse, und zwar erstens in Bezug auf die zur Nachfolge berechtigten Personen, 9. Methode und Form der Nachfolge (als Fortsetzung der ersten Wirkung), 10. Zweite Wirkung: Rechte des jeweiligen Inhabers, 11. Dritte Wirkung: Beschränkungen des jeweiligen Inhabers, insbesondere das Veräußerungsverbot, 12. Vierte Wirkung: Auf dem Familienfideikommiß ruhende Lasten, 13. Rechte und Klagen des Anwärters, 14. Beweis des Familienfideikommisses, 15. Verwandte Erscheinungen (Primogenitur und Majorat), 16. Auflösung.

III. Analyse von *Knipschildts* Traktat

1. Ursprung, Bezeichnung und Definition des Familienfideikommisses

Knipschildt beginnt mit einer Beschreibung der Geschichte der Fideikommisse generell bis *Justinian* (1.9)[50], in der die Fideikommisse als Einrichtung des *ius gentium* bezeichnet werden (1.10). Dann folgt die Definition nach Inst. 2, 23, 12 (1.12): „Dicuntur fideicommissa, quod fidei haeredis, vel alterius, a quo quid relinquitur, disponens committit, ut aliquid det vel faciat alteri“. Vom römischen Familienfideikommiß ist nicht die Rede. Anschließend geht *Knipschildt,* ohne die Verbindung klar zu machen, zu den Stammgütern der Germanen über, die im Titel des Werkes als identisch mit Familienfideikommissen bezeichnet worden sind (1.13). Sie werden eingerichtet zur Erhaltung eines „Fürstlichen, Gräflichen, Freyherrli-

49 Oben Fn. 44.

50 Die in Klammern in den Text eingefügten Zahlen beziehen sich auf Kapitel und Summarien nebst Randnummern des Werkes von *Knipschildt,* „1.9“ bedeutet also Kapitel 1, Nummer 9 im Summarium und als Randnummer.

chen, Adelichen Stammes und Namens". Diese Familienfideikommisse müssen von anderen Gütern verwandter Art sehr genau unterschieden werden, die ebenfalls nicht veräußerlich sind (1.14). Dem wird die Veräußerungsfreiheit nach „jus civile commune" entgegengestellt (1.16).

In 1.17 wird erwähnt, daß es neben Stammgütern auch Stamm-Häuser (gemeint ist Stammburgen) gebe. *Knipschildt* sagt, auch bezüglich dieser seien „fideicommissa familiarum" möglich. Danach spricht *Knipschildt* nur über die Namen bestimmter Adelsfamilien und den Begriff der adeligen Familien, die solche Familienfideikommisse begründen können. Kapitel 1 endet mit einer Definition speziell für das Familienfideikommiß (185): „... fideicommissum familiae ita definiri poterit, quod sit donatio quaedam ab instituente ea lege facta, ut bona proximioribus eodem gradu, vel seniori in familia, ad eius conservationem perpetuo ac ordine successive deferantur ...".

2. Einteilung und Arten

Im zweiten Kapitel schildert *Knipschildt* die verschiedenen Arten der „fideicommissa familiae". Diese können sein: *realia, personalia, expressa, tacita, universalia, particularia, simplicia et soluta, pura et conditionata, propria et impropria, conventionalia et ultima voluntate constituta, revocabilia vel irrevocabilia, perpetua vel temporalia, reciproca et mutua.* All das läßt sich mit Digestenstellen zu Legaten und Fideikommissen und mit Literaturzitaten belegen, wobei eindeutig die Italiener, von den Glossatoren angefangen, vorherrschen, mit dem Schwergewicht auf Consilienschreibern des 16. Jahrhunderts. So bleibt das – kurze – 2. Kapitel rein romanistisch. Unter anderem verweist *Knipschildt* in für seine Darstellung typischer Weise beim „fideicommissum reale" auf D. 31, 88, 15, wo der Wortlaut einer Einsetzung zitiert wird (hier die lateinische Übersetzung des griechischen Originals): „Volo autem domus meas nec venumdari sed integras manere ipsis et filiis nepotibusque in sempiternum". Im Zweifel handelt es sich nach *Knipschildt* stets um solch ein ewiges „fideicommissum familiae reale" (2.3 und 42). Hierfür werden aber nur Literaturstimmen zitiert: *Castro, Alexander, Simon de Praetis* und *Menochius.* Das zeigt aber, daß die von *Knipschildt* behandelte Materie ein fest etablierter Gegenstand der gemeinrechtlichen Rechtswissenschaft war.

3. *Causa efficiens:* Mögliche Begründer und Stifter

Das dritten Kapitel beginnt *Knipschildt* mit einleitenden Bemerkungen über die Einsetzung eines Familienfideikommisses und behandelt ausführlich die Personen, die eine solche Einsetzung vornehmen können. „Causa efficiens" ist der Wille des Einsetzenden. Es kommt mehr auf die Absicht an als auf die gebrauchten Worte. Deswegen kann im Prinzip jeder, der ein Testament errichten kann, der Verträge schließen und Schenkungen machen kann, also „quilibet paterfamilias“ auch ein Familienfideikommiß errichten (3.8 und 9). Soweit herrscht wieder die romanistische Theorie vor.

Im einzelnen muß *Knipschildt* dann aber doch folgende möglichen Personen als Begründer eines Familienfideikommisses mit unterschiedlichen Befugnissen erörtern: Kaiser (3.11), Könige (3.19), Fürsten, Herzöge, Grafen und Barone (3.28). Alle natürlich nur, soweit sie Güter zur freien Verfügung haben, was, wie sich aus den angeführten Beispielen ergibt, normalerweise nicht der Fall war, weil alle Güter bereits durch Gesetz oder frühere Verfügungen gebunden waren.

Weiter werden als Begründer diskutiert: Reichsunmittelbare und mediatisierte Adelige (3.31), aber auch jeder freie Bürger (3.32), sowohl der Paterfamilias als auch ein Filiusfamilias (3.42), und schließlich auch Frauen, selbst wenn sie verheiratet sind (3.46 - 51). Das Ganze stützt Knipschildt ab mit Hinweisen auf die Testierfreiheit und die Befugnis, Schenkungen zu machen, sowie mit dem D. 41, 1, 9, 3 entnommenen Satz, es stimme nichts mehr mit der natürlichen Vernunft überein, als dem Willen desjenigen, der seine Sache auf einen anderen übertragen wolle, Geltung zu verschaffen (3.32).

Umstritten war aber, ob auch eine „familia privata“ eine Primogenitur anordnen konnte (3.34). Geistliche können für ihr Privatvermögen einen Familienfideikommiß anordnen. Das gilt für den Papst, Kardinäle, Erzbischöfe und Bischöfe und einfachere Priester sowie Kanoniker und Mönche vor Ablegung der Profeß (3.35 - 41).

Wer sein Vermögen nicht selbst verwalten kann, kann natürlich auch keinen Familienfideikommiß errichten. Das gilt für Minderjährige, unter Vormundschaft stehende Personen, Geisteskranke, entmündigte Verschwender (3.52 - 60). Die Befugnis fehlt auch dem Verwalter fremder Vermögen, dem Nießbraucher, dem Ehemann hinsichtlich der Mitgift, dem Witwer bei Eingehen einer zweiten Ehe in Bezug auf den Nachlaß der ersten Frau und dem Vasallen (3.61 - 65).

4. Mögliche Begünstigte

Ebenso muß der Kreis der Personen festgelegt werden, zu deren Gunsten ein Familienfideikommiß angeordnet werden kann. Auch hier gilt das Prinzip, daß jeder begünstigt werden kann, der auch Rechte aus einem Testament, einem Vertrag und einer Schenkung erwerben kann (4.1). *Knipschildt* bemerkt aber, daß Familienfideikommisse in der Praxis in erster Linie für adelige Familien errichtet würden, deren Erhaltung im Interesse des Staates liege (4.2). An zweiter Stelle folgen die Patrizier (4.4). Es macht keinen Unterschied, ob der Bedachte Paterfamilias ist oder unter väterlicher Gewalt steht (4.11). Schließlich meint *Knipschildt,* daß man sogar für private oder „plebeische“ Familien ein Familienfideikommiß stiften könne (4.24).

5. Einem Familienfideikommiß zugängliche Güter

Was Objekt eines Familienfideikommisses sein kann, wird in Kapitel 5 dargestellt. Der Grundsatz ist, daß ein Familienfideikommiß nur angeordnet werden kann für Grundstücke und Grundstücksbestandteile sowie für Objekte, die rechtlich mit Grundstücken gleichgestellt werden (5.1 - 4). Die interessanten Fragen betreffen die Gleichstellung von beweglichen Gegenständen und Rechten mit dem Grundvermögen. Hier besteht eine enge Parallele zum Lehnrecht. Gegenstand kann nicht nur das gesamte Grundvermögen sein, sondern auch einzelne Teile. Nach diesen Maßgaben können Gegenstand eines Familienfideikommisses sein: Eine Erbschaft als solche mit allen unbeweglichen und beweglichen Sachen, die dazu gehören (5.7); andere Vermögensgesamtheiten wie Herzogtümer, Markgrafschaften, Grafschaften, Baronien und ähnliche Herrschaften und Rechte, an denen ein Lehen begründet werden kann (5.14 und 16), und somit schlechthin die Herrschaft über ein Territorium (*superioritas territorialis)* (5.15); weiter Regalien, Jurisdiktionen, Zoll und Steuer, noch nicht eingezogene Bußen und Strafen, das Recht zur Konfiskation, Zehnte, Kammer-Zölle (5.25), langfristige Renten aus Grundstücken wie Erbzins und Erbpacht; Forderungen aus einem Rentenkauf, Forderungen, die sich auf Grundstücke beziehen (5.33), Dienstbarkeiten, Nießbrauch, Jagd- und Fischrechte, Mühlen, Inseln, Heerlager und Befestigungsanlagen nebst dazugehörendem Material, Burgen und befestigte Städte, Häuser, Landgüter, Wälder, Steinbrüche, Weinpressen, Leibeigene als Teil des Grundstücks (5.70), Eisern-Vieh (5.71), zum Kauf von Grundstücken bestimmtes oder aus dem Verkauf erzieltes Geld (5.72 und 78), Erb-Gelder (Abfindungsansprüche bei Erbteilung). Bei all diesen Objekten lautet die Begründung, daß sie rechtlich wie Immobilien behandelt werden müssen. Gegenstand eines Familienfideikommisses können aber auch Wertgegenstände sein wie Gemmen, Perlen, Halsketten aus Gold und Silber, Schwerter und andere wertvolle alte Waffen sowie Pokale, soweit sie sämtlich dem Ruhm der Familie dienen (5.81 und 100); Erbpachtrechte (Emphyteuse) (5.84)[51]; Gegenstände im Eigentum des Erben nach Inst. 2, 20, 4, D. 31, 26 und C. 6, 42, 25 (5.89) und sogar eines Dritten (5.91); zukünftige Gegenstände, die nach dem Tode des Errichters des Familienfideikommisses von den Erben und ihren Abkömmlingen erworben werden (5.94). Nicht möglich ist die Errichtung eines Familienfideikommisses an kirchlichen Gütern (5.103) und Lehnsgütern (5.104), Emphyteusen (5.118, anders 5.84), und am gesetzlichen Erbteil (5.119).

6. Art und Weise nebst Form der Errichtung

Das umfangreiche Kapitel 6 gilt der Form der Errichtung. Die Errichtung durch Testament ist der durch einen Vertrag vorzuziehen, weil Verträge leicht auch wieder gelöst werden können und testamentarische Veräußerungsverbote eine stärkere

---

[51] Dazu auch Kapitel 12, Randnummer 121.

Wirkung haben als vertragliche. Außerdem wäre ein Universalfideikommiß durch Vertrag nicht möglich. Das Testament kann schriftlich oder mündlich errichtet werden. Erforderlich sind fünf Zeugen. Es reicht auch ein Codizill. Dafür werden zitiert: *Codex, Faber, Carpzov, Peregrin, Fusar* und der Reichsabschied über die Notare von 1512 (6.17 - 18). Umstritten ist, ob sich auch regierende Herren mit Jurisdiktionsgewalt der feierlichen Zeugenform bedienen müssen. *Knipschildt* empfiehlt die Einhaltung der Form jedenfalls den *Principes inferiores* (6.21). Einfache Schriftform genügt allerdings für das Testament eines Vaters zugunsten seiner Söhne (6.22). Auf bestimmte Worte kommt es nicht an, solange nur der Wille feststeht („modo de voluntate constet") (6.26). Unklar bleibt aber, wie die Einsetzung durch Brief („epistola") gemeint ist (6.27). *Knipschildt* läßt aber auch die Errichtung durch Vertrag („contractus", „pactum") unter Lebenden zu (6.25, 29), etwa durch einen „Burg-Frieden" unter Brüdern (6.32) oder durch Ehevertrag (6.33), das jedoch nur hinsichtlich einzelner Gegenstände (6.35), weil man sich durch Vertrag nicht für immer der Veräußerungsbefugnis begeben kann (6.43). Davon gibt es allerdings wieder eine Ausnahme für die gegenseitigen Erbverträge der Adeligen (*confraternitates* = Erbverbrüderungen), die sowohl nach *ius commune* als auch nach „generali Germaniae consuetudine" (6.44) wirksam sind.

Ein Familienfideikommiß konnte weiterhin durch eine Schenkung errichtet werden (6.57), und zwar trotz des generellen Verbotes einer schenkweisen Verfügung über alle gegenwärtigen und zukünftigen Güter. Diese Stelle ist bezeichnend dafür, daß *Knipschildt* stets versuchen mußte, seine Regeln mit dem allgemeinen Privatrecht in Übereinstimmung zu halten. Nicht ganz klar wird aber, was *Knipschildt* mit einer Errichtung kraft Gewohnheit gemeint hat (6.74). Es ging ihm an dieser Stelle wohl mehr um die gewohnheitsrechtliche Ausgestaltung der Nachfolgeregelung, die nicht nur erstgeborene Söhne, sondern auch Frauen begünstigen konnte (6.77). Das gleiche gilt für das, was Statuten bewirken konnten (6.80). Hervorhebenswert ist, daß sogar eine Begründung durch „praescriptio", d. h. durch Ersitzung, in Betracht kam (6.82).

Familienfideikommisse konnten nicht nur durch ausdrückliche Erklärungen, sondern auch indirekt, durch Zeichen (einen Wink), stillschweigend und sogar kraft Vermutung errichtet werden. All das spielte wohl hauptsächlich bei der Auslegung von Testamenten eine Rolle (6.86 ff.).

Auf gesetzliche Pflichterbteile (*legitima)* war bei der Errichtung Rücksicht zu nehmen (6.148 ff.), ebenso auf die den Töchtern zustehende Mitgift *(dos)* (6.186). Insgesamt war also dafür zu sorgen, daß auch stets die jüngeren Geschwister beiderlei Geschlechts versorgt wurden (6.210). Auch auf die Gläubiger war Rücksicht zu nehmen, d. h. vom Familienfideikommiß mußten zuerst die Schulden abgezogen werden (6.240).

Schriftform war aber bei allem erforderlich (6.242). Dazu kam die Bestätigung durch den Kaiser (6.245). Diese war jedenfalls bei Erbverbrüderungen fürstlicher Familien erforderlich (6.246). Damit ist die Vermutung von Hofmeister, *Knip-*

schildt habe gerade eine selbständige Theorie des Familienfideikommisses aufgestellt, um die kaiserliche Bestätigung als überflüssig erscheinen zu lassen, widerlegt.

Einzelne Modalitäten konnten durch den Stifter festgelegt werden (6.251). Das wichtigste war die Bestimmung der Person des jeweils Berechtigten. Dabei herrschte das Prinzip der Primogenitur eindeutig vor. Eine Teilung des Familienfideikommisses war verboten (6.300). Bei der Begründung wurde oft das Veräußerungsverbot eigens hervorgehoben (6.332). Doch ist nicht ohne weiteres einsichtig, warum das Veräußerungsverbot einer besonderen *causa* bedurfte (6.350), um nicht ein bloßer Rat zu sein. Das Verbot der Veräußerung verhindert die Eigentumsübertragung auch ohne Rücksicht auf die Kenntnis der Beteiligten.

Im Prinzip waren die Familienfideikommisse ewig, wie die Familie selbst (6.380). An dieser Stelle ist bei *Knipschildt* nicht die Rede von der von *Justinian* angeordneten Limitierung auf vier Generationen[52]. Gewillkürte zeitliche Beschränkungen waren aber zulässig. Dem Berechtigten konnte auch die Auflage gemacht werden, eine aus einer bestimmten Familie stammende Person zu heiraten (6.385). *Knipschildt* mißbilligte schließlich die umstrittene Regel, wonach zum Eintritt in das Recht nur zugelassen werde könne, wer sich gemäß dem Willen des Errichtenden zu einer bestimmten Religion oder Konfession bekenne (6.391 - 458). Eine Publikation des Familienfideikommisses hielt *Knipschildt* nicht für erforderlich (6.458).

7. Zweck

Vom Zweck der Familienfideikommisse handelt Kapitel 7. Zweck ist die Bewahrung des Rufes und des Glanzes (*splendor)* der Familie und ihrer Güter als der Grundlage des Staatswesens (7.5). Dazu ist, wie breit ausgeführt wird, ein gewisser Reichtum Voraussetzung, ohne den Adel nicht denkbar ist (7.6 ff.). Aber dieser Adel muß eben auch erhalten bleiben. Daher dient das beim Familienfideikommiß vorherrschende Prinzip der Primogenitur dem gemeinen Wohl (7.59). Der Erhaltung des Adels dienen aber auch Erbverbrüderungen (7.60), Erbverzicht der Frauen (7.61), Stifte zur Aufnahme der jüngeren Geschwister (7.62), Veräußerungsverbote (7.69), Lehnsauftragungen (7.70), Retraktsrechte (7.73) sowie Abfindungen der Töchter (7.76). Zur Erhaltung eines adeligen Geschlechtes konnte der Papst sogar einen adeligen Mönch zeitweise von seinen Gelübden dispensieren (7.80). All das belegt den Nutzen von Familienfideikommissen, die zwar die Ausnahme sind (7.81 - 84), aber doch wegen ihres öffentlichen Nutzens im Zweifel durch weite Auslegung der Regeln des *ius commune* als „favorabilia" möglichst aufrecht zu erhalten sind (7.85).

52 Dazu: *Söllner* (Fn. 33).

8. Wirkung der Familienfideikommisse, und zwar erstens in bezug auf die zur Nachfolge berechtigten Personen

Mit Kapitel 8 beginnt die Darstellung der Wirkung der Familienfideikommisse. Als erste Wirkung *(effectus)* bezeichnet *Knipschildt* das Recht zur Nachfolge in das Familienfideikommiß. Zur Nachfolge berechtigt sind in erster Linie die Agnaten, d. h. die Blutsverwandten im Mannesstamm. Berechtigt sind zunächst die vom Stifter Benannten einschließlich der zur Zeit der Stiftung noch nicht geborenen Kinder (8.9). Auch enterbte Personen bleiben im Sinne der Berechtigung zur Nachfolge in das Familienfideikommiß Agnaten (8.16). Und dazu zählen auch die Verwandten in der Seitenlinie. All das ist immer nur mit Hilfe ständiger Anleihen beim Erbrecht und beim Lehnrecht darstellbar. Oft wird nicht klar, welche konkrete Lage *Knipschildt* vor Augen hat. Dann verselbständigt sich das theoretische Räsonnement.

Die Rolle der Geistlichen war umstritten. *Knipschildt* sprach sich in Bezug auf Klosterangehörige gegen die Berechtigung zur Nachfolge aus (8.28), nicht aber bei Weltgeistlichen (8.43)und auch nicht bei den Angehörigen der Ritterorden (8.88). Maßstab für alle Lösungen ist immer „familiae et agnationis splendor et conservatio" (8.71). Aber das führt nicht zum Ausschluß von Junggesellen (8.92) und Hermaphroditen, die überwiegend mänlich erscheinen (8.96). Dieses Thema nimmt *Knipschidt* zum Anlaß für generelle Bemerkungen zur gesellschaftlichen Stellung der betroffenen Personen. Da erfährt man etwa, daß in Athen Junggesellen an einem bestimmten Tage von Frauen um den Altar geschleift und gegeißelt wurden. Neben solchen Hinweisen fehlt es aber oft an der Mitteilung von Rechtstatsachen. Zweifel bestanden auch daran, ob in irgendeiner Weise Behinderte vom Familienfideikommiß auszuschließen seien. *Knipschildt* diskutiert folgende Behinderungen: Stummheit, Taubheit, Blindheit, Stottern, Schielen, Lahmen, Buckel, Schwächlichkeit, Feigheit und Häßlichkeit (8.99). Dazu kommen noch die Geisteskranken – *furiosi et mente capti* – (8.113).

Frauen sind von der Nachfolge ausgeschlossen, weil sie mit der Heirat die Familie des Vaters verlassen und in die ihres Gatten eintreten (8.127). Doch bemerkt *Knipschildt,* es bestehe eine große Kontroverse darüber, ob dieser Ausschluß rechtens („de jure") sei. Deswegen widmete er dem Thema eine ausführliche Behandlung unter Erörterung des Pro und Contra (8.135). Interessant ist, welche Juristen in dieser Diskussion aufgetreten sind. Für die Gleichstellung der Frauen werden zitiert: *Justinian* mit zahlreichen Stellen aus dem *Corpus iuris, Dinus, Rolbag* (einer der Hauptzeugen), Altes und Neues Testament, *Corn. Agrippa, Tacitus, Tiraquellus, Eusebius, Plinius, Solinus, Petrus, Jacobus, Baldus, Bartolus, Pandolphus Colemus, Diodor,* viele Geschichtsschreiber, die etwa von Königinnen berichten usw. Insgesamt ist das ein sehr schönes und gut mit Beispielen belegtes *Plädoyer* für die generelle Gleichwertigkeit und Gleichberechtigung der Frau (bis 8.172).

Trotzdem entschied sich *Knipschildt* letztlich mit ausführlich vorgetragenen und vielen Zitaten belegten Argumenten dafür, daß der vom Stifter oder durch Statut angeordnete Ausschluß „angemessen dotierter“ Frauen rechtmäßig sei (8.173 - 290). Unter anderem wird dabei erörtert, daß auch in ein von einer Frau eingesetztes Familienfideikommiß nur Männer nachfolgen könnten, weil Mütter ihre Söhne mehr zu lieben pflegten als ihre Töchter (8.255 - 259).

Nach Absolvierung des Themas „Frauen“ geht es weiter mit den nichtehelichen Kindern (8.291) und Problemen der Legitimation (8.327), die nicht zur Nachfolge berechtigt, Adoption (8.399) sowie Einkindschaft (8.436), die ein Recht zur Nachfolge gewähren. Ausgeschlossen sind weiter die Kinder aus morganatischen Ehen (8.440), Häretiker (8.447), Abtrünnige, Atheisten und Apostaten (8.449) sowie auch Blasphemiker (8.450), Personen, die wegen Mäjestätsbeleidigung verurteilt worden sind (8.451), Aufrührer, Verbannte, Verräter, Meineidige, Fälscher, Mörder (insbes. jemand, der den vor ihm Berechtigten getötet hat), Räuber, Straßenräuber, Strauchdiebe, Meuchelmörder, Kirchenschänder, Brandstifter, Fahnenflüchtige, Spione, Landstreicher („Herrenlose“), „Hecken-Reuter“ und „Hecken-Fischer“ (8.468). Dazu kommen aber endlich auch Adelige, die ihnen unwürdige Berufe ausüben, wie Maler, Architekt, Klempner, Schneider, Schuster, Schankwirt, Koch, Bäcker, Müller, Barbier, Bademeister, Schmied usw. (bis 8.472).

9. Methode und Form der Nachfolge (als Fortsetzung der ersten Wirkung)

Nach den zur Nachfolge generell berechtigten Personen muß immer noch als Teil der ersten Wirkung des Familienfideikommisses die Berechtigung zur Nachfolge im Einzelfall beschrieben werden. In erster Linie waren die Anordnungen des Stifters maßgebend (9.1). Im übrigen erfolgte die Bestimmung nach den Regeln des gemeinrechtlichen Intestaterbrechts (9.7 - 9). Lehnrecht wurde nicht angewendet. Das gemeine Recht war daher auch als Leitlinie maßgebend, wenn die Anordnungen des Stifters interpretiert werden mußten. In dieser Hinsicht waren zahlreiche Zweifelsfragen zu diskutieren. Daran fällt auf, daß offensichtlich die Anordnung der Primogenitur keineswegs die Regel war. Auch eine Bindung für nur zwei Generationen scheint nicht selten gewesen zu sein (arg. 9.11).

Aber nicht alles ließ sich in Analogie zum gesetzlichen Erbrecht lösen. So wurde beispielsweise die Anordnung des Repräsentationsrechts nicht vermutet, was allerdings umstritten war (9.21 ff.). Wie stets ging es bei dieser Frage in erster Linie um die Berechtigung der Kinder des vorverstorbenen Sohnes neben ihren Oheimen (9.34). Ein spezielles und umstrittenes Problem war, ob der Enkel des verstorbenen Inhabers bei Vorversterben des ältesten Sohnes den Vorrang vor dem Zweitgeborenen hatte (9.62). Das war eine Frage, die im Verlaufe der Geschichte immer wieder bei der Nachfolgefrage in Königreiche von Bedeutung war[53]. In diesem Zusammenhang wird dann auch einmal die Goldene Bulle zitiert (9.65). Im Ergebnis ist *Knipschildt* als Konsequenz aus den allgemeinen Prinzipien der Repräsentation für den Vorrang des Enkels vor seinem Oheim (9.65). Die Fragen stellen sich ähnlich, wenn nach dem Tode des kinderlos verstorbenen Erstgeborenen die Kinder des vorverstorbenen Zweitgeborenen mit dem Drittgeborenen zusammentreffen (9.71).

Für den Fall, daß der Einsetzende die „nächsten Erben" berufen hat, ist die Frage diskutiert worden, ob beim kinderlosen Versterben eines Inhabers die nächsten Erben des Einsetzenden oder die nächsten Erben des letzten Inhabers gemeint sind. *Knipschildt* entschied sich nach Referat der für und wider vorgebrachten Argumente für die nächsten Erben des Begründers. Das auch an vielen anderen Stellen verwendete Argument dafür war, daß jeder neue Berechtigte sein Recht nicht im Erbwege vom letzten Inhaber herleitete, sondern nach den Regeln des Familienfideikommisses vom ursprünglichen Begründer (9.77)[54].

In diesen Zusammenhang gehört schließlich auch die Frage, ob ein Familienfideikommiß gemäß Novelle 159 nicht über den vierten Grad in gerader Linie oder die vierte Generation hinaus erstreckt werden dürfe. *Knipschildt* sprach sich gegen jede Beschränkung nach Generationem aus (9.103). Für die Widerlegung der Novelle 159 schloß sich *Knipschildt Cujas* an und ergänzte, diese Novelle gehöre zu denen, bei deren Abfassung Bestechung im Spiele gewesen sei (9.119)[55]. So gilt im Ergebnis die Anordnung eines Familienfideikommisses *in perpetuum.*

10. Zweite Wirkung: Rechte des jeweiligen Inhabers

Nach *Knipschildt* erwirbt der jeweilige Inhaber Eigentum („dominium"), was sich in erster Linie daran zeigen soll, daß ihm nach D. 22, 1 (de usur.) 42 die gezogenen Früchte zustehen (10.1). Außerdem werden weitere das Fideikommiß generell betreffende Stellen aus dem *Corpus iuris* zur Unterstützung des Eigentums des jeweiligen Inhabers herangezogen. Belegen läßt sich auch aus dem *Corpus iuris,* daß der Eigentümerstellung der Umstand nicht entgegensteht, daß der Berechtigte bei seinem Tode die Sache in vorbestimmter Weise weiterzugeben hat. Die Folge davon ist auch, daß dem Inhaber die „Rei vindicatio" zur Verfügung steht.

Trotzdem gibt *Knipschildt* zu bedenken, ob der Inhaber nicht eher Nießbraucher („fructuarius") als wahrer Eigentümer („verus dominus") (10.5.) sei, mit „dominium utile" und nicht „directum" (10.9), entschließt sich aber letztlich für wahres Eigentum (10.10). Allerdings kann der Begründer auch anordnen, daß stets der aktuelle Inhaber Nießbraucher ist, während der nächste Aspirant Eigentümer ist und sein Eigentum mit dem Erwerb der Sache an den dann folgenden nächsten Anwär-

53 Vgl. Shakespeares Drama *King John.*

54 Unten Kapitel 16, Randnummer 169.

55 *Söllner* (Fn. 33).

ter verliert. So soll es nach *Molina* bei den spanischen Majoraten der Fall gewesen sein (10.18). Aber auch dafür lassen sich typischerweise Texte aus dem *Corpus iuris* anführen, nämlich die nur entfernt verwandte Konstitution C. 5, 14, 11 und die in der Tat einschlägige *lex* D. 33, 2, 19.

Beim Tode des Inhabers geht das Familienfideikommiß ohne weiteres sofort auf den Nächsten über (10.19), denn der Begründer hat mit Wirkung für alle späteren Inhaber ein Sachenrecht begründet. Demnach ist die *rei vindicatio* für den Erwerber das Mittel der Geltendmachung seines Rechts[56]. Das vergleicht *Knipschildt* unter anderem mit dem Erwerb eines Vindikationslegates und auch mit dem unmittelbaren Erwerb einer Erbschaft nach römischem Recht (10.21) gemäß D. 47, 2, 44, 2 *in fine* und D. 47, 2, 65 (64). Auch das ist typisch für die Verwendung des römischen Rechts zr Erläuterung rechtstechnischer Vorgänge. Dasselbe soll auch *Molina,* der meistzitierte Autor, gesagt haben (10.23). Weniger eindeutig ist für *Knipschildt,* daß gleichzeitig der Erwerber auch „ipso iure" Besitzer wird. Als Zeuge dafür läßt sich nur *Molina* zitieren. *Afflictis* und *Tuschus* waren anderer Ansicht (10.24 - 25).

Wichtigstes Recht des Inhabers ist das Nutznießungs- und Fruchtziehungsrecht (10.33). Unter den Nutzungsrechten werden besonders hervorgehoben: Jagdrecht und Fischereirecht (10.79, 84), Taubenzucht, Waldnutzung nach dem Maßstab eines „bonus paterfamilias" (10.89), Einziehung des Zinses für ausgegebene Emphyteusen und Zinsgüter, Ausbeutung von Steinbrüchen, Kalkgruben, Gold- und Silberminen sowie Bergwerken (10.96), Ausübung der Territorialherrschaft (*superioritas territorialis)* und der Jurisdiktion in vollem Umfang mit Gesetzgebungsbefugnis und Steuererhebung über Burgen und Städte (10.100). Hierfür kann *Knipschildt* aber keinen Beleg anführen außer einem Hinweis auf sein eigenes Buch über die Ritterorden.

Umstritten ist, ob das Patronatsrecht („jus patronatus") beim Erben bleibt oder ebenfalls dem Nachfolger in das Familienfideikommiß zusteht (10.106). Im Zusammenhang damit stehen die Rechte am Familiengrab (10.113). Im Ergebnis stehen dem Berechtigten, gleich dem römischen *fideicommissarius* alle Rechte eines „diligens pater familias" zu (10.121).

11. Dritte Wirkung: Beschränkungen des jeweiligen Inhabers, insbesondere das Veräußerungsverbot

Eines der umfangreichsten Kapitel (S. 401 - 524) ist dem Veräußerungsverbot und sonstigen Einschränkungen der Rechte des jeweiligen Inhabers als der dritten in der Reihe der Wirkungen des Familienfideikommisses gewidmet. Das Veräuße-

56 Für Näheres zur *rei vindicatio* verweist *Knipschildt* häufig auf Kapitel 13, Randnummer 62.

rungsverbot sollte bewirken, daß das Gut dem nächsten Berechtigten jeweils ungeschmälert restituiert werden konnte (11.2). Da es um eine Kette von Anwärtern geht, hilft auch die Zustimmung des nächsten Berechtigten nichts (11.3). Da eine Veräußerung des Familienfideikommisses „contra naturam" wäre, muß sie bei der Begründung auch nicht ausdrücklich angeordnet werden (11.8). Die Art und Weise der Begründung des Veräußerungsverbotes hat aber doch Bedeutung für die Rechtsfolgen eines Verstoßes. Ist das Verbot ausdrücklich ausgesprochen worden, sei es durch Testament oder durch Gesetz, dann ist eine Veräußerung ohne weiteres nichtig, eine Eigentumsübertragung erfolgt dann nicht (11.14). Der nächste Berechtigte kann sofort vindizieren (11.15). Wenn das Verbot aber durch Vertrag eingeführt worden ist, bleibt nach einer viel vertretenen Ansicht eine Eigentumsübertragung möglich und der Berechtigte erwirbt lediglich eine Schadensersatzklage (11.15). Als Grund dafür wird aus dem allgemeinen Vertragsrecht angeführt, daß ein Vertrag nicht die Sache selbst, die Gegenstand des Vertrages ist, erfaßt, sondern nur die Person des Vertragspartners bindet (11.16). Und hier gilt auch, daß wer ein factum schuldet, sich durch Interesseleistung befreien kann (11.22)[57]. Das soll nach dieser Meinung nur dann nicht rechtens sein, wenn der Vertrag beschworen worden ist. Gegen diese Ansicht wendet sich *Knipschildt* aber und beweist, daß eine jede dem Verbot zuwiderlaufende Veräußerung unwirksam ist (11.30).

Wirksam bleibt allerdings trotz einiger Bedenken die Begründung einer Verpflichtung zur Übertragung (11.37). Danach ist aber ein Kaufvertrag trotzdem nichtig. Denn der Kauf ist für *Knipschildt* eine Veräußerung. Durch den Kaufvertrag wird das Eigentum übertragen (11.38). Nichtig sind weiter auch die im Folgenden aufgeführten Akte, wobei allerdings in den Details vieles streitig war und auch durchaus zahlreiche Ausnahmen zugelassen wurden. Nichtig sind demnach: Schenkung (11.43), Leistung an Zahlungs statt (11.47), Verpfändung und Hypothekenbestellung (11.52), Einsatz bei einer *fideijussio* (11.59), Tausch (11.64) – der allerdings vom Begründer zugelassen werden und von den Anwärtern als nützlich gestattet werden kann –, Hingabe als Mitgift (11.78), Veräußerung mit Besitzkonstitut (11.80), Verkauf gegen Rente (11.83), Abtretung – mit Ausnahme der Abtretung an den Zweitgeborenen wie im Falle von Esau (11.88), Abschluß eines Vergleichs, sowohl in Form einer „transactio" (11.90) (mit Ausnahmen zur Streitbeilegung auf Anordnung des Richters) als auch eines „compromissum" (11.109), Begründung eines Nießbrauchs (11.117), Verkauf gegen Rente in der Form des „Gültkaufs" (11.128). Aus allem ergibt sich, daß der jeweilige Inhaber die Bedingungen des Familienfideikommisses nicht ändern darf (11.131 und 149). Auch darf das Familienfideikommiß nicht anderen zum Lehen gegeben werden (11.134) oder zur Emphyteuse (11.136). Sogar Vermietung jeder Art ist untersagt (11.138), ebenso die Überlassung als Bittlehen (*precarium*) (11.148).

---

57 *Tilman Repgen*, Vertragstreue und Erfüllungszwang in der mittelalterlichen Rechtswissenschaft, Paderborn, 1994.

Unter bestimmten Umständen sind jedoch gewisse nachträgliche Änderungen möglich. So ist der letzte Anwärter in seiner Verfügung frei, wenn nach ihm kein Anwärter mehr denkbar ist (11.151), wenn alle Betroffenen zustimmen und wenn ein Inhaber das Gut vermehrt hat (11.152,153).

Eines der Hauptprobleme ist der Gegensatz zwischen der generellen Freiheit zu Verfügungen von Todes wegen und der Bindung an das Familienfideikommiß (11.154 - 202). Hier kommt es letztlich darauf an, ob der Stifter eine feste Nachfolgeordnung vorgeschrieben hat oder einfach die Familie bedacht hat. In letzterem Fall bleibt ihm Spielraum innerhalb der Familie.

Das Veräußerungsverbot erfaßt auch die Widmung zu religiösen Zwecken (11. 203), wie die Mitnahme beim Eintritt in ein Kloster (11.205) oder beim Entritt in eine militärische Hierarchie (11.206) oder als Gegengabe für etwas, das dem Begründer gewährt worden ist (11.207). Es genügt nicht, daß der Veräußerungswillige das Gut vor einem geplanten Verkauf zunächst seinen Verwandten anbietet (11.208). Selbst der Fürst kann das nicht erlauben (11.215).

Trotz allem gab es eine Anzahl von Konstellationen, unter denen eine Veräußerung des Familienfideikommisses möglich war. Das war der Fall bei Überschuldung des Begründers oder seines Nachlasses. Auch muß der Inhaber eine Mitgift bestellen (11.234) und bestimmte Verfügungen zugunsten der Kirche vornehmen können (11.281). Verfügungen sind auch möglich zur Vermeidung der Verletzung von Pflichtteilsrechten (11.309) oder Unterhaltsansprüchen (11.310), zur Bezahlung des Studiums von Söhnen (11.321), zum Freikauf von Kindern, die in die Hände von Barbaren gefallen sind (11.332), zum Zwecke der Erhaltung des Gutes insgesamt (11.346), für die Reparatur und Erneuerung des Gutes (11.347), für den Erwerb von Dingen, die für die Erhaltung der Gesundheit des Inhaber erforderlich sind (11.351).

Eine Veräußerung ist auch möglich, wenn das Verbot nur bestimmte Personen trifft (11.356). Während des Schwebens der Bedingung soll eine Veräußerung ebenfalls möglich sein, wenn das Familienfideikommiß unter einer Bedingung hinterlassen worden ist (11.357). Wirksam ist auch die in Unkenntnis des Familienfideikommisses gutgläubig erfolgte Veräußerung (11.358) sowie eine mit Zustimmung aller Betroffenen erfolgte, was eine in den Einzelheiten besonders umstrittene Frage war (11.379). Die Veräußerung kann auch – gleichsam vorab – an diejenigen erfolgen, die sowieso berufen sind (11.417). Ganz generell war eine Veräußerung auch dann gestattet, wenn es für das Gut von Vorteil war und der Kaufpreis für andere, nützlichere Dinge aufgewendet wurde (11.441). Das war insbesondere der Fall, wenn die Erträge gering waren (11.445) und die einzelnen Bestandteile unbrauchbar (11.446). Das Gleiche galt, wenn der gemeine Nutzen es erforderte (11.447) oder zu vermuten war, daß der Begründer in der gegebenen Situation die Veräußerung gestattet hätte (11.449). Früchte und Erträge konnte der Inhaber sowieso veräußern (11.450). Auch gegen persönliche Verpflichtungen bestanden keine Bedenken (11.452), ebensowenig gegen Verkäufe aus Not (11.453).

Falls die Verpflichtung dahin ging, an den Nächsten zu restituieren „quod supererit“, war der Inhaber sogar frei in seiner Disposition über drei Viertel des Gutes (11.469).

Bei einer nach diesen Prinzipien gestatteten Veräußerung waren aber gewisse Kautelen einzuhalten. Zuerst mußten die schlecht zu erhaltenden und keine Früchte erbringenden Bestandteile veräußert werden (11.485). Bewegliche Sachen mußten vor Grundstücken veräußert werden (11. 486). Veräußert werden durfte nur das unbedingt Notwendige (11.487). Den nächsten Anwärtern war ein Vorkaufsrecht einzuräumen (11.488). Bei allem war möglichst die Erlaubnis eines Superior einzuholen (11.493). *Knipschildt* empfahl die Einhaltung weiterer Vorsichtsmaßregeln: Daß man die Zustimmung der Verwandten einhole, daß man nicht an einen „Potentior“ verkaufe, von dem man die Sachen nicht zurückbekommen könne, daß man nur mit einer Rückkaufsklausel verkaufe usw. (11.494). Was aber einmal wirksam verkauft ist, bleibt für die Zukunft frei vom Familienfideikommiß.

12. Vierte Wirkung: Auf dem Familienfideikommiß ruhende Lasten

Von den mit einem Familienfideikommiß verbundenen Lasten, von *Knipschildt* als der vierte Effekt bezeichnet, handelt das 12. Kapitel. Obwohl das Familienfideikommiß in gewisser Weise eine Schenkung darstellt und einen reinen Gewinn bildet, ist es doch mit bestimmten Lasten verbunden, insbes. solchen, die auf dem Grund und Boden ruhen, weil Nutzungen und Lasten stets zusammen gehören. Daher muß der Inhaber als erstes ein Inventar errichten (12.8). Er muß eine Kaution wegen der ordentlichen Behandlung der Güter stellen (12.21), muß Steuern und Abgaben zahlen (12.44), muß anhängende Prozesse weiter führen (12.52), alle Gegenstände unversehrt erhalten (12.55) und verursachte Schäden ersetzen (12.60). Der Inhaber ist zur Restitution an den Nachfolger verpflichtet (12.71). Der Umfang der Restitution wird im einzelnen genau festgelegt. All das ist begründet, weil der Besitzer nicht „simpliciter et irrevocabiliter“ Eigentümer ist, sondern nur „revocabiliter“ (12.77).

13. Rechte und Klagen des Anwärters

In Kapitel 13 werden die Rechte des Berechtigten oder genauer des Anwärters, d. h. die ihm zustehenden „Actiones“, erörtert. Das Prinzip ist, daß der Berechtigte, bevor ihm das Gut „verbaliter“ restituiert worden = übergeben worden ist, keinerlei Rechte an dem Gut hat (13.1). Das bedeutet, daß er das Gut nicht aus eigener Machtvollkommenheit in Besitz nehmen kann, sondern es aus der Hand des Erben entgegennehmen muß (13.2). Davon gibt es jedoch eine Reihe von Ausnahmen, die im Ergebnis das Prinzip völlig entwerten. Ausnahmen gelten nämlich, wenn der Begründer den Berechtigten ermächtigt hat, das Gut selbst in Besitz zu nehmen

(13.6), wenn es keinen Erben gibt oder der Berechtigte gleichzeitig Erbe ist, wenn der Erbe selbst den Besitz nicht ergreift, wenn der Erbe dies duldet, wenn das Recht des Berechtigten eindeutig ist, wenn sich der Verpflichtete verborgen hält oder im Verzug ist, wenn das Familienfideikommiß nur bestimmte einzelne Teile der Erbschaft umfaßt, wenn der Erbe bei einem Universal-Familienfideikommiß das Gut veräußert hat sowie wenn die Restitution auf Grund einer „pia causa" zu erfolgen hat. Der Erbe kann gezwungen werden, die Erbschaft anzutreten, um die Restitution vornehmen zu können (13.17).

Wichtiger sind die Klagen und Rechte, die dem Berechtigten nach Restitution bzw. Inbesitznahme des Familienfideikommiß zustehen. *Knipschildt* unterscheidet zwölf verschiedene Klagen.

Deren wichtigste wiederum ist, für den Fall, daß das Familienfideikommiß durch Testament begründet worden ist, die der Rückforderung („revocatio") dienende „actio personalis ex testamento", die dem Berechtigten dann zusteht, wenn die dem Familienfideikommiß unterworfene Sache gegen den Willen des Begründers veräußert worden ist[58]. Wem diese Klage im einzelnen zusteht und wem nicht, wird ausführlich erläutert (13.20 - 13.59). In erster Linie dient sie natürlich den nach dem Willen des Begründers zur Nachfolge in das Familienfideikommiß berufenen Personen, die schon in Kapitel 9 behandelt worden sind. Dabei spielen auch wieder generelle Regeln eine Rolle, wie z. B., daß natürlich der das Gut nicht zurückfordern kann, der es selbst verbotswidrig veräußert hat (13.27). Es folgt die Liste derer, gegen die die Klage gerichtet werden kann. Das sind in erster Linie die beschwerten Erben und diejenigen, die etwas veräußert haben. Der Berechtigte muß aber erst den Tod des Veräußerer abwarten, es sei denn, die Veräußerung war ausdrücklich verboten (13.33). Die Klage ist eine persönliche Klage und richtet sich nicht gegen den Erwerber des Gutes, „quia personalis actio non sequitur personam", wie *Knipschildt* mit einem Digestenzitat belegt (13.35).

Weitere Klagen des Berechtigten sind die folgenden (13.60): Die „hereditatis petitio", falls die Erbschaft Gegenstand des Familienfideikommisses ist, eine Klage aus Vertrag bei einem durch Vertrag begründeten Familienfideikommiß, die *rei vindicatio* gegen jeden Besitzer. Die *rei vindicatio* war von besonderer Bedeutung. Sie stand dem Berechtigten auch dann zu, wenn das Gut erlaubterweise verkauft worden war, der Berechtigte jedoch bereit war, im Wege der Ausübung eines Retrakts den Kaufpreis zurückzuerstatten (13.70). Bei verbotenem Verkauf mußte der Kaufpreis nicht zurückerstattet werden, doch hatte dann jedenfalls der gutgläubige Käufer einen Anspruch wegen Eviktion gegen den Veräußerer, wie es allgemeinen Lehren entsprach. Weiter hatte der Berechtigte eine Klage aus einer Hypothek, einen einklagbaren Anspruch darauf, daß der beschwerte Erbe seine Erbschaft auch antrat, einen Anspruch auf eine „missio in bona" und die Interdikte „quorum bonorum" sowie „uti possidetis" und schließlich auch ein Recht auf ein Mandat des

58 Zu diesem Verbot und seinen Ausnahmen vgl. Kapitel 11.

Reichskammergerichts. Letzteres ist einer der weniger häufigen Fälle, in denen *Knipschildt* ein deutsches Gesetz zitierte.

14. Beweis des Familienfideikommisses

Bei dem Streit über einen Familienfideikommiß konnte einmal die subjektive Berechtigung streitig sein (14.3). Es kam aber auch ein Streit über das Bestehen des Familienfideikommiß in Betracht (14.43) sowie über die Zugehörigkeit eines umstrittenen Gutes zum Familienfideikommiß.

Bei der persönlichen Berechtigung kamen weithin die generell verwendbaren Beweismittel zum Zuge. *Knipschildt* diskutiert folgende Beismittel: Vermutungen und Indizien für das Bestehen einer Verwandtschaft (14.9), Zeugen, Urkunden, Waffen und Wappen („Schild und Helm"), der Ruf („fama") des Berechtigten (der auch beim Beweis des Adels generell zugelassen war), die allgemeine Meinung und Reputation, Matrikel (in die Studenten, Soldaten, Kaufleute, Notare etc. eingetragen wurden), Geschichtsbücher und Chroniken, Denkmäler, Inschriften auf Gräbern, Steinen und Wänden, Stammbücher, „Geburtsbriefe" (d. h. Geburtsurkunden) und rechtskräftige Urteile.

Streitig konnte zweitens aber auch das Bestehen des Familienfideikommisses sein (14.43). Hierfür gab es folgende Beweismittel: Testament oder Errichtungsurkunde, Geständnis der Gegenpartei, das Faktum einer Erbteilung nach dem Prinzip eines Familienfideikommisses (14.51), Urteile, eine seit Menschengedenken bestehende Überzeugung, Observanz und Vermutungen, wie sie schon bei der Errichtung eine Rolle gespielt hatten (6.88).

Unter Umständen mußte auch drittens mit den im wesentlichen gleichen Mitteln bewiesen werden, daß gerade das streitige Gut zum Familienfideikommiß gehörte (14.56). Und schließlich erörtert *Knipschildt* noch die Notwendigkeit des Beweises, daß Veräußerer und Erwerber Kenntnis vom Familienfideikommiß gehabt hatten (14.59).

15. Verwandte Erscheinungen (Primogenitur und Majorat)

An einem Familienfideikommiß verwandten Erscheinungen stellt *Knipschildt* folgende vor: Primogenitur, Majorat, Lehen, Erbverzicht, Erbverbrüderungen, Ganerbschaften, Erbgüter und Stammgüter, Frauen von der Erbfolge ausschließende Statutargesetze, allgemeine zeitlich beschränkte und Frauen nicht ausschließende Fideikommisse, den Kindern aus erster Ehe bei Wiederheirat „verfangene" Güter sowie Mitgift. Das englische „entail" und das schottische „tailzie" hat *Knipschildt* offenbar trotz seiner Vertrautheit mit der Literatur fast aller europäischen Länder nicht gekannt[59].

16. Auflösung

Das abschließende sechzehnte Kapitel behandelt die Beendigung von prinzipiell auf ewigen Bestand gerichteten Familienfideikommissen. Ein Familienfideikommiß endete natürlich mit dem Untergang aller davon erfaßten Güter (16.11). Das Gleiche gilt für den Untergang der Familie (16.17). Ein durch Testament eingerichtetes Familienfideikommiß kann wie ein Testament widerrufen werden, aber eben auch nur wie ein Testament (16.39 - 82). Im Zusammenhang damit erörterte *Knipschildt* viele Einzelfragen von Testament, Erbvertrag, gemeinschaftlichem Testament, Schenkung von Todes wegen usw.

Danach folgen Fallgestaltungen, bei denen der aktuelle Inhaber sein Recht verliert, so daß der nächste Anwärter zum Zuge kommt. Das war der Fall bei strafweiser Beschlagnahme des Vermögens. Allerdings war es für diesen Fall umstritten, ob das Familienfideikommiß auf den nächsten Anwärter übergehe oder an den Fiskus falle (16.83)[60]. In dieser Frage entschied sich *Knipschildt* nach ausführlicher Diskussion des Für und Wider für den Erhalt des Gutes in der Reihe der Anwärter (16.306). Die Anschlußfrage war, ob die zu konfiszierenden Güter nicht wenigstens zu Lebzeiten des Delinquenten wie ein Nießbrauch dem Staate zustünden (16.370). Aber das verneinte *Knipschildt* und sprach sich für den sofortigen Eintritt des Anfalles an den nächsten Berechtigten aus (16.377). Etwas anderes galt allerdings, wenn der Begründer des Familienfideikommisses sich selbst eines Verbrechens schuldig machte (16.389) oder der Delinquent der letzte in der Reihe der Anwärter war (16.391).

Unklar bleibt die Wirkung einer Eviktion (16.85). Persönlicher Verlust konnte auch unter Umständen durch Verjährung eintreten, falls nämlich der Berechtigte sein Recht vernachlässigte (16.86). Wer verbotenerweise das dem Familienfideikommiß unterliegende Gut veräußerte, verlor sein Recht (16.100)[61]. Das Recht aus einem Familienfideikommiß endete auch durch Verzicht (16.119), dessen Voraussetzungen und Folgen jedoch im einzelnen sehr unterschiedlich ausgestaltet waren und kontrovers diskutiert wurden. Zum Beweis der Möglichkeit des Verzichts weist *Knipschildt* unter anderem auf den Thronverzicht der *Kaiser Diokletian* und *Maximian*, von *Kaiser Lothar I.* und von *Kaiser Karl V.* zu Gunsten seines Bruders *Ferdinand* hin (16.129). Das bedeutet aber, daß der Verzicht immer nur Wirkung für den Verzichtenden persönlich hatte, so daß mit dem Verzicht und nicht erst mit dem Tode der nächste Anwärter zum Zuge kam. Seine Beispiele bezog *Knipschildt* mit Vorliebe aus der Geschichte der großen Staaten und Herrschaften. Ob aber die angeführten Reiche und Länder wirklich Familienfideikommisse waren, ist doch sehr fraglich.

---

59 Dazu oben im Text bei Fn. 6.

60 Dazu näher 16.271 ff. für den Fall der Konfiskation.

61 Zum Verbot im einzelnen Kapitel 11.

Die Berechtigung endete weiter auch bei Mißbrauch durch den Berechtigten (16.133) und wenn ein Inhaber gegen irgendwelche Bedingungen und Auflagen verstieß (16.144). Hierbei war es umstritten, ob die Zuwiderhandlung gegen die Regeln des Familienfideikommisses nur, wie sich *Knipschildt* ausdrückte, dem Vater schadete oder auch dem Sohn (16.152). *Knipschildt* führte, wie üblich mit der von ihm nicht geteilten Meinung beginnend, zuerst die Gründe an, die für den Ausschluß aller sprechen, die ihr Recht von dem wegen Mißbrauchs ausgeschlossenen Berechtigten ableiten könnten. Das Hauptargument war, daß wenn jemand von der Erbfolge ausgeschlossen würde, auch seine Abkömmlinge von der Erbfolge ausgeschlossen würden. Für die von ihm vertretene Gegenansicht, die auch die herrschende gewesen sein sollte, führte *Knipschildt* D. 31, 69, 3 (16.160) und andere allgemeine Erwägungen an. Der Hauptgrund dafür war aber, daß nach der Konstruktion des Familienfideikommisses der jeweilige Berechtigte sein Recht gerade nicht im Wege der Erbfolge von seinem unmittelbaren Vorgänger ableitete, sondern von dem ursprünglichen Begründer des Familienfideikommisses (16.169)[62].

Das Familienfideikommiß endete vollständig beim Ausfall oder bei Nichterfüllung einer Bedingung (16.181), beim Ablauf der festgesetzten Zeit (16.183) sowie durch ein die Beendigung aussprechendes Urteil (16.190). Insbesondere die Beendigung durch Urteil wirkte für alle Zukunft (16.194). Das galt allerdings dann nicht, wenn der Inhaber einen Scheinprozeß geführt hatte, um das Gut aus der Bindung an das Familienfideikommiß zu befreien (16.197). Ein solcher Prozeß konnte nach *Knipschildt* keine Wirkung entfalten. Für die auflösende Wirkung eines solchen auf einem Scheinprozeß beruhenden Urteils hatte sich aber auf Grund seiner prinzipiell gegenüber „tailzies" kritischen Haltung der Schotte Stair ausgesprochen[63].

Zur vollständigen Beendigung führten bei *Knipschildt* weiter ein mit der Infamie verbundenes Verbrechen des Inhabers (16.199) und eine unwürdige Lebensführung der Anwärter (16.200). Besondere Probleme wurden durch eventuelle Teilungen aufgeworfen (16.201), die aber nicht völlig unzulässig waren (16.226). Wenn der zur Nachfolge Berufene eine dem Familienfideikommiß unterliegende Sache kaufte, verzichtete er insoweit auf das Familienfideikommiß.

Ein umfangreicher „Index rerum et verborum" beschließt *Knipschildts* Buch. Dieser Index liefert erneut den Beweis dafür, daß sich *Knipschildt* immer möglichst eng an die gemeinrechtliche Theorie anschließen wollte. So finden sich in diesem Index Prinzipien wie „Omne recessus a jure communi est odiosus et stricti juris" (7.84), „Publica salus suprema lex est" (8.213).

---

62 Ebenso auch 9.77, 11.405 ff. und 16.312. Die gleiche Diskussion wurde auch in Schottland geführt, so *Stair* (Fn. 21) II, 3, 58, S. 383.

63 *Stair* (Fn. 21) II, 3, 58, S. 383. Vgl. oben bei Fn. 25.

IV. Schluß

Das bleibende Verdienst des mit regelrechtem Bienenfleiß verfaßten Traktates von *Knipschildt* war die Gewährleistung eines vollständigen Überblicks über alle wesentlichen Rechtsfragen des Familienfideikommisses und die Einfügung aller einschlägigen Normen in den wissenschaftlichen Begriffsapparat der gemeinrechtlichen Wissenschaft. Ein großer Vorteil des Traktates ist es, daß *Knipschildt* nicht nur für alle Fragen Regeln anführt, sondern daß er diese Regeln aus einem oft höchst unübersichtlichen Bestand von Kontroversen sorgfältig herausarbeitet. Oft mußte er allerdings für seine Lösungen beim Lehnrecht und bei den Hausgesetzen des Hochadels mit ihrem Prinzip der Primogenitur Anleihen machen. Die rechtspolitische Tendenz ist eindeutig. *Knipschildt* wollte das Familienfideikommiß fest im Bestand der Normen des Privatrechts verankern, weil er an die Notwendigkeit dieser Einrichtung glaubte, und zwar nicht nur als ein Instrument der Freiheit des Eigentümers. Wichtiger waren für *Knipschildt* vielmehr stets die Belange der adeligen Familien. In zahlreichen Kontroversen gab das Argument, die für die Familie insgesamt nützlichere Lösung sei vorzuziehen, den Ausschlag. Grundsätzliche Kritik, die es ja schon in der Zeit vor *Knipschildt* gab, wurde von ihm überhaupt nicht zur Kenntnis genommen. So war das Buch in der Lage, noch in der zweiten Hälfte des 19. Jahrhunderts in allen wesentlichen Fragen den geltenden Rechtszustand wiederzugeben[64].

---

64 *Otto von Gierke* (Fn. 47) 250.

SIBYLLE HOFER

Treuhandtheorien in der deutschen Rechtswissenschaft des 19. Jahrhunderts

Zur Verwendung von historischen Rechtsinstituten in der Zivilrechtsdogmatik

Die Treuhandtheorien, die im 19. Jahrhundert von der deutschen Zivilrechtswissenschaft entwickelt wurden, waren schon mehrfach Thema eingehender Untersuchung. Hinsichtlich der Aspekte, unter denen die Analysen erfolgten, lassen sich zwei Ansätze unterscheiden: Zum einen wird die Treuhand als exemplarischer Fall der Auseinandersetzung zwischen romanistischer und germanistischer Zivilrechtswissenschaft gesehen[1]. Im Mittelpunkt steht dann die Konstruktion der Rechtsposition des Treuhänders. Diese Perspektive wurde lange Zeit auch in Arbeiten zum geltenden Recht verwendet, wie eine Bemerkung von *Haemmerle* zeigt: „Es ist in Juristenkreisen zur Übung geworden, Abhandlungen über die Treuhänderschaft mit rechtshistorischen Betrachtungen einzuleiten. Im besonderen wird dabei Gewicht auf säuberliche Trennung zwischen dem römischen Institut der fiducia und der deutschrechtlichen Einrichtung des Treuhänders gelegt; bei der ersteren Form – so sagt man – werde der Treuhänder in Hinsicht auf das Treugut nur obligatorisch gebunden, während bei letzterer eine dingliche Beschränkung des Eigentumsrechtes eintrete"[2]. Wenn auch heute solche historische Einleitungen bei Untersuchungen zur Treuhand nicht mehr üblich sind, so wird doch mit dem gängigen Begriff „fiduziarische Treuhand"[3] immer noch die erwähnte Unterscheidung vorausgesetzt.

In eine andere Richtung gehen demgegenüber die Darstellungen von *Coing*. Bezeichnend für seinen Ansatz ist der Titel eines Aufsatzes aus dem Jahr 1973: „Die

---

[1] So *G. Otten,* Die Entwicklung der Treuhandtheorie im 19. Jahrhundert, 1975, mit Schwerpunkt auf der germanistischen Seite sowie *W. Asmus,* Dogmenschichtliche Grundlagen der Treuhand: Eine Untersuchung zur romanistischen und germanistischen Treuhandlehre, 1977, mit dem Versuch, Abweichungen innerhalb der romanistischen bzw. germanistischen Treuhandlehre herauszuarbeiten und damit nachzuweisen, daß der Gedanke einer jeweils einheitlichen Treuhandlehre unzutreffend sei.

[2] Verhandlungen des 36. Deutschen Juristentages, Band 1, 1930, S. 635.

[3] Vgl. *K.-H. Schramm,* in: Münchener Kommentar zum Bürgerlichen Gesetzbuch, Band 1, 3. Auflage, 1993, Rz. 29, 34 vor § 164; *P. Bassenge* in: O. Palandt, Bürgerliches Gesetzbuch, 55. Auflage, 1996, Rz. 34 zu § 903; *J. Gernhuber,* Die fiduziarische Treuhand, Juristische Schulung 1988, 355 ff.

Treuhandtheorie als Beispiel der geschichtlichen Dogmatik des 19. Jahrhunderts"[4]. Die Treuhand wird hier als Modell einer „eigentümlichen Verknüpfung zwischen Rechtsgeschichte und Rechtsdogmatik" im 19. Jahrhundert angeführt[5]. Diese Verbindung beschreibt *Coing* dahingehend, „daß man aus dem geschichtlichen Stoff definierte dogmatische Rechtsfiguren gewann, die sich in der Gegenwart anwenden ließen"[6]. Dies methodische Vorgehen wird als „begriffsjuristisch" gekennzeichnet[7].

Für die folgende Darstellung soll dieser zweite, von *Coing* verfolgte Ansatz den Ausgangspunkt bilden. Die Analyse der Texte steht unter der Fragestellung, wie im 19. Jahrhundert Treuhandtheorien von Romanisten und Germanisten entwickelt wurden und welche Bedeutung dabei historischen Quellen zukommt. Ziel ist eine Überprüfung der Ansicht von „geschichtlicher Dogmatik". Die Vorstellung von einer Ableitung der Rechtsfolgen aus Begriffen[8] wird dabei widerlegt durch die Beachtung des Weges, der zu den Bezeichnungen „fiduziarische Geschäfte" und „germanistische Treuhand" geführt hat. Und gleichzeitig zeigt eine Untersuchung der Elemente, über welche Rechtsgeschichte und moderne Geschäfte verbunden werden, daß nicht „überhistorische" Rechtsbegriffe zur Lösung aktueller Fragen[9] dienten.

I. Die romanistische Seite

1. *Regelsbergers* Theoriebildung

„Die Theorie vom fiduziarischen Rechtsgeschäft war ein Werk der Pandektistik; Regelsberger hatte sie aus der Fiducia des römischen Rechts entwickelt". *Coing* weist mit dieser Bemerkung[10] *Regelsberger* das Verdienst zu, die Theorie des fiduziarischen Rechtsgeschäfts und damit „die wichtigste Grundlage des deutschen Treuhandrechts" „geschaffen" zu haben[11]. Die Methode soll durch einen Rückgriff auf die altrömische *fiducia* gekennzeichnet sein[12]. Eine Überprüfung dieser Ansicht bezüglich *Regelsbergers* methodischen Vorgehens setzt zunächst voraus, seinen Gedankengang genauer zu verfolgen.

---

4 RabelsZ 37 (1973) 202 ff.

5 RabelsZ 37 (1973) 202.

6 RabelsZ 37 (1973) 203. Ebenso *idem.*, Die Treuhand kraft privaten Rechtsgeschäfts, 1973, S. 37. Vgl. auch *Mayer-Maly,* der die *fiducia cum creditore* als Beispiel fur „die Wiederkehr von Rechtsfiguren" anführt: JZ 1971, 2

7 RabelsZ 37 (1973) 207, 209. Vgl. auch *S. Lammel,* Die Haftung des Treuhänders aus Verwaltungsgeschäft, 1972, S. 5.

8 So *Lammel* (Fn. 7) 5; der Gedanke klingt auch bei *Coing,* RabelsZ 37 (1973) 205 an.

9 Siehe *Coing,* RabelsZ 37 (1973) 203.

10 *Coing,* Treuhand (Fn. 6) 47.

11 *Coing,* Treuhand (Fn. 6), S. 35; vgl. auch RabelsZ 37 (1973) 205.

12 Vgl. auch *Coing,* Treuhand (Fn. 6) 37 und RabelsZ 37 (1973) 205.

(a) „Fiduziarische Geschäfte"

Die für das Thema „Treuhand" relevanten Äußerungen von ***Regelsberger*** finden sich in einem Beitrag zur Zessionslehre aus dem Jahre 1880[13]. Einleitend heißt es dort: „Wiederholt hat die Gerichte die Frage beschäftigt, ob der Schuldner befugt sei, der Forderung des Cessionars mit der Behauptung zu begegnen, die Cession beruhe auf Simulation"[14]. Dies damals aktuelle Problem des Zessionsrechts nimmt *Regelsberger* zum Anlaß für eine grundlegende Untersuchung über „die Geltendmachung der rechtlichen Mängel des Cessionsvorgangs durch den Schuldner"[15]. Er unterscheidet dazu anfechtbare und nichtige Vereinbarungen[16]. Hauptbeispiel einer nichtigen Zession ist die *Simulation,* denn „das simulierte Rechtsgeschäft erzeugt anerkanntermaßen die rechtlichen Wirkungen nicht, worauf es seiner äußeren Erscheinung nach gerichtet ist"[17]. Für die Beantwortung der Ausgangsfrage, ob dem Schuldner in einem solchen Fall Einredemöglichkeiten zustehen, wendet sich *Regelsberger* dem „Wesen der Simulation"[18] zu, welches er folgendermaßen bestimmt: „Wer ein Rechtsgeschäft simulirt, nimmt ein der äußeren Erscheinung nach auf eine bestimmte rechtliche Wirkung gerichtetes Geschäft vor, ohne den Willen, diese rechtliche Wirkung herbeizuführen, aber in der Absicht, in Andern die Meinung von der wirklichen Errichtung dieses Rechtsgeschäfts zu erwekken"[19]. Zur Verdeutlichung wird die Simulation dann im folgenden von „verwandten Erscheinungen"[20] abgegrenzt. Als solche nennt *Regelsberger* den *Schleichweg* und: das *fiduziarische Geschäft.* Diese beiden Geschäftsgestaltungen unterscheiden sich nach *Regelsbergers* Bestimmung von der Simulation am Punkt des Verhältnisses von Wille und Erklärung. Sei es für die Simulation kennzeichnend, daß die Parteien „das erklärte Rechtsgeschäft nicht wollen"[21], so stehen beim Schleichweg sowie beim fiduziarischen Geschäft gemäß *Regelsbergers* Definition „Wille und Erklärung des Handelnden in Einklang"[22]. Beim *Schleichweg* werde das Rechtsgeschäft jedoch „zur mittelbaren Erreichung eines Erfolgs benützt, welchen das

---

13 Zwei Beiträge zur Lehre von der Cession; AcP 63 (1880) 157 ff. Später erwähnt *Regelsberger* die fiduziarischen Rechtsgeschäfte nochmals in zwei weiteren Arbeiten: 1.) Die Handelsgeschäfte. Allgemeine Grundsätze; in: W. Endemann (Hg.), Handbuch des deutschen Handels-, See- und Wechselrechts II, 1882, S. 409 ff.; 2.) Pandekten I, 1893, § 141, S. 518 - 520.

14 AcP 63 (1880) 157.

15 So der Titel des 1. Teils der Beiträge. Der hier nicht interessierende 2. Teil handelt „Ueber die rechtliche Natur des in Folge einer gesetzlich gebotenen Cession übertragenen Anspruchs"; S. 200 ff.

16 AcP 63 (1880) 163.

17 AcP 63 (1880) 168.

18 AcP 63 (1880) 169.

19 AcP 63 (1880) 171.

20 AcP 63 (1880) 169.

21 AcP 63 (1880) 171.

22 AcP 63 (1880) 173.

Gesetz entweder überhaupt nicht oder nur unter bestimmten Voraussetzungen gestattet"[23]. Demgegenüber kennzeichnet *Regelsberger* das fiduziarische Geschäft dahingehend, daß die (erklärte und gewollte) Vereinbarung unter der Voraussetzung stehe,

> „daß derjenige, welchem dadurch eine gewisse rechtliche Macht geschaffen wird, seine Stellung nur zu einem bestimmten, nicht zu allen dadurch ermöglichten Zwecken ausnützen werde"[24].

Zur Verdeutlichung dieser abstrakten Bestimmung nennt *Regelsberger* einige Beispiele derartiger Geschäfte, die zum Teil dem römischen Recht, zum Teil aktuellen Gerichtsentscheidungen entnommen sind:

> „es wird Eigenthum zu Pfandzwecken übertragen (*Gai.* II, 60)[25],
> eine Expromission zum Zweck der Schuldaufhebung vorgenommen (L. 91 de solut. 46, 3)[26],
> dem Vermögensverwalter die Stellung eines Mitgläubigers eingeräumt (adstipulation *Gai.* III, 110, 111, 215, 216)[27],
> die Verpflichtung als Selbstschuldner zum Zweck der Bürgschaft eingegangen (*Seuffert's* Arch. XXX. Nr. 89)[28],
> ein Wechsel zur Sicherheit für eine künftig mögliche Forderung ausgestellt (Sicherheits- oder Depotwechsel, Seuffert XIII. Nr. 158[29] ...)"[30].

In dieser Aufzählung und den daran anschließenden Ausführungen liegt das Zentrum von *Regelsbergers* Beschäftigung mit der Treuhand, die im Rahmen sei-

---

23 AcP 63 (1880) 173.

24 AcP 63 (1880) 172.

25 Dieser Fall darf nicht ohne weiteres mit der am Ende des 19. Jahrhunderts heftig diskutierten Sicherungsübereignung gleichgesetzt werden. Der Unterschied liegt allerdings nicht in der Besitzverteilung. Der Fiduziar bei der von *Gaius* angesprochenen Eigentumsübertragung zu Pfandzwecken erhielt zwar grundsätzlich den Besitz an der Sache, aber eine Rücküberlassung an den Schuldner war möglich (siehe *Gai.* Inst. II, 60). Insofern konnte die Situation derjenigen bei einer Sicherungsübereignung mit Besitzkonstitut entsprechen. Der Unterschied zwischen der römischen Rechtslage und derjenigen am Ende des 19. Jahrhunderts wird jedoch durch die gesetzliche Anordnung des Faustpfandprinzips (§ 40 Reichskonkursordnung, 1879 in Kraft getreten) begründet. Die Sicherungsübereignung rückt dadurch in die Nähe des Schleichweges (*infra* Fn. 61) und scheidet dann aus der Gruppe der fiduziarischen Geschäfte aus.

26 Nach dieser Digestenstelle kann eine Befreiung des Schuldner von einer Verbindlichkeit dadurch erfolgen, daß sich der Gläubiger von einem Dritten das von jenem Geschuldete versprechen läßt (im einzelnen umstritten, siehe *Kretschmar*, ZSS (RA) 38 (1917) 317 ff.).

27 Den Adstipulator bestellt der (Haupt-)Gläubiger als Vertrauensmann für die Einziehung einer Forderung. Jener erhält dafür die Stellung eines (Neben-)Gläubigers.

28 In einem Darlehnsvertrag wird ein Dritter als Mitempfänger und Mitschuldner aufgeführt; es besteht jedoch zwischen ihm und dem Darlehnsgeber die Verabredung, daß der „Mitschuldner" nur wie ein Bürge haften soll.

29 Ein Wechsel wird zur Sicherheit des Wechselnehmers für Verbindlichkeiten übertragen, die der Acceptant ihm gegenüber aus anderen Rechtsgeschäften hat.

30 AcP 63 (1880) 172.

nes Aufsatzes insgesamt nur knapp zwei Druckseiten ausmachen. An die soeben zitierte Liste von Beispielsfällen schließt sich zunächst eine terminologische Klärung an:

> „Ich möchte für diese Rechtserscheinungen die Bezeichnung fiduziarisches Geschäft vorschlagen, wofür wir in den Quellen einen Vorgang haben“[31].

Regelsberger lehnt also seine Wortwahl ausdrücklich an die von *Gaius* (Institutionen II 60) erwähnte altrömische *fiducia cum creditore* an. Die Zusammenfassung der einzelnen Fälle zu einer Fallgruppe unter der Bezeichnung „fiduziarische Rechtsgeschäfte“ begründet *Regelsberger* dabei folgendermaßen:

> „Charakteristisch ist für dasselbe [sc. das fiduziarische Geschäft] das Mißverhältnis zwischen Zweck und Mittel. Zur Erreichung eines bestimmten Erfolgs wird eine Rechtsform gewählt, welche mehr gewährt, als zur Erzielung jenes Erfolgs erforderlich ist; zur Sicherung des Gebrauchs wird die Möglichkeit des Mißbrauchs in den Kauf genommen“[32].

Regelsbergers Beurteilung der Rechtsfolgen fiduziarischer Geschäfte ergibt sich aus dem Zusammenhang seiner Ausführungen. Wie gezeigt, entwickelt *Regelsberger* fiduziarische Geschäfte als Abgrenzung zu simulierten Geschäften. Der Unterschied betrifft das Verhältnis von Wille und Erklärung und damit als weitere Folge auch die Gültigkeit der Geschäfte. Weil Wille und Erklärung nicht übereinstimmen, seien simulierte Vereinbarungen unzulässig. Demgegenüber beeinträchtige eine fiduziarische Gestaltung die Wirksamkeit der Abrede nicht, denn hier werde die Erklärung vom Willen gedeckt[33].

Angewandt auf das Thema seiner Abhandlung, die Zession, stellt *Regelsberger* der Simulation zwei fiduziarische Gestaltungen gegenüber. Letztere lägen vor bei der (gewollten und erklärten) Übertragung einer Forderung mit der Verabredung, daß der Zessionar diese Stellung nur besitzen solle, „um das Geschuldete für Rechnung des Cedenten beizutreiben“[34]. Gleiches gelte für die Verabredung, daß „die Forderung lediglich zur Kompensation verwendet werden soll“[35]. *Regelsberger* gibt zu, daß im Einzelfall die Entscheidung, ob eine derartige fiduziarische Gestaltung oder eine Simulation vorliegt, schwierig sei[36]. „Im Zweifel“ will er eine Übereinstimmung von Wille und Erklärung, d. h. ein fiduziarisches zulässiges Geschäft annehmen[37].

---

31 AcP 63 (1880) 173.

32 AcP 63 (1880) 173.

33 Für die Ausgangsfrage, ob der Zession Einreden entgegengehalten werden können, bedeutet dies konkret, daß der Schuldner nur im Fall einer (echten) Simulation, nicht jedoch bei der fiduziarischen Zession Einreden hat; AcP 63 (1880) 175, 177. Anders nur, wenn der Zedent die fiduziarische Zession gerade deswegen vornimmt, um Einreden abzuschneiden, AcP 63 (1880) 179.

34 AcP 63 (1880) 177.

35 AcP 63 (1880) 197.

36 AcP 63 (1880) 180, 183, 197.

An diesem Punkt geht *Regelsberger* dann nochmals über sein eigentliches Aufsatzthema hinaus und „erprobt" die „früher entwickelten allgemeinen Grundsätze" auch noch an dem Eigentumsindossament zu Inkassozwecken, welches zwar „keine Cession ist"[38], jedoch einen weiteren aktuellen Fall darstellt, in dem um die Berechtigung von Simulationseinreden gestritten wurde[39]. Dabei wird deutlich, wie ernst *Regelsberger* das Kriterium des Willens nimmt. Er zieht nämlich aus der Übereinstimmung von Wille und Erklärung bei fiduziarischen Geschäften die Konsequenz, daß das Geschäft genau mit den Rechtsfolgen wirksam werde, die vereinbart worden seien, d. h. mit einem Machtüberschuß für eine Partei. So betont *Regelsberger* für das Eigentumsindossament zum Inkasso die „juristische Folgerung", daß dem Indossanten beim Konkurs des Indossatars kein Aussonderungsrecht zustehe, da er das Eigentum am Wechsel vollständig aufgegeben habe. Der Indossant habe nur die zivilrechtlichen Forderungen aus dem Mandat[40].

Dieser Überblick führt zu einem ersten Ergebnis hinsichtlich *Regelsbergers* Methode. Mehrere Einzelfälle werden zu einer Fallgruppe unter der Bezeichnung „fiduziarische Rechtsgeschäfte" zusammengefaßt. Dies geschieht über das Auffinden eines Kriteriums, das allen Fällen gemeinsam ist. Ist *Regelsbergers* Vorgehen damit begriffsjuristisch? Dies ist zu verneinen, soweit mit dieser Kennzeichnung die Annahme verbunden ist, daß Rechtsfolgen aus dem Oberbegriff der fiduziarischen Geschäfte abgeleitet werden[41]. Die Rechtsfolgen (Zulässigkeit des Geschäfts, Umfang der Rechte der Parteien) werden von *Regelsberger* keineswegs aus dem Begriff „fiduziarische Rechtsgeschäfte" abgeleitet. Sie ergeben sich vielmehr als Folge einer Abgrenzung von zulässigen und unzulässigen Verabredungen, die sich allein am Willen der Parteien orientiert.

(b) Regelsbergers Vorbilder

Wenn *Coing* davon spricht, daß *Regelsberger* die Theorie der fiduziarischen Rechtsgeschäfte „entwickelt" bzw. „geschaffen" habe, so ist intendiert, daß *Regelsbergers* Ausführungen ein originäres Element enthalten[42]. Um dies beurteilen zu können, wird ein Blick auf den unmittelbaren Diskussionszusammenhang not-

37 AcP 63 (1880) 180.

38 AcP 63 (1880) 181. Das Eigentumsindossament zu Inkassozwecken wird ausführlich S. 180 - 193 behandelt. Bei diesem Geschäft wird ein Wechsel (vollständig) übertragen. Dabei wird jedoch vereinbart, daß der Indossatar seine Position nur zur Einkassierung nützen soll. Für solche Fälle wäre es nach dem Wechselrecht an und für sich möglich, die Beschränkung des Indossatars auf dem Wechsel zu vermerken („nur zum Inkasso"). Dies entsprach jedoch nicht dem Handelsbrauch (vgl. nur *Werthauer*, Der fiduciarische Indossatar und die Einrede des dolus; Grünhuts Zeitschrift für das Privat- und öffentliche Recht der Gegenwart 13 (1886) 587).

39 Nachweise vgl. *ROHG*, Entscheidung v. 9. 4. 1877, ROHG-E 6, S. 56 ff.

40 AcP 63 (1880) 187 f. Anders später in Pandekten (Fn. 13) 519.

41 So ausdrücklich *Lammel* (Fn. 7), 5.

wendig, in dem Regelsbergers Aufsatz steht. Dafür genügt nicht der Hinweis, daß die Darstellung aktuelle praktische Fragen der Zeit betraf[43], sondern es kommt auf die Lösungen an, die vor dem Erscheinen von *Regelsbergers* Abhandlung für diese Fälle diskutiert wurden. Dabei sind weniger gerichtliche Einzelfallentscheidungen als vielmehr Versuche, eine grundsätzliche Klärung zu erreichen, von Interesse. Derartige Versuche unternahmen das Reichsoberhandelsgericht (ROHG) in einer Entscheidung des Jahres 1872 und sechs Jahre später *J. Kohler* im Rahmen eines Aufsatzes. Auf beide Ansätze nimmt *Regelsberger* ausdrücklich Bezug[44]. Als weiterer für *Regelsberger* wichtiger Anknüpfungspunkt[45] sind im übrigen Ausführungen von *R. v. Jhering* im zweiten und dritten Band seines „Geist des römischen Rechts" zu beachten.

(aa) ROHG 1872

Mit seinen ausführlichen Bemerkungen bezüglich des Eigentumsindossaments zu Inkassozwecken greift *Regelsberger* 1880 ein Thema auf, zu dem das ROHG 1872 eine vielbeachtete Entscheidung getroffen hatte. Das Gericht wandte sich in der damaligen Urteilsbegründung gegen die Auffassung, daß „jede Incongruenz des gewollten materiellen Verhältnisses und der durch den Erklärungsakt begründeten wie gewollten Rechtswirkung" als Simulation anzusehen sei[46]. Stattdessen wird eine Unterscheidung zwischen „echten" und „unechten" Simulationsfällen[47] eingeführt, die *Regelsberger* dann auch als Ausgangspunkt für seine Darstellung wählt[48]. Das Unterscheidungskriterium soll nach dem ROHG – wie später bei *Regelsberger* – der Wille der Parteien hinsichtlich der Rechtsfolgen sein: Bei der *echten* Simulation wollten die Parteien nicht das erklärte Rechtsgeschäft, sondern ein anderes oder gar keines[49]. Bei einem Eigentumsindossament liege daher eine Simulation vor, wenn die Parteien vereinbart haben, daß das Eigentum der Wechselurkunde und das Forderungsrecht beim Indossanten verbleiben sollen[50]. Anders bei den *unechten* Simulationsfällen. Hier sei das erklärte Geschäft durchaus gewollt. „Der Eigenthumsindossatar soll, wie erklärt ist, Eigenthümer des Wechsels und Wechselgläubiger werden; seine gleichzeitig gewollte Verpflichtung: nicht für eigene, sondern für Rechnung des Indossanten die Wechselforderung geltend zu

42 *H. Dölle*, Juristische Entdeckungen, nennt das Treuhandgeschäft eine Erfindung, verbindet damit aber keinen bestimmten Erfinder, in: Verhandlungen des 42. Deutschen Juristentages, Band II, 1958, B 16.

43 So *Coing*, RabelsZ 37 (1973) 204.

44 AcP 63 (1880) 169 (ROHG); Anm. 6, S. 170 f. und *passim* (*Kohler*).

45 Siehe AcP 63 (1880) 173.

46 ROHG, Entscheidung v. 9. 4. 1872, ROHG-E 6, S. 58.

47 ROHG-E 6 (n. 46) 61.

48 AcP 63 (1880), 169 / 170.

49 ROHG-E 6 (n. 46) 57.

50 ROHG-E 6 (n. 46) 58.

machen, schließt Ersteres nicht aus“[51]. Rechtlich steht nach Ansicht des ROHG nichts im Wege, „für einen beschränkten Zweck ein über denselben hinausgreifendes Mittel zu wählen“[52]. Auch mit seiner Charakteristik der Zweck-Mittel-Diskrepanz konnte *Regelsberger* also direkt an das ROHG anknüpfen. Im übrigen weist das Gericht auf weitere Fälle mit diesem Merkmal hin: „Zum Zwecke bloßer Verbürgung kann eine Solidarhauptschuld eingegangen, zum Zwecke der Gewährung von Pfandsicherheit der Weg der Eigenthumsübertragung, zum Zwecke der Bevollmächtigung der Weg der Cession wie des Eigenthumsindossaments gewählt werden ...“[53]. Auch der Gedanke eines allgemeinen Grundsatzes für verschiedene Fallgruppen lag somit in der Entscheidung des ROHG bereit.

(bb) *J. Kohler*

Die vom ROHG getroffene Unterscheidung zwischen echter und unechter Simulation differenziert *J. Kohler* 1878[54] weiter, indem er die Frage nach einer eventuellen Unwirksamkeit wegen Gesetzesumgehung stellt. Zur Terminologie ist dabei anzumerken, daß *Kohler* diejenigen Fälle, die das ROHG als „unechte Simulation“ kennzeichnet, „verdeckte“ Geschäfte nennt[55]. Zu diesen bemerkt er: „... wer ein verdecktes Geschäft abschließt, der will das Geschäft mit allen seinen Rechtsfolgen, er will es aber zu ökonomischen Zwecken, welche dem Geschäft selbst oder seinen Rechtsfolgen nicht homogen sind“[56]. Derartige Geschäfte seien nicht ausnahmslos zulässig. Es gebe nämlich Gesetze, welche „die Erreichung eines bestimmten ökonomischen Resultats selbst verbieten“[57]. Ist ein solches untersagtes ökonomisches Resultat der Zweck eines verdeckten Rechtsgeschäfts, so werde dies dadurch unzulässig. Aus der Zweiteilung Simulation – verdeckte Geschäfte wird damit die Dreiteilung Simulation – zulässige verdeckte Geschäfte – unzulässige verdeckte Geschäfte.

Als Beispiele dafür, daß ein Gesetz „das Zweckstreben selbst trifft“[58], führt *Kohler* an: Gesetze, die den Erwerb von Schenkungen durch kirchliche Institute beschränken, erstrecken sich auch auf den Erwerb über Zwischenpersonen[59]; das Gesetz über Verbot der Winkeladvokatur betrifft auch die Zession von Ansprüchen an einen Winkler[60], und die Anordnung des Faustpfandprinzips macht den Verkauf

51 ROHG-E 6 (n. 46) 57/8.

52 ROHG-E 6 (n. 46) 54.

53 ROHG-E 6 (n. 46) 54.

54 Studien über Mentalreservation und Simulation; JhJb 16 (1878) 91 ff.

55 JhJb 16 (1878) 140.

56 JhJb 16 (1878) 141.

57 JhJb 16 (1878) 144.

58 JhJb 16 (1878) 146.

59 JhJb 16 (1878) 146 ff.

60 JhJb 16 (1878) 149.

mit Besitzkonstitut unzulässig[61]. Im Unterschied zu diesen Fällen sieht *Kohler* das Eigentumsindossament zu Inkassozwecken grundsätzlich als zulässig an. Dies ergibt sich aus seiner Feststellung, ein solches Vollindossament führe dazu, daß der Indossatar „vollkommener Gäubiger der Forderung" werde und unbeschränkt über den Wechsel verfügen könne. „Das Verhältnis zwischen Giranten und Giratar kann daher nur ein obligatorisches ... sein"[62].

Bei *Regelsberger* findet sich *Kohlers* Dreiteilung wieder: das (nichtige) simulierte[63] Geschäft – das zulässige fiduziarische – das zwar nicht simulierte aber trotzdem unzulässige Geschäft (der „Schleichweg"). Und auch bei *Regelsberger* dient die Gesetzesumgehung als Abgrenzungskriterium zwischen den fiduziarischen Geschäften und den Schleichwegen[64]. Der Blick auf das ROHG und *Kohler* ergibt somit für *Regelsbergers* Theoriebildung folgendes: Die Abgrenzung der fiduziarischen Rechtsgeschäfte zur Simulation hat Vorläufer. Sie entspricht inhaltlich genau derjenigen von *Kohler.* Auch hinsichtlich der Fallgruppenbildung und der Annahme einer Zweck-Mittel-Diskrepanz konnte *Regelsberger* auf Vorbilder zurückgreifen. Ebenso hatten *Kohler* und das ROHG bereits die Zulässigkeit derartiger Geschäfte herausgestellt und deren Rechtsfolgen nach dem Willen und der Erklärung der Parteien bestimmt. Als neu erscheint danach allein *Regelsberger*s Bezeichnung als „fiduziarische Geschäfte". Damit war ein positiver Name gegenüber ‚unechte Simulation' oder ‚zulässiges verdecktes Geschäft' gefunden. Allerdings kann man auch an diesem Punkt einen unmittelbaren Anhalt bei *Kohler* finden. Dieser spricht nämlich beim Vollindossament zu Inkassozwecken von „fiduziarische[r] Eigenberechtigung" des Indossatars[65]. Wenn *Regelsberger* diesen Ausdruck dann zur Kennzeichnung einer größeren Gruppe von Fällen einführt[66], liegt

61 JhJb 16 (1878) 151 f. Vgl. oben Fn. 25. Ebenso später *Bähr,* Urteile des Reichsgerichts 1883, S. 52 ff.; *Hellwig,* AcP 64 (1881) 369 ff. Bei der Diskussion über Sicherungsübereignungen geht es um Gesetzesauslegung im Zusammenhang mit der Frage der Gesetzesumgehung. Sicherungsübereignungen wurden von der herrschenden Ansicht nicht als fiduziarische Geschäfte im Sinne von *Regelsberger,* sondern als Schleichwege eingeordnet. *Regelsberger* selbst (Pandekten [Fn. 13], 519; Handelsgeschäfte [Fn. 13], 410) entscheidet diese Frage nicht eindeutig.

62 JhJb 16 (1878) 150. Unzulässig ist das Geschäft nach *Kohler* aber dann, wenn dadurch dem Wechselschuldner Einreden abgeschnitten werden, die zu einem Erlöschen seiner Schuld gegenüber dem Indossanten geführt hätten.

63 Von *Regelsberger* auch – abweichend von *Kohlers* Sprachgebrauch – „verdecktes Geschäft" genannt; siehe AcP 63 (1880) 173, Anm. 7.

64 In dem Aufsatz des Jahres 1880 wird dies nur nebenbei erwähnt (AcP 63 (1880) 174; vgl. aber auch S. 173, soeben zitiert bei Fn. 23). Deutlicher wird die Bedeutung der Gesetzesumgehung dann aber zwei Jahre später von *Regelsberger* in einer Arbeit über das Handelsgeschäft (Fn. 13) herausgearbeitet, S. 410.

65 JhJb 16 (1878) 149. Vorher weist *Kohler* im übrigen auf die *fiducia cum creditore* und die *fiducia cum amico* als Beispiele dafür hin, daß die juristische Gestaltung nicht mit dem wirtschaftlichen Zweck übereinstimmt (S. 142, 149).

66 Diese Bezeichnung verbunden mit der Lehre Regelsbergers setzte sich schnell durch (vgl. *Coing,* RabelsZ 37 (1973) 206 mit weiteren Nachweisen). Für den Bereich des Wechsel-

darin wahrscheinlich der Grund, daß sein Vorgehen heute mit dem Etikett „Begriffsjurisprudenz" versehen wird.

(cc) *Jhering*

„Fiduciargeschäfte" hatte vor *Kohler* und *Regelsberger* schon *Jhering* im Zusammenhang mit einer Abgrenzung von zulässigen und unzulässigen Gestaltungen von Rechtsgeschäften behandelt[67]. Bei *Jherings* Ausführungen ist jedoch zu beachten, daß seine Terminologie und Abgrenzung nicht mit *Regelsberger* übereinstimmt. *Jhering* unterscheidet zwischen „Scheingeschäften" und „simulierten Geschäften". Simulierte Geschäfte werden gleichbedeutend auch als „Schleichwege des Lebens" bezeichnet. Unterscheidungskriterium ist für *Jhering,* ob es sich um einzelne Gestaltungen durch die Parteien (dann Schleichweg / Simulation) oder um Schöpfungen des Verkehrs bzw. der Jurisprudenz, d. h. um rechtlich anerkannte Gestaltungsformen (dann Scheingeschäft) handelt[68]. Die Scheingeschäfte sind danach nicht aufgrund einer Inhaltsüberprüfung zulässig, sondern unanfechtbar wegen gewohnheitsrechtlicher Sanktion[69]. Als Beispiel solcher Scheingeschäfte führt *Jhering* die *fiduciae causa* abgeschlossenen Geschäfte[70], vor allem die *coemptio fiduciae causa*[71] und die *arrogatio fiduciae causa*[72] an. Allgemeine inhaltliche Kennzeichen dieser „Fiduciargeschäfte"[73] entwickelt *Jhering* nicht. Er stellt nur deren Zulässigkeit im Unterschied zu simulierten Geschäften fest.

rechts war dabei bedeutsam, daß *L. Goldschmidt* 1882 seine Ansicht, daß bei einem Eigentumsindossament zu Inkassozwecken der Indossatar Eigentümer wird, damit begründete, daß dies Eigentumsindossament als „fiduziarischer Akt" alle erklärten Rechtsfolgen nach sich ziehe (ZHR 28 (1882) 82 f.; zu *Goldschmidts* früherer Ansicht [der Indossant bleibt Eigentümer] ZHR 8 (1865) 326 f. Zur Wirkung der Bezeichnung von *Goldschmidt* und *Regelsberger* vgl. nur *Werthauer,* Grünhuts Zeitschrift für das Privat- und öffentliche Recht der Gegenwart 13 (1886) 635).

67 Siehe Geist des römischen Rechts II 2, 5. Auflage, Leipzig, 1894, S. 518; III, 5. Auflage, Leipzig, 1906, S. 277.

68 Geist III (Fn. 67) 290; vgl. auch S. 295, wo *Jhering* gegenüberstellt: „Scheingeschäfte des Rechts" – „Schleichwege des Lebens".

69 Geist III (Fn. 67) 283.

70 Geist II 2 (Fn. 67) 530.

71 Geist III (Fn. 67) 284 ff., 291, 292. Unzutreffend ist die Bemerkung von *Coing,* Treuhand (Fn. 6) 35, Anm. 21, daß *Jhering* die *fiducia* nur „beiläufig" erwähne. *Coing* berücksichtigt dabei allein Geist III § 57 (nur auf diesen verweisen *Regelsberger,* AcP 63 (1880) 173; *Kohler,* JhJb 16 (1878) 140, Fn. 1 ausdrücklich), nicht aber den für diese Frage wichtigeren § 58.

72 Geist III (Fn. 67) 298 f.

73 So Seitenüberschrift Geist II 2 (Fn. 67) 531.

2. Rechtsgeschichte und Dogmatik

Die Bezeichnung „fiduziarische Rechtsgeschäfte", die von *Regelsberger* geprägt wurde und für die Vorbilder bei *Jhering* und *Kohler* zu finden sind, leitet zum nächsten Gesichtspunkt über. Wie eingangs referiert, hat *Coing* an den Treuhandtheorien des 19. Jahrhunderts die „eigentümliche Verknüpfung zwischen Rechtsgeschichte und Dogmatik" hervorgehoben. Sie sollen ein Beispiel für „die Rückgewinnung der geschichtlichen Rechtsideen für die Gegenwart" und für die Vorstellung von „überhistorischen" Rechtsbegriffen sein[74]. Auf den ersten Blick scheinen *Regelsbergers* Ausführungen diesen Gedanken zu bestätigen. Wird doch mit der Bezeichnung „fiduziarische Rechtsgeschäfte" sprachlich an ein altrömisches Rechtsinstitut angeknüpft, das schon im *Corpus iuris civilis* keinen Platz mehr erhalten hatte[75]. Doch auch hier lohnt eine genauere Untersuchung. Die entscheidende Frage dabei lautet: Wie kommt *Regelsberger* von der *fiducia* zu den fiduziarischen Rechtsgeschäften? Es gilt diejenigen Elemente der *fiducia* aufzufinden, denen bei *Regelsberger* die Brückenfunktion zukommt, das altrömische Rechtsgeschäft mit den modernen Gestaltungen zu verbinden.

Coings Ausführungen deuten dabei eine gewisse Übereinstimmung im methodischen Vorgehen der Juristen nach 1850 an[76]. Dies fordert auch einen vergleichenden Blick auf andere Arbeiten aus der zweiten Hälfte des 19. Jahrhunderts, in denen die *fiducia* ebenfalls eine Rolle spielt. Dieser Gesichtspunkt führt zu einer Reihe von Untersuchungen: *Huschke,* „Ueber die usucapio pro herede, fiduciae und ex praediatura", 1848[77]; *A. v. Scheurl,* „Zur Usucapionslehre", 1854[78]; *H. Dernburg,* „Das Pfandrecht nach den Grundsätzen des heutigen römischen Rechts" I, 1860[79]; *H. Degenkolb,* „Ein pactum fiduciae", 1870[80]; *P. Krüger,* „Eine mancipatio fiduciae causa", 1870[81]; *A. F. Rudorff,* „Ueber die baetische Fiduciartafel", 1872[82].

Unter dem hier interessierenden Gesichtspunkt, wie rechtsgeschichtliche Ergebnisse für die aktuelle Dogamtik verwendet wurden, sind rein historisch angelegte Arbeiten jedoch nicht ergiebig. Dies betrifft die Werke von *Degenkolb, Krüger* und *Rudorff,* die sich anläßlich des Fundes eines Bronzetafelfragments (1868) mit der *fiducia* auseinandersetzen. Im Vordergrund dieser Ausführungen standen die Fragen, ob das gefundene Tafelfragment Teil eines Formulars oder die Beurkundung

---

74 RabelsZ 37 (1973) 203.

75 Erwähnung nur bei *Gaius,* Institutionen, II, 59 f.; III, 201.

76 RabelsZ 37 (1973) 202 f.

77 Zeitschrift für geschichtliche Rechtswissenschaft 14 (1848) 145 ff., 229 - 267.

78 In: Beiträge zur Bearbeitung des römischen Rechts II 1, Erlangen, 1854, S. 29 ff., 36 - 46.

79 Insbes. S. 7 - 26.

80 ZRG 9 (1870) 117 - 179, 407 - 409.

81 In: Kritische Versuche im Gebiete des römischen Rechts, Berlin, 1870, S. 41 - 58.

82 ZRG 11 (1873) 52 - 107.

eines konkreten Geschäfts darstelle, wie der Text zu ergänzen und ob das *pactum fiduciae* Teil der Manzipation oder eine Nebenabrede gewesen sei. Diese Bemühungen, welche darauf abzielten, die Gestalt von römischen *fiducia*-Geschäften zu rekonstruieren, eignen sich nicht für eine Untersuchung des Verhältnisses von Rechtsgeschichte und Dogmatik in der Rechtswissenschaft des 19. Jahrhunderts. Es bleiben somit die Werke von *Huschke, Scheurl* und *Dernburg*.

(a) Scheurl, Huschke

Bei *Huschke* und *Scheurl* erfolgen die Ausführungen zur *fiducia* im Rahmen von Erörterungen, welche die Ersitzung (*usucapio)* betreffen, wobei vor allem *Scheurls* Überlegungen auf das geltende Ersitzungsrecht gerichtet sind. Die Ersitzung ist im übrigen auch der Gesichtspunkt, unter dem *Gaius* in seinen Institutionen auf die *fiducia* zu sprechen kommt[83]. Die Darstellungen der *fiducia* durch *Huschke* und *Scheurl* werden nun üblicherweise herangezogen, wenn es darum geht, den Gedanken einer (einheitlichen) romanistischen Treuhandtheorie – im Sinne einer Vollrechtsübertragung mit allein schuldrechtlich wirkender Abrede[84] – zu überprüfen[85]. Dabei wird jedoch nicht berücksichtigt, daß beide Juristen gerade keine Treuhandtheorie entwickeln. Das Bestreben von *Huschke* und *Scheurl* geht vielmehr dahin, ihre Vorstellungen über Voraussetzungen der Ersitzung mit der Gaiusquelle (Institutionen II, 59) in Einklang zu bringen. Nach *Gaius* besteht für denjenigen, der eine Sache einer anderen Person fiduziarisch übertragen hat, die Möglichkeit, diese Sache (rück)zuersitzen (*usureceptio)*. Daraus ergibt sich als Problem für die Ersitzungslehre, daß hier die Möglichkeit einer *Usucapio* beschrieben wird, bei der die sonst notwendigen Voraussetzungen (Titel, *bona fides)* anscheinend nicht vorliegen. *Stintzing* eröffnete 1852 eine Debatte um die Rangfolge von Titel und *bona fides* als Ersitzungsvoraussetzung, wobei er die *Usureceptio* in seine Argumentation einbaute[86]. *Scheurl* schließt sich dem an und argumentiert gegen die Subjektivität der herrschenden Lehre[87]. Der Titel sei das Haupterfordernis, die *bona fides* spiele nur eine Rolle, soweit es an der „justitia" des Titels fehle[88]. Diesen Gedanken will *Scheurl* auch bei der *Usureceptio* (also der Ersitzung fiduziarisch übertragener Gegenstände) nachweisen: „Sie ist nur formell, nicht aber auch materiell eine Usucapion ohne Titel und bona fides. Materiell hat sie ihren Titel darin, daß ja ohnehin der Usurecipient wieder Eigenthümer werden soll, und seine bona

---

83 Institutionen II, 59 ff.

84 Vgl. nur oben bei Fn. 2 im Zitat von Haemmerle.

85 Siehe *Asmus* (Fn. 1) 82 ff., 145; *F. Wubbe,* Usureceptio und relatives Eigentum, T.R. 28 (1960) 13 ff., Anm. 66, S. 36.

86 *R. Stintzing,* Das Wesen von Bona fides und Titulus in der römischen Usucapionslehre, Heidelberg, 1852, S. 16 ff.

87 Usucapionslehre (Fn. 78) 29.

88 Usucapionslehre (Fn. 78) 54.

fides liegt in der That darin, daß er bei dem Bewußtsein, die Sache sei für ihn formell eine fremde, materiell sie doch mit Recht als ihm fortwährend gehörend, als Stück seines Vermögens betrachtet"[89]. *Scheurl* stützt seine Ansicht, daß auch bei der *Usureceptio* die Elemente Titel und *bona fides* vorliegen, somit auf eine enge Verbindung des Treugebers zum Treugut. Diese Argumentation hat Konsequenzen für die Darstellung der *fiducia,* bei der dann ebenfalls die Beziehung des Fiduzianten zur Sache betont wird: „... wer fiduciam contrahit cum creditore, will diesem nur ein eventuelles Verkaufsrecht in Beziehung auf die Sache und ein unbedingtes Recht, sie zu vindiciren, geben; beide [sc. der Fiduziant bei der fiducia cum amico und derjenige bei der fiducia cum creditore] aber wollen ihre Sachen nicht aus ihrem Vermögen weggeben; das besondere, in der fiducia liegende Anvertrauen besteht wesentlich darin, daß sie den Empfängern zutrauen, sie werden die ihnen übergebenen Sachen fortwährend als fremde Vermögensstücke betrachten, an welchen sie nur ein einstweiliges formelles Eigenthumsrecht haben"[90].

Für das hier interessierende Verhältnis von Rechtsgeschichte und Dogmatik ergibt sich folgendes: *Scheurl* beschäftigt sich nicht mit einer eventuellen Bedeutung der altrömischen *fiducia cum creditore / amico* für die Erklärung moderner Rechtsgestaltungen. Er versteht die Gaiusstelle als Darstellung des Rechts einer vergangenen Epoche. Eine Verbindung zum geltenden Recht entsteht nur dadurch, daß die Gaiusinterpretation als „Beweismittel"[91] für die Aufstellung von Ersitzungsvoraussetzungen eingesetzt wird. Dieses Vorgehen bedeutet eine Umsetzung der von *Scheurl* ausdrücklich formulierten Vorstellung, daß jedes Rechtsinstitut „sogleich bei seinem ersten Erscheinen die Keime seiner ganzen nachherigen Entwicklung vollständig in sich getragen hat"[92]. Aus diesem Grund ist es für *Scheurl* wichtig, die von *Gaius* erwähnte Ersitzung fiduzierter Gegenstände in die Begründung seiner Ansicht über das geltende Ersitzungsrecht einzubinden.

(b) Dernburg

Einen eigenen Paragraphen widmet *H. Dernburg* der altrömischen *fiducia* in seinem Werk „Das Pfandrecht nach den Grundsätzen des heutigen römischen Rechts" (1860)[93]. Dabei hebt er hervor, daß diese Vorform des Pfandrechts durch zwei

---

[89] Usucapionslehre (Fn. 78) 40.

[90] Usucapionslehre (Fn. 78) 37 / 8. Ähnlich *Huschke,* der aus der sprachlichen Bedeutung von *fiducia* (Vertrauen) die Konstruktion entwickelt, daß die Hingabe des Treuguts nur anvertrauensweise geschehe, der Empfänger daher, obgleich er formell das volle Recht an dem Gegenstand hat, doch materiell es als ein fremdes ansehen müsse (Usucapio [Fn. 77] 232).

[91] *Scheurl,* Usucapionslehre (Fn. 78) 36.

[92] Usucapionslehre (Fn. 78) 30, insoweit im Unterschied zu *Stintzing,* der im einzelnen überprüft, ob Grundsätze, die für das alte Recht gefunden wurden, auch für den gegenwärtigen Rechtszustand gelten, siehe Bona fides (Fn. 86) 36, 123.

[93] *Dernburg,* Das Pfandrecht nach den Grundsätzen des heutigen römischen Rechts, Band 1, Leipzig, 1860, § 2, S. 7 - 26.

Rechtsverhältnisse gekennzeichnet sei: ein Eigentumsrecht des Gläubigers und ein persönliches Gegenrecht des Schuldners[94]. Der Gläubiger habe volles und unbeschränktes Eigentum an der fiduzierten Sache und damit die volle Dispositionsbefugnis über diese erhalten[95]. Der Schuldner sei dagegen Inhaber eines rein persönlichen Anspruchs auf Rückübertragung der Sache bei Zahlung der Schuld gewesen[96].

Dernburgs ausführliche Erörterung der *fiducia* fällt etwa im Vergleich mit der großen Darstellung des römischen Pfandrechts von *Bachofen* auf. Letzerer widmet dem alten Institut nicht einmal einen eigenen Abschnitt, sondern erwähnt es nur gelegentlich[97]. Ein Erklärungsansatz für *Dernburgs* Betonung ergibt sich, wenn man die Bedeutung untersucht, welche die *fiducia* im Rahmen seiner Pfandrechtsdarstellung hat. *Dernburg* kommt nämlich im Laufe seiner Ausführungen noch einmal auf dies Rechtsinstitut zurück, und zwar in dem Abschnitt, welcher dem „Charakter des Pfandrechts" gewidmet ist[98]. Gerade der Charakter, d. h. die rechtliche Einordnung des Pfandrechts – dingliches oder obligatorisches Recht oder Mischform –, war ein zentraler Diskussionspunkt im 19. Jahrhundert[99]. *Dernburg* schließt sich in diesem Streit der älteren Meinung an, daß „das Pfandrecht als ein Recht dinglicher Herrschaft" zu betrachten sei[100]. Im Rahmen seiner Begründung für diese Stellungnahme findet sich dann der Verweis auf die *fiducia:* „Unbestreitbar aber erhielt der Gläubiger bei der fiducia das Recht dinglicher Herrschaft über die Sache, die ihm zur Sicherung seiner Forderung überlassen wurde. Ist es nun glaublich, daß die römische Jurisprudenz dem später gebildeten Vertragspfand eine ganz verschiedene juristische Auffassung zu Grunde legte ... ? Dergleichen lag der praktischen Weise römischer Juristen fern, vielmehr bewährte sich ihr richtiger Takt gerade darin, daß sie das Vertragspfand durchaus der alten fiducia insofern nachzubilden suchten, als nicht materielle Gründe entgegenstanden"[101]. Die *fiducia* dient hier als Argument im Streit des 19. Jahrhunderts um die Rechtsnatur des Pfandrechts. Ähnlich wie bei *Scheurl* steht dahinter der Gedanke einer kontinuierlichen Entwicklung.

Unter der Fragestellung „geschichtliche Dogmatik" ist es von Bedeutung, sich klarzumachen, warum die *fiducia* hier bei der Darstellung des geltenden Pfandrechts[102] erwähnt wird. Die Antwortet lautet: Beide Rechtsinstitute haben eine ver-

---

94 *Dernburg* (Fn. 93) 11.

95 *Dernburg* (Fn. 93) 8, 11. Ebenso *Puchta,* Cursus der Institutionen, 4. Auflage, Leipzig, 1853, § 247, S. 732.

96 *Dernburg* (Fn. 93) 9, 11, 24.

97 Das römische Pfandrecht I, Basel, 1847, ausdrücklich zur Verwendung der *fiducia* dort S. 1 / 2.

98 *Dernburg* (Fn. 93) 96 ff.

99 Siehe dazu *W. Wiegand,* Zur Entstehung der Pfandrechtstheorien im 19. Jahrhundert, Zeitschrift für neuere Rechtsgeschichte 1 (1981) 1 ff. mit weiteren Nachweisen.

100 *Dernburg* (Fn. 93) 105

101 *Dernburg* (Fn. 93) 110.

gleichbare Funktion. Besonders deutlich wird diese Verbindung bei *Puchta.* In seinem „Cursus der Institutionen" bestimmt er zunächst die „allgemeine Natur des Pfandrechts", womit er dessen „allgemeinen Inhalt" meint: „Es wird dem Gläubiger ein Gut angewiesen, durch dessen Verwerthung er seine Befriedigung, wenn sie nicht von dem Schuldner erfolgt, finden soll"[103]. Als eine juristische Form (unter anderen[104]), in der dieser Zweck erreicht werden kann, wird dann die *fiducia* behandelt. Ihre rechtliche Gestaltung wird dabei an den „Intentionen des Pfandrechts" gemessen[105]. Über diese Intentionen des Pfandrechts kann somit die *fiducia* mühelos in eine Reihe mit den aktuellen Verpfändungsformen gestellt werden. Die Verbindung zwischen historischem Rechtsinstitut und aktuellem Pfandrecht geschieht hier somit nicht etwa durch „überhistorische" Rechtsbegriffe, sondern über gemeinsame ökonomische Funktionen.

(c) Regelsberger

Eine Verbindung zwischen Rechtsgeschichte und Dogmatik, wie sie soeben für die Pfandrechtsdarstellungen herausgearbeitet wurde, kann *Regelsberger* für die von ihm unter der Bezeichnung „fiduziarisch" zusammengefaßten Fälle nicht vornehmen. Denn diese Gestaltungen dienen unterschiedlichen Zwecken. So nennt *Regelsberger* neben dem Pfandzweck für andere fiduziarische Geschäfte die Zwekke der Schuldaufhebung, der Bürgschaft oder der Sicherung künftiger Forderungen[106]. Dabei versucht er nicht, einen gemeinsamen Sicherungszweck herauszuarbeiten, der vor allem bei den von ihm erwähnten Inkassofällen auch nicht immer vorliegen dürfte. *Regelsberger* verbindet die unterschiedlichen Fälle stattdessen ausdrücklich über „das Mißverhältnis zwischen Zweck und Mittel". Um den Charakter dieser Verbindung – und damit *Regelsbergers* Umgang mit den römischen Quellen – deutlicher werden zu lassen, sollen als Kontrast schließlich noch diejenigen Bemerkungen herangezogen werden, die *P. Oertmann* zehn Jahre nach *Regelsberger* zur modernen Bedeutung der *fiducia* gemacht hat.

Oertmann[107] unterscheidet strikt zwischen der römischen *fiducia* und den modernen Fiduziargeschäften. Für das römische Institut wird darauf hingewiesen, daß

---

102 Auf S. 98 hebt *Dernburg* (Fn. 93) hervor, daß die „Doppelnatur der fiducia" auch beim Pfandrecht wiederkehre. Wenn der Gegensatz auch nicht mehr so schroff sei, so seien doch auch hier die beiden Seiten für eine theoretische Untersuchung scharf zu trennen. In diesem Sinn übernimmt er dann für seine Pfandrechtsdarstellung die Zweiteilung, welche er für die *fiducia* herausgearbeitet hat: 1. Dinglicher Charakter, 2. Verpflichtung aus Contract.

103 *Puchta* (Fn. 95) § 246, S. 726, 727.

104 *Puchta* (Fn. 95) § 247. Danach werden *pignus* und Hypothek dargestellt, §§ 248 f.

105 *Puchta* (Fn. 95) 732, 730.

106 *Regelsberger,* AcP 63 (1880) 172. Siehe oben bei Fn. 25 ff.

107 Die Fiducia im römischen Privatrecht. Eine rechtsgeschichtliche Untersuchung; Berlin, 1890. Mit den modernen fiduziarischen Geschäften beschäftigt sich *Oertmann* im Ausblick auf den letzten drei Seiten.

es zu ganz unterschiedlichen ökonomischen Zwecken dienen konnte[108]. Die Einheit dieses Rechtsinstituts habe „auf der formellen Einheit eines rechtlichen Entstehungsaktes beruht“[109]. Demgegenüber seien die modernen fiduziarischen Geschäfte im Sinne von *Regelsbergers* Bestimmung juristisch höchst unterschiedlich einzuordnen[110]. Es bestehe lediglich eine einheitliche „wirtschaftliche Natur“[111]. *Oertmanns* Fazit lautet dann: „Die fiducia ging und nimmer kehrt sie wieder“[112]. Mit dieser Bemerkung wird eine Verbindung zwischen der *fiducia* und den aktuellen „fiduziarischen“ Geschäften abgelehnt. Als Grund ergibt sich ein enger Blick auf die jeweilige Geschäftsform. Trotz dieser strikten Trennung sieht *Oertmann* an anderer Stelle Parallelen zwischen den alten und neuen Fiduziargeschäften. Er stellt nämlich fest, daß der moderne Handelsverkehr auf derselben Stufe wie der altrömische stehe[113]. So wie die antiken Geschäfte auf Treu und Glauben gebaut worden seien[114], so liege bei den modernen fiduziarischen Geschäften „ihre innere Einheit in dem wirklichen *Vertrauen* auf den Gegner“[115]. Allerdings unterscheidet *Oertmann* dann, daß diese Gestaltung im heutigen Verkehr freiwillig erfolge, während sie früher eine „dura necessitas“ gewesen sei[116]. So wird letztlich auch nicht über das Merkmal „Vertrauen“ bei *Oertmann* eine Verbindung zwischen *fiducia* und modernen Geschäften hergestellt.

Oertmanns Beispiel zeigt, daß eine Verbindung von modernen Geschäften und *fiducia* bei einem genauen Vergleich der Geschäftsformen nicht möglich ist. *Regelsberger* dagegen blickt bei der *fiducia* weder auf den Pfandzweck noch auf die konkrete Geschäftsform. Auch das Merkmal „Vertrauen“ erscheint bei ihm nicht als zentraler Punkt[117]. Stattdessen ist für *Regelsberger* die juristische Technik wichtig: „Zur Erreichung eines bestimmten Erfolgs wird eine Rechtsform gewählt, welche mehr gewährt, als zur Erzielung jenes Erfolgs erforderlich ist“[118]. Die *fidu-*

---

108 *Oertmann* (Fn. 107) 82 f.

109 *Oertmann* (Fn. 107) 258.

110 Z.B. Eigentumsübertragung, Forderungsabtretung, Indossament von Wechseln im Unterschied zur einheitlichen Form im römischen Recht: *mancipatio* mit Fiduciarklausel; dazu S. 72 ff.

111 *Oertmann* (Fn. 107) 258.

112 *Oertmann* (Fn. 107) 257.

113 Den Gedanken von Stufen der Wirtschaftsentwicklung übernimmt *Oertmann* von *W. Arnold,* den er auch S. 177 zitiert. Zu *Arnold* siehe *Kroeschell,* Ein vergessener Germanist des 19. Jahrhunderts, in: Festschrift für H. Krause, 1975, S. 253 ff.

114 *Oertmann* (Fn. 107) 177, 257..

115 *Oertmann* (Fn. 107) 83, Fn. 1 (Hervorhebung im Original).

116 *Oertmann* (Fn. 107) 83, Fn. 1.

117 Er erwähnt dies Element nur nebenbei, ohne den Terminus „Vertrauen“ überhaupt zu verwenden: „Nicht selten wird von den Parteien bei der Erklärung eines rechtsgeschäftlichen Willens die Herbeiführung derjenigen Rechtsfolge gewollt, worauf die äußere Erscheinung hinweist, aber in der Voraussetzung, daß derjenige, welchem dadurch eine gewisse rechtliche Macht geschaffen wird, seine Stellung nur zu einem bestimmten, nicht zu allen dadurch ermöglichten Zwecken ausnützen werde“ (AcP 63 (1880) 172).

cia ist ein Geschäft, in dem die vereinbarten und die gewollten Rechtsfolgen in einem (zulässigen) Verhältnis eines Mehr und Weniger stehen. Das ist die Gestaltung, die *Regelsberger* dann auch in anderen Geschäften wiederfinden kann. Damit zeigt sich in *Regelsbergers* Bezeichnung bestimmter Fallgruppen als „fiduziarische Geschäfte" ein anderer Umgang mit den Quellen als bei *Dernburg* und *Oertmann*. *Regelsbergers* Sicht ist durch ein höheres Maß an Abstraktion gekennzeichnet. Alte und neue Geschäfte werden unabhängig von ihrem Inhalt allein aufgrund einer parallelen juristischen Technik verbunden.

In diesem Zusammenhang erklärt sich auch der zunächst überraschende Umstand, daß sich bei *Regelsberger* keinerlei nähere Ausführungen zur *fiducia* finden. *Regelsberger* setzt sich nicht mit den Eigentumsverhältnissen an der fiduzierten Sache nach römischen Recht auseinander und verweist auch nicht auf die diesbezüglichen Überlegungen von *Scheurl, Huschke* oder *Dernburg*, die ihm sicher bekannt waren. Dieses Vorgehen ist ein weiterer Beleg gegen die Annahme, daß bei *Regelsberger* Rechtsfolgen aus Begriffen abgeleitet werden[119]. *Regelsberger* benötigt keine Darstellung der dinglichen bzw. schuldrechtlichen Wirkungen der altrömischen *fiducia*, da er die Rechtfolgen der modernen fiduziarischen Geschäfte gerade nicht aus diesem alten Institut übernimmt, sondern stattdessen selbständig (nach dem Willen der Parteien) feststellt[120]. Ebensowenig entnimmt er im übrigen die „Legitimation"[121] der fiduziarischen Geschäfte aus der *fiducia*.

Wenn es einerseits für *Regelsbergers* Umgang mit der *fiducia* bezeichnend ist, daß er zeitgenössische Untersuchungen über Einzelheiten dieser altrömischen Rechtsform nicht erwähnt, so ist es andererseits ebenso aufschlußreich, auf welche Abhandlungen er sich ausdrücklich stützt. Der einzige Literaturhinweis, den *Regelsberger* im Zusammenhang mit seinen Ausführungen zu fiduziarischen Rechtsgeschäften gibt, führt zu *Jhering*[122]. *Jhering* bestimmt aber gerade, wie später *Regelsberger*, die Bedeutung der römischen *fiducia*-Geschäfte unabhängig von deren ökonomischem und juristischem Inhalt: „Die Scheingeschäfte[123] und Fiktionen sind ebensowenig wie die starren Formeln des Prozesses etwas dem römischen Rechte Eigentümliches, sie wiederholen sich auf einer gewissen Kulturstufe überall, wofür insbesondere die Geschichte des englischen Rechts die lehrreichsten Beispiele liefert; mit Zurücklegung derselben sterben sie mehr und mehr ab, bis sie sich endlich völlig verlieren. Diese Wahrnehmung muß die Überzeugung in uns hervorrufen, daß nicht die Frage nach dem *Ursprung*, der äußeren historischen Entstehung, sondern die nach dem *Grunde* der Scheingeschäfte die eigentlich entschei-

118 AcP 63 (1880) 173.

119 Vgl. im übrigen oben unter I. 1 (a).

120 Siehe oben unter I. 1. (a).

121 So *Lammel* (Fn. 7) 5.

122 AcP 63 (1880) 173.

123 Fiduziarische Geschäfte sind in Jherings Terminologie Scheingeschäfte, siehe oben I. 1. (b) (cc).

dende ist"[124]. *Jherings* Antwort auf diese Frage lautet dann, daß der Grund solcher Geschäfte in dem Bemühen zu sehen sei, „neu auftauchende Bedürfnisse des Lebens mit den vorhandenen Mitteln zu befriedigen"[125]. *Jhering* interessiert hinter den konkreten römischen fiduziarischen Geschäften deren Funktion im Rechtssystem: „Die *Funktion* des Scheingeschäfts ist eine *rein technische,* Erreichung eines vom Recht selber gebilligten Zweckes durch eine etwas gewaltsame Anwendung der vorhandenen Mittel, – die Scheingeschäfte waren juristische Notlügen"[126]. Wenn auch hier ein Vergleich über „Funktionen" erfolgt, so wird damit doch ein ganz anderer Sinn verbunden als derjenige, der oben für die Pfandrechtsdarstellungen herausgearbeitet wurde. Wie bei *Regelsberger* spielt bei *Jhering* der inhaltliche Zweck des Rechtsinstituts keine Rolle. Im Unterschied allerdings zu *Regelsberger* kommt es *Jhering* auch nicht auf die Gestaltung eines Mehr und Weniger an, sondern ihm geht es um die Verbindung zwischen modernen Lebensgestaltungen und (älterem) positiven Recht durch bestimmte juristisch-technische Mittel.

II. Die germanistische Seite

1. Rechtsgeschichte und Dogmatik

(a) Schultze

Für die germanistische Seite werden üblicherweise die Arbeiten von *Alfred Schultze* denjenigen von *Regelsberger* gegenübergestellt: „Die germanistische Theorie der Treuhand, wie sie heute noch im Rahmen der deutschen Treuhandlehre eine Rolle spielt, ist jedoch von Alfred Schultze geschaffen worden"[127].

Anknüpfend an das soeben für *Regelsberger* analysierte Verhältnis von Rechtsgeschichte und Dogmatik soll dieser Punkt nun auch bei *Schultze* untersucht werden. Allerdings ist *Schultzes* erste Arbeit zur Treuhand (1895) rein historisch angelegt. Sein Buch „Die langobardische Treuhand und ihre Umbildung zur Testamentsvollstreckung" behandelt die Zeit vom 8. bis zum 13. Jahrhundert. Wenn *Schultze* dabei einer „Umbildung" der Treuhand während dieses Zeitraums nachgeht, erzielt er jedoch ein Resultat, das durchaus eine Weiterführung der Ergebnisse bis auf die Gegenwart ermöglicht. Er stellt nämlich fest, daß „das Institut in seinem Keim dasselbe geblieben ist"[128]. Daß *Schultze* auch tatsächlich an eine Übertragung seiner Gedanken auf die Situation am Ende des 19. Jahrhunderts denkt, zeigt sich, wenn er zu Beginn der Abhandlung betont, daß der in seiner

---

124 *Jhering,* Geist III (Fn. 67) 289 (Hervorhebung im Original).

125 *Jhering,* Geist III (Fn. 67) 290.

126 *Jhering,* Geist III (Fn. 67) 282 (Hervorhebung nicht im Original).

127 *Coing,* Treuhand (Fn. 6) 49.

128 *Schultze,* Die langobardische Treuhand und ihre Umbildung zur Testamentsvollstreckung, Breslau, 1895, S. 173.

Untersuchung erarbeitete germanische Rechtsgedanke „für die Dogmatik des heutigen Instituts" der Testamentsvollstreckung zu verwerten sei[129]. Damit nimmt er Bezug auf die aktuelle Debatte um die Lehre von der Testamentsvollstreckung[130]. *Schultze* sieht offensichtlich den „Keim", den er für die langobardischen Treuhand herausarbeitet, auch für aktuelle Rechtsfragen als entscheidend an. Dies bestätigt sich dann auch in seiner späteren Abhandlung „Treuhänder im geltenden bürgerlichen Recht" (1901)[131]. *Schultzes* Ziel ist es dort, die „deutsche" bzw. „germanische" Treuhänderschaft „als wirklich bereits [sc. im BGB] vorhanden nachzuweisen"[132]. Dabei ist für ihn die „germanische" Treuhand gleichbedeutend mit den Ergebnissen, die er für das langobardische Recht erarbeitet hat[133].

Die Entwicklungslinie, die hier angesprochen wird – langobardischer Salmann, Testamentsvollstrecker im 13. Jahrhundert, Testamentsvollstrecker iSd BGB[134] –, legt es nahe, an eine Verbindung zwischen Rechtsgeschichte und Gegenwart zu denken, wie sie zwischen *fiducia* und Pfandrechtsdarstellungen[135] festgestellt wurde. Tatsächlich läßt sich in *Schultzes* Ausführungen erkennen, daß die langobardischen Salmannen und die späteren Testamentsvollstrecker vergleichbare Funktionen hatten. *Schultze* arbeitet denn auch ausdrücklich die Zwecke der Einschaltung von Salmannen im Bereich der Vergabungen von Todes wegen heraus[136]. Überhaupt ist der Blick auf die „Funktionen" der Salmannen vor allem seit der Untersuchung von *Stobbe*, der es sich gerade zum Thema gestellt hatte, die „Funktionen" aufzuzeigen, welche man im Mittelalter durch Salmannen erreichen wollte[137], eine bekannte Perspektive in der Germanistik[138]. Aber diese Parallele im Bereich der Funktion wählt *Schultze* gerade nicht zum Ansatzpunkt für seine Darstellung der Treuhand. Er schiebt diesen Gedanken sogar ausdrücklich beiseite: „Die hier versuchte Gliederung der Zwecke [sc. die mit der letztwilligen Treuhand verfolgt wurden] erbringt Gesichtspunkte, die auch in der Folge im Auge zu behalten sind. Sie eignet sich aber *nicht* als Grundlage für den juristischen Aufbau des

---

129 *Schultze* (Fn. 128) 2 f.

130 *Schultze* bezieht sich ausdrücklich auf die Debatte zu diesem Thema beim 21. deutschen Juristentag 1889; *Schultze* (Fn. 128) 1. In den Referaten des erwähnten Juristentages wurde die Rechtsstellung des Testamentsvollstreckers als Amt bzw. als Vertreter des Nachlasses oder der Erben diskutiert (siehe die Referate von *G. Hartmann, v. Cuny).* Der Gedanke eines besonderen begrenzten dinglichen Rechts, den *Schultze* später vertritt, findet sich dort nicht.

131 *Schultze,* Treuhänder im geltenden bürgerlichen Recht, JhJb 43 (1901) 1 - 104.

132 *Schultze,* JhJb 43 (1901) 28.

133 Vgl. *Schultze,* JhJb 43 (1901) Fn. 14, S. 11.

134 Auf der Testamentsvollstreckung liegt das Schwergewicht von *Schultzes* Ausführungen zum BGB, S. sogleich unter II. 2.

135 Siehe oben I. 2 (b).

136 *Schultze* (Fn. 128) 46 ff.

137 *Stobbe,* Ueber die Salmannen, ZRG 7 (1868) 405 - 438, 407.

138 Siehe auch *Schultze,* JhJb 43 (1901) 8.

Instituts“. Für diese Frage soll ein anderer Aspekt entscheidend sein: „Dafür sind massgebend vielmehr die juristischen *Mittel*, die zur Erreichung jener Zwecke gewählt sind“[139]. Dieser Gedanke führt *Schultze* dazu, seine Ausführungen auf die Rechtsmacht und die Pflichten der Treuhänder zu konzentrieren[140]. Die Parallele zwischen langobardischer Treuhand und Testamentsvollstreckung wird dann dahingehend beschrieben, daß die Rechtsmacht in gleicher Weise gestaltet wurde, nämlich als dinglich beschränktes Eigentum[141]. Als Ergebnis ist somit festzuhalten, daß *Schultze* auf die juristische Gestaltung der Geschäfte abstellt, obgleich bei dem von ihm behandelten Fall der Salmannen und Testamentsvollstrecker ein Funktionszusammenhang besteht.

(b) Beseler

An diesem Punkt sollen auch auf der germanistischen Seite zum Vergleich andere Arbeiten zum Thema treuhänderischer Rechtsgestaltungen herangezogen werden, bei denen sich die Frage nach dem Verhältnis zwischen Rechtsgeschichte und Dogmatik verfolgen läßt. Dies gelingt bei *Georg Beseler*. Während andere Autoren sich rein historisch mit den mittelalterlichen Salmannen beschäftigen[142], veröffentlicht *Beseler* neben solchen Überlegungen[143] 1845 einen Aufsatz „Von den Testamentsvollziehern“[144], den er mit Blick auf „die Aufgabe der [sc. zukünftigen] Ge-

139 *Schultze* (Fn. 128) 51.

140 *Schultze* (Fn. 128) 51, 173; vgl. auch *idem*, JhJb 43 (1901) 9.

141 Bei der Auslegung langobardischer Quellen stützt sich *Schultze* dabei auf die Konstruktion, welche *H. Brunner* 1885 zu den Landschenkungen der Merowinger und Agilolfinger herausgearbeitet hatte. Nach *Brunner* standen derartige Schenkungen unter einer Zweckbestimmung, so daß bei Eintritt bestimmter Bedingungen, z. B. dem Tod des Beschenkten, ein Rückfall der geschenkten Sache erfolgte. (Landschenkungen, in: *Brunner*, Forschungen zur Geschichte des deutschen und französischen Rechts, 1894, S. 10, 22, 24). Für den Fall der langobardischen Treuhand nimmt *Schultze* entsprechend eine bedingte Eigentumsübertragung an den Treuhänder an. Die Bedingung sieht er dabei in der Vereinbarung, daß das Eigentum an den Treugeber zurückfällt, wenn der Treunehmer das Treugut nicht entsprechend dem vereinbarten Zweck verwendet, oder dieser Zweck aus irgend einem Grund unerfüllbar wird (*Schultze* (Fn. 128) 87, 211; Verweis auf *Brunner* S. 86 f. Zur Rechtsstellung der späteren Testamentsvollstrecker dort S. 181 ff. mit etwas anderer Bestimmung des Zwecks als bei der langobardischen Treuhand S. 183).

142 Hervorzuheben sind hier: *W.E. Albrecht*, Die Gewere als Grundlage des älteren deutschen Sachenrechts, 1828, § 23 („Gewere zu treuer Hand“); *Stobbe*, ZRG 7 (1868) 405 ff.; *A. Heusler*, Institutionen des deutschen Privatrechts I, 1885, § 49 („Die Salmannen“). Des weiteren beschäftigte sich eine Würzburger Dissertation von *H. Lammer* 1875 mit dem Thema „Das Recht der treuen Hand nach deutschem Recht“, wobei auch aktuelle Rechtsfragen erwähnt wurden. Alle diese Werke spielen keine Rolle bei *Schultzes* Darstellung der germanischen Treuhand.

143 Die Lehre von den Erbverträgen I, Göttingen 1835, § 15 f.: „Von den Vergabungen durch Salmannen“.

144 ZDR 9 (1845) 144 ff.

setzgebung"[145] schreibt. Bei den Ausführungen zur rechtlichen Stellung der Testamentsvollstrecker verwendet *Beseler* auffallend häufig den Ausdruck „Prinzip". Er will die „Lehre von den Testamentsexecutoren, wie sie sich im heutigen gemeinen Recht darstellt, principienmäßig" entwickeln[146]. Er sucht „ein allgemeines Princip ..., um das ganze Institut in seinem inneren Zusammenhange mit juristischer Sicherheit und Consequenz darzustellen und zu beurtheilen"[147]. Aus dem Prinzip sollen sich der Ursprung und die Rechtfertigung der Gewalt ergeben, die dem Testamentsvollstrecker zugemessen wird[148]. Als derartigen Grundgedanken nimmt *Beseler* dann die „Testierfreiheit" an[149]. „Vermöge der freieren Stellung der testamentarii factio im heutigen Recht [könne] der Testator die Vollstreckung seines Testaments von der Person des Erben trennen und sich von einem besonders dazu berufenen Dritten formell repäsentiren lassen"[150]. Aus dem Grundsatz der „formellen Repräsentation" begründet *Beseler* dann den Umfang der Befugnisse des Testamentsvollstreckers und seine Stellung zu Dritten[151].

Auch an *Beselers* Konstruktion interessiert hier vor allem, ob sich eine rechtshistorische Herleitung feststellen läßt. In seinen Ausführungen zu den Erbverträgen hatte *Beseler* die Vermutung geäußert, daß das Institut der Testamentsexekutoren aus dem Gebrauch der Salmannen bei den Vergabungen von Todes wegen hervorgegangen sei[152], wobei „das leitende Princip in dem Institut der getreuen Hand zu suchen ist"[153]. Wenn diese Ausführungen an eine Entwicklungslinie von den Prinzipien des Salmannenrechts zu denjenigen der Testamentsvollstreckung im 19. Jahrhundert denken lassen, so steht dem *Beselers* ausdrückliche Negation dieser Annahme im Aufsatz des Jahres 1845 gegenüber: „Die Befugnis des Executors, sich in den Besitz des Nachlasses zu setzen, läßt sich nicht aus der Stellung des Salmanns, der die Gewere zur getreuen Hand hatte, ableiten; denn zwischen beiden besteht *nur ein rechtshistorischer Zusammenhang*, der für eine practische Deduction zu dem Zweck, geltende Rechtsregeln zu gewinnen, *keinen* Anhalt gewährt"[154]. Der historische Zusammenhang allein rechtfertigt es somit für *Beseler* nicht, Prinzipien für die rechtliche Gestaltung eines Instituts aus früheren Rechtsordnungen zu übernehmen. Allerdings ist gerade hinsichtlich der Testamentsvoll-

145 ZDR 9 (1845) 222.

146 ZDR 9 (1845) 222,3.

147 ZDR 9 (1845) 172.

148 ZDR 9 (1845) 174.

149 ZDR 9 (1845) 174.

150 ZDR 9 (1845) 180.

151 ZDR 9 (1845) 186, 194, 209, 216, 218.

152 *Beseler* (Fn. 143) 284

153 *Beseler* (Fn. 143) 288.

154 ZDR 9 (1845) 211 (Hervorhebungen nicht im Original). Vgl. dort auch S. 169: „Auf die voigteiliche Grundlage, welche die Testamentsexecutoren in älteren Stadtrechten hatten, dürfen wir für das heutige gemeine Recht freilich kein Gewicht mehr legen, da sich darin nur für die geschichtliche Betrachtung des Instituts ein Anhalt gewinnen läßt ...".

strecker festzustellen, daß *Beselers* Prinzip für deren Rechtsstellung inhaltlich genau demjenigen entspricht, welches er für das mittelalterliche Recht entwickelt hat. Ausgehend von dem Institut der Salmannen und der Vogtei stellt *Beseler* nämlich für die älteren Stadtrechte fest, daß dort nur eine formelle, nicht eine materielle Repräsentation des Erblassers durch Mittelspersonen angenommen wurde[155]. Entsprechend hatte er für das ältere deutsche Recht herausgearbeitet, daß der Salmann nicht das Eigentum am Grundstück, sondern nur die Befugnis erhielt, diese Sache zu übertragen[156]. Das „Wesen" dieser Rechtsgeschäfte will *Beseler* dabei in dem „auf den Salmann gesetzten Vertrauen (fiducia)" sehen[157], womit das Vertrauen gemeint ist, daß der Salmann das Grundstück tatsächlich an einen Dritten überträgt[158]. *Beseler* setzt hier den Gedanken der treuen Hand zu einer bestimmten Rechtsgestaltung in Beziehung: nicht Eigentum wird übertragen, sondern allein die Befugnis, bestimmte Geschäfte über das Vermögen eines anderen abzuschließen. Mit dieser „formellen Repräsentation" begründet er dann aber nicht allein die Stellung der mittelalterlichen Salmannen, sondern ebenso diejenige der Testamentsvollstrecker nach aktuellem Recht. Genau diese Verbindung von Treuhand mit einer bestimmten Konstruktion, und zwar einer Konstruktion, welche durch die begrenzte Übertragung von Eigentumsrechten gekennzeichnet ist, findet sich dann, wie gezeigt[159], später bei *Schultze* wieder.

2. *Schultzes* Theoriebildung

Auffallendes Kennzeichen von *Schultzes* Darlegungen zur Treuhand ist die Entwicklung einer „germanischen" Treuhand in Abgrenzung zur „römischen" Treuhand[160]. Ist *Regelsberger* bekannt wegen der Einführung der Bezeichnung „fiduziarische Rechtsgeschäfte", so liegen die Fernwirkungen von *Schultze* in der Gegenüberstellung zweier Treuhandformen. Auch hier ist das methodische Vorgehen beachtenswert, wobei diesem Punkt eine besondere Bedeutung als Hintergrund moderner Treuhandlehren zukommt.

---

155 ZDR 9 (1845) 152 f., 154 f.

156 *Beseler* (Fn. 143) 267. Zum Zusammenhang mit der Vorstellung von der Unzulässigkeit von Stellvertretung, *Otten* (Fn. 1) 60; *Asmus* (Fn. 1) 176 ff.

157 *Beseler* (Fn. 143) 267.

158 Beseler (Fn. 143) 281 ff., wo sich Beseler mit den Folgen eines „treulosen Salmanns" beschäftigt.

159 Siehe soeben unter II. 1 (a).

160 Siehe JhJb 43 (1901) 6 Überschrift: „Unterschied zwischen römischer und germanischer Treuhandschaft". Dieser Ansatz war am Ende des 19. Jahrhunderts wieder aktuell durch *Gierkes* strikte Gegenüberstellung von deutschem und römischem Recht in seinem Vortrag über die soziale Aufgabe (1889). *Schultze* führt diese Abgrenzung erstmals für die Treuhand durch. Diese Rechtsfigur spielte vorher bei den prinzipellen Abgrenzungen zwischen römischem und deutschem Recht, z. B. von *C. A. Schmidt,* 1853, keine Rolle.

Schultze überschreibt den § 13 seines Werkes über die langobardische Treuhand: „Die germanische fiducia im Gegensatz zur römischen fiducia". An diesem Titel ist zweierlei bemerkenswert: Zum einen werden die römische *fiducia* und ein germanisches Rechtsinstitut in Zusammenhang gebracht. Diese Verbindung erscheint so eng, daß auch das germanische Institut als „fiducia" bezeichnet wird. Auf der anderen Seite wird das Verhältnis der beiden Formen als „Gegensatz" beschrieben. Diesen – scheinbaren – Widerspruch gilt es zu klären.

(a) Der Gegensatz zwischen fiducia und Treuhand

„Dort [sc. bei der römischen fiducia und den modernen fiduziarischen Geschäften] äussert sich die beschränkende Wirkung der Zweckbestimmung nur auf obligatorischem, hier [sc. bei der langobardischen Treuhand] schon auf dinglichem Gebiete!"[161] *Schultzes* Ansatzpunkt bei die Unterscheidung ist also derselbe wie bei der Verbindung von Rechtsgeschichte und aktueller Dogmatik: die Konstruktion der Verfügungsmacht für die Person, der ein Gegenstand fiduziarisch übertragen wurde. Nach der als römisch bezeichneten Konstruktion erhält der Fiduziar volles Eigentum; die Verabredung, die Sache nur zu bestimmten Zwecken zu gebrauchen, wirkt allein obligatorisch. Im anderen Fall, der sog. germanischen Treuhand, besteht nur ein beschränktes dingliches Recht des Fiduziars.

Mit dieser Kurzformel ist scheinbar alles über den Unterschied zwischen römischer *fiducia* und germanischer Treuhand gesagt. Es gilt jedoch, hier noch einen zusätzlichen Aspekt zu beachten, der durch den Blick auf die juristische Konstruktion leicht verdeckt wird. Die Gegenüberstellung der Gestaltungen von Verfügungsmacht erweckt nämlich den Eindruck, daß damit jeweils dieselbe Fallgruppe erklärt werden soll. Diese Annahme ist jedoch nicht zutreffend. Allerdings entwickeln sowohl *Regelsberger* als auch *Schultze* ihre Ansichten für den Fall des Eigentumindossaments zu Inkassozwecken[162]. Hier stehen sich die beiden Treuhandtheorien tatsächlich direkt gegenüber. Es sollte jedoch nicht übersehen werden, daß sich die übrigen „Anwendungsfälle"[163] treuhänderischer Rechtsgestaltung im geltenden Recht, die von *Regelsberger* und *Schultze* genannt werden, keineswegs decken. Bei *Regelsberger* sind dies die Eigentumsübertragung zu Pfandzwecken und der Sicherheits- oder Depotwechsel[164]. *Schultze* führt dagegen an: die fiduziarische Stiftung[165], Sammlung von Beiträgen[166], das Vollgiro zum Inkasso[167], die

---

161 *Schultze* (Fn. 128) 105.

162 *Regelsberger*, siehe oben I. 1. (a); *Schultze*, JhJb 43 (1901) 46 ff.

163 *Schultze*, JhJb 43 (1901) 32.

164 Pandekten (Fn. 13) § 141, 518, Handelsgeschäfte (Fn. 13) 409.

165 *Schultze*, JhJb 43 (1901) 32 ff. *Regelsberger* spricht später in seinen Pandekten (Fn. 13) im Abschnitt über Stiftungen ebenfalls vom „Fiduziar" (S. 342 f.). Dieser Gedanke war in den 90er Jahren des 19. Jahrhunderts aktuell durch *Kohlers* Abhandlung „Ueber das Recht der Stiftungen", AcP 3 (1890) 228 ff., 268 - 292 („Fiduciarische Stiftungen"). 1880 scheint

Pflegschaft[168], das Hypothekenbankgesetz[169] und schwerpunktmäßig die Testamentsvollstreckung[170]. Dem entspricht die Verschiedenheit der Sachverhalte, welche die Quellen regeln, auf die sich *Regelsberger* für seine Wortwahl und *Schultze* für seine Konstruktion stützen: eine Vorform des Pfandrechts einerseits und eine solche der Testamentsvollstreckung andererseits. Die unterschiedlichen Konstruktionen bezüglich der Rechtsmacht des Treuhänders werden also jeweils für sehr verschiedene Fälle eingesetzt[171]. Diesen Umstand verdeckt *Schultze* mit seiner allgemeinen Formulierung eines Gegensatzes der Treuhandtheorien.

Dieser Befund wird durch die Beobachtung bestätigt, daß demgegenüber inhaltlich vergleichbare Fälle auch vergleichbare Konstruktionen bei Romanisten und Germanisten finden. Besonders plastisch zeigt sich dies in *Jherings* Parodie „Im juristischen Begriffshimmel" (1884). Dort wendet der Besucher dieser phantastischen juristischen Geisterwelt entsprechend der geltenden Dogmatik gegen eine Ergänzung der römischen Testamentsformel ein: „Mir scheint das zu passen wie die Faust auf das Auge. Der familiae emtor, der die Formel spricht, will ja gerade betonen, daß er nicht Eigentümer, sondern, um mich eines Ausdrucks des germanischen Rechts zu bedienen, nur Treuhänder, Salmann werden, die Erbschaft nur in seine Obhut und Verwaltung nehmen will ..."[172]. Treuhänderschaft in Form einer beschränkten Verfügungsmacht wird also auch für das römische Recht in Fällen anerkannt, die Ähnlichkeit zur Testamentsvollsteckung aufweisen[173]. Umgekehrt erwähnt *Schultze* auch Fälle der Vollrechtsübertragung im langobardischen Recht, die gerade zu Verpfändungszwecken erfolgten[174]. Deutschrechtliche und romanistische Treuhand werden also im 19. Jahrhundert für unterschiedliche Fallgestaltungen entwickelt, die heute in einem einheitlichen Treuhandbegriff zusammengefaßt werden.

(b) Die Verbindung zwischen fiducia und Treuhand

Hat sich somit ein tiefgreifender Gegensatz zwischen romanistischen und germanistischen Fallgruppen der Treuhand gezeigt, stellt sich die Frage nach dem *ter-*

Regelsberger jedoch nicht an diese Fälle gedacht zu haben, und auch in den Pandekten erfolgt kein Querverweis bei der Darstellung fiduziarischer Geschäfte.

166 *Schultze*, JhJb 43 (1901) 35 ff.

167 *Schultze*, JhJb 43 (1901) 46 ff.

168 *Schultze*, JhJb 43 (1901) 58 ff.

169 *Schultze*, JhJb 43 (1901) 96 - 102.

170 *Schultze*, JhJb 43 (1901) 64 ff.

171 Eine Rechtsübertragung, die (auch) im Interesse des Treuhänders erfolgt, ist ausdrücklich nicht *Schultzes* Thema; siehe JhJb 43 (1901) 2.

172 *Jhering*, Scherz und Ernst in der Jurisprudenz, 13. Auflage, 1924, S. 267,8.

173 Auf eine Ähnlichkeit zwischen dem *familiae emtor* und den Treuhändern nach germanischen Rechts weist auch *Schultze*, JhJb 43 (1901) 7 hin.

174 *Schultze* (Fn. 128) 97 ff., 102 f.

tium comparationis, das *Schultze* berechtigt, römische und germanische Treuhand überhaupt zu vergleichen. Als solcher verbindender Gedanke ergibt sich derjenige der Treue, „fiducia im weitesten Sinne“[175]: „Es wird jemanden eine Rechtsmacht zu eigenem Recht übertragen, bei deren Gebrauch er sich ganz oder doch zum Theil durch ein fremdes Interesse, das des Gebers oder das eines Dritten, leiten lassen soll: man erwartet von ihm den dazu erforderlichen Grad von Uneigennützigkeit und Treue: die Hand, die empfängt, wird als eine treue Hand (manus fidelis) vermuthet“[176]. Dieser Gedanke ist nach *Schultze* sowohl bei beschränkter Verfügungsmacht wie bei der Vollrechtsübertragung an einen Treuhänder zu finden. Die „langobardisch-germanische fiducia“ und die römische *fiducia* sowie die „modernen fiduziarischen Geschäfte“ sind „demnach *Unterarten derselben Kategorie*“[177]. Deswegen können sie einander auch gegenübergestellt werden[178]. Die Bedeutung von *Schultzes* Arbeit ist vor allem in dieser Kategorienbildung zu sehen. Über die langobardische Treuhand hinaus entwickelt er eine allgemeine Treuhand über die Elemente *fides* und Treue. Damit ist *Schultze* Wegbereiter für die moderne umfassende Treuhandtheorie, in der unterschiedliche juristische Gestaltungen mit unterschiedlichen Rechtsfolgen zusammengefaßt werden.

III. Ergebnisse

Eine Durchsicht der Werke des 19. Jahrhunderts, die treuhänderische Rechtsgestaltungen zum Gegenstand haben, ergibt, daß dieses Thema auf zwei Ebenen diskutiert wurde. Darstellungen, die allein historische Formen der Treuhand behandeln, sind von solchen Arbeiten zu unterscheiden, in denen die Beschäftigung mit diesen Formen im Zusammenhang mit der Behandlung aktueller dogmatischer Fragen erfolgt. Die rein historischen Ausführungen zur *fiducia* von *Degenkolb, Krüger* und *Rudorff* sowie zu den Salmannen von *Albrecht, Stobbe* und *Heusler* sind im Hinblick auf die Entwicklung von Treuhandtheorien nicht von Interesse. Sie sind allein über die Begriffe „fiducia“ und „treue Hand“ mit der Debatte, wie Treuhandfälle im geltenden Recht zu beurteilen sind, verbunden. Inhaltlich wird von den genannten Juristen kein Bezug zur Rechtslage ihrer Zeit hergestellt. Auf der anderen Seite wird die *fiducia* nicht allein im Rahmen von dogmatischen Arbeiten, die Treuhandkonstellationen gewidmet sind, behandelt. Die *fiducia* hat bei *Dernburg* Bedeutung für die Pfandrechtsdarstellung, bei *Scheurl* und *Huschke* dagegen für die Begründung der Ersitzungsvoraussetzungen.

---

175 Siehe *Schultze* (Fn. 128), 95, 105. Angedeutet wurde dieser Gedanke vorher schon bei *Oertmann,* siehe oben I. 2 (c).

176 *Schultze* (Fn. 128) 96; ähnlich *idem,* JhJb 43, 1.

177 *Schultze* (Fn. 128) 105 (Hervorhebung nicht im Original).

178 So ausdrücklich *Schultze* (Fn. 128) 105.

Treuhandtheorien entwickeln gegen Ende des 19. Jahrhunderts *Regelsberger* und *Schultze.* Zunächst veröffentlicht *Regelsberger* 1880 seine Ausführungen zu „fiduziarischen Geschäften“. Sein Beitrag betrifft aktuelle juristische Fragen wie z. B. die Zession und das Eigentumsindossament zu Inkassozwecken. 15 Jahre später beginnt *Schultze* mit der Entwicklung einer „germanischen“ Treuhandtheorie, die er 1901 auf das geltende Recht überträgt.

Das Beispiel der Treuhand erweist sich als überaus aufschlußreich im Hinblick auf juristische Theoriebildung und den Umgang mit der Rechtsgeschichte im 19. Jahrhundert. Unter diesem Gesichtspunkt wurden die Werke von *Regelsberger* und *Schultze* von *Coing* dargestellt. Nach genauer Untersuchung der Texte müssen *Coings* Ergebnisse jedoch differenziert und modifiziert werden. Unzutreffend ist vor allem die Kennzeichnung als Begriffsjurisprudenz. Dieses allgemein in Rechtsgeschichte und Dogmatik schnell verhängte Etikett für die Rechtswissenschaft der zweiten Hälfte des 19. Jahrhunderts[179] hat in seiner ersten[180] zeitgenössischen Verwendung durch *Jhering* 1884 die Bedeutung von Lebensferne: Ein „sich an sich selber berauschendes Denken“ das nicht Halt mache vor einem Resultat, „das mit dem Zweck der Anwendung des Rechts völlig unvereinbar ist“[181]. Ähnlich wird heute „Begriffsjurisprudenz“ meist dahingehend beschrieben, daß „der Zweck, der mit einem Institut verfolgt wird“, bei der Konstruktion nicht berücksichtigt werde[182]. Anlaß und Ergebnis der Treuhandtheorien des 19. Jahrhunderts entsprechen diesem Bild in keiner Weise. Sowohl *Regelsberger* als auch *Schultze* knüpfen an aktuelle Rechtsfragen an[183]. Dabei geht es beiden Juristen darum, für die von den Parteien beabsichtigten Zwecke eine geeignete juristische Gestaltung aufzuzeigen. Hinsichtlich ihrer Ergebnisse genügt der Hinweis darauf, daß *Coing* selbst beiden Juristen das Verdienst zuspricht, eine Theorie entwickelt zu haben, die auch in der heutigen Treuhandlehre noch eine Rolle spielt.

Auch der Gedanke, daß Rechtsfolgen aus Begriffen abgeleitet werden, findet bei den Treuhandtheorien des 19. Jahrhunderts keine Stütze. Dies hat insbesondere die Analyse von *Regelsbergers* Ausführungen gezeigt. Allerdings steht bei *Schultze*

---

179 Vgl. nur *Wieacker,* Privatrechtsgeschichte der Neuzeit, 2. Auflage, 1967, S. 433 ff.; *Schlosser,* Neuere Privatrechtsgeschichte, 6. Auflage, 1988, S. 128 ff.

180 Siehe *Rückert,* Modernisierung des Handelsrechts im 19. Jahrhundert, ZHR (Beiheft) 66 (1993) 22.

181 Im juristischen Begriffshimmel, in: *Jhering* (Fn. 172), 362 f., 358.

182 *Coing,* Europäisches Privatrecht II, 1989, S. 47; ähnlich auch *ders.* Grundzüge der Rechtsphilosophie, 5. Auflage, 1993, S. 253. Vgl. auch *W. Wilhelm,* Zur juristischen Methodenlehre im 19. Jahrhundert, 1958, S. 82 ff., der Begriffsjurisprudenz dadurch gekennzeichnet sieht, daß die „reale gesellschaftliche Funktion“ der Rechtsinstitute nicht berücksichtigt wird.

183 *Regelsbergers* Ausgangspunkt ist die Rechtsprechung seiner Zeit zur Simulationsfrage (siehe oben I.1.(a)) und *Schultze* verweist am Beginn seines Werkes über die langobardische Treuhand auf die aktuelle Debatte über die Stellung des Testamentsvollstreckers (siehe oben II.1.(a)).

die juristische Konstruktion der Rechtsmacht des Treuhänders im Vordergrund. Und *Regelsberger* interessiert sich für die juristische Technik. Wenn aber Ausführungen zur juristischen Gestaltung von Geschäften und deren Rechtsfolgen als „Begriffsjurisprudenz" verstanden werden, muß dann nicht jede dogmatische Überlegung unter diese Bezeichnung fallen?

Coing bezeichnet die Methode der Rechtswissenschaft der 19. Jahrhunderts aber auch als „historische Rechtsvergleichung": „Sieht man einmal von den Besonderheiten ab, welche die deutsche Treuhandtheorie aus der Eigenart der deutschen Rechtswissenschaft empfangen hat, so stellt sie sich als Ergebnis einer Methode dar, die man als *historische Rechtsvergleichung* bezeichnen könnte"[184]. Dieser Gedanke ist für das Verständnis, wie Rechtsgeschichte und Dogmatik verbunden wurden, ergiebig[185]. Denn er macht auf die Frage aufmerksam, über welche Elemente diese Vergleichung erfolgt. Anknüpfungspunkt für eine moderne Rechtsvergleichung – etwa zwischen anglo-amerikanischem trust und deutscher Treuhand – ist die „tatsächliche Funktion [der Rechtsinstitute] im Rechtsleben"[186]. Der Aspekt der Funktion führt für die historischen Institute *fiducia* und Salmann zum Pfandrecht bzw. zur Testamentsvollstreckung. *Dernburgs* Ausführungen liefern ein Beispiel für eine derartige historische Vergleichung. Daneben hat sich jedoch gezeigt, daß im 19. Jahrhundert auch andere Ansätze für eine Verbindung zwischen Rechtsgeschichte und Dogmatik genutzt wurden. *Regelsberger* und *Schultze* stützen sich gerade nicht auf einen derartigen Funktionsvergleich. *Regelsberger* blickt bei der *fiducia* auf die juristische Technik, *Schultze* auf die juristische Konstruktion der Rechtsmacht des Salmannen. Daneben findet sich der Gedanke von Prinzipien (*Beseler)* und der Anpassung von Rechtsinstituten an veränderte Verhältnisse (*Jhering).* Es zeigt sich somit, daß die Rechtsgeschichte offensichtlich in ganz unterschiedlicher Weise in dogmatische Argumentationen eingebracht wurde.

---

184 *Coing,* RabelsZ 37 (1973) 209 (Hervorhebung nicht im Original).

185 Dabei ist es allerdings notwendig, auch an diesem Punkt den Gedanken aus der bei *Coing* bestehenden Verbindung mit Begriffsjurisprudenz und überhistorischen Rechtsbegriffen zu lösen; siehe *Coing,* RabelsZ 37 (1973) 209, *ders.,* Europäisches Privatrecht II (Fn. 182) 48. Im letztgenannten Werk spricht *Coing* für das 19. Jahrhundert nicht mehr von „historischer Rechtsvergleichung". Stattdessen wird diese Methodenbeschreibung allein für die Arbeit der Juristen der Rezeptionszeit verwendet: Europäisches Privatrecht I, 1985, S. 15, 26.

186 So *H. Kötz* in seiner rechtsvergleichenden Darstellung, Trust und Treuhand: Eine rechtsvergleichende Darstellung des anglo-amerikanischen trust und funktionsverwandter Institute des deutschen Rechts, 1963, S. 18.

JOACHIM RÜCKERT

Kontinuität und Diskontinuität in der Treuhandforschung

I. Die Problemzugriffe der deutschen Treuhandforschung

Mein Beitrag versteht sich als eine Art Zugabe[1]. Anders als die hier vorgelegten wichtigen Forschungen zu Trust und Treuhand, faßt er nicht diese Gegenstände selbst ins Auge, sondern die Treuhandforschung und davon auch nur die in Deutschland. Das soll nicht bedeuten, daß ich einen Forschungsbericht geben will, der in diesem Kreise unnötig wäre. Aber es gibt etwas, was an diesen vielen wissenschaftlichen Büchern interessant ist, außer, daß man sie eben liest und verwendet, daß man feststellt, ob ihre Quellen richtig erschlossen und analysiert sind und ob ihre Ergebnisse zutreffen oder nicht. Jeder weiß, daß manche Bücher, obwohl sie keineswegs schlecht sind, doch irgendwie langweilig und „out" wirken – es gibt also noch ganz andere Faktoren beim Umgang mit Forschungsbüchern als richtig und falsch, und gut und schlecht. Natürlich ist mit „out" auch nicht an Bücher zum geltenden oder nicht mehr geltenden Recht gedacht, sondern gerade auch an Geschichtsbücher. Von Zeit zu Zeit schreibt man diese Bücher bekanntlich um – eine merkwürdige Vorstellung. Man sagt sogar, die Geschichte werde umgeschrieben. Bleibt die Geschichte nicht immer gleich? Ich glaube, dieses Umschreiben gilt sogar für die Rechtsgeschichte noch mehr als für die allgemeine Geschichte. Was geschieht dabei eigentlich?

Der Vorgang hängt vor allem damit zusammen, daß es bei jeder Geschichtsarbeit immer auch um *Kontinuität und Diskontinuität* geht, um das Verhältnis zur Gegenwart. Immer wieder ist es die Frage, ob man die Geschichtsstoffe im Museum pflegt oder Ruine werden läßt, ob man ihnen treu bleibt oder sich von ihnen abwendet. In der Rechtsgeschichte berührt die Entscheidung Museum oder Ruine den Geschichtsschreiber besonders intensiv, weil man unmittelbar mit einmal wirklich gewesenen Wertungen zu tun hat, die einmal bestimmte Konfliktlösungen prägten. Zudem haben sich die juristischen und realen Vorgänge wenigstens im Bereich des Privatrechts zum Teil erstaunlich stabil gehalten. Die alten Konfliktentscheidungen lösen also sehr direkt unmittelbare Vergleiche und eigene Wertungen aus. Die alten Fälle und Stellungnahmen sprechen auch die neuen Juristen oft unmittelbar an. Das alles prägt die Problemzugriffe.

---

[1] Ich danke *R. Zimmermann* für nachhaltiges Interesse, Geduld und informelle Gelegenheit für diesen kleinen Vortrag.

Aber lassen Sie mich einige Beispiele untersuchen und vorstellen für das, was mir unter dem Stichwort Kontinuität und Diskontinuität in der *Treuhandforschung* interessant erscheint. Diese Perspektive scheint mir natürlich auch nicht folgenlos für die gemeinsame Arbeit über Trust und Treuhand. Denn die historischen Gegenstände lassen sich bekanntlich nicht von der Methode isolieren, mit der man sie erforscht. Bisweilen, so hat man behauptet, folgt die Forschung relativ plötzlich ganz neuen Paradigmata, ohne daß man dafür eigentlich eine entsprechende Veränderung des Forschungsobjekts feststellen könnte.

II. Das Beispiel *Alfred Schultze* (1901 und 1895): Begriffsbetonung im Dienst des Gegenwartsrechts

Ein erstes Beispiel ist eine Arbeit von *Alfred Schultze.* Er war Professor für Rechtsgeschichte und Oberlandesgerichtsrat in Jena, etwa um 1900. Diese Verbindung von Rechtsgeschichte und zivilistischer Rechtspraxis ist ein deutsches Phänomen mindestens seit *Savigny. Schultze* hat ein oft als epochemachend bezeichnetes Buch über „Die Langobardische Treuhand und ihre Umbildung zur Testamentsvollstreckung" geschrieben – schon 1895[2]. 1901 schrieb er einen großen Aufsatz über „Treuhänder im geltenden bürgerlichen Recht"[3] – also zum BGB, dem soeben in Kraft getretenen „Bürgerlichen Gesetzbuch für das Deutsche Reich". Der Aufsatz ist bemerkenswert gegliedert in A: Allgemeines, B: Anwendungsfälle, C: Schluß. Die Treuhandfälle sind also „Anwendungsfälle" eines Allgemeinen. In der Tat geht *Schultze* von einem gesetzesunabhängigen Begriff der Treuhand aus und sucht von hier aus Anwendungsfälle im BGB. Ich will das keineswegs als unsinnig, deduktiv oder illegitim bezeichnen[4]. Wichtig ist mir nur, daß *Schultze* unter „A: Allgemeines" nicht etwa eine allgemeine Treuhanddefinition aus dem BGB oder aus der Rechtssprechung zum geltenden Recht entwickelt, sondern

1. den Begriff von Treuhand ohne Nachweis und ohne weitere Einführung niederschreibt, dann
2. den Unterschied zwischen römischer und germanischer Treuhand beschreibt und
3. den Grund dieses Unterschiedes fixiert.

Was will er damit? Was ist die Logik dieses Vorgehens? – es geht um Kontinuität. Er schreibt:

---

2 *Alfred Schultze,* Die Langobardische Treuhand und ihre Umbildung zur Testamentsvollstreckung (= Gierkes Untersuchungen zur deutschen Staats- und Rechtsgeschichte, 49), Breslau, 1895, XII und 233 Seiten.

3 In: JhJb 43 (1901) 1 - 104.

4 Die Kritik als deduktiv war lange Zeit stehendes Thema, erscheint aber nicht durchweg als treffend, vgl. dazu den Beitrag von *S. Hofer* in diesem Band.

> „Es ist einleuchtend, daß die germanische Gestaltung, da sie die Unstimmigkeit zwischen Zweck und Rechtsmacht des Treuhänders vermeidet, dem Treugeber eine sehr viel größere Sicherheit verschafft, und daher die Empfehlung zu sehr viel ausgedehnterer und anhaltenderer Verwendung giebt als die römische Gestaltung. Thatsächlich hat sich denn auch der Treuhandgedanke in den germanischen Rechten um vieles fruchtbarer und lebenskräftiger erwiesen als im römischen Recht, wo er nach Erfüllung seiner entwicklungsgeschichtlichen Mission fast ganz zurückgetreten ist" (S. 12 f.)[5].

Lebenskraft und entwicklungsgeschichtliche Mission stehen also zur Debatte. Tatsächlich läuft *Schultzes* Aufsatz darauf hinaus, die germanische – wohlgemerkt nicht: die germanistische – Treuhand als aktuell nützlich und rechtlich möglich trotz des neuen BGB zu empfehlen. Wesentliche praktische Fragen diskutiert *Schultze* gar nicht, z. B. ob es nur auf den Treugeber ankommen soll und warum nicht auch auf Dritte und deren Sicherheit, etwa beim Konkurszugriff. Er argumentiert vielmehr positiv mit einer „germanischen Gestaltung" und negativ mit einer „Unstimmigkeit", die vermieden werde (S. 12). Die germanische Gestaltung der Treuhand war ihm die sogenannte dingliche Beschränkung, das auflösend bedingte Eigentum des Treuhänders im Gegensatz zum römischen Volleigentum. Wie kommt *Schultze* zu dieser Sicht einer germanischen Gestaltung?

Die *langobardische* Gestaltung des 6. bis 8. Jahrhunderts hatte er in seinem Buch von 1895 historisch dargestellt. Eine Kontinuität von dorther über die rund tausend Jahre bis 1895, als die Lombardei italienisches Österreich war, lag freilich nicht unmittelbar auf der Hand. Den Ausbau der langobardischen Gestaltung zu einer germanischen Gestaltung begründet *Schultze* 1901 in einer einzigen Fußnote auf Seite 11 mit den Worten „Es gilt das gleiche für die übrigen germanischen Rechte". Er nennt dafür drei Quellen. Sie sind zeitlich gestreut über fünf Jahrhunderte zwischen den Jahren 865 und 1366 und örtlich von der Bretagne über Konstanz nach Halle – genau bis zu unserem Tagungsort. *Germanisch* war daran also eigentlich nichts. Denn die germanische Zeit setzte man damals wie heute bis maximal in das 6. Jahrhundert an. Germanisches Recht als Forschungs-*Problem,* wie es heute gesehen wird, war freilich noch kaum Thema[6]. Und wie ist die spezifische Gestaltung als *auflösend bedingt* und *dinglich* bei den Langobarden zu verstehen? „Auflösend bedingt" war eher verständlich auch über die Zeiten hinweg. Aber „dinglich"? Die Antwort steht gewissermaßen bei *Maitland* 1905:

---

5 Diese Seitenangaben beziehen sich auf *Schultze,* JhJb 43 (1901) 1 ff.

6 *Karl Kroeschell,* Germanisches Recht als Forschungsproblem, in: Festschrift für H. Thieme, 1986, S. 3 - 19, jetzt auch in *idem,* Studien zum frühen und mittelalterlichen deutschen Recht, 1995, S. 65 - 88; wesentliche Bemerkungen zum Thema mehrfach bei *S. Gagnér,* etwa in: La storiografia giuridica scandinava ..., a cura di P. Grossi, Milano, 1988, S. 72 f. u.ö., und *idem,* Zielsetzungen und Werkgestaltung in Paul Roths Wissenschaft, in: Festschrift für Hermann Krause, 1975, S. 276 - 450; neuere Diskussion bei *J. Rückert,* Die Rechtswerte der germanistischen Rechtsgeschichte im Wandel der Forschung, ZSS (GA) 111 (1994) 275 - 309; sehr lehrreich jetzt die vorzügliche Untersuchung von *Andrea Siems,* Das Bild der deutschen Rechtsvergangenheit und seine Aktualisierung im „Dritten Reich" (= Fundamenta Juridica, 31), Baden-Baden, 1996.

„Wenn ich für meine Person von einem ausländischen Freunde gebeten würde, ihm in einem Worte zu sagen, ob das Recht des englischen Destinatars (jener Person, für welche Eigentum in Trust gehalten wird) *dinglich* oder *obligatorisch* ist, so wäre ich geneigt zu antworten: ‚Ich kann das nicht sagen. Wenn ich sagte, sein Recht sei dinglich, so wäre das unrichtig. Wenn ich sagte, es sei obligatorisch, so würde ich dadurch etwas Falsches vermuten lassen. Bei endgültiger Analyse könnte das Recht obligatorisch erscheinen, aber für viele praktische Zwecke von großer Bedeutung ist es so behandelt worden, als wenn es dinglich wäre, und in der Tat, man spricht gewöhnlich davon und denkt daran so, als ob es Eigentum wäre'"[7].

Die langobardischen Rechtsexperten hätten wohl ähnlich geantwortet.

Schultzes Kontinuität wird also aufgebaut durch seinen großzügigen Umgang mit solchen Basisbegriffen wie germanisch und dinglich. Sie liegt in diesen Begriffen, aber auch nur in ihnen. Mir erscheint sie als ein Trugbild. Die Konstruktion ist übertrieben, historisch wie dogmatisch. Für *Schultze* war offenbar entscheidend, daß er genau damit den germanischen Ansatz als „um vieles fruchtbarer und lebenskräftiger" (S. 13, auch 20) erwiesen zu haben meinte.

Bei der Erarbeitung des *Bürgerlichen Gesetzbuches* hat man sich an mehreren Stellen mit Anträgen zugunsten treuhandähnlicher Rechtsfiguren auseinandergesetzt, sie aber überall abgelehnt. Beim *Auftragsrecht* verwies man nach längerer Argumentation auf die Wahlmöglichkeiten mit direkter oder mittelbarer Stellvertretung und befürchtete bei einer „Vermischung der beiden Institute ... große Unklarheit" und vor allem ein Störung des Kredits, „wenn die Gläubiger einer Person nicht mehr sicher wären, daß das Vermögen, welches sich äußerlich als ihr gehörig darstellte, auch rechtlich entsprechend behandelt würde"[8]. Auch beim *Stiftungsgeschäft* bevorzugte man die „Formalisirung des Stiftungsgeschäfts"[9]; ebenso wurde für die *„fiduziarische Stiftung* in Form der Schenkung" mit eingehender Begründung der Formzwang jedenfalls für das Schenkungsversprechen festgehalten[10]. Im Sachenrecht wurde die hypothekarische Sicherung von *Inhaberpapieren* auf den Namen und mit Eintragung eines Treuhänders diskutiert und eine „verschiedene juristische Auffassung der Rechtsverhältnisse des Treuhänders" in diesem Fall festgestellt[11]. Man ließ hier die Eintragung der in der Praxis bereits üblichen Treuhandposition aus speziellen Erwägungen zu. Im Erbrecht diskutierte man bei der *Testamentsvollstreckung* ausführlich „die geschichtliche Entwicklung des Instituts der Testamentsvollstreckung" seit dem „altdeutschen Institute des Treuhänders und des Salmanns". Ausdrücklich wollte man jedoch „mit Rücksicht auf das Ver-

---

7 *F. W. Maitland,* Trust und Korporation, Zeitschrift für das Privat- und öffentliche Recht der Gegenwart 32 (1905) 1 - 76, 6.

8 Protokolle der Kommission für die zweite Lesung des Entwurfs des Bürgerlichen Gesetzbuchs, 7 Bde., Berlin, 1897 - 99, Band II, S. 364.

9 Protokolle (Fn. 8) Band I, 590.

10 Protokolle (Fn. 8) Band I, 34.

11 Protokolle (Fn. 8) Band III, 674 f.

kehrsbedürfnis ... von der Gewährung eines kausal bedingten Verfügungsrechts Abstand nehmen", um die dingliche Lage zweifelsfreier zu halten. „Es bleibe demnach nichts anderes übrig, als dem Vollstrecker ein absolut freies Verfügungsrecht zu gewähren, da jede andere Schranke die Gefahr nahe lege, daß die Erreichung des Zweckes der Testamentsvollstreckung, den letzten Willen des Erblassers zur Durchführung zu bringen, erheblich erschwert werde"[12]. Der Gesetzgeber hat sich also sehr intensiv und an den wichtigsten praktischen Punkten mit Treuhand befaßt. Er tat dies keineswegs begriffsjuristisch und durchaus geschichtsbewußt. Er hat sich bewußt gegen etwas wie eine „germanische" (*Schultze*), richtiger: „altdeutsche" (BGB-Diskussion), Kontinuität entschieden.

III. Das Beispiel *Franz Beyerle* (1932): ewige Grundformen als bleibende Substanz, aktuelle Lehre und Fingerzeig für die Zukunft

Mein zweites Beispiel lenkt den Blick auf ein berühmtes kleines Buch des Rechtshistorikers und Privatrechtlers *Franz Beyerle*. Es entstand 1931 / 32 aus seiner Antrittsrede bei der Übernahme seiner Professur in Frankfurt am Main. Das Büchlein spielt eine prominente Rolle in der deutschen Treuhandliteratur, die es immer respektvoll als gewissermaßen genial zitiert. Sein Titel lautet „Die Treuhand im Grundriß des deutschen Privatrechts"[13]. Für die Antrittsrede eines Rechtshistorikers ist das ein merkwürdiger Titel: Welches deutsche Privatrecht, welchen Grundriß meint er? Denn *Beyerle* meint nicht etwa das geltende Privatrecht, also das Bürgerliche Gesetzbuch von 1900. Vor 1900 gab es in Deutschland bayerisches, badisches, württembergisches, hessisches, sächsisches, preußisches und anderes Privatrecht, aber auch ein deutsches? Das war sehr umstritten. Um 1300 andererseits, im Ausklang des großen juristischen 12. Jahrhunderts mit seinen Rechtsbüchern, gab es zwar einen Sachsenspiegel und einen Schwabenspiegel, viel Kaiserrecht, viel Kanonisches Recht und auch einiges Stadtrecht – aber ein deutsches Privatrecht? Aus einer gemeinsamen deutschen Rechtsquelle?

Für *Beyerle* liegt in alledem kein Problem. Er sucht abseits von diesen schärfer gestellten Fragen „einen dem altdeutschen Recht und seinen eigenen Baugedanken wirklich gemäßen Grundriß seiner Darstellung" (S. 48)[14]. Er geht ohne weiteres von einer mittelalterlichen Formkraft aus: „Mit kühner Schöpferkraft gab sich die mittelalterliche Welt, seit sie bei Sinnen ihres eigenen Lebens war, aus dem schlichten Formenschatz ihres Alltags heraus ein Normgehäuse, das die reichgestaffelte und durchgegliederte Gesellschaft in großen konstruktiven Maßen und Formen umgab und ihren Sinngehalt zu organischem Ausdruck brachte" (ebda).

---

12 Protokolle (Fn. 8) Band V, 280 f.

13 *Franz Beyerle*, Die Treuhand im Grundriß des deutschen Privatrechts, Weimar, 1932, 48 Seiten.

14 Diese Seitenangaben beziehen sich auf *Beyerle* (Fn. 13).

Auch *Beyerles* Beitrag ist getragen von einem starken Kontinuitätsappell. Er fährt nämlich fort:

> „Wenn die Meisterwerke der Romanik und Gothik für den gegenwartsverwurzelten Baumeister trotz allen Abstands der Formensprache doch ein ewig Neues sind und bleiben: sollte nicht auch die lebensstarke Rechtskultur unseres Mittelalters wenigstens dem aufgeschlosseneren Gegenwartsjuristen doch eine eindrucksvolle Lehre und ein oft genug entscheidender Fingerzeig für Zukunftswege werden können?"

Obwohl *Beyerle* die Distanz zum Mittelalter deutlich bewußt ist, und obwohl er seinen Apell zurücknimmt auf „Lehre" und „Fingerzeig", betont auch er die Lebensstärke und damit die Kontinuität und mit besonderer Emphase. Sein Argument ist nicht mehr Schultzes „germanische Gestaltung", sondern allgemeiner und subtiler die „eindrucksvolle Lehre". Das „Eindrucksvolle" und die „Lehre" liegen freilich weniger in den Quellen als in *Beyerles* Interpretation. Er sieht nämlich im deutschen Privatrecht eine überzeitliche Trias von „Grundformen persönlicher Verkettung" (S. 16 ff.), das heißt, eine „Dreizahl wesentlichster Typen: Synallagma, Gesamthand und Treuhand" (17). In diesem subtil gespreizten Text – „wesentlichst" will das Wesentliche noch steigern – wird Treuhand also zu einer ewigen *Grundform.* Geschickt werden Entwicklungsstufen gebildet, um die offensichtlichen Unterschiede im Verlauf von tausend Jahren plausibel und passend gerichtet zu verbinden. Und geschickt wird die Innenseite der Treuhand, das heißt die Zweckabrede, für wesentlich erklärt – gegen Schultze, der sonst als meisterhaft bezeichnet wird. Auf diese Weise betrifft der offensichtliche „Wandel der Außenseite" (15) eben nur die Außenseite und darf als ein bloßer „Formwandel" (15) begriffen werden, der die Substanz unberührt läßt. Man muß nur noch in diesem äußeren Wandel „das Grundverhältnis" (15) richtig erfassen, um im „Innenverhältnis ... geschichtlich das Wesentlichere" zu erkennen. In diesem Sinne ist das Innenverhältnis „gleichsam der feste Fußpunkt im Wandel der Außenformen" (8).

Die Treuhandgeschichte zerfällt also in ein „äußeres Rechtskleid" (8) und das geschichtlich Wesentlichere und „Wesentlichste". Die ganze Rede und Schrift ist von dieser Sprache durchzogen, die einer spezifischen Grammatik folgt. Es ist ein sprachlich-logisches Hexenkabinett, das *Beyerle* hier vorführt. Aus harmlosen Wendungen wie innen – außen, wesentlich – wesentlicher – wesentlichst, Außenseite – Formwandel usw. wird eine substantielle Perspektive. Auf diese Weise kann der Kern der Treuhand bleiben, und nur die Schale ist verschieden. Diese Perspektive produziert also auf subtilere Weise als bei *Schultze* das Gleiche – Kontinuität.

IV. Das Beispiel *Otto Stobbe* (1868): Fälle und Funktionen gestern und heute

Eine dritte berühmte Abhandlung bietet ein ganz anderes Bild von Treuhandforschung. *Beyerle* hatte viel von „funktionell" und „Funktion der Rechtsfigur"

(15) gesprochen. Er wollte diese Funktion „genetisch, das heißt aus der Lebenslage verständlich machen". Diese kryptische Formel steht im Rahmen der Konjunktur des Lebens und der Wirklichkeit in der Rechtswissenschaft seit 1900[15]. Während bei *Beyerle* das Stichwort „Funktion" also eine etwas kryptische Verweisformel auf „Leben" bedeutet, hatte man es 1868 schon einmal ganz anders verwendet. Gemeint ist *Otto Stobbe,* wieder ein Rechtshistoriker und Privatrechtsjurist, tätig in Leipzig etwa um 1860. Er schrieb 1868 „Ueber die Salmannen" – lapidar und klar schon im Titel. Ihm kommt es „hauptsächlich" darauf an, „nachzuweisen, in wie verschiedenen Fällen man Salmannen hinzuzog, und welche verschiedenen Funktionen man durch ihre Vermittlung zu erreichen suchte"[16].

Stobbe spricht eine ganz andere Sprache, man spürt eine ganz andere Forschungsweise. *Stobbe* geht es um „nachweisen", um Fälle und konkrete Funktionen dabei – und so führte er es durch, aufschlußreich und grundlegend bis heute, von Urkunde zu Urkunde, von Fall zu Fall, vorsichtig erklärend. *Stobbe* hat kein Kontinuitätsproblem bei seiner Quellenauswahl, bei seiner Quellenanalyse und bei seinen aktuellen Folgerungen. Das bedeutete übrigens nicht, daß ihn die Kontinuitätsfrage nicht berührt hätte. Kein anderer als er hat das vor *Gierke* maßgebende „Handbuch des deutschen Privatrechts" begründet, pünktlich zum „Neuen Reich" seit 1871 und zuletzt in 3. Auflage in fünf Bänden seit 1893.

V. Bilanz: Kontinuitätsfeststellung, Gleichheitsbehauptung und *ceteris paribus.* Die Methode vergleichender Funktionsanalyse in Rechtsvergleichung (*Hein Kötz* 1963) und Rechtsgeschichte

Was will ich mit diesen drei berühmten Beispielen[17] belegen? Ich will damit nicht zeigen, daß Kontinuität eine verfehlte Fragestellung wäre. Allerdings scheint die Kontinuitätssuche besondere Gefahren mit sich zu führen. Sie führt offenbar leichter auf historische und methodische Abwege und Auswege, als wenn man sich mit Distanz und Diskontinuitäten bescheidet. *Stobbes* Untersuchungen überzeugen noch immer; von *Schultze* und *Beyerle* kann man das nicht sagen. Lassen sie mich dies auf den meines Erachtens entscheidenden theoretischen Punkt bringen.

---

15 Meisterhaft dazu *Karl Engisch,* Die Idee der Konkretisierung in Recht und Rechtswissenschaft unserer Zeit, 1953, 2. um ein Nachwort ergänzte Auflage 1968; vgl. zur Weimarer Lage auch *J. Rückert,* Richtertum als Organ des Rechtsgeistes: die Weimarer Erfüllung einer alten Versuchung, in: K. W. Nörr, B. Schefold und F. Tenbruck (Hrsg.), Geisteswissenschaften zwischen Kaiserreich und Republik: Zur Entwicklung von Nationalökonomie, Rechtswissenschaft und Sozialwissenschaft im 20. Jahrhundert, Wiesbaden, 1994, S. 267 - 313, 306 ff.

16 *Otto Stobbe,* Ueber die Salmannen, ZRG 7 (1868) 405 - 438, 406 f.

17 Ein viertes müßte sein die große Arbeit von *Wolfgang Siebert,* Das rechtsgeschäftliche Treuhandverhältnis: Ein dogmatischer und rechtsvergleichender Beitrag zum allgemeinen Treuhandproblem, Marburg, 1933, XXXXII und 439 S.

Kontinuitätsbehauptungen sind ein Fall von *Gleichheitsbehauptungen*. Die Achillesferse des Gleichstellens, also auch des Verbindens mit dem Bande der Kontinuität, ist die *ceteris – paribus – Bedingung*. Dazu mein letztes Beispiel – auch ein berühmtes Buch über Treuhand.

Ich meine die brillante Dissertation, „Trust und Treuhand: Eine rechtsvergleichende Darstellung des anglo-amerikanischen trust und funktionsverwandter Institute des deutschen Rechts", von *Hein Kötz*[18]. Der Name des Autors wird Ihnen schon sagen, daß dies keine rechtshistorische, sondern eine rechtsvergleichende Arbeit ist. Auch *Kötz* schreibt über „Funktionen", wie schon der Titel ausweist. Sein gemeinsamer Nenner sind „funktionsverwandte Institute". Wie *Stobbe* hundert Jahre zuvor in historischer Perspektive zu den Salmannen, schreibt *Kötz* konkret zu Fallgruppen in horizontaler Vergleichung mit dem anglo-amerikanischen Recht. Schon ein Blick in seine Gliederung zeigt prägnant die Gedankenführung nach „Hauptfunktionen". Es geht dort um den Trust „als Mittel langfristiger Nachlaßbindung", als „Mittel der Vermögenswidmung zu gemeinnützigen Zwecken", als „Mittel der Vermögensverwaltung zugunsten von Personenmehrheiten", als Mittel „der Zuweisung fremder Geschäftserfolge an den Berechtigten" und als Mittel „der Rückabwicklung fehlerhafter Vermögensverfügungen" – so die zentralen Abschnitte und Überschriften im 3. Kapitel. Rechtsfiguren werden hier als Mittel zur Lösung von praktisch-juristischen und ökonomischen Aufgaben verstanden. Aber *Kötz* beschränkt sich nicht auf die isolierte Funktionsanalyse, er bietet etwas Zusätzliches, er vergleicht die Funktionserfüllungen, nicht nur die Normen[19]. Der gemeinsame Bezugspunkt bei seinem Vergleichen ist seine Art von Funktionsbetrachtung. Diese Funktionsbetrachtung meint nicht wie die erwähnte *Beyerles* eine entwicklungsgeschichtliche Funktion der Rechtsfiguren, sondern ähnlich wie bei *Stobbe* die praktisch-juristische Funktion dieser Rechtsfiguren. Sie sollen bestimmte gesellschaftlich-ökonomische Aufgaben lösen. Diese Vergleiche gelingen *Kötz* vorzüglich aufklärend und wirken trotz des erheblichen Abstraktionsniveaus nicht künstlich. Im deutschen wie im anglo-amerikanischen Recht lassen sich die Rechtsfiguren gleichermaßen als Mittel zur Lösung analoger Aufgaben verstehen. Viel schwieriger wäre ein solches Vergleichen in Richtung langobardische oder germanische oder deutschrechtliche Treuhand. Warum? – nicht wegen der historischen Distanz allein. Aber offenbar ist bei *Kötz'* Gegenständen die *ceteris-paribus-Bedingung* im wesentlichen erfüllt. Englisches, amerikanisches und deutsches Recht der Jahre vor 1963 sind sinnvoll vergleichbar, wenn man nur die Funktionsfallgruppen geschickt genug wählt und genau genug auf die praktischen Ergebnisse achtet, die erreicht werden sollen oder nicht erreicht werden sollen. Die prozessua-

---

18 *Hein Kötz*, Trust und Treuhand: Eine rechtsvergleichende Darstellung des anglo-amerikanischen trust und funktionsverwandter Institute des deutschen Rechts, Göttingen, 1963, 174 S.

19 Wie sehr man sonst im Normvergleich steckenblieb, zeigt etwa eine an sich informative Arbeit wie die von *J. F. P. Töndury*, Die Treuhand in rechtsvergleichender Darstellung, Zürich, 1912.

len, ökonomischen, sozialen und anderen Randbedingungen von Trust und Treuhand ändern offenbar an den wesentlichen juristischen Lösungsmöglichkeiten und Lösungszielen nichts. Deutschland, England und die U.S.A. sind in diesem Punkte vor 1963 ähnlich genug. Andererseits erweisen sich zu weit gespannte Vergleiche über die *ceteris-paribus-Bedingung* hinaus an diesem Beispiel als lebensgefährlich bzw. spekulativ. Die UdSSR von vor 1963 oder China sind eben nicht einbezogen – und auch nicht „The Louisiana Private-law System: The Best of Both Worlds"[20]. Genau am *trust* zeigt sich hier die etwas vertrackte Mischung von Kontinuität und Diskontinuität, die entsteht, wenn ein *Civil-Law*-System Trust-Elemente importiert[21].

Wie sieht es aus, wenn man die Vergleichung von der Horizontale über den Kanal und das große Meer in die *Vertikale* wendet, also in die historischen Gefilde bis hin zu den Römern? Es ist klar, daß ähnliche Fallgruppen existieren, wir haben es vielfach gehört. Man kann vergleichen, man kann Kontinuitäten und Diskontinuitäten diskutieren. Aber es ist auch klar, daß ein Blick auch nur auf die prozessualen Bedingungen, auf die performance-Frage, ab ca. 1800 wesentliche Divergenzen offenbart, zu England wie zur gesamten Epoche davor. Und es ist auch klar, daß der juristische Kontext von Trust und Treuhand sich im Laufe der geschichtlichen Vorgänge sehr wandelt. Die *ceteris-paribus-Bedingung* ist hier im wesentlichen nicht gegeben. Während für England, die U.S.A und Westdeutschland vor 1963 man sich mit der Vermutung begnügen kann, daß die Verhältnisse im wesentlichen ähnlich sind, muß für diese fernen historischen Zeiten das gerade Gegenteil behauptet werden: Es gilt die *gegenteilige Vermutung*. Die alten Worte bedeuten meist ganz anderes, obwohl sie vielfach gleich klingen. Trust und Treuhand waren z. B. Instrumente, um Rechtsunsicherheiten zu beseitigen oder ständische Grenzen zu umgehen, im Lehenrecht; oder um Mängel an Rechtsfähigkeit zu überwinden, die der ständischen Gesellschaft sehr vertraut waren; oder um Verhältnisse auf Dauer zu stellen gegenüber einer sehr unsicheren Rechtsumwelt und Allgemeinumwelt. Wird aber die Rechtssicherheit stark verbessert, etwa durch zentrale verläßliche Justiz, durch klare Gesetzestatbestände und / oder gesicherte Judikatur, durch eine geschulte Juristenprofession usw., so wird diese Art von Trust und Treuhandfunktion uninteressant. Mindestens verlagert sie sich in Spezialprobleme. Für das BGB in Deutschland nahm man genau diese umfassende Rechtssicherheit als gegeben in Anspruch und konnte in der Tat von ihr ausgehen. Die erwähnten Bemerkungen in den Protokollen zur Beratung des BGB mögen als Beleg genügen.

Andere und neuere Trusts und Treuhandschaften waren z. B. eine Art kautelarjuristische Erfindung zur Kreditsicherung wie die Sicherungsübereignung. Solche Treuhandschaften sind immer noch aktuell, Geld wird weiter gebraucht. Dem deutschen Gesetzgeber gelang deren Bändigung und Kanalisierung in gesetzlichen Tat-

---

20 Nach dem Titel von *Joachim Zekoll*, (1995) 10 Tulane European and Civil Law Forum 1 - 30.

21 Dazu *Zekoll* (Fn. 20) 21 - 27.

beständen nicht, ein Hauptbeispiel ist die Sicherungsübereignung. Hier kommt es dann unter neuen Bedingungen zu sehr ähnlichen Rechtsproduktionen, die gleichwohl in ganz verschiedenen juristischen Kontexten verwendet werden und von diesen abhängen.

Mein kleiner Gang durch berühmte Beispiele der deutschen Treuhandforschung mag also fünf Punkte verdeutlicht haben:

- zum einen als kleine Forschungsgeschichte die berühmten *Beispiele* selbst;
- zum zweiten drei bis vier verschiedene *Arten* historischen und rechtsvergleichenden Zugriffs;
- zum dritten die *methodische Eigenart* von Kontinuitätsfeststellungen;
- zum vierten die spezifischen Gefahren dieser Feststellungen wegen der schwierigen Überprüfung der *ceteris-paribus-Bedingung* und
- zum fünften und vor allem, die für ein nichtdeutsches und gar englisch-amerikanisches Publikum ziemlich fremde *Methode,* Kontinuität zu ermitteln. Man behauptet, das ewige und lebenskräftige Wesen gewisser Rechtsformen gefunden zu haben – direkter bei *Schultze,* subtil bei *Beyerle,* gleich zeitbedingt und brüchig bei beiden.

Diese Technik der Kontinuitätsherstellung ist eine fachwissenschaftliche Erbschaft kontinentaler metaphysischer Philosophie, die so ihren großen Systemen immer wieder eindrucksvoll die erwünschte Einheit geschaffen hatte. Man muß sie ernst nehmen, weil sie sehr ernsthaft gerade im deutschen Wissenschaftsbereich und sogar in der an sich praktisch nüchternen Jurisprudenz verwendet wurde und wird[22]. Aber philosophische Verbindungs- und Gleichstellungsmethoden dürfen nicht unbesehen auf wissenschaftliche Forschungfragen übertragen werden.

---

22 Es sei gestattet, auf einen Titel hinzuweisen, dem man es nicht ansieht, daß er eine Charakteristik solcher Forschungslogik enthält, *J. Rückert,* „Das gesunde Volksempfinden" – eine Erbschaft Savignys?, ZSS (RA) 103 (1986) 199 - 247, hier besonders 224 - 235; weitergeführt in *idem,* Der Rechtsbegriff der Deutschen Rechtsgeschichte in der NS-Zeit: Der Sieg des „Lebens" und des konkreten Ordnungsdenkens, seine Vorgeschichte und seine Nachwirkungen, in: J. Rückert und D. Willoweit (Hrsg.), Die Deutsche Rechtsgeschichte in der NS-Zeit, ihre Vorgeschichte und ihre Nachwirkungen, 1995, S. 177 - 240.

ANDREAS RICHTER*

German and American Law of Charity in the Early 19th Century

I. Introduction

German and American law of charity in the early 19th century were worlds apart. The German law of charity came under the influence of the systematic reorganization of private law undertaken by the Historical School under the guidance of *Friedrich Carl von Savigny.* The American counterpart gives us some idea of how the Americans dealt with their English legal heritage after the Revolution and, in particular, how they dealt with that unique English legal institution, the charitable trust. The Revolution gave the young republic – at least theoretically – a choice between the common law and the civil law[1]. In spite of all the differences, there is a common feature which makes a comparison of German and American law of that period attractive: distinct intellectual movements in both countries laid the bases of modern private law and the modern law of charity. It was the formative era (*Pound)* of modern private law[2]. It brought about the concepts of the foundation and the charitable corporation. The Historical School vigorously transformed the Natural law heritage of German private law by reinterpreting the ancient sources of Roman law and by adding elements of idealistic philosophy[3]. In the former co-

* I am greatly indebted to *Henry Hansmann, John Simon* and *Reinhard Zimmermann* for their unfailing support and stimulating encouragement. I would like to thank the Yale Law School for allowing me to spend four months at the School in the summer of 1997 in order to do research on this paper. I would also like to extend my thanks to the members of the International Law Staff of the Yale Law Library for their friendly and efficient help. Financial support was kindly provided by the *Arbeitskreis Wirtschaft und Recht im Stifterverband für die Deutsche Wissenschaft e.V.*, Essen.

1 Cf., on the use of continental legal materials and their influence on the American legal system, *Richard H. Helmholz,* The Use of the Civil Law in post-Revolutionary American Jurisprudence, (1992) 66 Tulane L.R. 1649 ff.; see also *Peter G. Stein,* The Attraction of the Civil Law in Post-Revolutionary America, (1966) 52 Virginia Law Review 403 ff.

2 Cf. *Lawrence M. Friedman,* A History of American Law, New York, 1973, pp. 17 ff., 24.

3 Cf. *Franz Wieacker,* A History of Private Law in Europe, trans. *Tony Weir,* Oxford, 1995, pp. 286 ff.; on the reception of the Historical School in the United States see the study by *Mathias Reimann,* Historische Schule und Common Law: Die deutsche Rechtswissenschaft im amerikanischen Rechtsdenken, Berlin, 1993. The reception started in the period after the Civil War. During the period of time that this paper deals with there was hardly any intellec-

lonies, we encounter a self-confident group of judges whose approach to the common law and judicial law-making *Llewellyn* aptly called the "grand style"[4]. This paper will take a look at the development of the law of charity in the early 19th century. Why did the Historical School introduce the distinction between the legal form of the foundation and the form of the corporation, while American law favoured one legal institution, namely the charitable corporation?

II. Common European Roots of the Law of Charity

In spite of the differences in the 19th century, we should not forget that the German and the Anglo-American legal system share common European roots in this field. These roots are mainly to be found in Roman and Canon law[5]. The Church urged the faithful to seek their salvation by bequeathing part of their wealth to the support of "pious causes", *piae causae* in the words of the Justinianic *Codex*[6]. Many privileges were granted to the charitable legacy and various charitable organizational forms[7]. These privileges were denied to the private legacy[8]. For example, no charitable legacy was allowed to fail because it was too indefinite, and gen-

---

tual exchange between the protagonists of the Historical School and the American post-Revolution jurisprudence. A noteworthy exception is *Savigny's* reference to *Story's* work on the conflict of laws. Cf. *Knut Wolfgang Nörr*, The European Side of the English Law, in: Helmut Coing and Knut Wolfgang Nörr (eds.), Englische und kontinentale Rechtsgeschichte: ein Forschungsprojekt, Berlin, 1985, p. 29.

4 *Karl N. Llewellyn*, On the Good, the True, the Beautiful in the Law, (1942) 9 University of Chicago L.R. 224 ff. The exceptional nature of the period after the Revolution until the beginning of the Civil War is stressed by almost all legal historians. Cf. *Grant Gilmore*, The Ages of American Law, New Haven, 1977, pp. 19 ff.; *Morton J. Horwitz*, The Transformation of American law, 1780 - 1860, Cambridge Mass., 1977, pp. 1 ff.

5 Cf. the paper by *Robert Feenstra* in this volume. On trusts and trust-like devices in Roman law, see *David Johnston's* chapter in the present book.

6 *Feenstra* (n. 5) text at n. 15; *Reiner Schulze*, Stiftungsrecht, in: Handwörterbuch zur deutschen Rechtsgeschichte, vol. 4, Berlin, 1990, cols. 1980 ff.; *Helmut Coing*, Geschichte, in: Werner Seifart (ed.), Handbuch des Stiftungsrechts, München, 1987, § 5 nn. 18 ff.; *Hans-Rudolf Hagemann*, Die Stellung der piae causae nach justinianischem Recht, Basel, 1953, pp. 15 f.; *Joseph Kohler*, Über das Recht der Stiftungen, Archiv für Bürgerliches Recht 3 (1890) 277 ff.

7 See the chapter by *Reinhard Zimmermann* in the present volume at II. 2.

8 The rule "nemo pro parte testatus ..." was inapplicable in the case of *dispositiones ad pias causas*. Cf. *Coing* (n. 6) § 5 n. 21 with reference to *Andreas Tiraquellus*, De privilegiis piae causae tractatus (1560) and *Wolfgang Adam Lauterbach*, Collegium theoretico-practicum ad quinquaginta Pandectarum libros (1706 - 14); *Zimmermann* (n. 7) at II. 2 and III. 3 a). For German law, see *Dieter Pleimes*, Irrwege der Dogmatik im Stiftungsrecht, Münster / Köln, 1954, pp. 15 f.; *Otto von Gierke*, Das deutsche Genossenschaftsrecht, vol. 3, Die Staats- und Korporationslehre des Altertums und ihre Aufnahme in Deutschland, Berlin, 1881, pp. 760 ff. For English law, see *Gareth Jones*, History of the Law of Charity: 1532 - 1827, Cambridge, 1969.

erous rules of construction were developed to cure the uncertainty[9]. This European unity which originally existed at least intellectually was challenged by the Reformation, especially in the case of English law, and by the rise of the absolutist state[10]. But as *Robert Feenstra* rightly reminds us, "*a* foundation concept has been employed from the 12th to the 20th century"[11].

III. The German Development

1. The Medieval and Early Modern Period

It is difficult to present a clear picture of the legal status of foundations in German law. Especially in the field of trust and *Treuhand,* German legal historiography has long been bedeviled by ideological splits between the *romanistische, germanistische* and *kanonistische* schools of thought[12]. However, it is now widely recognized that a whole variety of various legal forms were used for charitable purposes during the medieval and early modern period[13] . Sometimes the fund would be administered by the church, a monastery, a town, a corporation or individual administrators. In general, the law of charity was to be treated in the context of the various corporations[14]. Little attempt was made to systematize the law or to integrate it into one legal institution[15]. Neither the Prussian *Allgemeines Landrecht* nor the Austrian *Allgemeines Bürgerliches Gesetzbuch* presented a cohesive picture[16]. In practice, the Catholic and the Protestant Churches alongside with the Territorial States played a dominant role in the administration of charities until the secularization in 1803. The more the influence of the Church waned during the era of Absolutism and the Enlightenment, the more the bases of the law of charity became questionable[17] .

---

9 *Jones* (n. 8) p. 5; for other examples see *Zimmermann* (n. 7) at II. 2 and III. 3 a).

10 For continental law, cf. *Feenstra* (n. 5) at IV.

11 *Feenstra* (n. 5) in the introductory paragraph.

12 Cf. *Zimmermann* (n. 7) at III. 1; the paper by *Sybille Hofer* in this volume, especially at II. 2 a); *Giseltraud Otten,* Die Entwicklung der Treuhandtheorie im 19. Jahrhundert, Dr. iur. thesis, Göttingen, 1975, *passim.*

13 *Feenstra* (n. 5) at I.

14 *Hermann Eichler,* Die Verfassung der Körperschaft und Stiftung, Berlin, 1986, pp. 9 ff.

15 *Otto von Gierke,* Deutsches Privatrecht, vol. 1, Leipzig, 1885, pp. 646 ff.; *Eichler* (n. 14) 43; *Schulze* (n. 6) cols. 1987 f.; *Helmut Coing,* Europäisches Privatrecht, vol. II, München, 1989, pp. 338 f.; *Hans Liermann,* Handbuch des Stiftungsrechts, Tübingen, 1963, pp. 235 ff.; *Michael Borgolte,* Die Stiftungen des Mittelalters in rechts- und sozialhistorischer Sicht, ZSS (KA) 105 (1988) 82, 83, 85.

16 Cf. *Liermann* (n. 15) 185 - 190, 247; *Eichler* (n.14) 37 - 44; *Josef Baron,* Das deutsche Vereinswesen und der Staat im 19. Jahrhundert, Dr. iur. thesis, Göttingen, 1962, pp. 19 - 24.

17 According to *Pleimes* (n. 8) 15, most German treatise-writing focused on the role of the churches and the interpretation of Catholic and Protestant Church law until around 1800.

2. The *Städel* Case

The uncertainty of the law of charity was brought to the fore when the validity of the will of a rich Frankfurt merchant called *Johann Friedrich Städel* was disputed by his next-of-kin in 1817[18]. *Städel* had left his estate to a foundation which had not yet been established. He appointed a number of friends as administrators of the foundation and executors of the will[19]. The testator stipulated that the foundation should be an entirely independent institution and that the administrators had the power to appoint their successors. *Städel,* who had been an amateur art enthusiast, gave the money for the erection of an art gallery and an art school. The will contained minute provisions for the operation of these institutions[20].

Städel's next-of-kin challenged the validity of the will on various grounds. What followed must have been one of the longest and most expensive trials in 19th century Germany. The *Städel* case raised a plethora of legal questions starting with the question whether the plaintiffs had sued the right party. Did they have to sue the art institute or the administrators? The court files remained ambiguous in this respect. Moreover, it was unclear which law was applicable. Local law in Frankfurt had changed several times between the drafting of the will and the testator's death. More importantly, *Städel* had not sought the consent of the city government. It was unclear whether such a consent was a legal prerequisite for the foundation of an independent institution. Much depended on whether this foundation was a *dispositio ad pias causas.* Of course, it was not in a strict sense, because the promotion of the arts was a purely secular purpose. But, arguably, it could still be a privileged purpose by analogy. The court realized the complexity of the matter and did what most German courts would have done at the time. It sent the files to various German law schools to have some eminent German law professors examine the case and clarify the intricacies of the German law of charity. This was an example of the well-established principle of *Aktenversendung,* and thus the *Spruchkammern* (judicial chambers) of almost all German law schools gave opinions[21]. Unfortunately, these opinions differed greatly and, in due course, more opinions were asked for in order to clarify the previous set of opinions. This procedure went on for eleven years and convinced the parties to settle out of court[22]. The *Städel* case had added a grain of confusion to the doctrinal hotchpotch.

---

18 For an overview of the trial see *Hans Kiefner,* Das Städel'sche Kunstinstitut, in: Quaderni fiorentini 11 / 12 (1982 / 83) 339 ff.; *Liermann* (n. 15) 243 ff.

19 *Kiefner* (n. 18) 344.

20 *Kiefner* (n. 18) 344.

21 *Kiefner* (n. 18) 351 ff.

22 Still early enough to avoid the entire estate being used up in legal fees. In spite of its painful birth process, the art gallery, as well as the arts school, feature prominently in Frankfurt's cultural life today.

3. The Role of *Friedrich Carl von Savigny*

When *Savigny* set out to write his seminal work, "Das System des heutigen Römischen Rechts", in the 1830s, the law of foundations was still unsettled[23]. It is unlikely that *Savigny* had previously been involved in the *Städel* litigation[24]. But he had to deal with the topic in the second volume of the "System" in which he set out to explain the law of persons on the basis of the sources of Roman law[25]. Instead of immersing himself in the details of the *Städel* litigation *Savigny* confined his discussion to a footnote. Moreover, he added, the question of state consent for the erection of an entity with legal personality was only one aspect in the adjudication of the *Städel* case; the other aspects are as irrelevant here as the result of the respective doctrinal disputes[26]. *Savigny* practices his own advice by leaving aside the vast contemporary literature on the status of foundations. Instead, he posits "that in our modern law charitable foundations are as much individual legal persons as are corporations, but it would be erroneous to classify them as corporations or to apply the legal institutions devised for corporations to foundations"[27]. It is thus that the Historical School can rightly claim the authorship for the modern concept of the foundation with its two prongs[28]: the foundation is a legal institution distinct from corporations. Secondly, foundations can have legal personality. *Savigny* supported the viewpoint of his close friend *Heise* who had been the first to suggest that funds *(Sachgesamtheiten)* could be conceptualized as legal persons alongside collective bodies *(Personengesamtheiten)*[29]. The *Sachgesamtheiten* which *Heise* had in mind were the endowment of a foundation, the *fiscus* or the *hereditas iacens*, which described the position of the estate after the testator's death and before the actual heir was known[30]. This was in 1816 and *Heise* was still influenced by Natural law writing on the subject[31]. Other authors agreed with *Hei-*

---

23 *Liermann* (n. 15) 233 ff.

24 Even though it is possible that *Savigny* was still a member of the *Spruchkollegium* when the *Königlich-Preußische-Universität zu Berlin* was asked to give an opinion. The chamber gave its opinion in June 1827 at which time *Savigny* was sick and preparing a trip to spas in Bohemia and Italy: *Kiefner* (n. 18) 352.

25 It is still not entirely clear why *Savigny* put so much stress on Roman law. Cf. *Joachim Rückert*, Idealismus, Jurisprudenz und Politik bei Friedrich Carl von Savigny, Ebelsbach, 1984, p. 57.

26 *Friedrich Carl von Savigny*, System des heutigen Römischen Rechts, vol. 2, Berlin, 1840, p. 277, fn. c).

27 *Savigny* (n. 26) 272.

28 Cf. *Robert Feenstra*, L'Histoire des Fondations, T.R. 24 (1956) 385, 388, 443 ff.; *Eichler* (n. 14) 43; *Schulze* (n. 6) cols. 1987 f.; *Coing* (n. 15) 338 f.

29 *Arnold Heise*, Grundriss eines Systems des Gemeinen Civilrechts zum Behuf von Pandecten-Vorlesungen, 2nd ed., Heidelberg, 1816, pp. 21, 23. *Heise* is generally remembered as the first scholar to have expressly applied the Pandectist system; see *Wieacker/Weir* (n. 3) 296.

30 On the *hereditas iacens*, see *Zimmermann* (n. 7) at V.

se's thesis, and the existence of foundations with legal personality was posited by some professors in the *Städel* litigation[32] . *Savigny* explained part of the confusion in the *Städel* case with the fact that the term *Stiftung* had not been reserved for the institution with legal personality[33]. After *Savigny* had given his seal of approval to the concept of the foundation with legal personality, most of the controversy about the status of foundations in German law came to an end[34]. Once again, *Savigny* turned out to be the founder of modern German private law[35]. Indeed, *Savigny's* concept of the memberless foundation as opposed to the corporation with members was received in many parts of Europe in the second half of the 19th century[36]: not only in Switzerland and Austria but also in Spain and Italy[37].

Why was *Savigny's* doctrine so effective? Mainly because *Savigny* was the first to develop an overall theory of legal personality in which each legal institution such as the corporation or the foundation found its logical place: a "closed system of institutions and rules"[38]. Even his opponents from the Germanist school like *Beseler* and *Gierke* accepted the systematic framework of his theory, although they disagreed vehemently with *Savigny* on political grounds[39]. *Savigny's* pathbreaking

---

31 *Wolfgang Henkel*, Zur Theorie der juristischen Person im 19. Jahrhundert, Dr. iur. thesis, Göttingen, 1972, pp. 49 ff.

32 *Pleimes* (n. 8) 72 ff.

33 *Savigny* (n. 26) 269.

34 Cf. *Pleimes* (n. 8) 79; *Liermann* (n. 15) 237 f. This fact highlights *Savigny's* importance as a scholar of private law. The systematization of private law was his true strength. Cf. *Rückert* (n. 25) 57 ff.; *Reinhard Zimmermann*, Savigny's Legacy, (1996) 112 L.Q.R. 576 ff.

35 *Helmut Coing*, Savignys rechtspolitische und methodische Anschauungen in ihrer Bedeutung für die gegenwärtige deutsche Rechtswissenschaft, in: Dieter Simon (ed.), Gesammelte Aufsätze zu Rechtsgeschichte, Rechtsphilosophie und Zivilrecht, Frankfurt / Main, 1982, vol. 1, p. 178. For a biographical sketch of *Savigny's* life, see *Erik Wolf*, Grosse Rechtsdenker der Deutschen Geistesgeschichte, 4th ed., Tübingen 1963, pp. 467 ff.

36 *Feenstra* (n. 28) 388: "... Allemagne, qui semble bien être la patrie de la 'fondation – personne juridique' opposée à la corporation ...".

37 For the reception in Austria, see *Wilhelm Brauneder*, Von der moralischen Person des ABGB zur juristischen Person der Privatrechtswissenschaft, Quaderni fiorentini 11 / 12 (1982 / 83) 272 f.; for the reception in Spain and Latin America, see *Ramon Badenes Gasset*, Las fundaciones de derecho privado, Barcelona, 1960, pp. 68 ff.; for the European reception, see *Coing* (n. 15) 353.

38 *Wieacker / Weir* (n. 3) 343.

39 The similarities between *Savigny's* treatment of legal persons and *Beseler's* are striking. See *Georg Beseler*, System des gemeinen deutschen Privatrechts, vol. 1, Leipzig, 1847, pp. 349 ff. Citing from *Savigny's* System des heutigen römischen Rechts, *Beseler* took over the stress on *Vermögensfähigkeit* (p. 350), the distinction between corporation and foundation (p. 351, pp. 383 ff.) and the systematic treatment of the subject as a *Rechtsinstitut* (p. 349). A minor systematic difference is that *Beseler* still treats the *hereditas iacens* as a legal personality (pp. 351 f.). However, *Beseler's* treatment of the *hereditas iacens* reveals to what extent *Savigny* ranked far superior as a systematic thinker. *Beseler* concludes his treatment of the subject by saying that "even though the legal personality of the *hereditas iacens* is not entirely without practical relevance, the institute has only minor importance, and therefore, in a sys-

theory still serves as the intellectual starting-point of every debate in modern German private law about legal personality[40].

4. *Savigny's* Theory of Legal Personality

Savigny rejected the Natural law concept of legal personality[41]. There are three striking differences between his theory of legal personality and the doctrine of *persona moralis*[42]. Firstly, Natural law had integrated individuals and collective bodies in one single concept, the concept of *persona moralis*[43]. But *Savigny* strongly believed that a difference should be made between individuals and collective bodies[44]. Secondly, *Savigny* criticized Natural law for failing to distinguish clearly between moral and legal obligations of the individual and of collective bodies[45]. That is why – from a terminological point of view – he preferred the term *juristische Person* which had been introduced by his teacher *Hugo*[46]. And thirdly,

---

tematic treatment of legal personality ('principienmäßige Behandlung der Lehre von den juristischen Personen'), it is of no further interest" (p. 352). Cf. *Karl-Jürgen Bieback,* Die öffentlich-rechtliche Körperschaft: Ihre Entstehung, die Entwicklung ihres Begriffes und die Lehre vom Staat und den innerstaatlichen Verbänden in der Epoche des Konstitutionalismus in Deutschland, Berlin, 1976, p. 110; on the theory of the legal personality of the Germanist school see *Jan Schröder,* Zur Älteren Genossenschaftstheorie, in: Quaderni fiorentini 11 / 12 (1982 / 83) 399 ff.

40 *Werner Flume,* Savigny und die Lehre von der juristischen Person, in: Okko Behrends *et al.* (eds.), Festschrift für Franz Wieacker, Göttingen, 1978, p. 340; *idem,* Die juristische Person, Berlin, Heidelberg, New York, 1983, *passim; Karsten Schmidt,* Einhundert Jahre Verbandstheorie im Privatrecht, Hamburg, 1987, pp. 7 ff.

41 *Savigny* (n. 24) 240. *Savigny* does not expressly mention these reasons. Cf. *Malte Dieselhorst,* Zur Theorie der Juristischen Person bei Carl Friedrich von Savigny, in: Quaderni fiorentini 11 / 12 (1982 / 83) 319 ff.; *Henkel* (n. 31) 71 ff.; *Hermann Eichler,* Personenrecht, Wien, New York, 1983, pp. 329 ff.

42 The influence of Natural law and the Law of Reason on *Savigny's* views is still not satisfactorily explained. See *Rückert* (n. 25) 57.

43 *Helmut Coing,* Zur Geschichte des Privatrechtssystems, Frankfurt, 1962, p. 48.

44 On the dichotomy between individual and legal persons, see *Felix Schikorski,* Die Auseinandersetzung um den Körperschaftsbegriff in der Rechtslehre des 19. Jahrhunderts, Berlin, 1978, pp. 53 ff. Dichotomies feature prominently in *Savigny's* systematic thinking. Cf. *Rückert* (n. 25) 358 ff. on the "universal dichotomy" between private and public law (*Universalprinzip).*

45 This critique is also encapsulated in *Savigny's* subdivision of the general principle of law (*allgemeines Rechtsprinzip)* into a dual principle of life (*doppeltes Lebensprinzip),* one being political and the other technical. Cf. *Okko Behrends,* Geschichte, Politik und Jurisprudenz in F. C. v. Savignys System des heutigen römischen Rechts, in: *idem et al.* (eds.), Römisches Recht in der europäischen Tradition, Ebelsbach, 1985, pp. 259 ff.

46 *Theodor Viehweg,* Einige Bemerkungen zu Gustav Hugos Rechtsphilosophie, p. IX, in: *idem* (ed.), Gustav Hugo, Lehrbuch des Naturrechts 1819, (reprint) Glashütten im Taunus, 1971; *Henkel* (n. 31) 46 ff. On *Hugo's* contribution to the Historical School see *Wieacker/*

he found that the concept of *persona moralis* was too unclear in many respects. Even if an entity was characterized as a *persona moralis,* this would not entail any qualification as to whether legal obligations were those of the entity as such or of the members of the entity as individuals[47]. *Savigny* introduced a new theory of legal personality which distinguishes first of all between individuals (*natürliche Personen)* and legal persons (*juristische Personen).*

(a) Natural Persons (natürliche Personen)

"Each individual, and only the individual can have legal personality"[48]. *Savigny* was influenced by idealistic philosophy[49]. This explains to a great extent his criticism of Natural law and of the Law of Reason[50].The moral autonomy of the individual forms the philosophical basis of *Savigny's* definition of individual legal personality[51]. It also shines through in *Savigny's* concept of the law. "The law is the bulwark within which the existence and potential of each individual is assured free room for play"[52]. His understanding of law differed from that of the Natural law writers insofar as law no longer had the task of prescribing a set of moral rules for the individual but of securing an area of freedom for the individual in which he could operate independently of the will of anybody else[53]. It was because of *Savigny's* belief in the autonomy of the individual that he stressed the distinction between the individual person and the legal person.

(b) Legal Persons (juristische Personen)

Considering the new concept of individual personality as elaborated by the philosophy of the Enlightenment, it is clear that *Savigny* sees the scope of the legal person as much more limited[54]. In *Savigny's* system the legal person is an entity which artificially comes into being and is able to enter into legal relations[55]. It only

Weir (n. 3) 300 ff. On the academic relationship between *Hugo* and *Savigny,* see *Behrends* (n. 45) 270, fn. 25.

47 *Savigny* (n. 26) 329.

48 *Savigny* (n. 26) 2.

49 *Rückert* (n. 25) *passim.*

50 *Wieacker/Weir* (n. 3) 281 f.

51 To what extent his concept of law is influenced by *Kant* is disputed. *Rückert* (n. 25) 232 ff., 287 ff., 301 ff. sees *Savigny* as being more influenced by *Herder* and *Schelling;* sceptical about an influence by *Kant* is *Franz Zwilgmeyer,* Die Rechtslehre Savignys – Eine rechtsphilosophische und geistesgeschichtliche Untersuchung, Leipzig, 1929, pp. 39 ff., 53; *Behrends* (n. 45) 270.

52 *Wieacker/Weir* (n. 3) 282.

53 *Savigny*, System des heutigen Römischen Rechts, vol. 1, Berlin, 1840, p. 333.

54 Cf. *Coing* (n. 43) 48.

comes into being for legal purposes: in other words, legal persons are fictions of the law[56]. *Savigny* introduces two further subdivisions. Firstly, he distinguishes between those with a "natural" or "necessary" existence such as municipalities or villages and those with an "artificial" or "willed" *(willkührlich)* existence such as foundations and *Gesellschaften,* the German form of the Roman law *societas*[57]. The latter group concerns entities formed by private initiative. But a private process of creation does not necessarily mean that the legal person, once it has been formed, is to be classified as a private law institution. Furthermore, *Savigny* stressed the importance of the consent of a state authority for the creation of a legal person and such consent could transform the private initiative into a public law institution[58]. The second subdivision is the one between foundations and corporations. He tells us that corporations had a visible substance, namely their members, whereas foundations had no members and thus were legal persons without substance[59]. *Savigny* does not distinguish between corporations or foundations of private law and those of public law[60]. Finally, the state acting in private law matters would appear as the *fiscus*[61]. *Savigny* notes that it would lead to confusion if one were to conceptualize the state as a corporation[62].

5. The Foundation as a Legal Person

(a) Advantages of a Foundation with Legal Personality

Savigny's theory of legal personality brought about legal certainty[63]. Considering the *Städel* case, this was no minor achievement. The personification of an independent legal person meant that the law could be developed with a view to making sure that the purpose as set by the founder would be pursued by the administration of the foundation[64]. Legal certainty was further enhanced by *Savigny's* insistence

55 *Savigny* (n. 26) 239: The term "Vermögensfähigkeit" means the ability to enter into legal relations. The legal person can be a right-and-duty bearing unit. *Savigny* mentions the following legal relations *(Rechtsverhältnisse)*: obligations, property, acquisition through inheritance. See *Savigny* (n. 26) 239.

56 *Savigny* (n. 26) 240 f.

57 *Savigny* (n. 26) 242.

58 *Savigny* (n. 26) 277 f.

59 *Savigny* (n. 26) 243 f.

60 Concerning foundations, *Savigny* (n. 26) 280; or concerning corporations, *Savigny* (n. 26) 332.

61 *Savigny* (n. 26) 245.

62 *Savigny* (n. 26) 245.

63 *Savigny* (n. 26) 269.

64 This was a step which *Savigny* did not take himself but he paved the way for the future doctrinal development in that direction, especially under the influence of the Pandectists whose will theory was applied to the field of foundations.

upon official consent before a foundation could be erected[65]. Before giving its consent the state could exercise its discretion as to whether the particular foundation was desirable or not[66]. This system was even more effective because the new concept of the independent foundation with legal personality consumed the old concept of *unselbständige Stiftung* without legal personality[67]. *Savigny* had put forward very similar arguments when the Prussian Stock Corporation Act was considered in the Upper House of Prussia in 1843. According to Prussian law, the board of a stock corporation had to ask for a royal privilege to be recognized as a legal person. *Savigny* argued that this restrictive system should be kept under the new Act in spite of its impracticability because it forced the stock corporation to seek the royal privilege. This would allow the state to tie the granting of legal personality to conditions[68].

(b) A Comparison with Mühlenbruch

A comparison with *Christian Friedrich Mühlenbruch's* encyclopedic treatment of the *pia corpora* and the law of foundations in *Glück's Pandecten* will further underline *Savigny's* systematizing achievement[69]. *Mühlenbruch's* style is an example of the "elegant antiquarianism of yesteryear"[70] which *Savigny* had rejected from early on. Undoubtedly, *Mühlenbruch* was more of a specialist in the field than *Savigny,* for he had prepared the opinion of Halle law school in the *Städel* case[71]. In spite of the difference in style, the two men did share similar viewpoints. From the perspective of legal theory, *Mühlenbruch* shared *Savigny's* view that a specifically legal doctrine of legal personality had to be developed and that *Heise's* distinction between *Sachgesamtheiten* and *Personengesamtheiten* was the right starting-point[72]. As for legal politics, *Mühlenbruch* also posited that a legal person could only be created with the consent of the state[73].

Mühlenbruch discusses the law of foundations as a subheading in his treatment of the law of succession[74]. A testator had the right to name the poor or the sick as

65 *Savigny* (n. 26) 277 f.

66 *Savigny* (n. 26) 278 f.

67 *Pleimes* (n. 8) 72 ff., 94 f.

68 Cf. *Theodor Baums,* Einführung, in: *idem* (ed.) Gesetz über die Aktiengesellschaften für die königlich preußischen Staaten vom 9. November 1843, Aalen, 1981, p. 34.

69 *Christian Friedrich Mühlenbruch,* De heredibus instituendis, in: *Christian Friedrich Glück,* Ausführliche Erläuterung der Pandekten nach Hellfeld, continued by *Mühlenbruch,* vol. 39, Erlangen, 1837; vol. 40, Erlangen, 1838.

70 *Wieacker/Weir* (n. 3) 307.

71 *Kiefner* (n. 18) 367.

72 *Henkel* (n. 31) 54 ff.

73 *Mühlenbruch* (n. 69) 89 ff.

74 It is the chapter "De heredibus instituendis" in *Mühlenbruch* (n. 69) § 1438b, pp. 1 - 108.

heirs which would neither refer to any individual nor legal person but to the purpose as such[75]. *Mühlenbruch* adds that this was the reason why the Romans had developed special rules for the interpretation of *dispositiones ad pias causas*[76]. *Savigny* treats the law of foundations as a subheading of the law of persons and a private foundation of a *Stiftung* for him is just one of the various modes of the creation of the foundation. This allows him to discard the Canon law doctrines that had developed over time.

Mühlenbruch distinguishes minutely between the rules of the *pia corpora* and the secular law of foundations. It would be unthinkable to extend the "anomalous" privileges of the *pia corpora* to secular endeavors[77]. Rare exceptions had been made in the past[78]. Legacies for the promotion of schools had been accepted as *dispositiones ad pias causas*. But this was only done because of the close relationship between schooling and religion[79]. It would be inconceivable to allow a testator to found a university, just because he promoted learning[80]. It is worth noting in the passing that this was exactly what was done in England and the American colonies, the foundation of Harvard College by John Harvard (1650) being probably the most notable private foundation[81].

For *Savigny*, the distinction between *pia corpora* and secular foundation as presented by *Mühlenbruch* has only historical relevance[82]. As far as modern law is concerned, there is only one secular legal institution – the foundation – and it can be used for purposes such as the exercise of religion, learning or benevolence[83]. *Savigny* describes the historical process by which the set of recognized charitable purposes was extended to learning and by which the state had taken over the care for the poor[84]. And he concludes "that therefore, the exclusive relationship be-

---

75 *Mühlenbruch* (n. 69) 47.

76 *Mühlenbruch* (n. 69) 47.

77 *Mühlenbruch* (n. 69) 46.

78 *Mühlenbruch* (n. 69) 41.

79 *Mühlenbruch* (n. 69) 41.

80 *Mühlenbruch* (n. 69) 42.

81 Founded in 1636, "The President and Fellows of Harvard College", was incorporated in 1650: cf. *Irvin G. Wyllie,* The Search for An American Law of Charity, 1776 - 1844, (1959) 46 Mississippi Valley Historical Review 204; though it has to be added that the legal nature of the College was not classified as either private or public at the time of its foundation. This question only arose in the late 18th, early 19th centuries.

82 Even though *Savigny* generally stressed the importance of Christianity, he also shared some of the concerns of the Enlightenment about the power and wealth of the churches and monasteries. See *infra* text accompanying n. 143. On *Savigny's* religious attitudes, see *Behrends* (n. 45) 271 ff.

83 *Savigny* (n. 26) 244.

84 *Savigny* (n. 26) 271 f. The process of secularization had started with the Reformation: cf. *Liermann* (n. 15) 250 ff. However, *Liermann* stresses that it was only in the 19th century that legal doctrine took notice of this development: *Liermann* (n. 15) 252. These findings are supported by *Pleimes*' observation that most German treatise-writing focused on the role of

tween foundations and the Church, as we know it from the Justinianic law, had to be restricted"[85]. In brief, what *Savigny* presents us with is one universal legal institution which has shed its ecclesiastical roots.

(c) The Foundation as a Legal Institution (Rechtsinstitut)

Savigny integrated the various doctrinal strands into one concept. The direct reference to Roman sources allowed him to discard the tomes of contemporary literature and to refute all the minor variations which stood in the way of a general theory[86]. More importantly, it allowed him to interpret the fragmentary sources of Roman law freely and to remould the law, notwithstanding that the Romans did not know the abstract concept "legal person"[87]. *Savigny* was the first to develop the foundation as a distinct legal institution (*Rechtsinstitut)*[88]. And he was able to do so because he took a new methodological stance. His previous discovery of the *Rechtsinstitut,* a juristic emanation of idealistic philosophy, allowed him to reorganize the doctrinal material completely: "[t]he rule, as well as its counterpart in the statute, has a deeper ground in the understanding of the legal institution (*Rechtsinstitut),* and the organic nature of the legal institution becomes clear in the lively context of its components, as much as in its continuous development"[89]. There could be no better tribute to *Savigny's* genius than the fact that his critics took over his systematic framework. The similarities between the systematic elements of *Savigny's* theory of legal personality and the treatment of legal persons by the founder of the Germanist school, *Georg Beseler,* are striking[90]. *Beseler* takes over the symmetric juxtaposition of corporation and foundation[91]. He supports an integrated view of the foundation as a *Rechtsinstitut* by rejecting any subdivision into a secular *Stiftung* and *pia corpora*[92].

---

the churches and the interpretation of Catholic and Protestant Church law until around 1800: *Pleimes* (n. 8) 15.

85 *Savigny* (n. 26) 272.

86 On *Savigny's* method, cf. *Behrends* (n. 45) 262 ff.

87 *Feenstra* (n. 5) *sub* II.

88 On the concept of a legal institution and its significance for the development of German private law, see *Helmut Coing,* in: Staudinger, Kommentar zum Bürgerlichen Gesetzbuch, 12th ed., Berlin, 1980, Einl. 162 - 175, especially n. 165; see also *Behrends* (n. 45) 257 ff.

89 *Savigny* (n. 53) 9 f.

90 Cf. text accompanying n. 39.

91 *Beseler* (n. 39) 383 ff.

92 *Beseler* (n. 39) 384.

6. The Memberless Foundation and the Corporation

Feenstra points out the novelty of the concept of the Historical School: "[j]amais avant cette époque [sc. le début du XIXe siècle] on n'a considéré les fondations comme une seconde categorie de personnes juridiques à côté des corporations"[93]. *Savigny's* subdivision of legal persons into foundations and corporations is based on a purely formal distinction: corporations had members and foundations were without members[94]. In many cases foundations and corporations would be serving the same social function. *Savigny* himself admitted this in the case of universities, where some had to be classified as corporations and others as foundations[95]. But the purpose of an organization – whether it was for charitable or for business purposes – did not have any relevance for the system of private law[96]. *Savigny* was aware that there are cases where one cannot really distinguish between a foundation and a corporation[97], but this subtlety got lost when the Pandectists took over and perfected *Savigny's* system. With the *Begriffsjurisprudenz* and its formalistic theory of law[98] the distinction between corporations and foundations became axiomatic[99].

(a) The Foundation – An Invisible Legal Person?

Savigny chose the title "Foundations, or invisible legal persons" as a heading for the history of foundations[100]. *Savigny* stressed that *piae causae* were privileged by the Christian Emperors by their giving them legal personality wherever it was appropriate[101]. We now know that when *Savigny* stated this general proposition, he read too much into the Roman sources[102]. The Roman foundation was not an invi-

---

93 *Feenstra* (n. 28) 385.

94 *Savigny* (n. 26) 243 f. Again, this element of *Savigny's* theory of legal personality was taken over by *Beseler*. See *Beseler* (n. 39) 384 On the importance of such dichotomies in *Savigny's* systematic thinking, cf. *Rückert* (n. 25) 358 ff.

95 *Savigny* (n. 26) 245.

96 *Savigny* (n. 26) 240. Is this a contradiction of what *Savigny* had said in the introductory part about foundations? There he had specified a limited set of purposes for the foundation: exercise of religion, education, benevolence etc.: *Savigny* (n. 26) 244. This qualification gets more and more lost. *Beseler* draws the analogy between the *Familienfideikommiß* (a legal institute, somewhat similar to the private trust) and the private *Stiftung* for public purposes, by stressing the *voluntas testatoris* as the guiding principle behind the two institutes: *Beseler* (n. 39) 385 f.

97 *Savigny* (n. 26) 244.

98 *Wieacker/Weir* (n. 3) 341 ff.

99 *Liermann* (n. 15) 237 ff.

100 *Savigny* (n. 26) 262.

101 *Savigny* (n. 26) 269.

102 Cf. *Hagemann* (n. 6) 41, who emphasises that the modern terminology of foundation and corporation would be inadequate for use in the context of the Roman law sources.

sible legal person. Rather, it was invisible as a distinct type of legal personality as opposed to corporations. Let us recall *Feenstra's* findings on the subject: "For those types of charitable foundations where there is no visible substratum like a 'house' the texts certainly do not give any support to the concept of a foundation as a legal person, ..."[103]. The sources point more in the direction of "trust-like devices" and *Feenstra* adds that the "reluctance to recognize this simple fact has to be explained as doctrinal prejudice"[104].

(b) The Impact of the German Anstaltsstaat

When *Savigny* defined the foundation as a distinct type of legal personality, he "legalized" a general historical development. He supported the state's claim to dominate the intermediate powers of society along the lines of his organic understanding of legal history. *Savigny* does not distinguish between private and public law foundations or corporations[105]. Therefore, the term foundation is supposed to encompass not just private foundations as in the *Städel* case but, equally, all public institutions which were not completely integrated into the state, such as colleges, universities, hospitals or orphanages, but which had clearly lost their medieval corporate character. In many cases these institutions no longer had administrators who held some fiduciary or discretionary position because they were directly controlled by a church or the absolutist state[106]. *Savigny's* conceptualization of the universities is a particularly interesting one, for he acknowledges that universities used to be understood as corporations[107]. However, over time, *Savigny* tells us, these universities have become institutions of the state and thus have to be classified as foundations. He concludes that "they no longer appear to be corporations"[108]. And

---

103 *Feenstra* (n. 5) text at n. 15.

104 *Feenstra* (n. 5) text at n. 15.

105 Concerning foundations, *Savigny* (n. 26) 280; concerning corporations, *Savigny* (n. 26) 332. *Savigny* only makes a distinction with regard to their coming into existence, not their status once they are formed. On the question of public and private law in the context of his theory of legal personality, cf. *Schikorski* (n. 44) 106.

106 Much evidence of the truly revolutionary structural changes in the administration of charities is contained in a study by *Fries* on the Imperial City of Nuremberg. Cf. *Peter Fries,* Das Nürnberger Stiftungswesen vom Ende der reichsstädtischen Zeit bis zur Verwaltung der Stiftungen durch den Magistrat, etwa 1795 bis 1820, Dr. iur. thesis, Nürnberg, 1963. Because of its imperial status Nuremberg had retained much of its medieval legal culture. With its integration into Bavaria and the secularization and centralization under *Montgelas,* the administration of charities was completely turned upside down.

107 The corporate members were either the teachers or the pupils, see *Savigny* (n. 26) 245. On the structure of these universities, see *Helmut Coing,* Die juristische Fakultät und ihr Lehrprogramm, in: *idem* (ed.), Handbuch der Quellen und Literatur der Neueren Europäischen Privatrechtsgeschichte, vol. 2, 1. (Neuere Zeit 1500 - 1800), München, 1973, pp. 16 ff.

108 *Savigny* (n. 26) 245.

he remarks that the overall importance of corporations has waned because of the increasing central powers of the state[109]. The foundation of the Royal University in Berlin (1810) where *Savigny* would teach for most of his life demonstrates the point. *Fichte* had argued that the new institution should not be called a university but "Höhere staatliche Lehranstalt" to signal the break with the past[110]. *Savigny* acknowledges the same process of depersonification for the state. It would lead to confusion if one was to conceptualize the state as a corporation[111]. The State was just another *Sachgesamtheit,* although the supreme one[112].

This process of institutionalization (*Anstaltsbildung*[113] was more pronounced in the German territories than in other parts of Europe, especially in England[114]. After the Reformation, the three denominations – Catholic, Lutheran and Reformed – tried to consolidate their influence and spread their teachings by founding new centrally-controlled institutions or taking over the old ones[115]. This process of "confessionalization" (*Konfessionalisierung)* according to the principle *religio vinculum societatis* went hand in hand with the establishment of territorial states and was enhanced by the fact that the three Churches were competing[116]. Alongside

---

109 *Savigny* (n. 26) 248: "In recent times, the importance of central state power has lead to a decrease in the use of the corporation, as we have seen above (§ 86) with the example of the universities".

110 *Rudolf Vierhaus,* Friedrich Daniel Schleiermacher, in: Wolfgang Treue and Karlfried Gründer (eds.), Berlinische Lebensbilder: Wissenschaftspolitik in Berlin, Berlin, 1987, pp. 77 - 88. For *Fichte,* strict state supervision was a safeguard against the perceived maladministration (*Schlendrian)* of most German universities at the time. A very different position was taken by *Schleiermacher*, a Protestant pastor who was to become the first Dean of the Divinity School of Berlin University (1810 - 1815) and second Rector of the University in 1815. In this position he succeeded *Fichte. Schleiermacher* had argued for independence from any state intervention.

111 *Savigny* (n. 26) 245.

112 *Savigny* (n. 26) 245.

113 It is very difficult to find a proper translation for the term "Anstalt". Most dictionaries suggest the English words "establishment" or "institution". Be that as it may, the difficulty in translating the term "Anstalt" betrays a significant historic difference between German and English legal history.

114 Cf. *Hans Hattenhauer*, Europäische Rechtsgeschichte, Heidelberg, 1992, pp. 398 ff.

115 German structural historiography calls this Post-Reformation process (1555 - 1620) *Konfessionalisierung* (confessionalization). Cf. *Heinz Schilling,* Die Konfessionalisierung im Reich, Historische Zeitschrift 246 (1988) 1 - 45. The Reformed Church followed a different path but her influence in Germany decreased continuously over time. Cf. *Alexandre Ganoczy,* Calvinismus, in: Herder Staatslexikon, vol. 1, 7th ed., Freiburg, 1985, cols. 1073 ff.; *Schilling* (n. 115) 27 f., 40.

116 The term *Fürstenkonfessionalisierung* (princely confessionalization) tries to encapsulate this combination; see *Schilling* (n. 115) 11. It should be noted that English historiography uses the term confessionalization only with reference to the religious process and not the evolution of the state. *Liermann* (n. 15) 175 ff. describes how foundations came under the influence of the territorial states after the *Confessio Augustana* (1530), particularly in Protestant territories.

the evolution of the state, society was transformed from the personal and fragmentary structures which were characteristic during medieval times to institutionalized, territorial and abstract structures[117]. This is one of the reasons that Germany had a vast number of educational institutions from early on and why lawyers as loyal civil servants played such an eminent role in German society[118]. These processes were later taken over and completed by the absolutist state[119]. Therefore, in Germany, most intermediary powers were integrated into the state administration. What absolutism had not completed, was then completed by the secularization in the year 1803 on the basis of the *Reichsdeputationshauptschluß*[120].

(c) Savigny's Treatment of the Sources

Savigny approved of the process of state centralization, not so much by expressly saying so but by presenting a system where foundations are virtually integrated into the general administration of the state and where all corporations are closely supervised by the state. Prussia had even integrated the churches into its public administration[121].

The emphasis on Roman sources[122] to the neglect of the medieval tradition made it much easier for *Savigny* to conceptualize the historic development. *Gierke* later pointed out that *Savigny* – from a doctrinal point of view – was really borrowing from Canon law[123]. The Canonists played a much more important role in "la marche vers la personnification"[124]. We now know that the Romans had several kinds of juristic persons but did not theorize about them, especially not as a right-and-duty bearing unit[125] . Could it be that *Savigny* who wanted to support the claim of the state as the supervisor of all intermediary powers was not ready to deal with sources that supported the claim of the Church?

117 *Schilling* (n. 115) 6, 33.

118 *Schilling* (n. 115) 12 f.; *Coing* (n. 107) 3 ff. *Coing* analyses the same structural developments and takes universities and law schools as an example.

119 *Michael Stolleis,* Geschichte des öffentlichen Rechts in Deutschland, München, 1988, vol. 1, p. 402. *Stolleis* notes that the development of a legal system for the administration of the territorial states was a remarkable achievement for the period, but that German public law and legal philosophy failed to present a political theory of any importance.

120 *Liermann* (n. 15) 199 ff. The *Reichsdeputationshauptschluß* (25. 2. 1803) was the last legal act of the Holy Roman Empire. Some states such as Prussia did not want to wait until 1803 and started the confiscation of church property even before: *Liermann* (n. 15) 213.

121 *Liermann* (n. 15) 184 ff.

122 On *Savigny*'s treatment of the sources in the context of his theory of legal personality, see *Schikorski* (n. 44) 100 ff.

123 *Gierke* (n. 8) 279 f.

124 *Feenstra* (n. 5) text at n. 29. The term was used by the Belgian author *Pierre Gillet* in 1927.

125 *Feenstra* (n. 5) text at n. 13.

7. Private Associations, the Stock Corporation and the Private Foundation

The Enlightenment was opposed to foundations[126]. What needed to be done for *publica utilitas* was the task of the state and not of private organizations, be it foundations or corporations[127].

(a) Savigny's Rejection of Freedom of Association

Savigny shared this attitude as can be seen in his system, especially when he deals with the requirement of state consent before a foundation could be erected[128]. eed for state consent of legal personality is a leitmotiv of *Savigny's* theory of legal personality[129]. Apart from "necessary" legal persons such as the state or municipalities, contractual *(willkührliche)* legal personality could only be created by the "consent of the supreme power in the State"[130]. In other words, the creation of legal personality was not guaranteed as an act of freedom of contract[131]. *Savigny* was suspicious of any voluntary association. The systematic separation of foundation and corporation and the practical integration of foundations into the state administration diminished the politically undesirable associative sector.

Savigny recalls that the need for consent for the creation of a corporation was generally accepted. This was partly because of Roman law, and partly because of the possible threat to the state which freedom of association would entail[132]. *Savigny* stresses that such consent would not easily be given under Roman law. Political considerations required that the attempt to form a free association without state consent be punished as an *extraordinarium crimen*[133]. The Romans had the factious, politically threatening clubs in mind without specifying them more clearly, because "everybody knew anyway who was meant"[134]. Consequently, *Savigny* also argues that corporations need state consent to be dissolved, and they could even be dissolved without the consent of the members[135].

126 *Coing* (n. 6) n. 59 f.; *Liermann* (n. 15) 173 ff.

127 *Feenstra* (n. 5) text at n. 75.

128 *Liermann* (n. 15) 248 posits that *Savigny's* theory of legal personality was instrumental in establishing the general belief that the creation of a foundation required state consent.

129 *Liermann* (n. 15) 248.

130 *Savigny* (n. 26) 275.

131 *Savigny* (n. 26) 275.

132 *Savigny* (n. 26) 276.

133 *Savigny* (n. 26) 256 f.

134 *Savigny* (n. 26) 258.

135 *Savigny* (n. 26) 258 f.

(b) "Privileges" of Private Foundations and the Business Corporation

In the *Städel* litigation, some professors had doubted whether state consent was required for the creation of a foundation[136]. Some opinions in the *Städel* case posited that Roman law did not require state consent for the creation of *pia corpora*. Here is one of the few instances where *Savigny* rejects the approach of Roman law. Roman law was not relevant here for two reasons[137]. Firstly, because Roman law on this question was not glossed. Secondly, because the sources only dealt with church foundations and the Church itself required authorization and would also apply a supervisory jurisdiction over foundations. As this was no longer the case in modern times, state consent was needed[138]. Apart from the question of the interpretation of the Roman sources, *Savigny* gives four more reasons why even private foundations would need state authorization. Firstly, state consent was needed in order to increase legal certainty. Without an official act of authorization nobody would know whether something was a special fund which was legally protected, a problem of a legal person without a corporate existence[139]. Secondly, he refers to political reasons[140]. The danger of corporations would be generally admitted but the danger of foundations could be just the same. What about a well-endowed foundation for the dissemination of "state-threatening, irreligious, amoral teachings or books"? Should the state tolerate such an endeavor[141]? Thirdly, private foundations could compete with the State and such misunderstood charity was undesirable so that no state consent should be given[142]. Lastly, the dead-hand problem could not be controlled by state supervision alone. The creation of wealth without ownership interests had to be stopped right from the beginning[143].

The stock corporation and the foundation are somehow privileged in this authoritarian model[144]. *Savigny* stresses that it is a criminal offense to form an unauthorized legal person; even the attempt to do so is an offense. But this law should not apply to business corporations or foundations[145]. Nevertheless, he was in favour of strict state supervision over stock corporations and foundations as well as over cor-

136 *Savigny* (n. 26) 276.

137 *Savigny* (n. 26) 277.

138 *Savigny* (n. 26) 277.

139 *Savigny* (n. 26) 277.

140 *Savigny* (n. 26) 277: "political considerations".

141 *Savigny* (n. 26) 278.

142 *Savigny* (n. 26) 278 f.

143 *Savigny* (n. 26) 278 f. The dead-hand problem concerns the accumulation of wealth without ownership interests. Here *Savigny* offers some utilitarian thinking. The dead-hand problem was the main argument of the Enlightenment against foundations, with the argument being that the clergy would not put their assets to good use.

144 On *Savigny's* attitude towards the stock corporation see *Rückert* (n. 25) 185 and fn. 182; *Baums* (n. 68) *passim*.

145 *Savigny* (n. 26) 275.

porations, because – from a legal point of view – they were all to be treated as minors[146].

As far as the law of obligations and law of property is concerned, freedom of contract is the core value for *Savigny*[147]. But when we deal with collective bodies or contractual *(willkührliche)* legal persons, an authoritarian model is apparent and freedom of contract denied[148]. This is where *Savigny* and the protagonists of the Germanist school like *Georg Beseler* really differed[149]. The authoritarian orientation reveals *Savigny's* "political half-step of freedom of private law *(Privatrechtsli-bertät)*" which we can observe in other doctrines put forward by *Savigny*[150]. In the field of foundations, this half-step can be understood in a literal sense. In *Savigny's* system, the creation of a foundation is still an act of private law, but the body created is an entity which can be much better characterized as an administrative unit. Any liberal movement was viewed with suspicion[151]. While *Savigny* supported individual freedom in private law, he also maintained that true individual freedom would lead the individual to understand that it was necessary to belong to certain groups such as the family, the people or the state where there was no scope for individual or group autonomy[152]. He is very explicit on this point in his "System des heutigen römischen Rechts". The assumption of any autonomy of the members of a corporation meant the "tacit, arbitrary acceptance of an absolute democracy in the constitution of all corporations"[153]. *Savigny's* thinking reflects the tension between the enlightened vision of the autonomous individual and the romantic longing for the pre-French Revolution public order[154]. It was the tension of his time.

IV. English Law of Charity

Before the absolutist state, it was the Reformation which had challenged the intellectual unity of the law of charity in Europe. This was particularly true in England[155].

---

146 *Savigny* (n. 26) 325.

147 *Rückert* (n. 25) 186.

148 *Schikorski* posits that *Savigny's* theory of legal personality is ripe with contradictions. Cf. *Schikorski* (n. 44) 106 f. *Schikorski* is right insofar as the dividing line between public law and private law is blurred in *Savigny's* system. Cf. *Rückert* (n. 25) 358 ff.

149 See the chapter on autonomy in *Beseler* (n. 39) 94 ff.

150 *Rückert* (n. 25) 184 ff.

151 *Rückert* (n. 25) 224, with a list of terms which in *Savigny's* eyes were negative: Enlightenment, equality, basic rights, constitutional liberalism, Parliament, Republic, political people and formal guarantees.

152 *Rückert* (n. 25) 367 ff.; *Schikorski* (n. 44) 53.

153 *Savigny* (n. 26) 332. Cf. *Henkel* (n. 31) 135 ff.

154 The romantic element is especially stressed by *James Q. Whitman*, The Legacy of Roman Law in the German Romantic Era: Historical Vision and Legal Change, Princeton, 1990, *passim*.

1. The Reformation

The Reformation under *Henry VIII* (1491 - 1547) brought about a radical change in the administration of charities[156]. The process of secularization was more radical in England than in most German territories[157]. In spite of this early secularization, English law of charity has preserved its ecclesiastical roots much more than its Continental counterpart[158]. Canon law had a lasting effect upon the English law of charity, mainly because ecclesiastical courts exercised an extensive jurisdiction[159]. But even before the Reformation, the Court of Chancery had started to offer remedies to beneficiaries of trusts from about the middle of the 15th century[160] and to take over elements of the Canon law[161]. The privileges that Canon law had bestowed *on dispositiones ad pias causas* were extended to dispositions for purely secular purposes. Legacies for charitable purposes were integrated into the law of trusts, their privileges were confirmed[162]. The trust was a creation of equity[163] and equity as a distinct body of rules was informed by Canon law, in substance as well as in procedure[164]. A good example of the far-reaching effects of Roman-Canon law is the *cy-près*-doctrine[165] which still forms a corner-stone of the modern doc-

155 Cf., for the English development, *Eamon Duffy,* The Stripping of the Altars: Traditional Religion in England 1400 - 1580, New Haven, London, 1992, pp. 379 - 423 on the separation from Rome, and pp. 504 - 523 on the secularization of the law of succession.

156 Church property was confiscated or destroyed: *Duffy* (n. 155) *passim; Edith L. Fisch,* American Acceptance of Charitable Trusts, (1953) 28 Notre Dame Law Review 221 f.

157 *Hattenhauer* (n. 114) 424 ff.

158 Indeed, one could also argue that early secularization was crucial because after secularization the English law of charity enjoyed a much more continuous development than charity law on the Continent, which in some form or another came under the influence of the *Anstaltsstaat* in most European jurisdictions.

159 *Zimmermann* (n. 7) at III. 3 a); as well as *R. H. Helmholz's* chapter in this volume at II.

160 *Helmholz* (n. 159) at III. 2.

161 Cf. *Shael Herman's* paper in this volume.

162 There were three privileges. Firstly, a trust for non-charitable purposes is held to fail for want of beneficiaries or for indefiniteness. But in the case of charitable trusts the beneficiaries may be, indeed to a large extent must be, indefinite: *Morice v. Bishop of Durham* (1804), 9 Ves. 399; (1805), 10 Ves. 522. Secondly, property could be allocated for an indefinitely long period or forever for the accomplishment of charitable purposes. The rule against perpetuities did not apply to charities. Thirdly, the *cy-près*-doctrine was permitted to devote a legacy for charitable purposes to similar objects if it was impossible to execute the testator's wishes in a lawful manner. Cf. *Jones* (n. 8) 5.

163 On the interrelationship between the law of trusts and the equity jurisdiction, see *Michael Macnair's* chapter in the present book. On the law of trusts in England in the sixteenth century, see the paper by *Neil Jones* in this volume.

164 *Reinhard Zimmermann,* Cy-près, in: Iuris Professio, Festgabe für Max Kaser, 1986, p. 409.

165 The *cy-près*-doctrine allows one to apply a legacy for charitable purposes to similar objects if it is impossible to execute the testator's wishes in a lawful manner. Cf. *Jones* (n. 8) 5. Its etymological origin is seen in the law French of the early Middle Ages and the term

trine of charitable trusts[166]. In the 17th century, the English law of charity could already present a "sophisticated and mature doctrine"[167]. This was also the result of continuous legislative efforts: from the beginning of the Reformation (1532) up to 1698 (*William III*) thirty-five statutes concerning charitable trusts were enacted[168].

2. The Elizabethan Statute of Charitable Uses 1601

The two most significant statutes were the Poor Relief Act 1597[169] and the Elizabethan Statute of Charitable Uses 1601. The Poor Relief Act provided for the appointment of Charity Commissioners who were supposed to supervise the charities[170]. The powers of the Commissioners and of the Lord Chancellor were enhanced by the 1601 Act[171]. The Commissioners applied an inquisitorial procedure[172], another hint at the integration of Canon law. The Statute of 1601 contained a list of charitable purposes, mainly geared towards the relief of poverty but also "to find bows and arrows for children between the age of seven and seventeen ..., to maintain a public midwife within the parish ..., or to pay fees for decayed persons to go out of prison to treat with their creditors..."[173]. During the following twenty-four years the commissioners' investigations provided the factual basis for over one thousand decrees, each one of which concerned the administration of a particular charitable trust[174]. In the period from 1400 to 1601 *Gareth Jones* estimates that not more than one or two decrees affecting charitable trusts could have been issued by the Chancellor annually[175]. The Elizabethan Statute of Charitable Uses 1601 became the keystone of the law of charity, because it simplified the system and reduced it to an orderly form[176]. The Statute laid the doctrinal basis for the development of a *Rechtsinstitut* of the charitable trust, more than 200 years before such an attempt was made in Germany.

---

assez-près. Cf. *John N. Hazard*, The Juridical Status of Foundations in the United States, in: Fondazione Agnelli (ed.), The Fiscal and Juridical Status of Foundations, Torino, 1972, p. 366.

166 *Zimmermann* (n. 164) 395 - 415.

167 *Jones* (n. 8) 74.

168 See the survey in *Jones* (n. 8) xiv-xv.

169 39 Elizabeth I c. 3. Printed in: *Jones* (n. 8) 221.

170 *Jones* (n. 8) 23 ff.

171 *Jones* (n. 8) 39 ff.

172 *Jones* (n. 8) 23 ff.

173 *Jones* (n. 8) 27 - 29.

174 *Jones* (n. 8) 52.

175 *Jones* (n. 8) 52.

176 *Howard S. Miller*, The Legal Foundations of American Philanthropy 1776 - 1844, Madison, 1961, p. x.

V. The American Development

"When the American colonies were first settled by our ancestors ... they brought hither, as a birth-right and inheritance, so much of the common law, as was applicable to their local situation, and change of circumstances"[177]. Thus, the English law of charitable trusts as enacted in the various charity statutes and refined by the jurisprudence of the Court of Chancery formed the legal basis of philanthropy in the American colonies[178]. Nevertheless, the charitable trust did not play the same prominent role in the United States as it did in its birthplace. In the early 19th century, the charitable corporation became the main vehicle for charitable endeavours. Therefore, the American development shares one feature with the German one: the shift towards organizational forms with legal personality. But the difference between a memberless foundation and a corporation did not play any role in the United States. *Angell* and *Ames*, authors of the first American treatise on the law of corporations (1832)[179], tell us that this overall development was not limited to charities: "[i]n no country have corporations been multiplied to so great an extent, as in our own; and the extent to which their institution has here been carried, may very properly be pronounced astonishing"[180].

1. The "Checkered Career" of the Charitable Trust

The popularity of the charitable corporation has to do with the "curiously checkered career" of the charitable trust in the United States[181]. This was due to American hostility to English law and a special hostility to English equity after the Revolution[182]. The Virginian example demonstrates the point[183]. Virginia repealed all

---

177 *Justice Samuel Chase* in *U. S. v. Worrall* 2 U.S. (2 Dallas) 384, 394 (1798). This was a Circuit Court Opinion (C.C. Pa.).

178 *Wyllie* (n. 81) 203 ff.

179 *Joseph K. Angell, Samuel Ames*, A Treatise on the Law of Private Corporations Aggregate, New York 1972 (reprint of the 1st edition, Boston, 1832). The earliest English-language law books entitled "corporations" were published in 1702 and 1793 respectively: *Anonymous*, Law of Corporations (printed by Assigns of R. and E. Atkins, London, 1702); this book consists of briefs of cases arranged in chapters; *Stewart Kyd*, A Treatise on the Law of Corporations, 2 volumes, London, 1793. This was the first genuine treatise. *Kyd* was a barrister of the Middle Temple. The work of *Angell/Ames* is infinitely more clear than the work of *Kyd* and displays a strong willingness to rationalize the material, a good deal of which was English.

180 *Angell/Ames* (n. 179) 35.

181 *Friedman* (n. 2) 223. For more detailed studies, see *Stanley N. Katz*, The Politics of Law in Colonial America: Controversies over Chancery Courts and Equity Law in the Eighteenth Century, in: Donald Fleming and Bernard Bailyn (eds.), Law in American History, Boston, Toronto, 1971, pp. 257 - 284; and *William J. Curran*, The Struggle for Equity Jurisdiction in Massachusetts, (1951) 31 Boston University Law Review 269 - 296.

182 *Roscoe Pound*, The Formative Era of American Law, Gloucester, 1938, pp. 155 ff.; *Miller* (n. 176) xi; *Fisch* (n. 156) 222; *Peter Dobkin Hall*, A Historical Overview of the Private Nonprofit Sector, in: Walter Powell (ed.), The Nonprofit Sector, New Haven, London,

English statutes in the year 1792[184] which had a far-reaching effect. In 1819, the U.S. Supreme Court had to deal with the question whether a charitable trust could be formed at all under Virginian law[185]. The Court answered in the negative. Hart's gift to the Baptist Association failed because of the lack of legal personality of the Association[186]. Had it been an incorporated charitable corporation, there would not have been any problem. But the device of the charitable trust was not available because of Virginia's implicit repeal of the Statute of Charitable Uses 1601[187]. The decision was reversed by the Supreme Court in 1844[188] but it influenced American philanthropy by favouring the charitable corporation over the charitable trust, much to the chagrin of leading equity lawyers such as *Chancellor Kent* who asserted that *Chief Justice Marshall* had "thrown embarrassment" over the whole question of the powers of the courts of equity and that the Supreme Court had deprived equity courts of "some of the most interesting and meritorious trusts that can possibly be created"[189].

In Virginia, equity was unpopular because of anticlerical sentiments[190]. Further north, the Puritans also opposed equity, because it involved discretion and meant that a magistrate could judge by a personal standard instead of by the "standing laws" which the Puritans demanded in the Massachusetts Bill of Rights[191]. The

1987, pp. 3 f.; *R. Kent Newmyer,* Supreme Court Justice Joseph Story: Statesman of the Old Republic, Chapel Hill, 1985, pp. 293 f.

183 Cf. *Miller* (n. 176) 7 f.

184 General Act of Repeal (1792). Cf. *Marion Fremont-Smith,* Foundations and Government, New York, 1965, p. 37; *Wyllie* (n. 81) 206 f.; *Hall* (n. 182) 5; *Miller* (n. 176) 10.

185 *Trustees of the Philadelphia Baptist Association v. Hart's Executors* 17 U.S. (4 Wheaton) 1 (1819). Cf. Wyllie (n. 81) 208 ff.; Hall (n. 182) 5.

186 The Baptist Association was an unincorporated association. An unincorporated association was not able to take by devise, because English statutes which were still in force in Pennsylvania outlawed conveyances to unincorporated societies. Cf. *Wyllie* (n. 81) 214 f.

187 *Trustees of the Philadelphia Baptist Association v. Hart's Executors* 17 U.S. (4 Wheaton) 1, 38 - 39 (1819). Cf. *Wyllie* (n. 81) 206 f.; *Fisch* (n. 156) 225.

188 *Vidal v. Girard's Executor* 43 U.S. (2 Howard) 125 (1844).

189 *James Kent,* Commentaries on American Law, 4 vols., New York, 1826 - 1830, vol. II, pp. 231 f. *Kent's* statement found wide support. See *Angell/Ames* (n. 179) 101. On *Kent's* impact upon American law of the "formative era", see the recent article by *John Langbein,* Chancellor Kent and the History of Legal Literature, (1993) 93 Columbia L.R. 547 - 594. The article also includes biographical information.

190 A statement of the President of the Virginia Court of Appeals, *Henry St. George Tucker,* in the case of *Gallego's Executors v. Attorney General* 3 Leigh (Va.) 479 (1832) shows the anti-religious feelings. "The church, if made capable to take ... never can part with any thing and thus, like those sustaining powers in mechanics, which retain whatever they have gained, it advances with a step that never retrogrades". The anticlerical sentiments were in particular directed against the Anglican Church which was widely represented in some parts of Virginia. Cf. *Wyllie* (n. 81) 207; *Hall* (n. 182) 3 f.; *Miller* (n. 176) 7 f., 25.

191 "Each individual of the society has a right to be protected by it in the enjoyment of his life, liberty, and property according to standing laws". Massachusetts Bill of Rights (1780), § 10.

Puritans' call for a universal and unyielding rule did not go well with equity, because equity sought to mitigate the harshness of the common law rules[192]. All religious groups outside the Church of England such as the Unitarians[193], the Anabaptists[194], the Catholics[195] or the Jews remembered their experience in England where the Lord Chancellor had from time to time used his discretion to their disadvantage[196]. The legislation and jurisprudence against such "superstitious uses" contained traces of confessionalization in England. In *De Costa v. De Paz,* for example, a Jew had left money for establishing a Jesuba for reading the law and for instruction in the Jewish religion[197]. At the time, the advancement of the Jewish religion was illegal in England so that the *cy-près*-doctrine[198] had to be applied. *Lord Chancellor Hardwicke* held that the matter of the disposition of the money should be referred to the King for disposition under the royal prerogative. The King applied the gift to support an Anglican minister and to provide instruction in the Christian religion to the children of a foundling hospital.

Beside these concerns, there were also very practical considerations. The lack of a central court system meant that it was much more difficult to establish an equity jurisdiction[199]. The courts of Pennsylvania did not have equity jurisdiction as such until 1836 nor did the courts of Massachusetts have complete equity jurisdiction till the last quarter of the 19th century[200]. In these states, other courts handled, in a piecemeal fashion, those equitable matters considered necessary[201]. And very little legal literature was available[202]. The English textbooks were not very helpful because they failed to reduce the principles of the exercise of the Lord Chancellor's discretion to hard and fast rules. A positive light was shed on equity when *Joseph Story* published his Equity Jurisprudence (1836)[203]. The Americans relied heavily upon *Blackstone* who was not much of an expert on equity. *Blackstone* basically

192 *Pound* (n. 182) 155; *Carl Zollmann,* American Law of Charities, Milwaukee, 1924, pp. 72 - 78; critical *Curran* (n. 181) 278 f.

193 *Attorney-General v. Pearson* 3 Mer. 353 (1817).

194 *Attorney-General v. Eades;* cited in: *Att.-Gen. v. Cock* 2 Ves. Sen. 273, 274 (1751).

195 *Cary v. Abbot* 7 Ves. 490 (1802).

196 Cf. *Zollmann* (n. 192) 14 ff., 74 ff.

197 *De Costa v. De Paz* (1753) Chancery, 1754; 2 Swans 487.

198 On the *cy-près*-doctrine, cf. n. 165.

199 *Pound* (n. 182) 8: "In a country of long distances and slow and expensive travel, the common law system of central courts and a centralized bar imposed an intolerable burden upon litigants".

200 On Pennsylvania, see *Hall* (n. 182) 5; on Massachusetts, see *Hall* (n. 182) 4.

201 *Friedman* (n. 2) 47.

202 *Wyllie* (n. 81) 214.

203 *Joseph Story,* Commentaries on Equity Jurisprudence, as Administered in England and America, 2 vols., Boston, 1836. Cf. *Pound* (n. 182) 156. On the influence of *Story's* treatises on American law, see *A. W. B. Simpson,* The Rise and Fall of the Legal Treatise: Legal Principles and the Forms of Legal Literature, (1981) 48 University of Chicago L.R. 670 ff. On Story's contribution to equity, see *Newmyer* (n. 182) 289 ff.

reproduced *Lord Mansfield's* views on the relationship between equity and the common law[204]. *Lord Mansfield* had been advocating that the common law should absorb what was useful in equity[205].

2. The Advantages of Incorporation

In English law "the advantages of corporateness were never sufficiently overwhelming" to induce groups to give up the "freedom they possessed in managing their own affairs"[206]. The charitable trust and other trust-like devices helped to solve almost all practical problems of collective bodies. Corporateness on the other hand required a royal charter which was difficult to amend[207]. This disadvantage existed to a far lesser extent in the United States[208]. The controversial position of the charitable trust and of equity further favoured incorporation[209]. *Chancellor Kent* mentions six reasons why incorporation was sought. It would allow perpetual succession, to sue and to be sued, and to grant and to receive by a corporate name; to purchase and hold lands and chattels and to have a common seal[210]. Furthermore, incorporation meant that the society could make by-laws for the government of the corporation, and that it had the power to remove members[211].

Incorporation was further facilitated when several states, such as New York (1784)[212] and New Jersey (1786)[213], passed general incorporation acts. Pennsylva-

204 *William S. Holdsworth,* Blackstone's Treatment of Equity, (1929) 43 Harvard L.R. 1, 11.

205 *Holdsworth* (n. 204) 7 ff.

206 *James Baker,* The Inns of Court and Chancery as Voluntary Associations, Quaderni fiorentini 11 / 12 (1982 / 83) 38.

207 *Baker* (n. 206) 18 ff. For the procedure of incorporating a charitable corporation under English law, see *Stewart Kyd,* A Treatise on the Law of Corporations, vol. I, London, 1793, pp. 51 f.

208 *Angell / Ames* (n. 179) v.

209 On the federal level, it was only in 1844 with the Supreme Court decision in *Vidal v. Girard's Executors* 43 U.S. (Howard) 27, 11 Lawyer's Edition 205 (1844) that charitable trusts and charitable corporations were put on an equal footing. Cf. *Hall* (n. 182) 6.

210 The importance of the common seal was to allow the corporation to manifest its intentions. An ancient common law rule provided that a corporation could not manifest its intentions by any personal act or oral discourse, and that it spoke and acted only by its common seal. Cf. *James Kent,* Commentaries on American Law, 4 vols., New York, 1826 - 1830, vol. IV, p. 232.

211 *Kent* (n. 210) 224.

212 Concerning charitable corporations which would be for religious or charitable purposes: Session Laws, pp. 23 - 25, cited in: *Joseph Stancliffe Davis,* Essays in the Earlier History of American Corporations, vol. 2, Cambridge Mass., 1917, p. 16.

213 Laws (ed. 1797), ii, 879. In 1794, New Jersey provided similarly for "societies for the promotion of learning"; Session Laws, 950, cited in: *Davis* (n. 212) 16 f.

nia passed a similar act granting freedom of incorporation "for any literary, charitable, or for any religious purpose" (1791)[214]. New York, in 1796, and New Jersey, in 1799, extended the corporate privilege to library companies[215].

In *Terret v. Taylor, Justice Story* held that religious societies had a right to be incorporated, because eleemosynary purposes could better be secured and cherished by corporate powers; something which could not be "doubted by any person who has attended to the difficulties which surround all voluntary associations"[216]. The support of private corporations has been a constant theme throughout *Story* 's career[217].

3. The Charitable Corporation as an Incorporated Trust

In the American colonies and the Union after the Revolution, elements of the English law of charitable trusts and the law of corporations were taken to form the legal basis for charitable corporations. The courts relied on English law as presented by *William Blackstone* and *Sir Edward Coke*[218]. One has to take into account that the terminology used by the various courts is far from clear and that the law differed greatly from state to state or even city to city[219]. However, various elements confirm the tendency to integrate the rules of equity concerning charitable trusts into the common law of corporations: namely, corporate charters, the analysis of membership as fiduciary and the investment policy of charitable corporations.

(a) Corporate Charters

Some examples from the world of learning show the close relationship between the law of corporations and the law of trusts. The Massachusetts General Court incorporated "The Feoffees of the Grammar School of the Town of Ipswich" (1756)

214 Session Laws, 255. Pennsylvania Statutes at Large, xiv, pp. 50 - 53. *Miller* (n. 176) 16. In 1794, New Jersey provided similarly for "societies for the promotion of learning"; Session Laws, 950, cited in: *Davis* (n. 212) 16.

215 New Jersey Session Laws, 644; New York Laws (ed. 1887), iii, 695. Cited in: *Davis* (n. 212) 17.

216 9 Cranch 49 (U.S. 1815).

217 *Justice Story* wrote the decision in *Terret v. Taylor,* even before he got actively involved in the administration of charities. In 1819, *Story* became a member of the Board of Overseers of Harvard College and from 1825 onwards he served as a Fellow of the Harvard Corporation. Cf. *Story,* in: Dictionary of American Biography, vol. XVIII, 22 vols., New York, 1928 - 1958, p. 105. Newmyer (n. 182) 125 ff.

218 The first English treatise of the law of corporations (1793) is also heavily based upon *Sir Edward Coke's* Institutes and *Blackstone's* Commentaries on the Laws of England. See *Kyd* (n. 207) *passim.*

219 *Alfred Conard,* Corporations in Perspective, Mineola, 1976, pp. 134 f.

to administer a private bequest in the interest of public education[220]. Somewhat similar were incorporations for schools by the Virginia assembly[221]. Brown University grew out of a college with the name of "Trustees and Fellows of the College, or University, in the English Colony of Rhode Island, and Providence Plantations, in New England, in America"[222]. Other examples are "The Trustees of the Road and Ferries from Newark to the Road leading from Bergen point to Paulus Hook"[223]. In 1772, "The Trustees of the New York Society Library" were chartered[224]. A charitable bequest to trustees could be aided by the incorporation of the trustees, even though the testator had not provided for any such action[225]. The charters of eleemosynary corporations were drawn up to reflect the powers and the duties of the trustees[226]. Trusteeship had been used in a roughly similar way under English law[227]. Trust standards were applied when charitable corporations were dissolved[228]. Assets were not distributed to the members but had to be directed towards the charitable purpose[229]. Even though the charitable trust was not available in Pennsylvania[230], many of the principles applied by the chancery courts in England were recognized by common usage and held useful as an aid in defining charity[231]. Traces of this "merger" can be detected in the modern law of nonprofit corporations[232].

---

220 Massachusetts Provincial Acts, iii, 891 - 893, 951 - 953, iv, 806. Cited in: *Joseph Stancliffe Davis,* Essays in the Earlier History of American Corporations, vol. 1, Cambridge Mass., 1917, p. 83.

221 "Trustees and Governors" of Peasley's Free School (1756) and of Eaton's Charity School (1759), Statutes at Large (Hening), vii, 41 - 43, 317 - 320. Cited in: *Davis* (n. 220) 83. A further example from New Jersey: "The Trustees of the Free Schools of the Town of Woodbridge" (1769), New Jersey Archive, xviii, 1, 6. Cited in: *Davis* (n. 220) 83.

222 It was incorporated by the "Governor and Company" of Rhode Island in 1764. Another example is Dartmouth College. Dartmouth College was incorporated in the year 1769 as "The Trustees of Dartmouth College". Cited in: *Davis* (n. 220) 86.

223 The corporation was constituted by act of the New Jersey Assembly in 1765. The Corporation consisted of a self-perpetuating body of nine trustees. New Jersey Laws (Allinson), 276. Cited in: *Davis* (n. 220) 99.

224 Probably by the Governor of New York, after having been active for at least fourteen years. Act of Feb. 18, 1789, in Laws (ed. 1887), iii, 59 - 60. Cited in: *Davis* (n. 220) 101.

225 *Sanderson v. White* (1836) 35 Mass. (18 Pickering) 328, 29 Am. Dec. 591.

226 *Nelson v. Cushing* (1848), 56 Mass. (2 Cushing) 519, 529.

227 *Kyd* (n. 207) 179: "Where the succession, in the case of a charitable corporation, is vested in trustees, these, of course, have no interest, but are only employed as instruments to effectuate the purposes of the institution; ...".

228 *Kent* (n. 210) 252.

229 *Duke v. Fuller* (1838), 9 N.H. 536, 32 Am. Dec. 392; *Thomas v. Ellmaker* (1844), 1 Clark 502 (Pennsylvania.).

230 Because of the decision in *Trustees of the Philadelphia Baptist Association v. Hart's Executors* 17 U.S. (4 Wheaton) 1 (1819). *Philadelphia Baptist* was reversed by *Justice Henry Baldwin's* opinion in *Magill v. Brown* (Case No. 8.952) 16 Fed. Cas. (1833). Cf. *Wyllie* (n. 81) 213 ff.

231 *Zollmann* (n. 192) 55.

(b) Membership and Trusteeship

Many eleemosynary corporations had members. In most cases the membership was fiduciary in character. This means that members had no ownership interests, could not sell their membership right and that no assets could be distributed upon dissolution of the corporation. But the borderlines were sometimes blurry, and abuse occurred. A New York Statute from 1784 is instructive. When it became clear that a number of estates originally donated for the support of a religious society had passed into private hands, a statute mandated the election of trustees who would then have the power to manage the secular affairs of each congregation[233].

The fiduciary nature of membership in an eleemosynary corporation points to the close relationship between trust and corporation and to *Maitland's* pathbreaking studies in this field at the turn of the century. Drawing a comparison between the Continental European and the English development, *Maitland* concluded that "... the device of building a wall of trustees enabled us to construct bodies which were not technically corporations and which yet would be sufficiently protected from the assaults of individualistic theory. The personality of such bodies – so I should put it – though explicitly denied by lawyers, was on the whole pretty well recognized in practice"[234]. The consequence for American law is obvious. As long as the "wall" between the body of the corporation and its members was maintained, the charitable corporation in American law could work in an almost identical way to the charitable trust under English law and most of the doctrines of the charitable trust could be applied by way of analogy.

But not all doctrines were taken over. The history of the *cy-près*-doctrine[235] shows that the Americans chose those elements which suited their conditions[236]. The *cy-près*-doctrine had two elements: the royal prerogative one and the judicial one[237]. *De Costa v. De Paz*[238] was an example of the use of the royal prerogative element of the *cy-près* -doctrine under the assumption of a general charitable intention[239]. *Justice Story* admitted that it was "not easy to perceive", how "Courts

232 One of the questions which is still disputed is whether board members of a charitable corporation are to be treated like trustees or like board members of for-profit corporations. Cf. *Howard Oleck*, Nonprofit Corporations, Organizations and Associations, 4th ed., New York, 1980, p. 1206.

233 Cf. *Miller* (n. 176) 18. This was well before New York adopted a very restrictive charity policy in 1829.

234 *Frederic William Maitland*, Moral Personality and Legal Personality, in: H. D. Hazeltine (ed.), Selected Essays, Cambridge, 1936, p. 235.

235 On the *cy-près*-doctrine cf. n. 165.

236 Cf. *Joseph Story*, Commentaries on Equity Jurisprudence, as Administered in England and America, vol. 1, Boston, 1836, pp. 420 ff.

237 *Fisch* (n. 156) 229 ff.

238 See *supra*, text accompanying footnotes 197 and 198.

239 (1753) Chancery, 1754; 2 Swans 487.

of Equity could arrive at any such conclusion"[240]. In the new world, *Zollmann* tells us, "this doctrine, so far as it is prerogative, and perverts funds given in support of illegal or impractical charity from the founder's design, under pretense of carrying out his general intention, ..., has been cut off as a tumor..."[241]. Only judicial *cy-près* was retained in America[242].

(c) Trust Investment

Conceptualizing the foundation in the context of the law of trusts had repercussions on the legal questions which were discussed. For example, *Savigny* did not address the question of trust investment. The investment of endowment funds is still a question which is hardly ever mentioned in modern German textbooks on the law of foundations[243]. By contrast, trust investment has always been considered an important aspect of the law of charitable corporations in the United States. The investment of the endowment of Harvard College[244] was at issue in the case of *Harvard College v. Amory* (1830)[245]. The decision laid a new legal basis for trust investments by enunciating the "prudent investor" rule. It eased the restrictions on trust investments and even allowed trustees to invest in corporate stock[246]. In the United States, the law of trusts even informed the law of for-profit corporations in the 19th century, in particular with regard to fiduciary obligations of board members and officers of the corporation who were understood to be trustees[247].

240 *Story* (n. 236) 425.

241 *Zollmann* (n. 192) 75; *Fisch* (n. 156) 228 ff.

242 *Zollmann* (n. 192) 75 ff.; *Wyllie* (n. 81) 218 f.

243 In the leading German textbook on the law of foundations of 738 pages, trust investment is discussed on a general level in five sentences, the fifth sentence stating that no general rules exist: *Werner Seifart*, Vermögen und Ertrag, in: *idem* (ed.), Handbuch des Stiftungsrechts, München 1987, § 10, n. 28. German law was much more restrictive in terms of trust investments, and favoured government bonds over other investments. The inflexible trust investment rules lead to the loss of the endowments of virtually all foundations after the First World War (the state administration had encouraged foundations to purchase war bonds) and during the inflation of the Weimar Republic. Cf. *Liermann* (n. 15) 282.

244 Founded in 1636, "The President and Fellows of Harvard College", was incorporated in 1650. Cited in: *Davis* (n. 220) 84.

245 26 Mass. (9 Pickering) 446 (1830).

246 Cf. *Lawrence Friedman,* The Dynastic Trust, (1964) 73 Yale. L.J. 547 ff.

247 *Friedman* (n. 2) 450 ff. The Massachusetts or business trust further illustrates the "transplant" of trust law. The Massachusetts trust was an unincorporated association that carried on business in the form of a trust. Instead of stockholders there were "beneficiaries" and their interest was not called stock but "certificate of beneficial interest": *Friedman* (n. 2) 177.

4. The Law of Charity as a Branch of Private Law

The distinction between private and public law entities, which features so prominently in any modern Western legal system, had curiously little relevance in *Savigny's* theory of legal personality[248]. The situation was slightly different in England. As we know from *Kyd's* treatise on the English law of corporations (1793), under the common law, private foundations were not just understood as a private law matter as regards the formative act but also as regards the status of the created organization[249]. The situation was very similar in the United States. In his "Commentaries on American Law" *Chancellor Kent* stressed that the "mere act of incorporation" would not change a charity from a private to a public one. Moreover, referring to the popular use of the term "public charity", *Kent* points out that in legal terms we are dealing with a private corporation according to private law[250]. "But if the foundation be private, the corporation is private, however extensive the uses may be to which it is devoted by the founder, or by the nature of the corporation"[251]. Under the influence of *Justice Story,* American law perfected the private law conceptualization of charities[252].

Of course, historic factors played a major role, too. The considerable social, religious and economic diversity of American society led to an emphasis on private law institutions. Schooling arrangements can serve as an example. In the Middle Atlantic colonies, numerous religious sects and doctrines coexisted: Quaker, Catholic, Presbyterian, Baptist, Lutheran, Dutch Reformed, Methodist, Mennonite, and others. In spite of the atmosphere of religious toleration, it would have been difficult to reach a consensus on what a unitary public school system should look like and teach. Instead, Pennsylvania, New York, and their neighboring colonies relied on church-run and other voluntary-sector schools which were formed as charitable corporations[253].

---

248 See *supra,* text accompanying footnotes 105 and 150.

249 *Kyd* (n. 207) 51 with reference to 11 *Coke* 77. a, 78. a: "And it is said, by Sir Edward Coke, that the foundership is so inseparably incident to the blood of the founder, that it cannot be granted over, and that if a subject should grant his foundership to the King by deed inrolled, it would be a void grant". The King would only be regarded as the founder, if he had contributed some "possession" to the foundation: *Kyd* (n. 207) 51.

250 *Kent* (n. 210) 223. The distinction between private and public law corporations dates back to the late 18th / early 19th centuries. Cf. *Davis* (n. 220) 49.

251 *Kent* (n. 210) 222.

252 It is noteworthy that *Story* shared *Savigny's* concerns (see *supra* nn. 82 and 143) about wasted property (the "dead-hand" problem) in the hands of religious charities. See *Story* (n. 236) 436 f.: "And it deserves the consideration of every wise and enlightened American legislator, whether provisions, similar to those of this celebrated statute [sc. the English Statute of Mortmain and Charities of the 9th of Geo. II, ch. 36] are not proper to be enacted in this country, with a view to prevent undue influence and imposition upon pious and feeble minds in their last moments, and to check that unhappy propensity (which sometimes is found to exist under a bigoted fanaticism), the desire to gain fame, as a religious devotee and benefactor, at the expense of all the natural claims of blood and parental duty".

(a) The Transformation of the Visitorial System

These social and political trends had repercussions upon the law. First of all, we could point out the different character of the visitorial system. The visitorial jurisdiction over foundations is yet another element of the law of charity which has its roots in the Canon law[254]. It used to be vested in the Church and allowed it to inspect proceedings and to correct abuses[255]. In the American colonies, the visitorial jurisdiction was only in the hands of the state or the church, if the state or church had acted as founders of the eleemosynary corporation. At common law, donors could also exercise a right of visitation. For the private donor, there were two ways of exercising the visitorial power. The more usual method was to create an eleemosynary corporation and to draft a charter which conferred on the officers the full power of the management of the property[256]. But the chartering of a corporation was not necessarily a delegation to it of the visitorial power. It could also be reserved by the donor to himself or his heirs, or could be conferred on some other person[257].

In general, courts as such would not exercise a visitorial power but they could be called upon when the visitors, in the exercise of their power, acted contrary to law in a matter amounting in effect to a breach of trust. Then a court of equity could interpose[258]. If a donor exceeded his powers, he could also be prosecuted by the Attorney-General and removed as a visitor[259]. The situation was different in cases where no person was appointed as visitor[260]. The rule that equity had jurisdiction over all charitable trusts meant that courts could exercise their inherent power over charities[261]. It was said that unless charities could come into some tribunal; they were "without the pale of the law and at the mercy of the any one disposed to despoil them"[262].

Städel had aimed at creating a somewhat similar private supervisory system where the city of Frankfurt would only have some subsidiary supervisory power[263]

---

253 Cf. *Marc Bendick*, Education as a Three-Sector Industry, in: Burton A. Weisbrod (ed.), The Voluntary Nonprofit Sector, Toronto, 1977, pp. 116 ff.

254 *David Yale*, Headless Bodies at Common Law, Quaderni fiorentini 11 / 12 (1982 / 83) 42.

255 The Canon law system also existed in Germany. During the process of *Konfessionalisierung*, visitations were used with "iron consequence" to remove so-called heretics and ensure the loyalty of the administrators of colleges and universities: *Schilling* (n. 115) 30 f.

256 *Chambers v. Baptist Education Society* 40 Ky. (1 Ben Monroe) 215, 218 (1841).

257 *Allen v. McKean* Fed. Cas. no. 229, p. 497.

258 *Nelson v. Cushing* 56 Mass. (7 Pickering) 303 (1848).

259 *Hazard* (n. 165) 388.

260 *Story* (n. 236) 421.

261 *Story* (n. 236) 435.

262 *Burr v. Smith* 7 Vt. 241, 284, 29 Am. Dec. 154 (1835).

263 *Kiefner* (n. 18) 344.

but because of the definition of public matters as state matters such a scheme was no longer acceptable, even though such an arrangement would have been upheld in many parts of Germany until the 18th century[264].

The development in the United States was a very different one, even though church and state were closely interlinked in some of the American colonies, in particular those in New England[265]. The foundation of Yale College in 1701 was the act of private donors and the state[266]. Only when the State of Connecticut wanted to exercise a right of visitation did the question whether the corporation was private or public become relevant. The College under *President Clap* (1740 - 1766) was vehemently opposed to direct state supervision[267]. *Clap* not only won the battle against the state but also managed to sever Yale's links with the Church[268]. Henceforth, the private side of the foundation of the College, which had consisted in the giving of fourty folios by some private donors, was seen as the decisive act of foundation. *Chancellor James Kent,* himself a Yale graduate (B.A. 1781), stressed in a speech in 1831 the importance of the private donation[269] and applauded *President Clap's* achievement: "He grounded himself upon English authorities, in the true style of a well-read lawyer, and successfully contended that the first trustees and donors, prior to the charter, were the founders and lawful visitors, and that the right of visitation passed to the trustees under the charter, and then resided in the president and fellows"[270]. The decreasing influence of state and church went hand in hand with the increasing influence of the alumni[271]. Alumni gained significant influence over Yale[272], Williams[273], Dartmouth[274] and Harvard. "The Act in Relation to the Board of Overseers of Harvard College" provided that only the president and treasurer of Harvard College be *ex officio* members of the Board of Overseers. The other thirty members would be elected by the alumni[275].

---

264 Cf. *Fries* (n. 106) *passim; Dieter Pleimes,* Weltliches Stiftungsrecht – Geschichte der Rechtsformen, Weimar, 1938, *passim.*

265 *Miller* (n. 176) xi.

266 *George Wilson Pierson,* The Founding of Yale, New Haven, 1988, pp. ix ff., 253 ff.

267 *Pierson* (n. 266) 34 ff. *Clap* was Rector, later President of Yale College (1740 - 1766).

268 On the separation of state and church in Connecticut, see *John S. Whitehead,* The Separation of College and State, Columbia, Dartmouth, Harvard and Yale, 1776 - 1876, New Haven, London, 1973, p. 41. On the links between Yale College and the Congregational Church, see pp. 42 - 45. Many of the American universities were attached to a particular religious group: Harvard to the Unitarians, Yale and Dartmouth to the Congregational Church and Columbia to the Episcopalian Church (p. 82).

269 "These folios became the deserved objects of the respect and curiosity of a grateful posterity": *James Kent,* "An Address delivered at New Haven, before the Phi Beta Kappa Society. September 1831". Cited in: *Pierson* (n. 266) 38.

270 *Kent* (n. 269). Cited in: *Pierson* (n. 266) 38.

271 Cf. *Whitehead* (n. 268) 151 f., 192 f., 198 f., 206 ff.

272 Cf. *Whitehead* (n. 268) 214.

273 Cf. *Whitehead* (n. 268) 207 f.

274 Cf. *Whitehead* (n. 268) 215 ff.

(b) The Distinction between Public and Private Corporations

The First Amendment of the American Constitution had a similar "privatizing" effect. The clause outlawing the establishment of religion was intended, in the words of Thomas Jefferson, to erect "a wall of separation between church and state"[276]. Many religious groups in the colonies were originally formed as corporations[277]. The separation of state and church meant that these corporations had to be classified as private corporations[278]. In *Terret v. Taylor, Justice Story* rejected state confiscatory legislation by Virginia and held that the property of the Episcopal Church of Virginia was protected because of the private character of the corporation[279]. The distinction between a private and a public corporation was to be based on the origin of the endowment. The legislature could not "without the consent ... of the corporators" take property vested by the corporate charter"[280].

(c) A Declaration of Philanthropic Independence

Justice Baldwin's decision in *Magill v. Brown* (1833) paved the way for a new interpretation of the viability of the charitable trust in American law. *Baldwin* showed that the Supreme Court had erred when it assumed that charitable trusts were not enforced before the enactment of the Statue of Charitable Uses (1601)[281]. Therefore, charitable trusts could be enforced in Pennsylvania even though the legislature had not adopted the Statute of Charitable Uses. But *Justice Baldwin* did not content himself with legal history. In addition, he put forward a teleological

---

275 Cf. *Whitehead* (n. 268) 204 ff.

276 Jefferson's Works, vol. 16, Monticello ed., 1903, p. 281.

277 Some examples from Rhode Island in the 18th century: Charters were given to the Benevolent Congregational Society (1770), the Charitable Baptist Society (1774) and the Catholic Congregational Society (1774). Cf. *Davis* (n. 220) 78 ff.

278 *Justice Story:* "Consistent with the constitution of Virginia the legislature could not create or continue a religious establishment which should have exclusive rights and prerogatives, or compel the citizens to worship under a stipulated form or discipline, or to pay taxes to those whose creed they could not conscientiously believe": *Terret v. Taylor* 9 Cranch 43 (U.S. 1815).

279 *Terret v. Taylor* 9 Cranch 43, 49 (U.S. 1815).

280 *Terret v. Taylor* 9 Cranch 43, 49 (U.S. 1815).

281 *Justice Baldwin:* "The rule of the common law is recognized and well illustrated in the preamble to the 39 Eliz. c. 5, for the erection of hospitals, ..., by private persons, – the reason for which is declared to be, 'understanding and finding that such good law has not taken such good effect as was intended, by reason that no person can erect or incorporate any hospital' ..., but her majesty, or by her highness' special license, by letters patent .... The act then authorized the creation of incorporations by the deed of the founder enrolled in chancery, without any act of the crown, with full corporate powers and franchises and to make any by-laws not repugnant to the laws of the kingdom": *Magill v. Brown* (Case No. 8.952) 16 Fed. Cas., p. 421.

analysis of the case. He thought that it was "not conceivable that the Quaker settlers of this province should have introduced those laws of the mother country, which would incapacitate them as individuals or a religious society from taking, holding or enjoying property as a matter of rights without charter"[282]. *Baldwin* argued for a distinct charity policy tailored to the needs of American society. "It is the true principle of colonization", he observed, "that the emigrants from the mother country carry with them such laws as are useful in their new situation, and none other"[283]. This meant, for example, that the twenty-one charitable purposes listed in the Elizabethan Statute should be extended. *Magill v. Brown* was both an acknowledgment of American indebtedness to English law and a declaration of philanthropic independence[284]. This policy was later expressly followed by the Supreme Court in *Vidal v. Girard's Executor* (1844) with *Justice Story* presiding[285]. In the wake of the *Magill* and *Girard* cases a more and more liberal approach towards charitable endeavours gained ground in the United States[286].

5. Constitutional Protection of Charities

Savigny pleaded for complete public control over corporations and foundations[287]. Foundations even seemed to be part of the state administration. In the United States, we find a different picture. Charities were explicitly protected by the Constitutions of Pennsylvania (1776), Vermont (1777) Massachusetts (1780) and New Hampshire (1784)[288]. However, public control over corporations was an important issue, too. The Federal Constitution was silent on the protection of cha-

282 *Magill v. Brown* (Case No. 8.952) 16 Fed. Cas., p. 410.

283 *Magill v. Brown* (Case No. 8.952) 16 Fed. Cas., p. 448.

284 Cf. *Justice Baldwin* in *Magill v. Brown:* "If there was any part of the law of England which could be congenial to the spirit and policy of the colony, and likely to be adopted by a society of men who sought an asylum from persecution for religious opinion, it would be that which would afford the best protection in the enjoyment of their rights, privileges, immunities and estates as a religious society" (Case No. 8.952) 16 Fed. Cas., p. 409; *Wyllie* (n. 81) 219.

285 43 U.S. (2 Howard) 125 (1844). Although this decision did not affect the status of charitable trusts in states such as Virginia and New York. In New York, the charitable trust was only reintroduced after the failure of the Tilden trust in the 1890s following a set of legal reforms. Cf. *James Barr Ames*, Essays in Legal History, Cambridge Mass., 1893, pp. 286 ff.

286 *Chief Justice Gray:* "A charity ... may be more fully defined as a gift, to be applied ... for the benefit of an indefinite number of persons, either by bringing their minds or hearts under the influence of education or religion, by relieving their bodies from disease, suffering or constraint, by assisting them to establish themselves in life, or by erecting or maintaining public buildings or works or otherwise lessening the burdens of government": *Jackson v. Phillips,* 14 Allen 339, p. 356 (Massachusetts 1867).

287 *Savigny* (n. 26) 278 f.

288 *Wyllie* (n. 81) 205 f. These were mostly states, where there was a close relationship between the state's lawmakers and the leaders of their religious and charitable societies; *Miller* (n. 176) 15 f.

rities. But it provided that no state could impair the obligation of a contract. But what was a "contract"? The Supreme Court had to deal with this question in *The Trustees of Dartmouth College v. Woodward* (1819), one of the most publicized cases of the time[289].

The case arose because the General Assembly of the state of New Hampshire had amended the Statutes of Dartmouth College to the effect that the number of trustees should be increased from 11 to 21. The additional trustees were to be chosen by the government. In addition, the government planned to set up a Board of Overseers and to appoint 21 of its 25 members[290]. The College opposed these measures[291]. Before the Supreme Court, Dartmouth College was represented by a "galaxy of legal talent"[292]. In his argument for the College, *Jeremiah Mason* announced: "[p]ermit the legislature, in this instance, to abolish a charter of corporate privileges and there will be no ground left on which they can be restrained from abolishing patents of land. The great principle of security for private property will be destroyed"[293].

The Supreme Court supported this argument. *Chief Justice Marshall* delivered the majority opinion, *Story* entered a separate concurring opinion[294]. If it were a public corporation, then the state had a right to control it, even to the point of amending its charter. But the Court held that Dartmouth was a "private eleemosynary corporation", endowed with the capacity to take property on the faith of its charter. Therefore, the state had no general right of regulation but had to respect the charter of the corporation. No legislature was allowed to change the terms of any charter which a previous legislature had granted[295]. Again, it was *Justice Story* who advanced the private law conceptualization of the eleemosynary corporation. He held that "from the very nature of the case, therefore, there was an implied con-

---

289 17 U.S. (4 Wheaton) 518 (1819). The College was represented by *Daniel Webster*, one of America's leading advocates at the time. His biographer described the last minutes of Webster's four hour argument as follows: "Sir, you may destroy this institution; it is weak; it is in your hands ...". ..."It is, sir, as I have said a small college. And yet there are those who love it". At that point, according to Webster's biographer, *Chief Justice Marshall's* eyes were "suffused with tears", there was a "deathlike stillness" in the room; "it lasted for some moments; every one seemed to be slowly recovering": *George T. Curtis*, Life of Daniel Webster, vol. 1, 2nd ed., New York, 1872, pp. 169 f.

290 For a survey of the proceedings, see *Whitehead* (n. 268) 65 - 75.

291 The College lost the case in the courts of New Hampshire. For a full account of the proceedings in New Hampshire see *Timothy Farrar*, Report of the Case of the Trustees of Dartmouth College against William H. Woodward, Portsmouth, 1819.

292 *Whitehead* (n. 268) 67.

293 *Farrar* (n. 291) 52. For the original charter of Dartmouth College and its various amendments, see *Edward C. Elliott, Merritt M. Chambers*, Charters and Basic Laws of Selected American Universities and Colleges, New York. 1934, pp. 176 - 187.

294 There was another concurring opinion by *Justice Washington* and a silent dissent by *Justice Duvall*.

295 *Miller* (n. 176) 24.

tract on the part of the crown with every benefactor, that if he would give his money, it should be deemed a charity protected by the charter, and be administered by the corporation according to the general law of the land. As soon, then, as a donation was made to the corporation, there was an implied contract springing up, and founded on a valuable consideration, that the crown would not revoke, or alter the charter, or change its administration, without the consent of the corporation. There was also an implied contract between the corporation itself, and every benefactor upon a like consideration, that it would administer his bounty according to the terms, and for the objects stipulated in the charter"[296]. It was this construction of a corporate charter as a tripartite contract which allowed the Supreme Court to bring the charter under the contract clause of the Federal Constitution[297] and to strike down the statute of the legislature of New Hampshire[298]. In his Commentaries, *Chancellor Kent* stressed that in *Dartmouth College,* the Supreme Court had placed charitable corporations under the same constitutional protection as individuals[299].

Constitutional protection of charities was based on individual basic rights, not just the right of property as in *Dartmouth College*[300] but also the right of conscience and religious worship[301]. In *Magill v. Brown, Justice Baldwin* referred to the Bill of Rights which declared "it to be the natural and inherent right of all men to acquire, possess and enjoy property", and the Constitution which protected all members of society "in their persons and estates"[302].

These references to natural rights and to Natural law were frequent in this "age of discovery"[303] of American law[304]. *Roscoe Pound* accurately described the way in which the theological Natural law in early 19th century America was replaced

---

296 *The Trustees of Dartmouth College v. Woodward* 17 U.S. (4 Wheaton) 518, 689 (1819).

297 "No State shall ... pass any ... law impairing the obligation of contracts": Art. 1, § 10.

298 For a more detailed analysis of the decision, see *Austin W. Scott,* Education and the Dead Hand, (1920) 34 Harvard L.R. 7 ff.; *Miller* (n. 176) 21, 24, 42; *Whitehead* (n. 268) 67 ff.

299 *Terret v. Taylor* 9 Cranch 43 (U.S. 1815) 45; *Mason v. Muncaster* 22 U.S. (9 Wheaton) 454; *Society v. Town of New Haven* 21 U.S. (8 Wheaton) 480; *The Trustees of Dartmouth College v. Woodward* 17 U.S. (4 Wheaton) 518, 624 (1819).

300 "No subject shall be ... deprived of his property, immunities or privileges, put out of the protection of the law, exiled or deprived of his life, liberty or estate, but by the judgment of his peers or the law of the land": Art. 15 of the Bill of Rights. See also Arts. 2, 20, 23.

301 *Magill v. Brown* (Case No. 8.952) 16 Fed. Cas., p. 412; *Justice Baldwin:* "The view we feel constrained to take of the constitutions of 1701, 1776, and 1790 [sc. of the State of Pennsylvania], all of which remain in force so far as respect the rights of property, conscience, and religious worship is this: that all bodies united for religious, charitable or literary purposes, though without a written charter or law, are to be considered as corporations by prescription or the usage and common law, and entitled to all rights which are conformable to the customs of the provinces".

302 *Magill v. Brown* (Case No. 8.952) 16 Fed. Cas., p. 421.

303 *Gilmore* (n. 4) 19 ff.

304 *Pound* (n. 182) 22 f.

by a more political form of Natural law, in which an ideal of "the nature of American institutions" or the "nature of free institutions"[305] or the "nature of free government" was pursued[306]. The selective adoption of the *cy-près*-doctrine illustrates this point[307]. An example from judicial reasoning can be found in *Terret v. Taylor* in which the Supreme Court negated state confiscatory legislation[308]. *Justice Story* argued "that we think ourselves standing upon the principles of natural justice, upon the fundamental laws of every free government, upon the spirit and letter of the constitution of the United States, and upon the decisions of the most respectable judicial tribunals ..."[309]. The juristic creed of *Savigny* and the Historical School was a different one. As *Joachim Rückert* has shown, the terms basic rights, constitutional liberalism, Parliament, political people and formal guarantees had a negative connotation in *Savigny's* eyes[310]. In his "Interpretations of Legal History", *Roscoe Pound* stressed that the Historical School was a reaction to the previous era of Natural-law thinking and its "paper-constitution making and confident disregard of traditional political institutions ... which characterized the French Revolution"[311]. Hence, *Savigny's* adoption of an authoritarian model and his rejection of any notion of freedom of association as a "tacit, arbitrary assumption" of an "absolute democracy in the constitution of all corporations" which was the transfer of the "public law theory of popular sovereignty" into private law"[312]. He adds that such a mistaken doctrine could only have been thought out, because the Natural lawyers had failed to distinguish clearly between the shell of the corporation and its members[313]. In Germany, freedom of association was introduced in 1908 and then not even on a constitutional level[314].

VI. Conclusion

If we were to venture into the modern German law of foundations, we would – to put it euphemistically – encounter a maze of legislation and legal concepts. The law of foundations remains a "stepchild" of German private law[315]. This is a rare

305 Cf. *Holden v. James* 11 Mass. 396, 398, 403 - 405 (1814); *Justice Chase*, in *Calder v. Bull* 3 Dallas (U.S.) 386, 388 (1798).

306 *Benson v. Mayer* 10 Barb. (New York) 223, 244 - 245 (1850).

307 See *supra* text accompanying footnotes 241 f.

308 9 Cranch 49 (1815).

309 *Terret v. Taylor* 9 Cranch 43, 52 (1815).

310 *Rückert* (n. 25) 224.

311 *Roscoe Pound*, Interpretations of Legal History, New York, 1923, p. 12 f.

312 *Savigny* (n. 26) 332; see *supra* text accompanying footnotes 150 ff.

313 313 *Savigny* (n. 26) 332.

314 Cf. *Michael Stolleis*, Geschichte des öffentlichen Rechts in Deutschland, vol. 2, München, 1992, pp. 371 ff.; *Dieter Grimm*, Deutsche Verfassungsgeschichte 1776 - 1866, Frankfurt/Main, 1988, pp. 129 ff.

phenomenon in a legal system which rates order highly. Is this *Savigny's* legacy? Could it be that *Savigny*, the "epoch-making man", "the *Newton* of the science of law" could have failed in this field[316]? Was *Savigny's* approach an example of German lecture-room jurisprudence?

We must leave these questions unanswered, for it requires us to go into the details of modern German law. However, we can say that *Savigny's* legacy and the legacy of his time in this field are still alive. *Savigny*'s model of the foundation was an administrative law model with virtual integration into the state machinery[317]. It is noteworthy that in the entire theory of legal personality that *Savigny* presents, neither courts nor the administrators nor the beneficiaries of charities play any role. *Savigny* refused to look "beyond the legal form" of a corporation or foundation in support of individual rights[318] as the Supreme Court had done in the *Dartmouth College* case. Across the Atlantic, even corporations which were under state or church influence became more and more independent and private in character. A complex, often blurry, system of trustees, overseers, visitors and beneficiaries took root. Judges played a pivotal role in this development and in many of the judgments we find surprising elements of a "policy-oriented"[319] or "instrumental"[320] approach to the law.

Savigny aimed at creating a legal order which would be clear enough so that a judge could apply it in an almost mechanical way[321]. This explains why *Savigny's* theory of legal personality was based on a closed system of concepts[322] and why his theory with its axiomatic distinction between foundation and corporation had to be more formalistic than the American concept of a synthesis of the law of charitable trusts and the law of corporations which provided for flexibility to the

---

315 *Staudinger/Coing* (n. 88) Vorbemerkung 2 concerning §§ 80 - 88.

316 *Mathias Reimann*, A Career in Itself – The German Professoriate as a Model for American Legal Academia, in: *idem* (ed.), The Reception of Continental Ideas in the Common Law World 1820 - 1920, Berlin, 1993, p. 170, fn. 14, 17. *Reimann* cites from *James Montmorency*, Friedrich Carl von Savigny, in: John MacDonell and Edward Manson (eds.), Great Jurists of the World, vol. 2, Boston, 1914, pp. 561 ff.

317 See *supra* text accompanying footnote 327.

318 Cf. *Justice Baldwin's* insistence upon individual rights: "The rights of conscience were declared inviolable by the charter of privileges of 1701, granted by William Penn to the people of the colony. No person who lived quietly under the government and acknowledged one God, should be in any case molested, or prejudiced in his estate, because of his conscientious persuasion": *Magill v. Brown* (Case No. 8.952) 16 Fed. Cas., pp. 416 f.

319 *Gilmore* (n. 4) 34.

320 *Horwitz* (n. 4) 1 ff.

321 Besides, because of the lack of subjective rights on the part of the beneficiaries it would be difficult to see how a dispute could be brought to court. This circumstance also explains why there is relatively little case law on foundations in Germany as opposed to the United States.

322 On the idea of the legal system as a closed system of institutions and rules, cf. *Wieacker/Weir* (n. 3) 343.

detriment of legal certainty[323]. In spite of widespread political rejection of equity in the United States, the law of charity was based on substantive equity. The parallel with the pre-Historical School system is striking. The Natural law had achieved such flexibility by an interpretation "iuris et aequitatis ratione"[324]. The *Städel* case had shown the doctrinal weakness of this approach.

In *Savigny's* theory of legal personality neither fiduciary obligations nor trust-concepts play any role. One explanation could be that in the Pandectist system there was no longer room for "fettered ownership" or "trust-like devices" which are favored by a dual ownership concept[325]. *Savigny* and the Historical School played a crucial role in introducing a unitary property concept[326]. If trusteeship was not available, then administration by the state seemed to be a good alternative, much in the same way as the Austrian ABGB conceptualized the *hereditas iacens* in the hands of the probate court[327]. It was only at the end of the century with the works of *Kohler, Regelsberger* and *Schultze* that fiduciary concepts were considered again[328], even in the context of the law of foundations[329]. But by that stage, German private law and the BGB had more or less found its shape. Only common lawyers could have missed the trust in the BGB[330]. The administrative law model was not challenged during the time of the codification of the BGB, because the dominant view was that all foundations belonged to public law[331]. Consequently,

323 The formalistic side can be seen in the stress on membership as the distinguishing feature between foundations and corporations. Moreover, it can be seen in the fact that the charitable privilege is given to the specific form foundation (*Savigny)* and not to the activity of the organization irrespective of the organizational form (American law). Did *Savigny's* system only give an "illusion of certainty", as *Peter Stein* suggests it to be generally true for the method of the civil law? *Peter Stein,* Roman Law, Common Law and Civil Law, (1992) 66 Tulane L.R. 1591, 1596.

324 This was the formula suggested by *Lauterbach* with respect to executorship: *Zimmermann* (n. 7) at IV. Natural law applied the same approach to the law of foundations. Cf. *Pleimes* (n. 8) *passim.*

325 *Feenstra* (n. 5) at I.; *Whitman* (n. 154) 166 ff. Cf. *F. H. Lawson,* A Common Lawyer Looks at the Civil Law, Ann Arbor, 1955, p. 201: "Perhaps the greatest difficulty the civilians have in accepting the trust is caused by what I have come to regard as an English peculiarity logically detachable from the trust, namely, the distinction between the legal and the equitable estate".

326 Cf. *Wolfgang Wiegand,* Die Entwicklung des Sachenrechts im Verhältnis zum Schuldrecht, AcP 190 (1990) 112, 117.

327 *Zimmermann* (n. 7) at V. Of course, the striking difference is that the Austrian concept only applies during a transition period between the testator's death and the *Einantwortung* of the heir. In the case of charities there can not be a distinct owner, and, therefore, this concept results in the integration of foundations into the general state machinery.

328 Cf. *Hofer* (n. 12) *passim.*

329 *Kohler* (n. 6) 277 ff.

330 On the relationship between trust and *Treuhand,* see *Stefan Grundmann's* chapter in this volume.

331 Benno Mugdan (ed.), Die gesammten Materialien zum Bürgerlichen Gesetzbuch für das Deutsche Reich, vol. I (Einführungsgesetz and Allgemeiner Teil) Berlin, 1899, pp. 657 ff.

the *cy-près*-doctrine as codified in the BGB allows the administration not only to redirect the funds but also to dissolve the foundation[332]. Traces of this model can also be found in the foundation statutes of the various German Länder[333]. "Juristic theory", in the words of *Maitland,* had proved its "petrifying effect"[334].

The characterization of the German private law of foundations as administrative points to an additional explanation of why trust-like devices do not enjoy a prominent position in Continental European private law. Especially in the 19th century, many fiduciary functions were taken over by the state. Since then they have only been "reprivatized" in a rudimentary fashion. *Reinhard Zimmermann's* analysis of executorship in this volume provides another piece of evidence[335]. Even if these legal institutes have been reintegrated into the private law system, such integration is sometimes merely nominal and not substantial in character as in the case of the German law of foundations. Considering that the pre-19th century context and continuity of the law of charity had been lost with the Historical School, this is not surprising. Legal history could have made a change. Unfortunately, German historiography in the field of "trust and *Treuhand*" remained heavily ideological, and hence counterproductive[336].

---

332 § 87I BGB: If the realization of the purpose of the foundation becomes impossible or if it endangers the public good (*Gemeinwohl*). the administration can order a new purpose or dissolve the foundation. Such a decision qualifies as an administrative act. Judicial relief has to be sought before the administrative courts.

333 Modern German law of foundations is not uniformly codified. The BGB contains some fragmentary provisions (§§ 80 - 88 BGB). The German *Länder* have enacted foundation statutes which do not even share common definitions for such terms as "municipal foundation", "church foundation", "private law foundation" or "public law foundation". The definition of these concepts is still much debated in the literature. The most basic distinction between private and charitable trusts is only acknowledged in some foundation statutes. Moreover, the foundation statutes of various Länder apply the same law to public and private law foundations. See § 1 *Baden-Württembergisches Stiftungsgesetz;* art. 1 I *Bayerisches Stiftungsgesetz;* § 1 *Hessisches Stiftungsgesetz;* § 1 *Mecklenburg-Vorpommersches Stiftungsgesetz.* One foundation statute stipulates that the board of a private foundation can apply for the conversion of the foundation into a public law foundation (§ 20I *Rheinland-Pfälzisches Stiftungsgesetz).* Many more examples could be added.

334 *Frederic William Maitland,* Trust and Corporation, in: H. A. L. Fisher (ed.), Collected Legal Papers, vol. 3, Cambridge, 1911, p. 467.

335 *Zimmermann* (n. 7) at V. on the Austrian system of comprehensive and obligatory official estate supervision and also n. 166 (state supervision of estate regulation was recognized by some individual German territories) and n. 279 (with reference to the Nordic countries which seem to have replaced executorship by a system of official estate regulation).

336 Cf. *Michele Graziadei,* Changing Images of the Law in XIXth Century English Legal Thought, in: Mathias Reimann (ed.), The Reception of Continental Ideas in the Common Law World 1820 - 1920, Berlin, 1993, pp. 115 ff. The ideological tradition continued well into the 20th century. Two noteworthy examples are the studies by *Wolfgang Siebert,* Die rechtsgeschäftliche Treuhand – ein dogmatischer und rechtsvergleichender Beitrag zum allgemeinen Treuhandproblem, Marburg, 1933, and *Pleimes* (n. 8), written in 1938 and published after the War. Cf. *Feenstra's* (n. 28) review of *Pleimes'* work: "Pleimes a peut-être exagéré dans l'autre sens – les termes 'Irrwege' et 'Fehlkonstruktion' ne conviennent d'ailleurs pas

One could indeed raise the question of whether German law has developed the foundation as a distinct legal institution of private law. In spite of state supervision by the Attorneys-General or the Charity Commissioners, the Anglo-American law of charity represents a private law model. Noteworthy is the contractual analysis of a corporate charter as enunciated in the *Dartmouth College* case[337]. This contractual analysis leads to "subjective rights"[338] which allow individuals to initiate private law enforcement of the fiduciary obligations of the trustees of a charitable corporation. By contrast, in German law one searches in vain for such subjective rights[339]. The German law of foundations is characterized by the interrelationship between a public administration and the board of the foundation[340]. The administrative law character of the German law of foundations might also explain why the foundation form is used ever more rarely. In practice, it is superseded by the charitable association and the charitable limited liability corporation[341]. Neither form was developed for charitable purposes nor do these forms offer significant constraints against practices of abuse and personal enrichment[342]. Any trust concept would prohibit these abuses. But in good old Prussia there was no need for legal trusteeship. Prussia was fortunate enough to have a magnificent administration which would make sure that no abuses occurred.

---

tout à fait á l'historien du droit – mais son ouvrage nous aidera tout de même à nous débarasser de l'influence trop forte du Pandectisme allemand": *Feenstra* (n. 28) 444.

337 See *supra,* text accompanying footnote 298.

338 Examples for such subjective rights are rights of members or beneficiaries of a charitable corporation or even individual board members who have standing to sue. Of course, modern American law has no universal rule in this regard, among other reasons because the law of charitable corporations is state law. For an evaluation of modern American law in this field, cf. *Henry Hansmann,* Reforming Nonprofit Corporation Law, (1981) 129 University of Pennsylvania Law Review 497 ff.; *idem,* The Evolving Law of Nonprofit Organizations: Do Current Trends Make Good Policy?, (1989) 39 Case Western Reserve Law Review 807 ff.

339 Could this have to do with the theory that foundations cannot have members because of their "legal nature"? The right of membership *(Recht der Mitgliedschaft)* is the doctrinal focus of subjective rights in German organizational law: *Marcus Lutter,* Theorie der Mitgliedschaft, AcP 180 (1980) 84 - 159; *Karsten Schmidt,* Gesellschaftsrecht, 2nd ed., Köln, Berlin, Bonn, München, 1991, *passim.*

340 Cf. *Hagen Hof,* Stiftungsaufsicht, in: Werner Seifart (ed.), Handbuch des Stiftungsrechts, München 1987, § 11.

341 The two forms are the "gemeinnütziger Idealverein" and the "gemeinnützige Gesellschaft mit beschränkter Haftung". Cf. *Klaus Riehmer,* Körperschaften als Stiftungsorganisationen, Baden-Baden, 1993. In the Netherlands, which received the Pandectist doctrine of the foundation with legal personality, the foundation form is still very much used. Maybe even more so after two core elements of the German legal institution were shed in the Foundation Statute (1956) and the new chapter in the Burgerlijk Wetboek (1976): namely, the requirement of a minimum initial fund and the requirement of a state license. See *Feenstra* (n. 5) n. 99.

342 *Riehmer* (n. 341) 213 ff.

STEFAN GRUNDMANN

The Evolution of Trust and *Treuhand* in the 20th Century

Common Law authors often complain that lawyers on the Continent are reluctant to make the effort to understand the trust concept[1]. The same authors write about specific statutory forms of the trust's equivalent in the Germanic law family, the *Treuhand,* without quoting a single primary source: they treat the *Testamentsvollstrecker,* the testamentary executor who holds the powers of trustee, without reference to the German, Austrian, Swiss or Japanese Supreme Court or relevant doctrine in these countries[2]. Must we conclude from this neglect that trust and *Treuhand* have drifted still further apart in this century?

One main problem both in understanding and in conceptualizing trust and *Treuhand* is that contractual and property elements seem strangely intertwined in them. A second problem has long been equally well known. There is a great variety – mainly in civil law systems – among institutions that are functionally equivalent to trust or *Treuhand;* they serve similar purposes, but the technicalities of their juridical construction differ[3]. And indeed, three different answers to the question raised at the outset can be given depending on whether one considers the third party rela-

---

1 Cf., as regards only the most recent literature, *Donovan Waters,* The Institution of the Trust in Civil and Common Law, Recueil des Cours 252 (1995) 113, 420. *Otto v. Gierke's* saying has become famous: "I can't understand your trust" – quoted by *William Frederic Maitland,* Equity – a Course of Lectures, 2nd ed., 1936, p. 23. Other literature quoted hereafter: Peter Apathy (ed.), Die Treuhandschaft, Wien, 1995; *George Bogert,* Trusts, 6th ed., St. Paul, 1987; *Helmut Coing,* Die Treuhand kraft privaten Rechtsgeschäfts, München, 1973; *Stefan Grundmann,* Der Treuhandvertrag – insbesondere die werbende Treuhand, München, 1997; *Hein Kötz,* Trust und Treuhand – eine rechtsvergleichende Darstellung des angloamerikanischen Trust und funktionsverwandter Institute des deutschen Rechts, Göttingen, 1963; *Eugene Scoles, Edward Halbach,* Problems and Materials on Decedents' Estates and Trusts, 4th ed., Boston/Toronto, 1987; *Austin Scott, William Fratcher, Mark Ascher,* The Law of Trusts, 4th ed., 12 volumes (+ 4 Supplements 1991, 1992, 1994, 1996), Boston/New York/Toronto/London, 1987 - 96; *J.C. Shepherd,* The Law of Fiduciaries, Toronto, 1981; *Wolfgang Siebert,* Das rechtsgeschäftliche Treuhandverhältnis – ein dogmatischer und rechtsvergleichender Beitrag zum allgemeinen Treuhandproblem, Marburg, 1933.

2 See *Waters,* Recueil des Cours 252 (1995) 386 - 388.

3 Cf. *Kötz* (n. 1) especially pp. 40, 41 - 63, 97 - 114, 63 - 69, 114 - 120, 70 - 76, 120 - 125; *Adair Dyer, Hans van Loon,* Report on Trusts and Analogous Institutions, Hague Conference on Private International Law, Actes et Documents, 15th Session, The Hague, 1984, vol. I, ch. II (especially para. 57).

tionship (section I *infra)*, the contractual relationship between trustee or *Treuhänder* and settlor / beneficiary[4] or *Treugeber* (section II *infra)*, or trust and *Treuhand* as embedded in a whole range of functionally equivalent institutions (section III *infra*).

I. The Third Party Relationship as Starting Point

1. Characterization and Key Problems

Traditionally, and in Germany up to this day, the third party relationship or the property aspects of trust and *Treuhand* have been considered the crucial one[5]. This starting point is not astonishing in a world where "fear and fraud" have been regarded as the parents of the trust[6]. The examples in which trusts became instruments to hide the real intentions and to circumvent prohibitions are numerous, mainly in former centuries[7]; the preponderance of this type of trust examples is characteristic of formalistic legal systems in which the doctrine of circumvention and – more generally – of an interest-based approach is weak[8]. In the terminology

4 In Anglo-American law, lawyers are accustomed to thinking of the settlor and the beneficiary as different persons, whereas on the continent the contrary is true. The split has to do with the most common field of application of trusts – in decedents' estates – but the major tendencies in both systems can be explained without reference to this split. Therefore, whenever the term "settlor" is used hereinafter, unless specified otherwise it is meant to refer merely to a settlor who has established a trust – an *inter vivos* trust – for his own benefit.

5 For German speaking countries, see *Siebert* (n. 1) 2; as well as *Siegbert Lammel,* Die Haftung des Treuhänders aus Verwaltungsgeschäften – Zur Dogmatik des "Verwaltungshandelns" im Privatrecht, Frankfurt / M., 1972, p. 17; and in the last ten years: *Joachim Gernhuber,* Die fiduziarische Treuhand, Juristische Schulung 1988, 355; *Martin Henssler,* Treuhandgeschäft – Dogmatik und Wirklichkeit, AcP 196 (1996) 37; *Rolf Watter,* Die Treuhand im Schweizer Recht, Zeitschrift für Schweizerisches Recht 1995, 179, 219 - 236 (expert opinion for the Swiss Law Association [*Schweizer Juristentag]*) and even *Coing* (n. 1), who although stressing the importance of the contractual link (pp. 87 f.) treats the third party relationship in much more detail. Perhaps not surprisingly this is different when a practising lawyer describes problems of *Treuhand:* see *Manfred Umlauft,* Die Treuhandschaft aus zivilrechtlicher Sicht, in: Apathy (n. 1) 36 - 45.

6 *Attorney General v. Sands,* Hard. 488 (491), 145 E.R. 563 (Exchequer, 1668); and, among the numerous citations of this *dictum* in legal literature, *Bogert* (n. 1) 7, n. 10. The main early regulation concerning the element of form which was intended to guarantee disclosure and ban "fraud" was therefore named the Statute of Frauds, 29 Car. II, ch. 3 (1676), see *Scoles / Halbach* (n. 1) 304 f.; a similar view was expressed in Germany by *Friedrich Klausing,* Fiduziarische Rechtsgeschäfte – einschließlich Sicherungsübereignung, in: Rechtsvergleichendes Handwörterbuch für das Zivil- und Handelsrecht des In- und Auslandes, Berlin, 1930, pp. 368, 370.

7 See *Bogert* (n. 1) 8 - 10; *Grundmann* (n. 1) 11 - 14; *Paul Oertmann,* Die Fiducia im römischen Privatrecht, Berlin, 1890, pp. 124 f., 135 - 146; *Siebert* (n. 1) 30, 34, 44 f.

8 *Wolfgang Kunkel,* Römische Rechtsgeschichte – eine Einführung, 12th ed., Köln / Wien, 1990, pp. 85, 87; *Oertmann* (n. 7) 118; *Robert Schless,* Mittelbare Stellvertretung und

of micro-economics, one would treat these examples as cases in which externalities were caused.

The main issues discussed in third party relationships in this century both in the Anglo-American system and in the doctrine of *Treuhand* have been: (1) whether and under which circumstances creditors of the trustee or *Treuhänder* can seize the trust property without consent of the settlor or *Treugeber;* (2) whether and to what extent the trustee or *Treuhänder* can convey title to trust property to a purchaser if this is contrary to the trust instrument; and (3) the question of the personal liability of the trustee[9]. The two questions mentioned first are the most characteristic.

2. Effects of the Anglo-American Trust against Third Parties

In the Anglo-American system – despite a very detailed doctrine and jurisprudence – the main rule is well settled and relatively simple. The equitable interest of the settlor is treated as if it were a property right. Therefore the settlor can trace the trust property if it is seized by a personal creditor of the trustee (i.e. for a debt incurred for the benefit of the trustee and not of the trust)[10] and – in case of conveyance – against any third party who is not a *bona fide* purchaser for value[11]. The exceptions to this rule have for long been regarded as insignificant and can be neglected here. What is crucial for the historical view is that the main rule was already well established at the beginning of this century[12], and therefore one can safely state that, as far as third party relationship goes, there has been no significant change in this century in the Anglo-American system. This report can therefore concentrate on *Treuhand* and its effects as to third parties. Here, significant change can be found.

3. Lesser Effects of the *Treuhand* against Third Parties

(a) The Victory in Theory of a Purely Contractual Concept

At the turn to the 20th century one of the two major trends in Germany sought to reach the same result as had been reached in Anglo-American law by reference to

---

Treuhand, Leipzig, 1931, p. 17; also: *Scoles/Halbach* (n. 1) 13; this explains the title of *Austin Scott,* The Trust as an Instrument of Law Reform, (1921/22) 31 Yale L.J. 457. It might even be that feudal systems survived longer precisely because of the flexibility of the trust and *Treuhand* device which took away some of their rigidity in a key area: see, for a more detailed exposition, the contribution in this volume by *Karl Otto Scherner.*

9 For the majority of these questions see (for Germany) *Coing* (n. 1) ch. VIII (especially 161 - 183); *Siebert* (n. 1) 149 - 182.

10 See *Bogert* (n. 1) § 32; *Kötz* (n. 1) 30; *Scott/Fratcher/Ascher* (n. 1) §§ 2, 459.

11 See *Bogert* (n. 1) § 165; *Scoles/Halbach* (n. 1) 777 - 787 (with further material); *Waters,* Recueil des Cours 252 (1995) 277 f., 432 f.

12 *Bogert* (n. 1) 115, n. 81.

Germanic, more specifically Langobardien, sources[13]. The supporters of such a *deutschrechtliche* (Germanic) *Treuhand,* especially *Alfred Schultze,* used the condition subsequent as a technical device to arrive at this result. He interpreted the sources to state that any conveyance of trust property from the settlor to the trustee must be considered to have taken place under the condition subsequent that the limits imposed by the fiduciary relationship should be respected. Any violation of these limits or seizure contrary to these limits would therefore render the conveyance void[14]. However, the supporters of the opposite trend, the *römischechtliche* (Romanic) *Treuhand,* ultimately prevailed. It is true that the prevailing view would uphold an express stipulation of a condition subsequent[15] – a result which could be justified at least for claims by pointing to §§ 161, 883, 2113, 2215 of the German Civil Code[16]. An express stipulation was, however, necessary under this view and

---

13 For this tendency, the well-foundedness of its historical assumptions and the dispute about the two types of *Treuhand,* see in more detail the contribution to this volume by *Sybille Hofer.*

14 Developed by *Alfred Schultze,* Die langobardische Treuhand und ihre Umbildung zur Testamentsvollstreckung, Breslau, 1895, pp. 76 - 88. Among the supporters of a similar solution in more recent years is *Hans Schlosser,* Außenwirkungen verfügungshindernder Abreden bei der rechtsgeschäftlichen Treuhand, NJW 1970, 681, 684 f.; for precursors and subsequent evolution of this theory, see *Wolfgang Asmus,* Dogmengeschichtliche Grundlagen der Treuhand – eine Untersuchung zur romanischen und germanischen Treuhandlehre, Frankfurt / M. / Bern / Las Vegas, 1977, pp. 44 - 71, 152 - 246; *Coing* (n. 1) 47 - 50; *Siebert* (n. 1) 44 - 52, 213 - 232.

15 Solution developed by *Alfred Schultze,* Treuhänder im geltenden bürgerlichen Recht, IhJb 43 (1901) 1, 19 - 25; later confirmed by the German Supreme Court: BGH NJW 1962, 1200; 1986, 977; and: *Ernst Heymann,* Trustee und Trustee-Company im deutschen Rechtsverkehr, Festschrift für Heinrich Brunner, Weimar, 1910, pp. 473, 518 - 520; *Adalbert Raible,* Vertragliche Beschränkung der Übertragung von Rechten – eine Untersuchung zum Verhältnis von §§ 413, 399 2. Alt. BGB zu § 137 Satz 1 BGB, Tübingen, 1969, p. 181; *Rudolf Reinhard, P. Erlinghagen,* Die rechtsgeschäftliche Treuhand – ein Problem der Rechtsfortbildung (Referat), Juristische Schulung 1962, 41, 46; *Siebert* (n. 1) 215 - 219, 221 f.; *Wolfram Timm,* Außenwirkungen vertraglicher Verfügungsverbote?, JZ 1989, 13, 18 f.

16 The opposite view is equally strong, especially for cases in which the stipulation of a condition subsequent would render the conveyance to a third party void (if contrary to the trust instrument). The opposite view can invoke the principle that under German law any stipulated restriction of the powers of conveyance does not operate against third parties (§ 137 BGB): first *Richard Schott,* Über Veräusserungsverbote und Resolutivbedingungen im Bürgerlichen Recht, Festschrift für Felix Dahn, vol. III, Breslau, 1905, pp. 303, 324 - 333 and *Georg Hengstberger,* Stellvertretung und Treuhand im bürgerlichen Gesetzbuch – vorzüglich mit Rücksicht auf § 1189 BGB, Stuttgart, 1912, pp. 49 f.; later on *Werner Flume,* Allgemeiner Teil des Bürgerlichen Rechts II – Das Rechtsgeschäft, 4th ed., Berlin / Heidelberg etc., 1992, p. 363; *Hermann Haemmerle,* Empfiehlt sich eine gesetzliche Regelung des Treuhänderverhältnisses?, Verhandlungen des 36. Deutschen Juristentages 1930, vol. I, pp. 632, 689; *Schlosser,* NJW 1970, 684; and in tendency also: *Alfred Friedmann,* Empfiehlt sich eine gesetzliche Regelung des Treuhänderverhältnisses?, Verhandlungen des 36. Deutschen Juristentages 1930, vol. I, pp. 805, 833; *Claudia Scharrenberg,* Die Rechte des Treugebers in der Zwangsvollstreckung, juristische Dissertation Mainz, 1989, pp. 39 f. Some also hold that the stipulation of a condition subsequent cannot protect trust property from seizure by personal creditors of the trustee or *Treuhänder* (see § 26 of the German Bankruptcy Code): cf. *Hengst-*

such a stipulation was not deduced from the mere fact that the aims of the fiduciary relationship had been established[17]. *Schultze's* ideas were therefore not given effect in most situations.

(b) Some Traces of a Property Right Concept

The success of the trend which claimed inspiration in Roman law was not complete, however. One has not only to take account of the main issues discussed, i.e. the guidelines of discussion, but also of the results reached. There was a significant shift away from a concept that would treat the beneficial right in the trust property as a purely contractual one, a concept that had been taken for granted by *Schultze's* opponents.

The parameters of the discussion were fixed by *Wolfgang Siebert*. His monograph on *Treuhand*, probably the most important one in the first half of the 20th century, did not describe the duties incurred by both parties mutually, but investigated whether and to which extent the different technical constructions of a *Treuhand* were appropriate to produce the results intended also with respect to a third party[18]. Later on, this question remained the most important one in discussion. In most cases it has been treated as determined by the question of how closely the beneficial interest could be considered a property or quasi-property right (*quasidingliches Recht*)[19]. Some authors have characterized the beneficial interest even

---

berger (earlier in this n.) 49 f.; *Ernst Jaeger, Friedrich Lent*, Konkursordnung mit Einführungsgesetzen, 8th ed., Berlin, 1958, § 26 KO, no. 15; and in tendency also: *Scharrenberg* (earlier in this n.) 39 f.

17 BGH NJW 1984, 1184, 1185 f.; *Gerhard Anker*, Die Rechtsnatur des Treuhandverhältnisses – ein Beitrag zur Dogmatik des Treuhandwesens, juristische Dissertation Heidelberg, 1932, p. 53; *Helmut v. Kries*, Die Rechtstellung des Erwerbers bei treuwidrigen Verfügungen eines Treuhänders, juristische Dissertation Göttingen, 1965, p. 141; *Rolf Serick*, Eigentumsvorbehalt und Sicherungsübertragung, vol. III, Heidelberg, 1970, pp. 393 f.; *Siebert* (n. 1) 229 - 232 (exception for cases of direct transfer); *Ulrich Leptien*, in: Soergel, Bürgerliches Gesetzbuch mit Einführungsgesetz und Nebengesetzen, vol. I: Allgemeiner Teil (§§ 1 - 240) – HaustürWiderrufG, 12th ed., Stuttgart / Berlin / Cologne / Mainz, 1988, Vor § 164 BGB, no. 70; *Timm*, JZ 1989, 13, 19 f.; opposite view by *Schultze*, JhJb 43 (1901) 1, 23 f.; and later *Fritz Baur, Jürgen Baur, Rolf Stürner*, Lehrbuch des Sachenrechts, 16th ed., München, 1992, p. 621; *Schlosser*, NJW 1970, 684.

18 See *Siebert* (n. 1) 149 - 172, 219 - 223, 295 - 297, 325 f., 331 f., 407 f.

19 The terms used are *de facto* property (*wirtschaftliches Eigentum*) or quasi-property in most cases when discussing the right of personal creditors of the trustee to seize trust property: see RGZ 84, 214, 217; 127, 341, 344; 133, 84, 87; BGHZ 11, 37, 41; 61, 72, 76 f.; BGH WM 1969, 475; 1972, 383; *Ulrich Huber*, Die Rechtsstellung des Treugebers gegenüber Gläubigern und Rechtsnachfolgern des Treuhänders, Festschrift zum fünfzigjährigen Bestehen des Instituts für ausländisches und internationales Privat- und Wirtschaftsrecht der Universität Heidelberg, Heidelberg, 1967, 399, 411 f.; *Gernhuber*, Juristische Schulung 1988, 359; *Scharrenberg* (n. 16) 45 f. (but see also 121 f.); *Hans Schuler*, Die rechtsgeschäftliche Treuhand – ein Problem der Rechtsfortbildung (Korreferat), Juristische Schulung 1962, 50,

as a restricted right *in rem*[20]. Relatively few condemn these terms and categories outright[21].

The same shift can be seen in the major attempt to have *Treuhand* regulated by statute in the first half of this century.

Already during the legislative process of the German Civil Code before 1900 the question was raised by the Second Commission (and answered negatively) whether the *fiducia* should be tailored to accord with § 392II of the German Commercial Code. In commercial sales commission cases the Commercial Code gives the settlor a right to trace trust property if it was seized by a personal creditor of the trustee (and possibly also against any third party who was not a *bona fide* purchaser for value).[22] In the following years legislation was quite often called for[23], and both in 1912[24] and in 1936[25] the question was even discussed by the German

52; *Rolf Serick*, Eigentumsvorbehalt und Sicherungsübertragung – neue Rechtsentwicklungen, 2nd ed., Heidelberg, 1993, pp. 49 f.; *Siebert* (n. 1) 193; using property categories very explicitly: *Claus-Wilhelm Canaris*, Die Verdinglichung obligatorischer Rechte, Festschrift für Werner Flume, vol. I, Köln, 1978, pp. 371, 411 - 419.

20 *Otto v. Gierke*, Deutsches Privatrecht, vol. II: Sachenrecht, Leipzig, 1905, p. 600; *Reinhard/Erlinghagen*, Juristische Schulung 1962, 49; *Hellmuth Zimmermann*, Die sachenrechtlichen Beziehungen in der rechtsgeschäftlich begründeten Treuhand nach englisch-amerikanischem Rechte, Leipzig, 1930, p. 57 and *passim;* see also the anthology in *v. Kries* (n. 17) 123 - 132.

21 *Heymann* (n. 15) 529; and today: *Wolfram Henckel*, Haftungsfragen und Verwaltungstreuhand, Festschrift für Helmut Coing, vol. II, München, 1982, pp. 137, 138; *Jan Marwede*, Rechtsnatur und Aussenschutz des Trust und der Treuhand – zugleich ein Beitrag zur Dinglichkeit und zum System subjektiver Privatrechte, juristische Dissertation Bonn, 1972, p. 118.

22 See for this discussion: *Asmus* (n. 14) 283 - 288; *Giseltraud Otten*, Die Entwicklung der Treuhand im 19. Jahrhundert – die Ausbildung des Treuhandbegriffs des modernen Rechts, Göttingen / Zürich / Frankfurt, 1975, pp. 204 - 207; *Schultze*, JhJb 43 (1901) 1, 19 f.

23 See, especially, *Oskar Fischbach*, Treuhänder und Treuhandgeschäfte nebst Beiträgen zur Lehre vom Eigentum, von der Stellvertretung und vom Auftrag, Mannheim / Leipzig, 1912, p. 194: "Der Treuhandgedanke [mit echter dinglicher Wirkung gegenüber Dritten] hat sich auf germanistischem Boden zu voller Blüte entwickelt, von dort nur kann auch für die Gegenwart die weitere Entwicklungsmöglichkeit dieses Instituts kommen." Similar statements appear in: *Dreyer*, Das fiduziarische Rechtsgeschäft, Gruchot 40 (1896) 449, 456; *Hermann Schlegelmilch*, Über das Wesen des fiduziarischen Rechtsgeschäfts, juristische Dissertation Jena, 1904, p. 49, n. 74; *Schroeder*, DJZ 1901, 331 (note); *Paul Seidler*, Die Sicherungsübereignung, juristische Dissertation, Jena, 1904, p. 48.

24 *M. Salinger*, Empfehlen sich gesetzliche Maßnahmen in bezug auf die Sicherungsübereignung?, Verhandlungen des 31. Deutschen Juristentages 1912, vol. I, pp. 409, 501 (proposing a registration solution); cf., also, *Hansjörg Weber*, Reform der Mobiliarsicherheiten, NJW 1976, 1601 ff., n. 2 - 5.

25 *Friedmann*, Verhandlungen des 36. Deutschen Juristentages 1930, vol. I, p. 805 (especially 994 - 1009); *Haemmerle*, Verhandlungen des 36. Deutschen Juristentages 1930, vol. I, pp. 632 ff., (especially 695 - 706). There were many contemporaneous legislative initiatives in other European countries: see *Arthur Nußbaum*, Sociological and Comparative Aspects of the Trust, (1938) 38 Columbia L.R. 408 f.

Lawyers' Association (*Deutscher Juristentag*). In all cases the expert opinion – as with almost all prior authors – advocated rules treating the beneficial interest as a kind of property right. Parliament did not react to the demand for change and later the possibility of change in the statute seemed obsolete[26]. In the few cases, however, in which a specific statute on *Treuhand* actually was passed, as in Liechtenstein, the third party relationship was always the dominating point of discussion[27].

The same shift can nevertheless also be seen in the results reached for the *Treuhand* under German law – at least for the problem of seizure by personal creditors of the trustee. At the outset the solution of the German Supreme Court was as simple as under ordinary trust doctrine: a personal creditor of the trustee could not seize trust property properly ear-marked (and therefore distinguishable)[28]. This result was justified mainly because the possibility of seizure was considered a windfall for any personal creditor of the trustee[29]. Despite this, the court later changed its mind, and made the protection of the beneficial right dependant on whether the trust property seized had been transferred from the settlor to the trustee directly rather than from a third party[30]. This rule, however, nowadays constitutes only the

26 The most important attempt no longer advocates substantive change of the respective sections in the Civil Code: see *Hans-Joachim Musielak,* Entgeltliche Geschäftsbesorgung – empfiehlt es sich, die Geschäftstypen, die als entgeltliche Geschäftsbesorgung anzusehen sind, zusammenfassend zu regeln? Welche Regelungen wären dabei aus dem Auftragsrecht, dem Dienstvertrags- und dem Werkvertragsrecht zu übernehmen und wie wäre der neue Vertragstyp gegen diese Schuldverhältnisse abzugrenzen? Müßten bestimmte Geschäftsformen im Gesetz besonders ausgewiesen werden?, in: Bundesminister der Justiz (ed.), Gutachten und Vorschläge zur Überarbeitung des Schuldrechts, vol. II, Köln, 1981, pp. 1209, 1215, 1289 - 1316.

27 For this statute, see *Klaus Biedermann,* The Treuhänderschaft in Liechtenstein Law, Oxford, 1984 (translated from the earlier work in German – Die Treuhänderschaft des Liechtensteinischen Rechts, dargestellt an ihrem Vorbild, dem Trust des Common Law, Bern, 1981). For a similar project in 1992 in France – later given up – see *Henry Dyson,* The proposed new law of trusts in France, [1992] The Conveyancer 407.

28 RGZ 45, 80, 83 - 87 and especially RGZ 79, 121, 122 f. (principle of certainty, *Bestimmtheitsgrundsatz).*

29 RGZ 45, 80, 84; 79, 121, 123; *Coing* (n. 1) 178; *Heymann* (n. 15) 531; *Scharrenberg* (n. 16) 9, 46; *Gerhard Walter,* Das Unmittelbarkeitsprinzip bei der fiduziarischen Treuhand, juristische Dissertation Tübingen, 1974, p. 65.

30 RGZ 84, 214, 217; 91, 12, 16; 127, 341, 344 f.; 133, 84, 87; 153, 366, 369 f.; 160, 52, 59; BGH NJW 1959, 1223, 1224; BGH WM 1964, 179; OLG Köln ZIP 1984, 473, 475; *Friedmann,* Verhandlungen des 36. Deutschen Juristentages 1930, vol. I, 862, coined the term *Unmittelbarkeitsprinzip* (principle of immediacy of transfer) used nowadays; many authors still follow this doctrine: *Adolf Baumbach, Wolfgang Lauterbach, Jan Albers, Peter Hartmann,* Zivilprozeßordnung – mit Gerichtsverfassungsgesetz und anderen Nebengesetzen, 54th ed., München, 1996, § 771 ZPO, no. 22; *Dieter Liebich, Kurt Mathews,* Treuhand und Treuhänder in Recht und Wirtschaft, 2nd ed., Berlin / Herne (Neue Wirtschaftsbriefe), 1983, pp. 152, 156 (but see also p. 24 f., 474); *Hans-Christoph Maulbetsch,* Beirat und Treuhand in der Publikumspersonengesellchaft, Bonn, 1984, p. 131; *Rolf Serick,* Eigentumsvorbehalt und Sicherungsübereignung, vol. II, Heidelberg, 1965, pp. 81 - 84. For further specification of the cases in which immediacy of transfer was found to exist (putting trust property into a

undoubted minimum protection granted to the settlor's beneficial interests. In the 1950s the Federal Supreme Court (Bundesgerichtshof), followed by virtually all commentators, extended the protection to those cases in which the trust relationship was evident to third parties, especially those involving bank accounts held in trust by a notary public or a lawyer[31]. And in the scholarly literature this line of jurisprudence was generalized to all cases in which the trust relationship could clearly have been recognized by a third party[32]. Many authors nowadays even return to the line of jurisprudence of the *Reichsgericht* at the beginning of this century and – for the reason given – advocate that the beneficial interest be protected whenever the trust property can be distinguished from other assets (principle of certainty)[33].

Less far-reaching is the protection of the settlor against wrongful conveyances made by the trustee. In general, the standard for determining the existence of a *bona fide* purchase for value under German law is the absence of gross negligence (§ 932 of the German Civil Code). The standard applicable to acquisitions of trust property contrary to the trust instrument by conveyance to a third party is however different. The majority view, both in jurisprudence and in legal literature, is that the conveyance is void only if an intention to harm the settlor fraudulently can be imputed to the third party. This is not the case if the third party merely knew about the existence of the trust instrument, but did not induce the conveyance[34]. One can

---

bank account) or not to exist (damages for injury of the trust property by a third party; substitution of parts property), see *Grundmann* (n. 1) 312 - 314.

31 BGH NJW 1954, 190 (especially 191); BGH v. 7. 4. 1959, NJW 1959, 1223, 1225; 1971, 559, 560; BGHZ 61, 72, 79 (implicitly); OLG Köln ZIP 1984, 473, 475; BayObLG NJW 1988, 1796, 1797 f.

32 *Arwed Blomeyer,* Zivilprozeßrecht – Vollstreckungsverfahren, Berlin / Heidelberg / New York, 1975, pp. 153 f.; *Canaris* (n. 19) 411 - 419; *Gernhuber,* Juristische Schulung 1988, 361; *Maulbetsch* (n. 30) 131 f. (shares in limited partnerships held in trust); see also *Lammel* (n. 5) 9 f.

33 *Dieter Assfalg,* Die Behandlung von Treugut im Konkurse des Treuhänders – Rechtsvergleichende Studie zur Grenzbereinigung zwischen Schuld- und Treuhandverhältnis, Berlin / Tübingen, 1960, pp. 170 - 172, 178 - 181; *Uwe Blaurock,* Unterbeteiligung und Treuhand an Gesellschaftsanteilen – Formen mittelbarer Teilhabe an Gesellschaftsverhältnissen, Baden-Baden, 1981, p. 248; *Coing* (n. 1) 178 f.; *Grundmann* (n. 1) 315 - 323; *Hartmut Kümmerlein,* Erscheinungsformen und Probleme der Verwaltungstreuhand bei Personengesellschaften, juristische Dissertation Münster, 1971, pp. 135 f.; *Gaby Nickel-Schweizer,* Rechtsvergleichender Beitrag zum fiduziarischen Eigentum in Deutschland und in der Schweiz, Basel / Stuttgart, 1977, pp. 97 - 100; *Scharrenberg* (n. 16) 172 f., 176 - 179; *Walter* (n. 29) 150 - 153. In Austria this is the majority view: *Umlauft* (n. 5) 26 f.

34 RGZ 99, 142, 145; 153, 366, 370 f.; BGH NJW 1968, 1471; *Canaris* (n. 19) 421; *Peter Bassenge,* in: Palandt, Bürgerliches Gesetzbuch, 55th ed., München, 1996, § 903 BGB, no. 40; *Scharrenberg* (n. 16) 164; *Siebert* (n. 1) 159; *Leptien* (n. 17) Vor § 164 BGB, no. 69; *Klaus Hopt, Peter Mülbert,* Kreditrecht – Bankkredit und Darlehen im deutschen Recht, Berlin, 1989 (Sonderausgabe der Vorbemerkungen zu §§ 607 ff. BGB [Bankkreditrecht] und §§ 607 - 610 BGB [Darlehen] in: Staudinger, Kommentar zum Bürgerlichen Gesetzbuch mit Einführungsgesetz und Nebengesetzen 12th ed.), Vor § 607 ff. BGB, no. 193.

surely find good arguments in the legislative process before 1900 in favour of this position[35]. In an analysis based upon a weighing of interests, however, considering later legislative measures (as for instance the Basic Law of 1949) would make it easier to support a standard that looks to mere knowledge[36]. Any purchaser knowing of the breach of fiduciary duty would not acquire title. On rare occasions, the Supreme Court applied this standard implicitely by equating the standard of fraud with that of knowledge[37] and even sometimes explicitly for cases in a corporate setting[38]. Only few authors wish to adopt the gross negligence standard applied to the acquistion of property also in all cases involving the acquisition of trust property[39]. The justification for restricting the protection of the settlor in this field can be found in the German Civil Code: Its § 137 provides that any stipulated restriction of the powers of conveyance does not operate against third parties.

4. Differences in Concept

If it is therefore true that, as far questions of results in third party relationships go, trust and *Treuhand* converge at least partially in result, it is difficult to say the same for questions of conceptualization. In Anglo-American law the trust may well have stemmed originally from a purely contractual relationship and it may be that the right was a contractual one in the beginning which was given effect by Chancery or other courts of Equity against both the trustee and a third party. Today, however, the division in the judiciary has largely disappeared and these origins no longer influence the doctrine in the sense that the beneficial right in a trust must be treated as different from any other (restricted) right *in rem*[40]. In Anglo-American law no distinctions are made as to how far the protection of the beneficial interest extends, whereas the intensity of protection differs under the Germanic system from one problem to another[41]. This statement already gives a hint of the reality if one asks what the main differences in conceptualization are: Anglo-American law, on the one hand, treats the third party relationship as if specific property or some other restricted right *in rem* were involved. The German *Treuhand*, on the other hand, bestows protection on third party relationships only if specific legislative po-

35 See *B. Mugdan*, Die gesammten Materialien zum Bürgerlichen Gesetzbuch für das Deutsche Reich, vol. II (Recht der Schuldverhältnisse), Berlin, 1899, pp. 1 f. (Motive, p. 2 ff.).

36 *Grundmann* (n. 1) 328 - 331; *Huber* (n. 19) 415; *v. Kries* (n. 17) 88 f., 91 f.

37 RG JW 1925, 1635; also BGHZ 12, 308, 319 f.; see also *Huber* (n. 19) 410 - 414; *v. Kries* (n. 17) 19 - 22, 88 f.

38 BGHZ 12, 308, 310, 319 f.

39 *Kötz* (n. 1) 140 f.; *Reinhard/Erlinghagen*, Juristische Schulung 1962, 46.

40 *Bogert* (n. 1) §§ 2, 6, 7; *Waters*, Recueil des Cours 252 (1995) 274 - 278.

41 For the questions treated here for Austria, see *Umlauft* (n. 5) 36 f., 61 - 66; for Switzerland, see *Nickel-Schweizer* (n. 33) 97 - 100; *Watter*, Zeitschrift für Schweizerisches Recht 1995, 219 - 236.

licies can be found in one field or the other. Whether the settlor and beneficiary enjoys protection therefore depends on the specific statutory rules in each field seperately, as for instance § 43 of the German Bankruptcy Act which provides some protection also for contractual rights or § 137 of the German Civil Code which, to the contrary, renders any contractual restriction of the powers of conveyance inoperative against third parties. At the core of the question is always a process of weighing conflicting interests (of the settlor and the third party), taking as starting point the relative weight that Parliament has given to these interests in different areas of law[42]. In 1990 the question has therefore been raised whether *Treuhand* should be regarded as a part of property law in which some key principles of this field do not necessarily apply, that is: where party autonomy as to the content of the right is permitted and where no *numerus clausus* exists[43]. And later in the 1990s this has been carried still further by taking the characterization of the fiduciary relationship as a contractual one seriously. Under this view all third party effects (externalities) of the *Treuhand* are best characterized as third party effects of a contract, the contractual fiduciary relationship (*Treuhandvertrag)*, which have been approved implicitly by the legislature[44].

II. The Fiduciary Relationship

1. The Crucial Importance of the Fiduciary Relationship and Key Problem Areas

Much more direct mutual influence between trust and *Treuhand* doctrine can be found in the fiduciary relationship, the contractual aspect or *Treuhandvertrag*. In the terminology of micro-economics one would speak in this area about synergy effect. In highly a-formalistic, interest-driven legal systems like those of Germany and especially the United States it is in this field that the more intriguing problems can be found today. It is therefore not astonishing that in Anglo-American treatises more attention is devoted to the discussion of the contractual relationship nowadays than to the third party relationship[45]. The Restatement Third on Trusts, in its

---

42 *Grundmann* (n. 1) 305, 309 - 312, 315, 317, 319 f., 324 - 327, 328 f.; and in principle following this line of arguments: *Henssler,* AcP 196 (1996) 52 - 54, 62.

43 *Wolfgang Wiegand,* Die Entwicklung des Sachenrechts im Verhältnis zum Schuldrecht, AcP 190 (1990) 112 (especially 131 - 135): "Obligatorisierung der dinglichen Rechte".

44 *Grundmann* (n. 1) ch. 7.

45 See for the United States: *Bogert* (n. 1) §§ 10 - 14, 16 (third party relationship only §§ 9, 14); *Scoles/Halbach* (n. 1) §§ 9 - 19 (third party relationship only in parts of § 10 and 12); *Scott/Fratcher/Ascher* (n. 1) §§ 89 - 163 and especially §§ 163A-260 (third party relationship only in §§ 74 - 88.2, 261 - 329); and for Great Britain: *E. H. Burn,* Maudsley and Burn's Trusts and Trustees – Cases and Materials, London / Dublin / Edinburgh, 1990 (three chapters out of those not dedicated to one specific type [16 ff.] treat the fiduciary relationship, only one the third party relationship); *Graham Moffat/Michael Chesterman/John Dewar,* Trusts

first and up till now only part, also treats only questions of the contractual relationship (prudent investor rule)[46]. The disputed and contradictory results in many recent cases in this area also show the increased importance of the contractual relationship. One need point only to the control premium cases, the (corporate) opportunity cases, the prudent investor rule, or competition clauses applied after termination of the relationship to appreciate the point. Other indicators of the increased importance of the contractual relationship in trust or *Treuhand* settings are to be found in economics: Where there is discussion in the law related branch of economics, the law and economics movement, about trust and *Treuhand* it has always and almost exclusively been about the contractual relationship. As a matter of fact, not only is there no equivalent to the so-called Agency Theory[47] in the trust considered as a third party relationship[48], but Agency Theory has also become more and more one of the very few key discussion areas for law and economics. Moreover, if economic needs have driven the European Community to harmonization, certainly one of the two key areas in private law has been corporate and capital market law[49]. Here, the most spectacular proposals and successes have often been related to fiduciary relationships which follow exactly the normal rules of the con-

Law – Text and Materials, London, 1988 (specific chapters, for instance chapters 10 and 19, only for the duty to administer, none for the third party relationship; and in the remaining chapters clear preponderance of the problems of the fiduciary relationship). The same can be stated for the comparative law article by *Helmut Coing*, Rechtsformen der privaten Vermögensverwaltung, insbesondere durch Banken in USA und Deutschland – zugleich ein Beitrag zur Frage der Übernahme des Trustrechts, AcP 167 (1967) 99, which deals almost exclusively with problems of the contractual relationship.

46 American Law Institute: Restatement of the Law Third, Trusts – Prudent Investor Rule, as adopted and promulgated by the American Law Institute, St. Paul, 1992.

47 The basic studies are: *Eugene Fama*, Agency Problems and the Theory of the Firm, (1980) 88 Journal of Political Economy 288; *Eugene Fama / Michael Jensen*, Agency Problems and Residual Claims, (1983) 26 The Journal of Law and Economics 327; *Michael Jensen / William Meckling*, Theory of the Firm – Managerial Behaviour, Agency Costs and Ownership Structure, (1976) 3 Journal of Financial Economics 305; the first major transposition to a Law and Economics analysis is John Pratt / Richard Zeckhauser (eds.) Principals and Agents – the Structure of Business, Boston, 1985; few books of the Law and Economics Movement have been as influential as *Frank Easterbrook, Daniel Fischel*, The Economic Structure of Corporate Law, Cambridge, Mass. / London 1991, which mainly deals with agency problems; see also, for a specific area, *Ronald Gilson*, The Law and Finance of Corporate Acquisitions, New York, 1986 (supplements with *Reinier Kraakman*, 1988 ff.); in German literature, e.g., *Jürgen Reul*, Die Pflicht zur Gleichbehandlung der Aktionäre bei privaten Kontrolltransaktionen – Eine juristische und ökonomische Analyse, Tübingen, 1991, especially pp. 128 - 250.

48 Quite explicitly *Easterbrook / Fischel* (n. 47) 17: "The corporation's choice of governance mechanisms does not create substantial third-party effects ...".

49 For this area, see the classical treatise and compilation in *Marcus Lutter*, Europäisches Unternehmensrecht – Grundlagen, Stand und Entwicklung nebst Texten und Materialien zur Rechtsangleichung, 4th ed., Berlin / New York, 1996; for the second key area, the law of contracts, see *Stefan Grundmann*, Europäisches Schuldvertragsrecht – Kernmaterie des Europäischen Unternehmensaußenprivatrechts, Berlin / New York, 1998 (forthcoming).

tractual relationship in trust or *Treuhand* settings. The description of the problems of this relationship has often been somewhat harder for the Germanic law family, however, because the contractual, the fiduciary relationship is often discussed quite briefly at least for the traditional two-party *Treuhand* relationship. It is not sursprising, as a result, that the main streams of influence today run from the Anglo-American system to the Germanic – some even call the phenomenon a reception of law[50] – and from fiduciary relationships in the corporate setting to those in the traditional two-party *Treuhand* setting[51].

The main problem areas can easily be highlighted by describing the key elements of trust and *Treuhand* relationships: The trustee administers the assets for the benefit of the settlor[52]. The shortest condensation of the two elements of this phenomenon can be found in the often used German term of *Fremdverwaltung*. Because the trustee works *for the benefit* of the settlor, the first question to arise involves distribution of assets. And as the trustee *should make the decisions* – otherwise there would be no relief for the settlor – and as on the other hand the person primarily interested, the settlor, might want, or deserve to have control mechanisms, there is, secondly, a decision-making-process question raised. The solutions adopted in both areas do not seem to fit easily under a common roof. There is, however, still consent that the basic rule should ensure that the interests of the trustee do not determine the solutions adopted[53]. And complications always and only occur when interests of more than one settlor / beneficiary are involved. This leads to rules which vary in the different systems of law, i.e. the basic rule may be the same but the weighing of interests often leads to different results in different systems. Where there are specific differences, they are generally greater in the decision-making-process question than in the distribution-of-assets question.

---

50 See *Wolfgang Wiegand*, Americanization of the Law – Reception or Convergence?, in: Lawrence Friedman, Harry Schreiber (eds.), Legal Culture and the Legal Profession, Boulder / Oxford, 1996, 137.

51 For this second area, see III *infra*.

52 *Franz Beyerle*, Die Treuhand im Grundriss des deutschen Privatrechts, Weimar, 1932, p. 7; *Scharrenberg* (n. 16) 15; *Shepherd* (n. 1) 35 f. *et passim*.

53 Even the Chicago Law and Economics Movement which fosters solutions apparently contrary to this statement always stresses that these solutions allow enough gains for the trustees (in the corporate setting which they mainly address: for the managers or members of the board) to (over-)compensate the settlors / beneficiaries (the shareholders); see, for instance, for the insider dealing and corporate opportunity area, in which these questions first have played an important part: *Henry Manne*, Insider Trading and the Stock Market, New York, 1966, pp. 155 f.; *Dennis Carlton, Daniel Fischel*, The Regulation of Insider Trading, (1983) 35 Stanford Law Review 857, 870 f.; *Easterbrook / Fischel* (n. 47) 257 - 259; more in detail now: *Kai Lahmann*, Insiderhandel – ökonomische Analyse eines ordnungspolitischen Dilemmas, Berlin, 1994, pp. 109 - 118.

2. The Distribution-of-Assets Question

The basic rule just described is particularly well established for values well enough defined to have become vested rights in a legal system, such as property, patents or titles. In this area appropriating trust assets is clearly forbidden to the trustee. Here even a *meta*-rule exists, designed to guarantee the effectiveness of the basic rule and requiring the trustee to segregate and ear-mark trust property. This rule is well settled. It is invariably one of the first rules stated in trust law in the Anglo-American legal system[54]. It is, however, also beyond doubt in the Germanic legal system[55]. Indeed, it has found its way into some of the general conditions and legislation in the universal bank area[56], probably the major player in *Treuhand* settings. It is equally apparent in looking to the third party relationship: one duty owed by the trustee to the settlor is to make sure that his interests are best maintained in the third party relationship. Ear-marking may prove an effective device to this end[57].

The prohibition against appropriating trust property becomes more complicated once one defines values less narrowly, but rather functionally – something that seems virtually impossible in German-speaking literature[58], but which is done by

54 Restatement of the Law Second – Trusts 2d, as adopted and promulgated by the American Law Institute, 3 vols. and 2 appendices, St. Paul, 1959 and 1987 (Supplement 1995), § 179 (quoting about 60 decisions stating this rule since Restatement of the Law [First] of Torts, as adopted and promulgated by the American Law Institute, 4 vols., St. Paul, 1934, 1934, 1938, 1939); *Bogert* (n. 1) 359 - 362; *Kötz* (n. 1) 31; *v. Kries* (n. 17) 143; *Scott/Fratcher/Ascher* (n. 1) §§ 179 - 179.3 (quoting about 100 decisions). One of the most eloquent and impressive decisions justifying this rule still is *Chapter House Circle v. Hartford National Bank & Trust Co.*, 186 A. 543, 547 - 549 (Connecticut 1936); see also *Waters*, Recueil des Cours 252 (1995) 113, 431 f.

55 Very explicitly: *Klaus Mohr,* Der Treuhänder des Bauherrenmodells, juristische Dissertation Hamburg, 1987, pp. 144 f.; often the rule is mentioned only *en passant: Coing* (n. 1) 142 f.; *Harry Ebersbach,* Handbuch des deutschen Stiftungsrechts, Göttingen, 1972, p. 179; *Lammel* (n. 5) 141 f.; *Scharrenberg* (n. 16) 129; and: BGH KTS 1961, 140, 141. The opposite view in *Maulbetsch* (n. 30) 131 can hardly be upheld.

56 See general conditions of 1978 for accounts held in trust by lawyers, notaries public and public acountants – four different types with virtually identical content and with identical numbering: reproduced *by Adolf Baumbach/Klaus Hopt,* Handelsgesetzbuch – mit GmbH & Co., Handelsklauseln, Bank- und Börsenrecht, Transportrecht (ohne Seerecht) 29th ed., München, 1995, under (9). The new Code of Conduct in sec. §§ 31 - 34 of the Wertpapierhandelsgesetz (BGBl. 1994 I, p. 1749 [1758 f.]), the German Securities Exchange Act, does not contain an explicit segregation and ear-marking duty, but can be interpreted in this way: see *Ingo Koller,* in: Heinz-Dieter Assmann, Uwe Schneider (eds.), Wertpapierhandelsgesetz – Kommentar, Köln, 1995, § 33 WpHG, nos. 10 f.

57 *Grundmann* (n. 1) 345 - 347.

58 Here the definitions always are narrow and strict: see *Coing* (n. 1) 1 f.; *Liebich/Mathews* (n. 30) 55 - 58; *Bassenge* (n. 34) § 903 BGB, no. 33; *Siebert* (n. 1)102 f.; *Leptien* (n. 17) Vor § 164 BGB, nos. 58, 60; *Hermann Dilcher,* in: Staudinger, Kommentar zum Bürgerlichen Gesetzbuch mit Einführungsgesetz und Nebengesetzen, 12th ed., Erstes Buch – Allgemeiner Teil – §§ 90 - 240, Berlin, 1980, Vor §§ 104 - 185 BGB, no. 59; *Andreas v. Tuhr,* Der Allgemeine Teil des Deutschen Bürgerlichen Rechts, vol. II, 2nd part, Berlin, 1957, pp. 185 f.

quite a few authors in Anglo-American literature. There the question is raised whether the rules of fiduciary relationships only apply to vested rights or also (and with identical content in principle) to valuable information[59] and to valuable positions of influence and decision-making power[60].

At this point inevitably one has to discuss the foundations of the fiduciary duty or *Treupflicht,* the key duty in any trust or *Treuhand* relationship. There has been much discussion about this duty, but the elements of it remain rather diffuse. One has to keep in mind from the outset that the fiduciary duty of loyalty is defined in the relevant case law, at least in the core areas, as one which forbids the trustee to take any account of his own interests.[61] Two questions are of major importance: the justification of such a fiduciary duty and the distinction between different types of fiduciary duties.

For the conceptualiziation and justification of the fiduciary duty, the two major steps were taken only in this century. (That involving the third party relationship was taken much earlier[62].) The first was taken in the 20s and 30s of this century

---

Gernhuber, Juristische Schulung 1988, 355 f., seems to constitute an exception, but also treats only subjective and vested rights and not other possible values. One real exception, *Beyerle* (n. 52) 19 f., apparently has had no effect.

59 *Shepherd* (n. 1) 110, 113, 323 ff., especially 330; *Robert Clark,* Corporate Law, Boston / Toronto, 1986, p. 224, treats the taking of Corporate Opportunities under the title "Taking of Corporate Property" (but "in a nontechnical sense"). American jurisprudence is rich in this sense: see, among others, *Carpenter, Felis & Winans v. U.S.*, 108 U.S. 316 (1988) ("Newspaper had property right in keeping information confidential ... which was protected by statutes"); *Ohio Oil v. Sharp,* 135 F.2d 303, 306 - 307 (10th Ciruit 1943); for more material see *Gareth Jones,* Restitution of Benefits Obtained in Breach of Another's Confidence, (1970) 86 L.Q.R. 463, 464. Many decisions speak about "theft" or "stealing" of information: *Harry Defler Corp. v. Kleeman,* 243 N.Y.S. 2d 930, 934 (Appellate Division 1963); *Meinhard v. Salmon,* 164 N.E. 545, 547 (NewYork 1928). For historical parallels see *Bernhard Pfister,* Das technische 'Know How' als Vermögensrecht, München, 1974, pp. 34 - 36. There are, however, also quite a few statements to the contrary: *Paul Finn,* Fiduciary Obligations, Sydney / Melbourne / Brisbane / Perth, 1977, p. 132 ("... to call ... information property is merely to add yet another consequence to a decision taken for reasons quite unrelated to property considerations"); *Ernest Weinrib,* The Fiduciary Obligation, (1975) 25 University of Toronto Law Journal 1, 11 - 13 (appropriation of corporate opportunities is not forbidden because of parallels to taking of property but instead for reasons of policy in favour of protecting entrepreneurship); *E.I. Du Pont de Nemours Powder Co. v. Masland,* 244 U.S. 100, 102 (1917) ("unanalyzed expression of certain secondary consequences of the primary fact that the law makes some rudimentary requirements of good faith").

60 For the same kind of presumption as for valuable information, see *Shepherd* (n. 1) 110 ("... powers of the sort we have described are *in fact* a species of property"); and quite a few court decisions (see *Shepherd* (n. 1) 113), the leading case being *York v. Guaranty Trust,* 143 F. 2d 503, especially 512 (2d. Circuit 1944).

61 See *infra,* n. 70.

62 Conceptualization for the third party relationship seems to have taken place in the 18th century. For more detail see the contribution in this volume by *M. Macnair.* This chronological order is not astonishing, since flexibility in the third party relationship was the key element for the development of trust and *Treuhand* devices.

when it became established that fiduciary duties were completely distinct from other contractual duties – the leading case in the Anglo-American system being *Cardozo's* decision in *Salmon v. Meinhard*[63] and the key treatise in the German system being the one written by *Alfred Hueck*[64].

The second step was taken after World War II and mainly in legal literature, where a search for a general justification of this more stringent rule in fiduciary relationships occured. Even in the Anglo-American system a monograph led the way, something which is not astonishing given that a reasoned justification is a question of doctrine rather than of case law. For *Shepherd* two elements were decisive: that the trustee receives "powers", i.e. valuable assets (which, as can be deduced from the examples given, include valuable information or positions of influence and decision-making power), and that the transfer of these powers be made under a proviso, i.e. that the powers be "encumbered"[65]. For the fiduciary duty in the German *Treuhand* it is more difficult to identify the leading monograph because it is a monograph on the analogous relationship in corporate settings, i.e. the trust relationship between the board and the shareholders or between a controlling shareholder and his co-shareholders. *Wolfgang Zöllner* finds the key element in the power to influence the legal position of another person, a power conveyed to the fiduciary by the legal system (not necessarily by the other party) within a (pre-) contractual relationship (or another equally individualized legal relationship)[66]. In

63 *Meinhard v. Salmon,* 164 N.E. 545, 546 (New York 1928): "Many forms of conduct permissible in a workaday world for those acting at arm's length, are forbidden to those bound by fiduciary ties. A trustee is held to something stricter than the morals of the market place. Not honesty alone, but the punctilio of an honor the most sensitive, is then the standard of behavior."

64 Fiduciary duty has to be distinguished from the general duty of acting in good faith (§ 242 BGB): *Alfred Hueck,* Der Treuegedanke im modernen Privatrecht, München, 1947, pp. 12, 15 - 19; and before, but less explicit, *Alfred Hueck,* Der Treuegedanke im Recht der offenen Handelsgesellschaft, Festschrift für Rudolf Hübner, Jena, 1935, pp. 72, 74, 86 f.; later also the important treatises of: *Marcus Lutter,* Theorie der Mitgliedschaft – Prolegomena zu einem Allgemeinen Teil des Korporationsrechts, AcP 180 (1980) 84, 103 - 105, 122; *Ernst-Joachim Mestmäcker,* Verwaltung, Konzerngewalt und Rechte der Aktionäre – eine rechtsvergleichende Untersuchung nach deutschem Aktienrecht und dem Recht der Corporations in den Vereinigten Staaten, Karlsruhe, 1958, pp. 214 f.

65 *Shepherd* (n. 1) 35 - 42, 93 - 123; see also the criticism of his position by *Deborah DeMott,* Beyond Metaphor – an Analysis of Fiduciary Obligation, (1988) Duke Law Journal 879, 912 f.

66 *Wolfgang Zöllner,* Die Schranken mitgliedschaftlicher Stimmrechtsmacht bei den privatrechtlichen Personenverbänden, München / Berlin, 1963, pp. 341 - 356 and especially pp. 343 and 342: "Dem Maß der Einwirkungsmöglichkeit ... und dementsprechend der Stärke des ... Anvertrauenmüssens entspricht eine Pflicht zur Rücksichtnahme", i.e. the fiduciary duty (of loyalty), whereby one has to consider that "die Betrachtung ... hier nicht von der Anvertrauung durch den Betroffenen aus[geht], sondern von der Einräumung durch die Rechtsordnung." Forerunners of this idea are: *Erich Fechner,* Die Treuebindungen des Aktionärs – zugleich eine Untersuchung über das Verhältnis von Sittlichkeit, Recht und Treue, Weimar, 1942, pp. 76 f. (still invoking other elements as well); *Ernst-Joachim Mestmäcker,* Verwal-

essence both positions are identical because *Shepherd* also accepts the possibility that the proviso may be made by the legal system for the settlor and because both authors presuppose at least a (pre-)contractual relationship in which the trustee has received – again identical in essence – valuable positions *(Shepherd)* or the power to influence the legal status of the settlor *(Zöllner)*. *Zöllner's* line of ideas has become the prevailing view in Germany[67], *Shepherd* wrote for a less doctrinal system so that his theory attracted fewer followers (although it flows as an unnoticed undercurrent into main streams of case law). The examples he gives, however, are illuminating. They show that the mere holding of an influential position in a (pre-) contractual relationship does not justify the imposition of a duty of loyalty *(Interessenwahrungspflicht)* which would completely forbid the fiduciary to take his own interests into account: In adhesion contract cases, the enterprise clearly holds an influential position in a (pre-)contractual relationship and yet, it would be amazing if it was held to a fiduciary duty (of loyalty) as described above; the enterprise would be completely forbidden to take into account its own interests, i.e. it would have to further exclusively the interests of the other party. Therefore, it would not only be useless to formulate standard contract terms but even counterproductive. This is clearly not the law in either Germany or the Anglo-American legal systems which only try to restrict abuses of the enterprise's opportunity to further its own interests.

A division between duties based on the interests of one party alone, excluding taking the interests of the other into account, and duties where the interests of both parties have to be weighed can be found also in settings which, unlike adhesion contract cases, have uniformly been characterized as fiduciary relationships. Indeed, both within fiduciary or trust relationships and within *Treuhand* relationships a key distinction between *two types of duties* is established. In Anglo-American law a distinction has become accepted between a duty of loyalty and a duty of care. The key difference is that the second duty, where the fiduciary only has to come up to a standard of sound business judgement, applies only in absence of any conflict

---

tung, Konzerngewalt und Rechte der Aktionäre – eine rechtsvergleichende Untersuchung nach deutschem Aktienrecht und dem Recht der Corporations in den Vereinigten Staaten, Karlsruhe, 1958, pp. 214 f.; and even RGZ 132, 149, 163.

67 In the 1990s: *Meinrad Dreher,* Treuepflichten zwischen Aktionären und Verhaltenspflichten bei der Stimmrechtsbündelung – gesellschaftsrechtliche und zivilrechtliche Grundlagen, ZHR 157 (1993) 150, 154 f.; *Oliver Brändel,* in: Großkommentar Aktiengesetz, 4th ed., 2nd leaflet, Berlin / New York, 1992, § 1 AktG, no. 86; *Torsten Schöne,* Haftung des Aktionärs-Vertreters für pflichtwidrige Stimmrechtsausübung – Anmerkungen zu LG Düsseldorf WM 1991, 1955, WM 1992, 209, 212; *Wolfram Timm,* Treuepflichten im Aktienrecht, WM 1991, 482; *Johannes Weisser,* Corporate Opportunities – zum Schutz der Geschäftschancen des Unternehmens im deutschen und im US-amerikanischen Recht, Köln / Berlin / Bonn / München, 1991, pp. 133 f. (intertwining, however, several elements); but also BGHZ 65, 15, 19; 103, 184, 195. In the United States the same position can be found in *Harold Brown,* Franchising – a Fiduciary Relationship, (1971) 49 Texas Law Review 650, 664. For other approaches see *Grundmann* (n. 1) 135 - 140, 145 - 166.

of interests[68]. It may be difficult to determine which cases are which. However, once a relevant conflict of interests has been detected it is well established that a more stringent rule applies. For the *Treupflicht* the disctinction between altruistic and egoistic powers *(eigennützige und fremdnützige Befugnisse)* has also become universally accepted[69] and in the first case the fiduciary is completely forbidden to take into account his own interests[70].

The distinctions seem to coincide, but in fact do not. Both in cases of egoistic and in cases of altruistic powers conflicts of interests are possible. The business judgment rule therefore corresponds to what is called the prudent merchant's standard under German law (the prerequisite of *erforderliche Sorgfalt).* It is a standard completely beyond the range of application of a fiduciary duty or *Treupflicht* as distinct from a mere duty to act in good faith and not to breach contracts: The business judgment rule covers doing business where there are no possible conflicts of interest. Among the cases which do raise conflict of interest problems, there are some where decisions can be made by considering one's own interests, although the interests of others have to be taken into account to some extent, and there are others where one's own interests may not exercise any influence whatsoever. In the first setting it is asked by way of example whether a shareholder (who has the power to object) is obliged to accept a certain solution in a restructuring process of

---

68 American Law Institute: Principles of Corporate Governance and Structure: Restatement and Recommendations, as adopted and promulgated by the American Law Institute, St. Paul, 1982 § 4.01, 6 - 76, 6 ff.; *Shlensky v. Wrigley,* 237 N. E. 2d 776, 778 - 780 (Illinois Appeal Court 1968); *Harry Henn, John Alexander,* Laws of Corporations and other Business Enterprises, 3rd ed., St.Paul, 1983 (Supplement 1986), p. 662; *Hanno Merkt,* US-amerikanisches Gesellschaftsrecht, Heidelberg, 1991, no. 687; *Shepherd* (n. 1) 48 f.; *Elliott Weiss,* Economic Analysis, Corporate Law, and the ALI Corporate Governance Project, (1984) 70 Cornell L.R. 1, 13 - 26.

69 See the commentaries in all areas: *Robert Fischer,* in: Großkommentar HGB – vol. II, 2nd part, §§ 105 - 144, 3rd ed., Berlin, 1973, § 105 HGB, no. 31b; *Peter Ulmer,* in: Münchener Kommentar zum Bürgerlichen Gesetzbuch, vol. III: Schuldrecht – Besonderer Teil, 2nd part (§§ 652 - 853), 2nd ed., München, 1986, § 705 BGB, no. 184; *Bassenge* (n. 34) § 903 BGB, no. 35; *Erich Steffen* and *Otto Friedrich v. Gamm,* Das Bürgerliche Gesetzbuch – mit besonderer Berücksichtigung der Rechtsprechung des Reichsgerichts und des Bundesgerichtshofes, vol. II, 4th part (§§ 631 - 811), 12th ed., Berlin / New York, 1978, § 662 BGB, no. 8 and § 705 BGB, no. 17 respectively; *Walther Hadding,* in: Soergel, Bürgerliches Gesetzbuch mit Einführungsgesetz und Nebengesetzen, vol. IV: Schuldrecht III (§§ 705 - 853), 11th ed., Stuttgart / Berlin / Köln / Mainz, 1985, § 705 BGB, no. 59; *Dilcher* (n. 58) Vor §§ 104 - 185 BGB, no. 60. The distinction has been developed at an early date by *Schultze,* JhJb 43 (1901) 2, and for corporate law, by *Max Hachenburg,* Aus dem Rechte der Gesellschaft mit beschränkter Haftung, LZ 1907, 460, 466. It has been taken up by the important treatises of the 1930s: *Alfred Hueck,* Festschrift für Hübner (n. 64) 72, 79 f.; *Siebert* (n. 1) 99 - 101, 169 f.

70 *Hueck,* Festschrift für Hübner (n. 64) 72, 75 f.; already RGZ 121, 294, 296; as well as BGH WM 1972, 383 f.; today this is virtually undisputed: see *Fischer* (n. 69) § 105 HGB, no. 31b; *Lutter* AcP 180 (1980) 84, 93; *Mestmäcker* (n. 66) 214 f.; *Ulmer* (n. 69) § 705 BGB, no. 184; *v. Gamm* (n. 69) § 705 BGB, no. 17; *Ernst Keßler,* in: Staudinger, Kommentar zum Bürgerlichen Gesetzbuch mit Einführungsgesetz und Nebengesetzen, Zweites Buch – Recht der Schuldverhältnisse – §§ 652 - 740, 12th ed., Berlin 1991, Vor § 705 BGB, no. 49.

the corporation[71]. An example for the second setting occurs where a controlling shareholder appropriates a corporate opportunity that belongs to the corporation. Here it is only the interest of the corporation which is relevant, and no weighing of interests has to take place.

A third step would be to identify an element which clearly distinguishes the two types of duties, which are so distinct in legal effect. This element recently has been proposed to be added to those put forward by *Shepherd* and *Zöllner*[72]. The type of fiduciary duty of loyalty that excludes the fidiciary from taking into account his own interests applies only and whenever the transfer of the valuable asset or the power of disposition to the trustee is gratuitous. Gratuitous promises often lead to rules based only on the interests of one of the two parties (the "donor") and are not the result of a process of weighing the interests of both parties.

In most distribution of assets questions it is easy to decide whether the assets were given for consideration or not. And it is therefore not astonishing that the rules can so easily be transposed from one country to another.

In the restructuring example the shareholder cannot be asked to disregard his own interests completely, because, by paying for the stock, he gave consideration for his power to take a proportional part in decisions. A complete disregard of his own interests can be required only if this person did not give any consideration for the asset to which the decision refers.

The trust or corporate opportunity doctrine can easily serve as an example. This doctrine is old in the Anglo-American legal system, even older than U.S.-American law itself: already in 1726 the appropriation of a trust opportunity by the trustee was held to be illicit because the trustee had not given any consideration for receiving this opportunity[73]. The trust concept came to the fore later on also in corporate opportunity cases[74] – with the sole difference that in corporate law cases it is more difficult to ascertain whether the fiduciary got the information gratuitously (in his role as a representative) or not (as an individual, independent of this role).

71 See the famous *Girmes* case, BGHZ 129, 136.

72 For this idea see *Grundmann* (n. 1) ch. 5.

73 *Keech v. Sandford*, 25 E.R. 223 (1726). Many discussions of trusts take this decision as a starting point; see, for example, *Weinrib*, (1975) 25 University of Toronto Law Journal.

74 See the leading cases: *Blake v. Buffalo Creek Railroad Co.*, 56 N.Y. 485 (1874); *Lagarde v. Anniston Lime & Stone Corp.*, 28 So. 199, 199 and 201 (Alabama 1900); and more recently: *General Automotive Manufacturing Co. v. Singer*, 120 N.W.2d 659, 663 (Wisconsin 1963); *Miller v. Miller*, 222 N.W.2d 71, 78 (Minnesota 1974); *Science Accessories Corp. v. Summagraphics Corp.*, 425 A.2d 957, 958 f. (Delaware 1980); as well as *Victor Brudney, Robert Clark*, A New Look at Corporate Opportunities, (1981) 94 Harvard L.R. 997, 1001 f., 1023; *Paul Carrington, Dan McElroy*, The Doctrine of Corporate Opportunity as Applied to Officers, Directors and Stockholders of Corporations, (1959) 14 The Business Lawyer 957, 958; *Notker Polley*, Wettbewerbsverbot und Geschäftschancenlehre – eine Untersuchung am Beispiel der Geschäftsleitung von US-Corporation und deutscher GmbH, Baden-Baden, 1993, pp. 38, 48 f.; *Weisser* (n. 67) 1, 77.

The controlling shareholder who gets information about an opportunity from the corporation has paid just as little as a manager or a member of the board. They are all completely compensated for what they invested (capital or work) by the agreed-upon returns (dividends or salary, bonus etc.). The aspect of gratuitous transfer is clearly the same; and even in the United States where many cases have been decided against the corporation[75] it has never been suggested that weighing its interests against those of the management, control shareholder etc. would be appropriate in these cases[76]. It has only been suggested that in the absence of any interests of the corporation, these persons might take the opportunity. And the key question is under what circumstances interests of the corporation can be considered to exist or not. In German law the necessity of this doctrine has been felt only recently because the most important types of trustees and fiduciaries economically speaking face an extensive prohibition against competing. When the doctrine began to influence German law, however, it was developed in strict parallelism to Anglo-American doctrine and jurisprudence[77]. This not only shows the importance of gratuitous transfer for evaluating the acts of a whole range of different trustee-fiduciaries. It also demonstrates that in the distribution-of-assets question, where a clear and simple key principle can be applied, solutions are easily transposed from one legal order to the other. This is not astonishing. In principle the trustee has to ascertain the best solution for the settlor in the distribution-of-assets question. What is best is a question of applied economics and therefore does not radically change from one country to another in a today's globalized economic world[78].

3. The Decision-Making-Process Question

The fiduciary's duty not to take into account his own interests can be seen also in the legal rules for the decision making process. Under German law the result is relatively clear-cut: The settlor has the right to any information at any time about the trust property and its administration (§ 666 of the German Civil Code)[79] and

---

75 See *Pat Chew*, Competing Interests in the Corporate Opportunity Doctrine, (1988/89) 67 North Carolina Law Review 435, 452, n. 53 (about 50% of the decisions in favour of the management, controlling shareholder etc.).

76 So far the only important opponents to this view, the Chicago School (see *supra* n. 54), have not had any influence on the case law in this respect.

77 See the first two monographs in this area: *Polley* (n. 71); *Weisser* (n. 67); and criticizing this fact: *Thomas Paefgen*, Die Geschäftschancenlehre – ein notwendiger Rechtsimport?, Die Aktiengesellschaft – Zeitschrift für das gesamte Aktienwesen 1993, 457 (especially 462 - 464).

78 Globalization leads to converging and often identical basic duties in the contractual relationship: *Waters*, Recueil des Cours 252 (1995) 408 - 410.

79 See BGHZ 41, 318, 320 f. The only exceptions are cases of abuse and cases in which the question does not directly concern trust affairs: *Hans Hermann Seiler*, in: Münchener Kommentar zum Bürgerlichen Gesetzbuch – vol. III: Schuldrecht – Besonderer Teil – 2nd

may also issue any order regarding the trust property at any time (§ 665 of the German Civil Code)[80]. The model is one of an informed settlor who would have to suffer the economic consequences of his own decisions and who is therefore free to decide. In the absence of a directly pertinent order, the trustee makes the decisions autonomously.

This model cannot be found in trust doctrine. Neither with respect to the settlor's right to information nor with respect to his right to give orders it is apparent. This may be due mainly to the fact that trusts normally involve three or more persons and on the side of the settlor at least two (settlor and beneficiary). Wherever this is true, the rule that the interests of the trustee have to be completely neglected cannot be applied fully because the interests of settlor(s) and beneficiary or beneficiaries have to be weighed. In two-party relationships, however, the rules for the decision making process under German law seem remarkably well-founded if one takes private autonomy seriously. This leaves open the question of how best to treat trust and *Treuhand* relationships involving a plurality of settlors and beneficiaries.

III. Trust, Corporation and the so-called *Quasitreuhand*

Traditional trust doctrine would seem incompatible with a number of the statements made so far because some of the examples given have not concerned trusts but other fiduciary relationships instead. The split between them has lost its importance in the contractual relationship, however, and was therefore rightly neglected in the section dedicated to it. The split has more to do with the third issue raised, in which the trust is seen as one institution among others, functionally equivalent. There are quite a few sub-questions to this question: among these, common law writers often focus on the question of whether the legal systems on the Continent do not rather tend to "personification" instead of emphasizing the trust's inherent flexibility[81]. By comparing trust and corporation, however, they implicitly raise a second and perhaps even more fundamental question. This has to do with the number of settlors and beneficiaries. It asks whether there is only one, or more than one, and, in the event of the latter, whether these settlors or beneficiaries may even have structurally diverging interests.

Part (§§ 652 - 853), 2nd ed., München, 1986, § 666 BGB, no. 7. Moreover, without being asked, the trustee has to give any crucial information which might change the settlor's general perspective on the trust property: see *Seiler*, § 666 BGB, no. 5; *Heinz Thomas*, in: Palandt, Bürgerliches Gesetzbuch, 55th ed., München, 1996, § 666 BGB, nos. 2 f.; *Roland Wittmann*, in: Staudinger, Kommentar zum Bürgerlichen Gesetzbuch mit Einführungsgesetz und Nebengesetzen Zweites Buch – Recht der Schuldverhältnisse – §§ 652 - 7041, 3rd ed., Berlin, 1995, § 666 BGB, nos. 4 f.

80 See RGZ 106, 26, 31; BGH WM 1971, 158, 159 f.; 1984, 1443 f.; NJW 1991, 2139; *Seiler* (n. 79) § 665 BGB, no. 1, 14 f.; *Thomas* (n. 79) § 665 BGB, no. 3; *Wittmann* (n. 79) § 665 BGB, no. 1 - 3, 8.

81 See, recently, *Waters*, Recueil des Cours 252 (1995) 421 - 427.

1. Trust v. Personality or Flexibility v. Registration?

The trust has certainly survived both because of its flexibility and because it offers an alternative to registration and state control. The question raised may therefore be important in law reform on the Anglo-American side[82], but *de lege lata* it concerns mainly the legal systems on the Continent.

Under German law *Hein Kötz* has singled out three institutions which serve needs satisfied by the trust in the Anglo-American world: the *Testamentsvollstreckung* and *Nacherbschaft,* which are used to control succession to property for several legatees (and typically for many years), the *Stiftung* which serves to collect and administer funds for charitable purposes, and the general *Treuhand* by which an estate is administered for the benefit of one or more persons[83] [84]. The latter, the general *Treuhand,* is as open, flexible and exempt from any state control as the trust. The other forms, specifically regulated by the legislature, often are called *Quasitreuhand*[85]. In most cases, however, they are not subject to registration[86] and the fiduciary duty of loyalty is exactly the same as in general *Treuhand* relationships[87].

---

82 For a change in trust law via statutory amendment, see the discussion in *Waters,* Recueil des Cours 252 (1995) 421 - 427.

83 *Kötz* (n. 1) 40 f., and for the different institutions in detail: 41 - 63 and 97 - 114; 63 - 69 and 114 - 120; 70 - 76 and 120 - 125.

84 There is in this area, however, – as in any country with a highly developed capital market – a specific form of *Treuhand* as well, the Mutual Fund, which has been subject of harmonization in the Community: Council Directive of 20 December 1985 on the coordination of laws, regulations and administrative provisions relating to undertakings for collective investment in transferable securities (UCITS) (85 / 611 / EEC), Official Journal 1985 L 375 / 19.

85 *Friedmann,* Verhandlungen des 36. Deutschen Juristentages 1930, vol. I, 827; and later, by way of example, *v. Kries* (n. 17) 50; *Liebich/Mathews* (n. 30) 48; for criticism, see *Coing* (n. 1) 97 f.

86 This is true for the *Testamentsvollstreckung,* which is specifically regulated, but otherwise – like any trust – subject to state control only insofar as a probate court can be invoked. This is also true for one of the two types of *Stiftung,* the *unselbständige Stiftung* regulated by §§ 525, 2194 BGB (see *Kötz* (n. 1) 114 - 120; and *Coing* (n. 1) 57 - 59; *Schultze,* JhJb 43 (1901) 32 - 35, 35 - 46). The only important exception is the incorporated type of *Stiftung* (regulated by §§ 80 - 88 BGB): it has to be registered, but constitutes only an alternative to the *unselbständige Stiftung* which allows the parties to opt against personal liability of the administrative body.

87 For the registred *Stiftung* see, for instance, arts. 10, 12, 15, 25 of the *Stiftungsgesetz* of Bavaria of 26. 11. 1954, BayGVBl. 1954, p. 301; and *Ebersbach* (n. 55) 102 f. For the *Testamentsvollstrecker:* RGZ 75, 299, 302; BGH WM 1967, 25, 27; *Michael Schmidt,* in: Erman, Handkommentar zum Bürgerlichen Gesetzbuch – 2 vols., 9th ed., Münster, 1993, § 2216 BGB, no. 1; *Hans Brandner,* in: Münchener Kommentar zum Bürgerlichen Gesetzbuch, vol. VI: Erbrecht (§§ 1922 - 2385) – Beurkundungsgesetz (§§ 27 - 35), 2nd ed., München, 1989, § 2216 BGB, no. 2. The *unselbständige Stiftung* is considered to constitute an example of general *Treuhand* in any event: RGZ 105, 305, 306; *Coing* (n. 1) 57 - 59; *Harm Peter Westermann,* in: Erman, Vor § 80 BGB, no. 3; *Arnold Liebisch,* Das Wesen der unentgeltlichen Zuwendungen unter Lebenden im Bürgerlichen Recht und im Reichssteuerrecht, Leipzig, 1927,

Therefore the split between general *Treuhand* and the specific forms of *Treuhand (Quasitreuhand)* regulated by the legislature is of prime importance only for the third party relationship. Here virtually all specific forms of *Treuhand* do not enjoy the restricted degree of protection of the general *Treuhand*, but rather a protection comparable to that of Anglo-American trusts: trust property can be traced and recovered if it is seized by a personal creditor of the trustee and – in the case of voluntary conveyance – against any third party who is not a *bona fide* purchaser for value[88].

The multitude of institutions therefore has less to do with the search for incorporation ("personification") and state control than with the desire to offer a specific regime, largely *ius dispositivum*, for each one of several important sub-tasks. In the contractual relationships the law has upheld in all regimes the same basic fiduciary duty of loyalty. In the third context, these specific regimes enjoy a level of protection Parliament did not wish to give to such an open institution as the general *Treuhand*, primarily to avoid a regime of "fear and fraud".[89] The difference between Anglo-American trust and the Germanic family of institutions, ranging from the general *Treuhand* to the many specific forms of *Treuhand*, is therefore over-rated. One can even say that under German law the basic duty in the contractual relationship is virtually the same as in the Anglo-American trust and that the level of protection of the beneficial interest in the third party relationship is virtually the same both in the Anglo-American trust and in the forms of *Treuhand* specifically regulated by Parliament. The main difference is therefore that the German legislature wanted to pick the situations in which full protection in the third party relationship would be given. The general institution of *Treuhand* was therefore left at a somewhat lower level of protection, to be defined by doctrine and jurisprudence.

2. Unity or Pluralism of Interests on the Side of the Settlor and Beneficiary

It makes an important difference in delineating the appropriate duty of loyalty whether there is a single settlor or several, who may even have structurally diver-

---

p. 23; *Schultze*, JhJb 43 (1901) 32 - 35; *Matthias Cremer*, in: Staudinger, Kommentar zum Bürgerlichen Gesetzbuch mit Einführungsgesetz und Nebengesetzen, Zweites Buch – Recht der Schuldverhältnisse – §§ 433 - 534, 13th ed., Berlin, 1995, § 525 BGB, no. 13. The same is true, for instance, for mutual funds because of an explicit rule in § 10I of the German Investment Companies Act (*Gesetz über Kapitalanlagegesellschaften*).

88 See, for all important specific types of *Treuhand* regulated by the statute, *Grundmann* (n. 1) 33 ff.

89 The decisive argument in the legislative process against fullest possible protection was that otherwise general trust in the ownership of goods could be impaired: see *Mugdan* (n. 35) 950 (Protokolle, p. 2310): "... der Kredit könne erheblich gestört werden, wenn die Gläubiger einer Person nicht mehr sicher seien."

ging interests. In the first case it is simple to deduce clear results from the principle that the self-interest of the trustee / *Treuhänder* may play no part in trust administration. This is so because, where this obtains, no weighing process is necessary. This is true for the distribution of assets and in my view also for the decision making process. The same, however, is no longer true for a situation in which several settlors exist. Their interests have to be weighed and results of such weighing may be quite diverse.

An example dealing with the distribution of assets may be illuminating. As far as the fiduciary relationship (and not the third party relationship) goes, the board of a corporation is clearly subject to exactly the same type of duty of loyalty as the trustee is. Therefore, where corporate capital increases, the board must completely ignore its own interests. The result of weighing the interests of the shareholders (settlors) can, however, lead to a different result: German corporate law held the ratio of the respective shares almost sacrosanct and therefore contained a mandatory preemptive right which could be excluded only *ad hoc* and under very narrow circumstances[90]. In American corporate law the preemptive right is typically determined by the charter of each corporation[91]. The corporation may therefore choose whether it might seem more attractive to investors-shareholders to invest in a corporation where measures dealing with capital increase do not risk delay at the hands of a small shareholder who abuses his power. It may equally decide that this risk appears to be more important to potential shareholders than the risk that their stock will be diluted in a capital increase. The German legislature recently did rate the risk of abuse as more important than in former legislation: The pre-emptive right is no longer mandatory if the capital increase amounts to no more than 10 per cent of the stated capital and a price near the stock market price is paid (new § 186III of the German Stock Corporation Act).

Weighing interests of several settlors becomes even more difficult in questions involving the decision making process. A whole variety of results may be reached, the poles of which *Hirshman* has described as "voice" or "exit". Nevertheless the underlying principle remains unchanged: The interests of the settlors alone must decide the question of which solution is to be chosen[92]. And if there is variety it is not only to be found between different legal systems but also within each of them. The model of the specific type of close corporations regulated in German law (*Ge-*

---

90 For these circumstances see: BGHZ 71, 40, 44 - 46; later BGHZ 83, 319, 321; BGH WM 1992, 2098, 2100; *Grundmann* (n. 1) 460 - 465; *Heribert Hirte,* Bezugsrechtsausschluß und Konzernbildung – Minderheitenschutz bei Eingriffen in die Beteiligungsstruktur der Aktiengesellschaft, Köln / Berlin / Bonn / München, 1986, pp. 15 - 30, 76 f. and *passim; Marcus Lutter,* in: Kölner Kommentar zum Aktiengesetz, vol. V, 1st issue – §§ 179 - 220 AktG, 1990, 2nd ed., Köln / Berlin / Bonn / München, § 186 AktG, nos. 60 - 64 ("in principle not disputed").

91 *Henn / Alexander* (n. 68) 662; *Merkt* (n. 68) nos. 412 - 417.

92 *Albert Hirschman,* Exit, Voice and Loyalty, Cambridge, 1970, pp. 39, 102 - 105 and *passim.*

sellschaft mit beschränkter Haftung) would thus be one of extensive voice, the model of the mutual fund one of mere exit[93].

Is there then only divergence between trust and *Treuhand* where a plurality of settlors is involved? The answer may be that, contrary to what was said for third party relationships, the results may differ considerably, but that there remains a common strand in questions of conceptualization. The first point of convergence is that in both legal systems there are more and more authors who see that the basic rule remains the same whether there is only one settlor or more than one, who perhaps even have structurally diverging interests. Rules can and should be transposed from one scenario to the other[94]. The second crucial point common to both legal systems is that more and more authors have sought to define those situations in which an absolute duty of loyalty exists. This has occured not only in traditional *Treuhand* and trust cases but also in very complex corporate settings. They normally isolate situations in which a person did not give consideration for the assets or for a position of influence and decision making power. This again, has provoked very similar solutions in leading cases, for instance in the question of control premiums, the surplus a controlling shareholder can (and another shareholder cannot) earn when selling his stock. It is difficult to conclude that any consideration was given for the surplus (over the proportional price) because the investment in the beginning was exactly proportional. Both leading cases in the United States and the proposal for a Council Directive of the Community take this as main argument. They make sure that all shareholders are treated equally[95].

IV. Trust and *Treuhand* Irreconcilable?

Trust and *Treuhand* traditionally are seen as irreconcilable concepts. This is mainly due to a restricted viewpoint – often comparatists look primarily to the

---

93 See the summary in *Grundmann* (n. 1) 278 - 280.

94 The most important step in this field in Germany was taken when the Federal Supreme Court applied the fiduciary principle in a generally unmodified way also in the context of public stock corporations *(Aktiengesellschaften)* and here also among shareholders: BGHZ 103, 184 (esp. 194 f.); and again: BGH NJW 1992, 3167, 3171; very radical today is the *Girmes* decision: BGHZ 129, 136. A theory for the transposition of the pertinent rules from one scenario to the other in: *Grundmann* (n. 1) 268 - 284, 421 - 481. In the United States one may point for instance to the important role the trust concept played when the corporate opportunity doctrine was developed.

95 See *Jones v. Ahmanson & Co.*, 460 P.2d 464 (California 1969); *Perlmann v. Feldmann,* 219 F.2d 173, 178 (2d Circuit 1955); and even for Delaware: *Rabkin v. Philip Hunt Chemical Corp.*, 498 A.2d 1099, 1106 f. (Delaware 1985). Art. 4 of an Amended Proposal of 14 September 1990 for a Thirteenth Council Directive on Company Law concerning takeover and other general bids, Official Journal 1989 C 64/8 and 1990 C 240/7; later modified: COM (95) 655 final (now Arts. 3 and 10). For the development of the argument in more detail, see *Grundmann* (n. 1) 465 - 467, 475 - 481; and, for a law and economics analysis, see *Reul* (n. 47) 127 - 250 (both with further references).

third party relationship – and also to overestimating the fact that several different institutions serve trust purposes on the Continent.

Trust and *Treuhand* seem irreconcilable mainly in the third party relationship, and even here this appearance is true only in part: The results for the main questions are virtually identical as far as cases of trusts are concerned and those cases of *Treuhand* specifically regulated by statute. Only the "common law" *Treuhand* on the Continent offers less protection in third party relationships. The concepts, however, tend to differ more and more indeed, because the proprietary characterization of the beneficial interest is now universally accepted in the common law world whereas the contractual characterization of the beneficial interest has gained ground on the Continent.

In the contractual relationship the basic duty of loyalty is virtually identical – in both results and concept. It is still, however, equally disputed in common law and on the Continent, what elements justify a duty to neglect own interests completely. Such a duty exists only when the trustee / *Treuhänder* received the value transferred without giving consideration. The gratuitous nature of the transfer justifies that such a duty be imposed by the law. And this element can be tested also in more complex situations, namely relationships with a plurality of settlors.

It is this difference between cases where there is only one settlor and those where a plurality of settlors are present which counts more than the often mentioned difference between the flexibility of the common law trust and the more regulated and corporate type of relationship that exists on the Continent. In fact this difference creates structurally identical problems both in the common law and on the Continent: A plurality of settlors makes weighing of interests necessary. The results may therefore vary quite substantially in these cases. The basic duty of loyalty, however, is the same as it is in traditional trust and *Treuhand* cases when only one settlor is involved. This duty holds the trustee to a purely "altruistic" standard, i.e. he has to neglect his own interests completely. This is justified by the gratuitous nature of the transfer.

MAURIZIO LUPOI

Trusts and Civilian Categories (Problems Spurred by Italian Domestic Trusts)

I. "Domestic" Trusts

The 1984 Hague Convention on the law applicable to trusts and on their recognition concerns not only trusts corresponding to the English model, but any legal relationship which falls within the definition given by article 2 of the Convention. Almost every legal system contains instances of such legal relationships[1]; most lawyers would not consider them to be "trusts", either in their respective countries or from a comparative standpoint, and yet they *are* "trusts" for the purposes of the Convention.

It follows that, short of some interpretative device, the provisions of the Convention referring to "States which do not have the institution of the trust"[2] can apply to only a handful of States, while it is plain that the draftsmen of the Convention meant to cover most of the non-common law systems. Such is the case, for instance, with article 13, under which "No State shall be bound to recognize a trust the significant elements of which, except for the choice of the applicable law, the place of administration and the habitual residence of the trustee, are more closely connected with States which do not have the institution of the trust or the category of trust involved". The trusts in question may appropriately be called "domestic" trusts[3].

The scholar of trusts in an international context, then, has only two choices: either he goes by the literal meaning of the provisions or he takes account of the preparatory works of the Convention and rephrases the expression to read "States which do not have the institution of the trust *as an institution of general application*". The first solution is unduly restrictive and might jeopardize the application of the Convention. The second solution, at the price of clumsy wording, fulfils the

---

1 See *Maurizio Lupoi,* Effects of the Hague Convention in a Civil Law Country, in: Paul Jackson, David C. Wilde (eds.), The Reform of Property Law, Aldershot, 1997, p. 222, § 3, where the notion of the "shapeless trust" is set out.

2 Articles 5, 6, 13.

3 I would discourage romance language speakers against translating "domestique" or "domestico". The terms "interne" and "interno" would appear to be much more appropriate.

objectives of the draftsmen and aligns itself to the common understanding, so that, in my submission, it should be preferred.

Therefore, under article 13, domestic trusts may be refused recognition, since their basic objective elements are connected with countries "which do not have the institution of the trust as an institution of general application"[4].

I will not repeat here the reasons supporting my position that citizens of the so-called "non-trust" countries which have ratified the Convention[5] are entitled to form "domestic" trusts governed by a foreign law[6] – be it the law of another ratifying country or *any* foreign law[7] – and that article 13 is no more than a safeguard clause, quite properly inserted in the Convention to prevent possible *abusive* domestic trusts from being recognised; hence my submission that article 13 is no bar to the recognition of domestic trusts generally[8].

Of course, and in spite of the title of the Convention, there is no such thing as the "recognition" of a trust. Properly expressed, the Convention binds the ratifying States to *give effect* to the foreign law by which a trust is governed. Many questions have been voiced by Italian scholars once the domestic trust theory began gaining acceptance[9]. It is well-known that the civilian mind is given to building bridges over rivers well before there is any need to cross them; therefore, one might discard the whole of this paper, where some of those questions will be canvassed, as a futile exercise, and then totally unsupported by authority. Before doing so, however, there is a finer point to explore.

---

4 There may be instances of countries where, in spite of the absence of a general notion of trust, specific arrangements are upheld which correspond to one of the known categories of trust on the English model.

5 A non-trust country is properly a country "which does not have the institution of the trust *as an institution of general application*".

6 *Supra* n. 1, § 4.

7 Depending upon whether the ratifying State has availed itself of the reservation made possible under article 21 of the Convention. Italy has expressed no reservation, nor has the United Kingdom.

8 It might be appropriate to point out that Italian courts have had twice the opportunity to question the soundness of my position and have in both instances allowed a "domestic" trust to operate in Italy. The Tribunale of Milan has approved the decision by the shareholders of an Italian company to issue debentures guaranteed by a Jersey trust of Italian real estate (also the trustee was Italian): see *Paul Matthews,* Italian trusts for debenture holders, (1997) 11 Tolley's Trust Law International 20. The Tribunale of Genoa has homologated the incorporation of a limited company where the sole shareholder was a Maltese trust (with an Italian settlor and Italian beneficiaries; and the trust property was cash which the settlor had in an Italian bank); it is interesting to note that in this case the Court required to inspect the trust deed before granting its approval of the incorporation of the company. I should add that there have been many instances of domestic trusts established in Italy in the last few years: one of the latest has been a charitable trust formed by a leading Italian bank. See further n. 39, *infra.*

9 It must be pointed out that at the time of writing this paper the domestic trust theory is far from being the generally held view.

II. The Comparative Law Issue

Contrary to all private international law instruments, the Hague Convention is *one-sided:* civilians have to apply common law rules but very seldom do common lawyers have to apply civilian rules. In spite of the very broad spectrum of the legal relationships covered by the Convention, in most instances their governing law will not belong to the civil law world. The original thrust of the Convention was to make the life of *common law* trustees simpler in *civil law* countries. From a purely legal standpoint, the final outcome of the Convention turned out to be somewhat different because any notion of "foreign" or "international" trusts was eliminated during the proceedings of the Hague Conference. However, operational effects have reinstated the dominance of the common law element and they must now be reckoned with: foremost among them the formation of domestic trusts by citizens of "non-trust" (usually, civil law) countries, which subject them to a foreign law. It will usually be a law following either the English model or the newly-developed international model[10]. As the Lord Chancellor had enthusiastically forecasted[11], the Convention is bringing about a unilateral flow of rules and legal concepts from the common law into the civil law systems.

The Convention, however, is not concerned with the transfer of assets to trustees nor with what the trustees do as trustees towards third parties: the former is to be governed by the law applicable to gifts, contracts, wills and other unilateral dispositions, the latter by the law applicable to the trustees' conduct (e.g. *lex commissi delicti, lex contractus,* etc.); nor is the Convention concerned with taxation[12]. *Partiality* must then be added to one-sidedness and, having done this, one can easily see whence the *comparative law issue* stems: if *some* of the rules concerning trusts are taken from a living legal system and placed in the hands of foreign judges (and taxing officers) an unfathomable host of problems is bound to ensue.

The fashionable (but equally unreliable) analogy drawn between the trust and a rocket with its launcher (the Convention was said to have ignored the launcher, i.e. the transfer of assets to trustees, and dealt with the rocket, i.e. the trust) should have been extended to the encounters of the rocket in open space, for whoever is in charge of applying the (domestic) rules prevailing there must by necessity take stock of the type of rocket, its mission, its crew, and so forth: in short, *understand* a foreign rocket, built by a foreign manufacturer under foreign guidelines. That can be achieved only by using the (domestic) methods of measurement and by test-

10 The notion of "international model" as well as its characters in comparison with the English model are put forward in *Maurizio Lupoi,* Trusts, Milan, 1997, Ch. IV.

11 When moving in the House of Lords the Second Reading of the Recognition of Trusts Bill: "... a convention which, in effect, allows us to export to civil law countries, first the concept of the trust ...". 482 House of Lords Official Report, 939 (4th December 1986).

12 Art. 19: "Nothing in the Convention shall prejudice the powers of the States in fiscal matters".

ing the (domestic) legal concepts, since the domestic rules cannot be applied on any different basis.

If, leaving analogies aside, we went back to proper legal expressions, we would not be faced with the now-fashionable theme of "transplants" nor with the old theme of "reception": a *foreign* law is made no less foreign by the fact that it governs a *domestic* trust; even more so when the governance is a very partial one, for, as noted above, other aspects of the same relationship, namely the transfer of assets to trustee, tax matters and the acts performed by trustees, are governed by a different law. All this calls for an unusually thorough understanding of the foreign law and for its careful "translation" in domestic or indigenous terms.

This is not the usual exercise with which comparative lawyers are familiar, that of *explaining;* nor is it the equally familiar one of finding the rule of law governing a specific set of facts in different jurisdictions. Facts and law are here inextricably intertwined and a foreign legal category, that of "trust", is the pivot on which the (domestic and by necessity comparative) legal analysis must turn.

Foreign legal categories can no longer be used as such in this unprecedented context, where legal *expressions* must adhere strictly to domestic law, for otherwise the required points of contact with the conceptual framework of the domestic law would go amiss – and how could the life of a domestic trust progress if it were tainted by such an original sin?

The *comparative law issue,* therefore, concerns the process whereby the rules of the foreign law governing a domestic civilian trust are *expressed* in terms and through the use of categories which belong to the domestic legal system.

III. Trust Instrument and Transfer of Assets to Trustees

1. From Agreement to Unilateral Disposition

A civilian can hardly omit asking whether a trust is a contract or a unilateral act, especially because civilian countries which provide for institutions a comparative lawyer would without question declare to be equivalent or homologous to trusts regularly place them in the contractual area, with the noteworthy exception of Liechtenstein[13]. Upon learning that trusts are not contracts, the civilian would ap-

13 "Ist ein Treuhänder nicht durch einen Vertrag unter Lebenden, sondern durch Treuhandbrief oder Testament, bestellt worden ...": Liechtenstein, Personen- und Gesellschaftsrecht, art. 903; see also articles 907 and 917 (and cf. *Rolf Watter,* Die Treuhand im Schweizer Recht, Zeitschrift für Schweizerisches Recht 1995, 181 ff., 194 - 197). Compare with the Israeli Trust Law (trans.), sect. 2: "A trust is created by Law, by a contract with a trustee or by an instrument of endowment". Gift or will are the sources of the *fideicomiso* in Venezuela: Ley de fideicomisos, art. 4; see also Panama, Law No. 1 of 1984, art. 10, ii co.; Louisiana Trust Code, § 1733; Peru, Ley general de bancos, art. 319; Québec, Code civil, art. 1262; Argentina, Ley 24.441, art. 3. Ecuador, Código de Comercio, art. 410 and decree of 26 August 1993,

pear to have two basic options: first, to define trusts as unilateral acts; second, to hold that while trusts may well not be *contracts* in English law they might none the less be *contrats* in French law or *contratti* in Italian law. In either case, the civilian cannot avoid having to explain what a trust is in civilian terms, for these would be the semantic and legal references on which his definition would eventually depend. The peculiar comparative law issue identified at the end of the previous section now connects with the customary comparative law challenge: there is no explaining a foreign law unless one's own is also explained and the two explanations interact with each other, so that in the end both laws come to be better known than before.

Let us explore the theory of non-contractual unilateral disposition first, whence we shall be drawn into the contractual area.

A paramount unilateral structure can certainly be seen in the declaration of trust where settlor and trustee coincide[14], and also in testamentary trusts. *Inter vivos* express trusts where settlor and trustee are different persons might easily be placed in the contexts of unilaterality[15], were it not for the fact that the role of the trustee is obviously not the same as in testamentary trusts. A testator writes down his dispositions and passes away peacefully, while a living settlor has to deliver the trust assets to the trustee – and how can he do that, unless the trustee accepts delivery and, moreover, accepts it subject to the terms of the trust?

In discussing the *inter vivos* express trust in which settlor and trustee are different persons, the contractual versus unilateral aspects cannot be dismissed by simply stating that a trustee, far from not having to accept a contractual proposal does not even have to accept his appointment; that has nothing to do with the absence of a contractual relationship, for there are contractual relationships, both in the common law and in the civil law, which call for no acceptance and no outward sign of consent.

I would submit that the *earliest* trusts, however one wants to identify them, arose out of agreements. They grew from that same conceptual framework which was much later investigated by the latest German Pandectists and approved, for instance, by the Swiss Federal Tribunal in 1905[16]. Trusts were conveyances coupled

---

art. 41 allows a *fideicomiso* (in commercial matters) to be contained in an *instrumento público cerrado,* so that the "trustee" will not come to know its terms until the document can be read.

14 I cannot find any basis for the position taken by *John H. Langbein,* The Contractarian Basis of the Law of Trusts, (1995) 105 Yale L.J. 625, 672 - 675, that the self-declared trusts do not belong to the modern forms of trust.

15 If one were minded to propose a complete picture to civilians, implied trusts ought to be considered. Constructive and, to a lesser extent, resulting trusts are the subject of much discussion in the common law world; therefore, one could not call them into play unless a prior selection were made of the possible viewpoints and an explanation provided of the one selected by the writer.

16 See *Luc Thévenoz,* La fiducie en droit suisse, Zeitschrift für Schweizerisches Recht 1995, 257 ff., 264 - 268; and *Sybille Hofer's* paper in this volume.

with a side-agreement or at times a proper nominee agreement (in today's parlance)[17]. All that Equity did was to make the side-agreement or the nominee agreement, neither of which was a "contract" actionable at common law[18], binding not only on the feoffee (something which Continental civilians also achieved – indeed, Roman law had already gone as far) but on third parties as well (modern civil law has stopped short of this result). Conveyances belonged to the common law, side agreements and nominee agreements were taken up to Equity. While the latter were bilateral, the former, like wills, were by definition unilateral; conveyances were thought of as *grants* and shared the unilateral characteristic with the *vestitura* and the transfer of *gewere* (which, be it said incidentally, was a well known structure throughout Europe before the school of Natural law got the upper hand). All the problems of classification which are encountered nowadays in a comparative law setting stem from the conceptual gap between contracts and conveyances.

2. The Unilaterality of the Conveyance

The unilaterality of the conveyance meant, among other things, that the feoffor, just like a testator, was free to lay down any condition he wished (the "words of limitation") and to convey either his own estate or any legally recognized estate carved out of his own. All this was done unilaterally and perceived as unilateral, but, even when a conveyance was made *in trust*, it had nothing to do with the trust. The trust did not and does not affect the estate or the conveyance thereof; that is why one can confidently assert that the settlor actually parts with his interest in favour of the trustee (or with that interest that he conveys to the trustee) and can thus contrast trusts with agency, mandate, and so forth. In the fullness of the history of the trust, clauses reciting or setting out the terms of a trust came to be inserted into the terms of the conveyance itself; hence, trusts came to share the unilateral nature of conveyances as of wills. What had been a fundamentally "contractual" institution never entered the area of contracts and merged with the non-contractual and unilateral structure of the conveyance. Therefore, in the subsequent history of trust law and in the myriad of rules which evolved trusts were treated as unilateral dispositions.

One has to tread warily in matters where the procedural issues are as important as substantive ones, if not more so. One must also be careful not to superimpose

[17] See, for instance, the codicil to the will of John of Gaunt (1399): "jeo Johan ... ay puchacez et fait purchacer a mon eops diverses seigneuries, manoirs, terres ..." (from *Frederic W. Maitland*, Selected Essays, ed. H. D. Hazeltine, G. Lapsley, P. H. Winfield, Cambridge, 1936, p. 160).

[18] It is of the greatest importance to keep in mind, not so much that no action lay at common law – which is a truism, but that those agreements did not find their way into the legal category of "contract" – and could not, for there was not at that time a general contractual action at common law.

purely conceptual constructions upon events which have an acknowledged root in the history of the forms of actions and of the shaping of Equity jurisdiction. Recent attempts to re-write the history of trusts fail for lack of historical insight and for a biased and simplistic conceptual approach[19]. The least that one can do, in this climate, is to restrict any generalization to its strictest limits. As far as express *inter vivos* trusts are concerned, I would submit that their remaining outside the area of contracts and their characterization as unilateral dispositions was caused by two factors: a general one, the analogy with testamentary trusts; and a specific one, the insertion of trust terms into conveyances.

3. Trusts of Personality

Conveyances, however, concern real property. When trusts of personalty came to acquire importance one could no longer hinge the trust structures on the conveyance, because there was obviously none. Delivery instead of conveyance, however, means contract instead of grant, bilateral arrangements instead of unilateral dispositions. The importance of trusts of personalty is a relatively modern occurrence and there can be little doubt that nowadays they represent the most frequent type of trust, and in the international context nearly the only one[20]. At the same time, unselfish trustees of old have almost disappeared. Certainly none can be found in the world of international trust companies. Lastly, trusts are increasingly formed by people living within legal systems where trusts are not an acknowledged structure which, as is often said, accompanies one's life from birth to death. People who do not easily understand the relationship between settlor and trustee nevertheless require the formation of trusts, almost invariably trusts of personalty, either through domestic trusts (mainly if not only in Italy, for the time being) or much more commonly through offshore trusts[21].

Trusts of personalty bring back the essentials of the primaeval trusts, in that the *agreement* between settlor and trustee (the *pactum conventum* of the *formula Betica,* the later *pactum fiduciae)*, the legal relevance of which had dissolved as a consequence of the inclusion of trusts in conveyances, comes to the fore and claims an independent status. But surely there cannot be diverse trust theories on how trusts come to life, depending on the type of asset involved. Moreover, whatever the theory is, testamentary trusts must fit within it.

It should come as no surprise if the Pandectist view recalled above were capable of explaining those aspects of the English trusts which I am canvassing. Indeed, it would only prove a point which has never been taken seriously enough by English

---

19 See the essay cited *supra* n. 13.

20 I am referring here to the so-called offshore trusts or, more appropriately, to trusts governed by laws of the international model (see *supra* n. 9).

21 The assets of such trusts are quite often offshore entities.

scholars, namely the civilian origin of trusts[22]; for the sources on which the 19th century Pandectists founded their views were the same as those with which the Chancellors were familiar.

Civil law systems are far from uniformity on the structure of the transfer of property rights. Just to mention two basic and well-known aspects, the German *Abstraktionsprinzip* has no corresponding concept in French or Italian law[23], while the great weight of the theory of *causa* in France and Italy has no counterpart in German law[24]. In spite of this, it may be possible to express in civilian terms how a trust comes about if one is prepared to work on the assumptions which I have just submitted on the conceptual framework of trusts in English law.

4. The Creation of a Trust, from a Civilian Perspective

From a civilian perspective, two aspects of express trusts must be carefully distinguished: the institution of the trust and the transfer of the asset to the trustee.

First, the institution of a trust, which we may legitimately call "the act of trust" (unfamiliar though this terminology may be to common lawyers), is a *unilateral* legal act or *Rechtsgeschäft* or *negozio giuridico* which sets out the intentions of the settlor: it is a *programme*[25]. Such unilateral act may or may not be in writing, may or may not take the shape of a formal trust instrument, and may be executed by the settlor and the trustee together or by the settlor alone. Acceptance by the trustee does not transform the act of trust into a *contract* between settlor and trustee, although in many civilian systems the existence of an *agreement* would be acknowledged. Also, from a purely conceptual standpoint, there are civilian systems which admit of contracts in which only one party is bound[26], but that is precisely where a purely nominalistic approach would prove fruitless. The basic reason why one has to stress the unilaterality of the trust *Rechtsgeschäft* or *negozio giuridico* (which, incidentally, has the advantage of covering the unilateral declarations of trust as well) is to ensure that civilian *fiduciary* notions do not creep in, as has hap-

22 See, however, *David Johnston,* The Roman law of Trusts, Oxford, 1988, *passim;* and at pp. 227 - 232 on the Roman rule of the *bona fide* purchaser without notice. Equally little studied are the canonical roots of the equitable rules; but see, in this volume, the papers by *R. H. Helmholz* and *Shael Herman.* (Additional references are in *Lupoi* (n. 9) 237 - 241.).

23 French civil code, art. 1131; Italian civil code, art. 1325 n.2.

24 With reference to the transfer of ownership of movables, see the seminal treatment by *R. Sacco,* Introduzione al diritto comparato, 4th ed., Turin, 1990, Ch. III, § 9; on *causa* see *Konrad Zweigert, Hein Kötz,* Einführung in die Rechtsvergleichung, vol. II, 2nd ed., Tübingen, 1984, pp. 92 ff. and recently *Reinhard Zimmermann,* Das römisch-kanonische ius commune als Grundlage europäischer Rechtseinheit, JZ 1992, 8 ff., 16 - 18.

25 A mere programme or a binding programme: this will be discussed in the following section.

26 These have nothing to do with the unilateral contracts of the common law.

pened in the now-abandoned French draft law on the *fiducie*[27] or in the German or Swiss *Treuhand*. Indeed, most civil lawyers, even those who have taken it upon themselves to write on trusts, do not appreciate that trusts *cannot* be contracts, in civilian terms, because typically settlors have no action against trustees. Of course, settlors can reserve rights in their favour against the trustee and, if so, can sue to enforce them; that, however, does not belong to the essentials of the trust. The act of trust is, in its essence, a *unilateral programme of divestiture*. Once that is clear, the classification of the act of trust, in civilian terms, as a unilateral act or a unilateral contract has only to do with the heavens (or the clouds) of national legal conceptualization. We shall see in the next section when proper bilateral contracts may assist in the formation of a trust, which would nevertheless remain an essentially unilateral act.

Second, the transfer of assets to the trustee constitutes the performance of the programme set out in the act of trust. It may be brought about by conveyance or by delivery or in whatever other form the law governing the transfer of the assets prescribes. In those systems which require a *causa*, the *causa* of the transfer will be the act of trust[28], while in others the trust instrument itself will allow the trustee to acquire a good title and therefore to be in a position to defend it, also against restitutionary measures.

The distinction between the act of trust and the transfer to the trustee should not be blurred by the fact that very often the two occur in the same document and, moreover, in a document which may plainly appear to be a contract[29]. That is a mere accident, as is shown by the fact that *additional* assets may be transferred to the trustee at a later time with reference to the terms of the trust laid down in the original instrument[30]. Moreover, third parties may transfer assets to the trustee of an already existing trust; that cannot be explained unless acts of trust and transfers of assets are considered as independent from each other and as fulfilling different functions (a typical instance is the charitable trust). A final reason to keep this distinction at the heart of the civilian understanding of the notion of trust is that it easily encompasses the testamentary trust, thus allowing all express trusts to share the same basic structure. In a testamentary trust the transfer of assets to the trustee is necessarily subsequent to the setting out of the terms of trust in the will, the unilaterality of which is of course beyond discussion.

The testamentary trust raises the difficult problem of secret trusts. There we find another instance of the distinction I am proposing, for the institution of the secret

---

27 Which began as follows: "La fiducie est un contrat".

28 Under prevailing Italian legal theory, that is called a "causa esterna". This notion is not used to give legal validity to an obligation (the traditional function of *causa)* but to justify an act of disposition.

29 That is to say, a contract transferring the trust property to the trustee.

30 This is a very common occurrence in commercial trusts, discussed in the following section.

trust is not accompanied by any transfer of assets, and indeed it cannot be. The assets will reach the secret trustee after the death of the secret settlor as a consequence of his will or by the rules of intestacy. The act of trust is here an *agreement* between secret settlor and secret trustee[31], whereby the secret settlor lays down his *programme* (which will be implemented, if at all, by a specific bequest or by intestacy. It is relevant that secret trusts on intestacy were known already in Roman law[32]. The existence of an agreement between secret settlor and secret trustee would appear to contradict the unilateral nature of the act of trust; that is not so, as a deeper examination of the notion of agreement and a clarification of the relationship between (bilateral) contracts and trusts will show.

IV. Contracts, Gifts and Trusts

A very quick search of the law reports will show that most trust cases coming before the courts do not concern family trusts or, according to the old and now outlived expression, settled land; they concern commercial trusts.

English textbook writers underplay the commercial uses of trusts, and they usually treat the transfer of assets to trustees as if it were a "gift". One questions whether this could apply to those commercial trusts, where the settlor is under an *obligation,* voluntarily incurred, either to form a trust, to contribute something to it, to declare himself a trustee, or to conduct its business so that certain assets become owned by a trustee[33]. In all those instances, the settlor is actually *performing the contract* whence his obligation arose: would that come under the heading "gift"? To be sure, there is no consideration for the transfer given *by the trustee* to the settlor, and yet the civilian mind (and, I should have thought, the common lawyer's mind as well) balks at recognizing this as a gift.

Of course, the civilian distinguishes between *liberal* transfers and *gratuitous* transfers and is accustomed to thinking that contracts may exist without consideration, donation being the most obvious example. One readily acknowledges that the unilateral structure of the English-shaped conveyance, modelled, as already noted, upon the grant, favours the use of the notion of "gift" as an illustrative way of describing more generally the transfer of something without a *quid pro quo.*

---

31 An express acceptance by the secret trustee is not required; acquiescence by silence is enough: *Moss v. Cooper* (1861) 1 John & H. 352, at p. 366, per *Page-Wood V.-C.*

32 Inst. II, 23, 10: "Praeterea intestatus quoque moriturus potest rogare eum ad quem bona sua legitimo iure, vel honorario pertinere intellegit: ut haereditatem suam totam, partemve eius, aut rem aliquam, veluti fundum, hominem, pecuniam, alicui restituat".

33 Among recent cases: *Re ILG Travel Ltd* [1995] 2 Butterworth's Company Law Cases 128; *Saipem* v. *Rafidain Bank* [1994] Company Law Cases 253; *Stephens Travel Service International* v. *Qantas Airways* (1988) 13 N.S.W.L.R. 331.

From a civilian standpoint, all this is most disturbing. Some civilian donations may not be seen as gifts by a common lawyer: consider the *donatio sub modo,* when the *modus* should take away most or all of the economic value of the asset and be regarded by a common lawyer as a contract with a condition subsequent; but consider that certain types of trusts have been looked upon in South Africa as *donationes sub modo*[34]. Moreover, not all common law gifts are civilian donations, either because the *animus donandi* is lacking or because, and this is a point of extreme importance in tax matters, the settlor has no intention of conferring any benefit upon the trustee[35]. Additionally, many civilian systems have developed the concept of indirect donation, which would fit well with the family trust model (as recently held by the French *Cour de cassation*)[36].

Where do we stand, then? Not only is "gift" an unmanageable term, one which must be done away with in a comparative connection, but also the *agreement* between settlor and trustee must now be revisited from a different perspective.

The commercial practice recalled at the beginning of this section has one invariable feature: a contract is entered into by the "prospective settlor" with a party having an interest in the coming of the trust into being. The subsequent coming into being of a trust is an act of performance of the contract. The trust may thus be regarded as an offspring of the contract, but the latter does not provide a legal basis for the former, which in English law needs none. Nothing changes in the procedure by which a trust is created[37], and yet the existence of a contract brings about one obvious shift: the settlor will not dispose of property of his free will, as one is accustomed to thinking in the traditional framework of family trusts, he will do so because he abides by a contractual engagement he himself has made.

The contract lies, therefore, outside the sphere of trusts and the difference between the arrangements we are discussing and the civilian *fiducia* can be seen immediately. The "prospective settlor" contracts in the former case with an interested party, in the latter with the fiduciary. Be it a *fiducia cum creditore* or a *fiducia cum amico,* the contract is but the side-agreement which the Pandectists saw as contrac-

---

34 Cf. *H. R. Hahlo,* The Trust in South African Law, (1961) 78 South African Law Journal 195, 202 - 205; *Ben Beinart,* Trusts in Roman and Roman-Dutch Law, in W.A. Wilson (ed.), Trusts and Trust-like Devices, London, 1981, p. 167, 185; cf. *Honoré and Cameron,* Honoré's South African Law of Trusts, 4th ed., Cape Town, 1992, pp. 25 - 33.

35 That is why the prevailing Italian scholarly writings hold that no Gift Tax is due on Italian domestic trusts. Although I fathered this opinion, I would now think that transfers of assets to charitable trusts should fall within the tax (and then be recognized as exempt if the charitable trust in question complies with the requirements of Italian law governing exemptions from Gift Tax in favour of non-profit bodies and other entities).

36 *Cass.* 20 February 1996, in JCP, 1996, n. 22647.

37 As noted in the preceding section, it does not matter if the trust instrument is included in the contractual document or is in a separate document. Actually, in most instances a trust instrument proper will not be required, at least under English law, because the trusts I am discussing now do not usually concern land.

tually *limiting* the fullness of the transfer to the fiduciary[38]; quite properly so, since the party receiving the asset and the party with whom the contract had been made were necessarily the same. The English Chancellors saw this when they characterized trusts as "secret confidences". Here is where the roads of Equity and civil law meet and also where they part, as can be seen by the unending discussions in the civil law on the *Missverhältnis zwischen Zweck und Mittel* and on the allied theme of the *Simulationstatbestand:* none of this has ever been a concern of the English lawyer.

Several strands of legal tradition wind together and varied consequences ensue. The agreements between settlors and trustees range from the unselfish grants of land to the use of Franciscan Friars to the all-encompassing contracts between international trust companies and wealthy shipowners for the benefit of their latest wives and the children begotten with them (with the attendant paraphernalia of protectors, letters of wishes, and offshore entities). Unless "trust" is to become a word devoid of any technical meaning, unfortunately a very real possibility, those contracts must be regarded as a travesty of trusts. They may well be *fiduciary contracts,* entitled to recognition as such, but they are not English-model trusts.

The early agreements between settlors and trustees were the functional equivalent of the subsequent trust deeds; but once the non-contractual and unilateral nature of the trust instrument was recognized (and it matters very little if that was by a twist of legal history without conceptual basis) it was too late to retrace the steps of the development of the trust. The relevance of the agreement between settlor and trustee, ousted from the realm of contract in English law, but firmly rooted in the civil law, found its recognition in the realm of Equity, whence it cannot depart. New types of agreements have appeared in the common law and these are proper contracts. They place themselves one layer below the two-level structure outlined in the previous section (trust instrument, transfer of assets) and make it clear to the civilian that the days when trusts were essentially voluntary grants have disappeared. Unilateral they remain, even if one single document included all three levels, just as unilateral is any act of performance – nothing has changed, and yet new features have appeared which have broadened the scope of the trust and have made it even more enticing to the civilian[39].

---

38 It is little-known that a long line of Italian precedents has recognized the so-called "fiducia statica", first propounded by *Nicola Lipari,* Il negozio fiduciario, Milan, 1984, pp. 153 ff., 303 ff., 390 ff. and now *Nicola Lipari,* Fiducia statica e trusts, in: Ilaria Beneventi (ed.), I trusts in Italia oggi, Milan, 1996, Ch. VII, § 1. The "*fiducia statica*" is no less than a unilateral declaration of trust; for a full examination of the relevant case law, see *Lupoi* (n. 9) 548 - 568.

39 Addition to n. 8: While this book was in print the Tribunale di Lucca handed down the first Italian judgment in the matter of domestic trusts and upheld their validity. The case concerned a testamentary trust by an Italian (domiciled in the United States) over assets part of which were located in Italy and for Italian beneficiaries (the testator's daughter and her children): Trib. Lucca 23rd September 1997, Foro italiano, 1998, I, 2007 (the domicile of the testator played no role in the reasoning of the court).

GEORGE GRETTON

Scotland: The Evolution of the Trust in a Semi-Civilian System[1]

I. Introduction

1. Defining the Trust

To write the history of a legal institution, of a *Rechtsinstitut,* is to presuppose an institution for which a history can be written. Thus the present controls and rewrites the past, by reconceptualising it. That is a truism, but it bears repeating. In the case of the trust, the problem is acute. It is not merely the question of modern categories being projected into the past, and reorganising the past. There is another dimension, which is that "trust" in itself is an Anglo-American concept. To look for the trust, to look for its history, is already to think in a certain way. To identify what are commonly called "trust-like devices" is already to accept the trust as a discrete legal institution, along with "person" or "obligation" or "action" or "right" or "delict" or "succession".

"If a foreign friend asked me to tell him in one word whether the right of the English *Destinär* (the person for whom property is held in trust) is *dinglich* or *obligatorisch,* I should be inclined to say: 'No, I cannot do that. If I said *dinglich,* that would be untrue. If I said *obligatorisch,* I should suggest what is false. In the ultimate analysis the right may be *obligatorisch,* but for many practical purposes of great importance it has been treated as though it were *dinglich,* and indeed people habitually speak and think of it as a kind of *Eigenthum'.*" Thus *Maitland*[2], on the ambiguous nature of the trust. English law does not readily fit into civilian pigeonholes. That is legitimate[3]. But one must beware of the converse. It does not follow that a system which has the trust must have an English pigeonhole for it[4]. Thus

---

[1] I would like to thank Almira Delibegovic, Murray Earle and Emma Williamson, who helped in the checking of references etc., and John Finlay, who located documents in the Scottish Record Office.

[2] *H. A. L. Fisher,* Collected Papers of Frederic William Maitland, vol. III, 1911, p. 326 ("Trust and Corporation").

[3] Though this sort of thing can be overstated. Already in *Maitland's* time the *Treuhand* seems to have had something of the ambiguity of the English trust, while the modern German *Anwartschaftsrecht* looks like equitable ownership. Something similar is true of the position of the creditor in *Sicherungsübereignung.*

Professor Fratcher's formulation in the International Encyclopaedia of Comparative Law[5] is unacceptable:

> "The interest of a beneficiary is also a property interest in the subject matter; it is not a mere personal or contract claim against the trustee. Neither trustee nor beneficiary has a mere *ius in re aliena.* In other words, the interests of both the trustee and the beneficiary in the subject matter are interests *in rem*".

This, true only of the Anglo-American systems, seeks to impose a certain conception as a matter of universal definitional validity. Indeed, one may ask whether it is even true of those systems: the European Court of Justice has held that the right of a beneficiary in *English* law is *not* a real right[6]. In Québec law, not only does the beneficiary not have a real right, but the trustee does not have one either[7]. In South African law a *bewind* is classified as a kind of trust, though the trustee has no real right[8].

This paper is a historical one, but the conceptual issue cannot be dodged. Thus if one describes trust as an arrangement under which one person manages assets for another, then all developed legal systems have the trust, and Scots law has had it from the earliest times. If it is defined more narrowly as such an arrangement, but with the added feature that the assets are vested in the administrator, then again one encounters such "trusts" almost universally, and again Scots law has had them from the earliest times. If one defines trust as involving a division of ownership into legal and equitable, then Scots law does not have the trust at all. These conceptual issues are particularly vital in delving into the origins of the trust. If you are looking for something, it makes sense to know what it is you are looking for. One needs

---

4 Cf. *H. R. Hahlo,* The Trust in South African Law, (1961) 78 South African Law Journal 195.

5 Vol. VI, Ch. 11. Though I consider the formulation unacceptable, I hasten to express my highest admiration for its author.

6 *Webb v. Webb* [1994] E.C.R. 1 - 1717, interpreting art. 16 of the Brussels Convention. The expression *droit réel* in the English text becomes "right *in rem*". (That is unsatisfactory for Scots law, where the correct translation of *droit réel* is "real right.") While the *Webb* case is in line with Scots law, the Scots lawyer may be permitted to regret that *Advocate-General Darmon* seemed unaware that English law does not extend to the whole of the United Kingdom.

7 "Le patrimoine fiduciare, formé des biens transférés en fiducie, constitue un patrimoine d'affectation autonome et distinct de celui du constituant, du fiduciaire, ou du bénéficiare, sur lequel aucun d'entre eux n'a de droit rééł." (Official translation: "The trust property, consisting of the property transferred, constitutes a patrimony by appropriation, autonomous and distinct from that of the settlor, trustee or beneficiary, and in which none of them has any real right".) (Code civil of Québec, art. 1261.) This formulation can be traced to the work of *Pierre Lepaulle.* It comes close to making a trust a juristic person, an idea for which much could be said.

8 Trust Property Control Act 1988. On the history of the South African trust, see *Tony Honoré,* Trust, in: Reinhard Zimmermann, Daniel Visser (eds.), Southern Cross: Civil Law and Common Law in South Africa, 1996, pp. 850 ff.

not only to be clear about concepts, but also to treat names with circumspection. For instance, the fact that the term "trust" first appears in the 17th century does not mean that trusts first appeared in the 17th century. They might have existed earlier, without the name. But equally, they might not have evolved until later, for the word "trust" can be used where there is no trust. In fact, in my view the trust – in the sense which I am about to explain – did indeed develop in that century. But that fact cannot be inferred solely from the introduction of a particular word. Nothing is more familiar than the fact that the term "trustee" is often applied, even in legal usage, to those who are not, in the accepted sense, trustees at all, such as company directors. Indeed, curators, tutors and judicial factors are expressly included under the definition of "trustees" in the Trusts (Scotland) Act 1921[9].

The problem of defining what is meant by trust is a difficult one both for Scots law[10] and indeed at an international level[11]. I give here what is I think the modern Scots concept[12]. Our law knows no division between law and equity, and so the Anglo-American approach is of no relevance. Trust involves the administration of assets by one person (or more, jointly) for another person or group of persons. That relation is a fiduciary one: every trustee is a *fiduciarius,* i.e. must act in the interests of the beneficiary to the exclusion of his own. But there must be more than that: the assets must be vested (in some sense) in the trustee: it is for this reason that company directors, commercial agents. judicial factors and so on are not strictly trustees[13]. Vesting in what sense? This too is a difficult area. *Lord Stair* in a passage which has had a powerful formative influence on the development of the concept, writes that "the property of the thing intrusted, be it land or moveables, is in the person of the intrusted, else it is not proper trust"[14]. The trustee is owner, albeit a *nudus dominus.* What sort of right do the beneficiaries have? A personal right against the trustee[15]. Just as the trustee's ownership is an odd sort of owner-

---

9 Section 2. *Charles Forsyth,* Principles and Practice of the Law of Trusts and Trustees in Scotland, 1844, of which more later, divided trusts into "proprietary" and "accessory", the latter being "trusts" where the trustee did not acquire *dominium.* It is an interesting approach, but did not establish itself, the latter category being regarded as cases of fiduciary obligation but not trust. *Forsyth* subverted his own idea by placing some trusts which were in fact proprietary under the accessory category.

10 Some of my own thoughts are briefly sketched in an essay, Trust and Patrimony, in: H. L. MacQueen (ed.), Scots Law into the 21st Century: Essays in Honour of W. A. Wilson, 1996.

11 See the Hague Trusts Convention, adopted into U.K. law by the Recognition of Trusts Act 1987.

12 As seen by the writer. Others might not analyse the trust in quite the same way, and they might accordingly see its history differently.

13 In certain exceptional cases, however, assets may become vested in such persons, at which point they may become trustees in the full sense.

14 *James, Viscount of Stair,* The Institutions of the Law of Scotland, ed. *D. M. Walker,* 1981, I, 13, 7.

15 This formulation works better for private than for public trusts.

ship, but ownership none the less, so the beneficiary's personal right is an odd sort of personal right, but personal none-the-less. If the beneficiary has a right to particular assets, his right is still personal not real. A right *ad rem* is not real but personal. This way of looking at the trust is probably made necessary by the fact that whilst Scots private law is "mixed" in the sense that it derives both from the *ius commune* and from the English traditions[16], the degree of mixture varies from area to area, and Scots property law, both moveable and immoveable, is for the most part unmixed, and belongs to the *ius commune*[17]. As such, it takes the civilian framework of personal and real rights as its starting point, the latter being divided into *dominium* on the one hand and *ius in re aliena (ius in re minus quam dominium)* on the other, this being itself subdivided into particular nominate kinds – a *numerus clausus* of real rights. Trusts have to be located in this framework. The rights of the parties must be either personal or real. That it is perfectly possible to locate trusts in a civilian system of property law – albeit with certain stresses – is not always fully appreciated at an international level. It is sometimes imagined, both by those from the Anglo-American tradition and by others, that trusts of necessity bring in equity, and therefore cannot be understood in *ius commune* terms. That is not true[18], as the Scottish example shows. Indeed, Scots law is of comparative interest in that it adopted a more or less full system of trusts into a civilian system of property law at an early stage. Some other countries with similar systems have done the same, but Scotland was the first.

But we have still not finished sketching the concept. All that has so far been said could be achieved without any special *Rechtsinstitut,* by means of the law of contract. X can transfer property to the ownership of Y and contract with Y that Y will administer it in such-and-such a way. That is simple contract. If X asks Y to administer for Z, then Z can be given title to sue by the *stipulatio in favorem tertii.* Is this trust? It could be so called, but it can be built up solely from the bricks of the law of voluntary obligations[19]. As late as 1866 a judge could say that "the law of trusts has always been treated as part of the general principles of contracts, and the obligations upon the trustee, and the rights of the truster and the beneficiaries as against him, have been given effect to on the ground of contracts"[20]. But this is doubtful as a historical proposition, for trust has been considered a distinct institution from the time of *Stair.* It is also doubtful conceptually. For a distinctive institu-

---

16 Not to mention a good deal of home-grown law.

17 The *ius commune* comprises not only the mediaeval and modern transformed Roman law, but also other elements, such as feudal law. Scotland is the last country in the world which retains feudalism in any real sense: see *K. G. C. Reid,* Property Law in Scotland, 1996. But as the feudal element has declined, the civilian element has increased in importance.

18 Unless one makes it true definitionally, but that seems unhelpful.

19 More or less. Modern trust law, with its ability to confer, extinguish and transfer rights without the consent or even knowledge of the beneficiary, who may even be unborn, probably goes beyond even the maximum that could be achieved by the *stipulatio in favorem tertii.*

20 *Lord Barcaple* in *Gordon v. Gordon's Tr.* (1866) 4 M. 501, at 535.

tion, something more than contract is needed. That something more is the separation of Y's estate into an ordinary patrimony and a trust patrimony. (The word "patrimony"[21] is better than "estate"[22], but none-the-less "estate" is the word commonly used.) The effect of this is wonderful: because of the separation ordinary assets are (in general) immune to creditors of the trustee as trustee, while, even more important, trusts assets are (in general) immune to the creditor of the trustee as an individual. Those immunities could not be achieved merely by contract[23]. Moreover, since the trust property forms a distinct patrimony, real subrogation takes place, so that if a thing is sold, the price forms parts of the patrimony, and *vice versa* for purchases with trust money. The net effect is to make a trust into something very like a separate juristic person, and some theorists[24] have argued that it should be so conceptualised. Be that as it may, Scots law has never taken this step, though, as will be seen later, it has come close to it for public trusts.

The fact that a trust can function as a virtual juristic person has led to its use in some countries as a trading enterprise, the "directors" being the trustees and the "shareholders" being the beneficiaries. This has never happened in Scotland to any substantial degree.

2. The Influence of English Law

One of the central questions in any attempt to study the history of the trust must be the extent of English influence. It is a question of considerable difficulty, which will be discussed below, but it may be as well to summarise here the conclusions which will be reached. The origins of the trust remain uncertain, and while it must be presumed that English law had some influence – the adoption of the English name is suggestive – the evidence does not support the theory of anything like a reception of English trust law, and, indeed, it is hard to prove *any* substantial degree of English influence before about the middle of the 19th century, by which time the institution had long been established. There is a certain tendency to assume that the trust *must* have come from England. One remembers *Maitland's* remark that the trust was "the greatest and most distinctive achievement performed by Englishmen in the field of jurisprudence"[25]. To trace the trust from anywhere

---

21 The discussions of the concept of patrimony which took place on the Continent in the 19th century were largely ignored in Scotland. In my opinion this has caused difficulties in the development of the concept of trust, and, indeed, difficulties in other areas.

22 "Estate" is cluttered by other senses, such as landed estates and the English doctrine of "estates in land."

23 Particular creditors might, of course, agree to restrict their rights of enforcement, but the nature of the trust is that the immunities arise *ex lege,* and are (in general) good against all creditors, consenting or not.

24 Such as *Pierre Lepaulle.* See, e.g., his Traité theorique et pratique des trusts, 1932.

25 *F. W. Maitland,* The Unincorporate Body, in: *idem,* Selected Historical Essays, 1957, p. 129.

else than England seems as implausible as to suggest that golf originated in Italy. But the close association of the trust with English law is misleading. Trust-like devices have developed in other systems[26]. (Indeed the expression "trust-like" is a loaded one, suggesting that the "real" institution is the English trust.) There would be nothing particularly surprising if Scots law had developed the trust wholly independently. As a matter of fact there was some English influence, but in the formative period its degree seems to be rather slight. More substantial English influence starts about the 1840s, by which time the trust was already old.

II. Origins

1. 19th and 20th Century Ideas as to Origins

"In Scotland, the origin of trusts is co-eval with the law of the land. For being a part and parcel of the civil law, on which the law of Scotland is based, they were necessarily introduced ...". Thus writes *Forsyth* in the first book devoted to the law of trusts, published in 1844[27]. Earlier he writes that the trust derives from the *fideicommissum* of the Roman law[28]. *Forsyth* also says that the *English* law of trusts has the same origins, a convenient view if one wishes, as *Forsyth* did, to cast the Scots law of trusts in an English mould. The question of whether the origins were the same became something of a point of dispute. In 1868 *Lord Westbury,* an English judge sitting in a Scottish case, stated that "the doctrine of trusts has the same origin and rests on the same principles both in Scots and English law, and it is desirable that it should be developed to the same extent in both systems"[29]. *Westbury's* agenda seems clear. One should, however, not necessarily bracket *Westbury* with *Forsyth. Westbury* might not have agreed that the trust originated in *fideicommissum*[30]. It became important for those concerned with the autonomy of Scots law to assert the independence of the Scottish law of trusts from the English law. That meant accepting *Forsyth's* thesis as to the antiquity of trusts and their civil

---

26 Most obviously the *fiducia* and *fideicommissum* of Roman law and the *Treuhand* of German law; on which see the papers by *David Johnston* and *Karl Otto Scherner* in the present volume.

27 *Forsyth* (n. 9) 9.

28 *Forsyth* (n. 9) 3.

29 *Fleeming v. Howden* (1868) 6 M. (H.L.) 113, at 121. Nothing was more common in 19th century House of Lords appeals coming from Scotland than for the judges to discover, to their convenience, that the Scots law on a certain point was the same as the English law. However, one must sympathise: their position was an impossible one. For a study of great value (despite its populist title) see *Andrew Dewar Gibb,* Law from over the Border, 1950.

30 However, some English authors of the 17th and 18th centuries traced the trust to *fideicommissum. William Blackstone,* Commentaries on the laws of England, London, 1765 - 1769, vol. II, pp. 327 - 328, compares the trust to *fideicommissum* and hints that there might be a connection.

origin, but rejecting the English connection. "The history of the origin and development of the law of trusts in Scotland is not at all the same as the history of the origin and development of the law of trusts in England" asserted *Lord Normand* in 1955[31]. "The origin of trusts is very different from its origin in England" said *Lord Reid* in 1971[32]. *T. B. Smith* in 1962 was prepared to follow *Forsyth* and *Normand*[33]. *Smith's* essay, interesting and valuable though it is, is not precisely a historical one. Indeed, only one serious attempt has ever been made to look at the origins of the trust, by *Burgess* in 1974[34].

2. The 17th Century and Before

The term "trust" came into use in the course of the 17th century. That fact takes us only so far: the trust might have existed without the name already in 1600, or might by 1700 have not yet been born, despite the use of the name. As to the latter doubt, it can be laid to rest at once. The discussion of trust in *Stair's* Institutions is admittedly (to modern eyes) brief, fragmentary and unsatisfactory, but it would be difficult to deny that this is the trust. Nor does the trust vanish after *Stair:* the texts writers keep it in view, and the courts decide cases. The modern broad river can be traced back, without interruption, to the narrow stream of *Stair,* and on the way certain tributaries are to be found. But if we move back before *Stair* the stream ends. But there is no sudden source or fountain. Rather there are wetlands which, in the course of the 17th century, form into a flow. To anticipate conclusions, the trust, in something like the modern sense, emerged in the course of the 17th century. Before looking to see what actually happened in the 17th century, let us look back before its start.

3. Pre-17th Century Private Arrangements

Examples of trust-like arrangements where X and Y agree that Y should hold property, corporeal or incorporeal, for X, go back a long way. All the examples given in this section may be categorised as trusts or not according to taste. They could be categorized as purely contractual arrangements.

---

31 *Camille & Henry Dreyfus Foundation v. I.R.C.* [1956] A.C. 39 at 47.

32 *Allan's Trs. v. Lord Advocate* 1971 S.C. (H.L.) 45, at 53.

33 *T. B. Smith,* Trusts and Fiduciary Relationships in the Law of Scotland, in: *idem,* Studies Critical and Comparative, 1962, p. 200.

34 *Robert Burgess,* Thoughts on the Origins of the Trust in Scots Law, (1974) Juridical Review 196. I am indebted to this pioneering essay, even though there are things in it with which I disagree. The standard texts on trust law, for example that of *W. A. Wilson, A. G M. Duncan,* Trusts Trustees & Executors, 1st ed. 1975, 2nd ed. 1995, also have some incidental historical material.

In his Legal History of Scotland[35] *D. M. Walker* writes that "the practice developed among landowners in the 15th century of conveyancing estates to patrons' relatives or friends in trust"[36]. He cites no authority or examples, but such conveyances may have been common. Whether they should be classified as trusts depends on what is meant by trust. Certainly in the 15th and 16th centuries it was common to have "trusts" of moveables, X holding for Y. Irritatingly, the sources generally fail to disclose why such arrangements were entered into. Here are some examples[37].

(i) In 1492 Lord Johnne Kennedy makes over to Sir Johnne Kennedy "twa hundreth merkis to the utilitie and profit of Jane Kennedy his dochter"[38] to be paid to her upon her marriage[39]. The expression "utility and profit" is one which seems to have been something of a standard one.

(ii) In 1498 Janet Innes sues Patrick Gordon for 100 merks, being the value of unspecified goods which her father "deliverit til Georg of Gordoun, bruther to the sade Patrik, quilk ressavit the sadis gudis fra hir sade fadir to hir utilitie and profitts"[40]. It is noteworthy that the action is not against the "trustee" but against a party who was the successor of the "trustee" and who is described as an "intromettour." This is, curiously, a feature to be found in some other early cases of trust or quasi-trust, such as *Lady Stanipath v. Her Son's Relict and Bairns*[41]. According to later concepts, one would wish to know whether the defender was *in bona fide* and what had been the *causa* whereby he acquired the property, but the early reports are tantalisingly brief.

(iii) In *Spittell v. Urquhart,* a case of 1532, as reported by *Balfour*[42], it was held that "gif ony man ressave in keiping ony infeftment of landis ... to be deliverit to him to quhom the samin was maid and gevin, and beand requirit be him to deliver the samin, refusis, postponis and delayis to mak deliverance to him thairof, he may

35 Vol. II, 1990, p. 687.

36 *Walter Ross* says much the same in his immensely valuable Lectures on the Law of Scotland, vol. II, 1792, p. 334.

37 These examples have been gathered rather at random. A survey of the sources, such as protocol books, suggests that such examples were not particularly common.

38 It is unclear which John Kennedy she is the daughter of.

39 Protocol Book of James Young 1485 - 1518, ed. Gordon Donaldson, 1952, p. 121.

40 Acta Dominorum Concilii, vol. II, p. 131. *D. M. Walker,* Equity in Scots Law, (1954) Juridical Review 103 ff., 141, cites this case as being perhaps one of trust. *Professor Walker* also there cites as a trust case *Rollock v. Hamilton* (1560) Balfour's Practicks 198. This, however, seems to be a simple case of deposit, though it is striking that the term "utilitie and proffeit" is used.

41 (1624) Durie 141.

42 *James Balfour of Pittendreich,* Practicks, ed. P. G. B. McNeill, Stair Society vols. 21 and 22, 1962, p. 198 of the first volume. As noted by *Burgess* (*supra* n. 34), *Balfour's* report is possibly not accurate, but for present purposes what a distinguished lawyer thought in 1579 is as important as what the court decided in 1532.

be callit and convenit to refound, content and pay to him the haill proffeits of girs, pasturage of cattell, or of ony uther gudis quhatsumever quhilkis he micht have had of the saidis landis ...".

(iv) In 1540 Alexander Forester wishes to repay £ 100, seemingly secured on land. He "warns" his creditor, David Forester, to appear at the altar of St Giles Church at a certain day to receive the money. The latter does not appear, so Alexander Forester pays the money to Thomas Marjoribanks "to the utilitie and proffit" of David Forester[43].

(v) In 1542 Alexander Mortoun is going off to fight the invading English. He expects to be killed in action. He conveys his land to his son, Alexander the younger. If he does return alive, his son is to reconvey. Otherwise, his son is to hold for the heirs and assignees of his father[44], though the lands are to burdened by provisions for the daughters (i.e. sisters of Alexander the younger), Isabella, Janet, Margaret and Elizabeth[45].

(vi) In 1551 Eduard Maxwell, a minor, is due an annuity from Robert Maxwell of £ 40 per annum. Sir John Maxwell, seemingly Eduard's curator, arranges that Robert should to pay the money to John Glendonyn "to the utilitie and profett" of Edward[46].

(vii) In 1580 James Mosman pays Andro Lamby £ 1200 which the latter is to pay to Alaxander King for the benefit of Barbara Troupe. Lamby fails to do this and Troupe sues[47].

The term "trust" had not yet come into use. These examples are all trust-like, but one should hesitate before calling them true trusts. It is to be noted that the chapter in *Balfour's* Practicks from which *Spittell v. Urquhart* is taken deals with the contract *de deposito*, and the very next case reported is of deposit of moveables. There can be no doubt that one of the roots of trust law was the contract of *depositum* which was varied in such a way as to involve not only the transfer of possession but also the transfer of ownership. If the depositee was contractually authorised not merely to hold but also to deal with the asset in relation to third parties (which would often be necessary for simple reasons of convenience) then a further contractual element entered, namely that of *mandatum*. The institutional writers tend to characterise trust as a combination of deposit and mandate[48]. This

---

43 Scottish Record Office MS. No. CS 6/14 fol 46v. Thomas Marjoribanks was one the leading lawyers of the day. For a similar example from 1549, see The Protocol Book of Sir Alex Gaw 1540 - 1558, ed. John Anderson, 1910, p. 8.

44 Presumably the son himself will be the heir.

45 Protocol Book of Sir Alexander Gaw (n. 43) 3.

46 Protocol Book of Mark Carruther 1531 - 1561, ed. R. C. Reid, 1956, pp. 47 - 48.

47 Register of the Privy Council, vol. III, p. 271. The report does not give the original wording. *D. M. Walker,* Legal History of Scotland, vol. III, 1995, p. 207, calls this a case of trust.

has often caused puzzlement, because no one now would adopt such a conceptualisation, since deposit and mandate are not conveyances. But if one approaches the matter from the standpoint of early practice, in which property was transferred subject to contractual conditions, the characterisation is an appropriate one, and indeed the only real hurdle is to realise that the deposit is an irregular one, in that ownership passes[49]. The significance of the characterisation, in *Stair* and other writers, of trust as being a combination of mandate and deposit is that it lends support to the view that trust cannot be regarded simply as a 17th century import from England. There is a continuity going back before 1600.

Of course, the pre-1600 examples might themselves reflect English influence, and to some extent they probably do. For instance, one sometimes comes across the very English word "use", as in a case of 1523/24, where the defender, Johne Mure, is averred to have owed money to Margret Ruderford "to the use and profit" of her daughter Kathryne Wallace[50]. To what extent English influence before 1600 can be identified is unclear. My impression is that that influence was slight. The word "use" may indicate linguistic more than doctrinal influence, and there was no reception of the English doctrine of uses in any developed sense.

Burgess[51] sees as a possible precursor the *resignatio in favorem* which was one of two methods[52] by which land could be transferred from X to Y. What happened is that X surrendered the land to his superior, with the latter regranting it to Y. In a sense one could see X as the truster, Y as the beneficiary, and the superior as trustee.

Finally, it should be noted that in some situations where "trust" might have been used, one does not find it. In 1557 Oswald Porteus intends to go abroad for a considerable time. He will leave behind in Scotland "twa zoung barnis callit Marion Porteous and Margaret Porteous, his dochtaris, being pupillis in thair minoritie and les age and thair moder decessit". Oswald conveys certain tacks (leases) to them, to be retrocessed to him if he returns alive, while at the same time he makes his friends Patrik Nicolsoune and William Porteus "actouris factouris rewalris and gidaris" in respect of the tacks[53]. To a modern eye it might have been simpler to assign the tacks to Nicolsoune and Porteus direct, in trust. That was not done.

48 Notably *Stair* (n. 14) II, 12, 17. This view was asserted as late as 1879 by a Lord President of the Court of Session (*Lord Inglis* in *Cunningham v. Montgomerie* (1879) 6 R. 1333). One might suppose that the trust/deposit relationship was especially Scottish, but it can be found in English law too. *Blackstone* (n. 30) 451 calls bailment a trust.

49 *Burgess* (n. 34) 202 questions the role of mandate in the history of trust, saying that prior to *Stair* mandate was unknown. But with respect that is simply not the case.

50 Scottish Record Office MS. No. CS 5/34 fol. 86v (11 February 1523/24). Interestingly, the action against Mure is by the daughter, i.e. the "beneficiary".

51 See *supra* n. 34.

52 The other was the charter of confirmation.

53 Protocol Book of Gilbert Grote 1552 - 1573, ed. W Angus, 1914, p. 26.

4. *Fideicommissum* and Roman Law

In Roman law *fideicommissum* was an institution where X, by testament, conveyed assets to Y under obligation to convey to Z. Y was the *fiduciarius*[54] and Z the *fideicommissarius.* This institution[55] went through a long course of development. In the *ius commune* it combined with *substitutio* to form fideicommissary substitution, which is arguably a major source of the Scottish talizie (entail). But that is a story that cannot be pursued here. *Stair* repeatedly compares the trust to *fideicommissum*[56], and the word has been used in other countries to mean trust[57]. As has already been seen, the origin of the Scots law of trust has frequently been attributed to *fideicommissum. Burgess* controverts that view. He argues[58] that "what Stair is doing is attempting to fit the trust into the framework of Roman ideas and principles and that he is finding that it does not fit precisely into either mandate or deposit or *fideicommissum.* This, in other words, is an acknowledgement, if any were needed, that the trust in Scotland had an origin and development independent of Roman ideas and institutions". *Burgess* sees the partial reception of Roman law as having taken place in the late 17th century, by which time, he argued, the trust was already established. But the partial reception cannot be pinned down to any particular period. It has been pervasive over the centuries. It began much earlier than the late 17th century and indeed continues to the present day[59]. *Fideicommissum* was a concept which lawyers had always been familiar with. *Stair,* in comparing trust with *fideicommissum,* was articulating an established idea. Already before *Stair* an executry was called *fideicommissum*[60], though it was not until later that executry and trust came together.

There is one case, in 1717, when a *fideicommissum* was held to exist as a distinct institution.[61] Here a marriage contract provided that on the eventual death of the bride's father she would take certain sums from his estate to pay over to her own future children, but to keep the money if she had none. One of her sons eventually sued her for his share. He was successful, and the case was called "fidei-commiss." The delatinised form suggests long linguistic usage. But this seems to be the only

54 This term was also used to describe the "trustee" in the institution of *fiducia,* but that was a two-party arrangement (either *cum amico* or *cum creditore)* and seems to have disappeared by the time of *Justinian.*

55 On which see *David Johnston,* The Roman law of Trusts, 1988 and his contribution to the present volume.

56 For example, at (n. 14) IV, 6, 2 and IV, 45, 21, but elsewhere also.

57 For example, Mexico, where trust is called *fideicomiso.*

58 See *Burgess* (n. 34) 202, with particular reference to *Stair* (n. 14) IV, 6, 2 and 3.

59 Especially if we speak of the partial reception of "Civil" rather than "Roman" law.

60 Thus in *Southall v. Cunninghamhead* (1657) Eng. Judg. 49 we read that "all the *dominium* he [the executor] has is *fideicommissum.*" (Incidentally, *Stair* was not counsel in this case.) I would imagine that earlier examples of this idea could be found.

61 *Seton v. Pitmeddon* (1717) Mor. 4425.

reported case of the kind. It may be that *fideicommissum* had an extensive life as a half-accepted institution, not quite distinct from, nor quite merged with, trust. At all events, the time when the traditional trust-like arrangements were emerging into the trust was precisely the time when lawyers were using *fideicommissum* as a way of modelling the emerging institution. Thus *fideicommissum* was one of the sources of the trust. Whether its role was marginal or something more substantial would be hard to say.

5. The 17th Century

Williamson v. Law, decided in 1623[62], is sometimes said to be the first reported case on trusts. It is indeed the earliest case in which one finds the terminology of trust in the report. But *Williamson v. Law* is less important than it seems. The report does speak of "trust". However, *Durie's* Reports were not published until 1690. The dates of *Alexander Gibson of Durie's* birth and death seem to be unknown, but he became a Court of Session judge in 1621 and it was his grandson who edited and published his reports in 1690. By that time the trust was already established. Might the editor have succumbed to conceptual anachronism? The original papers in this case[63] suggest that this might be so. A bond was payable to Dickson[64]. Williamson paid Dickson to assign it to him, and she did so, but for reasons which do not appear he arranged for the assignee to be named not as himself but as his nephew, Law. Law later denied that he held the bond for Williamson. Hence the action[65], which was by Williamson's executor. The word "trust" is not used[66]. The expression used is that the assignation was "to the behuif utilitie and proffeit" of Williamson. The case seems to be simply another example of the traditional private arrangements described above. It may be classified as a trust, but so may earlier cases. Even if one is interested in terminology rather than doctrine, the case is of limited significance since it seems not to have used the word "trust"[67]. One might equally – and equally inconclusively – argue that it must have been a trust case because it uses the word "behoof", and "for behoof of" is (at least since the late 17th century) a synonym for "in trust for".

62 1623 Durie 54.

63 Scottish Record Office MS. No. CS 7 / 371 fol 46r – 49v.

64 The original papers show that this "Dickson" was Janet, sister of the celebrated George Heriot.

65 Proof of trust (or "trust") has been a major theme in the 17th century, as later.

66 Except at 48v of the MS. where Williamson is said to have been "trusting." It should be added, that the fact that "trust" is not used in the original papers does not necessarily mean that it was added by the editor in 1690. It is possible that *Durie* used it in his own manuscript report, which has not survived.

67 I have not been able to locate the original papers in what is sometimes said to be the second reported trust case, decided the year after Williamson, namely *Lady Stanipath v. Her Creditors* (1624) Durie 141.

It would not have been surprising if *Williamson* had in fact been a case of trust in the fullest sense. In 1603 *Elizabeth* of England died, and her successor was the Scottish King, *James VI.* He left Edinburgh for London, and never returned. The Union of the Crowns had begun, to be followed in 1707 by the Union of the Parliaments. The effect of the Union of the Crowns was substantial. We know that intercourse between the two kingdoms increased. We know that many prominent Scots spent much time in London. To some extent they doubtless picked up the idea of the trust. But the evidence suggests that English influence at this stage was slight. Indeed, for the period before the Civil Wars I have come across only one example which can be so categorised[68], namely the creation of George Heriot's Trust, one of the largest, possibly the longest-running, of Scottish trusts, for it was founded in 1623 and still flourishes today[69]. Heriot was an extraordinarily successful businessman. Though he settled in London, he never forgot his native city, and shortly before he died he established the educational trust which bears his name. The trust was established by two deeds, the first being an *inter vivos* conveyance of 3 September 1623 and the second his testament of 10 December 1623[70]. Both make over assets to Edinburgh City Council, to establish a school "in imitatione of the publict pios and religious work foundat within the Citie of London callit Chrystis Hospitall". The deed is generally in Scottish style. Of course, even in London Heriot would have had access to Scots lawyers. But there are some intriguing anglicisms. In the testament we read: "I give and devyse unto the said Provest ... [71] quho are namit and appointit as feoffeis in trust in this behalf". "Devise" is an English term, but what follows is more dramatic. "Feoffees", to give the word its more usual spelling, is purely English, and Heriot's testament is probably the only Scottish deed in which the word has ever been employed. Linguistically, all we have here is a dead-end, but the word, appearing in a Scottish deed, is evidence of contact and influence. "Feoffies *in trust*", as a phrase, is truly striking. Heriot and his advisers, who evidently included Scots lawyers, must have been confident that this expression would be understood in Edinburgh. But the two deeds are also full of Scots terminology too, and the word "mortification" is repeatedly used[72].

It is possible that there was English influence during the Cromwellian occupation in the 1650s. During this period Scotland was in part governed by English officials and some judges were English. Scots lawyers had to handle legislation based on the trust concept. Thus on 12 April 1654 an Act was passed dealing with certain lands which had been confiscated by the Government for political reasons.

---

68 Of course, this may reflect the inadequacies of my researches.

69 I am grateful to the George Heriot Trust Office in Edinburgh for permission to examine their records.

70 See *William Steven,* Memoir of George Heriot with the History of the Hospital founded by him in Edinburgh, Edinburgh, 1845.

71 That is to say, the Council.

72 For mortification, see III. 7 *infra.*

The title is "An Ordinance for settling the Estates of Severall Excepted Persons in Scotland in Trustees to the Uses herein expressed"[73], and the Act itself is drafted very much in the terms of English law. We know that the word "trust" begins to be used in cases increasingly often after the Restoration, and we know that *Lord Stair,* who was appointed to the bench in 1657 and thus sat with English judges, was the first jurist to deal with trusts as such. But attractive though this theory is, evidence is sparse. One might expect to see the trust emerging in the decisions of the Cromwellian court which was in fact though not in name the Court of Session[74]. But these show no trace of trusts. It is a striking silence.

That there was some degree of formative influence coming from England in the 17th century would be hard to deny, and it seems to be associated with the accession of *James VI* to the English throne in 1603 and with the Cromwellian occupation of Scotland in the 1650s. But all this does not amount to a "reception" of English trust law. It would, indeed, be a defensible position, on the evidence which we have, to say that nothing was borrowed except the name[75].

As the reign of *Charles II* continued, the trust established itself as an institution. Two significant cases are *Livingston v. Forrester*[76] in 1664 and *Mackenzie v. Watson*[77] in 1678, both of them holding that where property is held in trust it is immune to the diligence (execution) of the ordinary creditors of the trustee[78]. If this immunity is the single most important distinguishing feature of the trust as a separate legal institution, one might say that with these cases the trust had emerged from gestation into the light of day. However, doctrinal history has an irritating habit of refusing to be neat. It is far from certain that in these cases the beneficiary succeeded because of the trust. At that time it was still arguable that diligence (forced execution) was subject to *any* third-party *ius in personam ad rem acquirendam.* It was also arguable that it was subject to *no* third party personal right. Long after these cases the question of immunity remained to some extent in doubt. The modern law is that diligence is in general not subject to third party personal rights, but there are some exceptions, notably rights arising out of trusts and certain other personal rights. (Exactly which is arguable[79].) But this was unclear in the 17th century. Moreover, *Stair,* who reported both cases, does not in his Institutions cite *Mackenzie,* and though he cites *Livingston* he does so only in connection with an-

---

73 APS vol. 6, part ii p. 821; *C. H. Firth, R. S. Tait,* Acts and Ordinances of the Interregnum, vol. II, p. 884.

74 The reports (cited as "Eng. Judg.") were eventually published in 1762.

75 Another example of the gradual introduction of the term: the Act 1633 c 6 which deals with mortifications refers to those "entrusted" with the administration of the mortifications. As will be seen later, mortifications were public trusts.

76 (1664) Mor. 191 and 10200; 1 Stair 232.

77 (1678) Mor. 10188; 2 Stair 607.

78 I would guess that *Stair* sat on both cases, but this is to speculate.

79 *Niall Whitty* has suggested the term "protected personal rights".

other point of law[80]. Though to the modern eye these cases seem of the first importance, contemporary observers perhaps saw differently.

Stair is the first jurist to deal with trust. But one should not overlook the place of trust in *Dirleton's* Doubts[81]. For instance he observes that "a backbond declaring a trust, with an obligement to denude, hath been found to be binding even against an assigny and arrester. And so it seems to be better than an assignation, which requires intimation to complete it"[82]. It is an acute remark, showing that the nature of trust was being looked at carefully[83]. Again, he asks: "A right being granted to one, his heirs and assigneys, for the use and behoof of another person and his heirs, whether the casualties of ward, marriage etc do fall by his decease, and with respect to the person infeft, or to the person to whose behoof the right is granted"[84]. This again is an acute question. The fact that the question was an open one suggests that trusts of land held ward were uncommon (the casualties of ward and marriage related only to wardholding) since otherwise it would presumably have become settled. The question also suggests that the parallel question for other tenures, such as the casualty of relief in feufarm, must already have had a settled answer, though if so I have not found it. (The 19th century practice seems to have been that casualties were a matter for agreement between the superior and the vassal-trustees. The trustees could hardly avoid reaching such agreement if they wished to obtain public infeftment, since that would require a charter by progress from the superior[85].)

One final observation is that in the 17th century there developed a conveyancing device called entry by adjudication on a trust bond. This was a means by which an heir could obtain entry with the superior in a manner different from the ordinary methods, which were *clare constat* and service. The heir granted a fictitious bond to a friend, who held it in trust[86], but who acted as if he were creditor to the heir. By this means the heir obtained what was called a tentative title. The device is said

---

80 *Stair* (n. 14) III, 2, 47.

81 *Sir John Nisbet of Dirleton,* Doubts and Questions in the Law, 1698. Presumably it was composed between his retirement in 1677 and his death in 1687. *Walker* writes of *Dirleton* that "[a]t a time when bad men were common, he was one of the worst" (*D. M. Walker,* The Oxford Companion to Law, 1980, p. 882.). But he had a talent for law. It is curious that much the same could be said for some other distinguished Scottish jurists of the early modern period, such as *Balfour of Pittendreich* in the 16th century and *Mackenzie of Rosehaugh* in the 17th. *Stair* himself might be cited.

82 *Dirleton* (n. 81) 215.

83 It is in general true for modern law, except that a transferee from a trustee will normally be protected.

84 *Dirleton* (n. 81) 215. *Sir James Steuart of Goodtrees,* Dirleton's Doubts and Questions in the Law of Scotland Resolved and Answered, 1715, pp. 317 - 8, says that if the fact of the trust enters the infeftment then the casualties attach to the beneficiary, or, to use *Dirleton's* word, the *usuarius.*

85 See *A. M. Bell,* Lectures of Conveyancing, 3rd ed., 1882, p. 1146.

86 I.e. the creditor held the bond in trust for the debtor.

to have been invented by *Thomas Hope* about 1630[87]. But the subject has not been researched and details are obscure[88].

6. Proof of Trust

Many of the cases of the 17th century concerning trusts or arrangements similar to trusts turn on the question of proof[89]. The alleged trustee denies the fact of trust and claims that he holds the assets absolutely. No written acknowledgement of the fact of trust exists. One issue which faced the courts was whether there should be any restrictions as to mode of proof. The cases culminated in *Higgins v. Callander*[90] in 1696, in which it was held that no restrictions existed, but that such restrictions ought to exist. "The Lords thought the evidences and presumptions of trust very strong; yet, on the other hand, such exorbitant and implicit trusts were not so favourable as to deserve encouragement, being oftentimes used as blinds to intrap and defraud; and, therefore, wished there were an Act for the future, that no trust should be otherwise proveable but by writ or the intrusted party's oath". That wish was promptly granted by the passing of the Blank Bonds and Trusts Act 1696[91], the first enactment on trust law[92]. It is an interesting question whether this Act was influenced by the English Statute of Frauds of 1677[93] which restricted proof of trust of land, requiring writing. However, there seems to be no evidence bearing on the question, either one way or the other.

III. History since the 17th Century[94]

1. Some Uses of the Trust

The trust is an institution of remarkable flexibility, which can be made use of in many different ways. In the 17th and 18th centuries, however, its uses were very limited. Perhaps the only two common ones were both connected with insolvency.

---

87 *Hope,* who was Lord Advocate, seems to have been an ingenious conveyancer, for he is also credited with the invention of the unbreakable tailzie (entail).

88 See, e.g., *Alexander Duff,* Treatise on the Deeds and Forms used in the Constitution Transmission and Extinction of Feudal Rights (commonly called Duff's Feudal Conveyancing), 1838, pp. 489 ff.

89 *Williamson v. Law* in 1623 (*supra* n. 62) is an example.

90 (1696) Mor. 16182. *Stair* was not involved in this case, having died the year before.

91 c 25.

92 *C. R. A. Howden,* Trusts Trustees and the Trusts Acts in Scotland, 1893, p. 6, calls the Act 1617 c 14 "the first legislative recognition of trusts in our statute book." But this requires the eye of faith.

93 29 Car. II c 3.

94 Inevitably this part must be highly selective.

The first was the practice whereby creditors would assign their claims to one of their number who would then enforce on behalf of everyone.[95] This had the advantages of speed and convenience. The assigned debts were held in trust by the assignee. The device can also be found in Roman law. (The *missio in bona* in favour of a *magister.)* It seems to have been rare by the end of the 18th century. The second was the trust deed for behoof of creditors. This was initiated by the debtor himself. He chose someone to act as his trustee, and conveyed to him most or all of his assets, in trust for his creditors, the trust purposes being realisation and distribution. This arrangement continues to flourish today, and indeed in 1985 received a measure of statutory encouragement[96]. In 1772 came the first of a long line of Bankruptcy (Scotland) Acts providing for the judicial sequestration of the estate of a bankrupt and its vesting in a trustee for realisation and distribution[97]. The vast history of bankruptcy law cannot be explored here, but the device of making the administrator a trustee was continued through successive statutes, notably the Bankruptcy (Scotland) Acts of 1856[98], 1913 and 1985.

There were other miscellaneous uses. In *Workman v. Crawford*[99] land was disponed to secure a debt. (This was an example of what was later to be called the *ex facie* absolute disposition[100].) The disponee was regarded as a trustee[101]. In many cases one comes across assignation of debt to a trustee to do diligence against the debtor. These may be examples of the device mentioned earlier (creditors assigning to a *magister)*, but some of them look as if the assignee is acting only for that cedent and not for others. If so, it is puzzling[102].

---

95 *John Russell,* Theory of Conveyancing, 1788 – admittedly not a work of the first rank – observes (at p. 337) that "hitherto, trust rights in Scotland have been chiefly confined to the security of creditors, and the expediting of the affairs of bankrupts." The meaning of the first category is uncertain, but probably refers to the *ex facie* absolute disposition.

96 Bankruptcy (Scotland) Act 1985, s. 59.

97 12 Geo. 3 c 72. Later this statute was, rather curiously, given the official short title of the Bills of Exchange Act 1772.

98 19 & 20 Vict. c 19.

99 1672 Mor. 10208; 2 Stair 121

100 That is to say, ownership was vested in the creditor as a security, the debtor having a personal right to a reconveyance on payment of the debt. This was not a true right in security – neither *pignus* nor *hypotheca* – because in a true security there are two real rights in one thing: the debtor has *dominium* and the creditor a *ius in re minus quam dominium.* In an *ex facie* absolute disposition there is only one real right, *dominium,* and it is the creditor who has it. However, if an owner purported to convey ownership to a creditor, but the deed revealed that it was intended as security, it took effect as *hypotheca.* This device is effectively the same as *fiducia cum creditore.*

101 This established itself as the law. For a later example, involving an *ex facie* absolute assignation, see *Purnell v. Shannon* (1894) 22 R. 74. Much the same result has been arrived at in German law, where the debtor in a *fiducia cum creditore (Sicherungsübereignung)* is protected in the event of the creditor's insolvency.

102 For example see *Craig v. Carbiston* (1677) Mor. 16174; 2 Stair 571; *Ogilvie v. Lyon* Mor. 16200; K. & W. Dict. 2, 477. In *Mackenzie v. Watson* (1678) Mor. 10188; 2 Stair 607,

Ante-nuptial marriage contracts are, of course, of considerable antiquity, but originally made no use of trusts. In the course of the 18th century it began to be the practice to appoint "trustees" who had the right to enforce the provisions. But nothing was vested in them, and so they were (to modern eyes) not trustees at all. There was evidently a problem as to whether such persons had title to sue: in *Hill v. Hunter* in 1766[103] it was held that they did. Later in the century there was a further development: the idea that the marriage contract should convey to trustees[104]. This idea was, one suspects, borrowed from England. It made rapid progress and during the 19th century the trust arising out of marriage contracts became one of the main uses of the trust. The old idea of unvested "trustees" continued side-by-side with the new system long into the 19th century[105]. It seems that the modern division of trusts into *inter vivos* and *mortis causa* only came into existence in the 19th century, since before that time there were no *mortis causa* trusts. Trusts were either purely *inter vivos* or, if intended to operate after death, nevertheless established *inter vivos*.

In the 19th century liferents (usufructs) increasingly became organised as trusts, so that instead of ownership being vested in the fiar and a subordinate real right being vested in the liferenter (usufructuary), a three-handed arrangement was devised, with ownership being vested in trustees, and the rights of fiar and beneficiary being personal rights against the trustees. This proved much more convenient, if also more expensive, and "proper" liferents of the old sort are today rare, though by no means unknown. Since lawyers are general employed to draft the documents, and since lawyers are commonly appointed trustees with the right to charge for their services, there was a natural motivation on the part of the legal profession to recommend trust liferents. The same motivation had doubtless operated to widen the use of trusts in other fields[106].

2. Proof of Trust[107]

The issue of proof of trust, which was such a dominant one in the 17th century, was not laid to rest by the 1696 Act. The Act became one of the main topics of

we are told that the creditor assigned the claim in trust because he was "unwilling to distress Elphinston [the debtor] his own name" [ie in the name of the creditor / cedent.]

103 (1766) Mor. 16207

104 See *Russell* (n. 95) 337, where it is said that trusts were seldom used except for creditors but that its use of trust in marriage contracts was a very new invention.

105 See, e.g., Complete System of Conveyancing (commonly called Juridical Styles), 3rd ed., 1826, vol. I, p. 179, and *Duff* (n. 88) 426 - 7.

106 This sort of thing tends never to become public, but in my own experience I can confirm that lawyers are not unaware of their own interest. Nevertheless, this aspect should not be exaggerated.

107 A valuable account of the law, prior to the repeal of the 1696 Act in 1995, is given in chapter 4 of the first edition of *Wilson / Duncan* (n. 34).

trust law, and generated a great deal of case-law. The Act was brief and left plenty of scope for dispute. It naturally exposed itself to ceaseless assaults by disgruntled litigants, and many subtle exceptions to it gradually grew up through case-law, giving rise to a maze of decisions full of artificial distinctions. The Act seems never to have commanded universal approval, because it enabled fraudulent trustees in certain cases to embezzle with impunity. When the Act was repealed in 1995[108] there were no mourners.

The Act dealt with *proof* of trust rather than with *constitution* of trust, which was perhaps not a happy plan[109]. Since the courts eventually held that the restrictions on proof applied only to some litigants and not others[110], it could lead to "limping" trusts, i.e. trusts which existed for some purposes but not others. The question as to whether the Act applied as between husband and wife gave rise to much dispute and was never finally settled[111]. Similar issues arose as between partners. The Act also generated much case-law about whether it applied to all trusts or only some. The Act spoke of trusts which arise out of a "deed of trust", and so those asserting the existence of a trust had an incentive to argue that their particular trust did not arise out of a "deed". Much subtle learning evolved on this point. For instance, registered company shares were held to fall under the Act[112], but not registered Treasury Bonds[113]. Again, the view came to be accepted that the Act applied only where the truster had consented to the taking of the title in the name of the trustee. That principle, reasonable in itself, generated much case-law, in which the courts had to decide what amounted to true "consent" in a multitude of different contexts.

3. Immunity to Creditors

The doctrine that trust assets are immune to creditors began to emerge in the 1660s and 1670s: see *Livingston v. Forrester*[114] and *Mackenzie v. Watson*[115]. But as has already been observed, the doctrine was by no means fully established at that time, or for long after, though in retrospect the trend was clear. In 1717 we find

108 Requirement of Writings (Scotland) Act 1995.

109 Though the repeal of the Act left no mourners, there are those who would like to see restrictive rules on the creation (as opposed to proof) of trusts.

110 The first case seems to be *Elibank v. Hamilton* (1827) 6 S. 69. It may be added that it is doubtful whether this approach is consistent with the wording of the Act.

111 *Anderson v. Anderson's Tr.* (1898) 6 S.L.T. 204 held that the Act did not apply but this was later doubted, e.g., in *Adam v. Adam* 1962 S.L.T. 332.

112 *Anderson v. Yorston* (1906) 14 S.L.T. 54.

113 *Beveridge v. Beveridge* 1925 S.L.T. 234.

114 (1664) Mor. 10200; 1 Stair 232.

115 (1678) Mor. 10188; 2 Stair 607.

another case, *Bannerman*, in favour of immunity[116]. *Bankton*, writing in 1752, says that immunity exists if the trust is constituted in writing but not otherwise[117]. He cites, not *Livingston* and *Mackenzie* or *Bannerman*, but *Street v. Hume*[118] and *Boylstoun v. Robertson*[119], cases whose status as trust cases is marginal[120]. *Erskine* does not discuss the question of immunity at all. There was a school of thought that merely personal rights of third parties, even by way of trust, should never prevail against diligence. Matters were still in dispute in 1803 when *Wylie v. Duncan*[121] was decided. That case held, or seemed to hold, that heritable property was not immune unless the fact of trust appeared in the title itself. *Bell*[122] adopted that view, and in the 19th century the law finally became settled: beneficiaries always won against creditors of the trustee, with one important exception. The exception was that if (a) the property in question was heritable (immoveable), and if (b) the trust was latent, meaning that the publicly recorded title did not reveal the trust, then creditors prevailed over beneficiaries. A final attempt was made to deny the immunity doctrine in *Gordon v. Cheyne* in 1824[123]. Here it was argued that the position of the trustee in sequestration was like that of a *bona fide* purchaser: the attempt failed. In 1891, in *Heritable Reversionary Co. v. Millar*[124], an attempt was made to deny the exception mentioned above, i.e. the rule that a latent trust of land is not good against creditors of the trustee. The Court of Session reaffirmed the now settled view. But the House of Lords reversed[125]. Although it is evident that the Court of Session was right and the House of Lords wrong[126], the decision established itself, and has even been enshrined in statute, at least for sequestration[127]. (In diligence and liquidation the rule remains a common law one.)

---

116 Bannerman v. Masters of Queen's College (1710) Mor. 16187; Forbes 420. It should be noted that though this case is classified in Morison's Dictionary under the head of "Trust" that word itself does not appear in the report.

117 *Lord Bankton*, An Institute of the Laws of Scotland, 1753, I, 18, 15.

118 (1669) Mor. 15122; 1 Stair 616.

119 (1672) Mor. 15125; 2 Stair 54.

120 Stair (n. 14) 1, 12, 17 calls *Boylstoun* (which he cites as *Roiston)* a trust case.

121 (1803) Mor. 10269; Ross's Leading Cases, vol. III 1849, p. 134. This was a case of sequestration rather than diligence.

122 *G. J. Bell*, Commentaries on the Law of Scotland and on the Principles of Mercantile Jurisprudence, 1810, 1, 301.

123 5 Feb. 1824 Fac. Coll.

124 (1891) 18 R. 1166.

125 (1892) 19 R. (H.L.) 43.

126 It is apparent that the House of Lords was much under the influence of English law. The Scottish judge, *Watson*, was anglicised to a high degree.

127 Bankruptcy (Scotland) Act 1985, s. 33(1)(b).

4. Powers

What can trustees do? Can they buy? Sell? Lease? Originally such questions were regarded as being primarily a matter for the deed of trust to regulate, though courts were ready to imply powers in appropriate cases[128]. Both cases cited below were public trusts, for at first the issue seemed to crop up much more with public than with private trusts. One reason for this is probably that whereas public trusts are usually permanent, and thus liable to throw up such problems eventually, private trusts tended to be short-lived, since the long-term family trusts were almost unknown before the 19th century. Although the court was prepared to find implied powers, it was more reluctant to grant, under the *nobile officium,* powers which were neither express nor implied[129]. It was not until 1861 that the first statute was passed to confer powers on trustees. This Act[130] gave power to resign and to assume new trustees. Like its successors it was suppletive rather than imperative, so that the power was merely presumed, and could be excluded by the terms of the trust itself. Then appeared the Trusts (Scotland) Act 1867, which, with amendments and supplementary legislation, was to last until replaced by the Trusts (Scotland) Act 1921, which, however, was largely a consolidating measure. The 1921 Act, with amendments and supplementary legislation, remains in force today. The 1867 and 1921 Acts gave presumed powers of sundry sorts, such as power to sell both moveable and immoveable property, to grant leases, to appoint factors and law agents, to invest (but subject to restrictions), and so forth[131].

The word "powers" has always been used in connection with trustees, as with companies. But whereas acts *ultra vires* of a company are at common law void[132], acts *ultra vires* of trustees have, it seems, never been so conceived. Such acts have been regarded as acts in breach of the obligations of the trustees to the beneficiaries, and thus potentially voidable at their instance[133], but not void. The expressions "powers" and "vires" are thus arguably misleading, but have generally been used.

---

128 E.g., *Magistrates of Edinburgh v. Binny* (1694) 1 Fount. 635, Mor. 9107, where trustees were held entitled to grant leases, and *Merchant Co. of Edinburgh v. Governors of Heriot's Hospital* 9 Aug 1765 Fac. Coll., Mor. 5750, – a decision which was to have an impact on the local history of Edinburgh – where it was held that trustees had an implied power to feu.

129 *Forsyth* (n. 9) 168 states that the court in his time would not grant powers. This was confirmed in *Kinloch Petitioner* (1859) 22 D. 175, where the court refused to confer power to borrow.

130 24 & 25 Vict. c 84.

131 These Acts also deal with matters other than powers of trustees. For instance, they provide for the court supervision of trusts by the court. It must be stressed, however, that these statutes do not form a code of trust law. To a large extent the law of trusts remains unenacted.

132 This may be an oversimplification, but the law of persons is remarkably undeveloped.

133 But since the Trusts (Scotland) Act 1961 even voidability is usually excluded.

5. English Influence after 1700

As has already been indicated, evidence of English influence before 1700 is slight, and is also slight until well into the 19th century. There are occasional hints. In *Drummond v. McKenzie*[134] we find a reference to "equitable title" and "legal title" which suggests that by 1758 English trust law was not unknown. But English authorities on trust law are almost never cited before the 1840s. Even *Bell*, who was not averse to citing English cases, does not cite English authorities on trust[135], though he does use the term "beneficial interest", which is presumably of English origin.

In 1844 appeared The Principles and Practice of the Law of Trusts and Trustees in Scotland by *Charles Forsyth*, "advocate and barrister-at-law". This was the first work to be devoted to trusts, and in many ways is admirable[136]. Whether its introduction of English law is to be admired is a matter on which opinions may differ. Whereas before 1844 English authorities were not cited by authors, of the 1600 or so decisions cited by *Forsyth*, about 890 are English. *Forsyth* says[137] that he does not regard English cases as being, strictly speaking, of true authority, but rather as being "notes or illustrations". But this qualification had no influence. The book was a tidal wave from a calm sea. One may even speak of a partial 19th century reception of English trust law. In *A.J.P. Menzies*, Law of Scotland affecting Trustees, published in 1913[138], about 44 per cent of cases cited are English. In *A. MacKenzie Stuart*, The Law of Trusts, published in 1932, 40 per cent of cases are English. But the flood gradually lessened. In the standard modern text, published in 1995[139] the proportion of English cases falls to 14 per cent[140].

---

134 (1758) Mor. 16206; Kames Sel. Dec. 203.

135 Principles of the Law of Scotland, 4th ed., 1839, the last by *Bell* himself. It is striking that by the time this classic work reached its 10th and last edition in 1899 (ed. W. Guthrie) about 98 per cent of the cases cited are still Scottish. English authority is equally absent from the Commentaries.

136 His statement (at p. 12) that "the right of the beneficiary has never in Scotland been acknowledged as a positive, vested, equitable and co-existent right, as distinguished from the legal right of the trustee, as in England" has often been quoted with approval, and whether one likes or dislikes the particular formulation, the underlying thought was as true then as it is true now.

137 At p. ix.

138 2nd ed. The first edition appeared in 1893.

139 *Wilson/Duncan* (n. 34) 2 ed. 1995.

140 *John (Lord) McLaren*, The Law of Wills and Succession, 3rd ed. 1894, deals with trusts at some length, but citation figures would be problematic since the work deals to a large extent with succession, as to which the citations would be almost purely Scottish. Oddly, a minor work, *Howden* (n. 92) has only about 11 per cent of its citations English, even though this was the time of maximum English influence, in trusts as in other areas of law. In *K. McK. Norrie, E. M. Scobbie*, Trusts, 1991, a student text, 22 per cent of citations are English.

It would be natural to conclude that there was a sort of 19th century reception of English trust law and that it began with *Forsyth.* But doctrinal history maddeningly refuses to do what you expect it to do. The strange fact is that *in the courts* English authorities have played a surprisingly small role: a much smaller role than they have played in the Scottish textbooks. One would naturally suppose that the case-law of the 1830s would have contained few English citations and the case-law of the 1850s many. But that is not what one finds. Certainly, in the 200 or so trust cases reported in the 1830s I have not seen a single English citation[141]. In two or three cases there is a reference to an English textbook, for instance *Earl of Strathmore v. Earl of Strathmore's Trs.*[142] which cites "Randall on Trusts, Accumulations Etc.". But in the 1850s the picture is only slightly different[143]. It is difficult, for various reasons, to compile reliable statistics, but perhaps 95 per cent of the trust cases in that decade cite no English authority. The picture does change in subsequent decades, but less so than one might expect, especially since the late 19th and early 20th centuries are generally thought of as the high-water mark of English influence. I am puzzled: the impression one gets from the books and the impression one gets from the case-law going through the courts are not easy to reconcile[144]. But the difficulty should not be overstated: the second half of the 19th century is clearly a period in which English authority is influencing the Scottish courts in trust cases, and that influence continued well into the 20th century.

Forsyth made great use of *Thomas Lewin,* A Practical Treatise on the Law of Trusts, the second edition of which appeared in 1842. This was a standard English text, which survived in successive editions until 1964[145]. His liking for *Lewin's* book is reflected to some extent in the cases[146]. Indeed, in the Scottish cases, what one finds is that where English authority is cited, what is cited is a textbook rather than a case. One can understand why: the text writers turned the bewildering riot of English trust law into something that could be understood, or half-understood, by those who did not practice before the Court of Chancery. *Lewin* was always the first choice[147]. *Snell* on Equity never made an impression north of the border[148],

---

141 Except cases dealing with other matters. Thus in a case involving shipping law and trust, English cases are likely to be cited on shipping law.

142 (1830) 8 S. 530.

143 There are some striking cases. Thus *Cochrane v. Black* (1855) 17 D. 321 and *Laird v. Laird* (1858) 20 D. 984, both involving a trustee's failure to invest as directed, bristle with English authority.

144 One possible solution is that English influence is to be found more in the landmark decisions. But this is speculative.

145 16th ed, ed. W. J. Mowbray. The 1st edition appeared in 1837.

146 E.g., *Ross v. Allan's Trs.* (1850) 13 D. 44.

147 The final edition of *Lewin* even makes it to the list of "Authorities Cited" at p. xciii of *Wilson/Duncan* (n. 34) 2nd ed. 1995. A search on the S.L.T. database 1893 - 1995 revealed 21 cases in which Lewin was cited. The citations continue: the latest (from LEXIS) is an unreported case of 1st March 1996, *Lutea Trustees Ltd. v. Orbis Trustees Guernsey Ltd.* The number is lower than that for citations of *Chitty* on Contracts (33 cases) but many of the latter

perhaps understandably, because it covers equity in general, and not just trusts. *Lewin* was canonised by *Forsyth*[149].

When English cases are cited, they are sometimes out of date in the country of their origin[150]. One example would be *Soar v. Ashwell*[151], an English case which even in its prime was not of profound importance, and which in England has long been forgotten except by the dustiest of scholars, but which ekes out a sad but vigorously malignant life in Scotland[152].

To some extent English influence was confined to particular topics. Thus it was natural that cases turning on the Thelluson Act[153], which dealt with accumulations and applied both sides of the border, should cite English authority[154]. Another example, and a more interesting one, concerns the question of whether a trustee can, as an individual (other than as a beneficiary), have relations with the trust, for instance by buying from it or by charging it for his professional services. The basic idea of fiduciary duties is already in the civil law: "Tutor rem pupilli emere non potest: idemque porrigendum est ad simila; id est ad curatores procuratores et qui negotia aliena gerunt"[155]. Cases of conflict of interest can be found at least as early as 1712[156]. But the English rules proved tighter than the native ones[157], and were imposed by the House of Lords in two cases in particular, *York Buildings Co. v.*

---

are recent, and whereas *Lewin* went out of print more than 30 years ago *Chitty* continues in successive editions. Moreover, in the pre-1893 period, which at present is not computer-searchable, it is evident that there were many citations of *Lewin* and probably none of *Chitty*.

148 A combined LEXIS and S.L.T. search reveals since 1893 only three citations of *Snell* namely, *Southern Cross Commodities Property Ltd v. Martin* 1991 S.L.T. 83 and *Kennedy v. Begg Kennedy & Elder Ltd* 1954 S.L.T. (Sh. Ct.) 103, *Roger (Builders) Ltd v. Fawdry* 1950 S.C. 483.

149 The Signet Library bought twelve of the sixteen editions, the missing ones being the 2nd, the 4th, 5th and 6th. Edinburgh University Library, curiously, acquired only the 2nd (1842) and the 5th (1867). (Of course the Advocates Library, as a library of deposit, took all editions.)

150 An essay could be written on this theme for Scots law as a whole. English lawyers are surprised to see dead English cases living on, like the ghosts in *Homer's* Hades.

151 [1893] 2 Q.B. 390.

152 The example is curious, but it is also shocking, because not only is *Soar v. Ashwell* wholly irrelevant to Scots law, but it is in fact irreconcilable with it. Doctrinal history has its quirks so astonishing as to tax belief.

153 39 & 40 Geo. III c 98.

154 For instance *Muir's Trs. v. Jameson* (1903) 10 S.L.T. 70. Eventually the Thelluson Act was replaced by separate legislation in both jurisdictions. For Scotland see the Trusts (Scotland) Act 1961 s. 5.

155 D. 18, 1, 34, 7 (A tutor cannot buy a thing belonging to his ward; this rule extends to other persons with similar responsibilities, that is curators, procurators and those who conduct another's affairs).

156 *Wright v. Wright* 1712 Mor. 16193.

157 For an interesting and valuable account of the Scottish rules, see *Lord Neaves* in *Aitken v. Hunter* (1871) 9 M. 756.

Mackenzie[158] in 1795 and *Home v. Pringle* in 1841[159]. The latter decision was regarded as so demonstrably a case of judicial legislation that the Court of Session treated it as exactly that, and declined to give it retrospective effect[160]. I am unaware of any other instance in which the Court of Session has responded in this manner to legislation from the House of Lords. But the Court of Session was, in other respects, only too willing to accept the English rules[161]. The House of Lords naturally tended to turn to English law unless wholly inappropriate. A quotation from *Lord Lindley* in 1902[162] illustrates the attitude: "It is so well settled that there is no conversion of land into money, or of money into land, if the trust for conversion is not imperative, that it is quite unnecessary to cite authorities on the point. They will be found collected in Lewin on Trusts, 10th ed, pp. 1158 and 1163".

But it would not be true to say that the House of Lords imposed English law in a blanket way. Very likely it would have done so if it had had the opportunity, but the number of trust cases going to it was limited. Moreover, a good deal of English influence was through counsel pleading before the Court of Session, and snatching at what authority they could find that favoured their position. For instance in a case in 1905[163] we read: "Argued for the respondent: – The reclaimers had no direct claim against the trust estate: Lewin on Trusts 11th ed. p 779; McLaren on Wills 3rd ed. sect. 2296; *Worral* [1802] 8 Vesey 4; *Hall* [1842] 1 Hare, 571; *Staniar* [1886] 34 Ch. D. 470. . . . The reclaimers could have no higher right than their principal: *Pelly* [1851], 1 De Gex, M. & G. 16". Although it was often the case that English authorities were more often cited to than by the court, this was not always so. For instance in a case in 1907 we find English authority much cited from the bench. It is noteworthy in this case that even the "Scottish" cases cited are often House of Lords decisions based on English law[164].

158 (1795) 3 Pat. App. 378.

159 1841 2 Rob. 384

160 See notably *Miller's Trs. v. Miller* (1848) 10 D. 765.

161 See for instance *Gray Petitioner* (1856) 19 D. 1, where the fees of the celebrated law firm of Dundas & Wilson were disallowed because a partner was a trustee of the trust. I cannot refrain from quoting the opening words of the report: "Lord Justice Clerk: It is better at once to fix the principle applicable to this case. In *New v. Jones* (1 Hall & Twells 632) . . .".

162 *Lord Advocate v. Sprot's Tr.* (1901) 4 F. (H.L.) 11, at 19.

163 *Ferme, Ferme & Williamson v. Stephenson's Trs.* (1905) 13 S.L.T. 236.

164 *Hay's Trs. v. Baillie* 1908 S.C. 1224; (1907) 15 S.L.T. 494. The authorities cited are: *Crichton* (1828) 3 W. & S. 329; *Cobb's Trs.* (1894) 21 R. 638; *Williams v. Kershaw* [1835] 5 Cl. & F. 111; *Pemsel's Case* [1891] A.C. 531; *Morice v. Bishop of Durham* [1804] 9 Ves. 399; *James v. Allen* [1817) 3 Mer. 17; Lewin on Trusts, 11th ed., 1904, p. 763; *Hagan v. Duff* [1889] 23 L.R. Ir. 516; *Hill v. Burns* (1826) 2 W. & S. 80; *Millar v. Black's Trs* (1837) 2 S. & M. 866; *In re Best* [1904] Ch. 354; *In re Sutton* [1885] 28 Ch.D. 464; *Williams v. Kershaw* [1835] 5 C.L. 1 F. 111; *In re Jarman's Estate* [1878] 8 Ch.D. 584; *In re Rilands* [1881] W.N. 173; *Ellis v. Selby* [1836] 1 M. & Cr. 286; *Duncan v. Blair* (1900) 3 F. 274 and (1901) 4 F. (H.L.) 1; *Grimond's Trs* (1904) 6 F. 285 and (1905) 7 F. (H.L.) 90; *Cocks* [1871] L.R. 12 Eq. 574; *Baird's Trustees* (1888) 15 R. 682.

One last example will suffice to illustrate the sort of thing that sometimes (but not particularly often) happened: in a case in 1908[165] we read this submission by counsel:

> "The lenders had a duty to enquire as to the application of the money when it appeared from the terms of the will that the trustees' power to borrow was limited, and there was a real burden (*In re Rebbech,* 1894, 63 L.J. Ch. 596; *Horn v. Horn,* 1825; 2 Simon and Stuart, 448; Lewin on Trusts, p. 530). Whether or not that duty was upon him in the above circumstances, it certainly was upon him when he knew that the money was not to be applied to trust purposes (*Corser v. Cartwright,* 1875, L.R. 7, E. and I. App. 781; *Howard* v. Chaffer, 1863, 32 L.J. Ch. 686, at p. 695). It must be assumed that the appellants knew of the burden on the heritage, if their solicitor knew, that was sufficient to affect them with knowledge (*Watkins v. Cheek,* 1825, 2 Simon and Stuart, 199)".

It is not possible to pursue these matters further. It remains only to add that as the present century has advanced, English influence has tended to decline. No particular landmark can be identified, though *Inland Revenue v. Clark's Trs.* in 1939[166], holding a beneficial right to be simply a type of personal right, stands out. It is striking that a leading English House of Lords case such as *Barclays Bank v. Quistclose Investments*[167], decided in 1970, has never been cited in a Scottish court. One suspects that had it been decided in 1870, it would, by 1897, have been cited many times[168].

I have left to the last what is perhaps the most important question: did English influence bring about an English understanding of the trust? Did equity arrive? One reason for the importance of the question is that the legal / equitable division is difficult or impossible to integrate with a civilian system of property law[169]. The answer is, in general, negative, as can be seen from the case just cited, *Inland Revenue v. Clark's Trs.* But there has often been some wobbling. *A. Mackenzie Stuart* in his standard text of 1932[170] states in his very first paragraph that in a trust the "estate is owned by two persons at the same time" and that a trust is something which is enforceable "in a court of equity". One suspects that even in the anglicising 1930s many readers must have gasped.

---

165 *Buchanan and Another v. Buchanan's Trustees* (1908) 16 S.L.T. 421. The version at 1909 S.C. 47 is slightly different.

166 1939 S.C. 11.

167 [1970] A.C. 567

168 It is cited in both the 1st (1975) and 2nd (1995) editions of *Wilson/Duncan* (n. 34), an example of how an English case may reach Scottish texts without reaching the Scottish courts.

169 Though see *supra* n. 3.

170 *A. Mackenzie Stuart,* Law of Trusts, 1932.

6. Doing the *Watson* Wobble

A more remarkable wobble was that of *Lord Watson* in *Heritable Reversionary Co. v. Millar*[171]. Here he said that "an apparent title to land or personal estate[172] carrying *no real right*[173] of property with it, does not, in the ordinary or in any true legal sense, make such land or personal estate the property of the person who holds the title". The reason I have separated this into a distinct paragraph is that while this is not Scots law, it is not English law either. For if English law accepted the concept of a real right[174], it would presumably say that the trustee had such a right, for in English law the trustee has "ownership in law". For English law, there is a *duplex dominium.* By contrast, for *Lord Watson,* ownership was undivided, and solely in the beneficiary. (Scots law also agrees that property is undivided, but locates it in the trustee.) If, for *Lord Watson,* the trustee had no real right[175], what did he have? A personal right of some sort. An obvious difficulty for this curious theory is that if the trustee was not owner, he could not transfer ownership: *nemo plus ad alium transferre potest quam ipse habet. Lord Watson* gets round this neatly by saying that "a true owner who chooses to conceal his right from the public and to clothe his trustee with all the indicia of ownership is thereby barred from challenging rights acquired by innocent third parties". The law reports contain few odder theories. Although the theory – if one can so dignify it – is not English law, it is surely English-influenced. *Lord Watson* wanted to make the beneficiary the equitable owner. The theory did not establish itself.

7. Mortification, Charities, Public Trusts and Foundations

Thus far this paper is concerned chiefly with private trusts. But what of public trusts? Their history is, if anything, even older than that of private trusts, under the name of mortification. This word is liable to confuse, for before the reformation it meant both a public trust and a form of tenure. Parallel to the military tenure of wardholding *(feudum militare)* and the commercial tenure of feufarm and the urban tenure of burgage there was the ecclesiastical tenure of mortification. Land was infeudated to the church to hold for *preces et lachrymae.* In other words, masses

171 (1892) 19 R. (H.L.) 43.

172 Meaning moveables. *Watson's* choice of the English term is significant.

173 Emphasis added.

174 It has a concept of rights *in rem* – presumably the Latin term is used to distinguish the concept from that of *real* property, by which is meant immoveable property – but this is not the same as the civilian concept of a real right. For example an English trust beneficiary often has a right *in rem.*

175 One possibility is that by "real" right he meant not *real* right but right of an *immoveable* nature. The basis for this argument is that in the same sentence he uses *personal* to mean *moveable,* so that one might expect him to use *real* to mean *immoveable.* But this interpretation makes no sense.

were to be said for the soul of the founder and (sometimes) other souls too. This was a form of tenure but it was also an incipient trust. With the Reformation in 1560, saying masses for the dead came to be regarded as popish superstition, and mortification as a tenure came to an end. But already before the Reformation mortification had come also to mean any transfer of property (regardless of tenure) for ongoing public good, such as education or the relief of poverty, and such mortifications, if not popish in their tendency[176], survived the Reformation[177], and new ones were created. The usual practice was to grant land, or (perhaps more commonly) a perpetual income from certain land, to a church or to a burgh council[178], or at all events to trustees *ex officio*[179] which thus became a trustee of the fund, and obliged to use it appropriately[180]. Mortifications for universities were sometimes given direct to the university, but sometimes to independent trustees[181]. The word "mortification" is no longer in general use, but many older public trusts still have the word as part of their name[182].

Over the centuries mortifications gave rise to a trickle of case-law, but jurists had little interest in them. The Institutional Writers say little. It may even be asked as to whether the category of public trust existed at all until the 19th century. In other words, the question is whether lawyers conceptualised public and private trusts as being two branches of the same tree. If one looks at the Institutional Writers one might be inclined to a negative answer. They deal with trusts as private trusts only, and public trusts are either not dealt with or classified as mortifications without reference to trust. Nevertheless, the answer is affirmative. For instance, a case in

176 Some originally popish ones also survived. In 1477 land in St Monans was burdened by a form of annualrent in favour of "friars predicators". Presumably this was for masses for the dead, but at some stage the benefit was transferred to the University of St Andrews, and it was still in existence when litigated in 1762, though its existence caused surprise. See *University of St Andrews v. Creditors of Newark* 1762 Mor. 10171.

177 Thus *Magistrates of Edinburgh v. Binny* (1694) 1 Fount. 635, Mor. 9107, involves a 15th century mortification made by the Bishop of Aberdeen to Edinburgh City Council for the education, discipline and training of delinquent youths in Edinburgh.

178 For example Heriot's Hospital, discussed above.

179 E.g., *Leslie and Black Petitioners* 8 June 1819 Fac. Coll. where a "foundation and mortification" was established in 1659 in favour of the Earl of Wemyss, and the minister and members of the kirk session as "patrons". Other examples abound, e.g. *Anderson, Petitioner* (1857) 19 D. 329.

180 Such earmarked funds, when vested direct in a public body, are sometimes held on public trust, and sometimes are merely part of the general assets to be employed for public purposes. The distinction tends to be unimportant, and in many cases it would be hard to say into which category a particular mortification belongs.

181 For instance, *Magistrates of Aberdeen v. University of Aberdeen* (1877) 4 R. 48 (H.L.) involved a mortification in which a benefactor wished to found a chair in the University of Aberdeen, and to that end transferred assets to Aberdeen City Council for behoof of the university (early 17th century).

182 The term "mortification" is used in a trust set up in 1873: see *McCrie's Trs, Petitioners* 1927 S.C. 556. Probably later examples could be found.

1752[183] involved a benefaction for education in a parish. Five trustees were nominated. This is evidently a public trust. Or again, in 1686 Viscount Tarbet establishes a trust for the poor of Tarbet: "We ... Dispone, Give, Grant, Annailzie,[184] Dot[185] and Mortifie ... to ... the very Reverend Mr Andrew Ross, now Minister at Tarbet, and the present elders of the Kirk at Tarbet, and their Successors in the said Ministry and Eldership (in Being for the Time) as Trustees and Fide-Commissaries for the Use and behove of the Poor ..."[186]. The draftsman evidently had no doubt that here mortification, public trust, and *fideicommissum* coincided. And as we have already seen, the language of trust was used by Heriot, or his lawyers, in 1623.

Continental lawyers often ask where, in English (or Scots) law, the "foundation" is to be found – the *fondation* of French law or the *Stiftung* of German law. Whereupon the English (or Scots) lawyer looks rather blank. It is a problem typical of what motivates the study of comparative law. Though the question is too large and too complex to be considered here, a few remarks may be made. Continental foundations are earmarked funds, and are normally for public purposes, though certain private foundations have also existed. Some are separate juristic persons[187], while others are simply public trusts (the German *unselbständige Stiftung).* The foundation is thus much the same as the mortification[188]. It is curious that the mortification more or less developed, in certain particular cases, into separate juristic personality. Thus in 1765 the Court of Session seems to have accepted that Heriot's Trust – originally established as an *unselbständige Stiftung* with the City Council as trustee – had evolved into a "community," a term which, in context, means a juristic person. Again, in 1637 John Cowan established a mortification to establish an almshouse for the poor. The burgh council were to be the "patrons", which is to say a governing body, but the immediate management was to be in a "preceptor or master". How was the property vested? Not, curiously, in the burgh council, but in the preceptor. Moreover, it seems to have been vested in him not personally but in his capacity as preceptor, so that as preceptors came and went no change to the title was needed. This looks very like a juristic person. In 1868 and 1874 statutory provisions were introduced to bring about the same result for most public trusts, so that a conveyance to the first trustees was deemed a conveyance to all future trustees[189]. That turned most public trusts into virtual juristic persons. Some public

---

183 *Campbell v. Campbell* (1752) Kames Sel. Dec. 35; Mor. 16203.

184 Alienate.

185 Endow.

186 See *George Dallas of St. Martins,* System of Styles, 1697, p. 833. Unlike a modern styles book, this contained chiefly actual deeds.

187 Having no members.

188 Indeed, the two words were sometimes used as synonyms, as where a "foundation and mortification" were established in 1659 for the poor of the parish of Largo. See *Leslie & Black, Petitioners,* 8 June 1816 Fac. Coll.

189 Titles to Land Consolidation (Scotland) Act 1868 s. 26 and Conveyancing (Scotland) Act 1874 s. 45 (both still in force).

trusts converted into actual juristic persons[190]. Indeed, many foundations having the status of juristic persons are (confusingly but revealingly) called "trusts". Many are incorporated under the Companies Acts, a practice that is doubly strange, since such "companies" are not only not trusts but not companies either[191]. (Most other countries have legislation allowing the grant of personality without the absurdity of creating a pseudo-company.) Some are incorporated by other means: a well-known example is the National Trust for Scotland[192]. Of course, there are also many foundations which are juristic persons without the word "trust" in their title.

"Charity" as a legal term seems to be of English origin, and yet another aspect of English influence in the 19th century. I have not noticed its use before *Forsyth* in 1844, and even he merely has an index entry reading: "Charitable trusts: see Mortifications"[193]. But by the end of the 19th century "mortification" was fading and "charity" had become dominant. Nowadays a charity and public trust are concepts which largely overlap, but do not coincide. There are charities which are not public trusts, because they are not in the form of a trust, and there are public trusts which are not charities, because, although for public benefit, they do not promote charitable purposes. Whether a foundation (trust or not) is a "charity" matters mainly for tax purposes, though there are other consequences also[194]. Whether "mortifications" were limited to what we now call charity is, perhaps, to ask an anachronistic question.

One final remark. The law of mortifications or foundations – which is to say the law of public trusts and of juristic persons dedicated to the promotion of a public good – has not attracted much academic attention in Scotland. The Institutional Writers say little. Later writers mention public trusts, but as an addendum to private trusts. The category of foundation, straddling the division between trust and juristic person, has been recognised with little more than a nod. Our legal system has been impoverished thereby. Much needs to be done[195].

---

190 See, e.g., *Scott's Hospital Trs Petitioners* 1913 S.C. 289. The same happened to the Heriot Trust itself: 6 & 7 Guilelmi c 25. For some background see *Incorporated Trades of Edinburgh v. Governors of Heriot's Hospital* (1836) 14 S. 873.

191 Except in the purely technical sense that they are companies for the purposes of the Companies Acts.

192 26 Geo. V & 1 Edw. VIII c ii (local and private statutes). Incidentally, it had previously been incorporated (with its "trust" title) under the Companies Act 1929.

193 *Forsyth* (n. 9) 508.

194 For instance, the Law Reform (Miscellaneous Provisions) (Scotland) Act 1990 contains provisions about both "charities" and "public trusts".

195 The Law Reform (Miscellaneous Provisions) (Scotland) Act 1990, and the publication of C.R. Barker (ed.), Charity Law in Scotland, 1996 may indicate a change in the wind.

8. Constructive Trusts

Constructive trusts are those arising by implication of law *(ex lege)* rather than by the intention, expressed or implied, of the parties *(ex voluntate)*. To what extent Scots law has the constructive trust is uncertain: the answer seems to be that it has them but only to a very limited degree, and that most of the categories of constructive trust in English law are not recognised in Scotland. To a great extent, cases which in England are constructive trusts are in Scotland handled under the concepts of contract, delict, express trusts and, perhaps especially, unjustified enrichment[196]. The term "constructive trust" began to arrive in the late 19th century. *Forsyth*, writing in 1844, has a section devoted to "Trusts by Operation of Law"[197] but the term "constructive trust" is not mentioned. I have not located its arrival with accuracy, but by the late 19th century it was common[198]. That is to say, the term was common. As already indicated, the term was on the whole being used to describe situations which were not in fact constructive trusts. Mention must be made of *Jopp v. Johnston's Tr.* in 1904[199] in which English authority was accepted – one might say received – on a large scale[200]. Curiously, this case, though often enough cited, has had less influence than one might have expected. Likewise, when *Lord Westbury* made his famous remark in 1868[201] that "an obligation to do an act with respect to property creates a trust" the consequences might have been dramatic, for this proposition – broadly true in English law – would turn much of Scots law upside down. But the remark was, for the most part, politely ignored. The soil of Scots law is constantly sown with English seeds, but some do not germinate, while some germinate but do not thrive[202].

---

196 For an extended study see my own, Constructive Trusts, (1997) 1 Edinburgh Law Review 281 and 408. This however is only partially historical.

197 *Forsyth* (n. 9) 382 ff.

198 Thus it is used both in *Howden* (n. 92) and in *A. J. P. Menzies*, Law of Scotland Affecting Trustees, 1st ed., 1893.

199 (1904) 6 F. 1028.

200 In particular this case performed the remarkable feat of accepting *Re Hallett's Estate* (1880) 13 Ch. D. 696.

201 *Fleeming v. Howden* (1868) 6 M. 113 (H.L.), at 121.

202 One possible analysis of *Sharp v. Thomson* 1997 S.L.T. 636, 1997 S.C.L.R. 328, is that the House of Lords decided that upon delivery of the disposition the sellers held in constructive trust for the buyers. That would be like (though not the same as) the English doctrine. However, the language of trust was not used. It is doubtful whether any coherent *ratio* can be found in this decision.

9. *Frog's Creditors v. His Children*[203]

Curiously, one situation which perhaps should be classified as constructive trust has always been treated as a special doctrine. This is the doctrine in *Frog's Creditors v. His Children*[204] in 1735 and *Newlands v. Newlands' Creditors*[205] in 1794. Some background is needed, and a curious background it is. In the 18th century – and perhaps before – it was often desired to convey property to X for his lifetime and then to his children. How could this be done? To convey to X with a destination (i.e. a *substitutio*[206] to the children) was possible but capable of being defeated by "evacuation." A tailzie (entail) was possible but cumbersome, expensive and inflexible. The obvious solution, to a modern conveyancer, would be to dispone to trustees to hold for X in liferent (usufruct) and to the children in fee. What is curious and instructive is that this solution seems simply not to have occurred to 18th century conveyancers. They attempted a direct conveyance to X in liferent and his children in fee. But that obviously could not work, since the owners were at the time of the conveyance indeterminate. When I write "obviously" I hope I am not being anachronistic, but surely even at that period the impossibility was clear enough. What happened if the attempt was made? In the leading case of *Frog's Creditors v. His Children*[207] it was held that the effect was to give ownership to X. Undeterred, and rather like lemmings, conveyancers continued, but now added the word "allenarly"[208] to the liferent. The courts decided that the word had to be given effect to. But it was still obvious that "a fee cannot be *in pendente*" to use the traditional maxim. So in *Newlands* it was held that the effect would be to give *dominium* to X (and to that extent following *Frog*) but subject to what was a sort of trust to hold for himself in liferent and his children in fee. This was called the doctrine of the "fiduciary fee". One might argue that this was best classified as implied *fideicommissum*. But nobody did. I speak in the past tense, because such conveyances are never now used, but the rule in *Newlands* in fact eventually received statutory blessing and is in substance still law[209].

10. Resulting Trusts and the Doctrine of the Radical Right

A resulting trust arises where the trust's purposes have been exhausted but some trust property remains. In that case the trustees hold on trust for the truster, though

203 For a valuable study, see *Wilson/Duncan* (n. 34) Ch. 6.

204 (1735) Mor. 4262. The similarity to the English decision – once a leading one – of *Shelley's Case* (1581) Co. Rep. 93b, 76 E.R. 206, is striking.

205 (1794) Mor. 4289.

206 The history of *substitutio* in Scots law has yet to be written.

207 (1735) Mor. 4262.

208 Meaning "only."

209 Trusts (Scotland) Act 1921 s. 8.

the doctrine is modified in the case of charitable trusts[210]. A resulting trust seems today to be conceptualised as simply an implied trust purpose. The term is English, and the first use of it I have noticed is a case in 1841[211]. The contingent right of the truster is often called his "radical right"[212]. According to one theory, the "radical right" was not an ultimate contingent beneficial right, but rather ownership itself. According to this strange theory, a transfer of ownership failed if intended to create a trust. The truster remained owner, and the trustee acquired a real right less than ownership. This idea was of course contrary to the view of *Lord Stair*, was hardly reconcilable with conveyancing practice, and suffered from all sorts of internal muddles and inconsistencies, but nevertheless existed as a sort of alternative doctrine for a long period. Its origins can be traced back to a case in 1734[213]. It took vigour from a case of 1801[214], and reached its high-water mark in *Gilmour v. Gilmours* in 1876[215]. But even at that period it was never fully accepted, and it gradually went into decline. Today it is almost, though not quite[216], forgotten[217].

11. Executry

The executor is a character who did not exist in Roman law but who became more or less universal in mediaeval Europe, Scotland included[218]. The executor is obviously like a trustee, in that he holds property for others. Whether an executor actually becomes a fiduciary owner is, however, rather an obscure question, which has attracted surprisingly little discussion. The decree of confirmation issued by the commissary[219] says nothing about ownership. In an example from 1878 the commissary "give and commit to ... full power to uplift, receive, administer, and dispose of the said Personal[220] Estate and Effects, grant discharges thereof, if need-

210 Where the English doctrine – with a law-French name – of *cy-près* will mean that new charitable purposes must be found.

211 *McLeish's Trs v. McLeish* (1841) 3 D. 914, where *Lord Moncreiff* quotes it, as an unfamiliar term, from *St Barbe Tregonwell v. Sydenham* (1815) 3 Dow. 194.

212 Though this term has also been used in senses unconnected with the law of trusts.

213 *Snee & Co. v. Anderson's Trs* (1734) Mor. 1206.

214 *Campbell of Edderline* (1801) Mor. Appendix to "Adjudication", no. 11.

215 (1876) 11 M. 853.

216 One sees its ghost in *Norrie / Scobbie* (n. 140) 35.

217 The only full study of this curious doctrine is my own article, Radical Rights and Radical Wrongs, 1986 Juridical Review 51 and 192.

218 The history of executry in Scotland has been little studied. A valuable article however is *A. E. Anton*, Mediaeval Scottish Executors, 1955 Juridical Review 129. See also the chapter by *Reinhard Zimmermann* in this volume.

219 The Commissary is the successor of the pre-Reformation Official. See *S. Ollivant*, The Court of the Official, Stair Society vol. 34, 1982. Today the post is always held by the sheriff.

220 A curious anglicism. The meaning is "moveable." Until the Succession (Scotland) Act 1964 the executor's role was confined to the moveable property, though he could also be made a trustee of the heritage.

ful pursue therefor, and generally ever other thing that to the office of Executor nominate is known to belong"[221]. The wording in use in the 1990s is almost identical[222]. Space does not permit discussion of this complex subject.

One curious feature of Scots law, in a European context, is that an executor is used in both testate and intestate cases. In the former case the term used is executor-nominate, and in the latter, executor-dative. The executor-dative is appointed by the court.

Stair seems not to classify executors as trustees. But once the category of trust was established, it was unsurprising that executry should be subsumed under it, and this had happened by the time of *Erskine,* who writes[223] that "executors are trustees for all interested in the executry". Likewise *Bell* writes[224] that "where an executor has been confirmed ... he is trustee for the heirs and legatees and creditors[225] of the deceased". But executry was not brought into the definition of "trust" for the purposes of the various Trusts (Scotland) Acts until 1900[226]. This applied to executors-nominate. Executors-dative were included only from 1964[227]. It should perhaps be added that an executor's liability to creditors of the defunct has always been limited to the estate: this is one of the most obvious trust-like features of executry. Despite the views of the Institutional Writers, *Lord President Inglis* in 1872[228] said that "[a]n executor is not a trustee in the sense of being a depository. A trustee has to hold as a depository; not so an executor, who has to administer, not to hold .... An executor is ... a debtor to with a limited liability, but he nothing else than a debtor, and the creditors of the deceased, and the legatees who claim against him, do so as creditors". This remark is of course muddled[229], but it shows that the view of executry as trust had not wholly prevailed. Again, in 1912 *Lord Dunedin*[230] said of the executor that "emphatically he is not a trustee"[231]. But although such remarks are occasionally still quoted, they do not seem

221 Edinburgh Commissariot, 27 June 1878, estate of Peter Hepburn. From my collection.

222 For an example from 1613, which again is silent as to ownership, see *P. Goudesbrough,* Formulary of Old Scots Legal Documents, Stair Society vol. 36, 1985, p. 17.

223 *John Erskine of Carnock,* An Institute of the Law of Scotland, 1773, III, 9, 42.

224 *Bell* (n. 122) 2, 80.

225 This theory eventually did not prevail. The majority view is that the heirs and legatees are trust beneficiaries, but the creditors are simple creditors. But this is a long and complex story which cannot be told here. Incidentally, *Bell* was keen on this sort of idea. He also argued that any debtor, on becoming insolvent, becomes a trustee for his creditors. This idea too did not establish itself. (For discussion, see *Nordic Travel Ltd. v. Scotprint Ltd.* 1980 S.C. 1.)

226 Executors (Scotland) Act 1900 s. 2.

227 Succession (Scotland) Act 1964 s. 20.

228 *Jamieson v. Clark* 1872 10 M. 399.

229 Both executors and other trustees hold. Both executors and other trustees administer, subject to certain limitations. The claims of legatees and of creditors are quite distinct.

230 By some considered to be a great judge.

to be taken very seriously. Executry is regarded as trust, but a special sort, to which some special rules apply[232].

Finally, though lack of space allows only the briefest mention, something must be said of the trust disposition and settlement. This was in effect a testament, whereby the testator conveyed everything to trustees, the legacies being converted into trust purposes. The trustees would be declared executors of the moveables. The deed developed during the 18th century, its origins being an *inter vivos* trust having a *mortis causa* purpose.

IV. Current Law

Compared with some areas of law, such as family law, the law of trusts has not changed very much in this century. Legislation such as the Trusts (Scotland) Act 1921, the Trusts (Scotland) Act 1961, the Trustee Investments Act 1961 and the Law Reform (Miscellaneous Provisions) (Scotland) Act 1990, have been concerned with the adjustment of points of detail. There has been a steady flow of case-law, but little of it has been of the first importance. One current issue which certainly is important but which remains uncertain – which has been little studied academically and which awaits a proper treatment by a good court – is the use of trusts as commercial security, the idea being to make the debtor a "trustee" for the creditor, thereby circumventing all the usual rules about registration, delivery, publicity, and real rights, which public policy has bestowed on conventional rights in security. The point, of course, is that the right of a beneficiary prevails over the creditors of the trustee[233]. Another current issue, which has attracted more academic attention, is that of constructive trusts[234]. But in general one can say that trusts have not attracted as much academic interest as one might have expected. *Wilson & Duncan*[235] is an impressive work, but there has been little in the journals. Such as there has been has often been of an anglicising tendency. No one is or has ever been quite sure whether trusts are, in the great map of the law, to be assigned

231 *Talyor v. Ferguson* 1912 S.C. 165.

232 One oddity which cannot be discussed here is that for some, but not all, purposes the executor is deemed to be *eadem persona cum defuncto.*

233 The main study of this issue is my own, Using trusts as commercial securities, 1988 Journal of the Law Society of Scotland 53.

234 See *R. Burgess,* The Unconstructive Trust?, 1977 Juridical Review 200, 201; *A. Wilson,* The Constructive Trust in Scots Law, 1993 Juridical Review 99; *Kenneth Norrie,* Proprietary Rights of Cohabitants, 1995 Juridical Review 209 (arguing for the use of constructive trusts in sexual relationships, on the lines developed in England, the Commonwealth and the U.S.A.); *Gretton,* (1997) 1 Edinburgh Law Review 281. Though my regard for *Professor Norrie* is extremely high, I cannot agree with his article. Even the term "proprietary rights" is to be regretted.

235 *Wilson/Duncan* (n. 34).

to property, or obligations, or persons, or perhaps form a continent of their own. To anyone interested in how the trust can fit in to a system some of whose roots are civilian and which does not know "equity" Scots law has much to offer, but the truth is that in the Year of Grace 1997 Scots law is still not quite sure how it wants to handle the trust[236].

236 I conclude with two examples of how even distinguished authors have found the trust so baffling as to lead them into absurdity. (1) *D. M. Walker* in his Principles of Scottish Private Law, 4th ed., 1989, vol. IV, p. 4, writes that the trustee has "full legal right of property." At p. 218 he writes that the beneficiary has "full legal right of property". (2) *Lord McLaren* (*J. McLaren*, Wills and Succession, 3rd ed., 1894, a leading work) wrote that trust is "quasi-contract" (at para. 1508). What trusts have to do with the law of quasi-contract it is perhaps better not to enquire.

List of Contributors

Joseph Biancalana, M.A., J.D., is a Professor of Law in the University of Cincinnati College of Law

Robert Feenstra, Dr. iur., Dr. iur. (h.c.) mult., is Emeritus Professor of Roman Law in the University of Leiden

Michele Graziadei, Dr. iur., is Senior Researcher and Acting Professor of Law in the University of Torino

George L. Gretton, LL.B., W.S., N.P., is Lord President Reid Professor of Law in the University of Edinburgh

Stefan Grundmann, Dr. iur., Dr. phil., LL.M., is Professor of Private Law and Business Law in the University of Halle-Wittenberg

Richard Helmholz, A.B., LL.B., Ph.D., Dr. iur. (h.c.), is Ruth Wyatt Rosenson Professor of Law in the University of Chicago

Shael Herman, M.A., J.D., is Professor of Law at Tulane Law School, New Orleans

Sibylle Hofer, Dr. iur., ist wissenschaftliche Assistentin an der Universität Frankfurt / Main

David Johnston, M.A., Ph.D., is Regius Professor of Civil Law in the University of Cambridge

Neil Jones, M.A., LL.M., Ph.D., is a University Assistant Lecturer in Law in the University of Cambridge

Klaus Luig, Dr. iur., ist Professor für Privatrecht, Römisches Recht und Neuere Rechtsgeschichte an der Universität Köln

Maurizio Lupoi is Professor of Comparative Legal Systems in the University of Genoa

Michael Macnair, M.A., B.C.L., D.Phil., is a Senior Lecturer in Law at Lancaster University

Andreas Richter, B.A., LL.M., is a Ph.D. candidate in the University of Regensburg

Joachim Rückert, Dr. iur., ist Professor für Juristische Zeitgeschichte und Zivilrecht an der Universität Frankfurt / Main

Karl Otto Scherner, Dr. iur., ist Professor für Bürgerliches Recht, Deutsche und Europäische Rechtsgeschichte an der Universität Mannheim

Harald Siems, Dr. iur., ist Professor für Deutsche Rechtsgeschichte, Geschichte des Kirchenrechts, Geschichtliche Rechtsvergleichung und Bürgerliches Recht an der Universität Erlangen

Reinhard Zimmermann, Dr. iur., LL.D., LL.D. (h.c.), is Professor of Private Law, Roman Law and Comparative Legal History in the University of Regensburg

MIX
Papier aus verantwortungsvollen Quellen
Paper from responsible sources
FSC® C105338

Printed by Libri Plureos GmbH
in Hamburg, Germany